CONTEMPORARY

INDONESIAN-ENGLISH

DICTIONARY

CONTEMPORARY

INDONESIAN-ENGLISH

DICTIONARY

A Supplement to the Standard Indonesian
Dictionaries with Particular Concentration
on New Words, Expressions, and Meanings

by
A. ED. SCHMIDGALL-TELLINGS
and
ALAN M. STEVENS

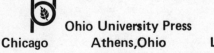
Ohio University Press

Chicago Athens,Ohio London

Library of Congress Cataloging in Publication Data

Schmidgall-Tellings, A. Ed.
    Contemporary Indonesian-English dictionary.

    Bibliography: p.
    1. Indonesian language—Dictionaries—English.
I. Stevens, Alan M., joint author.   II. Title.
PL5076.S34   499'.221321   80-20994
ISBN 0-8214-0424-5 clothbound
ISBN 0-8214-0435-0 paperbound

To our wives:
Oemi and Jackie

PREFACE

The form of Malay used in the Indonesian archipelago was already different from peninsular Malay when, on October 28,1928, a nationwide youth congress held in Jakarta named Bahasa Indonesia, the Indonesian Language, as the national language. Since August 17, 1945, when Indonesia declared its independence, the language has changed rapidly, especially in the area of vocabulary. Adaptation to the modern world in the areas of politics, social development, science and the like, have expanded the lexicon either from native sources or from borrowings, the latter from Sanskrit, English and (to a lesser extent) Dutch. Wide-scale borrowings from regional languages and dialects, particularly Javanese and Jakarta Malay, have also taken place.

It has been difficult for modern Indonesian dictionaries (either monolingual or bilingual) to keep up with this influx of new words and meanings. In the years since the publication of Echols and Shadily, *Indonesian-English Dictionary,* Cornell University Press 1964, and A. Ed. Schmidgall-Tellings, *Indonesian-English Supplemental Word List to Existing Dictionaries,* Lembaga Administrasi Negara 1964, it has become increasingly difficult for foreigners (and even for Indonesians who are out of touch with the mass media) to read Indonesian publications and to understand some portions of the spoken language. With this in mind, we have collected material from recent newspapers, periodicals and scholarly publications written by Indonesians as well as from recorded conversations. We have included here roots, derivatives, compounds, expressions and meanings which do not appear in Echols and Shadily. In some instances we have expanded on the explanations of words which do appear in that dictionary but which we thought needed greater clarification. All illustrative sentences and phrases are from the original sources.

This dictionary is, therefore, intended as a supplement to the existing Indonesian-English dictionaries, and with the exceptions mentioned above we have tried not to include material which already appears there. The organization of this work follows that of Echols and Shadily: root, idioms, derivatives (in the same order) and compounds.

How to use this dictionary

1. Orthography

Indonesian has three different sounds represented by the letter *e*: (1) the *é* which sounds more or less like the *a* in *make,* (2) the *è* which sounds like the *e* in *red* and (3) the unstressed *e* which sounds like the *e* in *open.* These three *e*'s are not specifically indicated in printed matter, such as newspapers, magazines, books, etc. Here we have indicated them by using the acute (') and the grave (`) for (1) and (2) respectively. These differences are only indicated in the main entry, however. In determining the diacritic mark for the various *e*'s, we have, among others, consulted the *Kamus Ejaan Bahasa Indonesia Standar, Edisi Pertama,* Jakarta, Mei 1973, 588 pages; this edition published by the *Panitia Pengembangan Bahasa Indonesia* of the *Departemen Pendidikan dan Kebudayaan* was circulated in a limited circle.

There is, however, a great deal of dialect variation between the vowels *é* and *è*, and the reader should not assume that the vowel we have indicated is the only one possible.

Foreign words whose pronunciation does not follow from the Indonesian spelling have been italicized.

Since this dictionary is not intended to be a complete listing of all Indonesian words but rather a non–overlapping supplement to Echols and Shadily the user should look up words both here and in that work. This will involve working with both the older, pre–1972 orthography, and the newer, post-1972 (so-called *EYD: Ejaan Yang Disempurnakan* 'perfected spelling') orthography. Equivalents are given below.

pre–1972	EYD
ch	kh
dj	j
j	y
nj	ny
sj	sy

The pre–1972 orthography also used the *angka dua,* a raised number 2, to show reduplication while the EYD writes out the reduplication in full, e.g. *buku²* vs. *buku-buku.* The older spelling also wrote the prepositions *di* and *ke* as part of the following word; the newer writes them separately.

The old orthographic system is still retained in many personal names and in abbreviations and acronyms.

Javanese words spelled with *dh* (or *ḍ*) and *th* (or *ṭ*) are frequently spelled with plain *d* and *t* when borrowed by Indonesian. For example, *thok* (or *ṭok*) usually appears as *tok* in Indonesian. In this dictionary we have given both the spelling with the *h* and without the *h*. For example, *andap* and *andhap.* In many cases the spelling with *dh* or *th* is never actually used in Indonesian printed materials.

2. The *meN–* prefix

In this work we have included both standard and non–standard forms of the *meN–* prefix. Following Echols and Shadily's practice we have usually given only the *meN–* form and not the corresponding *di–* form. In some cases, however, we have given the *di–* form because we were not sure whether a *meN–* form existed or we were not sure of its pronunciation. The prefix *peN–* follows the rules for the standard forms of *meN–*. The forms of the *meN–* prefix are as follows:

If stem begins with	standard forms	non-standard forms
vowel	meng–	ng–
b	mem–	m– or nge–
c	men–	ny– (c is lost) or nc–
d	men–	n– or nge–
f	mem–	
g	meng–	ng– or nge–
h	meng–	
j	men–	n– or nge–
k	meng– (k is lost)	ng– (k is lost)
l	me– or	ng(e)–
	meng– (rare)	
m, n, ng, ny	me–	nge–
p	mem– (p is lost)	m– (p is lost)
r	me– or	ng(e)–
	meng– (rare)	
s	meny– (s is lost)	ny– (s is lost)
t	men– (t is lost)	n– (t is lost)
v	mem–	
w, y	me–	nge–
z	men–	

Foreign words, words beginning with prefixes and words beginning with more than one consonant in many cases keep their initial consonant instead of losing it according to the rules given above. E.g. *protes/memprotes* and *memrotes.* Words beginning with sequences of sounds that are similar to prefixes, once were prefixes, or are dead prefixes often also fluctuate between losing their initial consonant or not, e.g. *tertawa/mentertawakan* and *menertawakan.* Native words beginning with a single consonant, especially *k,* occasionally keep this sound instead of losing it, e.g. *kilat/meng-kilat.* Foreign words beginning with *s* often also have the forms *meng–* or *men–.* In this dictionary we have indicated the instances where the initial consonant is not lost by specifically including it in the form e.g. *kilat/ mengk–* for the example given above. One–syllable roots usually prefix the vowel *e* before adding a prefix ending with *ng,* e.g. *rem/mengerem, pengereman.* This *e* does not appear with other prefixes, however. The prefix *ber–* often occurs without *r* in some dialects, e.g. *besukaan, betelor.* In a few cases we find the suffix *–ni* instead of *–i,* e.g. *ngrasani.* The suffix *–in* corresponds to standard Indonesian *–i* and *–kan.*

3. Cross References

Cross references to words found in this dictionary are indicated by (s.). For example, *hingkang* (s.) HENGKANG. Cross references to Echols and Shadily are indicated by (S.). For example, *mengehendaki* (S.) MENG-HENDAKI. If a cross reference is to a phrase, the word under which the reference is to be found is not in parentheses. For example, (s.) RUMAH (BENTUK KOPEL) means look for the phrase under *rumah.*

4. Symbols

The use of a comma in parentheses (,)—immediately followed by a word or phrase indicates that the word(s) following the comma can be substituted for the word immediately preceding the parentheses; thus, *hidup rukun.damai,* to live in harmony (,concord), means that the equivalent of *hidup rukun.damai* is either 'to live in harmony' or 'to live in concord'; *tertangkap basah (,tangan),* caught red-handed (,in the act), means that either *tertangkap basah* or *tertangkap tangan* can be translated by either 'caught red–handed' or 'caught in the act.'

Parentheses containing a portion of a word or a word by itself are used to indicate that the portion concerned may be omitted without changing the sense, i.e. *tidak (men)jadi soal* means the either *tidak menjadi soal* or *tidak jadi soal* may be used without a difference in meaning.

- repeats the main entry and ~ refers back to the nearest form. For example, under **abang** we have - *sopir* = *abang sopir* and under **adat** there is **ng-** and then *Mobilnya* ~ = *Mobilnya ngadat.* A dot marks the boundary between parts of a reduplication or parts of an affixed compound, e.g. -.- means a reduplication of the main entry and ~.~ means a reduplication of the nearest form.

5. Variant pronunciations

Since many words, especially colloquial words, have variant spellings or pronunciations we have given some of the possible variants below. The reader should be aware that only one of these variants may appear in this or other dictionaries, and should be prepared to look up the word in both places, if necessary.

a) native words: *h* is present or absent; *hati* or *ati.*

a or *e* as the last vowel of a root and/or suffix; *garam* or *garem, didiamkan* or *didiemken.*

i or *e; periksa* or *pereksa.*
final *k* or final vowel; *kalau* or *kalok; masa* or *masak.*
au or *o; pulau* or *pulo.*
ai or *e* or *ek; capai, cape* or *capek.*
words containing a consonant plus
r or *l* may also appear with an *e* in between; *berantas*
or *brantas; telaten* or *tlaten.*

b) non–native. This list contains only the most common ones.
dh and th are replaced by *d* and *t* respectively.
f or *v* is replaced by *p.*
v is replaced by *f.*
kh is replaced by *k* or *h.*
g is replaced by *h.*
dz is replaced by *j* or *z.*
z is replaced by *s.*
dl is replaced by *d* or *r.*

6. In general any negative can be replaced by any other negative. If we have *tak*, for instance, it can usually be replaced by *tidak, ndak, nggak, kagak,* etc. and vice–versa. This is not true, however, in affixed compounds where only *tidak* or *tak* can occur, e.g. *ketidakstabilan* or *ketakstabilan.*

7. Abbreviations

abbrev.	abbreviate(d)
adj.	adjective
bhw	bahwa
blm	belum
bln	bulan
col.	the Dutch colonial period
coll.	colloquial
cp.	compare
dgn	dengan
dlm	dalam
dpt	dapat
dr	dari
drpd	dari pada
e.o.	each other
esp.	especially
euph.	euphemism
fig.	figuratively

geol.	geology
gramm.	grammatical term
hrs	harus
Jap.	Japanese
Jav.	Javanese
jur.	juridical
k.o.	kind of
kpd	kepada
mil.	military
naut.	nautical
o.	one
o.a.	one another
opp.	opposite
o's	one's
o.s.	oneself
pron.	pronounced; pronunciation
s.	see (cross reference to a word in this dictionary)
S.	See (cross reference to a word in the dictionary of Echols and Shadily)
sbg	sebagai
sbl	sebelum
sdh	sudah
sl.	slang
s.o.	someone
s.o.'s	someone's
spt	seperti
spy	supaya
s.t.	something
Sund.	Sundanese
tdk	tidak
tgl	tanggal
th	tahun
thd	terhadap
tlh	telah
ttg	tentang

utk   untuk

v.i.   intransitive verb
v.t.   transitive verb

yg   yang

BIBLIOGRAPHY

Badudu, J.S. KAMUS UNGKAPAN BAHASA INDONESIA. Cetakan II. Bandung: Penerbit C.V. Pustaka Prima, Jl. Bukit Dago Selatan 27, 1975.

Chaer, Abdul. KAMUS DIALEK JAKARTA. Jakarta: Penerbit Nusa Indah, 1976.

Coolsma, S. SOENDANEESCH-HOLLANDSCH WOORDENBOEK. Derde druk. Leiden: N.V. A.W. Sijthoff's Uitgeversmaatschappij, [?].

Crockett, Jeffery R.D. INDONESIA: ABBREVIATIONS AND ACRONYMS USED IN INDONESIAN PUBLICATIONS. 3750 Northampton Street, North West, Washington, D.C. 20015.

Drewes, G.W.J. WOORDENLIJST JAVAANSCH-NEDERLANDSCH (A companion Publication to EENVOUDIG HEDENDAAGSCH JAVAANSCHE PROZA). Leiden: E.J. Brill, 1946.

Echols, John M. and Hassan Shadily. AN INDONESIAN-ENGLISH DICTIONARY. Second Edition, Fourth printing. Ithaca and London: Cornell University Press, 1970.

Horne, Elinor Clark. JAVANESE-ENGLISH DICTIONARY. New Haven and London: Yale University Press, 1974.

Iskandar, Teuku. KAMUS DEWAN. Kuala Lumpur: Dewan Bahasa dan Pustaka Kementerian Pelajaran, 1970.

Jansz, P. PRACTISCH JAVAANSCH-NEDERLANDSCH WOORDENBOEK met Latijnsche Karakters. Derde, verbeterde en veel vermeerderde uitgave, voor den druk bewerkt en voortgezet door P. Ant. Jansz. Semarang, Soerabaia, Bandoeng, 's-Gravenhage: N.V. Boekhandel en Drukkerij v/h G.C.T. van Dorp & Co., [1906].

Kähler, Hans. Band 5. WÖRTERVERZEICHNIS DES OMONG DJAKARTA. Berlin: Verlag von Dietrich Reimer, 1966.

Karow, Otto und Irene Hilgers-Hesse. INDONESISCH-DEUTSCHES WÖRTERBUCH/ KAMUS BAHASA INDONESIA-DJERMAN. Wiesbaden: Otto Harrassowitz, 1962.

La Dage, John. KAMUS ISTILAH PELAJARAN/DICTIONARY OF NAUTICAL TERMS. Djakarta: Akademi Ilmu Pelajaran, 1962.

Mörzer Bruyns, A. KAMUS SINGKATAN DAN AKRONIM JANG DIPERGUNAKAN DI INDONESIA/GLOSSARY OF ABBREVIATIONS AND ACRONYMS USED IN INDONESIA. Jakarta: Penerbit/Publisher: Ichtiar, Djl. Madjapahit 6, 1970.

Mulder, Niels. MYSTICISM & EVERYDAY LIFE IN CONTEMPORARY JAVA. Singapore University Press, 1978.

Pamoentjak, M. Thaib gl. St. KAMOES BAHASA MINANGKABAU-BAHASA MELA-JOE-RIAU. Batavia: Balai Poestaka, 1935.

Pamuntjak, K.St., N.St. Iskandar dan A.Dt. Madjoindo. PERIBAHASA. Tjetakan Kedelapan. Djakarta: Dinas Penerbitan Balai Pustaka, 1961.

Panitia Pengembangan Bahasa Indonesia. KAMUS EJAAN BAHASA INDONESIA STANDAR. Edisi Pertama. Jakarta, Mei 1973.

Pigeaud, Th. JAVAANS-NEDERLANDS HANDWOORDENBOEK. Groningen-Batavia: J.B. Wolters' Uitgeversmaatschappij. N.V. [1938].

Poerwadarminta, W.J.S. Diolah kembali oleh: Pusat Pembinaan dan Pengembangan Bahasa Departemen P dan K. KAMUS UMUM BAHASA INDONESIA. Jakarta: P.N. Balai Pustaka, 1976.

Poerwadarminta, W.J.S. en A. Teeuw. INDONESISCH-NEDERLANDS WOORDEN-BOEK. Tweede, bijgewerkte druk. Groningen/Djakarta: J.B. Wolters, 1952.

Schmidgall-Tellings, A. Ed. INDONESIAN-ENGLISH SUPPLEMENTAL WORD LIST TO EXISTING DICTIONARIES. Jakarta: Lembaga Administrasi Negara, 1964. DENBOEK. Tweede, bijgewerkte druk. Groningen/Djakarta: J.B. Wolters, 1952.

Schmidgall-Tellings, A.Ed. KASIP (KAMUS SINGKATAN INDONESIA PERTAMA). Tjetakan Pertama. Djakarta: P.T. Suluh Indonesia, 1955.

Tair, M.A. and H. van der Tas. KAMUS BELANDA. Belanda-Indonesia/Indonesia-Belanda. Djakarta: Timun Mas, 1957.

VĀK, 1964, No. 6–Poona: Deccan College.

van der Tas, H. KAMUS HUKUM BELANDA-INDONESIA. Djakarta: Timun Mas N.V., 1956.

van Pernis, H.D. WOORDENBOEK BAHASA INDONESIA-NEDERLANDS. Groningen/ Djakarta: J.B. Wolters, [1950].

Wilkinson, R.J., A.E. Coope and Mohd. Ali bin Mohamed. AN ABRIDGED MALAY– ENGLISH/ENGLISH–MALAY DICTIONARY. Pocket Edition. London: MacMillan and Co. Limited, 1963.

Wojowasito, S. and W.J.S. Poerwadarminta. KAMUS LENGKAP INGGERIS-INDO- NESIA/INDONESIA-INGGERIS, Tjetakan ke 1. Djakarta: Penerbit Hasta, [1972].

Wolff, John U. BEGINNING INDONESIAN, Part One and Part Two. Cornell Univer- sity, Southeast Asia Program, Ithaca, New York, 1977.

Zain, Sutan Mohammad. KAMUS MODEREN BAHASA INDONESIA. Djakarta: Penerbit Grafica, 1960.

A. Ed. Schmidgall-Tellings
Alan M. Stevens

Falls Church, Virginia
Queens College and the Graduate Center,
City University of New York

CONTEMPORARY
INDONESIAN-ENGLISH
DICTIONARY

A

a ahh (hesitation).

à at. – *Rp. 1.000,–* at Rp. 1,000.00.

aäla dynasty. – *Tang* Tang dynasty.

aam (s.) AM.

aau ow! ouch!

aba peng- *(,pemegang -) genderang* drum major(ette).

abai *tdk - dr* to be always (on the alert).

abaimana the lower orifices of the body, anus.

abang I 1 form of reference for lower-class workers, such as, – *sabit rumput* grasscutter. – *sopir* car driver. 2 intimate and respectful epithet for some prominent persons of Jakarta background. – *Jakartè* the male counterpart of *nonè Jakartè*.

abang II red(dish brown). –.– *lambé* lipservice.

abangan I Javanese who are nominally Moslem but who adhere to pre–Moslem Javanese beliefs.

abangan II roof gutter.

abaran (psychological) inhibition. – *renjana* emotional inhibition.

abau a large swamp tortoise.

abc and **ABC** *tdk tahu samasekali –...* don't have the faintest idea about...

abdi slave. peng- *masyarakat* public servant. peng-an dedication. *penuh* ~ dedicated. - *dalam (,dalem) kraton* royal servant. -.*dalemisme* serfdom. - *masyarakat* public servant.

abd(u) 1 slave. 2 servant.

abelur crystal.

abèn (me)ng-(kan) to cremate. peng-an cremation.

abérasi aberration, deviation.

abet 1 appearance. 2 behavior.

abid pious, godly.

abidin adorers of Allah.

abidun adorer of Allah.

Abil Abel.

abiturièn high school graduate.

abjad 1 white. 2 clear.

abjadiah alphabetical.

ablatif ablative.

abnormal abnormal. ke-an abnormality.

abnormalitas abnormality.

abolisi meng-kan to abolish.

abon a meat dish of fried meat reduced to fibers.

abonemèn to have a subscription (,season ticket). *Saya – bus,* I have a bus commuter ticket.

aborsi abortion.

abortus abortion. peng-an aborting.

abrak mica,

abrakadabra abracadabra.

abreg se-.- (s.) SAK.A(M)BREG. A(M)BREG.

ABRI [Angkatan Bersenjata Republik Indonesia] Armed Forces of the Republic of Indonesia. ke-an (adj.) armed forces. *dlm lingkungan* ~ in armed forces circles. meng.–.kan to place (the Department of Religious Affairs) under the Armed Forces of the Republic of Indonesia.

abrikos apricot.

ABS [Asal Bapak Senang] (s. ASAL (BAPAK SENANG). di.-i to be flattered. meng.-.kan to flatter s.o.

absèn not present. *tak pernah - dr* never free from. *daftar* -an attendance list.

absènsi roll call.

absès abscess.

absis abscissa.

absolusi absolution.

absolut absolute.

absolutisme absolutism.

absorbsi and **absorpsi** meng- to absorb.

abstè(i)n abstain (from voting). ke-an abstention.

abu diper-kan to be cremated. – *blarak* dried–coconut–leaf powder (used as a cleanser).

abuh –.–an 1 swollen. 2 swelling. *sakit* ~ dropsy, oedema.

abus very little, a trifle.

ac and *AC* (pron. a-sé) air-condition(ed). *kamar* - an air-conditioned room. ber-

to be air-conditioned. *ruangan kerja* ~
an air-conditioned office.

acak *secara* – at random. **di-.-** to be
messed up.

acan (not) a single.

acancut taliwanda (,**taliwondo**) (s.)
CANCUT TALIWANDA.

acara – *bebas* an unprepared (,unsche-
duled) program. – *padat* a full schedule.

acarya a suggested Indonesian academic
degree comparable to the M.A. degree.

acc [(from the Dutch) accoord; pron.
asésé] approved, agreed. **meng–kan**
to approve.

aceuk older sister.

acir ng- 1 to dash off. 2 stiff and vertical.
–.-**an** to run fast.

aco –.-**an** reckless.

acu *bagaikan* **se–an** it's a perfect fit.
karangan –**an** bibliographical references.

acuh – *tak* – apathetic. **ke- tak –an**
indifference. *baginya tdk menjadi*
–**an** he does not care.

acung meng–kan: ~ *ibu jarinya* to raise
o's thumb (as a sign that s.t. is good).
~ *jari berbentuk huruf V* to give a
V(ictory) sign. ~ *telunjuk* to raise
o's hand.

ada – *nyawa* – *rezeki* the future will look
after itself. *Sdh* – *pukul tujuh?* Is
it now already seven o'clock? *A-*
setengah jam saya tertahan, I was
held up (by the train) for about half an
hour. – *sedia* available. – *apa?* what's up?
what's going on? what's the matter?
– *orang* (this seat is) occupied, taken.
– *yg merah,* – *yg biru* some of them are
red and some are blue. – *saja yg...*
there's always o. who..., there are always some who...*Anak.anak tdk* – *yg*
tahu, None of the children knew it.
ber- *pd jalan yg tepat* to be on the right
track. **ke–an**: ~ *badan* physical conditions. ~ *berhati.hati* deliberation.
~ *cuaca* weather conditions. ~ *darurat*
emergency situation. ~ *darurat perang*
martial law. ~ *dpt masuk* accessibility.
dlm ~ *jalan* in running condition (of

car, army tank, etc.). ~ *kahar* unavoidable circumstances. ~ *kodrati* natural
state. ~ *luarbiasa* abnormality.
~ *malang* adversity. ~ *memaksa* state
of emergency. ~ *tdk menentu* uncertainty. ~ *terpaksa* emergency situation.
~ *yg nyata* (,*sebenarnya*) reality.
keber–an 1 presence. 2 wealth. **meng–.**
ng– to invent (stories, etc), exaggerate,
overdo. **peng–an** 1 supplies. 2 stockpiling.
se–nya whatever you have, whatever
there is. *makannya* ~ they ate whatever
was available. ~ *saja yg...* there's
always o. who..., there are always
some who... *Mesti* ~ *saja yg mau jadi*
sukarelawan, There are always bound
to be volunteers. – *tidaknya* the presence or absence of, the existence or
non–existence of. –**nya**: *tdk* ~ the absence of. *Demikianlah agar Tuan*
(,*Saudara ,Anda) maklum* ~, (epistolary) Such so that you know the state
of affairs, i.e. such is the situation.
–.-: ~ *saja!* (exclamation suggesting
that words fail one) never at a loss for
words! *A* ~ *saja zaman sekarang ini!*
Really, the times we live in...! *Orang*
ini ~ *saja!* This guy is just too much!

adab ber– to be courteous.

adalat righteousness, justice.

Adam Adam. *anak* (,*bani*) – mankind.
nabi – the common ancestor of all men.

Adan 1 Eden. 2 Aden.

adang peng–an surprise attack.

adap I (s.) HADAP.

adap II (*nasi*) –.-(**an**) k.o. ceremonial
(rice dish).

adaptasi adaptation.

adas fennel. – *pulosari* (or, *biji* – *manis*)
anise.

adat traditional law or custom; unwrit-
ten rules of behavior covering a large
gamut of matters, such as, inheritance
rights, landownership, ceremonies of
birth, marriage and death, times and
methods of sowing rice, etc. **ng–** 1 to
adopt a bad habit (such as, for instance,
a horse which is treated too hard and
has adopted the habit of becoming

lazy), be moody. *Isterinya suka ~* ,
His wife is apt to be moody.
Mobilnya ~, His car has whims (i.e.
it does not run, move). 2 temper
tantrums.

adati traditional

adegan - *ranjang* sex scene (in film).

adèh *ber-* to trot.

adem - *ayem* quiet and calm.

adempauze a breathing spell.

adhési adhesion.

adhyaksa magistrate. *A- Dharma Karini*
the women's association of the office
of the public prosecutor.

adi I splendid, excellent. *batu setengah -*
semi-precious stone. *logam -* precious
metal. **ng-** *sariro* [to beautify o's body
(,appearance)] i.e. to make up, by
putting on cosmetics, etc. *-.busana*
haute-couture.

adi II and **adhi** 1 younger brother (,sister).
2 spouse. 3 the shortened form *di.* is
used for younger brother *(di.mas)* or
younger sister *(di.ajeng).*

adi III - *bangkit* reveille.

adiatèrmik adiathermic.

adib respectful.

adicita ideology.

adigang, adigung, adiguna to rely (too
much) on o's strength (,power), authority and knowledge.

adik *-.kakak* brothers and sisters.

adikodrati supernatural.

adil *dgn tdk* **di-i** without trial. **peng-an**:
di dlm (,muka) dan di luar ~ in and
out of court. *menghadapkan ke
depan ~* to summon before the court.
P~ Ekonomi Court for Economic Delicts.
P~ Landreform Court for Land Reform
Delicts. *P~ Militer* Court Martial.
P~ Negeri District Court. *P~ Subversif*
Court for Subversive Delicts. *P~ Tinggi*
Tribunal of Appeal. **per-an**: *bantuan ~*
judicial assistance. *~ singkat* summary
procedure (in court).

ad interim ad interim, temporary. *jabatan
itu akan* **di.-.kan** *kpd menteri lain* the
position will be given to another minister on a pro tem. basis.

Adipati title conferred by the Netherlands
Indies government on a *Bupati.*

adiratna pekaca 1 pure lotus jewel.
2 girl.

adiwarna resplendent.

administratif and **administratip** administrative.

administratur 1 administrator. 2 (in
estate) estate manager.

admiral admiral.

admisi admission (to college, etc.).

adon ke-an doughy. **-an** paste.

adopsi adoption.

ad rèm to the point.

adrénalin adrenalin.

adreng eagerness.

adrès *buku -* directory. *mesin -* addresso-
graph.

Adriatik Adriatic. *Lautan -* Adriatic
(Sea).

adu ber-: *~ dgn* to contend with.
~ hidung to collide head-on. *Kereta.api
dan bis ~ hidung di pagi buta*, A train
and bus were involved in a head-on
collision very early in the morning.
~ mata (,pandang) to exchange glances
(with a girl). *boleh* **di-** to be able to
hold o's own. **meng-** to sue, bring
legal action against. *~ bibir* to kiss.
~ kepandaian 1 to outdo o.a. 2 to
test o's ability. *~ nasib* to try o's
luck. **peng-***ayam* cock fight enthusiast.
peng-an 1 arraignment. 2 lawsuit.
- bagong boar fighting. *- bogem* to
punch e.o. *- fisik* tug of war
(between...). *- jotos* boxing match.
- kekuatan tug of war. *- mulut* dispute,
wrangling. *- urat leher* battle of wills.

aduh meng- to moan.

aduhai staggering (of prices), fantastic,
great. *- cakap* extremely good-looking.
dgn tarif yg - at fantastic rates.

aduk peng- *beton* concrete mixer. **ter-**
mixed up.

Advènt Advent.

Advèntisme Adventism.

aérobatik aerobatics. **ber -** to perform
aerobatics.

aérodinamika aerodynamics.

aéronot aeronaut.

aéronotika aeronautics. *Badan A- dan Angkasa Nasional* National Aeronautics and Space Administration, NASA.

aérosol aerosol.

aérostatika aerostatics.

aèstétika aesthetics.

af *harga - pabrik* price ex factory, i.e. free of charges to the purchaser until the time of removal from the factory.

afal conduct, behavior.

afdéling section, division, department.

afdlal and **afdol** excellent, outstanding. **meng-kan** to celebrate.

afiks affix. **peng-an** affixation.

afiliasi affiliation. **ber-** to be affiliated. ~ *dgn* to affiliate with.

afkir (s.) APKIR. **meng-kan** to declare unfit for services.

afschuif-systeem pass-the-buck system.

aga *orang Bali* - the original inhabitants of Bali.

agak I -nya it seems to me that.

agak II meng-.-kan pantatnya kpd to stick o's buttocks at.

agama ber- confessional. ~ *kpd uang* to serve Mammon. **ke-an** religious. *orang se-* co-religionist. - *animis* animism. - *belebegu* heathendom. - *Jawa* 'religion of Java,' i.e. a syncretic blend of religious beliefs. - *Katolik* Catholicism. - *Kristen* Christianity (i.e. Protestantism).

agamawi religious.

agel thread made from fan palm leaves.

agèn 1 representative. 2 newspaper dealer in neighborhood. **di-i** to be represented. *"Djakarta Lloyd" di pelabuhan Tegal ~ oleh N.V. "Sentasa,"* The "Djakarta Lloyd" is represented by "Sentasa," Inc. in Tegal port. **ke-.tunggalan** sole agency. **meng-i** to be an agent for. - *dagang* commercial agent. - *ganda* double agent. - *kepala* head agent. - *kuasa* agent holding a power of attorney. - *muda* subagent. - *penidur* sleeper agent. - *perjalanan* travel agent.- *perkapalan* shipping agent.

- *polisi* policeman. - *rahasia* secret agent. - *tunggal* sole agent. - *umum* general agent.

agènda agenda. **di-kan** to be a subject of discussion. *Usul tersebut akan diajukan kpd Badan Musyawarah utk ~,* The proposal will be submitted to the Consultative Body in order to be put on the agenda.

a.go.go. and **ago.go I ber-** to do 'a-go-go' dancing.

ago.go II [aksi gobak gonjeng] action (to eat) dried *sago* (instead of rice, since the Malay community in the Riau archipelago can't afford to buy rice any longer (1979).

agrèsi meng- to launch an aggression against.

agrèsif and **agrèsip ke-an** aggressiveness.

agun security, pledge. **meng-kan** to offer s.t. as security. **-an** 1 security. 2 guaranteed.

agung ke-an 1 prestige. 2 mastery.

Agustus ber-an to celebrate August 17th. **-an** the celebration of Indonesian Independence Day (August 17th).

ah The exclamation implies a mild protest: hey! (as a protest against s.o.'s teasing, etc.). *sdh -!* stop it! *tdk mau pergi - !* I don't *want* to go! *-, tdk apa.apa kok!* heck, it was nothing at all! *Saya pulang - !* I'm going *home!*

ah.ih.èh a sound indicating indecision.

ahli 1 (an) authority (on). 2 relative(s), people, = *ahlu(l): ahlulbait* the family; *ahlulkubur* the deceased. *bukan* - layman. *tenaga* - expert. *tak* **berke-an** and *tak mempunyai (,punya)* **ke-an** unskilled. **ke- negaraan** statesmanship. - *agronomi* agronomist. - *analisa intel(ijen)* intelligence analyst. - *anatomi* anatomist. - *anestesi* anesthetist. - *antropologi* anthropologist. - *arkeologi* archeologist. - *arsip* archivist. - *astronomi* astronomer. - *atom* atomic expert. - *bahasa* linguist. - *bakteri* bacteriologist. - *bangsa.bangsa* ethnol-

ogist. - *bangunan* architect.
- *barang.barang kuno* antiquarian.
- *batu* petrographer. - *bedah plastik* plastic surgeon. - *bedah tulang* orthopedist. - *bina wicara* speech therapist.
- *binatang* zoologist. - *biokimia* biochemist. - *biologi* biologist. - *bor* drilling superintendent (of oil company). - *botani* botanist. - *cangkok jantung* heart transplant specialist.
- *catur* chess master. - *cuaca* weatherman. - *demografi* demographer.
- *dgn dadu* crapshooter. - *dermatologi* dermatologist. - *disain* designer. - *dokumentasi* documentalist. - *ekologi* ecologist. - *ekonomi* economist. - *elektronika* electronic expert. - *epigrafi* epigrapher. - *farmasi* pharmacist. - *fisika* physicist. - *genetika* geneticist. - *geologi* geologist. - *gizi* nutritionist. - *hama* entomologist. - *hewan* veterinarian. - *hisab dan ruyat* an expert who, based on calculations and sighting of the moon, determines for Indonesia, Malaysia and Singapore, on which days Moslem holidays will fall. - *hortikultura* horticulturist. - *ilmu alam* physicist.
- *ilmu falak* occultist. - *ilmu keturunan* geneticist. - *ilmu manusia* anthropologist. - *ilmu pelikan* mineralogist.
- *ilmu pengetahuan* scientist. - *ilmu perbintangan* astronomer. - *ilmu urai* anatomist. - *jasad renik* microbiologist. - *kardiologi* cardiologist. - *kebatinan* mystical philosopher. - *kecantikan* beautician. - *k(e)riting rambut* hairdresser (for women). - *ketimuran* orientalist. - *kriminologi* criminologist.
- *kriya kraton* expert in traditional ways. - *listrik* electrician. - *logam* metallurgist. - *makan enak* gourmet.
- *makmal* laboratory worker. - *masak* chef. - *masalah.masalah Cina* sinologist. - *masalah.masalah Indonesia* indologist, student of Indonesia(n affairs).
- *mekanik* mechanic(al engineer).
- *mencopet* seasoned pickpocket.
- *mengenai Mesir* Egyptologist.

- *mesin* mechanical engineer. - *metalurgi* metallurgist. - *metrologi* metrologist, inspector of weights and measures. - *pahat (,patung ,pemahat patung)* sculptor. - *patologi* pathologist.
- *pemasangan pipa* pipe fitter.
- *pembangun (,bangunan) kota* town (,city) planner. - *pembikinan kapal* shipbuilder. - *pembuka tulisan.tulisan rahasia* cryptologist. - *penata warna* color consultant. - *pencegahan dan pengobatan penyakit tua* gerontologist.
- *pendidik* pedagogist. - *penduduk* demographer. - *pengamat telapak tangan* palmist. - *penggunaan tanah* soil scientist. - *pengobatan kaki* pedicurist. - *pengukuran kapal* admeasurer (of ship). - *penjinak bom* demolition (,bomb disposal) expert.
- *penjualan* sales manager. - *penyakit dlm* internist. - *penyakit kulit* dermatologist. - *penyakit telinga, hidung dan tenggorokan* (s.) THT. - *penyakit tumbuh.tumbuhan* phytopathologist, plant pathologist. - *perancang mode* dress designer. - *perbendaharaan* treasury accountant. - *perhotelan/ perestoranan* hotel/restaurant manager.
- *perpustakaan* librarian. - *peta* surveyor. - *petilasan* archaeologist.
- *pisah* analyst. - *politik* politician.
- *praja* administrative officer. - *purbakala* archaeologist. - *racun* toxicologist. - *radio* radioman. - *radiologi* radiologist. - *resensi* bookreviewer, critic - *röntgen* X-ray specialist.
- *ruang angkasa* space scientist. - *rumah* the family. - *sanggul* hairstylist.
- *sejarah* historian. - *senipidato* elocutionist. - *serangga* entomologist. - *sinologi* sinologist. - *sosiologi* sociologist. - *statistik* statistician. - *strategi* strategist. - *sulap* magician. - *tas(s)awuf* mystic. - *tehnik* technician. - *teknologi* technologist. - *teori* theoretician. - *terapi* therapist. - *tulisan kode* code expert. - *tulisan.tulisan kuno* epigrapher. - *tulisan tangan* graph-

ologist. - *ukur (tanah)* surveyor. - *urusan karyawan* personnel manager. – *urut* masseur. – *varuna* hydrographer. – *venereologi* venereologist.

ai I (personal pronoun).

a.i. (s.) AD INTERIM.

ainul yakin completely convinced.

air *tdk lalu* - watertight. - *matanya dilepasnya sepuas.puasnya* to weep o.s. out. *itu hanya - mentah* (fig.) that doesn't amount to much. *spt - soda* (fig.) short-lived enthusiasm. - *kali tdk selamanya banjir* life is not all beer and skittles. - *laut siapa yg garamin* selfpraise is no recommendation. - *susu dibalas dgn - tuba* return good for evil. *ada - ada ikan* o. can find means of subsistence in every country. - *beriak tanda tak dalam, berguncang tanda tak penuh* the empty vessel makes the greatest sound. - *diminum rasa duri* listless, spiritless, powerless. - *tenang menghanyutkan* still waters run deep. - *cucuran atap jatuhnya ke pelimbahan juga* like father, like son. *bagai - titik ke batu* cast pearls before swine. *bagai - jatuh ke pasir* it is like pouring water into a sieve, it is like wasting powder and shot. *bagai membandarkan - ke bukit* perform a Sisyphean labor. *menepuk - di dulang* it is an ill bird that fouls its own nest. *sambil menyelam minum* - killing two birds with o. stone. *sauk - mandikan diri* (fig.) stand on o's own legs. *spt - basuh* obtainable in abundance. *tak - talang dipancung (peluh diurut, hujan ditampung)* do o's utmost to obtain o's purpose. **per-an:** ~ *kepulauan* archipelagic waters. ~ *pedalaman* inland waters. **ter-i** to be irrigated. *banyak* –*nya* juicy. - *alur* wake (of ship). - *asin* brine. - *baptisan* baptismal water. - *bocor* oozing water. - *busi* water in a battery. - *daging* beef broth. - *garam* brine. - *gula* molasses. - *matang* boiled water. - *pendingin* coolant. - *pengadem* 'cooled water,' believed to make s.o. invulnerable. -.*peng–an* irrigation water. - *putih* boiled water. - *tapisan* filtrate. - *yg dipindahkan* displaced water.

Aisyiah and **Aisyiyah** the women's branch of the modernist, orthodox but reformist Moslem cultural organization *Muhammadiyah.*

aja (pron. ojo) don't. - *dumeh* don't get on your high horse just because you...

ajab astonishment.

ajaib wonderful, strange. - *di atas* - it was a miracle that. **ke-an** remarkableness, curiosity.

ajak I **meng–** to invite (to go with s.o.).

ajak II k.o. half-wild dog.

ajal - *samar* sudden death.

ajang place, site.

ajar I *sesudah tamat* **bel-** on graduation. **dibel-kan** to be taught. *Iwa Tirta berpendapat bhw anak.anak sebaiknya sejak kecil* ~ *menari,* Iwan Tirta is of the opinion that it is best that children be taught dancing from childhood on. **keterpel-an** intellectualism. **pel-** secondary (,high) school student. *Departemen* **Pemel-an** *ttg Indonesia dan Malaysia* Department of Indonesian and Malaysian Studies (in Australia). **–an** 1 warning. 2 dogma. *Dia tak makan* ~, He never learns. ~ *hidup* biology. ~ *kejadian dunia (,alam)* cosmogony. ~ *kesatuan (,serba tunggal)* monism. ~ *tujuan* teleology.

ajar II hermit, recluse.

ajeg 1 invariable, constant, steady, stable. 2 regular. *memeriksa dgn* - to check regularly. **ke-an** regularity.

ajèr to melt, dissolve; (s.) AJUR(.AJER).

aji I 1 incantation. 2 secret formulas. - *gineng* knowledge (,science) of sexual techniques. –**an** (s.) AJI I.

aji II - *mumpung* and *ng– pumpung* to avail o.s. of an opportunity, give free rein to o's passions. –*ning saliro soko busono* the fine coat makes the fine gentlemen; fine feathers make fine birds.

Aji No Moto M.S.G.

Ajisaka King Saka, an ancient monarch

alleged to have invented the Javanese calendar and alphabet.

ajnas miscellanies, sorts. *tuhfatul.-* (epistolary) the letter and the gifts which theoretically accompany it.

ajojing modern western dances. **ber-** to perform modern western dances.

ajubila (s.) AUDZUBILLAH.

ajuk meng- 1 to take soundings. 2 to gauge, probe.

ajur pulverized, crushed. *mundur kita -, mandeg kita ambleg* retreat is defeat. *-.ajer* to assimilate.

akadémisi alumni.

akal *masuk (,lintas ,lulus ,sampai) -* and *masuk di -* logical, acceptable. *kurang masuk -* inadmissible, unacceptable. *dlm waktu tak masuk -* in the incredible amount of time of. *- tak sekali tiba* Rome was not built in a day. *bertukar (,berubah) -* to lose o's mind. *banyak - yg buruk* crafty. *banyaknya -* inventiveness. *panjang -* crafty, tricky. *-.-an* invention, fabrication. *- busuk (,geladak)* a dirty trick. *- waras* common sense.

AKAN [Antar.Kerja Antar.Negara] 'International Interlabor.' **di-.kan** to be sent abroad to work (referring) to Indonesians who are going to work in Iran, Saudi Arabia, etc.).

akang 1 (older) brother. 2 term of address for husband.

akar form of reference for snake (in superstitious awe and veneration). *Sangat dlm* **ber-** *keyakinan itu, bhw ...,* So deeply rooted was the conviction that ... - *wangi* lavender.

akasia acacia.

akaunting accounting.

akèw Chinese lad.

akh just, in a word, in short, briefly. *Tubuhnya semampai. Giginya putih bersih. A-, menarik sekali.* She's slender. Her teeth are snow white. In a word, she's most attractive.

akhir ber- to finish, terminate, expire. *~ minggu (,pekan)* to spend the week-

end. **ber-kan** to wind up with. **meng-i** *masa bujangnya* to give up o's bachelorhood. **ter-** lately, recently. *-.-nya* in the course of time. *- kelaknya* sooner or later. *- minggu panjang* a long weekend. *- pekan* weekend.

akhli (s.) AHLI. *- penuh* postgraduate.

akibat effect, outcome. *-.- besar* far-reaching consequences. *sebab dan -* cause and effect. *sbg -* in consequence of, as a result of. **ber- jauh** to have far-reaching consequences. **ber-kan** to result in. **meng-kan** to have a certain effect. *pd -nya hanyalah satu* it comes to the same thing, it works out the same in the end. *- pengaruh* impact. *- sampingan* side effect.

akliah rational.

akonting accounting.

akor I (s.) AKUR.

akor II [anti korupsi] anticorruption. *kampanye -* anticorruption campaign.

akordion accordion.

akostik acoustics.

Akrab Scorpio.

akrédit meng-kan to accredit.

akrobat acrobat.

akrobatik acrobatics.

akromat achromate.

akronim acronym. *Surat Keputusan Penyerahan Perkara* **di.-kan** *menjadi SKEPPERA,* Surat Keputusan Penyerahan Perkara is acronimized as SKEPPERA.

aksa far off, remote. *masjid al.-* the remotest mosque, i.e. the mosque in Jerusalem.

aksara 1 script. 2 symbol, emblem. *- baur* monogram. *- Cina (,Tionghoa)* Chinese characters.

aksarawan literate (masc.).

aksarawati literate (fem.).

aksélerasi acceleration. **meng-** to accelerate.

aksèn stress.

aksèntuasi accentuation. **di-** to be emphasized.

aksèptabel acceptable.

aksèptan acceptor (of *aksep*).

aksèptasi acceptance.

aksi I anything undertaken to win a demand. - *ambalela* passive resistance. - *keong (,lambat kerja)* work slowdown. - *sefihak (,sepihak)* unilateral action. - *penerbangan (,udara)* flight activity.

aksi II chic, stylish. *buang (,pasang)* - to show off, make a show. *membuat* - to act in a play. **-nya** *saja!* showoff!

aksial axial.

aktentas *pengusaha* - a fake enterpriser. *perusahaan pelayaran* - a shipyard having a license to operate but not in possession of the necessary equipment to operate such a yard, a nominal (,fake) shipyard.

aktif *tak* - inactive. **ke-an** (and **keaktivan**) activity. **meng-kan** to activate. **peng-an** activation. *zat* ~ activator (a catalyst).

aktifis (s.) AKTIVIS.

akting (temporarily taking over the duties of s.o. else) acting. **ber-** to act (i.e. to perform on the stage). - *ketua* acting chairman.

aktiva assets.

aktivis (of the PKI, etc.) activist.

aktor - *intelèktual* 'moving spirit,' instigator.

aktuariil actuarial.

aktuaris actuary.

aku I *Sang A-* Ego. **meng-.-** to claim to be. **ng-nyè** so he claims. **peng-** confessor. **peng-an** testimony, evidence. ~ *dosa* (Roman Catholic) confession. ~ *iman* (Protestant) creed. ~ *penerimaan* acknowledgement of receipt. - *yg kedua* my alter ego.

aku II (s.) AKI.

akuaduk aquaduct.

akuarèl aquarelle.

akuarium aquarium.

akuisisi acquisition.

akuisme cult of the personality.

akumulasi accumulation.

akumulatif accumulative.

akumulator accumulator. - *kalor* heat accumulator.

akuntan - *publik* public accountant. - *swasta* private accountant (not work-ing for the government).

akunting accounting. - *manajemen* managerial accounting.

akupunktur acupuncture.

akupunkturis acupuncturist.

akur ke-an agreement. **meng-kan** *arloji* to set a watch right.

akurat accurate. **ke-an** accuracy.

akustik acoustics.

akut acute, critical.

akwal words (opp. deeds).

akwarèl aquarelle.

ala I 1 to. 2 in, on, upon. 3 according to. - *bisa* whatever is possible. - *kadarnya* 1 according to ability. 2 what is available. 3 modestly. 4 sufficient, appropriate. 5 bribe. *dan lain.lain* - *kadarnya* and other things as fit. - *sebentar* for a moment, for a short time.

ala II in the...style.

alabangka crowbar.

alaf one thousand.

alah I oh! hey!

alah II 1 subjected. 2 to succumb. - *bisa oleh biasa* theory is worsted by practice. - *kpd* to be susceptible to (a disease).

alam I *Syah A-* Lord of the Earth. - *dongeng* the realm of fables. - *haiwanah* the animal kingdom. - *kabir* macrocosm. - *kanak.kanak* the juvenile world. - *nabatah* the vegetable kingdom. - *pikiran* philosophy, way of thinking. - *raya* cosmos. *(restoran)* - *terbuka* open-air (restaurant).

alam II know. *wa Allahu* - and God knows best.

alam III flag, standard.

alamat I signal, mark. *dgn* - in care of, c/o. *Jika tdk sampai kpd -nya minta dikembalikan kpd... ,* in case of nondelivery please return to... *buku* - directory. - *darurat* address in case of need. - *kawat* cable address. - *samaran* cover address. - *surat* 1 the address on an envelope. 2 inscription.

alamat II ng- omen, augury.

alap ng- *berkah* to request prayers and

blessings for success.

alaram alarm.

alas -an excuse, alibi. - *kaki* footwear, shoes, foot covering.

alat I 1 equipment. 2 apparatus, appliance. 3 utensils. 4 organ, medium (of information). 5 means. 6 agency (of government). **per-an** ordnance. - *bagian* part (of a machine). - *bakar* caustic. - *bantu* 1 aid. 2 accessories. 3 auxiliary apparatus. - *bayar* means of payment, currency. -.- *berikut* accessories. - *bernafas* respiratory organs. -.- *besar* heavy equipment. - *bicara* organ of speech. - *bunyi.bunyian* musical instrument. -.- *cerna* digestive organs. - *cukur* shaving equipment. - *deteksi* 1 detector. 2 'sniffer' (for airplane passengers). - *elektronik* electronic device. - *hias* toilet articles. - *hias tutup dinding* wainscoting. -.- *hubungan semesta* mass communications media. - *indria* sense organ. -.- *kecantikan* cosmetics. -.- *kedokteran* medical equipment. - *kekuasaan* machinery of power. - *kelamin* sex organ. -.- *kelengkapan* organs (of State). - *kemudi* steering gear. -.- *keperluan* necessaries. - *kontrol* (means of) check. - *likwide* liquid assets. - *masak* kitchen utensils. -.- *mesin* mechanized equipment. -.- *mobil* car tools. - *musik petik* stringed instrument. - *musik tiup* wind instrument. - *napas* respiratory organs. -.- *Negara* 1 State apparatus. 2 (in the U.S.) G-men. - *negara penegak hukum* law-enforcing agency. -.- *olahraga* sports (,sporting) goods. - *pacu jantung* pacemaker. - *peledak* explosive device. - *peluncur roket* rocket launcher. - *peluncar torpedo* torpedo tube. - *pemacu jantung* pacemaker. - *pemadam (busa)* (foam type) extinguisher. - *pemadam kebakaran* fire-extinguisher. - *pembantu* aid. - *pembantu instruksi* training aids. - *pembantu mendengar* hearing aid. -.- *pembayaran* 1 means of payment, money. 2 financial re-

sources. - *pembayaran sah* legal tender. - *pembesar* microscope. - *pembungkus* packing material. - *pemecah atom* atom smasher. - *pemerintah* governing authority. - *pemersatu* unifying instrument. - *pemodalan* means of financing. -.- *pemotong* cutlery. -.- *pemuat* cargo handling gear. - *pemutar kaset* cassette player. - *penakut* deterrent. - *pencari arah* direction finder. - *pencari ikan (elektronik)* (electronic) fishfinder. - *pencatat gempa (bumi)* seismograph. - *pencatat kebohongan* lie detector. - *pencatat kendaraan* traffic counter. - *pencatat radiasi* Geiger counter. - *pencuci baju otomatis* automatic washing machine. - *pendengar* listening device. *memasang* - *pendengar* to put on earphones. -.- *pendengaran* auditory organs. - *pendingin* freezer. - *penetas* incubator. - *pengaman* safety device. - *pengangkutan* means of transportation. - *pengatur hawa* air-conditioner. - *pengecap* organ of taste. - *pengering* desiccator. - *pengering baju otomatis* automatic dryer. - *penggali* excavator. - *penggempur atom* cyclotron. - *penggiling padi* rice milling unit. - *penghidu* olfactory organ. - *pengikat* binder. - *pengisap debu* vacuum cleaner. - *pengisi batu baterai* battery charger. - *penglihatan* organ of sight, visual organ. - *pengocok* shaker (for preparing cocktails). - *pengolah data* computer. - *pengontrol* (means of) check. - *penguat* amplifier. - *pengukur* measuring instrument. - *penulis* writing materials. - *penyejuk* air-conditioner. - *penyemprot gas mata* tear gas dispensing gun. - *penyulingan* destilator. - *peraba* tentacle. - *peraga anatomi* anatomic model. -.-*per-an* 1 supplies. 2 (mil.) equipment. -. *per-an kesatrian* (mil.) post equipment. - *perang* military equipment, war material. - *percepatan* accelerator. - *perekam (suara)* tape recorder. - *perekam penerbangan* flight recorder. - *perintis jalan* road

tracer. - *perjuangan* weapon. - *perkakas*
instruments, apparatus. - *pernapasan*
respiratory tract. - *persisi* precision
instrument. - *perum gema* echo sound-
er. - *pijat listrik* electric massager and
vibrator. - *pireng.pirsa* audio-visual
aids. - *potret* camera. -.- *produksi*
means of production, productive
resources. - *proyeksi* projector. - *rekat*
adhesive. - *revolusi* a tool of the
revolution. - *semir* lubricating apparatus. - *senjata* armament. - *serap* absor-
bing agent, absorption apparatus.
- *suling* distillation apparatus.
- *suntik* syringe. - *tenun* loom. - *tertib*
means of discipline. - *tiup* blowing
engine. - *tukar* medium of exchange.
- *vital* genitals.
alat II guest.
albas alabaster.
album album. - *sisipan* stock book
(for stamps).
albumen and **albumina** albumen.
aldubul *A- Akbar* Great Bear. *A- Asgar*
Lesser Bear, cynosure.
alégori allegory.
alégoris allegorical.
alem -an spoiled (of person).
alèrgi allergy.
alèrgis allergic. - *thd* allergic to.
alesduk neckerchief, scarf.
alfa alpha.
alfabèt alphabet.
Alfatékah the short prayer which precedes the Koran proper.
alf(u) thousand. *(Cerita) Alfa lailah wa
lailah* The 1001 Nights.
aliansi alliance. **ber-** allied.
alias otherwise named, nicknamed.
Alibaba 1 Ali Baba. 2 name for an
Indonesian who organizes a business
for foreign capitalists under the
cover of a national enterprise, front
man; (cp.) BABA.ALI.
alibi alibi. *memberi bukti ttg -nya*
to prove (,establish) an alibi.
alif first letter of the Arabic alphabet.
tegak berdiri sbg - bolt upright.
alifbata (the Arabic) alphabet.

alih ber- *haluan* to change o's tack,
switch to another subject. **meng-kan**
to distract. **meng- aksarakan** to transcribe. **meng- ba(ha)sakan** 1 to translate. 2 to interpret. **meng- ejakan**
to transcribe. **meng-hurufkan** *x menjadi
ks* to change the (letter) x into (the
letters) ks. **meng- kapalkan** to tranship.
meng- tugaskan 1 to send s.o. on a
tour of duty. 2 to transfer s.o. (from
military to civilian duties). **peng-
bahasa** translator. **peng- bahasaan**
translation. **peng-kapalan** transhipment. - *bahasa* 1 translator. 2 interpreter. - *kapal* transhipment. - *tugas*
1 tour of duty. 2 transfer.
alimèntasi alimentation, alimony.
alinéa paragraph.
alir *daerah* **peng-an** *sungai* catchment
area. **-an** *kebatinan* contemporary
mystical groups (,sects) practising
kebatinan mysticism.
aliterasi alliteration.
Aliyah (s.) SEKOLAH (ALIYAH).
Aljasair Algiers.
alkitabiyah biblical.
alkohol alcohol. *minuman tak* **ber-**
nonalcoholic beverages.
Alkus Sagittarius.
Allah - *subhanahu (wa taala)* God be
praised (and Most High). *-hu Alam*
God knows best. *-humma* O God!
all in everything included.
almalun the damned.
almarhum the deceased. **di-kan** to be put
to rest (as of business).
almari - *arsip* filing cabinet.
alokasi **meng-kan** to allocate. **peng-an**
allocation.
alokir meng- (s.) MENGALOKASIKAN.
alon.alon slow. - *asal kelakon* slow but
sure. - *tapi mantap* slow but steady.
alot difficult. *penyebaran modal asing
ke luar Jawa tetap* - the distribution of
foreign capital to the areas outside
Java remains difficult.
alpukan initiative.
altruis altruist.
altruisme altruism

Altur Taurus.

alup meng- to predict bad luck through sound (of howling dog). **meng-i** to lament over.

alur I - *laut* sea lane.

alur II plot (of a novel, etc.).

aluwung preferable.

am ...*-nya* ...*khasnya* ...in general ...in particular.

amai.amai - *panggaleh* retailers.

amaliah (adj.) charity.

aman meng-kan 1 to render harmless, apprehend. 2 (euph.) to imprison. ~ *senjata (api)* to release the safety catch.

amanat trust (territory). *A- Negara* State-of-the-Union-Message.

amandemèn (S.) AMENDEMEN.

amang meng-kan to threaten (with a weapon).

amantu bilahi I believe in God.

amar (jur.) dictum.- *ma'ruf nahi mungkar* the do's and don'ts. *melakukan - ma'ruf nahi mungkar* to expound what is correct and reject what is wrong. **-an** warning.

amat meng-.-i *terus.menerus* to put under continuous surveillance. **peng-** *Cina* China watcher. **peng-an** surveillance.

amatir *pemain* - nonprofessional player. *radio* - ham, amateur radio operator. **-an** amateurish.

amatirisme amateurism.

am.atman a man who has no self.

ambalan unit in the *Pramuka* Boy Scout Movement.

ambang *di - pintu* at hand. *berada di -...* to be about to..., be on the point of ...-ing.

ambaru campshed(ding), sheet piling.

ambasador ambassador.

ambata.rubuh in a body. *bersorak.sorai -* to applaud in a body.

ambeg I and **ambek** *-.parama.arta* and *-.paramarta* the ability to put important things first. **di-.paramaartakan** to be given (top) priority to. **peng-.para-maartaan** sense of priority.

ambeg II peng- moneylender.

ambèien hemorrhoids.

ambek (s.) AMBEG I.

amben abdominal belt, belly-belt (of horse).

ambèn couch (made of bamboo).

amber *batu* - amber.

amberuk (s.) AMBRUK.

ambet binder, bandage.

ambil *tdk - perhatian dgn* to pay no attention to. *ia tiada (mau) - tahu akan* he does not care a bit about. **meng-:** ~ *alih* to expropriate. ~ *bandingan ke* referring to, revert to. ~ *foto* to take a picture. ~ *gusar* to resent. *Disertasi itu* ~ *140 halaman,* The dissertation takes up 140 pages. ~ *hatl* 1 attractive. 2 to captivate. ~ *hawa sejuk* to take the air. ~ *ijazah* to obtain a diploma. ~ *ingatan* to pay attention to. ~ *jalan* 1 (to go) via. 2 (fig.) to take a course. ~ *kesempatan* to seize (,take ,avail o.s. of) the opportunity. ~ *ke-simpulan* to conclude. ~ *kias* to draw an analogy. ~ *langkah.langkah mundur* to retreat. ~ *muka* to flatter. ~ *nyawa* to kill. ~ *paedah dr* to profit (,benefit) by, take advantage of. ~ *panjang* to take the matter up. ~ *peduli* to pay attention to. ~ *per-bandingan dr* to learn a lesson from. ~ *posisi* to make a stand (against). ~ *putusan* to make a decision, decide. ~ *sikap* to strike an attitude. *dgn* ~ *tempat di* (by establishing its offices) in. ~ *tikungan tajam* to take a sharp turn. **-.meng-** to intermarry. **peng-:** ~ *inisiatip* initiator, promotor. ~ *ke putusan* decision maker. **peng-an:** ~ *alih* taking over. ~ *foto* 1 picture taking. 2 film shooting. ~ *keputusan* decision making. ~.~ *Pemerintah* (banking term) Government drawings. **ter-** *dr* derived from.

ambing (S.) OMBANG.AMBING.

ambisi ambition. **ber-** to have ambitions, be ambitious.

ambisius ambitious.

ambiya prophets.

ambleg to collapse.

ambreng.ambrengan strong-scented.

ambrin exhausted.

ambrol to break in two, break up, collapse.

ambruk to fall through, break down, fail. **ke-an** collapse, (down)fall.

ambulan(s) ambulance.

ambung *kehilangan daya* - (in aviation) to stall.

ambyar to fall apart.

ambyuk to swarm, flock.

amèn I ng- persistently.

amèn II (ng)- to go from house-to-house in order to give a (street) performance. *tukang* - and **peng-** street musician, k.o. troubadour.

Amérika the United States. **Ke.-.-an** Americanism. - *Latin* Latin America. - *Sentral (,Tengah)* Central America.

Amérikanisasi Americanization. **meng-kan** to Americanize.

Amérikanisme Americanism.

amfibi amphibious.

amful (s.) AMPUL.

amien (S.) AMIN.

amko k.o. *opelet.*

amma ba'dahu and furthermore, after that, and then (used in correspondence and speeches).

amoh in rags, worn out.

amoi Chinese gal.

amok (s.) AMUK.

among tani 1 countryman. 2 farmer.

amonia(k) ammonia.

Amor Cupid.

amoral amoral.

amorf amorphous.

amortisasi amortization. **meng-kan** to amortize.

ampang (Batak) large basket.

ampas - *buangan* waste product.

ampat (S.) EMPAT. *si A-* a rice variety, such as, *PB 5, PB 8,* etc.

Ampera [Amanat Penderitaan Rakyat] Message of the People's Sufferings (under President Soekarno).

ampir -an stopping off place.

ampitéater amphitheater.

amplasemèn 1 emplacement. 2 yard.

- *kereta api* railway yard. - *langsir* shunting yard.

amplop 1 envelope. 2 bribe. *penyakit -* bribery. **meng-kan** and **ng-in** to put in an envelope.

ampo edible earth.

amprok - *sama* to meet (accidentally).

amprung.amprungan to run away head over heels.

ampu *ditaruh di bawah* **peng-an** to be placed under guardianship.

ampuh effective.

ampul ampule.

ampun 1 grace. 2 excuse. *minta -* 1 to ask forgiveness. 2 have mercy (beggar's cry). *baunya minta -!* the smell is terrible! *tanpa -* mercilessly. **ke-an** *dosa* absolution. **-an** *umum* general pardon.

amput di-! darn!

amputasi meng- to amputate.

amra hog-plum (L. Spondias mangifera).

amuba amoeba.

amuk amuck. *Brebes* **di-** *lindu,* Brebes was swept over by an earthquake. **-an** *angin topan* raging storm.

ana I (personal pronoun).

anak I **ber-:** ~ *penak (,pinak)* 1 to have descendants. *Almarhum sementara itu tlh ~ penak, bercucu dan bercicit yg kini jumlahnya meliputi 72 keluarga,* In the meantime, the deceased has descendants, grandchildren and great-grandchildren, now amounting to 72 families. 2 to mount up (to). *Harga ini tiba.tiba ~ pinak menjadi Rp. 2.000,-,* All of a sudden, the price mounted up (or, was jacked up) to Rp. 2,000.00. **meng-.emaskan** to favor. **peng-tirian** treatment in a stepmotherly fashion. *Jawi* **per-an** Keling (,Tamil) born in Malacca. - *air* rivulet, mountain-river (brook). - *ajaib* prodigy. - *alamiah* 'natural child,' (euph.) illegitimate child. - *asuhan* trainee. - *bawang* figurehead. - *bayi* infant in arms. - *belasan th* teenager. - *bendungan* cofferdam. - *bengal* rascal, scoundrel. - *benua* subcontinent. - *bermasalah*

a problem child. - *brandal* rascal,
scoundrel. - *buah* 1 subordinate.
2 personnel, staff. - *buangan* foundling.
- *cangkokan* adopted child. - *corot* a
child born to elderly parents. - *cucu*
descendants. *A- Dalam* the new name
for the Kubus, a primitive and animistic
tribe, living scattered in the interior
of the border areas of Palembang and
Jambi. - *dara tua* old maid. - *dayung*
oar. - *didik* student. - *gedana.gedini*
child having brothers and sisters.
- *gobek* betelnut pounder. - *gundik*
child of a secondary wife. - *ingusan*
whipper-snapper. - *jari* finger. - *jenjang*
ladder step. - *kembar lima* quintuplets.
- *kembar Siam* Siamese twins. - *keparat*
accursed child. - *kolong* 1 illegitimate
child. 2 bum living under bridges
(in Jakarta). - *kompeni* (col.) soldier.
- *kota* satellite town. - *kukut* foster
child. - *luar kawin* illegitimate child.
- *mas* 1 teacher's pet. 2 favored person.
- *menengah* the second of three
children. - *ontang.anting* only child
(without brothers and sisters). - *partai*
affiliate (of political party). - *penak*
(,pinak) (s.) BERANAK PENAK
(,PINAK). - *perusahaan* branch office.
- *pesawat terbang* aircrew. -.- *pidak*
pedarakan the downtrodden, ignorant.
- *polah, bapak kepradah* if a child misbe-
haves, his father (,parents) is (,are) to
blame. - *pri(y)a* son. -.- *(yg) putus.*
sekolah dropouts. - *rakyat* child of
common people. - *saudara* 1 nephew.
2 cousin. - *singiang* imp, little devil.
- *sulur* offshoot. - *tuna sosial* juvenile
delinquent. - *wanita* daughter. - *wayang*
member of stage cast. - *yatim piatu*
orphan. - *yg berangkat besar* teenager.
- *yg disahkan* legitimized child. - *yg*
lahir dr perkawinan yg sah legitimate
child. - *yg lahir di luar perkawinan yg sah*
illegitimate child. - *yg lahir di luar*
nikah (,kawin) child born out of wedlock.
Anak II - *Agung* (in Bali) title used by
the male members of the Brahmanic

caste preceding personal names,
e.g. *Anak Agung Gde Agung.*
anarkis and **anarsis** anarchist.
anastési (s.) ANESTESI.
anatomi anatomy.
ancak offerings of food placed in a
basket for evil spirit. *membuang -*
to make such offerings.
ancam *di bawah* -**an** under duress.
ancang.ancang 1 first steps, introduction.
2 preparations.
ancer **di-**.- *saja antara th 1830-1860* just
put (,mark) it (i.e. the foundation of
the town of Labuhan Deli, Medan)
between 1830 and 1860. **di-**.-**kan** *pd*
tgl 17 Juni targeted for June 17.
-.- target, main outline. *harga* ~
pilot price. *tgl* ~ target date.
ancoa strong curse word: dammit!
ancok a large crossnet.
ancuk **di-** fuck you! fuck it! **ng-** to fuck.
andai **ber-**.- 1 to seek the opinion of.
2 to take for granted. **peng-an** (gramm.)
conditional. **per-an** assumption. -**nya**
suppose that.
andal **ke-an** reliability. *orang* -**an**
confidant.
andalan (in the *Pramuka* Boy Scout
Movement) a commissioner.
andap and **andhap** - *asor* humble (and
courteous).
andarah anaemia.
anderok slip (article of clothing).
andika you.
andil *mempunyai (,memiliki)* - *dlm*
to have a share in.
andok and **andhok** to hang out.
anè (s.) ANA.
anèh remarkable, noteworthy. - *di balik* -
most remarkable. - *tak* -, *heran tak*
heran it seems conflicting. -**nya** *ialah...*
the strange part of it is...
anéka **ber-.warna** assorted, variegated.
ke-an diversification. **meng-.jeniskan** to
diversify. **peng-.ragaman** diversification. - *macam* miscellaneous, assorted.
- *usaha tani* mixed farming. - *warna*
1 miscellaneous, assorted. 2 news
items.

anèkdot(e) anecdote.

anèksasi annexation. meng-(kan) to annex.

anémon anemone.

anèstési(a) anesthesia.

angan.angan: *dlm - saja* fictitious, illusory. *menjadi - saja* it remained an unfulfilled desire.

angat (s.) HANGAT. -.- *tahi ayam* short-lived enthusiasm.

angèk (s.) ANGAT. -.- *tahi ayam* (s.) ANGAT(.ANGAT TAHI AYAM).

angèl difficult. *gampang.gampang - kok* seems easy but it's hard.

Angelsaksis Anglo-Saxon.

anget (s.) ANGAT.

angga antler.

anggap di-: *nggak* ~ to be of little account, don't count for much. *Kalau nggak punya mobil, nggak ~,* Without a car, you don't count for much. *dlm* -an in imagination.

anggar I 1 hangar (for aircraft). 2 quay, wharf, shed.

anggar II ber- *pena* to be engaged in a paper war.

anggar III meng-kan to budget. per-an budgeting. -an committed (,earmarked) funds. *A~ Dasar* Articles of Association. *mata ~ yg menghabiskan uang* an item of loss (in a budget).

anggauta s. ANGGOTA. - *pencinta* supporter-member (of the outlawed PKI), next to the ordinary *anggauta* (member) and *calon anggauta* (aspirant member).

anggerèk (S.) ANGGREK.

anggit -an idea.

Anggorokasih Tuesday *Kliwon.*

anggota ber-kan to consist of ...members. *komisi yg ~ 40 orang* a 40-member committee. *Pesawat terbang itu anak buahnya ~ 5 orang,* The plane had a five-man crew. di-.-.pramuka.kan to be made a member of the *Pramuka* Boy Scout Movement. *Berapa* -nya? What's the membership? - *Dewan Harian Kotapraja* alderman. - *erpekad* a commando. - *gelap* a non-card carrying member. - *gerombolan* gangster.

- *keluarga* member of the family.
- *Kongres* (U.S.) Congressman. - *parlemen biasa* backbencher. - *pengganti* alternate. - *pengurus* board member, member of the committee. - *peserta* associate member. - *Senat* (U.S.) Senator. - *serikat buruh* unionist. - *tentara* soldier. - *tdk penuh* associate member.

anggrèk peng-an orchid raising.

anggrèkwan orchid grower.

anggu set. - *ungkapan* set of expressions.

angguk *menurut - kuda* to post (on a horse). meng- mengiyakan to nod affirmatively. *si* - the yes man.

anggup.anggip to nod.

anggur ng- 1 to be at loose ends. 2 idle, inactive. peng-an *terselubung (,tak kentara)* disguised unemployment.

angin *dpt* - there are indications. *tak dpt* - 1 to get no chance to. 2 to get the worst of it. *kagak hujan kagak -* and *nggak hujan nggak -* out of the clear blue sky. *ke mana - yg deras, ke situ condongnya* he will turn with every wind that blows. *menjalar ke seluruh penjuru -* to spread to all directions. ber- airy. *tlh ~* there are indications. ter-.- *ke telinga* to have come to o's attention. -.-an whimsical, fickle. *blm juga aku mendengar -.-nya* I have not heard a thing about it yet. - *kuat tiba.tiba* a gust. - *lesus* whirlwind, gale. - *semilir* soft blowing breeze. - *sepoi.sepoi basa* a soft breeze.

angkara ke-an 1 avarice. 2 rudeness.

angkasa meng- to take off.

angkasawan 1 (male) astronaut. 2 radio announcer.

angkasawati 1 woman astronaut. 2 female radio announcer.

angkat di- *dr* to be adapted from (a novel, etc.). meng-: *~ anak* to adopt a child. *~ ibu jari* to raise o's thumb. *~ langkah seribu* to run away. *~ muka* to look up. *~ tilpon* to pick up the 'phone. pember-an departure. *pelabuhan ~* port of dispatch. peng-an adoption (of a child). *~ bis* letter collection. *~ kerangka kapal* salvage. se-an of the same

generation. -an: *A~ Angkasawan* Air
Force. *A~ Bahari* Navy. *A~ Bersen-
jata* Armed Forces. *A~ Bhumiyam*
Army. *A~ Darat* Army. *A~ Kepolisian* Police Force. *~ kerja* work force.
A~ Perang Combat Forces. *- gelas* to
toast. *- kaki* to leave. *- koper* (fig.)
to (pack up and) clear out, make o.s.
scarce.

angker 1 dangerous. 2 holy, sacred.
3 inhabited by demons. 4 (adj.) ghost.
tempat yg - a haunted site. 5 forbid-
ding, unapproachable.

angkrèk (S.) ANGGREK.

angkring(an) a long pole carried hori-
zontally on o. shoulder with carrying
baskets at either end of the pole; (S.)
PIKUL(AN).

angkul.angkul yoke.

angku palo (in West Sumatra) village
head.

angkut *-an jenis IV* motor vehicles
comprising *minicars, bajajs, helicaks*
and *bemos.*

angler I 1 finished. 2 to finish.

angler II quiet, tranquil.

Anglikan Anglican.

Anglir Mendung name of a dance performed by four girls.

Anglisisme Anglicism.

anglo *- list(e)rik* 1 electric stove. 2 hot
plate.

anglong ng- (to talk) confusedly.

angop 1 a yawn. 2 to yawn.

angot 1 recurring. 2 to recur. 3 to
skyrocket. *-.-an* recurrent.

angpau alms, present.

angsana and **angséna** the ansenna tree
(L. Pterocarpus indica).

angsu meng- to gain knowledge.

angsur *-an pertama* down payment.

angus *- hati* 1 angry. 2 yearning.
-.- hati hendak ... to be eager to...

anhidrit anhydride.

anilin aniline.

anim [(from the Dutch) *ANIEM:*
Algemeene Nederlandsch-Indische
Electriciteits Maatschappij 'General
Netherlands Indies Electric Company']

1 electric company. 2 electricity.

animisma and **animisme** animism.

animo gusto, zest.

anjak ber-: *~ dr kursinya* to get up
from o's chair. *Hari memang sdh
~ malam,* Evening is closing in.
~ pulang to get ready to go home.
~ tua to get old.

anjang to visit s.o. **ber-:** *~ karya* to
make a field trip. *~ sana* to tour (an
area), make a tour of inspection.
- karya field trip. *- sana inspeksi*
inspection tour.

Anjiman *kapal -* an East Indiaman
(ship).

anjing I dog (as a term of abuse). *hidup
spt - dgn kucing* to be at e.o.'s throats,
bicker all the time. *bagai - beranak
enam* to be all skin and bones. *- biri.biri*
sheep dog. *- herder (,gembala Jerman)*
German shepherd dog. *- Nica* a running
dog of the *Nica. - pelacak* bloodhound.
- pembiak dog for breeding purposes.
- pembimbing tunanetra seeing-eye
dog. *- pengawal* guard dog. *- penjaga*
watchdog. *- perempuan* bitch. *- trah*
pedigree dog. *- tutul* Dalmatian.

anjing II *-.-* tree with edible fruit (L.
Cynometra cauliflora).

anjir (in Kalimantan) primary canal in
irrigation system.

anjlog and **anjlok** to go down, fall.
- dr rel to derail.

anjung *-an* platform (in airport).

annèmer (S.) ANEMER.

ano hesitation word when you can't
think of what to say; (s.) ANU.
Siapa yg - memukulnya? Who, er,
hit him? *Pak A-* Mr. What's-His-Name.
di-kan it was erred. **-nya** its er.

anoa a wild cow species found in the
Southern Celebes.

anoda anode.

anom 1 young 2 vice-. *bupati -* vice-
regent. *raja (,parabu) -* vice-roy.

anomali anomaly.

Anoman name of the (white) monkey
from the *Ramayana* epic.

anonim anonymous.

anonimitèt anonymity.
anonser announcer.
anorganik inorganic.
ansambel ensemble.
ansar helpers; the first converts to Islam.
ansor (s.) ANSAR.
ansyovis *(ikan)* - anchovy.
antah.berantah (S.) NEGERI(ANTAH. BERANTAH).
antali marble.
antamir meng- to take (the matter) up.
antan - *patah lesung hilang* it never rains but it pours; misfortunes never come alone; one misfortune rides on the back of another.
antar I meng-kan *tamu ke pintu* to show a guest to the door. peng- convoy. ~ *kata* preface. *tak* ter- undeliverable (of mail).
antar II di-.negarakan to be shipped between certain countries (esp. Indonesia, Malaysia and Singapore). di-. pulaukan to be transported from o. island to another. -.*angkatan* inter-service. -.*golongan* intergroup. -.*ilmu* interdisciplinary. -.*nasabah* correlation.
antara - *ada dgn tiada* hardly, barely. *blm* ber- *lama* not long after. memer-i (from *perantara*) and memper-i to act as mediator for, mediate. per-an: *dgn* ~ through (the intermediary of). *memberi* ~ *utk* to act as an intermediary for. - *lain.lain* among other things.
antariksa atmosphere.
antariksawan astronaut.
antariksawati woman astronaut.
antawacana and antawecana dialog.
anteb (S.) ANTEP.
antèk stooge, henchman, accomplice, running dog.
antem a blow with the fist; (S.) HANTAM. ber- to have a fistfight; (S.) BERHANTAM.
antèna antenna, aerial. - *menjadi satu dgn kaca depan* windshield antenna. - *tivi* TV antenna.
antèr.antèr very calm (,quiet).

anteré and anteri (s.) ANTRE.
anterpo entrepôt.
anti. 1 non-. 2 to be against. *Beliau - pd ketidakadilan,* He is against injustice. *Gerakan A- Kebodohan* (abbrev. GAK) Movement Against Ignorance (1977).
anti.gendut non-fattening.
anti.gorèsan scratch-resistant.
antik meng-kan to antique.
antisipasi anticipation. meng-(kan) to anticipate.
anti.trus antitrust.
antologi anthology.
antop belching.
antrasit anthracite.
antré (s.) ANTRI. -an waiting in line.
antreprenur entrepreneur.
antri (s.) ANTRE. ng- to stand in line, queue up. ~ *lift* to stand in line to get in the elevator. -an *panjang menunggu droping bensin dr Jakarta* a long line was waiting for the gas allocation from Jakarta.
antropologi anthropology. - *budaya* cultural anthropology.
antuk sting (of insect). *sdh* ter- *baru tengadah (,menengadah)* shut the stabledoor after the horse has been stolen.
antun *orang* - dude.
Antwèrpen Antwerp.
anu 1 such-and-such. *di kampung* - in such-and-such village. 2 a word to indicate a thing or person the name of which has slipped o's memory at the moment of speaking or which o. does not want to mention, what-you-may-call-it. -nya (euph.) his testicles.
anumert(h)a posthumous.
anut peng-: ~ *garis.keras* hardliner. ~ *politik bebas* neutralist. - *grubyuk* to follow others blindly.
anyep 1 cold. 2 tasteless.
anyes 1 cool. 2 cold (of water, in *kendi*).
anyir tasting (,smelling) of train oil.
apa what (k.o.) thing? to do what? *Hari - sekarang?* What day is it today? - *namanya (,itu)?* what-do-you-call-'em (,it)? *Saudara lagi -?* What are you

doing? *Saudara sakit -?* What's wrong with you? *Perlunya -?* 1 What do you want? 2 What's it for? *Mau -?* 1 What do you want? 2 (kids, while fighting) Come on, I challenge you. *Anak itu -mu?* What relation are you to that child? *bukan karena - melainkan...* simply and solely for.. *tdk (,tak) -(lah)!* it does not matter! never mind! *Wah, kok membeli buku Inggeris -!* Goodness, why have you gone through all the trouble to buy an English book! *Kenapa ndak bisa tidur? Minum kopi itu -!* Why couldn't you sleep? The reason was that I've drunk coffee! **di-.-kan**: *tdk ~ lagi* (they were) not bothered any further. *Orang tua tdk akan ~*, Nothing will be done to elderly people. **meng-** what's the matter with...? **ng-in** 1 what are you doing? 2 what are you going to do? *lelaki -an?* what k.o. a man is he? *-.-an lu?* (coll.) what's up? *ada -.-nya di balik peristiwa tersebut* there's s.t. behind that incident. *-.-* (after negatives) nothing. *~ saja* 1 something, anything. 2 something or other. *~ sajalah* whatever there is will do. *tdk ada ~* there was nothing afoot. *tdk ~* 1 there's nothing wrong, nothing in particular, nothing at all, perfectly all right. 2 it does not matter. *dia tdk ~* (that dog) isn't doing you any harm (it is good-natured). *mesti ada ~ dgn...* there must be s.t. wrong with... *dia bukan ~ saya* he is not my relative. *- iya (,ya)?* is that so? *- juga* anything. *A- lagi?* 1 What else? *Nonton - lagi?* What else did you watch (on the TV)? 2 What more do you want? *- saja* 1 everything. 2 what (did he say) as a matter of fact. 3 what all (plural). 4 anything at all. 5 whatever. *tindakan - saja* whatever measures. 6 all conceivable things. *"Mau minum -, Par?"* *"Ah, jangan repot.repot, San. A- saja."* "What do you want to drink, Par?" "Oh, don't trouble yourself, San. It doesn't matter (or, It's all the same to

me)." *- sajalah* anything will do. *- yg dikatakan (,dinamakan)...* the so-called... *-kah... maupun...* whether... or...

apalagi 1 furthermore, and on top of that. *- saya ini orang melarat* and on top of that, I'm poor. 2 to a much greater degree.

aparat *- penyaluran* distribution system.

aparatur machinery. *- bawahannya* its subordinated apparatus. *A- Negara* State Apparatus.

apartemèn apartment.

aparthèid apartheid.

apem (S.) APAM.

apes unlucky (day, etc.).

api *- dlm sekam* there is a snake in the grass. *- penyucian* purgatory.

apik attractive, chic.

apikultur apiculture.

apiwan fire fighter.

apkir di- to be declared unfit for use or service. **-an** condemnation (declared unfit for use).

aplikasi meng-kan to apply.

apolitik apolitical.

apoplèksi apoplexy.

aposisi apposition.

apostolik apostolic.

apostrof apostrophe.

apotéma apothem.

apotik per-an pharmaceutical.

appel (S.) APEL.

appèl *- bendera* flag ceremony.

aprésiasi appreciation. **meng-** to appreciate.

April Mop April Fool's joke.

a priori a priori, before examination or analysis.

aprok (s.) AMPROK.

apropriasi appropriation.

apus -.-an deceit, cheating.

aqidah faith.

ara *menanti - tdk bergetah* and *menanti - hanyut* an endless wait.

Arab Saudi Saudi Arabia.

arah I ber- *kpd* to be directed towards. **keter-an** guiding principles. **menye-kan** to direct s.t. towards. **peng-** director

(of a company). *panitia* ~ steering
committee. ~ *kata* narrator. **peng-an**
1 briefing. 2 directives. ~ *perusahaan*.
perusahaan negara directing State
enterprises. **se-** of the same direction
(,course). *kendaraan yg berjalan* ~
vehicles going in the same direction.
ter- guided. **-an** directions. - *gejala*
trend. - *jarum jam* clockwise. - *tindakan*
policy.

arah II fig. (L. Ficus glomerata Roxb.).

arak -.-**an** *mobil* motorcade.

aral - *melintang* unforeseen event.
Apabila (,Kalau) tdk ada - melintang
maka ... If all goes well ...

arang - *sdh terbakar jadi bara* what is
done cannot be undone. **per-an** charcoal brazier.

aransemèn arrangement.

aransir meng- to make arrangements.
peng- composer (person who composes
music).

aras -.-**an** don't feel like.

aréal area, acreage.

arèk child, offspring. - *Suroboyo* native
of Surabaya.

arem ng-: pe~. ~ rice-paddies turned over
to a retired village official as a pension.

aréna arena. - *parkir* parking lot.

argomèter taxi meter.

argumèn argument.

argumèntasi argumentation. **meng-kan**
to argue.

ari I *kulit* - epidermis, scarfskin.

ari II *ular* - k.o. poisonous snake.

ari III *tali* -.- umbilical cord.

aria I aria (melody in opera).

Aria II Aryan.

Aria III honorific title of a *Bupati*.

arif skilful. *hendaklah - bhw*... (the read-
der) should pay attention to the fact
that...

aring stinking, smelly.

Ario (s.) ARIA III.

arisan - *jedulan (,perkumpulan)* club
arisan, i.e. a lottery with neighborhood
wives who have formed an association
or a club.

aristokrasi aristocracy.

aristokrat aristocrat.

arit ng- to seek spare time employment
(particularly during office hours).

arivé (s.) ARRIVE.

Arjuna a heroic *wayang* character who
has many wives and mistresses; to
the older generation of Javanese he
is the model of the whole man.
- *Wiwaha* 'Arjuna's Wedding,' to the
celestial nymph, Supraba (an episode
of the *Mahabharata* and subject of an
old Javanese poem).

arkéologi archeology.

arkian furthermore, again.

aroma aroma.

aronotik aeronautical.

aronskèlk arum.

Arpah Mount Arafat.

arrivé well off, arrived (economically).

arsén(ikum) arsenic.

arsik fish in tomato and spices.

arsiparis archivist, filing superintendent.

arsir -**an** hatching (in drawing).

arsitèk di-i to be engineered. - *dalam*.
rumah interior designer.

arsitèktonis architectonic.

arsitèktur architecture. **di-i** to be archi-
tectured. *orde politik lama yg* ~ *oleh*
PKI the old political order architec-
tured by the Indonesian Communist
Party. - *landsekap* landscape architecture.

arso ng- the o. in front.

arta money. *A- Yasa* The Mint.

artha money. *A- Kencana* and (later)
A-karini name of the women's association of the Department of Finance.

arti *sdh ng-* (speaking of a bird, etc.)
tamed, domesticated. **se-** *dgn*
synonymous with. **-dua** ambiguity.
-.*penting* significance.

artikulasi articulation.

artileri artillery.

artis artist. - *film* film artist.

artistik artistic.

artona *(hama)* - pest which attacks
coconut trees.

arts physician, general practitioner.

arummanis (s.) HARUM MANIS.

arus - *lemah* weak (,low-tension) current.
arwah ghost (of deceased person).
aryaduta ambassador.
as I axle. *negeri-negeri* - the Axis (powers).
as II ace (in card deck). - *sekopong* ace of spades.
asa *hilang (,putus)* - to be disappointed.
Asad Leo.
asah.asih.asuh. to love, help, and cause harmony between o.a.
asainéring sanitation.
asal *A- Bapak Senang* anything goes as long as it pleases the *Bapak* (i.e. a certain mental attitude towards authority). *kembali kpd* - and *balik (,pulang)* - to return to o's origin. - *orang masuk diladeni* (in stores) every o. who comes in is served. - *saja (,aja)* anything goes. *Pakeannya - saja,* They wear any old thing. *Jangan - saja!* Don't do it in a slapdash manner! - *damai saja* peace at any price. - *mulaning (,usuling) dumadi* the origin of mankind. di-kan *oleh* to be caused by. se-*(dgn)* cognate, related. *bersifat* -.-an kitsch. -nya: *Dia ∼ dr mana?* Where is he from? Where does he hail from? *Kata ini ∼ dr...,* This word is derived from... ∼ *sama* to be cognate. - *muasal* origin(s).
asam *Bagaimana - garamnya?* How do you like it (the food)? *sdh banyak makan - garam* and *tahu - garamnya* 1 to know the ins and outs of. 2 to have a lot of experience. ke-an acidity. - *amino* amino acids. - *cuka* acetic acid. - *Kandih (,Padang)* pieces of dried black tamarind.
asap *Bagaimana ibu janda wartawan itu mempertahankan - dapurnya spy tetap bisa mengepul sehari.hari?* How does that newsreporter's widow make ends meet? ber- 1 smoky. 2 dim, misty. ber-.- to smoke. *Tiga buah gelas berisi kopi panas yg ∼,* Three glasses filled with steaming hot coffee. - *solar* carbon monoxide.
asbun [asal bunyi] 1 filibustering.

2 talk(ing) for the sake of talking.
ASEANEKA [Association of South East Asian Nations + (n)eka] Television arts programs of the five ASEAN nations: Indonesia, Singapore, Malaysia, Thailand and the Philippines.
asem (s.) ASAM. *A-!* Damn!
asèmbler (automobile) assembler.
asèmbling meng- to assemble.
asep (S.) ASAP. *bandeng* - smoked milkfish.
asesanti prayers.
asésé agreed! it's a bargain! (cp.) ACC.
asetat acetate.
aseton aceton.
ASI [air susu ibu] breast milk.
Asia 1 Asia. 2 Asian, Asiatic. *suasana* ke.-an an Asian atmosphere. - *Kecil* Asia Minor. - *Tenggara* Southeast Asia.
asil asylum.
asimétri asymmetry.
asimilasi ber- to assimilate.
asimtot asymptote.
asimut azimuth.
asin.asin a shrub with edible leaves.
asing - *maksud - sampai* things take another turn than o. expects. *tak - sbg* just (,exactly) as. *tak - lagi* familiar, not unknown. *sdh tak - lagi* already familiar. keter-an isolation.
asinyasi 1 order for payment. 2 draft.
asistèn I - *apoteker* pharmacist's assistant.
asistèn II assistant to a professor (BA). - *ahli* assistant to a professor (MA).
asitilèn acetylene.
asli aboriginal, native-born. *bahasa yg -* 1 primitive language. 2 original native language. *bangsa (,orang) -* autochthonous population. *karangan -* 1 o's own work. 2 authentic work. *kilo -* standard kilogram. *sifat -* innate quality. *warganegara -* autochthonous citizen. *warganegara bukan -* non-autochthonous citizen. -nya: ∼ *dr mana?* where are you from originally? *sesuai dgn ∼* (for) true copy.
asma I asthma.
asma II names (of God), name. *dgn -*

Tuhan in the name of God.

asmara - *ketlusuban iblis* diabolic love.

asmaradanta snow-white.

asmaragama the art of sexual relations.

asmarawan lover.

asoi posh;(s.) ASSO(O) I and ASYO(O)I.

asonansi assonance.

asongan (s.) PEDAGANG (ASONGAN).

asor inferior. **ke-an** humiliation, defeat.

asosial asocial.

asosiasi association, partnership. **ber-** 1 to associate (v.i.). 2 associated. **meng-kan** to associate (v.t.).

aspal *jalan* **ber-** an asphalted street. **peng-an** 1 asphalt pavement. 2 asphalting.

asparagus asparagus.

aspèk aspect.

aspèrsi asparagus.

aspiran aspirant.

aspirasi aspiration.

asprak appointment, engagement.

Aspri [Asisten pribadi] personal assistant.

Asrafil the archangel Israfel.

asrama hostel. **meng-kan** 1 to provide accommodation. 2 to encamp (troops). **peng-an** the stationing in barracks. - *biarawan* abbey. - *gundik.gundik* whorehouse. - *mahasiswa* college students' dormitory.

asri fine, pleasing to the eye. **ke-an** beauty.

assalam *-ualaikum warahmatullahi wabarakatuh!* peace be with you as well as Allah's (,God's) mercy and blessing!

asso(o)i (s.) ASYO(O)I.

assoy easygoing, relaxed and rather casual. -.-**an** launching out a bit, having a good time.

asta eight.

astabrata the eight virtues and personalities of the king (,sovereign ,chief of state).

astagapirulah and **astagfirullah** 1 Heaven forbid! O, my God! 2 No!

astakona ber- octagonal.

Astèng [Asia Tenggara] Southeast Asia.

astohpirulah (s.) ASTAGAPIRULAH.

astrada [asisten sutradara] assistant movie (,play) director.

astronomi astronomic(al).

astronotika astronautical.

asuh peng- *anak (,bayi)* babysitter. *di bawah* -**an** under the auspices of, sponsored by.

asumsi assumption.

asurador insurer.

asuransi di-kan to be insured. *jumlah yg ~* the sum insured. **per-an** insurance system. - *bendasraya* property insurance. - *bersama* mutual insurance. - *jiwa kumpulan* group life insurance. - *jiwasraya* life insurance. - *kecelakaan* accident insurance. - *kerugian* indemnity insurance. - *kesehatan* health insurance. - *kredit jiwa* credit life insurance. - *mobil* car insurance. - *selamat be(r)layar* insurance against total loss only. - *utk pihak ketiga* third-party liability insurance.

aswa horse.

aswad black. *hajar ul* - the black stone in the Kaabah (Mecca).

aswasada 1 equestrian. 2 cavalry.

asyhadu 1 testify. - *ilaha ila'llah* I affirm there is no God but Allah.

asyik I (ber)- *masyuk* to make love. - *(ber)bicara* talked animatedly. - *(dan) masyuk* 1 (deeply) in love with o.a. 2 a young couple. *sepasang* -.*masyuk yg tengah dilanda cinta* two lovers head over heels in love. *pasangan* -.*asyoi* lovers.

asyik II comfortably, snugly.

asyo(o)i swell, great. **ber-** to shout *'asyo(o)i.'*

Asyura the porridge mixture eaten on the 10th day of Muharram.

atang and **athang** to lie on o's back. *mobil truk terguling* **ng-** the truck flipped over.

atas di - exceeding, over. *Jumlah.jumlah di - Rp. 300,-* , Amounts in excess of Rp. 300.00. *di - segala.galanya* above all. *di - tanah* above ground. *tak dpt* **di-i** insurmountable. **di-.namakan** to be in the name of, in…'s name.

meng-.alam supernatural. **meng-i** *suara* to deafen, drown, shout out. **meng-.namai** to put (,issue) in the name of. **ter-i** can be overcome. **-.meng-i** to fight (,contend) for supremacy, contend for the mastery (also used regarding fantastic news).

atawa or.

athéis atheist. **ke-an** atheism.

atma soul.

Atmawan a male student of Atma Jaya University (Jakarta).

Atmawati a co-ed of Atma Jaya University (Jakarta).

atmosfir atmosphere.

atob (S.) ATOP.

atol atoll.

Atoni the native peoples of Indonesian Timor living mainly in the inland mountain areas.

atribut attribute.

atributif and **atributip** attributive.

atur *(di) dlm segala hal yg tdk di- atau tdk cukup di- dlm anggaran dasar ini, maka…* (i.e. a phrase from a memorandum of association) in all cases not or not sufficiently provided for by these articles of association… **meng-rambutnya** to do o's hair. **peng-:** ~ *angkutan udara* air traffic controller. ~ *farmasi* assistant pharmacist. ~ *lalu.lintas* traffic policeman. ~ *peledak* detonator. ~ *perjalanan* tour operator. ~ *sinar* searchlight handler. ~ *teknik radio penerbangan* radio flight mechanic. **peng-an** 1 adjustment. 2 arrangement. *mengadakan* ~ *dgn* to make (,effect) an arrangement (or, a settlement) with. ~ *haid* menstrual regulation. ~ *hawa* air conditioning. ~ *kembali* rescheduling. ~ *penundaan* rescheduling (of payments). **per-an:** ~ *dasar* articles of association. ~ *dua kamar* bicameral system. ~ *gaji (,upah)* salary scale. ~ *lalu.lintas* traffic regulation. *P*~ *Menteri* Ministerial Regulation. *P*~ *Pelanggaran Pelayaran* Rules of the Road. ~ *tatatertib* standing orders. ~ *tingkah.laku* rule of conduct.

aubade ceremonial song, anthem.

audiènsi *diterima* **ber-** *oleh* to be received in audience by.

audiovisuil audiovisual.

audzubillah, a'udzubillah and **aud(z)u billahi** 1 I take refuge with God. 2 damned. *a'udzubillah sulitnya!* damned difficult!

auk **meng-.ng-** to howl (of jackals).

aula auditorium, lecture-hall.

aulia saint.

Aus(s)i Aussie, Australian.

aut 1 out (in sports). 2 to get out (of a club, etc.).

autarkis autarchic.

aviasi aviation.

awa prefix equivalent to the English prefix de- and dis-. **meng-bulukan** to depilate. **meng-hutankan** to deforest. **meng-samakan** to dissimilate. **meng-tularkan** to decontaminate. **peng-buluan** depilation. **peng-hutanan** deforestation. **peng-samaan** dissimilation. **peng-tularan** decontamination. *-bulu* depilation. *-hutan* deforestation. *-sama* dissimilation. *-tular* decontamination.

awak - *sama* - and *sama.sama* - 1 among friends. 2 between you and me. **meng-i** to man (a ship, plane, etc.). *rendah* **peng-an** small of stature. - *pesawat (terbang)* aircrew.

awal first (chairman, etc.). *dr* - *sampai akhir* from beginning to end. **meng-i** to initiate.

awam - *badarai* the general public.

awang *main* **-an** *saja* to play (a musical composition) extemporaneously (,impromptu ,at sight ,on the spur of the moment).

awar average. - *khusus (,umum)* (in marine insurance) particular (,general) average.

awas (cautionary word) beware (of dogs, pickpockets, etc.)! *A-Anjing!* (on signboards) Beware of the Dogs! **peng-** caretaker. ~ *lalu.lintas udara* air traffic controller. ~ *penjualan* sales supervisor. **peng-an:** ~ *persenja-*

taan (,senjata) arms control. ~ *sosial* social control. -.*waspada* to be on the alert, be careful.

awé (s.) HAWE.

awèt di-kan to be preserved, be stuffed. *Seekor burung cendrawasih yg tlh* ~, A stuffed bird of paradise. **peng-** preserver. **peng-an** preservation.

awéwé 1 woman. 2 wife.

awig.awig (in Bali) *adat* regulations.

awignam astu (namas sidem) may it come true! may there be no obstacle!

awloh Allah; God.

awul.awul cotton waste.

awur keng-an recklessness. **ng-** aimlessly, thoughtlessly. ~.~**an** to act thoughtlessly.

awut ng- to do s.t. carelessly. -.-**an** 1 at random, blindly, haphazardly. 2 wild, disordered, messy (of hair).

AX *mobil* - a car for which the payment of import duties has been postponed temporarily.

ayah ber-kan to have ... as o's father. **se-**. *seibu* of the same blood.

ayal *tak* - *lagi* immediately, without delay. -.-**an** to linger, delay.

ayam *ikan* - chicken meat. *mati* - *saja* killed without much ado. *merdeka* - quasi free (,independent). *bagai* - *bertelur di padi* live in clover, live as merry as the day is long. - *alas* 1 woodcock. 2 woodhen. - *asing* (euph.) pork. - *bersiang* a skinned chicken. - *bertelur* layer (chicken). - *cabut tulang* galantine. - *goreng* fried chicken. - *hutan* 1 woodcock. 2 woodhen. - *isi (,kodok)* dressed chicken filled with stuffing. - *mutiara* guinea fowl. - *pedaging* broiler. - *pemacak mancanegara* foreign-raised, imported chicken used for crossbreeding with domestic chickens. - *penelur (,petelur)* layer (chicken). - *piaraan imperialis* running dog of the imperialists. - *potong(an) (,sembelihan)* fryer (chicken). - *ras*

a pedigreed chicken. - *red* Rhode Island Red (i.e. a breed of American chickens with reddish-brown feathers and a black tail). - *telur* layer (chicken).

ayan epilepsy. -**an** 1 epileptic. 2 to have (,get) epilepsy.

ayar pickpocket.

ayat -.- *peralihan* items running into the following year (bookkeeping).

ayem I calm, quiet, contented. *dgn* - in peace.

ayem II to feel secure.

ayeng.ayengan to roam around.

ayer (S.) AIR.

ayid slippery (of an eel).

ayom shaded, protected, guarded. **di-i** *oleh* under the aegis of. **meng-i** to protect. take care of. **peng-** 1 protector. 2 patron. **peng-an** aegis, protection.

ayu pretty, lovely, beautiful. *(em)bok* - and *(m)bakyu* 1 title of young ladies of lower standing. 2 form of address to an older woman.

Ayub Job.

ayun oscillation. *Mereka itu melanjutkan perjalanan dgn* -.*dengkul,* They continued their trip on foot. **se-** *dgn* in agreement with. -.*temayun* 1 swing. 2 ebb away (water). -**an** fluctuation, handle, oscillator, pendulum. ~ *tangan* motion (,movement) of the hand, gesture.

azam ber- resolute, determined.

azas se-: *organisasi* ~ (of political party) subsidiary. *ormas yg* ~ mass organization working in the same direction.

azimat *Lima A- Revolusi Indonesia* (under the Soekarno regime) The Five Talismans of the Indonesian Revolution.

azimut azimut. - *bintang* astronomical azimut. - *kontra* counter-azimut.

aziz dear, darling.

azza honored. -.*wa.jalla* may He be honored and glorified (of God).

B

ba I boo! *tanpa bilang - dan bu kpd* without uttering a word to.

ba II name of the second letter of the Arabic alphabet.

baada after. *-.hu* after that.

bab gate, door. *B- al Mandab* The Gate of Tears.

Baba.Ali Chinese businessman managing money held by Indonesian powerholders or anyone in joint commercial ventures with them; (cp.) ALIBABA.

babad *soto* - soup made with tripe.

babak I scene. **pem-an** periodization. *- pungkasan (,wasana)* (in sports) finale, final round.

babak II *membayar - belur* to pay through the nose. *- bundas* black and blue.

babak III *dlm - kedua* in the second reading (in Parliament).

babang gaping wide, agape.

babarpisan altogether, quite, completely.

babat *mem-* to ban (pedicabs from a certain street, area, etc.).

babè father. *B-* Big Daddy (i.e. the sobriquet for President Soekarno).

babi *- guling* (in Bali) roasted suckling pig. *- kecap* pork cooked in sweet soy sauce. *- panggang* barbecued pork. *- puter* roasted suckling pig.

Babil Babel. *menara -* the tower of Babel.

babon 1 mother ..., basic ..., family ...; original (text). 2 *(ayam) -* layer, laying hen.

baca *nggak* **ke-** illegible. **mem-** *bibir* to lip-read. **-an** *porno* pornographic literature.

bacik ship's captain.

backing (pron. bèking) (s.) BEKING **mem-i** to support **-.-an** (illegal) collusion.

*backing*isme influence (,power) peddling.

bacot snout.

bacul dull, spiritless, spineless. *ayam - a* cock that will not fight.

bacut *ke-* go past (time or place).

bada celebration at the end of *Ramadan*.

badai *- pasir* sandstorm. *- salju* snowstorm.

badak *dia berkulit -* he has a thick skin, he is thick-skinned. *- api* a fabulous rhinoceros. *- bercula dua* the two-horned rhinoceros (found on the Island of Sumatra). *- bercula satu* the one-horned rhinoceros (found on the Ujung Kulon Peninsula, Southwest Banten). *- hempit (,kerbau)* the Sumatran two-horned rhinoceros. *- raya* the Javanese rhinoceros (L. Rhinoceros sondaicus). *- tampung* the tapir.

badakong nice, pretty.

badal 1 substitute, deputy (in pilgrimages to Mecca). 2 agent (in business, the mosque).

badan board, bureau, organization. **ber-:** *aktris berumur 24 th dan ~ montok itu* the 24-year old shapely actress. *~ tampan* well-built. *- intelijen* intelligence agency. *B- Intelijen Pusat* Central Intelligence Agency, CIA. *B- Kerjasama Ekonomi utk Asia dan Timur Jauh* Economic Commission for Asia and the Far East, ECAFE. *B- Koordinasi Intelijen Negara* (abbrev. *BAKIN*) State Intelligence Coordinating Agency. *B- Koordinasi Penanggulangan Masalah Kenakalan Remaja dan Penyalahgunaan Narkotika* (abbrev. *Bakorlangtik*) Coordinating Board for Combating Juvenile Delinquency and Drug Abuse. *B- Musyawarah Desa* (abbrev. *Bamudes* or *BMD*) 'Village Consultative Body,' i.e. a legislative institution of a village administration. *B- Pemerintah Harian* Municipal Executive. *- penegak hukum* law enforcement agency. *- pengawas* supervisory board, trustees. *B- Pengawas Keuangan* State Audit Bureau. *- pengaduan* grievance board. *B- Penyelidik Persiapan Kemerdekaan* Independence Preparations Investigation Assembly. *B- Permusyawaratan Kewarganegaraan Indonesia* (abbrev. *Baperki*) Consulta-

tive Body for Indonesian Citizens (of mainly Chinese extraction). - *pimpinan* executive board, governing body.
- *sinoman* association of youngsters to render aid to villagers. - *usaha* business concern, undertaking.

badani(yah) bodily, corporeal, carnal.

badau k.o. fish. *bapak* - a leader who lives at the expense of his followers.

badé -an 1 enigma, riddle. 2 puzzle. ~ *saya ternyata betul* my guess (,conjecture) proved to be true. *spt* ~ enigmatic, puzzling, mysterious.

badèg liquor made from fermented cassava.

badi the evil influences (supernatural) haunting a place, animate being or corpse.

badog and **badhog** m- and nge- to gorge o.s., stuff o.s. -an chow, grub.

baduk 1 to nudge s.o. 2 to push against s.t.

badung I impudent.

Badung II Denpasar (Bali).

bagai se-: ~ *berikut* as follows. ~ *mestinya* as it should be, duly, properly.

bagaikan like.

bagaimana 1 how's it with …? what (did you just say)? 3 how do you like it? *B- kabarmu?* How are you doing? *B-kabarnya?* How's everything? What's new? *B- rasanya?* What does it taste like? *Anehnya* -? What's strange about it? - *kalau* … how about it if …, what do you think of … *Tapi - kalau hal itu memang benar adanya?* But how about it if this turns out to be indeed the truth? *B- kalau minum es kopyor?* What do you think of having a glass of *kopyor* ice? *B- nanti?* "How later? " This expression is used when you do not want to commit yourself: Let's see how things are a little closer to the time. (*noun +*) *yg* -? what kind of (noun)? *Pemecahan yg* -? What kind of solution? *-pun* anyhow, anyway; (stronger) *-pun juga. B-pun juga ditawar* …, No matter how he bargained … *B-lagi?* What can I do about it? How

can I help it? *Betul, Pak! Betul* -? Right, sir! What do you mean by 'right? ' *se- mestinya* as it should be, duly, properly.

bagak bold, daring.

bagan trapnet.

bagasi and *tempat - mobil* trunk (compartment in car for holding luggage, etc.). - *cangkingan* hand-baggage.

bag(h)al mule.

bagi di-.-kan to be subdivided. *tdk* ke-an *tempat* (in movie, hotel, etc.) filled to capacity. pem- *arus* current distributor, timer. pem-an *orang dlm* bribe. se-an *besar (,kecil)* most (,few) of. ter-.- *ke dlm* divided into. -an 1 allotment. 2 area, edge. *B~ Kendaraan* Motor Pool. *B~ Pembelian* Procurement Department. ~ *pinggiran* fringe areas. ~ *rahasia wanita* a woman's private parts. ~ *selatan kota* the south edge of the city. ~ *terlarang* private parts. -.- *rejeki* bribe. - *hasil* production sharing.

bah exclamation of scorn, disgust, contempt.

bahagi pem-an *kerja* division of labor.

bahak sea eagle, osprey.

bahala affliction.

bahan *besar kayu besar -nya, kecil kayu kecil -nya* cut o's coat according to o's cloth, live within o's income. - *bacaan* reading matter (,materials). - *baju* fabrics. - *bakar Elpiji* liquefied petroleum gas. - *baku* 1 (raw material) element. 2 component (,constituent) part, base (,initial, starting) material, base product. 3 prefabricated material. -.- *bagunan* building materials. - *ekspor* export products. - *galian* minerals. - *jadi* manufactured articles (,goods). -.- *(keperluan) hidup* necessities of life. - *keterangan* 1 data. 2 info(rmation). - *keterangan pokok* basic data. -.- *kimia* chemicals. - *mentah* raw materials. - *pangan* foodstuffs. - *pangan rohani* mental food. - *pelanting* rolling stock (of State Railways). - *pemanis* sweetener (like cyclamate). - *pembantu* auxiliaries, auxiliary materials, aids and appliances. - *pembunuh serangga* insecticide. - *pemikiran* food for reflection (,thought). - *penguat badan* tonic. - *perang kimia* chemical agents. - *perbandingan* comparative materials. - *pewarna* coloring matter. - *setengah-jadi (,olah)* semi-finished (,manufactured) goods. - *uang emas* gold bullion. - *ujian* examination paper(s). -.- *yg mudah terbakar* flammables.

bahara a weight = 3 *pikul* = 399 lbs.

bahari I *jaman* - time immemorial.

bahari II 1 sea. 2 maritime. **ke-an** seamanship.

bahariwan seaman.

bahasa - *menunjukkan bangsa* 'the language shows the people,' i.e. a tree is known by its fruit. *diam dlm seribu* - to be conspicuously silent. *tdk tahu* - not to understand etiquette, to lack manners. *Kalau* **di-** *kitakan artinya ...*, When translated (in our language) it means ... **ke-an** (adj.) language. - *asing* 1 (any) foreign language. 2 the Dutch language. - *daerah* regional language. - *gado.gado* a hodgepodge language. - *gerak* sign language. - *halus* a refined language. -.- *hidup* modern languages. - *ibu* mother tongue. - *Inggeris pasaran* pidgin English. - *isyarat* sign language. -.- *klasik* classical languages. - *kolot* archaism. - *lagu* tonal language. - *lapuk* archaism. - *pergaulan* colloquial language, common parlance. - *rahasia* cryptology. - *sehari.hari* colloquial language. - *sininya* its equivalent in the local (our) language. - *Tarzan* sign language.

bahaya alarm. **ber-** *bagi jiwa* perilous, involving risk of life. - *maut* danger of life, mortal danger. - *ranjau* danger of (land)mines.

bahènol chubby with a big behind (esp. referring to women).

baheula in olden times, long ago. *jaman (,zaman)* - the olden days. *th* - very old.

bahkan 1 more than that. 2 yes, and even. 3 on top of that.

bahnè because of, due to. *Bis BOM* -

kerasnya kebentur pohon, sdh jadi ringsek, Because it hit the tree so hard, the BOM bus was destroyed.

bahtera ship (poetic). - *(Nabi) Nuh* Noah's ark. - *negara* the ship of State. - *rumah tangga* the journey through life.

bahu I - *jalan* shoulder (i.e. either edge of a road).

bahu II - *desa* (s.) BAU (DESA).

bahureksa **mem-** to protect the Yogyakarta area (from ghosts or spirits which might inhabit the region).

bai'at allegiance, homage to religious (Moslem) leader; (s.) BAYAT. **di-** to be taken an oath of allegiance. **pem-an** taking an oath of allegiance.

baid *karib dan* - 1 near and far. 2 relatives and strangers.

baiduri cat's eye (precious stone).

baik 1 good-natured, kind-hearted. 2 sound (of make). 3 honest and respectable. 4 *diterima dgn* - to be received with a good grace. 5 - *dipakai* suitable for, appropriate to. *Dia berbicara bahasa Indonesia dgn* -, He speaks good Indonesian. *-lah* it would be best if. *jika cuaca* - weather permitting. *Sdr. ada* -? Are you well? How are you? -.., *demikian pula* 1 both ... and. 2 neither ... nor. -... *atau* ... both ... and ... - *dr tuan rumah, atau dr organisasi yg pekerjaannya berkaitan dgn usaha kita* both from the host, and from the organization whose activities are linked to our business. **ber-** *kembali* to reconciliate. **ke-an** 1 benefit. 2 interest. **mem-** 1 to improve, become better. 2 to clear up (of weather). **memper-i** *rekor* to break a record. **per-an**: ~ *menyeluruh* overhaul. ~ *nasib* improvement of o's lot. *Penyakitnya sdh agak* -**an,** He is on the way to recovery. *-(nya) kita ...* let's ... **-nya:** *ada* ~ it has its good side, it may be of some use. *ada* ~ *bila* it would be best if. *ada* ~ *kalau* we might (just) as well, it might be a good plan to. -.*buruknya* the good and bad points, the pros and cons. -.- carefully. *jaga* ~ take care.

orang ~ people from a good family,
respectable people. - *hati* to be kind
(-hearted). - *hati kpd* to be kindly
disposed towards, humor a person.
- *niat* to be in good faith.

bait *B-(h) Indonesia* 'Indonesia House,'
i.e. the local office of the Republic of
Indonesia in Mecca. *B-ullah* 'God's
house,' i.e. the Mosque in Mecca. *B-ul
Makdis* and *B- Mukadas* Jerusalem. *-ul
mal* community chest. *B- Rakhim* and
B-urrakhim 'House of the Merciful,'
i.e. the name of the Mosque on the
compounds of the *Istana Merdeka* in
Jakarta.

baja I dung, crap.

baja II dentifrice.

bajaj a three-wheeled Indian-manufactured
passenger car using a 1962 150-cc Italian Vespa scooter motor.

bajak I *dahulu - drpd jawi* 'the plow is
before the ox,' i.e. to put the cart
before the horse.

bajak II **mem-** 1 to hijack, skyjack. 2 to
pirate. **pem-** 1 hijacker, skyjacker. 2
pirate. **pem-an** 1 hijacking, skyjacking.
2 pirating. **-an** 1 hijacked, skyjacked.
2 pirated. - *udara* hijacker, skyjacker.

bajigur drink made from coconut milk,
water, coconut sugar and slices of
coconut.

bajik **ke-an** 1 good deed, kindness. 2
(guna) - (in the) interest (of). 3 *(nama)*
- good repute. 4 virtue, merit.

bajing - *lompat (,loncat)* (fig.) opportun-
ist(ic). - *loncat* thief who pilfers goods
from trucks. *taktik - loncat* hit-and-run
tactics.

baju *memelihara penyengat dlm* - cherish
(,nourish) a viper on o's bosom. *men-
cabik.cabik - di dada* 'to tear up a coat
on your chest,' i.e. to show off o's own
disgrace. *mengukur - di badan sendiri*
you measure other people's cloth by
your own yard. **ber-:** ~ *hijau* to be an
army man. ~ *putih* to be a civilian.
- *berenang* swim suit. - *dingin* 1 over-
coat. 2 winter clothes. - *hijau (,ijo)*
term of abuse for the Indonesian

soldier or, army in general. - *kemanten
(,kemantin)* wedding dress. - *kemeja* a
shirtdress (for women). - *kodian* ready-
made clothes. - *koran* American fancy
shirt with pictures of various newspapers. - *kotak.kotak* checked jacket.
- *monyet terusan* overalls (worn by
city bus drivers and conductors in
Jakarta). - *safari* short-sleeved dress
jacket for men (part of suit). - *terus*
gown, dress. - *zirah* armor.

bajul - *buntung* Don Juan, playboy.

bak I - *(tempat) mandi* large tub from
which water is scooped for bathing.

bak II a strip of cultivated ground in
sugarcane compartment or a strip
divided from a longer portion of land
by ditches.

bak III like.

bakal I - *isterinya* his wife to be. - *Presiden*
President-elect.

bakal II **-(an)** will (future tense). *Tindakan
apa yg* ~ *diambil oleh PWI?* What measures are to be taken by the Indonesian
Journalists' Association?

bakal III - *pelanting* rolling stock.

bakaloréat and **bakaloriat** baccalaureate
(degree).

bakar **pem-** arsonist. **pem-an** 1 arson.
2 combustion. ~ *diri* immolation.
~ *kapur* limekiln. **ter-** *habis* burned
down (of a building). - *diri* to immolate
o.s. - *hati* wrath.

bakarat baccarat.

bakat I (natural) disposition, competence,
skill. **ber-** accomplished. ~ *seni* artistic.
~ *utk celaka* accident prone. **pem-.pem-
baru** new talent (people who have
talent). - *bahasa* language aptitude.

bakat II 1 vestige, track, mark, remains.
2 pockmark. 3 (foot) print.

bak.bak.kur (s.) MAIN (BAK.BAK.KUR).

bakda after (a certain period). *B- Mulud*
name of the fourth Jav. month. *B-
Pasa* Jav. New Year.

bakdo (s.) BAKDA.

bakéro stupid! idiot! **di-** to be considered an idiot.

bakhil **ke-an** avarice.

bakhsis (s.) BAKS(Y)IS.
bako *mencari* - to look for a son-in-law (in order to provide descendants).
bakpao k.o. Chinese pastry resembling a bun, filled with pork or soybean mixture.
bakso a dish of Chinese origin consisting of meatballs and noodles in soup; (S.) BASO. **mem-** to eat *bakso*.
baks(y)is 1 alms. 2 tip (of money). 3 douceur. **mem-** to bribe.
baktau madam (i.e. a woman in charge of a brothel).
baktéri bacterium. - *bundar* coccus.
bakti ber- devout. **ke-an** 1 merit. 2 piety.
baku I standard. *harga* - standard price. **pem-an** standardization. - *emas* gold standard. - *pincang* limping standard.
baku II e.o., = *saling*. - *hantam* to come (,get) to blows. - *jotos* to fight. - *tembak* to fire at e.o. - *tolak* to push e.o.
bakul (usually, a female) vendor; (s.) MBAK (AYU BAKUL JAMU). *kaum -an* the vendors. - *kecil* retailer, retail dealer. - *obrokan* 1 (in Lamongan, East Java) a small rice broker. 2 (in other parts of Java) retailer. - *wedang* coffee vendor.
bakung (a large white-flowered) lily(-like plant) (L. Crinum Asiaticum).
balada ballad.
balah ber- to debate. **per-an** debate. *masalah (,pokok)* ~ crucial (,critical) point.
balai - *benih* seed bed. *B- Budaya* Art Gallery. *B- Harta Peninggalan* Probate Court - *kambang* an artificial island with a pavillion (reached by a bridge or walkway) in the center of a round pool surrounded by gardens. *B- Masyarakat* Community Center. - *percobaan* experimental (,research) station. *B- Pertemuan Umum* Convention Hall. *B- Prajurit* Soldiers' Center, Social Center for Soldiers. - *seni* art gallery. *B- Sidang* Convention Hall. *B- Yasa* State Railways Repair Shop (found in Surabaya, Yogyakarta, Manggarai, Semarang and Madiun). *B-*

Yudha War Room (in *Istana Merdeka*).
balairung audience chamber.
balas *atas dasar -.***mem-** on a quid pro quo basis. **pem-***dendam* avenger.
balèan (in Bali) (s.) DUKUN.
baléla rebellion. *sikap* - satyagraha.
balèt *penari* - ballet dancer.
baliho film-poster made of hardboard.
balik -... *bertanya* to ask ... in return. *"Bagaimana dgn demonstran? "* - *"Buana" bertanya,* "What do you think of the demonstrators? " asked "Buana" in return. *di* - indicating a high degree. *aneh di* - *aneh* extremely queer (,strange). *menurut cerita di* - *cerita, tatkala...* on hearsay. *senang di* - *senang* most pleasant. *di* - *awan* like walking on air. *Ia* **ber-** *tanya dgn suara makin tinggi,* He asked in turn with an increasingly high-pitched voice. **ke-annya** on the contrary. **mem-** to contradict o.s. *lanjut ke* **se-** and *lihat* **se-nya** please turn over (the page). **ter-** *kalang* run counter to. - *jalan* to return without having effected o's purpose. *Seringkali Yapto hrs - jalan dr mengajakku nonton,* Often Yapto had to turn back without taking me to the movies. - *nama* transfer of title. - *sifat poyang* atavism.
balistik ballistic. *proyektil* - *antarbenua* intercontinental ballistic missile.
balita [(di) bawah lima tahun] under the age of five years. *anak* - preschooler.
Balkan Balkans.
balok I counter for things which come in large blocks: block. *es batu empat* - four blocks of ice.
balok II chevron.
balok III 1,030 kilograms of morphine.
balola [barisan lonte lanang] gigolo front.
balon I round neon light. **pem-** balloonist. **-.-an:** *tlh jadi* ~ to be a plaything (,toy). *main* ~ to blow soap bubbles. - *kabel* captive balloon.
balon II whore.
balong fishpond.
balsem balm. **mem-(kan)** to embalm.
balur hides and skins.

balut **pem-** *wanita* sanitary napkin.

baluwarti circular brick wall surrounding *kratons,* esp. that of Surakarta.

bambam k.o. musical instrument.

bambu (in Aceh, North Sumatra) a measure of capacity equivalent to 2 liters.

bambungan (in East Java) vagabond, bum. *bocah* - a juvenile delinquent.

ban I (race) track.

ban II belt. - *arloji* watchband. - *berjalan* conveyor belt. - *hitam* black belt (in Karate).

ban III - *buta* a solid tire. - *hidup* a pneumatic tire. - *mati* a solid tire. - *mobil bekas yg divulkanisir* retreads. - *pejal* a solid tire. - *serap* a spare tire.

banal banal.

bancakan a joint religious meal for special occasions, such as, a birthday of a child, wedding, etc.

bancèt a rice paddy frog.

banci 1 homosexual. 2 homosexual prostitute. 3 an effeminate man.

band I (pron. **bèn**) (a musical group) band. - *tenar* a popular (music) band.

band II (pron. **ban**) (in radio) band. *radio transistor (dr) 1 (,3)* - a o. (,three) band portable (,transistor) radio.

Banda Aceh Kutaraja (the capital city of the Aceh Special Region).

bandar ditch. **per-an** port system. - *udara (antarbangsa)* (international) airport.

bandel **pem-** a stubborn person.

bandeng 1 k.o. milkfish (L. Chanos chanos), ordinarily kept in fishponds. 2 (in *tukang catut* jargon) a piece of good fortune. *Sekali pukul dpt* -, At a (,one) blow you receive a windfall.

banderol *harga pas* - the exact price shown on the tax stamp.

bandijzer (pron. **banèser**) hoop iron.

banding **pem-** (party) appellant. **per-an** comparative. ~ *kekuatan* balance of power. ~ *nilai* rate. *memgambil* ~ *dr* to learn a lesson from. *menurut* ~ *ukuran* to scale. *mengambil* **-an** *ke* with reference to, to revert to. *tak ada* **-nya** unequalled, unique.

bandit - *bertangan satu* slot machine.

banditisme banditism.

bandos (**be**)- sweets made from cassava.

bandot - *tua* 'an old billy goat' (i.e. a dirty old man). - *yg doyan lalap rumpat muda* 'a billy goat who likes a side dish of young grass' (i.e. an old rake who likes young girls).

bandrèk I a warming drink, made from heated (,boiled) water, sugar, ginger and other spices.

bandrèk II master (,skeleton) key. **mem-** to open (a door, etc.) with such a key.

bandung I (in Pontianak, West Kalimantan) houseboat.

bandung II *balai* - two halls connected by a passage. *telur dua* **se-** two yolks in one egg.

bang call to prayer.

bangau *setinggi.tinggi terbang* -, *surutnya ke kubangan juga* east or west, home is best. - *hitam* the black egret found in the Southern Celebes.

banget *Dan ini isu sih* **ke-an**! And this issue is indeed going too far!

bangga - *pd apa?* proud of what? **ke-an** *akan (,atas ,dgn ,karena)* pride in.

bangir very sharp (nose).

Bangkahulu *ketupat* - (fig.) a blow with the fist, push.

bangkai *besar* - tall, robust, sturdy. *menjemur* - *ke atas bukit* 'to dry a dead body in the sun on top of a hill,' i.e. to expose o's own shortcomings. - *kapal* the remains of a wrecked ship.

bangkang **mem-** to disobey, resist, strike work. *kaum* **pem-** the reactionaries. **pem-an** *sipil* civil disobedience.

bangkes **be-** to sneeze.

bangkit **mem-kan:** ~ *minat thd* to rouse interest in. ~ *perangsang* to annoy. **pem-:** ~ *selera (,nafsu makan)* apéritif, appetizer. ~ *(tenaga) listrik* 1 electrical power station. 2 electric generator. - *menentang neo.kolonialisme* to revolt against neo-colonialism.

bangkot I **-an** very old.

bangkot II diehard. **-an** totally committed.

bangku - *sekolah* (school)desk. *duduk di*

- *sekolah* at school.
Bangkulu (s.) BANGKAHULU.
banglo bungalow.
bango k.o. stork. - *putih* large egret.
- *tontong* certain large stork with a
long beak.
bangor naughty, mischievous.
bangpak unreliable, inferior (to).
bangsa 1 (member of a) category, class.
- *ajengan* the elite. - *bahar* a seafaring
nation. - *berwarna* colored people.
- *dewek* Javanese people (term used
for themselves). - *halus* supernatural
beings. -.- *jajahan* the colonial peoples.
- *pengembara* nomad(ic) people.
- *tempe* 'a beancake nation,' i.e. an
insignificant and small nation. -.-
ter(ke)belakang the underdeveloped
nations. -.- *yg sedang membangun* the
developing nations. -.- *yg tertindas* the
oppressed nations. 2 (member of a)
nationality, ethnic group. - *Babilon*
Babylonians. - *Mongol* Mongolians.
orang yg tak punya **ke-an** a stateless
person. *dan* **se-nya** and the like.
banjar (in Bali) hamlet association.
banjir **mem-** to flood. - *bandang* tremen-
dous floods. - *kiriman* flood unleashed
by heaven.
bank (pron. bang) **per-an** banking. *B-*
Bakulan Small Farmer's Bank. *B-*
Berlayar Floating Bank. *B- Dagang*
Negara Commercial State Bank. - *devisa*
(,devisen) foreign exchange bank. *B-*
Donor Darah Blood Bank. *B- Dunia*
World Bank. - *hipotek* mortgage bank.
- *milik negara* state-owned bank.
- *perniagaan* commercial bank. - *sirku-*
lasi bank of issue. *B- Tabungan Pos*
P.O. Savings Bank. - *tani* agricultural
loan bank.
bankir banker.
bantah **ber-** *pena* to practice polemics.
dgn tak **ter-kan** *lagi* irrefutably.
bantal **-an** *sekoci* boat chock. - *angin* air
cushion. - *s(e)tempel (,cap)* stamp pad.
Bantèng the election symbol of the Indonesian Democratic Party. *menusuk*
Ka'bah dan - to vote for the Moslem-

backed Development Unity Party and
the Indonesian Democratic Party.
banter *paling -* at the most, not more
than. *paling - Rp. 300.-* at most Rp.
300.00.
banting **ke-** *sama pakaiannya* not harmo-
nizing with his clothing. **mem-(kan)**
kaki 1 to stamp o's feet. 2 to march in
goose step. **pem-an** *harga* dumping.
- *stir* 'drastic turning of the steering
wheel,' i.e. the title of President Soekarno's message to the Provisional
People's Consultative Assembly on
April 11, 1965 calling for a more
radical turn away from the West.
bantras (S.) BERANTAS.
bantu **ber-an** subsidized. **di-tulis** *oleh* co-
authored by. **diper-kan:** ~ *kpd (,pd)* to
be detailed to, be assigned to assist.
pegawai tinggi ~ the senior official in
charge. **pem-** 1 abettor, backer. 2 auxiliary. 3 domestic servant. *P~ Jaksa*
Assistant Public Prosecutor. ~ *paderi*
acolyte. ~ *rumah tangga* domestic
(servant), household help. ~ *tindak*
pidana accomplice. **-an** aid, grant.
dgn ~ assisted by. ~ *ahli hukum* legal
aid. ~ *bathin* moral support. ~ *tembak-*
an fire support.
bantut **ter-** vain, futile.
banyak I to have much (,many). *dia -*
anak he has many children. *dia - uang*
he has much money. *saya - waktu* I've
a lot of time. - (+ a verb) (to perform
that activity) often, much, habitually.
Dia - minum bir, He is a habitual drinker.
kami mengucapkan **diper-** *terima kasih*
atas we offer you our best thanks for,
we thank you very much for. **ke-an:**
~ *orang* most people. *orang* ~ the
common man, man in the street.
se-.-nya 1 at most, maximum. 2 not
more than. **-nya** amount. *menurut* ~
quantitatively.
banyak II goose.
banyo banjo.
banyol **(be)-an** to joke, jest. **nge-** to make
jokes. **-an** *Aprilan (,Satu April)* April
Fool's joke.

banyu water. - *bening* 'clear water,' i.e. a mystical term peculiar to Javanese philosophical mysticism. It refers to peace in o's household, success in o's work or enterprise, cure for sickness, etc. It is not always in the form of water, but may be in that of a *slametan,* following an ascetic (religious) regimen, etc. The above can be achieved not just by the intermediary of 'an older person,' but by visiting holy graves, to beseech blessings from those buried there.

bapak ke-an fatherly. -.- (coll.) big shots (in a derogatory sense). - *angkat* step-father. *B- Kami* Our (Heavenly) Father. *B- Marhaenisme* Father of Marhaenism, President Soekarno. *B- Negara* Father of State, the President. - *mentua (,mertua)* father-in-law. *B- Pembentuk Negara* The Founding Fathers (in the U.S.). - *permandian* godfather. *B- Suci Paus* His Holiness the Pope.

Bapakisme 'Paternalism,' i.e. the concept of putting emphasis on father-and-son type relations in Indonesian bureaucracy, the unquestioning loyalty and obedience of inferior to superior.

bapang daddy!

bapèt 1 bad. 2 broke, penniless.

baplang - *melingker* protruding (moustache).

Baptis Baptist. *tanda* -an baptismal certificate.

bar bar (in hotel, etc.).

baraat - *surat kebebasan* (letter of) safe-conduct.

baragajul (s.) BAJUL.

barah abscess, tumor, ulcer, cancer.

barakatuh *wa* - and (God's) blessing.

barang I article, item. - *angkutan* goods by slow train. *mengirim sbg* - *angkutan* to send by (ordinary) goods train, send at freight train rates. - *bawaan* hand-luggage. - *bekas* second-hand goods. - *bergerak* personal property. - *bukti* exhibit (evidence in a Court), (documentary) evidence (in a lawsuit). -.-

bulk bulk cargo (,goods). - *cangkingan* hand-luggage. - *cepat* fast (,speed) goods. *mengirim sbg* - *cepat* to send by fast goods-train. - *dagang(an)* merchandise. -.- *dlm pelayaran (,perjalanan)* goods in transit. - *ekspor* export product. - *galian* mineral. - *ganti* substitute. - *gasakan* stolen goods. - *gerobakan* wagon (,truck- ,car-)load. - *(h)antaran* parcels. *mengirim sbg* - *(h)antaran* to send by passenger train. - *hutan* forest produce (,products). - *impian* wishful thinking. -.- *jadi* finished products. - *jaminan* gage, security. -.- *kebutuhan sehari.hari* daily needs. -.- *kelebihan* surplus goods. - *kelontong* drapery, soft goods; small wares. -.- *keperluan dapur* kitchen utensils. - *keperluan perang* war material. - *keperluan rumah tangga* household effects (,utensils). -.- *keperluan selama (,dlm) perjalanan* 1 wearing apparel. 2 traveling requisites. - *kesenian* art object. - *kiriman* parcels. -.- *konsumi* articles of consumption. - *loakan* junk. -.- *logam* metal wares. -.- *luks* luxury items. -.- *meledak* explosives. -.- *mentah* raw materials. - *modal* capital goods. - *nadirat* curio, bric-a-brac. - *niaga* commodity. -.- *pakai habis* expendable supplies. - *palen* small wares (,goods). - *pengganti* substitute. -.- *penumpang* passengers' goods. - *pindahan* personal effects. - *potongan* (general) cargo. - *purbakala* antiquities. - *romel* junk, rags. - *selundupan* contraband (,smuggled) goods. - *sepele* trivia, bagatelles. - *serbuan* spoils of war. - *sdh* manufactured articles, finished products. -.- *takbergerak* fixtures, immovables. -.- *tak bertuan* (usually in ports, warehourses) unowned property, property having no owner. - *tawanan* captured goods. -.- *temuan* lost property. - *tetap* real estate, immovable goods. -.- *timpa(h)an* (coll.) pilfered (,stolen) goods. -.- *yg akan segera habis dimakan (,dipakai)* expendables. -.- *yg dikenakan bea* dutiable

goods. -.- *yg memabukkan* intoxicants.
-.- *yg tak dpt dipakai lagi* obsolete
goods. -.- *yg tdk tahan lama pemakai-
annya* perishable goods. *bukan - baru*
it is not news. *baik - akar atau terlepas*
(in Medan) movables as well as immovables.

barang II se- (s.) SEMBARANG - *apa* all,
whatever. - *bilapun* any time. - *ke mana*
to wherever. - *sedikit* a little bit. - *sekali*
once. - *sekedarnya* 1 somewhat, in
some degree, a bit. 2 (to tell) a few
things. *beras - seliter dua liter* about
one or two liters of rice. *tdk ... - satu
(,se + counter)pun* and - *satu (,se +
counter)pun ... tdk* not even a single.

barang III code name for morphine.

barangan arsenic.

barat *3 B-* the three big western powers:
the United States of America, England
and France. **pem.B-an** (s.) PROSES
(PEMBARATAN).

baraya family.

bareng ber-an *waktu* synchronized, at
the same time, coinciding (with).
se-an *dgn* coinciding with.

barèt ber- to wear a beret. - *hitam* worn
by the Army Cavalry and the Police
Force Mobile Brigade. - *kuning* worn
by the Greater Jakarta College Students
Regiment Corps. - *merah* worn by the
Army Para Commando Regiment.
- *oranye* worn by the Air Commandos.
- *ungu* worn by the Navy Marines.

barikade barricade. **di-** to be barricaded,
be blocked.

baring I *jenazahnya* **di-kan** *di* his (mortal)
remains lie in state at.

baring II bearing. *Kita - matahari,* We are
taking a bearing of the sun. **-an** sextant.
mengambil ~ to take bearings.

baris I -.**ber-** marches and parades. **se-** *dgn*
abreast of. **-an:** ~ *belakang* (in soccer)
the backs. ~ *berkuda* cavalry. *B*~ *Drum-
band* Drum and Bugle Corps. ~ *merah*
communist troops. ~ *meriam* artillery.
~ *meriam yg bermesin* motorized artillery. ~ *pengawal* guards.

Baris II Balinese war dance for a male
solo dancer.

baromèter barometer. - *air raksa* mercur-
ial barometer.

barong I (s.) UDANG (BARONG).

barong II - *tagalog* an embroidered
Philippine shirt.

Barong III 1 a Balinese dance. 2 a myth-
ological animal in this dance.

barongsai and **barongsay** 1 male lion.
2 lion-shaped puppet carried by s.o.
inside it.

barso (in Medan) honey, darling.

barter barter.

baru just, just before (,now). *(sdh) ... -
... * it was (already) ... and only then
did ..., it was ... before ... - *+ number*
only ... (so far). - *... blm ... * just ... so
far, we haven't gotten to ... yet. *Ini -
nasinya saja. blm lauk.pauknya,* This
is just the rice so far, we haven't gotten
to the other dishes yet. - *ini* not until
now, for the first time. *-lah* and only
then, suddenly. - *mau* (just) about to.
- *saja* to have just (done s.t.), no sooner
... - *saja hendak (,mau) ...* to be about
to ... - *sekarang* not until now, only
now. - *setelah* not until, and only
then. *tdk* **ter-kan** nonrenewable.

Baruna Neptune.

barunawati 1 (Indonesian) seaman's wife.
2 *(B-)* name of the Association of the
Wives of Employees under the jurisdiction of the Directorate General for Sea
Communications.

barung squad in the *Pramuka* Boy Scout
Movement.

Barus a place in Tapanuli (Sumatra's
west coast). *kapur* - camphor (from
Barus), mothball.

barusan - *(berapa hari)* a short time ago,
not long ago, just.

barut ke-.- with cuts (,scratches).

barzakh *alam* - period between death and
judgment; Hades, realm of the dead.

barzanji *membaca* - to read from the life
of the Prophet.

basa.basi 1 lipservice. 2 conventionalities.

basah well-paid, lucrative; (s.) DOKTER
(BASAH). *habis* - soaking (,sopping)
wet.

basekat k.o. double-breasted coat.

baskara the sun.

baskèt basket.

baskom *pedagang (,penjual) kue* - female
street vendor who has a dual function;
during the day she sells food and during the evening her body.

basmi **pem-an** annihilation, eradication.
~ *malaria* malaria eradication.

baso **nge-** (s.) (MEM)BAKSO.

basoka bazooka.

basuo (S.) BERSUA.

Basyah and **Basyaw** Pasha.

bata - *klinker* (stone) clinker, brick. -an
(s.) GARAM (BATAAN).

Batak **ke.-an***nya* his Batak ethnic background.

batako hollow brick.

batal *dianggap* - to be considered void.
dinyatakan - to be declared null and
void, nullified.

batalyon - *zeni konstruksi (,tempur)*
engineer construction (,combat)
battalion.

batang I (tree) trunk. *cokelat* - chocolate
in bars. -an (student sl. in Jakarta) boy
friend. - *muat(an)* cargo boom. - *padi*
1 stalk (of the rice plant). 2 straw.

batang II -an ingot.

Batara - *Guru* the Upper God (mythology). - *Kala* in the Jav. belief system,
a spirit who takes away s.o.'s soul so
that he dies.

batas **keter-an** limitation. **pem-an** *kehamilan (,kelahiran)* birth control. -
kredit credit ceiling, line of credit.

baterai - *kering* dry-cell battery.

bathil false, untrue. **ke-an** iniquity.

bathin I *tekanan.tekanan* - nervous breakdown.

bathin II (in the Riau Archipelago) (s.)
KEPALA (ADAT).

bathlalhuriah Al Awal The First Hero of
Independence, i.e. President Soekarno.

bati **se-** united.

batik - *cap* hand-blocked batik through
the use of a copper stamp *(,cap)*, usually of low quality. - *tulis* hand-drawn
batik through the use of a copper
vessel with a spouted nib *(,canting)*,
more expensive than the *batik cap.*

batil (s.) BATHIL.

batin I 1 hidden, secret, real (meaning);
(the) deeper (sense of what o. is reading). 2 mental. 3 moral. 4 mystical
(power). 5 esoteric, mysterious. 6 psychic, medium. 7 the inner or spiritual
aspect of o's personal existence; inner-
man, the secret place where man and
'God' may meet; its instrument is the
rasa; (s.) BATHIN I. *Kalau tak dpt dgn
lahir dgn -*, If it does not go openly,
well then (do it) secretly. **ke-an** 1 the
practice of contemporary Javanese
mysticism as it appears in the *aliran
kebatinan.* 2 the culture of inner-man.
3 Javanese science. 4 the essence of
Javaneseness.

batin II 1 title of (village) heads in Jambi,
Lampung and Palembang; (s.) BATHIN
II. 2 head of a *kuria* (,district) in Tapa-
nuli. 3 head of a proto-Malay tribe in
Malacca (Western Malaysia).

batiniyah spiritual.

batu jewels (of timepiece). *lempar(kan)* -
sembunyi(kan) tangan and *melempar -
sembunyi tangan* not willing to admit
that o. has committed an act (or, a
crime). - *bara muda* brown coal, lignite.
- *cincin* semiprecious jewel. -.- *jam*
jewels of a timepiece. - *kantong kencing*
cystolith, urinary calculus. - *karang
bulan* moonrocks. - *kecubung* amethyst.
- *koral* corallite. - *kulansing* granite.
- *melintang* stumbling stone, obstacle.
- *penjuru (,pertama)* corner stone.
- *pecah* road metal. - *sandungan* stumbling stone, obstacle. - *senter* flashlight
battery. - *teker* flint. - *templek* broken
stones (,bricks), rubble. - *tepi* curb-
stones. - *ular* snakestone.

Batujajar training center, located 22 kilo-

meters from Bandung (West Java),
where soldiers are trained in parachute
jumping.

batuk 'anybody home?' -.-: *oplet yg
sdh pd* ~ broken down jeepneys with
'coughing' motors. *Gunung Merapi* ~
Mount Merapi (in Central Java) is
erupting. - *kambing* to cough excessive-
ly to draw attention. - *kering* phthisis.
- *klimis* (s.) TUK.MIS. - *lelah (,sesak)*
whooping cough. - *pilek* flu-like symptoms. - *rejan (,100 hari)* pertussis.

batur servant.

bau I - desa deputy village chief.

bau II -nya *setahun pelayaran* it stinks to
high heaven.

baur ber- to group together with. **mem-**
to assimilate (v.i.). *Cina WNA atau WNI
yg tak mau* ~ *bisa pilih Peking atau
Taiwan,* Chinese of foreign or Indonesian nationality who do not want to
assimilate may choose between Peking
or Taiwan. **pem-an** assimilation (of
population group).

baut - *solder* soldering iron.

bawa di-: *Dan beberapa kali malam hari
Lisa tlh ~nya makan ke restoran,* And,
several times during the evening Lisa
also agreed that she would go out to
eat with him in a restaurant. ~ *kabur*
to be carried off, be spirited away (by
thieves). ~ *karena* due to. ~ *lahir* innate,
inborn, congenital. *boleh* ~ *ke tengah*
to be able to hold o's own. *utk* ~ *bepergian* for your travels (a medicine). *mesin
tulis yg dpt* **di-**.- a portable typewriter.
di-kan to be staged, be put upon the
stage. **mem-:** ~ *acara* to direct the entertainment at a (musical) show, party
or the like. ~ *berahasia* to admit to the
secret. ~ *(ber)keliling* to show (,take)
s.o. around a place. *pandai* ~ *diri* easy
going. ~ *kabur* to run off with. ~ *kembali* to bring back. ~ *ke tengah* to put
forward. ~ *lari* to abduct. ~ *nama
beberapa kedutaan besar asing* to
implicate some foreign embassies.
~ *pulang* 1 to take home. 2 to bring

back. ~ *serta* to take along with o.
tdk ~ *sukses* unsuccessful. **mem-kan:**
~ *diri (,tabiat)* to know how to com-
port o.s. in society. ~ *politik* ... to
conduct a ... policy. ~ *tari* to give a
dance performance. -.**mem**- transporting. **pem-:** ~ *acara* M.C., master of
ceremonies. *(si)* ~ *bendera* flag carrier.
pem-an character, behavior. **sepem-
kaki** at random, haphazardly. **ter-** *oleh*
due to. **ter-**.- carried away, implicated.
kecil teranja.anja, besar ~ as the twig
is bent the tree is inclined. *Kepala
kampung itupun* ~ *juga dlm urusan itu,*
Even the village head was implicated in
that matter. **-an:** *sebuah tas jinjing* ~
T. a handbag carried by T. ~ *hidup*
way of life.

bawah di- perintahkan to be subordinated
to. **mem-i** to have under o's control
(,jurisdiction). **-an** 1 subordinate, un-
derling. 2 subdistrict. - *sadar* subcon-
scious(ness). - *umur* underage.

bawal silver pomfret (L. Pampus argen-
teus).

bawang *rusak* - *ditimpa jambak* to be
ruined by o's splendor. *(kelakuan)
anak* - rascal, ne'er-do-well. *menjadi
anak (,pupuk)* - to sit mum. *kueh* -
sticks formed of wheat flour, coconut
milk, eggs, onions and deep fried.
pemakan - quick-tempered. - *Bombai*
Bermuda onion. - *daun* leek. - *kotong*
without anybody doing anything about
it.

bawèl chatterbox, busybody.

bawon portion of harvested rice intended
for the paddy-harvester as k.o. premium;

baya *sdh* -, *tlh (agak)* -, *setengah* -, *seper-
dua* - and *tlh separuh* - well advanced
in years, i.e. 35 to 40 years of age.

bayak ke-an corpulence.

bayan village head.

bayang *hujan yg* **ter**- threatening to rain.
blm **ter**-.- there is no evidence yet of.
-an disguised. *kartel* ~ a disguised cartel. *di dlm* ~ *saja* only in o's imagination, false. *blm ada* ~*nya* not the

faintest trace of it was to be found yet. *kelihatan ~nya* there is evidence of. -.- silhouette. *ibarat ~ badan* inseparable, said of persons who are much seen in e.o.'s company. *tdk kelihatan ~nya* (he) was nowhere to be seen. *mengukur ~ sepanjang badan* cut o's coat according to o's cloth, live within o's income. *~ tdk sepanjang badan* having a champagne taste on a beer-drinker's pocketbook.

bayar *- tinggi* to pay a lot. *yg terlalu keliwat* **di-** *murah* grossly underpaid. **pem-an** *dgn jangka waktu* deferred payment. *tak* **ter-kan** couldn't be paid.

bayat *masa* **pem-an** initiation period (replaces hazing in Indonesian colleges).

bayata male freshman.

bayati female freshman.

bayèn to give birth to.

bayi *- tabung* test-tube baby.

bayonèt *dgn - terhunus* with fixed bayonet. *dgn ujung -* at bayonet point.

bayu a submissive pronoun of the first person.

bayun **pem-** the oldest (,firstborn) child. *putri ~ Sultan Adiwijaya* the oldest daughter of Sultan Adiwijaya.

bazir (s.) MUBAZIR. **pem-an** waste.

béa *- balik (,pindah) nama* transfer-of-title fee. *- ekspor* export duty. *- legalisasi* legalization fee. *- lelang* public auction dues. *- pemindahan hak* transfer-of-title fee. *- perambuan* beaconage.

béa.cukaiwan customs officer.

béaya **pem-** financier. **pem-an** financing.

bebangkes (s.) BANGKES.

bébas **di-kan**: *Mereka ~ dr pungutan bunga,* They got a grace period. *~ dr segala tuduhan dan tuntutan* to be discharged from further prosecution, dismissal of the summons (,action), *~ dr tugasnya* (a person has been) relieved of his task. *~ dgn perjanjian* to be paroled. **ke-an** freedom (exemption from arbitrary restrictions on a specified civil right, such as, freedom of speech, etc.). *~ beragama* freedom of

worship. *~ bergerak* freedom of movement. *~ di laut* freedom of the seas. *~ dlm hidup* permissiveness. *~ mimbar* academic freedom. *~ pers* freedom of the press. *memberi* **pem-an** *kpd Direksi* to discharge the Management. **pem-tugasan** discharge (from a function). *bekerja dgn -.leluasa* to work freely (without restraint).

bèbèk (bandit jargon) car, automobile. *spt - dengar geluduk* 'like a duck hearing the thunder,' i.e. to stare like a struck pig. *- Manila* (s.) MENTOG.

bèbèkisme following the leader blindly (like ducks in a row).

bebel dumb, stupid, goofy.

bebenah 1 to put in order. 2 to clear away, remove.

bebencé long-tailed nightjar.

bebenyut (s.) BELIBIS.

bebesran mulberry.

bébi baby.

bebidung **m-** to pester.

bebodor and **-an** clown, comedian, buffoon. *utk -an* jokingly.

bebogohan 1 mating. *sepasang cicak lagi -* a couple of mating wall lizards. 2 amusement (park).

bebotoh 1 rascal, rogue, scamp. 2 referee. 3 gambler.

bebotok *- ikan* fish cooked in banana leaves au bain marie.

bebrayan 1 to gather, assemble. 2 community.

bebuahan fruits.

bebuyutan ancestral, traditional.

béca(k) a form of man-pedaled, three-wheeled rear-driven pedicab that carries the passenger(s) in front of the driver, a bicycle-propelled rickshaw. **di-kan** to be turned into (or, used as) a pedicab. "**M-** *den*? " "Do you want to ride in a pedicab, sir? " *Joni* **se-** *dgn Yusuf,* Joni and Yusuf shared a pedicab. *- air* pedal-boat. *- dayung* any kind of pedaled *beca(k),* (opp.) *- mesin* any kind of motor-driven *beca(k).*

bècèng pistol.

becus *tdk -* incompetent.

béda mem-kan *mana yg benar, mana yg salah* to tell right from wrong. **pem-.–an** *bendera* flag discrimination. **per-an** *graduil (,tingkat)* difference in degree.

bedah pem-an: ~ *kosmetis* cosmetic surgery. ~ *plastik* plastic surgery. ~ *terbuka* open surgery.

bedak mem-i *jalan.jalan bopeng* to patch up potholed streets.

bedangkik stingy.

bedaya and **bedhaya** [pron. bed(h)oyo] a classical female dance, usually performed by nine dancers at a time, representing the nymphs of *Nyai Loro Kidul. B- Ketawang* dance symbolizing the sensual love between *Nyai Loro Kidul* and Sultan Agung (this dance may only be staged in the main front veranda of the palace, during a *jumenengan* and *wiyosan* ceremony of the prince).

bedebah *si* - stinker.

bèdèng -an seedbed.

bedil *menjual* - *kpd lawan* to foul o's own nest. -.-an *sumbat* popgun.

bedol and **bedhol** di- to be moved. *Sebelas desa di Gresik akan* ~, Eleven villages in Gresik will be moved (,relocated). **di-.-** to be pulled, drawn. **mem-** to relocate families, (esp.) away from the island of Java. ~ *brankas* to break open a safe. **M-** *Desa* to move a whole village. *ongkos* -an transportation costs.

Bedrijfsreglementeringsordonnantie Industrial Regulations Ordinance.

bè.èng very. *gede* - very big.

begadang (s.) GADANG I.

begandring meeting.

begasi (s.) BAGASI. *tempat* - trunk (of car).

Begawan title given to a religious ascetic of noble origin (it is esp. used for kings who have abandoned their throne to seek religious enlightenment).

begejil dwarf, gnome.

begini this is the way it is, it's like this, the point is this. *ceritanya* - this is how the story goes. **se-** of such a size (or, an amount). *Pesawat.pesawat* ~ *bia-*

sanya sanggup menempuh jarak maksimum 5 jam terbang, Planes of such a size can usually cover a distance of maximum 5 flight hours. *hanya* ~ only as much (,little) as this. -an like this, such as this. *menjadi* ~ to become a prostitute. - *hari* so early. - *ini* like this.

begitu as soon as, the moment ... - ... - ... and - ... *lalu (,lantas)* ... as soon as ... *B- saya melihat wajahnya,* - *saya lalu jatuh cinta,* As soon as I saw her face I fell in love. *kalau* - if that's the way it is. *memang* - it's always like that. - *rupa sehingga* ... in such a way that ... *(dgn)* - *saja* abrupt, offhand, without further ceremony. -lah 1 we have to take it as it comes, that's life. 2 yes, that's about the way it is. *"Yaaaa, -lah lebih kurang,"* "Yeeees, that's more or less the case." *Tina, -lah,* That's the way it is with Tina. *kenal.kenal -lah* to know s.o. slightly, be superficially acquainted with s.o. *Kok bisa -?* How is that possible? mem-kan and -an *dgn* to have sexual intercourse with *perempuan* -an prostitute. -.-(lah) so-so.

bégo stupid, simpleminded.

beguk 1 part of neck and jaw. 2 thyroid gland.

begundal accomplice.

bejo 1 luck. 2 to be fortunate.

bèk I 1 (administrative) district, ward. 2 head of a district (,ward). 3 (in Jakarta) office of village head.

bèk II (in soccer) fullback. - *kanan (,kiri)* right (,left) fullback.

bekakah I grilled. - *ayam* grilled, whole chicken, on the spit.

bekakah II the offering of a sacrifice in the month of *Sapar* (the second month of the Moslem year) to ward off epidemic diseases at the village of Gamping (Yogyakarta).

bekal I - *hidup* victuals. - *makanan* packed rations.

bekal II pem- (in the Hulu Sungai Tengah Regency, Kalimantan) village head.

bekantan k.o. monkey (L. Nasalis larvatus) only found in Kalimantan.

bekas ber- to leave a trace. *hilang lenyap tak* ~ to disappear without a trace. *B-Ibukota Negara Republik Indonesia* Yogyakarta. - *pakai* second-hand. - *reman* skid marks.

bekatul bran.

bekèn and **ke-** well-known, famous. *Haji Abdul Malik Karim Amarullah lebih ke- dgn panggilan (Buya) Hamka,* Haji Abdul Malik Karim Amarullah is better known by the name of (Buya) Hamka. **ke-an** fame. *yg -.-* celebrities.

bekicot k.o. large snail.

bekikuk crossbreed between a Bantam (fowl) and a *bekisar.*

bèking backing, clout. *Pemilik pabrik itu punya -,* The factory owner has a powerful friend, has protection from s.o. with power.

bekisar crossbreed between a Bantam (fowl) and a wild fowl (or, *ayam alas*).

beklééd (S.) BEKLEDING. *ahli -* upholsterer.

beklèiding (car) upholstery store; (S.) BEKLEDING.

bèklès backlash.

beko *sabun -* bar of soap, soap in bars.

bekoar (s.) KOAR.

beku ke-an coagulation. *dana tabungan di-kan* blocked savings fund. **pem-an** 1 coagulation. 2 freezing (of bank account) ~ *90% dr semua uang simpanan di bank.bank* the freezing of 90% of all deposits in the banks. - *kepolitikan* politically inflexible.

bekuk mem- to defeat.

bèl mem- and **menge-** to ring a bell.

bela (frequently confused with **béla**) **pem-** *(perkara)* counsel for the defense.

béla (frequently confused with **bela**) **pem-** apologist. - *diri* self-defense.

belacu calico.

belah I *kedua - pipi* both cheeks. **ber** *se-(.-)an* adjacent. **pem-an** fission. **se-:** *anak gadis* ~ *rumah* the girl next door. *rumah* ~ next door. **-an:** ~ *dunia* hemisphere. ~ *sisiran* part (of the hair). - *bumi* hemisphere. - *ketupat* lozenge-

shaped. - *rambut* part (of the hair).

belah II (in Gayo, Aceh) clan.

belaka mere(ly).

belakang *di -* 1 abaft. 2 (in a document) on the back, on (the) back of this. 3 at the back of. 4 behind o's back. *Kalau memberi sedekah jangan memaki.maki di -,* If you have given alms (to s.o.) don't use abusive language behind his back. *di - (buritan)* astern. *di - layar* (fig.) behind the curtains. *menyesal di - hari* will regret in the future. *keuangan yg seimbang di -nya* commensurate supporting funds. *paling -* recently. **keter-an** 1 arrears, backlog. 2 backwardness. **ter-** underdeveloped (country). *anak.anak* ~ *(mental)* (mentally) retarded children. **-an** (in newspapers) stop press. ~ *dikirim* (of letters) forwarded (on), redirected. *dlm th.th* ~ *ini* in the past years. *sampai waktu* ~ *ini* until recently (,lately).

belalang *mata - blm pecah, sdh hendak membuta* to go to bed with the chickens.

belanak *ikan -* the gray mullet (L. Mugil sp.).

Belanda 1 Netherlander, Dutchman. 2 any European or westerner. *bagai - minta tanah* 'like a Dutchman asking for land,' i.e. give him an inch and he will take an ell. *si -* a long haired, yellow-colored monkey with pointed nose, found in the Mahakam area of Kalimantan. - *Inggris* Englishman. - *Rusia* Russian. *(orang) - berkulit sawo matang* Eurasian, Dutch Indonesian. - *Didong* a full-blooded Dutchman. - *hitam serdadu* 'the black Dutch soldier,' i.e. 1 the Ambonese soldier. 2 the black Surinam negro with Dutch citizenship who during col. served in the Netherlands Indies army or police. 3 the South African negro who mainly served in the army of the Dutch East India Company. - *kertas* Indonesian who has become a Dutchman based on certain regulations.

Belandis native Indonesian with pro-

Dutch leanings.

belang spotted, variegated. -.*bonteng* streaked all over. *bahasa Indonesia yg -.bonteng campuraduk dgn bahasa daerahnya* an Indonesian language interspersed with regional dialects.

belangsak *hidup yg* ke- a difficult life.

belanja *hrs diberikan - terus* should be continuously provided with funds. *pandai* - knowing how to make ends meet. *tukang* - and **pem-** shopper. **per-an** shopping.

belantan club, cudgel, truncheon.

belantara scene.

belarak dried coconut leaf; (s.) ABU (BLARAK).

belas I *sejak (,utk)* -an *th* for scores of years.

belas II - *hati* compassion.

belasteran (s.) BLASTERAN.

belasting tax.

belat.belit *tanpa* - without beating around the bush, straight-forward.

belatung maggot, mite.

belau (in the interior of the Mahakam River area in Kalimantan) a mysterious human being or devil.

belebegu (s.) AGAMA (BELEBEGU).

belegur bang! (sound of the roar of guns).

belèh di- to be slaughtered.

belèid policy. - *pemerintah* government policy.

bèlèk -an conjunctivitis, pink-eye.

bèlèl to fade away (of color). *celana* - pre-washed (,faded) pants.

belèlètan to stick to. *Kuah gado.gado - di baju itu,* Some *gado-gado* sauce was stuck to the shirt.

belèr ke- to get cut by a sharp object.

beli *Ini saya* - *Rp. 1.000,* I'll give you 1,000 rupiahs for this. *dpt* **di-** *pd* obtainable from, on sale at. **pem-** *tunggal* single buyer. **pem-an** *di muka* previous purchase, buying futures. **ter-kan** can be bought.

belia youth(ful).

beliat (S.) BELIAK.

beliau person. *kedua - itu* both of them. -.- *(itu)* those gentlemen (derisively).

belibis whistling teal.

belida and **belido** a marine fish (L. Notopterus kapirat).

belija *jamaah* **pe-an** k.o. syndicate of traders in diamonds originating from Martapura (Kalimantan).

belimbing carambola, a sour star-shaped fruit, pale yellow and waxy; star-shaped if crosscut.

belit ber-.- to beat around the bush. **mem-** to complicate, make intricate (,difficult).

beliung adze.

belok prisoner's stocks. **mem-** to place in the stocks.

belongsong material (paper, bamboo, etc.) for wrapping fruits while still on the tree, to hasten the ripening.

bélot pem- defector.

beludru velvet.

beluk plague in rice (the stalk borer).

belum 1 not including, exclusive of. 2 still left out. 3 not quite, almost. 4 is not so much as. - + *reduplicated verb* still hasn't, though expected to by now. **se-:** ~ *dan sesudahnya* (in correspondence) in advance. *tahu* ~ to have advance knowledge. - *dewasa (,akil balig)* underage. - *lagi* not yet, not to mention, still not (although should have by now), not counting, we still haven't included. - *lama ini* the other day, recently. - *tentu* it's not necessarily the case that, it's not certain that. -.- *juga* still not (although expected to by now).

belus free to go in and out, unobstructed, loose in a socket.

belut *sbg - diketil (,digetir) ekor* 'like an eel the tail of which has been cut,' i.e. to dart off, be gone. *licin sbg -* as slippery as an eel. *spt - pulang ke lumpur* and *sbg - jatuh ke lumpur* to be in seventh heaven.

benah ber- *diri* to get ready (,prepared); (s.) BEBENAH. **ter-i** ready, fixed up.

benak mind.

benam mem-(kan) *uang* to invest money.

benar ke-an confirmation. *Utara* se-nya
true North.
bencana affliction. *dlm* - (to be) in danger.
benci - *aku!* How awful! Oh, no! - *akan*
(*,kpd ,thd*) to despise.
bèncong homosexual.
benda collateral. *tanah dan -.- yg ada di
atasnya* (in legal documents) the land
with the buildings (,structures) erected
thereon, with the buildings, structures
and erections thereon, and anything
built upon it, and its appendages. ke-an
collateral. - *angkasa* celestial body.
- *keras* a blunt instrument. - *langit tak
dikenal* unidentified flying object,
UFO. -.- *pos* stamps, postcards, etc.
- *terbang aneh* and - *terbang yg tak
dikenal* unidentified flying object,
UFO. - *tetap* real estate.
bendaharawan treasury officer.
bendalu 1 a mistletoe shrub. 2 parasitic
plant, parasite. 3 (fig.) sponger, parasite.
bendar ditch; (s.) SAWAH [(BER)BEN-
DAR LANGIT].
bendasraya indemnity insurance.
bendawi (adj.) material.
bèndel a bound volume of a magazine.
bendéra *kapal* ber- *Indonesia* an Indonesian flag ship. mem-i to welcome
with flags. - *biru* the blue flag hoisted
in coastal towns on the Island of Java if
it is too dangerous to land. - *kemudahan*
flag of convenience. - *penungkul* the
flag of truce. *B- Pusaka* the original
Indonesian flag.
bendésa village head.
bèndi (drug sellers' sl.) cops, police.
Ada -! The police are coming!
bèndiwan a driver of a *bendi* (,two-
wheeled horse-drawn cart).
bendo chopper.
bendoro master, lord.
bendung -an weir, barrage, embankment,
causeway. ~ *gelombang* breakwater.
~ *pelimpah* spillway. ~ *peti* cofferdam.
bener *yg -aja* don't did around, be serious.
bengal 1 conceited, opinionated. 2 dull,
unteachable. 3 mischievous. 4 incor-
rigeable.

bengeb and bengep swollen (of face, due
to beating, etc.).
bènggol (party) boss.
bengis - *bertimpal* -, *kejam berbalas kejam*
an eye for an eye and a tooth for a
tooth. ke-an austerity, rigor.
bengkak I mem- 1 to increase. 2 to expand.
bengkak II cancer. - *lapar* malnutrition,
oedema.
bengkalai work that still has to be done,
daily work. keter-an neglect. ter- 1 will
come to nothing. 2 got stuck. 3 mo-
tionless.
bèngkap boots, leggings.
bengkarung the skink.
bèngkèl - *las* welding plant.
bèngkèr bunker, casemate.
bèngkok garbled (of a newsitem). *pikiran*
- dishonest. - *hati* unreliable, undepend-
able.
bengkok 1 land tenure (i.e. land given in
usufruct to members of the village
administration as a k.o salary). 2 land
taken care of by a village head to
finance the village organization.
bèngkong *(tukang)* - circumcizer.
bengkuang jicamo (Mexico), k.o. vegetable.
bengok I water hyacinth (L. Eichornia
crassipes).
bengok II the mumps.
bengok III m- to shout, yell.
bengong 1 perplexed, bewildered, confused, taken aback. 2 to be absorbed
in thought. (me)m- *kagum* stupefied
from astonishment. nge-in to make s.o.
confused (,perplexed). - *terlongong.
longong* to stare blankly.
bèngot twisted, awry.
benguk peas.
bengut (s.) BENGOT.
bèni motorized *becak* using a Lambretta
(scooter) motor.
benih pem-an *buatan* artificial breeding.
bènsol benzol.
bentang -an span (of a bridge). ~ *tengah*
main span. - *alam* landscape. - *sungai*
span over a river.
bentar se-: *Seperempat abad adalah waktu*

yg tdk ~, A quarter of a century is not a moment of time. ~ *ya?* just a moment, please. ~ *antaranya (,lagi)* soon, before long. ~ *kemudian* shortly after. ~ *sore* this evening. ~... ~*(,kemudian)* ... now ... now (,then) ..., one moment ... the next ... *ala* ~ for a moment (,short time). *tidur barang* ~ to take a quick nap. *tiap* ~ every now and then. ~**an** for the time being. ~.~ from time to time.

bèntèng - *kuno* citadel.

bentèr (s.) IKAN (BENTER).

bentèt cracked but not broken through.

bentrok to conflict. -**an** clash, conflict. ~ *senjata* armed clash.

bentuk ber-: ~ *sel* cellular. ~ *tabel* tabular. **mem-**.*ulang* to reconstitute. -**an** style. *PKI* ~ *baru* the new-styled Indonesian Communist Party. - *hukum* legal form. - *kata* morphology.

bentur ber-(an) to clash. -**an** *kepentingan* conflict of interests.

benua - *hitam* Africa. *B- Kangguru* Australia. - *kecil* subcontinent.

be'ol to shit.

Bèos the downtown railway station in Jakarta.

Bèppan (during the Jap. occupation) the Japanese Special Task Unit within the 16th Army Headquarters which was responsible for counterintelligence and special operations.

bera (s.) BERO.

berabé 1 annoyance, trouble. 2 difficult, hard, troublesome, complicated, embarrassing. *membuat* - to make things difficult. *Kalau dua.duanya diam bisa -,* If both are quiet then there is the devil to pay. -**in** to complicate.

Berahman(a) a Brahmin.

Berahmani a female Brahmin.

beraksa I (s.) KUDA (BERAKSA).

beraksa II k.o. tree (L. Cassia fistula).

berambang (s.) BRAMBANG.

berandal ke-an mischief.

berangan (s.) BARANGAN.

berangas -**an** irascible, hot-tempered.

berani *dgn* **ke-an** *sendiri* on o's own initiative. *semakin* **mem-** increasingly daring.

berantas pem- *hama* pesticide.

berapa *jam (,pukul ,th ,tgl)* -? what time (,year ,date)? -, *ya* let me see, how much. - *lagi* how much more. *tiada - th lamanya* a few years later. *tak - kerap kali* not frequently any more. *Tdk - lama kemudian mobil berhenti,* Shortly after the car stopped. **be-** 1 various 2 a couple of, a good deal of, a good many of. *dlm* ~ *waktu yg akhir ini* for some time. **ke-** ...? how many (from a certain point) ...? *utk* ~ *kalinya* ...? how many times ...? **se-** as much as, as many as. ~ *dpt* as much as possible. *tdk* ~ not so (much, many), not very (much), not a great many, negligible, not to any extent. *tdk* ~ *jauh* not so far.

beras per-an (adj.) rice. - *Amerika panjang* rice consisting of long, slender grains, transparent, a bit cream colored. Grains remain separate after cooking. With all other types of rice, the grains stick together if rice is cooled after cooking. - *Belanda* rye. - *bersih* clean rice. - *bulu tumbuk* hand-milled rice. - *Cianjur* rice consisting of medium grains. - *fitrah* rice earmarked as an obligatory gift at the end of the Fasting month. - *gandum* bulgur-wheat. - *Irwin* a rice made from corn which after undergoing certain chemical processes no longer has the outer skin of its corn kernels. - *jatah [,drop(p)ing]* allocated rice. - *Jepang* rice consisting of small, nearly round grains resembling barley. - *kencur* mixture of powdered raw rice and medicinal roots for massaging. - *kepala* whole rice. - *kuning (,kunyit)* rice not yet ripe or that is yellow from improper drying. - *menir* very small broken rice. - *merah* red-brown colored rice. - *pecah kulit* and - *P.K.* rice with inner bran layer. - *pera* granular, dry rice. - *perelek* rice grains fallen out of sacks during transportation. - *putih* white rice; top-quality rice. - *Saigon* medium-grain rice. - *Saigon Bandung* slender, medium-grain rice. - *Siam* lower-grade, red-colored rice. - *sosoh (,tumbuk ,tuton)* home-pounded rice.

berat to favor. - *pd (,kpd)* to take a person's part, side with a person. *Kau lebih - padaku?* Do you lean more toward me? -*!* it's tough! - *ke atas (,puncak)* top-heavy. *tapol.tapol klas -* dangerous political detainees. *tdk* **berke-an** *atas* to have no objections to. **ke-an** drawback. *Saya tdk* ~ I don't care. - *atom* atomic weight. - *dugaanku* I'm sure that. - *hati* 1 to be afraid of, shrink from. 2 to incline to, care for, be in sympathy with. - *lidah* it costs a great effort (to say s.t.). *tdk - sebelah* unbiased.

berba [berlapis baja] armored.

Bèrber *orang -* Berber.

bercak -.- *merah* red marks on face.

berdikari [berdiri di atas kaki sendiri] 1 to be self-reliant. 2 to be self-supporting. **di.B-kan** to be made self-reliant. *Th 1967 P.N. Postel ~,* In 1967 the Postal and Telecommunications State Corporation will be made self-reliant.

berèken to figure out.

bèrem -**an** (grass) verge, verge (of the road).

berem (s.) BREM.

beremban - *peti* cofferdam.

berèngsèk (s.) BRENGSEK. **ke-an** lousiness (of traffic conditions).

bèrès fixed, settled; (s.) TAHU I. *sdh -!* (that's all) cut and dried! it's taken care of! no sweat! *kurang - ingatannya* he is not right in the head. **di-kan** (coll.) to be killed (be taken care of). *Komandan pemberontakan ~,* The rebel commander was killed. **pem-an** discharging (the Managing Board and Board of Directors from all proceedings as appear in the bookkeeping).

bergajul rascal, scoundrel, hooligan, villain. **ke-an** vandalism, hooliganism.

berhala animistic idol.

beri di-: ~ *angin* favored. ~ *beratap* (the house) was provided with a roof. ~ *berawalan* (such compounds) prefixed with (ber-). ~ *bergambar* (the book) is illustrated (by). ~ *berjangkar* (each corner of the boat) was provided with anchors. ~ *berkaki* (the signboard) was mounted on a stand. *Kalèng itu ~nya berlubang,* He made a hole in the can. ~ *bernama* to be called (,given a name). ~ *berpintu* to be provided with a door. ~ *bertali* (the dog) was roped. ~ *bertanda* to be indicated. ~ *bertitian* to be bridged (over). **mem-:** ~ *aval* (banking term) to guarantee (a bill). ~ *hukuman* to condemn. ~ *ingat* to warn, caution. ~ *kesan* to give an idea. ~ *keuntungan* profitable. ~ *kuasa* to authorize. ~ *malu* 1 to bring discredit upon. 2 to make s.o. look a fool. 3 to affront. ~ *muka* to be lenient, give in. ~ *semangat* to stimulate, inspire. **mem-kan** *suaranya* to cast (,give) o's vote. **pem-:** ~ *amanat* adviser. ~ *aval* (banking term) guarantor. ~ *kredit* lender ~ *tahu* notifier. ~ *tugas* principal. **pem-an** award, granting. ~ *amanat* mandate, commission. ~ *amnesti* granting of amnesty. ~ *grasi* granting of a pardon. ~ *kerja* procuring of employment. ~ *kuasa* delegation of authority. ~ *nasehat.nasehat perkawinan* marriage counselling. ~ *tugas* mandate, commission. **pem- tahuan** communication. ~ *barang masuk utk dipakai* entry for home use (i.e. a Customs document). ~ *resmi* legal notice.

berik brig (a ship).

beringas irritable, hot-tempered. **di-i** to be irritated.

beringin *B-* the elections symbol used by *Golkar* in the 1971 and 1977 general elections.

berita *blm* **ter-** (it) has not yet been reported. - *acara* official report, deposition. - *hasutan* seditious news. - *intel* news transferred through long-distance call. - *kapal* shipping intelligence. - *kawat* cablegram. - *kematian* notice of deaths. - *panji* banner headline (in

newspaper). - *panggilan ganda* multiple
call messages. - *pasar* market report. -.-
radio dengkul rumors. - *tendensius*
slanted news. - *terlambat* a belated
report (,news item).

berkas 1 lawyer's brief. 2 dossier.

berkèk *burung* - the snipe.

bèrko electric bicycle lamp.

bèrkolin trade name of a lightweight
fabric.

berlian ke-an brilliance.

bermis [beton ringan dr batu pamis]
light-weight concrete made from
pumice (used in home building).

bernga larva; (S.) BERENGA.

bero uncultivated, untilled.

berobot -.- (constant) rattling (of rifle-
fire). -.-an rat-tat-tat.

beroerte (pron. oe as oo in mood) stroke
(of apoplexy).

berok *turun* - hernia.

berondong *kena* - get shot. **mem-** to strafe.

berondongan popcorn.

berongsang to be in an angry mood.

beroti a horizontal lath, rung.

bersih - *dr stok* out of stock. **pem-** cleanser. ~ *gigi palsu* denture cleanser. - *desa*
annual purification of the village from
evil spirits.

bersit *cuma* se- only a little bit.

beruang - *kutub* polar bear. *si B- Merah*
the U.S.S.R.

beruaya (of prawns) to migrate in schools.

beruntusan covered with a rash, suffer
from 'German measles.'

besalèn 1 blacksmith's shop, forge.
2 *keris* making.

besar I 1 major. 2 to grow up. *Dia - di
Jawa,* He grew up in Java. *sdh* - grown
up. *Saya* **di-kan** *di Jakarta,* I grew up
in Jakarta. **mem-kan:** ~ *belanja* to
spend more than necessary. ~ *nafsu* to
give free rein to. ~ *suara* to raise o's
voice. **pem-.pem-** *kapal* the ship's
officers. -. *kecilnya* 1 size. *B-. kecilnya
telur tdk terlalu tergantung pd keturunan ayam,* The size of the eggs does
not depend too much on the pedigree
of the chicken. 2 amount. *Perhitungan*
-. *kecilnya sewa biasanya tergantung pd
...,* The calculation of the amount of
the rental usually depends on ... 3 extent. -. *kecilnya suatu kerusakan akan
ditentukan bersama oleh kedua belah
pihak* the extent of damage shall be
determined jointly by the two parties.
se- *nyata* as big as life. **-an** number,
figure. - *bangkai* sturdy.

Besar II the 12th (lunar) month of the
Moslem calendar. *Lembu* **B-an** the cow
given by the Sultan of Yogyakarta to
the poor and needy in his administrative area on the 10th of the Javanese
lunar month of *Besar* on the occasion
of *Idul Korban.*

besengèk curried chicken, meat, etc.

bèsèr incontinence of urine.

besèt abraded, rubbed off.

besi - *kejen* pig iron. - *p(e)lat* sheet iron.
- *tua* (fig.) of no use anymore. *menjadi*
- *tua* and **di- tuakan** to be scrapped.
pem- tuaan scrapping (of sunken ships).
- *tuang* cast iron.

beskup mem- to seize, confiscate.

bésok next. *bln September* - next September. - *atau lusa* one of these days.
- *malamnya* the next evening. **-nya** the
next morning. -.-**nya** 1 the day after
tomorrow. 2 later.

besot badly scratched. - *kulitnya* his
skin was chafed.

bestèk (in building construction) (tender)
specification.

bestèl pem-an mail delivery. ~ *expres*
special delivery.

bestik beefsteak.

bestral pem-an x-ray treatment.

bésuk (s.) BESOK.

besuk visit. **mem-** to visit.

besukaan (s.) SUKA.

besut -.-**an** outpourings.

bet - *(h)ilang* to disappear with lightning
speed.

BETA [Benda Terbang Aneh] UFO.

betah to feel at home. - *bicara* to be in a
talkative mood.

betapa (not followed by an adjective +
nya) how. - *banyak orang.orang Indo-*

nesia ... how many Indonesians ...
- *terkejutku ketika* ... how startled I
was when ... - *lagi (,pula)* 1 not to
mention, to say nothing of, let alone.
2 so much the more. - *tdk* why not.
-*pun* in any case, be that as it may.
Betara (s.) BATARA.
Betari a special title for female deities.
betatas sweet-potato plant.
beteging unyielding.
betik I news. **ter-** it has become (well-)
known. *ada kabar* ~ there is a report
abroad. ~ *di hati* it flashes into o's
mind. *tdk* ~ *ke luar* did not show it,
did not betray his feelings.
betik II -.- German measles.
betis *diberi - hendak paha* (if you) give
him an inch he will take an ell.
beton di- to be covered with concrete.
- *berbesi [,(ber)tulang]* reinforced
concrete. - *bis* concrete tube. - *mollen*
concrete mixer. - *pratekan* prestressed
concrete.
betonisasi the covering (of streets, etc.)
with concrete.
betot - *urat keras.keras* to debate heated-
ly, oppose vehemently. **ke-** pulled.
merasa hatinya spt ~ to be overjoyed
or saddened, very touched.
betul *bodoh -!* what a stupid thing!
sembuh - completely recovered. *tdk -!*
you're wrong! **ke-an:** *karena sesuatu* ~
by a coincidence. ~ *yg bertali.tali* a
coincidence. **mem-kan** *letak duduknya*
to twist and turn (in o's seat). *di* **-an**
1 off (the west coast of Kalimantan).
2 right in front of. *ada* **-nya** there's
some truth in it. - *tidaknya* the truth
(of some matter). *Pertanyaan ttg -
tidaknya desas.desus itu,* A question
regarding the truth of the rumors.
betutu - *bebek* duckling broiled in banana
leaf, a favorite at Balinese banquets.
bezètting **pèrsonalia** staffing.
bezuk visit. **mem-** to visit.
bh (pron. béha; the Dutch abbrev. for
'bustehouder') bra(ssiere).
Bhakti Wanita women's organization
which has under it the State Secretary

and 18 non-departmental institutions.
bharatayud(dh)a (s.) BRATAYUD(H)A.
Bhayangkara 1 The Police Force of the
Majapahit Kingdom. 2 The Police Force
of the Republic of Indonesia.
Bhayangkari 1 guardian. 2 name of the
Police Wives Association.
bhikhu, bhikku, bhikkhu and **bhikkshu**
(S.) BIKU.
Bhinnéka - Tunggal Ika motto of the
Indonesian State Coat of Arms, mean-
ning: Unity in Diversity. **ke-an** diversity. **ke-.tunggal.ikaan** 'unity-in-
diversity-ness.'
Bhirawa Anoraga motto of the *Brawijaya*
Division, meaning: Courageous but
Humble.
Bhra name of the *Majapahit* dynasty.
Bhrawijaya (also spelled: **Brawijaya**)
name of the army division stationed
in East Java.
Bhuda Buddha.
bi I in, on, with. -*hi* on (,with) him.
-*smillah* in the name of God (,Allah).
bi II contraction of *bihi.*
bia (S.) BEA.
biang - *keringat* German measles. - *kerok*
1 mastermind. 2 troublemaker. - *macet*
center of traffic jams.
biar I - *lambat asal selamat* better late
than never, slow but sure. - *d(ah)ulu!*
not for the present! - *mahal,* - *murah,*
tak akan saya beli be it cheap or expensive, I won't buy it. - *begitu!* leave it
as it is! - *nanti* so that (it) would be.
*dgn maksud - nanti dipenatukan oleh
pelayan* with the intention that (the
clothes) would be taken to the laun-
dryman by the bellboy. - *seketikapun*
not even a minute. -*pun begitu (,demi-
kian)* nevertheless. -*pun siapa* and
- *siapa saja* who(so)ever. - ... *maupun*
..., *maupun* ... -*pun* ... and *baikpun*
... -*pun* ... 1 both ... and ... 2 or,
-*(pun)* ... *atau* ... (or, - ... - ...) either
... or ... **-in** *saja* never mind, forget it.
-.**mem-kan** to be tolerant. **ter-** *(begitu
saja)* abandoned.
biar II -.-: *cacing* ~ intestinal worms (L.

Filaria loa) ~ *naik ke mata* 'the biar-
biar worm reaches your eyes,' i.e. a
pun on the meanings of **biar I** and
biar II, conveying the warning, 'If you
are not on your guard, you will have
reason to regret it.'

bias pem-an *sinar* diopter.

biaya *atas - saya* at my expense. - *batas*
marginal costs. - *hidup* cost of living.
- *inklaring* Customs fees. - *kawat* cable
charges. - *muat* shipping charges.
- *pemeliharaan* maintenance costs.
- *penagihan* cost of recovery. - *penginapan* hotel expenses. - *penyimpanan*
(safe-)custody fee. - *perawatan* nursing
expenses, hospital fees. - *perjalanan*
traveling expenses. - *siluman* bribes.

Bibel Bible.

bibik middle-aged woman of lower social
level.

bibir *kering dr* - already forgotten. - *meja*
table edge.

bibit 1 young employees. 2 the early
stages (of a war). 3 good sort. *kuda -*
stallion, stud horse. *-, bebet dan bobot*
1 Javanese saying referring to the three
elements taken into consideration for
a harmonious marriage: (equal) origin,
descent and position. 2 birds of a feather flock together. - *minyak wangi*
perfumery compounds.

bicara *angka.angka lain yg* - other telling
figures. *dgn tak banyak* - and *tanpa
banyak* - without much ado, without
making a great fuss. *memasang - ini.itu*
to talk about this and that. *saling tukar
- ttg* ... to enter into a conversation
about ... *Nama ini mungkin tdk banyak
(ber)- bagi pembaca,* This name probably does not mean much (,a thing)
to the reader. **ber-**: ~ *dgn* to talk with,
speak to (sometimes, - *pd*). ~ *di muka
mikropon* to go on the air. *fakta.fakta
yg* ~ bold facts. *fakta yg tlh* ~ *sendiri*
a fact that speaks for itself, that tells its
own story. *mereka blm* ~ *satu bahasa*
they're not yet on the same wavelength.
mem-kan *tempat* to make a reservation.
pem- *tamu* guest speaker. **pem-an** (tele-

phone) call. ~ *interlokal* long-distance
call. ~ *pembuka jalan* preliminary talks.
~ *(secara) blak.blakan* open talks. *S
dibawa ke* ~ *politik,* S was brought to
political discussions. *menjadi* ~ *ramai*
to become the topic of the day.

bida (in Northern Jakarta) collector of
sand (for building purposes).

bidadari angel, nymph, houri.

bidan - *perawat berijazah* registered
nurse, RN.

bidang area. **mem-i** to cover, deal with
(certain sectors in Parliament, etc. by
certain committees in which Parliament has been divided), subordinate
... sectors. - *kerja* field of operations.

bidar racing proa (of Palembang, South
Sumatra).

bidat (S.) BID'AH.

bidik -an a shot. ~ *tepat* a well-aimed shot.

biduk se- *dan setujuan* to work for the
same goals.

biduren urticaria.

biduri 1 opal. 2 quartz (semiprecious
stone).

biduwati (S.) BIDUANITA.

bigami bigamy.

bihari formerly, in former times. *baheula.-*
in former times, in olden times. *Indonesia: B- dan Kini,* Indonesia: Past and
Present.

bihun rice sticks made from shaped boiled
rice, dried.

bijaksana *Itu terserah kpd* ke-an *Tuan,* I
leave it to your discretion.

bijaksanawan wise man.

Bijblad (pron. bêblat) Supplement of
Statute Book.

biji *kena -nya!* 'grabbed by the balls!'
- *jakar* testicles. - *jambu mede (,mo-
nyet)* cashew (L. Anacardium occiden-
tale). - *longkong* chance(s), possibilities. - *pelir* testicles. - *sawit* palm
kernels.

bika ambon yellow, sticky cake, served
in wedges.

bikin di-: *Ayahnya sdh tdk ada. D~
lurahnya.* His father is already dead.
The village head cast a spell on

him. ~ *menurut ukuran* to be custom-made. **mem-kan** to make ... for. **pem-**
uang palsu counterfeiter (of money).
pem-an: ~ *pab(e)rik* manufacture,
fabrication. ~ *uang* coinage. **-an**:
~ *pab(e)rik* manufacture, make.
senyum ~ a simper.

biksu melepaskan **ke-an**nya to relinquish
o's Buddhistship.

biksuni Buddhist (female) priest.

bilal - *masehi* chaplain.

bilang *sonder - item.putih* and *sonder -.-*
(coll.) without saying a word. **ber-**:
~ *bln (,jam ,th)* for months (,hours
,years). ~ *kali* again and again, repeatedly. *hidup di desa* ~ *gobang, hidup di*
kota ~ *rupiah* (coll.) in the village people reckon by 2½-cent coins, in the
cities by rupiahs. *hanya* ~ *waktu saja*
(within) a short time. *boleh* **di-** mostly,
practically.

bilik cabin, compartment. - *kerja* office.
- *pencoblosan* voting booth. - *telepon*
umum public phone booth.

bilyèt 1 form. - *giro* transfer form. 2 card,
ticket.

bilyètris conductress (on *Bima, Mutiara*
and *Parahyangan* trains).

Bima I *Raden* - a *wayang* character.

Bima II [Biru Malam] the blue-colored
night express between Jakarta and
Surabaya.

Bimas [Bimbingan Masal (Swa Sembada
Bahan Makanan)] Mass Guidance for
Self-Sufficiency in Food, i.e. an agricultural program, introduced in 1965
and including promotion of fertilizer
use, high-yielding seeds and other
means of increasing crop yields; (s.)
INMAS. **pem-an** 'Bimasation.'

Bimasakti and **Bima Sakti** 1 Milky Way,
Galaxy. 2 the code name given by the
Gestapu/PKI to the *Lubang Buaya*
volunteers in their abortive coup
staged on September 30, 1965. 3
G-30-S troups with the assignment of
occupying the Jakarta Radio Station
and Telephone Exchange.

bimbing pem- thesis advisor. *guru* ~ teach-

er counselor. **B-an** *Kemasyarakatan*
dan Pengentasan Anak, Social Guidance
and Child Care.

bin *qualitative* + *bin* + *qualitative* forms
an affective expression indicating a
high degree: *ajaib - ganjil, aneh - ajaib,*
ganjil - ajaib and *heran - ajaib* extremely queer (,strange); *kalut - kacau* extremely confused; *serakah - tamak*
extremely greedy.

bina pem- 1 indoctrinator. 2 guest conductor (of the *Orkes Simponi Jakarta*
Jakarta Symphony Orchestra). 3 trainer for women noncommissioned officers in the Air Force who aspire to
commissions. ~ *bangsa* nation builder.
~ *kerta* social worker. ~ *perusahaan*
manager. **pem-an** 1 indoctrination.
2 building. ~ *bangsa* nation building.
3 formation. 4 management. ~ *kepega-*
waian personnel management. ~ *tenaga*
kerja manpower management. *B- Graha*
Executive Building. *B- Karya* Rehabilitation of the Unemployed. *Direktorat*
Jenderal B- Karya Directorate General
for the Rehabilitation of the Unemployed. *B- Marga* Highways. *Direktorat*
Jenderal B- Marga Directorate General
of Highways. *B- Mitra* 'Developing
Friends,' i.e. the name of a foundation
dealing with tourism. - *raga* body building. *Direktorat Jenderal B- Tuna Warga*
Directorate General of Correctional
Institutions. *B- Waluya* Health Care.
- *wismabumi* real estate.

binal naughty (eyes).

binaragawan body builder.

binasa ke-an ruin(ation), fall.

binatang I vermin. - *berkantong* marsu-
pial. - *buruan* game. - *kulit duri* porcupine. - *(me)lata* reptile. - *merusak*
vermin. - *yg bertulang belakang*
(,punggung) vertebrate.

binatang II brutal, ferocious.

bincacak and **bincacau** *anak* - witch child.

bingkai frame (of eyeglasses).

bingkis -an bribe. ~ *Lebaran* parcel given
to an influential person to mollify him
(on Lebaran day).

bingung *ke-an* completely confused.

bini - *gelap* illegal wife. - *muda* second and (usually) younger wife, concubine. - *piaraan* paramour, mistress. - *simpan* illegal wife. - *tua* first and (usually) older wife. -.-*an* 1 desirous of marrying. 2 illegitimate concubine.

binnen arrived (economically).

binomium - *Newton* Newton's binomial.

bint daughter of.

bintang *Ia dilahirkan dlm naungan* - *Leo,* She was born under the sign of Leo. *Gadis Amerika yg* **ber**-*Pisces ini ...,* This American girl born under the sign of Pisces ... **mem-i** to star in. - *tamu* guest star.

bintara - *dan tamtama* enlisted men.

binti.binti a small species of kingfisher.

bintrok sexy.

bintul.bahar mermaid.

bio Chinese temple.

biokimia biochemistry.

biologi biology.

bioritme biorhythm.

bioskop - *misbar (,openkap)* drive-in (theater). *tokoh* **per-an** movie magnate.

bir - *kalengan* canned beer.

birit the buttocks, ass. *lari* **ter-.**- to run helter-skelter, take to o's heels.

biro - *ahli* firm of surveyors. - *arsitek* architectural bureau. - *bangunan* builder's office. *B*- *Dunia Pandu Putra* Boy Scouts World Bureau. *B*- *Hubungan Masyarakat* Public Relations Office. - *konsultasi* consultation center. *B*- *Pengapalan Indonesia* Indonesian Cargo Control Agency. *B*- *Penyelidikan Federal* (The U.S.) Federal Bureau of Investigation. - *perjalanan* travel bureau, tourist office. - *perkawinan* matrimonial agency. *B*- *Pusat Statistik* Central Bureau of Statistics.

birokrat bureaucratic.

birokratisasi 'bureaucratization,' i.e. a system whereby leaders have become bureaucrats only responsible to their office, department, superiors and subordinates, so that they don't maintain relations with society at large.

biru *meninju mata orang sampai* - to give a person a black eye. - *kobalt* cobalt blue. - *muda* azure.

bis **per-kotaan** (adj.) city bus. - *antarkota* intercity bus. - *kota* city (,local) bus. - *malam* 'night bus,' i.e. a long-distance bus. - *tiga tingkat* 'three-level bus,' i.e. a passenger bus consisting of three types of passengers: 1 those squatting on top of the roof, 2 those having a seat, and 3 those standing.

Bis(s), bis(s) (pron. biiis, biiis) Bis, bis ...! Encore, encore ...! (a demand by the audience, shown by continued applause, for the repetition of a piece of music, etc.).

bisa I *ular* - a venomous snake.

bisa II 1 can, to know how (to). 2 to manage to (do), succeed in (do)ing. 3 to (do) in accordance with o's nature. *Macan* - *mengaum,* Tigers roar. *alah* - *oleh (karena) biasa* experience is the best teacher. - *saja* (they) can of course. *B*- *saja mereka datang ke Jakarta,* Of course they can come to Jakarta. - *sekali* very able (,clever). - *tidur?* did you sleep well? *paling* - at (the) most. *tdk* - *tdk* undoubtedly, absolutely. *Orang Indonesia tdk* - *tdk hrs menerima nasehat ahli.ahli asing,* Indonesians absolutely must accept the advice of foreign specialists. **se**-*mungkin* as much as possible. **se-.**- *if possible.* **se-(.-)nya** 1 to try o's best, to the best of o's ability. 2 if at all possible. *atas* -**nya** on o's own, independently. -.- possible.

bisbul (s.) BUAH (MENTEGA).

bisèktris bisector.

bisik -**an** inspiration. *menurut* ~ *hati (,kalbu)* to follow the dictates of.

biskop bishop. **ke-an** bishopric, diocese.

biskuit cracker. - *nasib* fortune cookies.

bismi in the name of.-*llahirrahmanirrahim* in the name of God, the Merciful, the Compassionate.

bismillah -*irrokhmanirrokhim* and -*ir. arahmanir.rahim* in the name of God, the Merciful, the Compassionate.

bisnis 1 business. 2 businessman, entrepreneur. *utk keperluan* - for business. *melakukan* - to carry on business, trade. *orang* - businessman. **ber-** to do business.

bissawab *wallahualam* - and God knows the truth.

bistik - *komplit* steak dinner.

bisu silent. *film* - silent movie. **bersi-** to behave as if o. were stupid.

bitumen 1 bitumen. 2 bituminous.

bius **pem-an** *lokal* local anesthetization.

biut obstinate, stubborn.

bivak bivouac. **ber-** to bivouac.

biwad(h)a to revere, venerate.

biyuh.biyuh exclamation of astonishment.

blacan (S.) BELACAN.

blaco (s.) BELACU.

blado broke, penniless.

blak.blakan straightforward, frank. *Mereka mengadakan tukar.pikiran secara* -, They had a straightforward exchange of views.

Blandis (s.) BELANDIS.

blandong teakwoodcutter working on a contract basis.

blandrèk **m-** (s.) BANDREK II (**mem-**).

blang.bleng (sound of) bomb explosions.

blangko blank.

blangkrèh in disorder, in the wrong place.

blantik I 1 trader in horses, buffaloes, chickens, ducks or weapons. 2 purchaser of items which after having been repaired, are sold again; (s.) BELANTIK.

blantik II **-an** *musik* musical firmament.

blasak **ke-** to get lost.

blaster **-an** 1 of mixed blood. *anak* ~ child of mixed blood. 2 a bird, the crossbreed between a *puter* and a *perkutut.*

blasur *pating* - to act in a hasty disorganized way.

bledèk lightning.

blegudrèk blood pressure.

blèjèt **di-i** to be robbed.

blèk **-an** in cans. *Korma itu dibelinya* ~, He bought the dates in cans.

blekèk little green heron.

blekok Chinese pond heron.

blèncong hanging oil lamp used in shadow play.

blendok resin.

blèndong foreign (non-Indonesian) homosexual.

bleng I sound of (bomb) explosion. - *lagi!* another bomb explosion!

bleng II salt water.

bléngah.bléngah and **bléngah.blèngéh** 1 pretty, yellowish-brown complexion. 2 pleasing in appearance (,facial features).

blèpot **-an** messy, muddy.

bletak bang!

bléwah k.o. cantaloupe.

blik (s.) BLEK.

blinger **ke-** 1 to get caught, be led astray, be deceived. 2 wrongheaded. *sikap. sikap yg serba* ~ completely wrongheaded attitudes.

blingsatan uncomfortable, worried, uneasy, restless, nervous. *Negeri-negeri Barat - melihat pembangunan militer RRC,* The western countries are uneasy at seeing the military development of the PRC.

Blitar city in East Java. *bahasa Inggeris* **-an** broken English.

bliyèr **m-** 1 to dissemble, sham, pretend, feign. 2 to behave (,answer) foolishly.

blobor **m-** to run (,flow) out (of liquid, paint, etc.).

blok *Rumah saya tiga - lagi dr sini,* I live three blocks away. **mem-** to block (a road). *sdh* **nge-** *ke Barat* (The Indonesian army) has already sided with the western bloc. - *bangunan* building block. - *komunis* the communist bloc. - *Sovyet* the Soviet bloc.

blokir **mem-** to freeze (a bank account). **pem-an** blockading, blocking. **-an** blockage.

bloknot notebook, note pad.

bloko suto (pron. of *blaka suta*) straightforward.

blong to fail, go out (of brakes). *Mobil itu mengalami kecelakaan karena* *remnya* -, The car met with an accident because the brakes failed.

blongkotan full-fledged. *anak Betawi* - a full-fledged Jakartan.

blo'on and **bloon** foolish, stupid. **ke-an** stupidity. **mem-i** to make a fool of s.o., trick.

blorok *si B-* and *Banteng B-* the 40-mm AA-gun used by the Indonesian freedom fighters around 1945.

blubut brazen, out and out. *Sorge memang seorang gombunis yg -*, Sorge was indeed a brazen commie.

bludag and **bludak m-** 1 to erupt. 2 fullbreasted.

bludas.bludus to go in and out without permission. *Armada Sovyet - di Samudera Indonesia,* Soviet fleets are secretly slipping in and out of the Ind(ones)ian Ocean.

bludrèk (high) bloodpressure.

blujin blue jeans. **ber-** to wear blue jeans.

bluk *-.-!* bang! (the noise made by falling heavy objects).

blur splash! (the noise made by jumping into water).

bluwok milky stork. *- sayap merah* painted stork.

bo'at and **boat** code name for morphine powder. **nge-** to use such a powder.

bobok *nina -!* rest, my baby, rest! hushaby baby!

bobol burst (of a dike), forced open. **ke-an** 1 loophole. 2 to be robbed. 3 to be penetrated. **mem-i** to penetrate and destroy.

bobot weight. **ber-** 1 to weigh. 2 serious, of high quality. 3 influential. *seniman. seniman* ~ artists of weight (,consequence ,importance). ~ *mati 3.992 ton* (a ship of) 3,992 dwt. *- atom* atomic weight. *- lawan* counterweight. *- mati* deadweight. *- punggah* shipping weight.

bobrok good for nothing, useless, weak. **ke-an** dilapidation.

bocah child. *- angon* shepherd. *- belasan th* teenager. *-.- cilik* small fry. *- ingusan* snotty kid. *-.- prasiswa* preschool children.

bocor 1 to bleed. 2 (fig.) to trickle out, filter through. 3 to suffer from diarrhea. **ke-an** *uang negara* (euph.) corruption of State funds. **mem-kan:** ~ *rahasia* to divulge (,expose) a secret. ~ *uang negara* (euph.) to corrupt State funds.

bodoh (pron. in a somewhat long-drawn out tone) what do I care! *bikin - sama* (coll.) to fool, make a fool of. *membuat diri -* 1 to play ignorant. 2 to behave like a fool. 3 indifferent. **di-i** to be insulted. **mem-** to play (,pretend) innocence.

bodol damaged, broken.

bodong counterfeited; (s.) GIRIK (BODONG).

bodor (s.) BEBODOR.

Boer (pron. as Boor) Boer.

boga food. **ber-** to eat.

bogèl insufficiently covered. *ayam -* chicken without feathers.

bogi buggy (a carriage).

bogoh *- pd* to like, be fond of; (s.) BEBOGOHAN.

bohok (s.) BUHUK.

bohorok foehn (on Sumatra's east coast).

bojo spouse.

bok *- ayu* (s.) AYU.

bokal beaker.

bokè(k) poor, without means, destitute.

bokji ear-shaped fungus.

bok(s) play-pen.

boksen 1 boxing. 2 to box.

boksit bauxite. **ber-** bauxite-bearing.

bola delivery boy. *- gada* baseball. *- kristal* crystal ball. *- lisut* softball. *- salju* snowball. *- tampar (,volley)* volley ball.

bolak round (of eyes).

bolak.balik *pikirannya -* 1 he weighs the pros and cons. 2 he is wavering. 3 restlessly roaming thoughts (of an insomniac). *diplomasi - Henry Kissinger* Henry Kissinger's shuttle diplomacy. *pesawat ruang angkasa -* space shuttle. **di-** *bagaimana juga* no matter how the matter is twisted (,turned).

bolèh 1 all right, I give assent. 2 yes. *"Mau pisang? " "B-."* "Would you like to have a banana? " "Yes." *-lah* 1 O.K.

2 it's good. *apa - buat?* what else can
we do? *mana -!* what a ridiculous
idea! what on earth are you talking
about! *- deh* all right, I give assent.
- diadu and *- dibawa ke tengah* to be
able to hold o's own. *- dikata(kan)
kosong* practically empty. *- juga* it'll
do, not bad. *akan tetapi sangat - jadi
bhw* ... but it might well be that ...
berke-an to have the ability. **ke-an**
ability, skill. **-an** passable, O.K. *di
antara mereka ada saja yg* ~ among
them (the female street sweepers)
there are always those who are not
bad to look at. *Ia berasal dr SMA yg*
~, He graduated from a passable
Senior High School.

boling bowling.

bolong I *uang -* coin with a hole in its
center.

bolong II *di tengah hari -* and *di siang -*
in broad daylight.

bolos cut, skip. *- makan dr kantin* to
skip eating in the clubhouse. **pem-an**
truancy.

bolotu sailboat (from the Central Celebes).

bolpèn ballpoint pen.

Bolsyewik Bolshevik.

Bolsyewis Bolshevist.

bolu kukus steamed, sweet, white cake
made of wheat flour; resembles a pile
of mashed potatoes on top of a cup-
cake.

bom pem- bomber. ~ *berat* heavy bomber.
~ *jarak.jauh* long-range bomber. ~ *raksasa B-25* the B-25 giant bomber. **pem-
an** *tukik* dive bombing. **pem-.atoman**
the dropping of the atom bomb. *-
bensin* Molotov cocktail. *- bersampul*
letter bomb. *- brisan* high-explosive
bomb. *- H* H-bomb. *- hidrogen* hydrogen bomb. *- Molotov* Molotov cocktail.
- napalm napalm bomb. *- nuklir* nuclear bomb. *- seks* sex bomb. *- zat air*
H-bomb.

bombardemèn bombardment.

bombastis bombastic.

bombon bonbon, candy.

bomoh medicine man, shaman.

bon I union. *B- Becak* Pedicab Drivers'
Union.

bon II di- (police term) to be tortured,
be maltreated.

bon III nge- to buy on credit.

bonafide 1 bona fide. 2 in good faith.

boncèng mem-i to follow, accompany.
barang -an goods clandestinely shipped
(i.e. not recorded in customs documents) by being sent along with other
goods.

bondan *kampung* police.

bondo capital (investment).

bondol *burung -* k.o. paddybird.

bondong se-.- in groups.

bonéka mem-kan *diri* to play the role of
puppet. *- salju* snowman. *- tali* mario-
nette.

bong I 1 Chinese grave. 2 Chinese graveyard.

bong II circumcizer.

bonggol I to drub, cudgel. **m-in** to trash.

bonggol II part of tree or plant just above
soil.

bongkar *toko.toko yg terkena -* stores
which have to be demolished (,torn
down). **mem-** to uncover, dismantle.
~ *sauh* to weigh anchor. **mem-.bangkir**
to turn over (,inside out). *- muat* loading and unloading. *- pasang* assembling.
- pasang senjata (mil.) weapon breakdown and reassembling.

bongkok *si B-* The Hunchback. 2 (fig.)
a pistol.

bongkrèk (s.) BUNGKIL. *tempe -* fermented beancake made with peanut
residue.

bongmèh di- to be felt out, be sounded
(a person).

bongsor to thrive. *anak (,bayi) -* a child
(,baby) who is thriving.

bonjol mem-in to defeat, beat (in sports).

bontot I youngest (child).

bontot II -an food supply wrapped in
leaves from the teak tree.

booking Saya *- ticket Malaysian Airline
System (MAS) utk pulang.pergi Medan-*

Penang-Medan, I booked a seat with MAS for a roundtrip Medan-Penang-Medan.

boom (pron. oo as o in go) Customs office.

boomklèrk Customs clerk.

boomzaken Customs business.

bo'ong 1 lie. 2 to lie.

bopèng potholed.

boper - *angin (,udara)* air buffer.

bor name-plate (on building).

borak insipid (of tobacco).

borang (application) form. - *langganan* subscription form.

Borbon Bourbon.

borboran bloody, blood-stained, covered with blood.

bordil brothel.

bordir (S.) BORDEL. **-an** embroidery.

borèh cosmetic, cream.

borg **di-kan** to be given as security.

boro.boro 1 let alone, much less. 2 instead of.

borok 1 abscess. 2 pothole.

boros **pem-an** squandering, extravagance.

boru (in the Batak area) daughter of the ... clan. - *Nasution* daughter of the Nasution clan *(,marga).*

bos boss (person who superintends others).

bosan - *dgn (,pd)* sick (,tired) of, satiated with. - *hidup* weary of life. *tdk* **-.-nya** untiring, unwearying.

bosé (s.) JAGUNG (BOSE).

botanikus botanist.

botelir steward (on board a ship).

boti.boti a sailing proa of the Buton islanders (South Celebes).

botik boutique.

boto(h) (to look) attractive, handsome, pretty.

botol *membawa - (minuman) sendiri* BYOB. **di-kan** to be bottled. - *dot* baby bottle - *udara* compressed air bottle.

boven *naar* - (to go) to the mountains (for relaxation or sexual fun).

bowong a person (= *wong,* Jav.) who pulls a plough to replace a water buffalo (= *kebo,* Jav.).

B.P.H. [Bendara Pangeran Harya] title for brothers of the Sultan of Yogyakarta.

br [boru] (s.) BORU; such as, *Dra. Christelina Rosica Tiurma Liz br Panggabean.*

B.R.A. [Bendara Raden Ayu] title for a married princess.

Brahmana a member of the first Hindu caste of priests (Bali).

B.R.Aj. [Bendara Raden Ajeng] title for an unmarried princess.

Braling (coll.) Purbalingga (a town).

brambang red onion.

brandal (S.) BERANDAL. **-an** troublemaker, juvenile delinquent.

brander burner.

branggah *tanduk* - wide-spread antlers.

branwir fire department.

bratawali (pron. brotowali) plant whose bitter-tasting leaves are used in folk medicine.

Bratayud(h)a a Jav. version of the heroic struggle between the five *Pandawas* and their cousins, the *Kurawas,* as described in the Indian epic poem, the *Mahab(h)arata.*

breg sound of s.t. heavy falling, thump!

brèidel **mem-** to ban, revoke its license. **pem-an** ban.

brem 1 rice brandy, a sweet sherry made from fermented black rice. 2 k.o. cookies made of fermented rice.

brèn brengun. **di-** to be brengunned.

brèndi brandy.

brengbrengan strong smelling.

brèngsèk 1 bad, evil, wicked, mean, rude. 2 arbitrary, high-handed, indescribable. 3 unfit for use, unserviceable. -*!* goddamn! *mobil* - a jalopy.

brenti (S.) BERHENTI.

bret *tangan panjang main - aja* it was a great day for pickpockets.

brevèt brevet.

bréwok long sideburns.

bridge bridge (the card game).

bri(e)fing briefing.

brigade *B- Anjing* K-9 Brigade. *B- Mobil* Mobile Brigade. *B- Satwa* K-9 Brigade. *B- Tempur* Combat Brigade.

brigadir brigadier. *B- Polisi* Police Brigadier.

brigidig **mem-kan** to shiver, quake (when telling a horror story).

brintik curly (haired).

Brahmana member of the first Hindu caste of priests (in Bali).

brikèt briquette.

bripèt (s.) BREVET.

brital brutal.

Britania Raya Great Britain.

Britis British.

B.R.M. [Bendara Raden Mas] title for a young unmarried prince.

brobot (s.) BEROBOT.

brojol to come out together.

brok **nge-i** to occupy.

brokat brocade.

broker broker.

brokohan a religious ritual in the form of a feast held in the area of Kebumen, Central Java.

brokoli *(sayur)* - broccoli.

bromocorah, bromo curah and **bromocurah** 1 riffraff, rabble, scum, underworld. 2 *(B-)* Robin Hood. 3 habitual criminal, recidivist.

brondol and **brondhol** 1 to moult, shed o's feathers. 2 to fall off.

brondongan salvo, (volley of) gunfire.

brongkos a vegetable side dish seasoned with *kluwak.*

bronjong (cylinder-shaped) large bamboo basket (for packing sugar, pigs, etc.).

bronkhitis bronchitis.

bros brooch.

brosot **mem-** to sneak out, slip away without beating the drum.

broti (s.) BEROTI.

brubuh *perang* - war of destruction.

bruder friar. **ke-an** Christian brothers' school. **-an** Catholic seminary school.

bruk sound of s.t. dropping down, plump!

brunèt brunette.

brus brush.

Brussel Brussels.

brutal impudent, impertinent. **ke-an** impudence, brutality.

bruto gross.

buah *sebab - dikenal pohonnya* a tree is known by its fruit. *- yg manis berulat di dalamnya* when the fox preaches, guard your geese. **mem-kan:** ~ *seorang bayi yg lahir muda* to give birth to a premature baby. ~ *uang* to yield income. **mem-.bibirkan** to discuss. **peman** conception (conceiving in the womb). ~ *sendiri lengkap* autogamy. *- adpokat (,alpokat ,alpukat)* avocado. *- apel* apple. *- (a)pokat* avocado. *- berangan* chestnut. *- ceri* cherry. *- karangan ulung* masterpiece (of an author). *- khuldi* the apple of Adam and Eve. *- leci* lychees. *- mahoni* a fruit used as an efficacious medicine against hypertension. *- mentega* ebony, butter fruit (L. Diospyros discolor). *- nona* custard apple. *- pelaga* cardamom (L. Amomum cardamomum). *- seri* cherry. *- (,hasil) usaha* the results of s.o.'s work.

bual *- basung* hot air.

buana world.

Buanawan reference used by the Jakarta-based daily "Berita Buana" in speaking about their newsreporters.

buang *lalu.lintas yg* **di-** *ke Pecenongan* the traffic which was diverted to Pecenongan (Street). **mem-:** ~ *hajat* to defecate. ~ *ingus* to blow o's nose. ~ *keringat* to work. ~ *laju* to slow down. *Pesawat mendarat,* ~ *lajunya di landasan dan akhirnya berhenti,* The aircraft landed, slowed down on the runway and finally came to a stop. ~ *mata ke* to look at. ~ *muka* to look back. ~ *muka kpd orang tua* to disregard o's parents. ~ *ongkos* to spend money, (fig.) to be fortunate. ~ *pandangan* to look back. ~ *penat* to take a break. ~ *sauh* to cast anchor. ~ *setir* to turn the steering wheel. ~ *senyum* to smile. ~ *tenaga* to work. ~ *tubuh ke laut* to plunge into the sea. *pergi* ~

to spend the pool. **mem-.-:** ~ *pandang* to look about. ~ *tingkah* to pose. **pem-an:** ~ *air* drainage. ~ *waktu* waste of time. - *angin* to break wind. - *hajat* to defecate.

buani universal.

buat ber- to act. ~ *aniaya* to play dishonest tricks. ~ *banyak* to do a lot. ~ *begitu* to act in that way. ~ *bodoh* to play the ignorant. ~ *curang* to be guilty of fraud, practice fraud. ~ *demikian* to act in that way. ~ *dosa* to sin. ~ *hal.hal yg lucu* to play jokes. ~ *iseng* to be unfaithful (marital infidelity). ~ *itu* to have sexual intercourse. ~ *korupsi* to be involved in corruption. *Ia dipecat dr jabatannya dan ditahan selama lima bln karena dituduh ~ korupsi,* He was removed from his job and detained for five months on the charge of being involved in corruption. ~ *lain* to act differently. ~ *nekad* to act in despair. ~ *salah* to be mistaken, err. ~ *sejauh* to go as far as. *Seseorang boleh ~ sejauh yg dpt ditanggung.jawabkannya pd dirinya,* Anyone may go as far as he can justify for himself. ~ *semaunya* to do just as o. likes. ~ *spt itu* to act like that. *Mereka ~ spt itu karena lapar,* They acted like that because of hunger. ~ *serong* to be unfaithful (marital infidelity). ~ *sesuka hati kita* to do what we like. ~ *yg berlebih.lebihan* to go over the line, exceed the bounds. *orang yg ~* an active person. **di-:** ~ *menurut ukuran* to be custom-made. ~ *panjang* to be taken up (of some matter). *Dgn langkah yg* **ku-.-** *saya masuk …,* I pranced into (that restaurant). **mem-:** ~ *foto* to take a picture. ~ *kesalahan* to make a mistake, commit an error. **pem-:** ~ *eskrim* ice cream freezer (the device). ~ *gaduh* troublemaker. ~ *kebijaksanaan* policy maker. **pem-an:** *dlm* ~ under construction. ~ *jalan* road construction. ~ *hujan kimiawi* cloud seedings. ~ *pab(e)rik* manufacture, fabrication. **-an** 1 made by. ~ *Jepang* Japanese made. *roket* ~ *sendiri* a self-made rocket. ~ *sini* locally made. 2 man-made. *danau* ~ a man-made lake. 3 work. *akan merintang* ~ for recreation. ~ *pab(e)rik* manufacture, make.

buaya *adakah - menolak bangkai* the fox may grow gray, but never good. *mencucurkan air mata -* to shed crocodile tears. *dasar - - juga* a cad remains a cad. *-Kemayoran* riffraff operating in the Kemayoran area (in Jakarta). *- stasiun* riffraff operating at railway stations. *- uang* money grabber, Shylock.

bubar *Sdh hampir* **-an** *sekolah,* School was almost over.

bubèng 1 nameless. 2 rascal.

bubrah to disperse, disintegrate.

bubuhan (in Banjarmasin) member (of political party).

bubuk code word used by drug traffickers to refer to various k.o. drugs. **pem-an** pulverization. *- kadal* lizard powder (L. Pulv. Maboyae multifasciatae), i.e. a traditional and efficacious medicine against eczema.

bubung mem- *tinggi* to skyrocket (of prices).

bubut I name for coucals and crow pheasants (L. Centropus eurycercus and Centropus bengalensis).

bubut II stay. *layar -* staysail. *tali* **-an** halliard. *- belakang* backstay.

budak *- lampau tua tdk* young fellow, stripling, youth passing into manhood. **pem-** slaveholder.

budal.badil to fall apart, collapse. *Bentrokan pikiran sedikit saja, bisa bikin rumahtangga -,* Just minor disagreements can wreck a household.

budanco and *budancho* squadcommander of the *Peta* during the Jap. occupation.

Budapès Budapest.

budaya mem- to become part of the mores. **mem-kan** 1 to civilize. 2 to institutionalize. **pem-an** civilization.

budayawan a cultured man, culturebearer.

budek deaf.

Budha Darma the Buddhist religion.

budheng the black long-haired monkey.

budi *Dia banyak lepas -,* He has put many

persons under an obligation. *tinggi -nya* he is of high character, he is high-minded. *B- Nurani Manusia* Social Conscience of Man. *B- Utomo* 'High Endeavor,' i.e. the 1908-grouping of Javanese medical students in Batavia (Jakarta) with the purpose of promoting Javanese cultural ideals.

budidaya I to strive after, aim at.

budidaya II commodity.

budidaya III cultivation. *kebon -* estate, plantation. **ke-an** estate, plantation. **mem-kan** to cultivate. **pem-an** cultivation. *- laut* sea farming, mariculture. *- tembakau* tobacco cultivation.

budiman wise man.

buduk mangy (of a dog).

bugil (s.) BOGEL. **mem-kan diri** to strip o.s. naked.

buhuk struma.

bujang pem- bachelor. *- serabutan* handyman, jack-of-all trades.

bujèt budget.

bujètèr budgetary.

bujubusèt good gracious (me)!

bujuk -an cajolery.

buka *- kata ... tutup kata* quote ... unquote. **keter-an** openness, candor. **mem-:** ~ *diri* to go public. ~ *(dr) lipatannya* to unfold. ~ *hutan* to deforest. ~ *ingatan kembali* to recall (to mind). ~ *kartu* to lay o's cards on the table. ~ *omongan* to begin (,start) a conversation, enter into a conversation. ~ *sandi* to decode. ~ *suaranya* to give o's opinion. **pem-** *selera* apéritif. **pem-an** *tanah* deforestation. **ter-** open-minded. *kami akan* ~ we'll be open-minded.

bukan *-saya!* (the popular formula to evade responsibility) 'not me' (when a superior shifts responsibility for having committed a mistake to his subordinate, and the latter shifts it to a still lower-rank subordinate, the last may say: *bukan saya!*, i.e. he has only followed the instructions of his higherups). *- tdk mungkin* it isn't impossible. *Itu macan (apa) -?* Is that

a tiger (or isn't it)? *-nya* (and) not ... (but s.t. else). *Para demonstran meneriakkan: "Berilah kami makanan,* ~ *pidato.pidato,"* The demonstrators yelled: "Give us food, (and) not speeches." ~ *tdk* it isn't the case that ... not. -.- absurd. *- orangnya* not the sort of man (to ...).

bukèt bouquet.

bukit pe-an hills.

bukrah 1 tomorrow. 2 mañana, at some indefinite time in the future.

bukti mem- dirikan to prove o's identity.

buku pem-an: ~ *kembali* reversing (,compensating) entry. ~ *muatan* cargo booking. *- babon* reference (book). *- bacaan komik* comic book. *- besar* ledger. *- catatan* notebook. *- cek* checkbook. *- daftar peserta* register of shareholders. *- ekspedisi* delivery book. *- harian* logbook. *- hijau* health certificate for *hajis*. *- jiplakan* plagiarized book. *B-Kuning* the yellow-colored booklet containing: (I) International Certificate of Vaccination and (II) Personal Health History. *- log* logbook. *- maneuver* bell-book. *- mutasi kantor polisi* police blotter. *- notes* notebook. *- olahgerak* bell-book. *- pelajaran* textbook, manual. *B- Pemilik Kendaraan Bermotor* Motor Vehicle Owners Book (owner gives car title, tax statements, etc. to police in exchange for this record book). *- penuntun* manual. *- picisan* dime novel. *- referens (,referensi)* reference (book). *- saku* pocket book. *- setoran* deposit book. *- tabungan* savings account book. *- tamu* guest book. *- tilpon* telephone director.

bulan *di ujung -* after the 20th of the month. *pengujung -* the last two days of the month. **ber-** *madu* to honeymoon. **mem-** to go to the moon. **mem-kan** to send (a spaceship) to the moon. *menjadi -.-an* 1 to be much talked about. 2 made fun of. *- ber* a month the name of which ends in *-ber* (the rainy months). *- Haji* the pilgrimage month. *- muda* the first half of the

month when o. still has some money.
- *Puasa* Ramadan. - *stor* month of payment. - *Suci* Ramadan - *tua* the second
half of the month when o. is running
short of money.

bulat **ke-an** *tekad* determination. *dgn* **se-**
hati with all o's heart. -.- (as a) whole.
- *berisi* fat. - *panjang* 1 cylindrical.
2 oval (table). - *penuh* fat. - *silinder*
cylindrical.

buldoser bulldozer. **di-** to be demolished
by bulldozer(s). **pem-an** demolition
by bulldozer(s).

bulé(k) white (person). *bahasa* - a western
language. *orang* - a white, westerner.

buletin bulletin.

Bulgaria *(negeri)* - Bulgaria. *orang* -
Bulgar(ian).

bulgur precooked, cracked wheat (imported from the U.S.).

bulian *kayu* - k.o. ironwood (L. Eusider-
oxylon Zwageri).

bulla (doctor's) diploma.

bulpar boulevard.

bulu - *tengkuk* (,*tengkuruk*) *kita berdiri*
it gave us the (cold) creeps, it made
our flesh crawl. *berganti* - 1 to moult,
shed o's feathers. 2 to change o's
attitude. *menunjukkan* - *dulu* to show
o's (real) colors. *membangunkan* - *roma*
and *meremangkan* - to make o's hair
stand on end. **ber-** *kasap* coarse-haired.
se- **dgn** similar to, of the same type as.
- *mink* mink (fur).

buluh *dlm* **pem-** *darah* intravenous.

bulus k.o. freshwater turtle. *main* -.-**an**
to play hide-and-seek.

bumantara (air)space.

bumbu seasoning. *yg banyak* -**nya** spicy.
- *penyedap makanan* flavoring (spices
added to a food to give it a certain
taste).

bumbung (in Bali) dance performed to
highlight a dinner party.

bumerang boomerang.

bumi *di muka* - *(ini)* (here) on earth.
antara - *dan langit* between the devil
and the deep blue sea. *tdk melihat lagi
di* - do not see any longer the cold

(,hard) facts. - *berputar dan jaman
beredar* times change and we are
changed in them. - *mana yg tiada kena
hujan* to err is human. *di mana* - *dipijak,
di sana langit dijunjung* 'where the earth
is stepped on, there the sky is respected,'
i.e. 1 When in Rome do as the Romans
do. 2 to obey all commands. **mem-** to
land. **penge-an** burial. **pem-**.**hangusan**
razing, scorching the earth. *B- Moro,*
(coll.) Morokrembangan, Surabaya;
the navy training center. *B- Perkemahan*
Camping Ground (of the *Pramuka* Boy
Scout Movement).

bumiah earthly, worldly.

bumper bumper (of automobile). -
belakang rear bumper. - *muka* front
bumper.

bumpet clogged (of ditch, o's nose, etc.).

bun dew. - *upas* a poisonous k.o. dew,
honeydew (found at the Diëng plateau
in Central Java).

bunda *B-(Suci)Maria* (The Virgin) Maria.

bunder (S.) BUNDAR. -**an** traffic circle.

bundet and **bundhet** entangled (of thread,
rope, etc.).

bunga I **ber-** *semangatnya* he is well
pleased. - *angin* a light breeze. - *ban*
tread (of tire). - *bangkai* snake plant,
devil's tongue, leopard palm (L. Amor-
phophallus titanum Becc.). - *kol* cauli-
flower. - *lotus* lotus. - *sedap malam*
(L. Polianthes tuberosa) long golden-
brown dried stems for soup and *jamu,*
various Indonesian herb medicines.
- *tiruan* artificial flowers. - *tulip* tulip.

bunga II (banking term) - *majemuk* compound interest. - *tdk berganda* and
- *tunggal* simple interest.

bungalo bungalow.

bungkam **ter-** *dlm seribu bahasa* maintained a stony silence.

bungker bunker, pillbox.

bungkil peanut residue after the oil has
been pressed out, k.o. linseed-cake.

bunian *orang* - invisible elves of the forest
(who can make people lose their way).

buntal *ikan* - the fox-fish, sea-porcupine.

buntil rasped and spiced coconut wrapped

in *tales* leaves.

bunting to be knocked up. **ke-an** pregnancy. **mem-i** to knock up.

buntu *Pikiran saya -,* My mind went blank. I was at a loss for what to do.

buntung *blm tentu untung* -**nya** it is not sure yet how it will turn out with him.

buntut - *Nalo* (unofficially) gambling on the 'tail' or the last two digits of the outcome. -**nya** 1 trailing after (him, it, etc.). 2 o. who is (left) behind. -.-**nya** the aftermath. - *kuda* pony tail.

bunuh mem- *waktu* to kill the time. **pem-**: ~ *jamur* fungicide. ~ *serangga* insecticide. **pem-an** carnage. ~ *besar.besaran* genocide.

bunyi ber- 1 to ring. *telepon* ~ the telephone was ringing. 2 to be heard. *Tapi sejak th itu kredit sepeda tak ~ lagi,* But since that year nothing more has been heard about credits (made available) for the purchase of bicycles. **mem-kan** *mercon* to let off fireworks. - *cina karam* (an infernal) noise, tumult. - *lanjut* (in phonetics) a continuant. - *luncuran (,pelancar)* (in phonetics) a glide. - *udara* aerophone.

bupati ke-an (S.) KABUPATEN.

buraken traditional dance of the Mamasa community, South Celebes, representing a prayer asking for luck; the dance is performed by 10 persons, including the drummer, ranging in age from 60 to 100 years.

buram obscure, dim, dark. **di-kan** to be obscured.

bureng dull, darkened. *pikirannya sdh -* he is nuts.

buri back, behind.

burit *di* - abaft. *dr* - astern. -**an** poop(deck). *berhaluan* ~ and *bergilir ke* ~ to be a henpecked husband.

Burjamhal Aries.

burjasmani ecliptic.

burjo [bubur (kacang) ijo] mung bean porridge.

bursa *B- Efek.Efek* Stock Exchange. - *gandum* corn exchange. - *saham* stock exchange. - *tenaga kerja* placement office.

buru ke-: ~ *cemas* worried (,afraid) ahead of time. *Belon sempet masak babè udè ~ pulang,* We hadn't had the time to cook yet since father got home ahead of time. **pem-**: ~ *jet* jet fighter (plane). ~ *mata.mata* spycatcher. **per-an** *ngedrèv* drive (i.e. a hunt in which game is driven toward stationary hunters). **ter-** *nafsu* impetuously, rashly, thoughtlessly, done with insufficient thought or care.

buruh *banyak (,sedikit) mempergunakan (,memakai)* - labor extensive (,intensive). - *borongan* pieceworker. -.- *darat* shore staff (of shipping company). - *halus* white-collar worker. - *kontrakan* laborer working on a contract basis. - *lepas* casual laborer. - *minyak* oil worker. - *musiman (,semusim)* seasonal worker. - *pelabuhan* dock worker. - *terlatih* skilled worker. - *upah.batas* marginal worker.

buruk - *muka cermin dibelah* it's an ill bird that fouls its own nest. **mem-** 1 to deteriorate. 2 deteriorating. *Apa* -**nya?** What is wrong with it?

burung - *terbang di pipis lada* don't count your chickens before they are hatched. *daun* - a shrub (L. Rhinacanthus nasuta Kurz). *Perhimpunan B- Indonesia,* Ornithological Society of Indonesia. - *cenderawasih (,dewata)* the bird of paradise. - *gagak* crow. - *gelatik* the Java temple bird, Java rice bird. - *gelatik Indo* (s.) BURUNG (GELATIK), but with white feathers. - *hong* phoenix. - *kaleng* starling. - *kuntul kepala merah* (in Irian Jaya) the eastern Sarus Crane (L. Grus antigone sharpii). - *maleo* a fowl species found in the Gorontalo area (North Celebes). - *merpati kebutan* race pigeon. - *merpati klepekan* decoy pigeon. - *nuri raja* (in Irian Jaya) the pesquet's parrot (L. Nestor pesqueti). - *ocehan* talking bird. - *perantau (,yg suka pindah.pindah)* migratory bird,

bird of passage. - *setan* (in some places of Central Java) pelican. - *sorga* the bird of paradise.

burwater boraic lotion.

bus - *air* river bus. - *omprengan* bus used illicitly to earn extra money.

busah ber- foam at the mouth (from talking a lot).

busana clothes, dress. *dlm keadaan tanpa* - in the nude. *Operasi B-* the operation launched in 1964 to clothe the Irian Jaya people in the hinterland. **ber-** 1 to be (,get) dressed. *Wanita.wanita Bali di desa.desa masih ~ yg bagian atasnya terbuka*, Balinese women in the villages are still dressed in such a way that the upper part of their body is uncovered. *wanita ~ terbaik* the best dressed woman. 2 to dress. **mem-kan** to clothe. - *prima* haute-couture.

busar *spt - Arjuna* 'like Arjuna's bow,' i.e. a simile for a beautiful arm.

busèt go to hell! confound it! dash it! damn it! (stronger) -.*bojong!*

busuk 1 carrion. 2 addled (of egg).

busung - *darah* aneurysm.- *kulit* anasarca.

busyèt (s.) BUSET.

buta I unacquainted with, unused to. *Sdh malam dan saya masih - samasekali keadaan Jakarta,* It was night and I was still completely unused to the Jakarta scene. *makan gaji -* to have a soft job, have a sinecure. *orang - kehilangan tongkat* 'a blind man who has lost his stick,' i.e. to be in a precarious situation. - *baru melek (,melihat ,celik)* to go (,run) hogwild. *tdk sepeser -* completely broke. *Cina -*

a *muhallil. si - baru melek* the person who runs hogwild. **ke-.hurufan** illiteracy. **mem-kan** *mata thd kenyataan* to ignore reality. - *akan* blind to. - *aksara* (S.) BUTA(HURUF). - *hati* unfeeling, insensible, heartless. - *huruf* ignorant. - *kemajuan* primitive (of tribes). - *larang(an)* myopia, nearsightedness. -*perasaan* insensible.- *politik* apolitical. - *senja* shortsighted, nearsighted. - *tuli* deaf and blind, ignorant.

buta II -.- a sea-shore tree (L. Cerbera odollam).

butarepan competition, rivalry, jealousy between spouses.

but.but the crow-pheasant.

butik boutique.

butir - *darah* blood corpuscle.

buto jockey (at bull race).

butongpai a Chinese system of self-defense (a blend of *kungfu* and *karate*).

butuh ke-an requirement(s). *~ akan tanah* greed for territory. *menurut ~* as circumstances require. *~ dan pengadaan* supply and demand.

butut unfit for use.

BUUD [Badan Usaha Unit Desa] k.o. cooperative village organization; aim: to establish a sort of cooperative village organization by organizing better availability of input, including credit, for all peasants and farmers concerned.

buwès (S.) REBEWES.

byar the lights all of a sudden lit up. - *pet* to go on and off (of a lamp). *neonnya - pet* the neon lamps go on and off. **di-kan** to be switched on (of electric light).

C

NOTE—In case the *c* in a word is pronounced differently from the *c* representing the former *tj*, the word has been printed in italics. In such cases, the *c* is pronounced *k* before *a, l, o, r, u* and *s* before *i, e, y*.

cabai *Siapa yg makan -, mesti dia sendiri yg kepedasan* (or, *dialah yg kepedasan*) 'He who eats pepper must suffer personally from the sharp, biting taste,' i.e. chickens come home to roost. - *merah* chil(l)i, red pepper.

cabang ber-: *pikirannya* ~ *(dua)* he is in doubt. ~ *dua* two-fold. **ke-an** branch. - *atas* the élite, top-level.

cabé (s.) CABAI. -.-**an** red flower-pecker. - *rawit* (fig.) small (person) but very active.

cabik pen- *karcis* ticket taker (in movie theater).

cabol (S.) CEBOL.

cabut -*!* bus conductor command to driver to start on last leg of the route. *Embargo minyak tlh* **di-,** The oil embargo has been lifted. **men-** *blokade* to lift a blockade. **pen-an:** ~ *hak.milik* expropriation. ~ *pengakuan* de-recognition.

cacad (S.) CACAT.

cacah *mesin* - perforating machine.

cacar - *teh* blister blight (a tea plant disease).

cacat *tiada* - *sedikit juga* unhurt. **ke-an** disablement. **men-i** to mutilate. **pen-an** stigmatization. *tak ada* -**nya** 1 blameless, flawless, beyond reproach. 2 that can do no harm, there is no harm in it, there is no harm in doing that. -.- *badan* bodily defects. - *mental* imbecile. - *veteran* disabled veteran.

cacengklok kneehollow.

caci -.*maki* 1 abuse, abusive language, sarcasm. 2 remark. 3 criticism.

cacing -**an** wormy. *obat (,jamu)* ~ worm medicine. - *gelang* ascariasis. - *gila* nymphomaniac.- *laut* serpula.- *segmen* annelid. - *tanah* earthworm.

cadang -**an:** ~ *diam* silent reserves. ~ *rahasia* secret (,hidden) reserves.

cadas 1 sandstone. 2 (in a broader sense) stone, rock.

cadik outrigger.

cadong (**me)ny-** to ask for s.t. ~ *dawuh* 'to ask for an order (,instruction) under superior directions,' i.e. to ask what o. has to do, wait around for instructions.

ca'em good-looking, beautiful.

cagak - *hidup* life annuity.

cagil men- 1 to disturb. 2 to bother.

cahaya - *udara* aurora borealis.

ca'ilah (an exclamation) my gosh!

cair to be watered down. *mencapai persetujuan sekarang, besoknya* - *lagi* today an agreement is reached and tomorrow it is watered down again. *menjadi* - *kembali (,lagi)* 1 (diplomatic relations) have been re-established. 2 (funds, earlier frozen) have been released, *Cepat atau lambat hubungan diplomasi RI.RRC akan* **di-kan,** Sooner or later the diplomatic relations between the Republic of Indonesia and the PRC will be thawed out. **men-kan** 1 to cash. ~ *cek perjalanan* to cash a traveler's check. 2 to release. ~ *uang* to release assets (earlier frozen). ~ *kekerasan hati para teroris* (psychiatrists tried) to mollify the terrorists (in their demands). -**an** *pembersih* cleanser (liquid).

cai siem (s.) CAISIM.

caisim and **caisin** mustard greens.

cak I brother, buddy. - *kopi* coffee seller.

cak II (S.) BECA(K).

cakakah sacred kingfisher.

cakalang skipjack (L. Katsuwonus pelamis).

cakap I ber- *perut* to ventriloquize.

cakap II ke-an attainments. ~ *bahari* seamanship. - *perawakannya,* - *benar rupanya, ia mempunyai rupa yg* - and *roman mukanya* - he is handsome.

cakar bersi-.-an to fly in e.o.'s face. *Mereka sedang* -.-**an** *satu sama lain,* They are at loggerheads.

cakera - *putar* turntable.

cakil character, guy.

cakim [calon hakim] aspirant judge.

cakra discus, weapon of the god Wishnu.

Cakrabirawa Soekarno's palace guard.

cakrawala horizon.

Cakrawa(r)ti Supreme Ruler.

Cakung the bonded warehouses at Cakung (Bekasi). **men-.-kan** to store imported goods in the Cakung bonded warehouses. **pen-an** the storing of imported goods in the Cakung bonded warehouses.

Cakungisasi the removal of imported goods from a ship moored at Tanjung

Priok (Jakarta), directly to the Cakung bonded warehouses (see above).

cakupan to hire a prostitute for the night.

caladi - *batu* pygmy woodpecker.

calo(k) 1 middleman, broker, agent. - *bis* person who looks for bus passengers (he gets a tip from the bus conductors for his services). - *kewarganegaraan* citizenship broker. - *paspor* passport broker. 2 hustler, tout.

calon fiance(e). - *anggota* (of a professional association) associate. - *harapan* (in U.S. presidential elections) favorite son. - *joki* apprentice jockey. - *mualim* deck cadet. - *perwira* officer cadet. - *prajurit* recruit. - *prajurit taruna* cadet recruit. - *raja* pretender to the throne. - *Wakil Presiden Gerald Ford* Vice President-designate Gerald Ford.

calui to be bribable.

caluk (in Palembang) a seasoning paste made from ground shrimp or fish, used as an ingredient for peppery sauce *(sambal)*.

Calung name of a welcoming dance to honor tourists disembarking at Cilacap.

cama [calon mahasiswa] prospective college freshman (masc.) who is undergoing hazing.

camar I *burung* - sea gull.

camar II greedy. - *uang* money-grubbing.

cambang sideburns.

cami [calon mahasiswi] prospective college freshman (fem.) who is undergoing hazing.

camplungan cesspool.

campur ber-: ~ *baur (,gaul)* to associate, mix, have social contact. ~ *dgn* mixed with. *sisa.sisa makanan* ~ *dgn minyak* the leftovers from a meal were mixed with oil. **di-** to be alloyed. **meny- ta-ngani** to interfere, meddle in. **-an** *Indonesia* a mixed Indonesian, part Indonesian.

camuk whore.

can chance. *banyak - yg dibuangnya* he has missed many chances.

canang *menjadi* - much-discussed, generally known.

cancut to tuck the end of the *kain* into the front of the waist band. - *taliwanda (,taliwondo)* 1 (only) dressed with a loincloth (for heavy work). 2 with united strength, with a united effort, with combined (,concerted) efforts. *Mari - taliwanda berusaha bersama mengatasi soal pangan,* Come on, let us jointly and with concerted efforts overcome the food problem.

canda *Jangan suka -!* Don't make fun! **ber-** capricious.

candak I and **candhak ny-** to catch (the train, etc.), be in time (for the train, etc.).

candak II - *kulak* a small loan to a vendor intended for use in purchasing goods for immediate resale.

candat -**an** (psychological) inhibition.

candi *(Roro Jonggrang) C- Prambanan* The Prambanan Hindu Temple near Yogyakarta (Central Java).

Candra Bhakti Panca Windu 'Forty-Year Devotional Superiority,' i.e. the name given to the 40th anniversary of the *PNI* (1927–1967).

Candrawilwatikta (s.) TAMAN (CANDRA WILWATIKTA).

candu prepared opium (cooked). -*nya orang Rusia pd teka.teki silang* the addiction of Russians to crossword puzzles. *biji.bijian* - poppy seeds. *bunga* - poppy (the plant). *penderita* **ke-an** *narkotik* drug addict. **ny-** to be addicted to. **pe-:** ~ *buku* bookworm (the person). ~ *film* film fan. ~ *narkotika* narcotic addict, pusher. **pen-:** ~ *bioskop* movie fan. ~ *ganja* pothead, pot smoker. ~ *morfin* morphine addict, morphinist. ~ *rokok* chain smoker. ~ *(sepak)bola* soccer fan. **peny-** (s.) PE(N)CANDU.

cangak heron. - *abu* gray heron. - *merah* purple heron.

cangcang to fasten, tie up, tether.

canggung *tidaklah - baginya* it is not difficult for him.

cangkelong (s.) CANGKLONG.

cangking (me)ny- to hand-carry (letters,

etc.). **-an** hand-, portable. *barang. barang*
~ hand-baggage. *generator* ~ portable
generator.

cangklong I any modern foreign-made
pipe.

cangklong II double bag worn over the
shoulder. **ny-** to carry s.t. (on a shoul-
derstrap) by o's side under o's arm.

cangkok graft. **men-** to tap, bug. **men-kan**
jantung to transplant a heart. **ny-** to
adopt (a child). **pen-an** transplant. **-an**
graft.

cangkriman enigma, puzzle.

cantèl I ny- to get stuck, cannot be released. *Sumbangan korban banjir masih
banyak yg~,* A lot of the contributions
for the flood victims still got stuck, i.e.
didn't get distributed.

cantèl II sorghum.

cantèng -an hand carried.

canthas ke-an boldness.

cantik - *molek* very pretty. *si* - the beauty.

canting a small copper vessel with a
spouted nib for applying melted wax
to fabric being batiked.

cantol ter- *pd* depends on.

cao to run away, get away in a hurry.

caos I to guard.

caos II to prepare (esp. food). - *dahar* to
prepare food (for the spirits).

cap I ten. *-tun* ten rupiahs.

cap II trade-mark (including a design,
picture or photograph). *C- Macan*
Tiger Balm.

capai *mudah dpt* **di-** 1 within easy reach.
2 easy to achieve. *yg blm pernah* **ter-**
all-time (high).

capgomèh and **Cap Go Mèh** '15th night
(of February),' a Chinese celebration
observed with pomp and gaiety.

capgotun fifteen rupiahs.

Capjigwéé December.

capjitunpoa twelve and a half rupiahs.

cap(e)lok men- to annex. **pen-an** annexation.

Capra Beetle name of the beetle species
found in the rice imported from Pakistan.

captain (in sports, with airlines, such as,
the Garuda Indonesian Airways, shipping companies, such as, the Djakarta
Lloyd) captain; (s.) KAPTEN.

cara ke-an modality. **se-:** ~ *bersudut*
angular. ~ *bertahap* in stages, phased.
~ *besar. besaran* massively. ~ *blak. blakan*
openly, frankly. ~ *buatan* artificially.
~ *diam. diam* covertly. ~ *dua. duaan*
privately. *pembicaraan* ~ *dua. duaan* a
private talk. ~ *gelap* clandestinely, illegally. ~ *G to G* from Government to
Government. ~ *lisan* orally, by word
of mouth, viva voce. ~ *mandiri* independently. ~ *naluri* instinctively.
~ *oglangan* by turns. *Suratkabar. suratkabar harian yg terbit di Yogyakarta
sejak hari Senin yl. tlh terbit* ~ *oglangan,*
The daily papers published in Yogyakarta have since last Monday been published by turns. ~ *padatnya* in short,
to be concise. ~ *perseorangan* in person, personally. ~ *rukun* harmoniously.
~ *sahabat* amicably. ~ *tambal. sulam* in
a makeshift way. ~ *teka. teki* enigmati-
cally, mysteriously. ~ *tersurat dan tersirat* verbatim et litteratim. ~ *timbal
balik* conversely. - *bekerja* working
method, procedure. - *bergaul* manners.
- *berpikir* attitude of mind. - *Chicago*
à la Chicago (i.e. violent). - *hidup* way
(,mode) of life. - *hidup menyendiri*
exclusivism. - *kuno* archaism. - *memasak*
cuisine. - *pembayaran* mode of payment. - *perjuangan* mode (,method) of
warfare, fighting method.

caraka courier. *C- Loka* the building
managed by the women's association
of the Department of Foreign Affairs.
- *yudha* (sometimes used for) military
attaché.

Carakawati name of the Foreign Office
Women's Association.

cari di- (in want ads) wanted (a salesgirl,
etc.). **men-:** *tugas* ~ *dan menyelamat-
kan* search and rescue task. ~ *duit* to
make a living. ~ *enaknya sendiri saja*
bent on self-interest only. ~ *gara. gara*

(,penyakit) looking for trouble. ~ *info sana.sini* to find out here and there. ~ *jalan gampang* to take the line of least resistance. ~ *jejak* to trace, track. ~ *keterangan (,tahu)* 1 to inquire. 2 to investigate. ~ *pekerjaan* to be after a job. ~ *tahu* to find out, discover. **pen-:** ~ *jejak* stalker, tracker. ~.~ *kemungkinan perdamaian* peace feelers. ~ *mangsa* hooker, prostitute, predator. ~ *untung* fortune seeker, adventurer. *Pusat* **Pen-an** *dan Penyelamatan* SAR (,Search and Rescue) Center. - *duit sendiri* to earn o's own money. - *iseng* to loiter (as a prostitute looking for business). *Di Jakarta ini orang sulit - kerja,* In Jakarta it is difficult for a person to find work. - *muka (kpd)* to cajole, wheedle, try to make up with s.o.

carik secretary (to a *lurah*).

cartal (s.) UANG (CARTAL).

carter pen- charterer. **pen-an** chartering. **-an** chartered. - *masa* time charter. - *sejalan* voyage charter. - *waktu* time charter.

carut - *marut* obscene language.

cas to charge (a storage battery). **men-** *accu* to charge a (car) battery. - *accu (,aki)* battery charger.

cas.cis.cus (opp. *nang.ning.nong*) - *berbahasa Belanda* to speak Dutch fluently (like a native-born Dutchman). **ber-** to speak a western language (Dutch and English) fluently.

casis (automobile) chassis.

cassète (pron. kasèt) 1 cassette. 2 cassette tape recorder; (s.) KASET. *membunyikan* - to play the cassette tape recorder.

cat men- *rambut* to dye o's hair. - *kuku* nail polish. - *penahanan api* fire-proof paint. - *rambut* hair dye.

catat men-.kumpulkan to take stock. **pen-:** ~ *rapat* minutes clerk. ~ *waktu* timekeeper. **ter-** recorded. **-an** *kaki* footnote.

cator [beca(k) (ber)motor] motorized *beca(k)*.

catu pen-an allotment.

catur I - *wangsa* the four castes in Bali. - *wulan* a quarter (of a year).

catur II pe- chess player.

catut pen- (ticket) scalper. **pen-an** *nama* the misuse of the name of. - *pantat* 'scalping of buttocks,' i.e. keeping seats warm in train compartments until s.o. shows up who is willing to pay a certain sum of money to the *tukang - pantat* who has illegally occupied the seat, with the only purpose of 'chasing him away' from 'his' seat which, in fact, is yours because you have already paid for it!

catutisme the 'art' of blackmarketing (,moonlighting).

cawé.cawé to join in what others are doing.

CC-PKI [Central Comite - Partai Komunis Indonesia] Indonesian Communist Party Central Committee.

ceban ten thousand (rupiahs).

ceblok I to crash (of aircraft).

ceblok II ny- to work under a mutual agreement whereby A. agrees with B. that, if he plants rice for A. free of charge, he will be entitled to cut the rice during harvest time for a certain wage, usually in the proportion 10:1 or 12:1 of the harvest.

cebur ny- to plunge.

cecah *sejak* **men-** *dunia* from o's childhood up. **men-kan** *kaki* to plant feet. **ter-** *ke* planted on, touched down on.

cecèng o. thousand.

cècèr *beras* **-an** rice sweepings, i.e. rice kernels swept up from the route between a port area and the warehouse in which the bales of rice have to be stored.

cecengklok (s.) CACENGKLOK.

cecéré 1 a small river fish [L. Rasbora argyrotaenia (Blkr)]. 2 cockroach. 3 commoner, small fry, worthless (,good-for-nothing) fellow.

cecongoran face, mug.

cèdok (s.) CIDUK.

cedra (S.) CEDERA. - *janji* (jur.) non-fulfillment.

cegah men- *perluasan* to nonproliferate. **pen-an** *penyakit* preventive medicine.

cèk I di- *kebenarannya* its authenticity was checked. **meng(e)-** (S.) MENCEK. **pen(ge)-an** check, control. - *pelancong* traveler's check. - *pos* postal check. - *wisata* traveler's check. - *(yg diberi tgl) mundur.* - *yg diberi tgl lebih kemudian drpd tgl penarikannya* and - *gantung* (in Medan) postdated check. - *yg tdk cukup dananya* check with insufficient funds, bad check.

Cèk II Czech.

cekak insufficient. *uangnya* - he has insufficient funds. - *aos (,aus)* clear and succinct, curt.

cekak(an) 0.08-gram package (the smallest package) in which morphine is clandestinely sold.

cekal men- to catch, seize.

cekalang *ikan* - (s.) CAKALANG.

cekam di- *ketakutan* to be seized by fear, fear-stricken.

cekar hard a-port or hard a-starboard (of steering wheel).

cekat - *dua tangan* ambidexterous.

cek.cek.cek clicking the tongue.

cèkcok ber- to conflict. - *mulut* wrangle.

cek.del frank, outspoken, openhearted.

cekèk *tarip* - *leher* cutthroat tariffs.

cekel (s.) CEKAL.

ceki *(kartu)* - small Chinese playing cards (120 in total).

cekiber flying lizard.

cekik pen- strangler.

cekikik *ketawa (,tertawa)* **-an** to giggle, chuckle.

ceking(.terèpès) scrawny, (very) thin, skinny.

ceklèk click (of camera).

cekluk ter- slip and fall.

cekok di-i 1 (a liquid medicine) has been forced down a child's throat. 2 (fig.) to be forced to swallow.

cekres *suara* - clipping sound (of scissors).

cekung ke-an concavity. - *benua* continental shelf.

cekur - *manis* a shrub the leaves of which are eaten as vegetables (L. Sauropus albicans).

celaka 1 disaster. 2 unlucky, inopportune. - *aku!* I'm out of luck! *dpt* - to meet with an accident. - *dan sengsara* affliction. - *duabelas (,tigabelas)!* what (a piece of) bad luck! **ke-an:** ~ *lalu.lintas* traffic accident. ~ *mobil* auto crash, automobile accident. **-nya** it's a pity that, unfortunately.

celana - *(be)renang* bathing suit. - *kolor* undershorts. - *komprang* broad, long pants. - *levis* Levi's. - *pangsi* black-colored pants (used in *silat*). - *pof* plus fours. - *puntung* shorts. - *sport pendek putih* white sports shorts.

celat men- to jump up.

celemèk apron.

celentang ter- to lie stretched out.

celingak.celinguk looking left and right.

celotèh ber- to talk nonsense.

Cèlsius centigrade.

celurut a variety of rat with a strong disagreeable odor.

cema ter- accused. **-an** 1 accusation. 2 allegation.

cemar men-i and **men-kan** to pollute. **pen-an** pollution. ~ *udara* air pollution. **ter-** polluted.

cemara I *ayam* - a chicken with needle-leaved feathers. - *Amerika* the casuarina tree with needles.

cemara II 1 wig, chignon. 2 pendant of horse hair (under the blade of a spear). 3 yak tail. 4 hairbun stuffed with fake hair.

cemas *ia menyatakan rasa* -*nya yg mendalam atas* he expressed his profound concern over.

cemberut 1 (to continue) unswervingly, unperturbedly. 2 sour (of face). - *asam spt cuka.biang* as sour as a lemon. **-an** sour face.

cèmè blind in o. eye. *si C-* the one-eyed man. *di negara orang.orang buta, si C- menjadi raja* in the kingdom of the blind the one-eyed man is king.

cemerlang men-kan to add luster to.

cemil se- a little bit.

cemol men-.- to grab with the whole hand.

cempaka a tree with strong-smelling yellow blossoms (L. Michelia champaka).

cempedak k.o. jack fruit (L. Artocarpus polyphema). *seorang makan -, semua kena getahnya* 'o. person is eating a *cempedak* and all are hit by its (sticky) sap,' i.e. o. rotten apple will decay a bushel.

cèmpin champagne.

cemplang 1 tasteless, without taste. 2 (fig.) in bad (,poor) taste. 3 insipid (food, remarks, anecdotes), expressionless, without expression.

cempor *lampu -* oil lamp.

cemprèng shrill, strident (noise).

cenal.cenil 1 elastically. 2 rhythmically. *seorang wanita dgn lenggang.lenggoknya yg -* a woman with her rhythmically swaying hips.

cenayang medium (the person).

Cendana President Soeharto's residence (in Jakarta).

cendawan *tumbuh sbg - habis hujan* and *tumbuh* men- 1 to mushroom. 2 mushrooming.

cenderawasih (s.) BURUNG (CENDERAWASIH).

cenderung - (,ke-an) *utk celaka* accident prone. berke-an to have the tendency to.

cèndol a cooling drink, prepared from rice flour, cut up and mixed with brown sugar and coconut milk.

cèng thousand. se- o. thousand (rupiahs).

cengar.cengir 1 to boast, brag. 2 to cry (of babies). 3 to grin, turn up o's nose, pull faces.

cèngbèng and **cèng bèng** (s.) CINGBING.

cengèk ny- shrill, reedy (of voice).

cengèngèsan to sneer, grin, (make a) grimace.

cènggo o. thousand and five hundred (rupiahs).

cengir meny- *spt kuda* to guffaw. ny- to grin, turn up o's nose, sniff (at). - *kuda* horse laugh, guffaw.

cengkar arid, infertile.

cengkau 1 agent, dealer, broker (in valuables). 2 matchmaking woman, pimp.

cengkèh per-an (adj.) cloves.

cengkeram men- to strangle, choke.

cengkerung alcove.

cengkir very young coconut.

cèngli stands to reason, plausible.

centangan place for stretching.

centil coquettish.

cèntral central, in: *Central Comite Partai Komunis Indonesia;* (s.) CC-PKI.

cèos men- to hiss (sound produced when striking a match). *geretan ~* the match hissed.

cep all of a sudden quiet. - *k(e)lakep* suddenly (they became) quiet. *menanti di-* k(e)lakepkan waiting for silence to be imposed upon.

cepak crew-cut.

cepat *lebih - lebih baik* the sooner the better. *siapa - siapa dpt* early birds get the worms. berke-an to have a speed of. *Kedua kendaraan itu ~ cukup tinggi,* The two cars moved at a substantial rate of speed. ke-an: *~ terbesar (,tertinggi)* top speed. - *panèn* quick yielding.

cepè(k) o. hundred.

cepèkcèng o. hundred thousand.

cepèng *tempat pelacuran kelas* -an a low-class brothel.

ceplas.ceplos (to tell s.t.) in plain terms, in down-to-earth language.

cèples to look exactly like.

ceplok fried egg.

ceplos ke-an *omong* to let o's tongue run away with o. men-kan *bola ke dlm gawang* to kick the ball into the goal.

cepo broke, without money.

cepuk tube (for toothpaste, etc.).

cerabut ter- degenerated.

cerah bright (of prospects).

cerai ber- divided, disconnected, apart. men-kan *atas sukunya* to divide (a word) into syllables. per-an: *~... dgn ... divorce ... from ... ~ lanreporem* a formal divorce based on the Agrarian Basic Law. -.*dahar.guling* judicial

(,legal) separation, separation from bed and board.

ceramah - *tamu* guest lecture.

cerang - *rimba* a clearing in the forest.

cerbung [cerita bersambung] serialized story.

cercah men-.- to cut up into little pieces. **-an** small piece.

cerèwèt 1 whimsical, capricious, wayward. 2 to bother, nag. 3 censorious, critical. 4 to have a ready tongue, have a tongue in o's head. 5 to talk too much. 6 to complain constantly. **ke-an** faultfinding, censoriousness, carping spirit.

cergam [cerita bergambar] comics.

cergas agile, nimble.

cèri (s.) BUAH (CERI).

ceria **pen-an** purification.

ceriga 1 doubtful, suspicious. 2 slow to decide, hesitant.

cerit(er)a *dgn tdk banyak* - stripped of all unnecessary verbiage, in a nutshell. *bukan - baru* it's not a new story, it's nothing new. *C-nya begini* ... The facts of the case are as follows ... **pen-** narrator, story-teller. - *bergambar* cartoons. - *bersambung* serialized story. - *bohong* hoax. -.- *burung mengatakan bhw* ... rumors have it that... - *rekaan* (prose) fiction. - *seribu satu malam* the Arabian Nights.

cerkan [ceritarekaan] (prose) fiction.

cerkrim [cerita kriminil] detective story.

cermai name of a tree with small, sour fruits, preserved and eaten as a side dish (L. Phyllanthus acidus).

cermin *buruk muka* - *dibelah* it's an ill bird that fouls its own nest. **be(r)-** *bangkai* (s.) BANGKAI. - *spion* outside rear view mirror.

cerocos and **ny-** 1 to pour (,stream ,flow) out, overflow. 2 the sound produced by red-hot iron when put in water. **-an** to pour, drip (profusely). *keringat ~ dr pori.pori badannya* the sweat poured out of his pores.

cerpelai mongoose.

certificaat certificate. *C- van Oorsprong*

(in trade and commerce) Certificate of Origin.

cespleng to hit the mark. *karikatur. karikatur yg* - cartoons which hit home.

cess 1 a tax, an assessment. 2 (in Indonesia) a surcharge on export products from plantations levied by the local regional government.

cètak **ber-kan** imprinted with. **di- semprot** to be spraypainted. **men-** to turn out (doctors, etc.), certify. **Per-an** *Uang* The Mint. **-an** graduate. - *kasa (,sablon)* screen printing.

cetèt men-.- *tangannya* to snap o's fingers while simultaneously making a soft sound to (usually) a turtledove, encouraging it to coo.

ceto.wélo.wélo crystal-clear.

cetus **pen-** *ide* sponsor, idea man, initiator.

cèwèk girl friend. **ber-.-an** to go looking for girls.

Cèwèng the code word used by the *PKI* to refer to the late Dr. Soebandrio.

CFW a dining and passenger railway coach.

chéongsam the traditional Chinese gown.

chi a weight used in drug traffic, about 3.8 kilograms.

chiak to eat. - *kopi* 1 amenable to bribery. 2 bribery.

Chili Chile.

chroom chromium.

chudancho company commander of the *Peta* during the Japanese occupation.

Chuo Sangi-in Central Advisory House (in the Capital City of Jakarta) during the Jap. occupation.

ci- (contraction of the Sund. cai: water, river) element in many place and river names in West Java, such as, *Cimahi* (a town) and *Citarum* (a river).

cialat too bad!

cicil **peny-an** paying out in installments.

ciduk **men-** to arrest. **ter-** arrested. **-an** grip, clutches. *Orang. orang itu berusaha melarikan diri dr ~ ABRI,* Those people attempted to escape from the grip of the Armed Forces.

ciek *ijazah* - *baduo* (in Sawahlunto, West

Sumatra) marriage certificate.

cigok **men-** *ke* to stick o's head into.

cihuuuiiii great! *Ceweknya -!* The girls were knockouts!

cik large quantity of morphine powder consisting of 3,000 *cekaks.*

cikal I 1 first-born, oldest child. 2 first (of s.t.). **ber-.bakal** *dr* to originate from. *-.bakal* first workers of land, founder of a village.

cikal II *kaleng* **-an** (coll.) tin scrap (,refuse), tinplate scrap (,cuttings).

cikalang (s.) CEKALANG.

cikar (s.) CEKAR. **pen-an** *kemudi* (on sea) = *banting s(e)tir* (on land).

cikarwan cart driver.

cikutan to hiccough.

cilu(k) bah! and **ciluuup … ba!** peeka-boo, i.e. a child's game in which s.o. hides his face behind a newspaper, etc. and says *"ciluuup"*, and then suddenly reveals it, calling: *"ba! "*

cim (s.) ENCIM.

cina **men-** to become Sinicized. **Pe-n** Chinatown. **per-an** (adj.) Chinese - *kebakaran jenggot* pandemonium.

cincau 1 a refreshing drink. 2 *(daun -)* plant (L. Cyclea berbata) the leaves of which can be squeezed out to become a viscous, gelatinous mass to form the main substance of the drink; some molasses syrup is added to taste.

cincin *- dlm rantai* chain link. *- emas* species of a snake. *- kawin* wedding ring.

cincing **men-** *kain* to hold up a sarong on o. side.

cincu 1 owner's agent on a (Chinese) ship. 2 ship's captain. 3 (in Aceh) bus con-ductor.

cindaku (in West Sumatra) were-tiger; (s.) CINDEKU.

cindé (mainly red) flowered silk fabric.

cindeku (in Banten) certain persons who can transform their body into that of a tiger.

cinderawasih (s.) CENDERAWASIH.

cindo (in Palembang) good-looking.

cing 1 uncle! 2 auntie!

Cingbing and **Cing Bing** Chinese version of "All Souls' Day" in early April.

cingcai to reach a settlement.

cingcong *tdk banyak* - easy going, not finnicky.

cino (S.) CINA.

cinse (in Jakarta, derogatory term for) a Chinese.

cinta *berseminya* - love in bloom. *- laut* seaminded. *- menyala.nyala* ardent love. *- monyet* calf (,puppy) love. *- pd pandangan pertama* love at first sight. *- pura.pura* hypocritical affection. *- segi.tiga* love triangle. *- sepihak* one-sided love. *- tak berbalas* unrequited love. *- udara* airminded.

cintamani a brilliantly golden-yellow snake, the finding of which betokens good fortune in love.

cintawan lover. *- agung* great lover.

cintrong (pun on *cinta*) love. *jatuh* - to fall in love. *mabuk - kpd* madly in love with, head over heels in love with.

cipoa 1 crooked, not straightforward, dishonest, swindling. 2 a lie. *tukang -* a crook, swindler.

cipok kiss. **men-** to kiss.

ciprat **ke-an** *(bagian)* to get o's slice of the pie.

cipta **pen-** *mode* fashion designer. (Direk-torat Jenderal) *C- Karya* (Directorate General of) Housing, Building, Plan-ning and Urban Development. *- sastra* literary work.

ciput cunt.

ciri **ber-kan** to be characterized by.

cita I chintz.

cita II **ber-.-** to long, desire, aspire, hope.

Citgwéé July.

citra image.

ciu (s.) CIYU.

cium **di-** *mobil* to be hit (,knocked down) by a car. **men-** to sniff out. ~ *adanya organisasi di bawah tanah* to sniff out a subversive organization. **- (an)** (snif-fing) kiss.

ciut **di-kan** *utk* to be narrowed down to, be limited to. **pen-an** shrinkage. ~ *luas* shrinkage of an area.

civic mission civic mission. **di-kan** to be used for civic mission purposes.

ciyu k.o. brandy extracted from fermented cassava.

ckk, ckk, ckk sound of clucking tongue.

clamit(an) greedy, grasping.

clash clash.

clearing (banking term) clearing.

cleguk gulp.

climèn simple (not elaborate, feast). *Perkawinan Anne cuma - saja,* Anne's wedding was very simple.

clingak.clinguk to look about everywhere (seeking, as if o. has lost s.t.).

clingus shy, timid, bashful.

clola.clolo to roam about.

clonèh *pating -* particolored, of various colors.

clurit small Madurese sickle-shaped knife. **di-** to be stabbed with such a knife.

coan profit, gain, advantage.

coba look (,see) here! say! **per-an** *asam* acid test. -.- experimental. *produksi ~* experimental (,pilot) production.

coblos **men-** and **meny-** to vote for. **pen-** and **peny-** voter. **pen-an** and **peny-an** voting. *~ tanda.gambar* voting by perforating an election symbol. **-an** general elections.

cocak(-rawa) the Indonesian thrush.

cocog and **cocok** 1 appropriate, suitable, proper. 2 adaptable. 3 settled, fixed. 4 to meet with (great) favor, tasty (of food), good, be appreciated. *selalu - masakannya!* she is an excellent cook!

cocor *- merah* (during the confrontation with the Dutch in the years 1945–1949) (coll.) the (Dutch) Mustang fighter plane.

cogok **ter-** erected (of stores, etc.).

cokèk a Jakarta dance.

cok(e)lat cocoa. **ke-.-an** brownish.

cokol **ber-** implanted, ensconced, lodged.

Cokordé (in Bali) name element placed before personal names, e.g. *Ida Cokorde Gde Mayun.*

colak.calik shuttle service.

colèk **di-** to be touched (with a finger).

colok **ke-** to get stuck in the eye. *dgn tdk*

meny- *(mata)* unobtrusively. *- mata* cynosure, center of attention.

colong **ny-** to steal. *~ petek* to falsify (,disprove) the prediction, turn out differently from the expectation. *Kanada bersedia tetap dlm ICCS sampai tgl. 31 Mei. Eh, ~ petek alias di luar dugaan.* Canada is prepared to remain in ICCS until May 31. Eh, this is contrary to expectations. *~ waktu* to get away (in a hurry). *sepeda motor -an* a stolen motorcycle. *-.-an* to steal left and right. *orang main ~ ceritera* people commit plagiarism left and right. *-.-* stealthily, clandestinely.

colot **ny-** to jump up.

Colt (pron. kol) a small Japanese-made suburban bus. **ber.-** to use a Colt (bus).

comat.comot to jostle e.o., elbow e.o.

combèr **ke-an** 1 open sewage ditch. 2 basin for household waste water. **pe-an** cesspool. **-an** sewer, drain.

combi *sebuah mobil - VW* a Volkswagen van.

combro(k) nourishment from cassava filled with *oncom. tukang -* person who produces this nourishment or sells it.

comité committee.

Commanders Call the meeting of commanders of *KODAM, KODAK,* etc.

Commanditaire Vennootschap a firm including o. or several partners whose liabilities go only as far as the amount of capital they have put into the company, while the managing partner(s) remain(s) fully responsible for the firm's liabilities.

comot **men-** 1 to take s.t. between the fingertips. *nasi* **pe-** a portion of cooked rice taken between o's fingertips. 2 to snatch with the fingertips. 3 to steal. **men-kan** to steal s.t. **-an** theft. *hasil ~* results of a theft.

congak.bong(k)ak arrogant.

congo pickpocket.

congti, Cong Tifu and **Cong Tipu** (in the Tanjung Priok port area, Jakarta) 1 thieves and small-caliber mafia-type people. 2 request for or collection of money under duress.

contoh -nya for instance.

copèt *Saya terkena* **pen-an,** I was pickpocketed. - *seks* sexual molester.

coplok **men-** to fire, kick out. **pen-an** dismissal (from office).

copot 1 gotten loose (of bike chain, teeth, buttons, pages in a book, etc.). *jantung saya mau -* my heart skipped a beat. 2 taken off (clothes). **men-** 1 to fire, kick out. 2 to take s.t. off, remove. ~ *kacamata* to take o's glasses off. **men-i** to snatch. ~ *arloji. tangan* to snatch a wrist watch. **ny-:** ~ *dr* to desert, leave [o's (political) party]. ~ *sebelum tamat* to drop out (of students). **pen-an** discharge (from office). - *hati* quite taken aback (with fright).

coprak **nge-** to keep on talking (,chattering), speak (,chatter) continuously.

cor **men(ge)-** to cast (metal). **peng-an** casting.

corak *pelbagai -* dan *banyak -nya* manifold, multifarious. **ke- ragaman** differentiation. - *pikiran* (mental) attitude, attitude of mind. *setiap daerah mempunyai - ragam tersendiri* each region has its own characteristics.

corat.corèt **men-** to put graffitti on.

corèng **men-** *di muka sendiri* to lose face, disgrace o.s.

corèt **men-** to write (slogans) on walls. ~ *kening sendiri dgn arang* to lose face, disgrace o.s.

coro 1 (a large species of) cockroach. 2 (in Indonesian nationalist circles during col.) spy, traitor.

corong **kemen-an** grandeur, pomp, splendor.

corps corps. *C- Baret Merah* The *RPKAD. C- Diplomatik* Diplomatic Corps, Corps Diplomatique. *C- Intendans Angkatan Darat* Army Quartermaster Corps. *C- Polisi Militer* Military Police Corps.

cover **meng-** to cover (a story).

cowèk and **cowèt** small saucer-shaped stone bowl for making *sambal.*

cowo(k) boy friend.

cowokan illegal retribution consisting of the levying of fish, k.o. tax.

CPM [Corps Polisi Militer] Military Police Corps.

c.q. [casu quo] or ... as the case may be. *Pelaksanaan semua Undang-Undang - Peraturan Pemerintah RI,* The implementation of all Laws or Government Regulations of the Republic of Indonesia as the case may be.

crat.crit *airnya -* the (tap)water drips.

criping potato chips.

crocos (s.) CEROCOS. **nrocos** to pour out. ~*lah info dr mulut perjaka itu* information poured out of the young man's mouth.

crossboys and *crossgirls* comparable to the British mods, Teddyboys, etc. *crossboys udara* 'air crossboys,' the epithet given to the unlicensed radio transmitters in Bandung.

crossmama and *crosspapa* an adult whose social and parental behavior lacks decorum and the proper sense of responsibility.

cs [cum suis] *-nya* o's friends, o's buddies. *Penerima.penerima kredit itu adalah ~ si direktur utama,* Those who receive credit are the 'buddies' of the chief director.

CSIS [Center for Strategic and International Studies] the Indonesian think tank leaning towards *Golkar.*

cuat **ber-an** to stick up all over. **men-** to shoot up. ~ *ke langit lepas* to rocket skyward (of 'Sabre' jets, etc.).

cu bik sen [cuma bikin senang] (in Manado) just for fun.

cucakrawa *(burung) -* yellow crowned bulbul (L. Pycnonotus zeylanicus).

cuci **pen-** *kaca* windshield washer. **peny-an** cleansing. - *darah* hemodialysis. - *gudang* warehouse sale. - *mata* 1 to eyeball. 2 girl watching. *di sinilah orang dpt ngopi sambil - mata* it's here that o. can drink coffee while watching girls. - *mulut* dessert. - *nama* to clear o's name. - *otak* brainwashing.

cucul to undress, take off (o's coat).

cudanco (s.) CHUDANCHO.

cuil se- very few. *Orang Betawi asli sdh tinggal ~,* There remain only a very few native Jakartans. *andil* ~ small parts.

cuka *minum - pagi hari* to get out of bed on the wrong side.

cukai *- bir* excise on beer. *- gula pasir* excise on (granulated) sugar. *- korek api* excise on matches. *- minuman keras* excise on spirits. *- minyak tanah* excise on kerosene. *- tembakau* excise on tobacco.

cukil -an extract (from book, document, etc.).

cukong (Chinese) wheeler-dealer, a term for the vastly wealthy Chinese financiers of key Indonesian political figures. men-i to back, finance, pay for (bad connotation). pen-an and per-an wheeling and dealing.

cukongisme wheeler-dealerism, wheeling-dealing.

cukup fairly, rather, sufficient. *blm - sebulan* not quite a month. *- sekian sajalah* that's enough. berke-an affluent; sufficient. *tak* men-i insufficient, inadequate. se-nya (to an) adequate (degree) for the purpose. -an good enough, fair. ~ *saja* just average, medium. *-.- saja* reasonable, moderate. *- jelas* self explanatory (legal). *- mutu* qualified. *- persenjataannya* armed to the teeth. *- ramai* rather busy. *- umur* 1 adult, mature. 2 obsolete.

cukur -an *selamatan* in which the hair of a 40-day old baby is cut. *- komplit* 'complete shave,' this includes not only a haircut, but also trimming of sideburns and mustache. *- krukat* (to have) a crew cut.

culak.culik various kidnappings.

culas crafty, dishonest. ke-an dishonesty.

culik I *si* ter- the kidnapping victim.

culik II female nocturnal cuckoo. *-.-* koel.

Cultuurstèlsel the force-crop "Cultivation System" by the Dutch colonial government (1830–1870).

cumadong and cumadhong (s.) CADONG.

- dawuh to wait for instructions (in a humble way).

cuman only, merely.

cumbu men-.rayu to sweet-talk, soft-soap, persuade with promises.

cuming only. *- gelar* a mere title.

cum suis 1 with his friends (,companions , associates). 2 with affiliates.

cundrik poniard.

cungkup (memorial) tomb in the shape of a house.

cunia barge, flat-bottomed ship.

cup mine! (word by which children lay claim to s.t.).

cupak (s.) (TEMPAT) PENGINANGAN.

cupang *ikan -* Siamese fighting fish.

cupet to be lacking in common sense. *seorang yg - pikiran* a narrow-minded person.

cuping *- sayap* flaps (on aircraft). *- telinga* ear lobe. *tdk memperlihatkan - hidungnya* didn't show up, didn't appear.

curah bulk. *Ia* di-i *kepercayaan kami,* He was given (,extended ,accorded) our confidence. *kecurigaan* di-kan *kpd* the suspicion fell on. men- to pour down (of rain). men-kan: ~ *perhatian thd* to pay attention to. ~ *tenaganya kpd* to devote o's energy to. pen-an *tenaga* devotion of energy. ter- *kpd* focused on. *- hujan* rainfall.

curang *tdk -* candid.

curi *-.-* stealthily, in a stealthy manner.

curiga 1 doubtful. 2 slow to decide. *- dgn* suspicious of. *dgn -* suspiciously. me-naruh *- atas* to be suspicious of. *merasa - atas* to become suspicious of.

curuk waterfall.

cus shut up!

cutbirahi pun on *cutbrai.*

cutbrai bell-bottom.

cuti vacation, holiday. *- bersalin* maternity leave. *- biasa* ordinary leave. *- di luar tanggungan Negara* leave without pay (for government employees). *- haidh* leave due to menstruation. *- hamil* maternity leave. *- luarbiasa* extraordinary leave. *- panjang* long

leave. - *sakit* sick leave. - *studi selama
setahun* a 1-year sabbatical (leave) (for
lecturers, professors).
CV a passenger car (in train formation).
CVPD [Citrus Vein Phloem Degenera-

tion] a disease which attacks citrus
plants.
cyak (s.) CHIAK.
cylinderkop pakking gasket.

D

da (S.) ADA.
daayah (Moslem) propaganda.
dabing dubbing. men- to dub.
dableg n- stubborn, obstinate.
dabyah nge- to hold o's ground, last long.
dada *Ini -ku, mana -mu?* a challenge to
fight. men- to accept with courage.
*Perpisahan! Inilah sebenarnya yg
segera ku-,* A farewell! This is in fact
what I soon have to accept with courage.
dadah drugs.
dadak n- suddenly. pen-an surprise
(attack).
dadali I and dhadhali *manuk* - k.o.
swallow.
dadali II name of a bird of prey, sparrow
hawk (almost as big as the *alap.alap*
and very wild).
dadap I k.o. tree (used as shade tree in
coffee estates).
dadap II *si D- dan si Waru* A and B (two
hypothetical persons).
dadar pen-an 1 touchstone. 2 (Spartan)
training center. 3 - *gulung* wheat flour
crepe; usually green in color; rolled
around a mixture of coconut and
brown sugar. - *telur* (S.) TELUR
(DADAR).
Dadu Aquarius.
daérah *rasa* ke-an provincialism. *D-
Aliran Sungai* (abbrev. *DAS*) Water-
shed. *D- Bebas Beca(k)* (abbrev. *DBB*)
Pedicab-Prohibited Zone. *D- Bebas
Militèr* Demilitarized Zone, DMZ (in
Vietnam). - *belakang* hinterland. - *ber-
bahaya* danger zone. - *dataran tinggi
tengah* the central highlands (in Vietnam). - *demilitarisasi* demilitarized

zone. - *desa* rural area. - *di mana terus
terjadi kekacauan.kekacauan* a chaos-
ridden area. - *(hawa) panas* tropics.
- *hijau* (*PKI*-term) an area in which the
army is strongly represented. - *hitam* a
red-light district. - *hukum* (territorial)
jurisdiction. *D- Istimewa Aceh* The
Aceh Special Region (in Northern
Sumatra). *D- Istimewa Yogyakarta*
The Yogyakarta Special Region (in
Central Java). - *jalur hijau* greenbelt.
- *kediaman* residential area. - *kericuan*
trouble spot. *D- Khusus Ibukota Jakarta Raya* The Greater Jakarta Special
Capital Region. - *kota* urban area.
- *merah* (*PKI*-term) an area in which
the Indonesian Communist Party is
strongly represented. - *militer* military
area. - *minus* an area that does not
grow enough to support itself. - *pemilihan (,pemungutan suara)* electoral
district, constituency. - *penghasil karet*
rubber producing area. - *penyekat*
bufferzone. - *perbatasan* frontier areas.
- *pertokoan* shopping center. - *pesisir*
1 coastal area. 2 (in Java) the regions
along Java's north coast. 3 (also, in
Java) the regions outside the principal-
ities (Yogyakarta and Surakarta).
- *pinggiran* 1 outskirts (of a city).
2 (in Jakarta, the city quarters) Pal
Merah, Kebayoran Lama, Tanggerang,
Kramat Pulo, Klender and Pasar Rebo.
- *putih* (*PKI*-term) an area in which the
Indonesian Communist Party is weak.
- *seberang* 1 (viewed from Sumatra)
Malaysia. 2 (viewed from Java) the
outer regions. *Menteri D- Seberang*
(The Dutch) Minister of Overseas

Territories. - *sedang* temperate zone. - *senja* twilight zone. *D- (Swatantra) Tingkat I* First Level (Autonomous) Region (i.e. the former *Propinsi* Province). *D- (Swatantra) Tingkat II* Second Level (Autonomous) Region (i.e. the former *Kabupaten* Regency). - *takluk* dependency, a subject territory that is not part of the ruling country. - *terjepit* pocket, enclave. - *terlarang* a prohibited area. - *tropika* tropics. - *yg banyak gangguannya* a trouble spot. - *yg bergolak* a hot spot. -*yg dikosongkan dr militer* demilitarized zone. - *yg tdk dikenal* terra incognita.

daérahisme regionalism.

daftar di- hitamkan to be blacklisted. **men-** to register o.s. **men-(kan).** *ulang* to reregister. **pen-** registrant. **pen-an:** *P~ Jiwa* (s.) CATATAN (SIPIL). ~ *tanah* land survey. ~.*ulang* reregistration. ~ *warga* (s.) CATATAN (SIPIL). - *angka* list of grades (in school). - *isi buku (,kitab)* table of contents (of a book). - *isian* form (to fill out). - *isian pertanyaan* questionnaire. - *nilai* (in school) examination results. - *pemilih* register (,list) of voters, electoral register. - *permintaan* questionnaire. - *takhadir* attendance list. - *tunggu* waiting list. - *upah* payroll.

dag.dig.dug sound of a palpitating heart (from fear). *hatinya* - he was rattled (,scared).

daga resistance. -.*dagi* insubordination, willful disobedience.

dagang ber- *kecil.kecilan* to carry on a small-scale business. *tak boleh* **diperkan** not negotiable. **pe-:** ~ *acung* peddler. ~ *antara* middleman, distributor. ~ *asongan* peddler, huckster. ~ *barang rombengan* junkman. ~ *(ber)keliling* peddler, huckster. ~ *besar* large merchant. ~ *eceran* retailer, small merchant. ~ *girlan* (in Bogor) street vendor. ~ *kaki.lima* sidewalk vendor. ~ *kecil* retailer, small merchant. ~ *menengah* middle class trader. ~ *minuman keliling* street vendor of drinks. ~ *pertengahan*

1 middle class man. 2 tradesman, shopkeeper. **per-an:** ~ *antar.daerah (,pulau)* inter-regional (,insular) trade. ~ *banyak pihak* multilateral trade. ~ *besar* wholesale trade. ~ *daging mentah* 'flesh' trade, i.e. prostitution. ~ *dlm negeri* domestic trade. ~ *eceran* retail trade. ~ *gelap* illegal trade. ~ *kecil* retail trade. ~ *komoditi penyerahan kemudian* commodities futures trading. ~ *luarnegeri* foreign trade. ~ *mengumpul* collective trade. ~ *multilateral* multilateral trade. ~ *penyaluran* distributive trade. ~ *sapi* (fig.) horse trading, traffic in votes. ~ *seberang laut* overseas trade. ~ *tetap* regular trade. ~ *transito* transit trade. ~ *tukar. menukar* barter trade. ~ *wesel* bill trading.

dagé gembus k.o. *tempe bongkrek* produced by the local people of Ranjeng (Brebes, Central Java).

daging - *asé* hash(ed meat). - *asin* salted (,pickled) meat. - *beku* frozen meat. - *cacah (,cincang)* (raw) ground beef. - *mentah* 'a piece of ass,' woman considered as sex object. - *merah* beef. - *numbu* 1 tumor. 2 polyp. - *sapi bakar* roast beef. - *susur* corned beef.

dah I (s.) DEH. Particle giving or requesting permission, agreement. *biar* - go ahead then, O.K.

dah II a greeting comparable to 'bye.'

dahaga thirst. *melepaskan* - to quench o's thirst.

dahriah (s.) KAUM (DAHRIAH).

dahulu (s.) DULU. *lebih* - in advance, ahead of time. *zaman* - past ages. **ber-.-an** to rush, hasten forward, speed. -.**men-** to contend (,fight) for supremacy, try to surpass e.o. *dgn* **men-i** *pengesahan* ... in anticipation of the ratification of ... **pen-** precedent. **pen-an** preliminary. **ter-:** ~ *dr itu* before, previously. ~ *drpd waktunya* premature. -.(-)**nya** formerly.

dahyang and **dhahyang** 1 the guardian spirit of a Jav. village. 2 a special title conferred upon *Durno* (2).

da'i 1 muezzin. 2 (Moslem) person who

conducts the *dakwah*, propagandist,
missionary.

da'i'ah 'o. more minute,' depending on
the context it can mean 'another
month' or, even longer.

daidan (during the Jap. occupation)
battalion.

daidanco and *daidancho* (during the Jap.
occupation) battalion commander of
the *Peta* with a rank somewhere between major and lieutenant-colonel.

daihatsu small Jap.-made public transportation vehicle.

dajal the complete term is: *al.masih al* -
the false Christ.

dakep *dgn tangan* **se-** with arms folded.

daki **pen-** (mountain) climber.

dakik bombastic, pompous.

Dakochan 1 Jap.-made, black monkey-
like inflated vinyl doll which clings to
o's arm. 2 (during the *Konfrontasi*)
nickname for Malaysia's Tunku Abdulrachman.

Daksinapati name of the college students
dormitory of the University of Indonesia at Rawamangun, Jakarta.

daktiloskopi dactyloscopy, fingerprinting.

daku **di-** to be acknowledged.

dakwa **men-** to indict. **-an** arraignment,
indictment.

dakwah the Islamic version of evangelism,
missionary activity. **pen-** missionary.

dalam - *beberapa hari terakhir ini* during
the last few days. - *usia 52 th* at the
age of 52. *dr* - from within. *sdh* - *(bln,
th)* as far back as (...). **ke-an** draft.
memper- *pengetahuannya (di)dlm ilmu
Public Administration* to increase o's
knowledge of Public Administration,
make a more profound study of Public
Administration. - *negeri* domestic.

dalang **n-** 1 to conduct a shadow-play
performance. 2 (fig.) to act like a
dalang.

dalem 1 His or Her, in talking about a
prince or princess respectively; very
respectful. 2 Your (very respectful).
3 the Sultan of Yogyakarta. 4 the
residence of a *bupati* or other digni-

tary, both the interior and the entire
building.

dalia (s.) KEMBANG (DALIA).

dalil *utk* - in support (,testimony) of.
pen- arguer.

dalini horbo water buffalo milk.

Dalu Aquarius.

daluwarsa due date. *tgl* - expiration date.
ke- to have expired.

dam greedy.

damai conciliation. *D- di atas Bumi* Peace
on Earth. **ber-** conciliatory. ~ *dgn* to
conciliate with. **pen-** peacemaker. **per-
an** conciliation. *tak* **ter-kan** irreconcilable, uncompromising.

damar dammar. - *mata kucing* the cat's-
eye dammar (,resin) (L. Hopea globosa
or Pachynocarpus Wallichii).

damba **pen-** *damai* peacemaker.

damen rice straw.

dampak impact.

dampar throne.

damping *duduk* **ber-an** to sit side by side.
(wanita muda) **pen-** (young woman)
escort. ~ *dlm hidup* partner in life.

damprat **men-** to call s.o. names.

dan -/*atau* and/or. - *sebagainya* et cetera.

dana *seluruh* - *dan daya* all funds and
forces. - *cadangan* reserve fund. *D-
Moneter Internasional* International
Monetary Fund. - *pensiun* retirement
fund. - *pensiun dan tunjangan* retirement and relief fund.

dandan **-an:** ~ *muka* make-up. ~ *rambut*
hairdo.

dang.dang.dut (s.) DANGDUT. **ber-** to
show 'dangdut' films.

dangdut k.o. music characterized by the
typical rhythm of the continuous beat
of a *gendang* (,drum) betraying Indian,
Arab and Malay elements. *film* - a film
with *dangdut* music accompaniment.
lagu.lagu berirama ndangndut melodies
geared to the dangdut rhythm. *Ratu
ndang.ndut* Ndang-Ndut Music Queen.
pe- dangdut singer.

dangé k.o. food made from sago.

dangkal **ke-an** *pikiran* narrowmindedness.
pen-an lowering (of water level).

dansa ber- *ago.go* to dance the go-go.
musik utk **di-kan** music to dance to.
pe- dancer.

danta *asmara* - beautiful white teeth.

Danu(h) Sagittarius.

danyang and **dhanyang** spirit of a place.

dapat men-: ~ *angin baik* 1 to have good
fortune. 2 to be favored. ~ *karun timbul* to be lucky. ~ *kemajuan* to make
progress. ~ *kepastian* to ascertain,
obtain assurances. ~ *kesulitan* to have
difficulties. ~ *malu* to lose face. ~ *promosi* to be promoted. ~ *sorotan* to be
spotlighted. ~ *tahu* to find out. **pen-:**
menurut ~*nya* in his opinion. ~ *.akhir
(fraksi)* (s.) STEMMOTIVERING.
~ *umum* poll. **pen-an** acquirement.
~ *perusahaan* operating revenue.

dapur cuisine. - *(di) kapal* caboose. - *koran
(,surat kabar)* (coll.) editorial board
(of a newspaper). - *tukang besi* blacksmith's workshop, smithy.

dar I - *.dor.dèr* sound of rifle-fire.

dar II - *ul aman* abode of peace (,security).
- *ulhar(a)b* non-Moslem countries. *D-ul
Islam* 1 Moslem countries. 2 a Moslem
rebel movement operating in the eastern
part of West Java and the southern
Celebes in the 1950's. - *ul salam* and
- *ussalam* abode of peace.

dara I *(burung)* - pigeon, dove. - *kipas*
fantail pigeon. - *putih* pied imperial
pigeon.

dara II - .- (sl.) homosexual.

darah *di dlm* - *dagingnya* through and
through, completely. *Dia memang
seorang penerbang di dlm* - *dagingnya,*
He is indeed a pilot through and
through. - *sbg ditampi* puffed. - *dalem*
related to the crown. **ber-:** ~ *campuran*
to be of mixed descent. ~ *dingin* phleg-
matic. ~ *panas* warm-blooded. ~ *politik*
to be politically motivated. **men- daging**
deeply rooted. **pen-an** bleeding. ~ *otak*
brain (,cerebral) hemorrhage. - *tinggi*
hypertension.

darat *suku D-* (in Pontianak, West Kalimantan) (euph.) the Dayak ethnic
group. *di* - ashore. **di-i** landed on (,at).

daerah "Samodra Badai" yg akan
~ *pesawat pendarat Apollo-12* the
"Ocean of Storms" on which Apollo
12's LEM is going to land. **men-** *darurat*
to make an emergency landing. **pen-an:**
~ *di bln* moonlanding. ~ *empuk (,lem-
but)* soft landing. ~ *perut* belly landing.
~ *senyap* (mil.) silent landing. **D-an**
Cina Mainland China.

daripada it's better than.

darma contribution to social or humane
ends or institutions. **men- bhaktikan**
to make a sacrifice.

darmakelana tourism.

darmawisata ber- to picnic, make a trip
to points of interest.

darul (s.) DAR II.

darum (S.) DARUN.

darurat ...- crash ..., emergency ... **ke-an**
state of emergency.

dasa -teen, 10 digit. - *th* decade. - *warsa*
1 decade. 2 tenth anniversary.

dasar - ... that's the way it is with ... *D-
manusia, sdh ngantuk, tidurlah mereka,*
It is inherent to the nature of men that
when they are sleepy, they go to bed.
tdk **ber-** *samasekali* completely un-
founded. **ber-kan** and **di-i** to be based
on. *perbedaan yg* **men-** a fundamental
difference. - *laut* seabed.

daster duster (the dress).

data data. - *pokok* basic data. - *statistik*
statistical data. -.- *tehnik* technical data.

datang 1 to fall (of night). *bila malam* -
when night falls. 2 - *kpd* to call on. *Dia
- kepadanya meminta pekerjaan,* He
called on him for a job. *Jam berapa
dia* -? When do you expect him? *air
tdk* - the water doesn't run (from the
pipe). **ber-an** to arrive, come (referring
to plural subject). *Ratusan detektip
dan mobil anti.peluru* ~, Hundreds of
detectives and bulletproof automobiles
arrived. **di-i:** *mudah (,sulit)* ~ easy
(,difficult) of access. *tempat.tempat
itu sukar* ~ those places are of difficult
access. **men-** coming, next. *tgl 21 Maret*
~ next March 21. *di waktu* ~ and *pd
masa* ~ in the future. *yg* **men-kan**

bahaya maut perilous, involving danger to life, dangerous. **pen-** 1 visitor. 2 arrival (the person). ~ *baru* newcomer. **pen-an** importation (of commodities). - *bln* to menstruate.

datar **D-an** *Tempayan* Plain of Jars (in Vietnam).

Dati (s.) DAERAH [(SWATANTRA) TINGKAT].

datu king. **ke-an** *Sriwijaya* The Sriwijaya Kingdom (of Sumatra).

Datuk (in the Minangkabau area, Central Sumatra) an honorific title, i.e. a *gelar* for people of high status or older people within the clan.

daun - *bawang* Chinese scallion, green onions. - *jeruk purut* citrus leaf. - *kemudi* afterpiece of rudder. - *prei* chives. - *salam* Jav. bay leaf.

daur - *hidrologi* hydrological cycle.

da'wah (s.) DAKWAH.

dawai string (of musical instrument).

dawet *(es)* - (s.) CENDOL.

daya *mengerahkan - dan dana* to mobilize funds and forces. *Pengawal gerbong yg diserbu tak* **ber-** *karena ancaman. ancaman penjahat,* The guard of the train coach which was attacked succumbed to the threats of the bandits. **ber-guna** useful. **men-gunakan** 1 to use. 2 to make effective. **pen-gunaan** effectiveness. - *capai* access. - *cium* (sense of) smell, olfactory sense. *kehilangan - cium* anosmia. - *gabung* affinity. - *gerak* mobility, drive, kinetic energy. - *guna perusahaan* industrial productivity. - *jangkau* broadcast area (of TV station). - *juang* fighting power. - *kata* motto, catchword. - *kejut* shock action. - *kerja* energy, potential forces. - *konsentrasi* power(s) of concentration. - *laksana* creativeness. - *lekat* adhesion. - *lenting* resilience. - *lihat* (eye-)sight, visual acuity. - *mampu* carrying capacity (of a road). - *pakai* consumptive capacity. - *pendorong* motivation. - *pengertian* comprehension. - *penghancur* destructive force (,power). - *produksi* productive power. - *pukau* appeal (of

a movie theater, etc.). - *pukul* striking power. - *samar* apparent capacity. - *serap* absorptive capacity. - *tahan* durability. - *tahan lama* stamina, (power of) endurance. - *tak sungguh* apparent capacity. - *tampung* occupancy rate. *D- tampung Hotel Bali Beach di Sanur sejak th 1971 sampai kini meningkat terus,* The occupancy rate of the Bali Beach Hotel in Sanur has since 1971 up to now shown a constantly upward trend. - *tangkap* apprehension. - *tarik* hauling power, haulage, traction, tensile force. - *tembak* fire power. - *(upaya)* expedient(s), makeshift(s), resource(s).

dayak (teenager sl.) a gatecrasher.

dayang chaperon(e).

Dayu truncation of *Idayu;* (s.) IDA (BAGUS). - *Dol(l)ar* epithet used in Bali for a prostitute from the Brahmanic caste who serves males paying in U.S. dollars.

dayung **men-kan** to pedal (v.t.). **se-sampan** in tune (with), in line (with).

DBM [Daerah Bebas Militer] Demilitarized Zone, DMZ.

dbp [di bawah pimpinan] directed, headed by.

debar **men-kan** *jantung* exciting, thrilling.

débarkasi debarkation.

débat **ber-** to argue (in detail). **pen-** debater.

Dé-bé-bé [from *DBB:* Daerah Bebas Beca(k)] Area from which pedicabs are prohibited. **men-kan** to prohibit pedicabs from.

debos **nge-** to sit idly.

debus (in Serang, Banten) performance in which the players show their invulnerability by stabbing themselves with sharp objects, eating glass fragments, cutting the tongue, rolling over barbed wire, etc.

début debut, first appearance (before the public).

dedak - *halus* chaff (a by-product of the milling of rice, consisting of a mixture of finely ground husks and bran).

- *kasar* husks (a by-product of the milling of rice, consisting of the outermost covering of the *gabah* grain).

dedalu mistletoe.

dedarè young (of chicken). *ayam* - a young rooster.

dedek (S.) DEDAK.

dedemenan sweetheart.

dedengkot big shot (,wheel). - *film* film magnate.

dederuk spotted-necked (,mourning) dove.

dèdèt *jual* - to sell to an employee and take payment out of his salary.

dédikasi dedication.

déduksi deduction.

dé-èskalasi de-escalation.

défènsif defensive. **ber-** to stand on the defensive.

Deferred Payment Khusus term used in Jusuf Muda Dalam trial (1966) in connection with financial favors granted to a number of firms.

défilé (mil.) review, parade. **ber-** to march.

définisi *tdk dpt* **di-kan** indefinable. **men-kan** to define.

définitif final, definitive.

défisit deficit.

déflagrasi deflagration.

défoliasi defoliation.

degan - *ijo* (young) green coconut.

degdegan 1 to be anxious (about s.t. that might happen) 2 to beat pitapat (of heart).

dégen foil.

degleng and **dhegleng** eccentric.

degup (heart)beat.

dèh The speaker urges the hearer to believe his statement. Gives or requests permission or agreement; (in statements) Really. This is really true; (in commands) I urge you to do this. *ayo* - 1 so long, 'bye. 2 come on!

déhidrasi dehydration.

dékagram decagram.

dekap ber- *tangan* with arms across.

dekat 1 close (in relationship, feeling). 2 near (in time). -, *di* -, - *dr (,dgn ,ke ,pd ,kpd)* next to, close (by). *di -nya*

near (it, them, etc.). **men-i** approaching, on the point of. **men-kan** *duduknya ke* to move close to. **pen-an** approach. - *jauh* irrespective of distance.

dèk(k)ing I cover(ing). - *emas* (in banking) gold-cover(ing), gold reserve.

dèking II protection (by important person) against arrest, etc. **di-i** to be protected.

déklamasi ber- to declaim, recite. **men-kan** to recite (v.t.).

dékor decor, scenery, scenes, settings.

dékorasi decoration. - *intern (,ruangan. dalam)* interior decoration.

dékoratif decorative.

dékrit *mengeluarkan* - to enact (,issue) a decree.

deksa well-built, in proportion to stature.

deksura to treat others with contempt.

deku ber- to kneel.

délégasi pen-an delegation (of s.t.).

delep men- to hide.

deles n- pure-bred, true-born. *Dia sebenarnya bukan orang Sala* ~, Actually, he is not a true-born Solonese.

délik delict, misdemeanor. - *kesusilaan* indecent assault.

delikan 1 peekaboo. 2 to play hide-and-seek.

délikat delicate, ticklish, requiring careful handling.

délinkwènsi delinquency.

dèlman a 2-wheeled horse-drawn carriage with the passenger seats right across the axle-tree and a small door at the back; the cabman sits on a bench placed parallel with the axle-tree in front of the passenger seats.

delu men- to be fed up. ~ *di dlm hati* to become fed up.

déma [dewan mahasiswa] college student council.

démagogi demagogy.

demam *orang* - fever patient. - *berdarah* dengue hemorrhagic fever, DHF, breakbone (,dandy) fever. - *emas* gold rush. - *keong* schistosomiasis. - *rematik* rheumatism. - *ternak* tick fever.

demang - *tani* (in Central Java) an agricultural district officer.

demi - *segi praktis saja* just for practical reasons. *seorang* - *seorang* o. after the other.

demikian - *Antara* (in news items) according to "Antara." - *mayjen S.* (in news items) so said Major General S. - *spy saudara (,anda) maklum(i)* and - *spy saudara (,anda) maklum adanya* (i.e. a typical closing sentence in letters) with this the above has been brought to your attention. *karena dgn* - ... because in this way ... *adalah* -: ... is as follows: ... - *dgn singkat arti* ... such, in brief, the meaning of ... *D-lah naskah ini dibuat di Jakarta* (in notarial instruments) In witness whereof this document has been drawn up in Jakarta. - + *a noun* + *memberitakan* and - + *a (pro)noun* + *mengatakan* according to (pro)noun...., - *suratkabar Al Hayat memberitakan* ..., according to the newspaper Al Hayat. *D- peninjau. peninjau mengatakan* according to observers. *se- rupa sehingga* in such a way that.

démilitèrisasi demilitarization.

démisionèr lame duck, continue pending replacement. **men-kan** *kabinet* to dissolve a Cabinet. **pen-an** *kabinèt* dissolution of a Cabinet.

dèmmo a 3-wheeled motorized vehicle powered by a German-made D.K.W. engine; the front wheel is steered by means of an elongated tubular handlebar on which controls for transmission and throttle are mounted. Brake and clutch are on the floor of the vehicle and are foot-operated.

démobilisasi demobilization. **men-kan** to demobilize.

démografi demography.

démokrasi ber- democratic. **men-kan** to democratize. **pen-an** democratization. *D- Pancasila* Indonesian-style democracy (based on the *Pancasila*). - *parlementer* parliamentary democracy. - *penindasan* pressure democracy. *D-Terpimpin* Guided Democracy.

démokrat democrat.

démonstran demonstrator. *kaum (,para)* - demonstrators. - *anti.perang* antiwar demonstrator.

démonstrasi demonstration. **di-** to be demonstrated against. - *terselubung* disguised demonstration.

dèmplon chubby, plump.

dèn - *ayu* (s.) RADEN.

dèncis (s.) SARDENCIS.

denda - *damai* conciliatory fine. - *darah* blood money.

dèndang *perut.perut yg tlh* **ber-** hungry stomachs.

dèndèng - *ragi dendeng* with seasoned grated coconut.

dengan - *harga $5,-- sebuah* at $5.00 apiece. - *ini* by this, hereby, herewith (I declare). - *sendirinya* it goes without saying that. - *suara nyaring* aloud. - *tdk malu.malu* 1 unprejudiced, unbias(s)ed, open-minded. 2 without reservation.

dengar men- *lewat radio* to hear over the radio. **sepen-an** it is learned (,understood) that ..., we learn that ...**ter-** audible. - *pendapat* hearing.

denger (s.) DENGAR.

dengkèng n- (airborne troopers term) arching the body.

dengkul *peluk* - to do nothing, sit idly. *uang yg* **di-** the money corrupted (,embezzled).

Dèn Haag (pron. aa as a in art) The Hague.

dènok and **dhènok** 1 chubby, fat girl. 2 young girl.

dentum *21 kali* **-an** *meriam* a 21-gun salute.

dénuklirisasi denuclearization.

dèpak and **dèbak men-** to fire, oust.

départemèn *D- Agama* Department of Religion.

Déperdag [Departemen Perdagangan] Department of Commerce.

Dèpkès [Departemen Kesehatan] Department of Health.

Dèpnakertranskop [Departemen Tenaga Kerja, Transmigrasi dan Koperasi] Department of Manpower, Relocation and Co-operatives.

dépo depot.

déponir men- (fig.) to slip s.t. under a blotter, push out of sight. pen-an slipping s.t. under a blotter.

déportasi deportation. men-kan to deport.

déposan depositor.

déposito deposit. men-kan to deposit (money). pen-an 1 deposit. ~ uang the deposit of money. 2 depositing.

depot (mil.) depot. - bahan bakar fuel depot.

deprok nge- to sit down.

Dèpsos [Departemen Sosial] Department of Social Affairs.

députasi deputation.

dèputi deputy (commander, etc.).

dera (corporal) punishment. men- to chastise, flog. ~ hukum to punish.

derajat se-: ijazah lain yg ~ another equivalent certificate. peserta ~ equal partner.

dèrèk men- to tow (a car). pen-an towing. - kambang floating crane (in harbors). - petikemas container crane.

derep (me)n- to assist in cutting rice in the field for a certain wage, usually in the proportion 4:1 of the harvest. pen- and tukang - assistant who does the above job.

dèrèt se- dgn abreast of. -an toko.toko arcade of stores. - hitung arithmetic progression. - ukur geometric progression.

dering telepon itu ber- the telephone was ringing.

derit squeak (of brakes, cars).

derita pen-: ~ bengek asthmatic. ~ paraplegia paraplegic. ~ penyakit demam fever patient. ~ penyakit gula diabetic. pen-an affliction. bila ~ sdh memuncak maka akan datanglah pertolongan the darkest hour is before the dawn.

dermaga jetty.

dermimil n- to mutter.

désa seorang wanita se-nya a woman of the same village. - swadaya, - swakarya and - swasembada names for the various stages of development of a village from low to high.

desah murmur.

desak ber-.- to crowd. men- mundur to push back.

désapraja village administration (,government).

désimal decimal. dibulatkan sampai 2 - rounded off to two decimals.

désimèter decimeter. - lipat folding decimeter staff.

desing men- to whistle, buzz.

desus di-kan to be rumored.

détail detail. men- detailed. memberikan keterangan ~ to give detailed information.

détaséring detachment (i.e. the sending of troops on special service).

détasir di- to be detached (i.e. sent troops on special service).

détèksi men- to detect.

détèktip detective.

détèktor - ranjau mine detector.

détèrjèn detergent.

détil (s.) DETAIL.

détonator detonator.

dévaluasi men-kan to devalue.

devisen and dévisen foreign exchange.

Déwa (in Bali) title of the male members of the Ksatriyas.

Déwakembar Castor and Pollux.

déwan D- Ekumini Oecumenical Council. D- Guru pd Perguruan Tinggi Kedokteran Faculty of Medicine. D- Harian Executive, Executive Committee (,Body), Working Committee. D- Komisaris (of an Inc. or Ltd.) Board of Directors. D- Kurator Board of Regents. D- Moneter Monetary Board. D- Negara (in Malaysia) Senate. D- Niaga Board of Trade. - parampara advisory council. D- Pengawas Keuangan Fiscal Auditing Office. D- Penyantun Board of Regents. D- Perancang Nasional National Planning Council. D- Pertahanan Nasional National Defense Council. D- Pertimbangan Agung Supreme Advisory Council, i.e. an organ provided for in the 1945 Constitution. D- Perusahaan Enterprise Council (under President Soekarno). D-

Pimpinan (of political party) Executive Council (,Board).

déwasa *anak.anak sdh menanjak* - the children have grown up. **ke-an** *mental* mentalage **kebelum -an** immaturity. **pen-an** (jur.) (declaring) of age.

déwasawan adult, grownup.

déwé and **dhéwé** to be different.

dèwèk and **dhèwèk -an** alone.

dèwi *D- Fajar* Aurora. *D- Fortuna* the goddess of fortune.

dhaif (S.) DAIF.

dhat (S.) ZAT.

dharma (s.) DARMA. *D- Pertiwi* the all-embracing Armed Forces Wives Association. *D- Wanita* federation of women's organizations encompassing 16 departments with the exception of the Defense and Security Department, state banking institutions, the Attorney General's Office and *Bhakti Wanita*.

dholim ke-an tyranny, oppression.

di 1 on. - *Senin* on Monday. 2 in. - *bln Juli* in July.

dia *Itu -!* 1 That's it (,him ,her)! 2 Precisely! Exactly! Just so! **men-kan** to treat contemptuously. -.- *juga* the very same people. - *orang* they.

diakritik diacritic(al).

dialèk dialect.

dialog ber- to have a dialogue. *D- Utara. Selatan* The North-South Dialogue [between 8 major non-communist industrial (northern) countries (the United States, Canada, England, France, Western Germany, Italy, Japan and Spain) and the (southern) Third World (comprising 19 nations from Latin America, Africa, Asia and the Middle East)].

dialooh (pron. oo as o in go) (s.) DIALOG.

diam kepen-an being a quiet person, reticence. -.-: ~ *makan dlm* unreliable. ~ *ubi (berisi)* still waters run deep. *dgn (,secara)* ~ unobtrusively, covertly. *secara* ~ *dan terang.terangan* covertly and overtly.

diamèter diameter.

Dian Ékawati name of the women's association of the Department of Information.

diaré diarrhea.

dibya (extraordinarily) excellent.

didaktik didactics. - *bahasa* language didactics.

didaktis didactic.

didèh and **didih** black pudding of coagulated blood.

didik *bersifat* **men-** educative, instructive. **pen-an** training, instruction. ~ *dasar* basic training. ~ *kawiryan* military training. ~ *kejuruan* vocational training. ~ *kekaryawanan* occupational education. ~ *kelompok* group education. ~ *keniagaan* business education. ~ *kewarganegaraan* civics. ~ *latihan kerja* on-the-job training. ~ *latihan pertempuran* combat training. ~ *para* airborne training. ~ *permulaan* preliminary training. *Dia* **-an** *Universitas Indonesia,* He is an alumnus of the University of Indonesia.

didong foreign, from abroad. *bahasa Belanda* - the Dutch patois spoken (by Eurasians) in Indonesia.

diesel diesel. **men-kan** to convert to diesel engines.

dieselisasi the introduction of diesel-powered locomotives.

diès natalis dies natalis, anniversary (of university, etc.).

diét diet.

diferènsial differential (calculus). *hitungan* - differential calculus.

diferènsiasi differentiation. **di-kan** to be differentiated.

diftéri diphteritis, diphteria.

digdaya and **digjaya ke-an** invincibility.

Digulis *bekas seorang* - a person formerly exiled by the Dutch to Boven Digul in Irian Jaya.

diit (s.) DIET.

dikir chant (God's Praises).

dikit slightly. *bisnya rusak* - the bus was slightly damaged. -.- every now and then.

diko spraypaint. **di-** to be spraypainted (a car).

diktat mimeographed (lecture) notes.

diktator **ke-an** dictatorship.
diktatur dictatorship.
diktèktif (s.) DETEKTIP.
diktum verdict.
dilalah corruption of Arabic *takdir Allah*
God predestination. **n-** and fate would
have it that ..., it so happened that ...,
chance would have it that ...... ~
masuk bersamaan dgn pengaruh hip-
pies, ganja, free sex dan sebagainya ...
it so happened that (this type of music)
entered (the Third World) at the same
time as the influence of hippies, marijuana, free sex and the like.
dilman (s.) DELMAN.
dim dim (of light).
dimènsi dimension.
dinamit **pen-an** blowing up (with dyna-
mite).
dinamo dynamo.
dinas *D- Aeronautika dan Angkasa. Luar*
NASA. *D- Investigasi Federal* FBI.
- malam (to work on) the night shift.
D- Pendidikan Masyarakat (U.S.) Board
of Education. *D- Pengawasan Udara*
Aircraft Warning Service. *D- Purbakala*
Archaeological Service. *D- Sekuriti*
Security Service.
dinasti dynasty.
dinding *D- Tangis* Wailing Wall.
diné 1 dinner. 2 dinner party. *- sinar*
lilin candlelight dinner.
dingding wooden or bamboo wall; (S.)
DINDING.
dingin **ke-an** chilliness. **pen-** 1 coolant.
2 cold-blooded person. **pen-an**: *masa* ~
cooling-off period. ~ *udara* air-cooling.
dingkik to keep watch secretly. **-.men-**
to check upon o.a.
dingklik and dhingklik footstool.
dini early. *sistim peringatan* - early warning system. **se-** *mungkin* as early as possible. *-hari* 1 the part of the day from
midnight to daybreak. 2 aurora.
dioksid *- arang* carbon dioxide.
diorama diorama.
dip [displaced Indonesian person] *orang -*
displaced Indonesian person, i.e. o. who
was taken out of Indonesia by the Jap-

anese during World War II.
dipati *adat* chief of the *Anak Dalam.*
diplomasi **ber-** to pursue diplomacy.
- badminton 'badminton diplomacy,'
referring to the PRC's pingpong diplomacy. *- bakmi* 'Chinese noodles diplomacy,' referring to the PRC's pingpong
diplomacy (from Indonesian viewpoint).
- ping pong pingpong diplomacy (of the
PRC).
diplomatik **ke-an** diplomatic.
Diponegoro the Jav. prince who led the
Java War (1825–1830) against the
Dutch.
dirèksi 1 board of management (,direc-
tors), 2 managing executive, director,
member of a board of directors.
dirèktiva directives.
dirèktorium governing board.
dirèktris 1 headmistress (of a school).
2 woman manager (of a factory, business, etc.).
dirèktur 1 headmaster (of a school),
principal. 2 director (of an institute).
3 manager (of a factory, business, etc.).
D- Amanat Delegate Member of the
Board of Supervisory Directors. *D-*
Jenderal Director General (of a Directorate General). *D- Pelaksana* Managing
Director.
dirga long (live).
dirgantara air space. **ke-an** (adj.) aerial.
minat (,semangat) - airmindedness.
diri o.s., in forming reflexive verbs, such
as, *mengkhususkan* - to specialize,
mengundurkan - to withdraw (o.s.).
pd - sendiri as such, in itself (,them-
selves). *seorang* - alone, by o.s. **ber-:** ~
di atas kaki sendiri (abbrev. *berdikari*)
1 to stand on o's own feet. 2 to be self-
reliant. ~ *di atas tanduk kesulitan* having to choose between two difficulties.
sdh ~ *di ambang liang kubur* to have
o. foot in the grave. ~ *di belakang*
layar to stay in the background. *terus*
~ *di luar garis* to stay aloof. ~ *urut*
and *urut* ~ to wait in line. ~ *sama*
tengah to be impartial. ~ *sendiri* to be
independent, self-sustaining. ~ *tegak*

to stand at attention. **pen-an** attitude. *ia tetap pd ~nya* he stuck to his guns. *~ sama tengah* impartial view. *tdk mudah goyang ~nya* he is steadfast. *menyatakan ~nya* to put forward o's views. **-nya** he, she (emphatic). *waktu ~ di Semarang* when he was in Semarang. *~ sendiri* 1 he himself (emphatic). 2 she herself (emphatic).

dirigèn conductor (of orchestra).

dirjèn [direktur jenderal] director general.

dirum [direktur umum] general director.

dirut [direktur utama] chief director.

disain design. **ber-** *artistik* with an artistic design. **di-** to be designed. **pen-** designer.

disainer designer.

disènteri dysentery. *- amuba* amoeba dysentery. *- basiler* basilary dysentery.

disimilasi dissimilation.

disiplin **di-kan** to be disciplined, be regimented. *langkah.langkah* **pen-an** disciplinary measures. *- bangkai* rigid discipline. *- diri* self-discipline.

disko disco. *musik -* disco music.

diskonto discount. *- wesel* bill discount.

diskotik discotheque.

diskrédit **men-kan** to discredit.

diskriminasi *- rasial* racial discrimination.

diskusi *- panel* panel discussion.

dispènsasi dispensation. *memberikan - kpd* to grant dispensation to.

distribusi **men-kan** to distribute. **pen-an** distribution.

distributor distributor.

ditèktif (s.) DETEKTIP. *- partikelir* private investigator.

ditjèn [direktorat jenderal] directorate general.

divèrsifikasi diversification. **men-kan** to diversify.

divisi (mil.) division *- baja [,(ber)lapis baja]* armored division.

DIY [Daerah Istimewa Yogyakarta] Yogyakarta Special Region.

Djojobojo (the pre-1972 orthography is retained here) king of Kediri (1135–1157), noted for his prophecies; up to now he is still considered to be the coming founder of a Messianic empire in which all Javanese will be happy and powerful.

DKI Jaya [Daerah Khusus Ibukota Jakarta Raya] Greater Jakarta Special Capital Region.

DL I a freight car (in train formation).

DL II (the pre-1972 orthography is retained here) Djakarta Lloyd.

dlèwèr *keringat yg* **-an** sweat that is dripping down.

doa **men-i** to bless s.t. *- sujud syukur* prayer of thanks.

dobel **men-kan** to double.

Doberai *Jazirah -* the former Vogelkop and Kepala Burung in Irian Jaya.

dobrak **pen-** *almari besi* safecracker.

dodol a confection made of coconut milk, palm sugar and sticky rice.

dodot I (s.) DEBUS.

dodot II ceremonial batik wraparound. *mengenakan -* to put on such a wraparound.

dogèr a dancing girl, usually part of the *lenong.*

dogmatis dogmatic.

doif 1 objectionable. 2 incapable, failing to meet requirements. 3 *(hina) -* poor, helpless; (S.) DAIF.

dok I (coll.) doc, doctor (vocative).

dok II dock. *naik -* to go into drydock. *- terapung* floating dock.

dokarwan *dokar* driver.

dokter *Jangan* **men-i** *diri sendiri atau keluarga anda!* Don't treat yourself or your family! *- ahli* specialist, specializing physician. *- ahli dlm ilmu kebidanan dan penyakit kandungan* obstetrician and gynecologist. *- ahli jantung* cardiologist. *- ahli kulit* dermatologist. *- ahli penyakit dlm* internist, internal medicine specialist. *- ahli tulang* orthopedist. *- anak* pediatrician. *- basah* highly paid physician. *- bedah* surgeon. *- bedah syaraf* neurosurgeon. *- gigi* dentist. *- gula* production manager, analytical chemist (in sugarmill laboratory). *- hewan* veterinarian. *- jaga* physician on duty (,call). *- jawa* prewar Indonesian physician graduated from the *STOVIA* in Jakarta.

- *jiwa* psychiatrist. - *kacamata* optician.
- *kandungan* abortionist. - *kering* low
paid physician. - *kuping* ear doctor.
- *langganan* family doctor. - *lokal* graduate of a private medical faculty who
has not yet taken/passed the State examination. - *mata* eye doctor, optometrist.
- *negeri* government physician. - *partike-*
lir private physician. - *pelabuhan* harbor
physician. *D- Piket* Physicians on Duty
(i.e. the name of a newspaper column).
- *pribadi* personal physician. - *spesialis*
kulit dermatologist. - *telinga* ear doctor.
- *umum* general practitioner.

dokteranda (s.) DOKTORANDA.

dokterandus (s.) DOKTORANDUS.

doktoranda before women's names, candidate for doctor's degree who has completed all work but the dissertation.

doktorandus before men's names, candidate for doctor's degree who has completed all work but the dissertation.

doktrin doctrine.

doku dough, money. *ngentit* - to steal
money.

dokumèntasi pen-an documentation.

Dokuritsu Jumbi Chosakai Independence
Preparations Investigation Committee;
(s.) PANITIA(PENYELIDIK PERSIAP-
AN KEMERDEKAAN).

dolan to make a trip (for pleasure).

dolar I di-kan to be converted to dollars.
-.*minyak* petro-dollar.

dolar II *pohon* - the (Hawaiian "Good
Luck") Ti plant.

dolarsèn cent of American dollar.

dolle Mina women's libber.

domba I old goat (older man who likes
young girls).

domba II *para* - the congregation.

domblong n- to stare openmouthed.

domèin domain, i.e. land belonging to
the government.

domestic capital capital belonging to the
pribumi, non-pribumi and foreigners
residing in Indonesia.

domèstik domestic.

dominasi men- to dominate.

Dominika (s.) REPUBLIK (DOMINIKA).

dominir men- (s.) MENDOMINASI.

domino domino. *main* - to play dominos.

domisili ber- to be domiciled.

dompèt case (for glasses).

domplèng and **dhomplèng** *sifatnya hanya*
- it's just a coincidence. **di-** *reklame* to
be decorated with advertisements (such
as, name plates on the roof top of stores,
etc.). **di-i** to be exploited. *tanpa ~ kepen-*
tingan.kepentingan perorangan atau
golongan without being exploited by
individual or group interests. **men-** to
go along. **n-** 1 to get a free ride. 2 to
sponge off s.o. *~ di rumah* to live (,re-
side, stay) with. *Mereka ~ di rumah*
famili atau kenalan, They stayed in the
house of relatives or acquaintances.
pen- illegal passenger.

dompol bunch, cluster. **se-** *buah kopi* a
bunch of coffeeberries.

Donal Bèbèk Donald Duck.

donat (s.) KUE(H) (DONAT).

dondang pe- backstay.

donder to fulminate (against), storm (at).
Ia kena - pacarnya, He was bawled out
by his girl friend. **di-** to be bawled out.

dong I Asserts strongly that what is said
is true; (in statements) The previous
statement or question was wrong or
implied the wrong answer. *This* is what
is really true; (in imperatives) What you
are (,were ,will be) doing is wrong. Do
this (instead); (in questions—rarely used)
Insistent question.

dong II (s.) DORANG.

dongan clan-mate. - *Sabutuha* Sabutuha
clan-mate.

dongbrèt (in Indramayu) woman street
dancer.

dongèng - *rakyat* folklore.

dongkèl to jimmy. **men-** to unseat, oust.
Maling itu ~ jendela utk masuk ke dlm,
The thief broke through the window to
enter the house. **pen-an** ousting.

dongkol I kemen-an annoyance. **men-**
offended, hurt.

dongkol II ex-, former.

dongkol III -an a retired person.

dongkrak n- 1 to jack s.t. up. 2 to line

up (trucks, etc.).

dongkrok and **dhongkrok** n- to slump, sit idly. 2 to be inactive.

dongpan class.

Don Kisot Don Quixote.

donor pen- donor. - *darah* blood donor.

dop cap. - *mobil* hubcap.

dopèrcis green peas.

dor bang! boom! **di**- to be shot. *Seorang anggauta polisi ~,* A member of the police was shot. *Penyelundup obat.obatan kpd pihak komunis akan ~ mati,* A smuggler of medicines to the communists will be executed. **-.-an** shooting. *D~ lagi di Siprus,* Again shooting in Cyprus.

dorang (Eastern Indonesia) 1 they. 2 their. 3 them.

dorèng marbled.

dorgok (s.) SENJATA (DORGOK).

dorong pen- motive. *mudah terpengaruh oleh* -an *hatinya* impulsive.

dosèn - *terbang* visiting professor (,lecturer) using an aircraft to reach the university where he has to lecture.

dosir dossier, files.

dosis dose. - *yg tepat* the right dose.

dosa ber- sinful. *(yg) tdk ~* innocent.

dot pacifier (for baby).

doti magic incantations.

douane (S.) DUANE.

Double Ten the anniversary of the People's Republic of China (October 10).

dowèr pouting, protruding (lips).

doyan - *makan* to have an appetite. - *ngobrol* to be talkative.

doyong 1 slanting, sloping. 2 inclined.

dozer bulldozer. *diterjang* - to be bulldozed.

DPP [Dada, Pinggang dan Paha] vital measurements.

draf I bolt.

draf II draft. - *bank* bank draft.

draimol(1)en merry-go-round, carrousel.

drainase drainage.

Drakula Dracula.

dramatari ballet.

dramatis dramatic.

drèi screwdriver (the device).

drh [dokter hewan] veterinarian.

dribel dribble. **men**- to dribble.

drop men(ge)- 1 to distribute (supplies, etc.). 2 to disembark. 3 to unload. **-.-an** supply distributions. **penge-an** distribution of supplies.

droping allocation.

drum drum. - *kotoran* trash barrel.

dua *antara kita* **ber**- privately. *mereka* **ber-an** the two of them. *Vietnam* **ke**- another Vietnam. **men**- ambivalent. **-nya**: *tak ada ~* unequalled, unrivalled, unparalleled. *Kehidupan malam Bangkok tak ada ~ di Asia Tenggara,* Night life in Bangkok is unparalleled in Southeast Asia. **-an** *wae* in private, privately, tête-à-tête. *dlm* -.- *hal* in both cases. - *arah (,nilai)* ambivalence.

duaja banner, standard (used in army regiments).

dualisme dualism.

dub (col. mil.) sergeant major.

dubang (red-colored) *sirih* spittle.

Dubes men-kan 1 to make s.o. ambassador. 2 to send s.o. to limbo.

duduk *menceritakan* - *soalnya* to tell how it all happened, tell all the facts of the case. **ke-an**: ~ *bawahan* subordination. ~ *komando* commanding position. ~ *kunci (,pengunci)* key position. **ke-pen-an** (adj.) population. **men-i**: ~ *posisi yg menonjol* to occupy a (pre)dominant position. ~ *tempat kedua* to be the runnerup. ~ *tempat kedua setelah* ... and ~ *urutan kedua sesudah* ... to rank second to ... ~ *tempat teratas* to rank first. **pen-**: *daerah yg padat (,rapat)* ~*nya* a densely populated area. *daerah yg tipis* ~*nya* a sparsely populated area. ~ *sdh melimpah.limpah* and ~*nya sesak (,padat)* overpopulated. -*nya* its fit (of clothing). - *perkara* the ins and outs of the matter. -.- to sit around. - *bertimpuh(an)* to sit with the legs turned to the right and bent back towards the body, while the left arm rests on the ground. - *lurus (,tegak)* to sit upright (,straight). - *semeja dgn* to sit at o. table with. - *terbengkalai* to do nothing. - *termenung* to be absorbed in thought.

duèl 1 duel. - *artileri* artillery duel. 2 collision. - *antara truk dgn kereta api* a collision between a truck and a train. **berdgn** (fig.) to collide with.

duga *hal.hal yg tdk dpt* **di-** *terlebih dahulu* unforeseen circumstances (,emergencies, contingencies). **pen-an** *pedoman* compass bearing. *beaya tak* **ter-** unforeseen expenses. *di luar* **-an** beyond expectations, unexpectedly.

dugal **n-** lawless, rowdy, naughty.

dugdèng and **dhugdhèng** magically invulnerable.

dugdèr and **dhugdhèr** folk festival on the evening prior to the Fast.

du-ileee (S.) DUILAH.

duit a copper Dutch coin of 1700–1847. *gampang* **di-kan** can easily be converted (,turned) into cash.

dukacarita and **dukacerita** tragedy.

dukacita *datang menyatakan* - *kpd* to condole with. *turut (,ikut)* **ber-** to offer condolences.

dukana 1 lustful, lascivious. 2 incontinent.

dukat ducat.

duku lanzon (L. Lansium domesticum).

dukuh **(pe)-an** hamlet (headed by a *kamitua*).

dukun 1 faith healer. 2 sorcerer, person who practices black magic. There are several k.o. *dukuns;* some concentrate on curing sick people, physically or psychologically; others give spiritual advice about all present or future human problems; yet others specialize in the performance of ceremonies and rituals. *Dukuns* are just practical healers or else they are sorcerers, commanding magic powers. Usually, o. *dukun* is competent in more than o. of the various specialized fields. - *bayi* midwife. - *pengantin* make-up artist for brides.

dukung *sbg* - *thd* in support of. **pen-** supporter.

Dul contraction for *Abdullah, Abdulrachman,* etc. - *Dakochan* nickname for Tunku Abdulrachman, Malaysia's Prime Minister during the *Konfrontasi.*

dulag name of the *bedug* beaten on *Lebaran* and at the end of the month of *Ramadan* when people are summoned to pay the *fitrah;* it is the same *bedug* as usual, only the name has been changed for this special occasion. **nga-** to beat on the *dulag.*

dulang **pen-** panner (for gold, etc.).

dulu (s.) DAHULU. *Saya pergi* -, I'm leaving ahead of time. *Siapa* - *siapa dpt,* First come first served (in advertisements). *dr* - *mula* from the very beginning. *tanpa memberi tahu lebih* - without giving advance notice. *Jangan mandi* -! Don't bathe just yet! -.- formerly, used to. *spt yg selalu kita lakukan* ~ like we formerly always did. **-an** to be (,go) ahead of s.o. else.

dulur 1 brother. 2 sister.

dum to dump (to sell in quantity at a very low price or regardless of the price).

dum.dum dumdum.

dumel **nge-** to grumble, grouch, murmur.

dungu mentally retarded.

dunia *dr* - *lalu ke akhirat* (faithful) unto death. - *ini tdk selebar daun kelor* and - *ini tdk selebar telapak tangan* (fig.) with time comes counsel. - *anak.anak* child world. - *binatang (,kehewanan)* fauna. - *hitam* underworld. *D- Ketiga* The Third World. - *leta* corrupt (,perverse) world. - *luar* outside world. *terputus dr* - *luar* cut off from the outside world, completely isolated. - *luaran* outside world. - *pedagang* mercantile (,commercial) world. - *persurat.kabaran* the press world. - *perusahaan* commerce and industry, industrial life. - *ramai* outside world. - *saudagar* mercantile (,commercial) world. - *selebihnya* outside world. - *tumbuh.tumbuhan* flora. - *usaha* business world.

duniawi mundane, worldly.

duniawi(y)ah 1 (s.) DUNIAWI. 2 the earthly things.

dupli(e)k reply by defense lawyer.
duplikat duplicate.
durhaka men-i to betray.
duri *jadi* - prickly.
durian a gray-green, soccer ball-size fruit which grows on 200-foot trees in Indonesia and other parts of Southeast Asia. The fruit has a pungent smell and taste. *dpt - runtuh* 'to get a fallen *durian,'* i.e. to be in luck, hit the jack pot.
durja appearance, look.
durjasa discredit, disservice.
Durna and **Durno** 1 *wayang* character. 2 the late Dr. Soebandrio 3 intriguer, schemer, plotter, agitator, double-tongued opportunist.
Durnois follower of the late Dr. Soebandrio.
Durno.isme Machiavellism.
dursila *tindakan* - illegal government action.
dus di- to be plated. ~ *emas* gold-plated.
dusel men- to snuggle up.
duta men.D- Besarkan 1 to make s.o. ambassador. 2 to send s.o. to limbo. - *besar berkuasa penuh* ambassador plenipotentiary. - *besar luar biasa dan berkuasa penuh* ambassador extraordinary and plenipotentiary. - *luar biasa dan berkuasa penuh* envoy extraordi-

nary and minister plenipotentiary.
duwegan young coconut.
DW a goods car (in train formation).
dwi bi, two-. **di- gandakan** to be doubled. **ke- artian** double meaning. **ke-bahasaan** bilingualism. **ke- mukaan** ambivalence. - *abad* bicentennial. - *arti* ambiguous. - *ba(ha)sawan* bilingual (person). - *bulanan* bimonthly (magazine). - *cakap* dialogue. - *dasawarsa* twenty-year period. *-fungsi* dual function. - *huruf* diphthong. -.*isteri* bigamy. *D-kora* [Dwi Komando Rakyat] People's Dual Command; the two commands were: (1) Strengthen the defense of the revolution; (2) Support the struggle for independence of the peoples of Malaya, Singapore and Borneo. - *kutub* bipolar. - *marga* two-way (traffic). - *minggu* two-week. - *muka* ambivalent. - *pekan* biweekly. - *purwa* (gramm.) reduplication of the first syllable of a word. - *th* biennial. *katakerja -transitif* benefactive verb (such as, *membelikan, membukakan,* etc.). *Sang D-warna* the Indonesian flag. - *windu* 1 sixteenth anniversary. 2 sixteen years. - *wulanan* bimonthly (magazine).

E

e (pause in speech) um!
èbèg *jaran* - (in Cilacap, Central Java) k.o. *kuda kepang.*
éboni ebony.
ècèng - *gond(h)ok* water hyacinth (L. Eichornia crassipes).
ècèr *warung* **peng-** (roadside) retail store.
éco tasty.
èdan - *kasmaran (,kesemaran)* head over heels in love.
èdar peng- *obat bius* drug trafficker.
édit meng- to edit. **peng-an** editing.
éditor editor.
édukasi education.
édukatip educative, instructive.

èfèk I -.- securities. *pembelian* ~ (banking term) purchase of securities.
èfèk II - *sampingan* side effect.
èf(f)èktip peng-an effectiveness.
èfisiènsi efficiency.
Égéa (s.) LAUT (EGEA).
égoisme egoism.
égrang stilts. *naik* - to walk on stilts.
eh and **èh** 1 (exclamation of disgust, rejection) ugh, damn it. *E-, jangan dekat.dekat saya!* Ugh, don't come near me! *E-, salah lagi!* Damn it, another mistake! 2 (exclamation of amazement, awe) wow! my! (s.) E.
èigen (pron. èikhen) *sebuah pavilyun dgn*

- *gemakken* a pavilion fitted with every comfort (or, conveniences of every sort).

éjawantah meng-kan to manifest. *dewa ng-* creator. **peng-an** manifestation.

éka one. **ke-an** *dan* **kean-an** unity and diversity. - *basawan* monolingual. - *marga* one-way (traffic). - *suku* monosyllabic. -*warsa* one-year.

Éka Dharma Santi name of the women's organization under the jurisdiction of the Department of Manpower, Resettlement and Co-operatives.

Ékadyasa name of the women's organization under the jurisdiction of the Department of Air Communications.

Ékaprasetia Panca Karsa Guidelines for Experiencing and Implementing the *Pancasila.*

ékologi ecology.

ékonom economist.

ékonométri econometrics.

ékonomi - *mikro* microeconomics. - *perusahaan* business economics, industrial economy.

èkor 1 aftermath. 2 last digit in a lottery number.

ékornia water hyacinth (L. Eichornia crassipes).

èks I exported from.

èks II ex-. - *Letkol Untung* ex-Lieutenant Colonel Untung.

èksakta natural/physical science.

èksekusi di- to be executed (to put to death).

èksekutif (adj.) executive.

èksèpsi (jur.) exception, demurrer, bar.

èksès excess.

èksibisi exhibition.

èksim eczema.

èksistènsialis existentialist.

èksistènsialisme existentialism.

èksit exit. *kalau gagal aku hrs* - if I flunk I'll have to leave school.

èksklusif exclusive.

èksklusivisme exclusivism.

èkskursi excursion, outing, trip.

èksodus exodus.

èksogami exogamy.

èksogén exogenous.

èksotik exotic.

èkspansif expansive.

èkspansionis expansionist. *politik* - expansionism.

èkspedisi expedition. - *botani* botanical expedition. *E- Kutub Selatan* Antarctic Expedition.

èkspeditur forwarding (,shipping) agent.

èkspérimèn experiment. **ber-** to experiment.

èkspérimèntasi experimentation.

èkspèr(t) expert.

èksplisit explicit.

èksploitasi *ongkos.ongkos* - working expenses.

èksplosi explosion.

èksplosif explosive.

èksplotasi exploitation.

èksponèn -.- *daerah* regional notables.

èkspor *negara.negara* **peng-** *minyak* oil-exporting nations. - *kayu.kayuan* lumber exports.

èkspose meng- to expose.

èksposisi exposition.

èksprès express.

èksprèsi expression. **meng-kan** to express.

èksprèsif expressive.

èksprèsionisme expressionism.

èkstase ecstacy.

èkstènsif extensive.

èkstènsifikasi extensification.

èkstradisi extradition. **meng-kan** to extradite.

èkstrak - *ganja* hashish.

èkstra kurikulèr extracurricular.

èkstra.parlemèntèr extraparliamentary.

èkstrim *dlm bentuk* -**nya** in the extreme.

èkstrovèrt extrovert.

ékumini oecumenical.

ékwivalènsi equivalency.

élaborasi elaboration. **meng-kan** to elaborate.

èlak peng- *wajib militer* draft dodger. *tak* **ter-kan** unavoidable.

elang - *laut* frigate bird. *E- Malindo* Malaysian-Indonesian Joint Air Operation Maneuvers.

élastisitèt elasticity.

élèktroda electrode.
élèktronik electronic.
élèktronika electronics.
élèktrotèknik electrotechnics, electrical
engineering.
éling to be sensible.
èlips ellipse.
èlipsis ellipsis.
èlipsoide ellipsoid.
élite - *pemimpin* the ruling élite.
elon meng-i to favor.
ELPIJI (the English pron. of *LPG,* standing for) Liquefied Petroleum Gas.
E.L.S. [Europese Lagere School] European Elementary School, grades 1
through 7 for Dutch-speaking children.
elu I (S.) LU.
elu II meng-.-kan to praise to the skies.
peng-.-an encomium, (words of) praise.
e-mam (children's language) to eat.
èmang of course, indeed, it is true, no
doubt, in (point of) fact, as a matter
of fact, certainly, be sure. - *benar*
indeed it's true. -nya 1 actually, really.
2 do you really think that …?
emas *menilai mana yg - mana yg loyang*
sift (,separate) the chaff from the
wheat (,grain). - *hitam* (fig.) petroleum.
embah - *Jawer* the invisible being in
charge of the Jatiluhur water reservoir.
emban meng- to bear. ~ *kewajiban* to
devote o.s. to a task selflessly. ~ *tang-
gung.jawab* to bear (,assume) the responsibility. peng-: ~ *Ampera* repository of the Message of the People's
Sufferings. ~ *tunggal* sole repository.
peng-an reposition.
èmbargo embargo.
èmbarkasi embarkation.
embun - *salju* frost. - *upas* (s.) BUN
(UPAS).
émigrasi emigration. meng-kan to cause
to emigrate.
émirat emirate.
émosionil emotional.
empan I -.*papan* (to act) with discretion
(considering to whom and where o. is
speaking).
empan II ng-in to feed.

èmpè.èmpè a Palembang (South Sumatra)
food.
empedu - *ayam* chicken gall (a folk cure
for malaria).
empèk 1 husband of mother's older sister. 2 older brother of o's father.
empèng pacifier, teething ring. ng- 1 to
chew on a pacifier. 2 to suck on the
nipple of a woman's breast which is
no longer producing milk. 3 to suckle
another woman's child. 4 (fig.) to be
still dependent on o's parents.
èmpèr - *lepau* coffee shop.
emping a chip similar to a potato chip
made from the meat of the seed of old
mlinjo; the meat is pounded flat, then
dried and fried.
emplèk - *wedang kopi* canvas-roofed roadside stall which sells hot coffee.
empok title for lower-class women from
Jakarta.
empot k.o. marine plant (that can make
a woman retain her youth).
empu (s.) MPU.
empuk simple, easy. *Cara paling - utk
memasukkan obat bius tersebut adalah
melalui diplomatic bag,* The most simple (and safest) way to bring in the
narcotics is via diplomatic pouch.
peng- *daging* meat tenderizer.
emut ng- to put s.t. in o's mouth to suck
on.
énak I *cuma tahu - sendiri saja* from selfish motives. - *dimakan* good to eat.
- *ya* 1 it feels good (stretching the mus-
cles)! 2 (sarcastic, to s.o. who didn't
show up for work) taking it easy, eh?
tdk - unsavory. *tdk* - *badan* not in good
shape (physically). *Badannya kurang -,*
He doesn't feel quite fit. *merasa tdk* -
(fig.) to feel bad. - *kepenak* 1 pleasure,
comfort. 2 amenities. *sikap* - *kepenak*
easy going. E-nya *mereka membayar
dgn dolar Amerika,* Most welcome was
that they paid in U.S. dollars. se-nya
as o. pleases.
énak II -.- unconcerned.
encèk uncle (younger brother of father).
para - dan encim Chinese married men

and women.

èncèng gondok water hyacinth (L. Eichornia crassipes).

èncèr watery, aqueous. *susu* - thin (,diluted) milk. *teh* - weak tea. - *otaknya* he is smart.

encim auntie (*encek's* wife).

encling (S.) KUDA (KEPANG).

èncok *kena* - to suffer from rheumatism.

endak 1 no. 2 not.

endap **meng-**: ~ *di gudang* (the goods) remained in the warehouse. *secara* ~.~ secretly, in secret. **peng-an** deposit. **-an** *darah* sedimentation rate. *main* -.- to play hide-and-seek.

endas and **endhas** head.

endon **ng-** 1 to come from another area or town. 2 to come from afar to stay over for some time. 3 to go and play soccer, etc. in another place, not in o's own home town. **peng-an** visit (from afar). *orang* **-an** 1 visitor from another area. 2 immigrant.

endong *pohon* - k.o. frangipani.

èndrin a rat poison. **di-** to be poisoned with *endrin*.

endus **di-** to be detected, be perceived, be sniffed out. *tdk* **ter-** *oleh bininya* (his fooling around with women) was not sniffed out by his wife.

enek 1 disgusting, unsavory, repulsive, sickening. 2 to be disgusted, loathe.

enèng petname for little girls.

énèrgi and **énèrji** energy. *krisis* - energy crisis. - *panas bumi* geothermal energy.

énèrjik energical.

énèrjètik energetic.

énèrsi (s.) ENERGI and ENERJI.

enes **ng-** sad, melancholy. *mati* ~ to die of a broken heart.

enggan unwilling, reluctant. *tak* - to have the guts to. -.- to hesitate, waver.

enggang (s.) PIPIT.

engkim wife of mother's younger brother.

èngko (from: & Co.) partner; (cp.) INGKU.

engko you.

engkoh older brother.

engkong grandfather.

engkuk **di-.-** to be grabbed by the neck and shaken.

eng(g)ro wholesale.

engso wife of older brother.

enjot to wobble.

ènsiklik encyclic(al).

ènsim enzyme.

ènsopor etcetera, and so forth.

entah I wish I knew. - *ya* gee, I don't know. *Namanya Dave* – - *apa nama belakangnya,* His name is Dave – his last name is irrelevant. - ... - ... and - ... *atau* ... either ... or ... *Kursi itu dibeli - oleh ayahnya - oleh kakeknya dlm pelelangan,* The chair was bought either by his father or by his grandfather in an auction. - *Garuda, Merpati atau apa saja* either Garuda (Indonesian Airways), Merpati (Nusantara Airlines) or whatever it is. - *benar* - *tdk* whether it is true or false. *dan* - *apa lagi* and so on, etc.

entak **meng-kan** *kedua belah kakinya* (mil.) to click heels. **-an** stroke (in typewriting, usually abbrev.: *ent/men* =*entakan semenit* ... strokes per minute).

entar soon. **-an** later. - *malam* later tonight.

entas **meng-kan** *anak* to raise a child till he becomes self-sufficient. **peng-an** *anak* child care.

énté you

èntèng **-an** willing to help.

enti (S.) NANTI.

entit **ng-** to steal.

èntitas entity.

èntog and **ènthog** Manila duck.

èntomologis entomologic.

èntot **ng-** to fuck.

èntrepot entrepot. - *umum* general entrepot.

enyah **peng-an** expulsion (of undesirables).

épidémi epidemic.

épigrafi epigraphy.

épisèntrum epicenter, epicentrum.

épolèt epaulet. *menyemat* - to fasten an epaulet. *penyematan* - the fastening of an epaulet.

epyur di-.-i to be lavished on s.o.

éra era.

èrbis (s.) MARKISA.

èrèk.èrèk (in Ujungpandang) lotto.

Éritréa Eritrea.

érobika aerobics.

érokomunis eurocommunist.

érokomunisme eurocommunism.

Éropa(h) die-kan to be Europeanized. - *Timur* East Europe.

érosi erosion.

érotik erotic.

èrpah long lease (75 years) of land out of the free domain.

èrpékad (pron. of) RPKAD.

èr.té [from *RT:* Rukun Tetangga] neighborhood association. *Aku tersenyum ke arah pak -,* I smiled in the direction of the neighborhood association head.

erti meng- *sendiri* to bribe. **peng-an** perception. *dlm* ~ *bhw* ... on the understanding that ...

eru the casuarine (L. Casuarina equisetifolia). *spt pucuk -* to set o's sail to every wind.

èrwé (s.) RW.

ès - *balokan* ice in blocks. - *buah* tutti-frutti. - *cipok* popsicle. -.*curai* ice plate (manufactured in the Banjarmasin fish harbor) used for cooling fish. - *gandul (,gantung)* shaved ice on a dried rice straw suffused with a sweet syrup. - *gepukan* crushed ice. - *gosok* shaved ice. - *kantong plastik* popsicle. - *kering* dry ice. - *kopyor* a beverage, consisting of the soft meat of a special variety of coconut, served with syrup and crushed ice cubes. - *mambo* popsicle. - *Petojo* block ice made in the ice factory located in the Petojo area of Jakarta. - *plastik* popsicle. - *puter* (Indonesian style) ice cream. - *setrup* cold beverage made with fruit syrup. - *Shanghai* a fruit cocktail mixed with sugared jelly covered with shaved ice. - *soklat* iced chocolate drink.

esa variant form of *sa* or *se* meaning 'one' in certain expressions. *membilang dr -,*

mengaji dr alif to start from scratch. *E- hilang, dua terbilang* motto of the Siliwangi Division stationed in West Java, meaning 'For each man fallen, two will spring up to replace him.'

èsdé and Ès Dé [from *SD:* Sekolah Dasar] Elementary School.

èséis essayist.

èselon echelon. - *atas* top echelons. - *I* (in a *Departemen* Ministry) the Directors General and Secretaries General - *II* (in a *Departemen* Ministry) the Directors.

èsèma and ès-èm-a [from *SMA:* Sekolah Menengah Atas] Senior High School.

esèmbling assembling.

èsèmpé and Ès Èm Pé [from *SMP:* Sekolah Menengah Pertama] Junior High School.

èser iron.

èsèr [from *SR:* Sekolah Rakyat] Elementary School.

ésèt the Indonesian/Dutch pron. of the two letters *E* and *Z* in *Economische Zaken* Department of Economic Affairs. *harga -* the official price [stipulated by the (Dutch) Department of Economic Affairs].

ès.ha [from *S.H.:* Sarjana Hukum] Master of Laws, LL.M.

ès.ka.ka.a [from *SKKA:* Sekolah Kesejahteraan Keluarga Atas] Senior High School for Domestic Sciences.

Èskimo Eskimo.

Èslandia Iceland.

ésok -annya the following day.

èstétis aesthetic.

étalase show window.

ètèk (S.) MAK (ETEK).

étèrni(e)t asbestos cement board, cement-asbestos board.

étikèt - *harga* price tag.

Étiopia Ethiopia.

étis ethical.

ètnis ethnic.

ètnografi ethnography.

ètsa etching (drawing).

éufoni euphony.

évangélis evangelist.

évolusi evolution. ber- to evolve.
èwah 1 (to be) fed up with (s.t.), (to be) sick of. 2 to be repelled by, dislike, hate, be tired of (s.t.), be bored. 3 antipathy.
éwé ng- and -an to fuck.
éwuh -.*pakewuh* ill at ease, (to feel) uncomfortable (,embarrassed). *karena orang Timur umumnya masih besar rasa -.pakewuhnya* since an Oriental, in general, still has a great feeling of embarrassment. *tdk -.pakewuh* without feelings of dislike.

èxtranéi external candidates.
èxtrauniversitèr college student group organized on the basis of a political, religious or other nonacademic affiliation.
éyang 1 grandfather. 2 grandmother. - *kakung* grandfather. - *putri* grandmother.
EYD [Ejaan Yang Disempurnakan] The Perfected Orthography (introduced on August 16, 1972). meng-kan to spell according to the new orthography.

F

Words not found under this letter should be looked for under P

fa. [firma] company.
fabel fable.
Factorij the Batavia-based office of the now defunct N(ederlandsche) H(andel) M(aatschappij), Netherlands Trading Company, directing its affairs in the whole of the Netherlands Indies.
fadzilat virtue, excellence.
fahombé stone-jumping sport of the Nias Islanders (on Nias off Sumatra's west coast); an activity once used to train young men for battle purposes and to prove a young man's fitness to marry. Now a tourist spectacle.
fajar aurora. - *menyingsing* sunrise. *ketika - menyingsing* at daybreak.
fakta ber- factual.
faktor - *penghambat* retarding factor. - *waktu* time factor.
faktuil factual.
faktur invoice.
fakultas o. of the major disciplines of an Indonesian university. *F- Ekonomi* (abbrev. *FE*) School of Economics. *F- Hukum dan Ilmu Pengetahuan Kemasyarakatan* (abbrev. *FHIPK* and *FH dan IPK*) School of Law and Social Sciences. *F- Ilmu Pasti dan Pengeta-*

huan Alam (abbrev. *FIPPA*) School of Mathematics and Physics. *F- Kedokteran* (abbrev. *FK*) Medical School, School of Medicine, Faculty of Medicine. *F- Kedokteran Gigi* (abbrev. *FKG*) School of Dentistry (, Dental Surgery). *F- Keguruan dan Ilmu Pendidikan* (abbrev. *FKIP*) School of Teacher Training and Pedagogy. *F- Sastera Universitas Indonesia* (abbrev. *FSUI*) School of Literature, University of Indonesia.
fakultatif and fakultatip optional.
fakultèt (s.) FAKULTAS.
Falantil the *Fretelin* army operating in Timor Timur.
falsafah philosophy. - *hidup* philosophy of life.
fam (in the Minahasa, North Celebes) family name.
famili 1 family. 2 relative. *dgn dalih dipanggil seorang -nya* under the pretext of having been called by a relative. *ada hubungan - dgn* to be related to. ber- *dgn* to be related to. per-an family relations.
familia family (a subdivision in the classification of plants).
fana temporary (opp. eternal). *dr negeri yg - ke negeri yg baka* from a perishable to an imperishable world, from

earth to heaven.
fanatisme fanaticism.
fantasi fantasy.
fantastis fantastic.
fara'idz religious obligations, (esp.) regarding the division of intestate property.
faraj vulva.
fardh(u) duty. *-ul ain* individual obligation. *-ul kifayah* collective obligation.
farji (s.) FARAJ.
farmakologi pharmacology.
farmakopé pharmacopoeia.
farmasi ke-an pharmaceutical.
fasid mem-kan to annul (marriage).
fasilitas facility. - *kredit* credit facilities.
fasis ke-an fascism.
fasisme fascism.
fastabikhulkhairat to compete in doing good deeds.
fatal fatal. - *bagi* fatal to.
fatamorgana fata morgana.
Fatayat NU Young Women's Organization of the Nahdlatul-Ulama party.
fatihah 1 the confession of faith. 2 the first *sura* of the Koran.
favorit favorite. **mem-kan** to favor.
fénoména phenomena.
féderalisme federalism.
féderalistis federalistic.
féderasi *Republik F- Jerman* Federal Republic of Germany.
féminisme feminism.
fénoménal phenomenal.
fénomin phenomenon (the person).
fèntilasi ventilation.
fèri ferry.
fermèntasi fermentation.
fètakompli fait accompli. **di-kan** to be confronted with an accomplished fact (a fait accompli).
fétor (in Nusa Tenggara) 1 village chief. 2 chief of an ethnic group.
fi in, at, upon, regarding. - *l.alam* on earth, in the world. *-sabilillah* (s.) SABIL and JIHAD.
fiasko fiasco.
figh (s.) FIKH.

figur person.
figuran an extra (actor), mute.
fihak kese-an bias, one-sidedness.
fikh law based on Moslem theology, Islamic jurisprudence.
filantrop philanthropist.
filateli philately.
filatelis philatelist.
filem (S.) FILM.
filharmoni philharmonic.
filing lottery prediction, hunch.
film memf-kan (s.) MEM(P)-KAN. - *biru (,cabul)* pornographic film. - *dokumenter* documentary (a documentary motion picture). - *gituan* pornographic film. - *mandarin* a Chinese film. - *perdana* film shown for a première.
filologi philology.
filologis philological.
filter filter (also, in cigarette); (s.) ROKOK (BERFILTER).
final final.
finansiil financial.
finèc and finèk financial-economic (matters).
firasat presentiment. - *jelek* a bad omen.
firma firm, i.e. a company in which the owners are fully responsible for liabilities of the company.
firman 1 order, command. 2 the word of God, apocalypse. *spt - Allah* in accordance with God's word.
fisik physical.
fisika - *terapan* applied physics.
fisikawan physicist.
fiskal fiscal.
fitnah backbiting. *kena* - to be slandered. **pem-** backbiter, slanderer. - *secara tertulis* libel.
flaai high on drugs.
flamboyan flamboyant tree.
flamingo *(burung)* - flamingo.
flat - *jejaka* bachelors apartment.
flèksibel flexible.
flèksibilitas flexibility.
flès (S.) PELES.
flin.flan (the denigrating form of) PLIN. PLAN.

flit an insecticide spray under the trademark Flit. **di-** to be sprayed with Flit, be flitted.

florèt foil, fencing sword.

flotila flotilla.

flu flu, influenza. - *celeng* swine flu. - *Hongkong* Hongkong flu.

fly (s.) FLAAI.

fly.over and **flypass** overpass.

fohte damp, oozing.

fokus focus. *menjadi - perhatian* to be in the center of interest, be in the limelight, command a widespread interest. **mem-kan** to focus. ~ *perhatiannya kpd* to focus o's attention on.

fondamèn foundation (of building, etc.).

fonds -.- securities (in banking).

fonémik phonemic.

fonétik phonetics.

fonétis phonetic.

fonologi phonology.

forklif forklift.

formalitas formality.

formasi appointment to government position.

format size, format. - *baku* standard size.

formatir premier-designate, i.e. a person appointed by the chief of state to form a cabinet of ministers.

formika formica.

formil ke-an formality.

formulasi mem-kan to formulate.

formulir form (to fill out). - *daftar barang bawaan penumpang* Customs declaration. - *lamaran* application form. - *pendaftaran* registration form.

forsir mem- to force (a person, door, lock, etc.), burst (the door), strain (o's voice).

fosil fossil. **mem-** to fossilize.

foto snapshot. **di-** to be photographed (,pictured). - *udara* aerial photograph.

fotografer photographer.

fotografi photography.

fotokopi memf-(kan) to photocopy.

fototustèl camera, (s.) TUSTEL.

fotowan photographer.

fragmèntaris *secara* - fragmentarily, scrappily.

fraksi faction, group in Parliament or in local councils which acts together (a *fraksi* may be a party, a group of parties, or of individuals), splintergroup (in Parliament).

frambusia yaws.

frasa (s.) FRASE.

frase phrase.

fregat frigate.

frékwènsi - *nada* audio-frequency. - *terdengar* audible frequency.

Frètelin [Frente Revolucionaria de Timor Leste Independente] Revolutionary Front for the Independence of East Timor; (s.) PRETELIN.

frikatif fricative.

friksi friction.

fronton hai-lai.

frustrasi frustration.

fufu (in the Minahasa, North Celebes) method for smoking fish.

fuli mace (of nutmeg).

fulus 1 money (often in an unfavorable sense). 2 covetous.

fumigasi fumigation. **di-** to be fumigated.

fundamèntil fundamental.

fungisida fungicide.

fungsi position. **mem-kan** to have s.t. function (as).

fungsionaris functionary, official.

fungsionil functional.

Funisia Phoenicia.

fuqoro wal masakin the poor.

fusi merger, amalgamation. **ber-** to merge, amalgamate (v.i.). **mem-kan** to merge, amalgamate (v.t.). **per-an** merger, amalgamation, fusion.

futur to end fasting (by eating, etc.).

futurisme futurism.

futuristik futuristic.

futurolog futurologist.

u yong hay egg foo yong.

G

G–30–S, G 30 S and G30S [Gerakan 30 September] The September 30 (1965) Movement.

gabag measles. -en to have measles.

gabah rice in the husk after threshing.

gableg and gablek to own, possess, have.

gabug and gabuk empty rice kernels, empty *gabah* grains.

gabung meng-kan *diri pd* to align o.s. with. peng-an *usaha* merger. ter- 1 affiliated. 2 connected (with), related (to). -an 1 fusion, merger. 2 federation. 3 association. 4 affiliation. ~ *otak* braintrust.

gacoan 1 companion, fellow. 2 sweetheart, love, dearest.

gacok and gacuk marble used in children's game which in the opinion of the player will make him win over the other participants.

gadang I be- (s.) BERGADANG.

gadang II meng- to expect, look forward to.

gading *tak ada - yg tak retak* no rose without a thorn; nothing is perfect.

gadis - *Aron* girl worker in Tanah Karo (Sumatra). - *bar* bar girl. - *kelinci* bunny (of Playboy Club). - *pemijit* massage girl. - *pengiring penganten* bridesmaid.

gado meng- to nibble at the accompanying dishes to a *rijsttafel* without the rice. - *saja!* just nibble a little bit! - *hati* to cause to feel unhappy, aggravating. -.- (fig.) a mess.

gaduh *tingkat -* noise level. -an loan.

gadung -an 1 false, fake. 2 self-styled, pretended, would-be. *pemimpin* ~ a bogus leader.

gaèt meng- to grab (a thief). ~ *barang dr (,di) toko* to shoplift. ~ *hatinya* to appeal to him (,her). ~ *langganan baru* to snare (,get) new subscribers (to a newspaper, etc.). peng- *barang di toko* shoplifter.

gaga (pron. gogo) non-irrigated (non-terraced mountain) rice field; (s.) PADI. - *rancah* rice cultivation on non-irrigated field.

gagah audacious. *masih* ber- still going strong, still in good shape. meng-i to rape.

gagak slender-billed crow.

gagal 1 undeveloped, abortive, misfired. *kudeta yg - di Indonesia* the abortive coup d'état in Indonesia. *kup yg -* the coup that misfired. 2 to be frustrated, not take place. ke-an a flop.

gagang I - *telpon (,tilpon)* telephone handpiece.

gagang II stalk of the paddy, straw.

gagas di-kan to be designed. peng- designer. ter- thought up.

gagu *Dia spt orang -*, He stood tongue-tied.

gahari moderate.

gaharu *sdh - cendana pula* to ask for the sake of asking.

Gaimusho Jap. Foreign Ministry.

gairah ambitious. ber-... ...-minded. ke-an 1 jealousy. 2 ambition. meng-kan *hati* 1 to charm. 2 charming. - *berdikari* the spirit of self-sufficiency. - *syahwat* sexual drive.

gairat (s.) GAIRAH.

gajah I term for the Police wreckers or tow trucks. - *laut* 'sea jumbo,' i.e. a 45-ton floating crane in Tanjung Priok port. *G- Mada* 1 the *Mapatih* of *Majapahit.* 2 (spelled Gadjah Mada) name of a university in Yogyakarta. - *terbang* 'flying jumbo,' the Boeing 747.

gajah II - *oling* k.o. batik pattern.

gaji meng- *pembantu* to hire a servant. peng-an pay. - *bermula* initial salary, salary to start. - *cuti* vacation salary. - *permulaan* initial salary. - *yg dibawa bersih ke rumah* take-home pay.

gajul (s.) BAJUL.

gak-ang mole cricket.

gakari task.

gala I **meng- premierkan** to show a film at a gala première.

gala II *main - asin* k.o. folk game.

gala III *G- Puspha Sena* 'Women Soldiers Training (,Indoctrination).' *G- Yudha* (mil.) Field Test.

galah *Matahari Bandung baru* **sepeng-**, It was just about 7 or 8 o'clock in the morning in Bandung.

galak provocative, aggressive, fanatic. **meng-kan** to encourage, promote. **peng-an** encouragement, promotion.

galang **peng-** member of the *Pramuka* Boy Scout Movement from 12 to 15 years, scout.

galau **per-an** overlapping.

gali **meng-** *keterangan* to elicit information.

galir loose, not fixed properly. *Pendirian-nya* **gular.-**, He trimmed his sails according to the wind.

galon gallon.

Galungan the Balinese New Year according to the *Wuku* calendar. It lasts ten days and occurs every 210 days; (cp.) NYEPI.

gamal *pohon -* (L. Glerycidea) a cheap and effective exterminator for *alang. alang* (L. Imperata cylindrica).

gamalisasi planting of *gamal* trees to eliminate *alang.alang*.

gambang (Jav.) xylophon-like instrument. *- k(e)romong Jakarta* Jakarta xylophone-like instrument.

gambar **meng-***mistar* geometrical drawing. **peng-** *peta* cartographer. **-an:** ~ *grafik* a graph. ~ *kepribadian* image. *- ejekan* caricature. *- kaca* slide (for projection on screen). *- komik* comic, a comic cartoon or strip of cartoons. *- lucon* caricature. *- telanjang* a pin-up picture.

gambir I 1 gambier (L. Uncaria gambir). 2 preparation made from the leaves of this plant which possesses strong astringent properties, a constituent part of the betel quid.

Gambir II *(Tanah Lapang) -* (coll.) Merdeka Square (in Jakarta).

gamblang plain, obvious, explicit. *masih - dlm ingatan kita* it is still fresh in our minds. **ke-an** clearness, distinctness. **meng-kan** to clarify.

gamblok **ng-** 1 to be attached to, hold on to. 2 to join.

gambus a 6-stringed Arab musical instrument resembling a lute.

gambut peat, fen.

gambyong a classical Jav. dance performed by women. **ng-** to perform that dance.

gamelan 1 (classical) Jav. musical instrument. 2 the ensemble of such instruments.

gamit **meng-** 1 to beckon with the fingers. 2 to solicit.

gampang *G-!* (pron. in a somewhat long-drawn out tone on the second vowel) I will cross that bridge when I come to it! *cari -* and *mencari -nya* to take the line of least resistance, take the easy way out. *G- marah, tapi - baik lagi,* He is quick to become angry, but also quick to recover. *Saya ini dikiranya -an apa?* Does he think that I'm easy? *secara -.-an saja* by shirking the difficulties. *utk -nya* to make it easy, give an easy example, for convenience ('sake). *-.- angel (,sukar)* not to be foreseen (,foretold), unpredictable, i.e. sometimes easy to please and sometimes not.

gamping limestone.

ganas cruel. **ke-an** barbarity.

gancang I 1 rapid. 2 nimble, agile.

gancang II (s.) GANGSANG.

ganda I *- campuran* (in tennis) mixed doubles. *- pria* (in tennis) men's doubles.

ganda II ambiguous. **ke-an** ambiguity.

gandapura a liniment containing as active ingredients: methyl salicyl, cayenne pepper, oil of clove, oil of peppermint, oil of turpentine, used for the relief of pain associated with arthritis and rheumatism.

gandarukam (s.) GONDORUKEM.

gandem good to eat.

gandèng *(dgn)* **ber-an** *tangan* arm in arm.

meng- to escort (a lady). **peng-an** docking (of spaceship). -an trailer.

gandes graceful, charming, elegant.

ganding -an appendix.

gandokan 1 to have a love affair. 2 unmarried couple.

gandringan meeting.

gandrum (s.) JAGUNG (CANTEL).

gandrung di-i *publik* to be in vogue with the public. **ke-an** *kpd* fondness for. **meng-i** to be devoted to, love. - *udara* air-minded.

gandul di-in *ngantuk* overcome with sleepiness. -an mass support. *suratkabar.suratkabar yg tdk mempunyai* ~ newspapers which do not have mass support.

gandum corn.

Ganésha in Hindu mythology, the fat-bellied elephant-headed son of Shiva; the Household God, or God of Prosperity.

gang I *G- Lokomotip* a rice trading center in Jatinegara (Jakarta).

gang II (pron. gèng) gang (i.e. a group of people).

ganggam - *bauntuik* right to use (land).

ganggang algae. - *laut* seaweed, sargassum.

ganggu *tak dpt* **di-** *gugat* unassailable. *hak yg tdk bisa* **di-** *gugat* inalienable right. **peng-** disturber. -an: ~ *serangga* insect nuisance. ~ *tikus* plague of rats. ~ *udara* atmospheric disturbance. ~ *ujar* speech impediment.

gangsang lustful, lascivious, concupiscent.

ganja marijuana, hashish. **ber-** to smoke pot (,marijuana).

ganjais potsmoker.

ganjak *Pendiriannya tiada* **ber-,** He has an unshakable viewpoint.

ganjal **meng-** to supplement. *sesuatu yg* ~ *di hati* a worry. **peng-.perut** anything to take the edge off of hunger.

ganjawan (s.) GANJAIS.

ganjel I prop, support; (s.) GANJAL. **nge-** to supplement. ~ *belanja hari ini* to supplement today's (kitchen) expenses.

ganjel II **meng-** *mata* to be an eyesore. **ng-** thorny (problem). -an 1 shim.

2 thorn in the flesh. *Okinawa ~ antara Jepang-AS,* Okinawa is a thorn in the flesh of Japan and the U.S.

ganjen coquettish.

ganjil extraordinary, exceptional, abnormal, eccentric, quaint. - *dr biasa* different from others. **ke-an** deformity, idiosyncrasy.

ganjur a rice plant disease.

gantang **meng-** *asap* to build castles in the air.

ganteng **ke-an** handsomeness. **ng-** (S.) GANTENG.

ganter **ng-** to produce loud steady sounds. *Burung prenjak itu menyanyi* ~, The warbler was singing loudly.

ganti **ber-** to turn. *Lampu lalu.lintas ~ merah,* The traffic light turned red. *secara* **ber-an** in rotation. **peng-:** *kpd* ~ to bearer. ~ *pelaku* stand-in. **peng-an** *warna* alternately colored. **per-an:** ~ *lampu merah ke ijo itu nggak seberapa lama* (of traffic light) the change from red to green does not take that long. *(pd)* ~ *th* (at) the turn of the year. *merayakan* ~ *th* to see the old year out, see the new year in. *sbg* **-nya** instead, as a substitute for. *sekarang - cerita saya* and now I want to tell about s.t. else. - *pesawat* to change planes. - *rugi* amends, compensation, recompense (for property taken by the State). - *tangan* (done) by another person.

gantol **meng-** to hook on to.

gantung **ber-** *tak bertali* up in the air, not firm. **di-** to be idle, be out of commission. *ratusan truk* ~ hundreds of trucks are idle. **keter-an** dependence. *saling* ~ interdependence, interdependency. **meng-** *diri* to hang o.s. **meng-kan** *diri dr (,kpd)* to depend on, be dependent on. **peng-:** ~ *mangkuk* cuphook. ~ *manusia* lyncher.

ganung heart of the kapok fruit.

ganyang **meng-** 1 to crush, destroy. 2 to eat. **peng-an** crushing.

ganyong k.o. reed (edible rhizome).

gap.gap (S.) DEGAP.DEGAP.

gaplè domino. **pe-** domino player.

gaplok meng- to spank.

gapura gateway, entrance.

gara.gara 1 commotion. 2 idea, instigation. *-mu!* it's your fault! *mencari -* to look for trouble, asking for trouble. *Ini -nya siapa ya?* Whose idea was this? Who's the wise guy?

garai (in West Sumatra) sorghum.

garam *sdh makan - dunia ini, sdh banyak makan -* and *banyak menelan - hidup* experienced, seasoned, well-versed. *- asam cuka* acetous salt. *- bataan* salt in briquets. *- curai* non-iodine containing salt.

garang aggressive.

garansi *- bank* banker's guarantee (,indemnity).

garasi di-kan to be put (,kept) in a garage.

Garba Ilmiah Alma Mater.

garbis a variety of melon; round, large, light yellow, very bland; in season January through March.

garda guard. *- depan* avant-garde, vanguard. *G- Nasional* National Guard (in the U.S.).

gardamunggu cardamon.

gardan differential gear.

gardu *- pembangkit* power house. *- telepon* telephone booth. *- transformator* transformer station.

garebeg celebration of the three big annual feasts: *Maulud, Bakda Pasa* and *Besar* in the *kratons.*

garèng I cicada, tree cricket.

Garèng II son of *Semar* and brother of *Petruk.*

garing crisp.

garis meng-.bawahi to underline. *dlm - besarnya* in broad terms, broadly speaking. *- edar matahari* ecliptic. *- hirarki yg bercabang dua* dual command. *- incang.incut* a crisscross of lines. *- keras* (in politics) hard-line. *baik menurut - lurus maupun - ke samping* both in the lineal and in the collateral line. *- menengah* diameter. *- pantai* coast line. *- pemisah (,pisah)* 1 partition (,dividing) line, line of division.

2 (between regions) boundary (,demarcation) line, line of demarcation. *- petunjuk* guide line. *- sipatan* building line, alignment. *- start* starting line.

garnisun garrison.

Garogol (bus conductor shouting announcing the name of the next stop) Grogol! (i.e. o. of Jakarta's suburban areas.

garuk ke- to be robbed. *Bank asing ~ ratusan juta,* Foreign banks have been robbed of hundreds of millions. **meng-** to arrest. **-an** arrest, capture.

garwa spouse. **ber-** *pd* to have...as o's spouse.

gas di- to be accelerated (of automobile). **meng-** to fumigate. **peng-an** fumigation. *- alam cair (,yg dicairkan)* liquefied natural gas, LNG. *- asam arang* carbon dioxide. *- bio* methane. *- bumi* natural gas(oline). *- lemas* choking gas. *- mudah terbakar* highly combustible gas. *- oksigen* oxygen gas.

gasak meng- to rob, steal. **-an** (s.) BARANG (GASAKAN).

gasang ke-an lasciviousness.

gasir *A* ke-an A's house was broken into.

gatal lustful, lascivious. **ke-an** lustfulness. *ia ~* (said of a woman) she has itchy pants.

gatèk -an 1 susceptible. 2 quick in learning.

gatra I constituent (in syntax).

Gatra II *- Loka* (s.) BINA GRAHA.

gatuk and **gathuk** comparison, connection.

Gatutkaca 1 a warlike figure from the *wayang purwa.* 2 a pilot. 3 the code name given by the *Gestapu/PKI* to the Air Force Base Guards. 4 the code name for Omar Dhani. 5 the *G-30-S* reserve troops.

gauk siren.

gaul ber- 1 to mingle with s.t. else. 2 to intermix (marriage), mix (cards). 3 allied, united. **meng-i** to have sexual intercourse with. *sang wanita yg sdh mereka -i* the woman with whom they had sexual intercourse. *luas* **per-annya**

he has a large circle of friends.

gaun ber- to wear a gown.

gaung response, reaction.

gaut peng-an profession, occupation.

gawai work, activities; (s.) GAWE.

gawal mistake, error. *sepandai.pandai tupai melompat, sekali - juga* it is a good horse that never stumbles.

gawat ke-an danger.

gawé -an job. *nyari* ~ to seek a job.

gaya ber-: ~ *pegas* elastic, resilient, springy. ~ *saran* suggestive. **di- barukan** to be given a new touch, be renovated. - *atom* atom power. - *gabung* affinity. - *gerak* motive power. - *kupu.kupu* (in swimming) butterfly stroke. - *pegas* elasticity, spring. - *pusaran* centripetal force. - *pusingan* centrifugal force. - *sentripetal* centripetal force. - *tarik* attractive power. - *udara* aerodynamic.

gayeng 1 pleasant, cordial. 2 in turn. *Empat orang yg nampak - mengadakan pembicaraan ini masing.masing dr kiri ke kanan...*, The four persons (in the picture) who are seen discussing in turn are from left to right...

GBHN [Garis-Garis Besar Haluan Negara] Perspectives of the Course of the Nation.

Gdé (in Bali) name element placed before personal names to indicate the first born child, such as, *I Gde Putu Wirata.*

gebah nge- to drive (,chase) away. *pedagang* -an streetvendor who sells on sidewalks without permission and is subject to being chased away at any time by local authorities.

gebaran vibration.

geblak ng- to fall backward.

gebrag I ber- and **meng-** to set about, engage in.

gebrag II meng- 1 to hit, give a blow to. 2 to attack. -an 1 a blow (with fist). 2 attack, charge, assault, raid.

gebrak (s.) GEBRAG.

gebu meng-(.-) 1 to exaggerate (s.t.). 2 exaggerated.

gebug (S.) GEBUK. **di-in** to be beaten (,thrashed).

gebyag -an performance, official presentation.

gebyah -uyah generalizing. **meng- uyah** to generalize.

gebyar glitter.

gecul 1 roguish, impish. 2 funny, comic.

gedana.gedini having brothers and sisters.

gedé I peng- and *orang* -an big shot.

Gedé II (s.) GDE.

gedebak.gedebur to palpitate (of heart).

gèdèg to shake the head. *membuat orang -.-* to make people shake their heads.

gedèmpol fat.

gedobos ng- to talk nonsense.

gedombrongan too large (,big) (of clothes).

gedong (S.) GEDUNG. *G- Dalam* The *BAPERKI* Headquarters in Bogor (West Java).

gedung - *apartemen* apartment building. - *bertingkat (,berlantai) satu (,dua ,dll)* a one- (,two-, etc.) story building. *G- Conefo* (under President Soekarno) Political Venues (*Conefo* stands for: [Conference of the New Emerging Forces]). - *flat* apartment building. - *induk* main building. - *jangkung* highrise. - *madat* (in Jakarta) 'opium building,' thus called owing to its function during col.; now, the building of the central administration of the University of Indonesia on Jalan Salemba Raya. - *olahraga* sport hall. - *peraih langit* skyscraper. - *perkantoran* office building. *G- Pola* Blueprint Hall (Jakarta, Jalan Pegangsaan Timur 56); from this site the proclamation of Indonesia's independence was made on August 17, 1945. *G- Saté* 'Barbecued Meat Building,' i.e. the epithet given by the population of Bandung to the Office of the Head of the First Level Area (the Governor's Office); it is also popularly known as *Kantor Gubernur Jawa Barat* (Office of the Governor of West Java) located at Jalan Diponegoro 22. - *yg menjangkau awan* skyscraper.

gegana 1 air. 2 sky, heaven. *Satgas G-*

[Satuan Tugas G-] task force comparable to the U.S.A.F. "Blue Angels," but a component of the national police.

gegar - *budaya* culture shock.

gegiris ng-i alarming, frightening, terrible.

gegisik foreland, forshore.

gegoakan 1 screeching. 2 to screech.

geguyon joke.

gejahan whimbrel.

gejala 1 trend. 2 phenomenon. -.- *permulaan* early symptoms.

gejos imperfect, defective.

gelabaran bemused with sleep.

gelagah a wild sugar cane (L. Saccharum glaga). - *ilalang* k.o. reed grass growing in watery places.

gelagapan 1 confused. 2 perplexed, flabbergasted.

gelagat 1 look, appearance, aspect. 2 sign. 3 symptom. - *yg kurang baik* an ominous situation. - *masa* conditions of the time(s), state of affairs. *melihat -nya* 1 there are indications (,signs) that, there is every indication (,appearance) that. 2 judging from the manner (,way) in which. 3 it looks as though, to all appearances.

gelak - *berguman* to smile, smirk, laugh with o's tongue in o's cheek. - *terbahak. bahak* and *tertawa* -.- to roar with laughter.

gelandang meng- to haul off to the police station. **-an** 1 to be unemployed. 2 a vagrant, tramp.

gelang - *besi* handcuffs. - *kaki* anklet. - *tangan* armlet. - *tretes* a bracelet bedecked with precious gems.

gelanggang G- *Balap Sepeda* Velodrome Sports Center. - *dunia* world forum. - *hidup* 1 society. 2 life. G- *Mahasiswa* College Student Center. - *olahraga* sports center. G- *Pembinaan Bangsa dan Persahabatan Antar Bangsa.Bangsa* (in Jakarta) Center for Nation Building and International Understanding. - *permainan anak.anak* children's playground. - *pertemuan* 1 society. 2 life.

G- *Remaja* Youth Center. G- *Samudra* Oceanarium. G- *Wanita* Exhibit of Articles made by Women.

gelantung *Pd pinggangnya* **ber-an** *Colt besar,* A large Colt (revolver) dangled from his hip.

gelap illegal, clandestine, covert, sinister. *habis - timbul terang* after rain comes sunshine; behind the clouds the sun is shining. - *samar muka* not be able to see o's hand before o's face. *bank -* illegal bank. *senjata -* illegal weapon. *taksi -* gypsy cab. *tokoh -* a sinister character (,figure). **peng-** embezzler. **peng-an**: *masa* ~ the dark ages. *melakukan* ~ to embezzle. **-an** darkness. *di ~ malam* in the darkness of the night. -.-**an** clandestinely. *bacaan porno yg beredar* ~ pornographic literature circulating clandestinely. - *temaram* pitchdark.

gelar I 1 designation. 2 alias, nickname. - *dokter* physician's degree. - *kebangsawanan* title of nobility. - *kesarjanaan* academic degree.

gelar II **diper-kan** to be performed, be staged. **pe-an** and **pa-an** performance (of play). *pa-an busana* fashion show. **per-an**: ~ *jazz* jazz concert. ~ *lukisan* exhibition of paintings. ~ *musik* orchestra.

gelatik Java temple bird.

gelayut **ber-an** to swing, hang (plural subject). *monyet.monyet besar* ~ large monkeys were swinging around.

gelédah meng- *(badan)* to frisk.

gelèdèk *sbg - di siang hari bolong* like a bolt from the blue.

gelembung **peng-an** expansion. ~ *wilayah industri* expansion of industrial areas. -.-**an** *paru* alveolus (of the lung).

gelepar meng- *di tempat* to hover (of aircraft).

geli amusing, pleasing. **meng-kan** disgusting. - *hati* amused, entertained.

gelimang *hidup dgn* **ber-** *uang* rolling in money. **ter-** all covered with (dirt).

gelinding meng- to taxi (of aircraft).

gelinjang to jump up and down. meng-
1 bright, flashy (colors). 2 to jump with
joy.

gelintir 1 a particle. 2 (unimportant)
group (of persons). *beberapa - importir*
o. or two importers *se-* a minute
fraction. ~ *manusia* a very few persons.

gelisah - *belia* restless.

gelitik meng- titillating. *asap sate ~
selera pejalan kaki* shishkebab smoke
was titillating to pedestrians.

gèlo foolish, silly.

gelombang meng- to come in waves.
- *mikro* microwave.

gelondong -an logs.

gelontor peng-an drainage.

Gelora [Gelanggang Olah Raga] Athletic
Stadium.

geluh clay, loam. *tanah* - loamy soil.

gelung meng-i to coil up (s.t.), wrap up.

gelut di- *pusing* overcome by dizziness.
di-i *sepi* to be engulfed in silence.

gemah ripah loh jinawi prosperous and
populous (flowing with milk and
honey).

gemak the Jav. (fighting) quail.

gemang 1 short and stout. 2 circular,
spherical.

gemar ke-an: ~ *akan* love for. ~ *membaca*
reading habit.

gemas meng-kan to pout (of lips).

gembèng inclined to weep easily.
cengeng - apt to cry at the slightest
provocation. *anak (,si)* - crybaby.

gembili (S.) KEMBILI.

gembira ke-an animation.

gembok meng- to lock with a padlock.

gèmbol -an parcel carried by s.o. in his
sash.

gembolo the larger variety of the *gembili*.

gèmbong (fig.) big wheel. *(macan)* -
the Bengal (,striped royal) tiger.

gembrobyos pouring out (of sweat).

gembrot 1 bulky, ponderous. 2 slobby.

gembung inflated. meng- to increase.

gembur bulky (of physique), flabby.

gemek (s.) GEMAK.

gemerutuk to clatter. *suara - rantai jang-*

kar yg diturunkan the clatter of the
dropping of anchor chains.

gemi.nastiti frugal and scrupulous.

gempa *daerah* ke-an seismic zoning.

gempal - *kukuh* sturdy.

gempor broken down.

gemriming a chilly feeling.

gemuk profitable (of a transportation
line). peng-an fattening (of calves).
- *kimplah.kimplah* heavy set. - *terokmok* chubby.

gemuruh tumultuous, boisterous, loud.

genah just, fair.

genap - *berumur*... exactly... years old.
- *200 th* a full 200 years.

gencar meng- to become incessant (of
shelling, etc.).

gencat ter- suspended, frustrated.

gencer nonstop (of shelling, etc.); (S.)
GENCAR.

gendam *tukang* - hypnotist.

gendar a Central Java delicacy made
from rice; (s.) KERAK (GENDAR).

gendeng stark, raving mad. *roda* -
flywheel.

Gending Sriwijaya courtdance (of
Palembang).

gèndong I peng- *jamu* a medicinal herb
dealer (the sellers are women carrying
their herbs in bottles in a basket on
their back).

gèndong II meng- to fuck.

gèndong III se-an 1/12 of the entire estate
in the form of land.

gendut ke-an corpulence.

gènèng popular (due to wealth).

génerasi - *muda kita* our young generation.
- *taruna* the younger generation.
- *wredda* the older generation.

génétika genetics.

genggam se- *kecil* a little bit.

gèngsi *turun* - to lose o's prestige.

gèngsot (western) dancing.

genit alluring, cute.

génitalia genitals. - *wanita* the female
genitals.

gènjah to ripen early.

gènjang 1 awry, crooked. 2 aslant, not

parallel. 3 out of line. - *genjot (,genjut)* zigzag.

genjot ng(eng)- and **n-** to pedal (a *becak*). **peng-** *pedal becak* pedicab driver.

genjrèt and **genjrit** *lari -* to take suddenly to o's heels.

gentar *dgn tak -* unafraid.

genting I meng- overacting

genting II -an isthmus.

gentingsenting hairsplitter.

gentong and **genthong** earthen pitcher for keeping a supply of water, *beras,* etc. handy. - *pendaringannya sdh mulai miring* he could no longer make ends meet.

gentus -an 1 a push. 2 (in soccer) head-ball.

géodési 1 geodesy. 2 geodetic. *pekerjaan -* geodetic activities. - *fisik* physical geodesy.

géofisika geophysics.

géofisikawan geophysicist.

géografi - *ekonomi dan sosial* economic and social geography.

géografis *letak -nya* its geographical location.

géoide geoid.

géolog geologist.

géologiawan geologist.

gepit meng- *rokok* to squeeze a cigarette.

ger ha-ha (interjection indicating laughter). **-.-an** to roar with laughter.

gerah ke-an to suffer from stifling heat (e.g. due to a threatening rain).

gerai *Rambutnya yg ter- bebas,* Her freely hanging-down (,unloosened) hair.

gerak ber-: *Jangan ~!* Freeze! *~ maju* (mil.) to advance. *~ mundur* to go astern. **ber-.-** *hatinya utk* he feels inclined to. **peng-:** *~ perobahan* agent of change. *~ utama* prime mover. **ter-** *hatinya* impressed by, feel drawn to. **-an:** *G~ Cina Komunis* Chicom Movement. *G~ Kebebasan Wanita* Women's Lib. *~ maju musuh* (mil.) hostile advance. *G~ Mahasiswa Nasional Indonesia* Indonesian National College Students Movement. *~ memisah*

separatism. *G~ Wanita Indonesia* Indonesian Women's Movement. *~ Zionis* Zionism. *sdh ada -.-nya* there are (positive) indications (,signs). - *jalan* hiking, walking. - *jalan orang. orang miskin* the poor people's march (in Washington, D.C.). - *lembam* slow-motion.

geranat peng-an attack with grenades. - *asap* smoke grenade. - *asap fosfor* white phosphorous grenade. - *brisan* high explosive shell. - *plastik* concussion grenade.

gerangan *apa -?* what on earth? what in the world?

gerayah to grope around. *tangannya -.- kpd amplop itu* his hand was groping around for the envelope.

gerayang di-i *maling* to be robbed. **meng-i** 1 to probe stealthily, case (the joint). 2 to steal.

gerbong - *ekor* the last train coach (in train formation). - *penumpang* railroad passenger car. - *restorasi* diner. - *tangki (minyak)* tank car.

gerbus di- to be hulled (of coffeebeans).

gerebekan scrimmage (in soccer).

geregetan (s.) GREGETAN.

geréja ke-an ecclesiastical. *G- Anglikan* Anglican Church. *G- Bethel Injil Sepenuh* Bethel Full Gospel Church of God. *G- Masehi Advent Hari Ketujuh* Seventh Day Adventist Church. *G- Ortodoks* Orthodox Church. *G- Pantekosta* Pentecost Church.

geréjawan churchgoer.

gèrèk peng- sugar cane pest.

geremet meng-i to infiltrate. **peng-an** nibbling away at.

gerèndèl (s.) GRENDEL.

gerendeng di-in to be snapped.

gerenjal.gerenjul ber- bumpy, rough, uneven (of road).

gerètan lighter. - *gas Ronson* Ronson butane lighter.

gergaji - *bermesin* chainsaw. *spt - dua mata* a double edged knife, the knife cuts both ways.

geriak.geriuk rumbling (of the stomach

from hunger).

gerilya - *perkotaan* urban guerrilla warfare. - *politik* political guerrilla warfare.

gerilyawan a male guerrilla fighter.

gerilyawati a female guerrilla fighter.

gerimis *siaran TV masih saja* - TV broadcasts are still blocked by interference ('snow').

gerincing **meng-kan** *pedang* and -**an** *senjata* saberrattling.

germo madam (woman in charge of a brothel), women vice boss.

gerobak - *barang* baggage cart (,trolley).

gerodak **meng-i** to rummage (in a box, etc.).

gerogot **meng-i** 1 to steal. 2 to make inroads on. *Jepang yg sdh ~ sebagian besar pasaran mobil Amerika dan Eropa memprogramkan produksi 250 ribu mobil listrik, th 1988,* Japan, which has made inroads on the greater part of the American and European car markets, has programmed a production of 250 thousand electric cars in 1988. **peng-** *uang* corruptor.

gerojog water falling. **meng-** to fall (of water).

gerombol **meng-** to come together, meet, assemble, gather.

gerontang (S.) GERANTANG. - *keling* threat with nothing to back it up.

gérontologi gerontology.

gerot.gerot *(ikan)* - a fish, the grunter (L. Pristipoma hasta).

gerpol [gerilya politik] political guerrilla warfare. **meng-** to launch political guerrilla warfare.

gerpolis *'gerpolist,'* i.e. an adherent of political guerrilla warfare.

gersang arid. **ke-an** barrenness, aridness.

gertak **meng-kan** *gerahamnya* to gnash o's teeth.

gerujug (s.) GRUJUG.

gerun *tiada* **ber-** to have no power. **meng-kan** awe-inspiring.

gerut.gerut (s.) GEROT.GEROT.

gesa **keter-an** haste.

gèsèk **memper-kan** *gerahamnya* to gnash o's teeth. **peng-:** ~ *biola* violinist.

~ *selo* cellist.

gèsèr **meng-** *(duduknya)* to move (o's seat). **per-an** tour of duty (in the army), transfer (from o. post to another to get rid of s.o.).

gesit active, alert. **di-kan** to be sped up, be speeded up.

Gèstapo Gestapo.

Gestapu [Gerakan September Tigapuluh] September 30 (1965) Movement.

Gestapuisme 'Gestapuism,' i.e. the actions and practices carried out by the *Gestapu.*

getah - *rokok* tar (of cigarette). - *susu* cream latex.

getar *yg* **meng-kan** *seluruh dunia* world-shaking. -**an:** ~ *laut* seaquake. ~ *seismik* seismic tremor. ~ *tektonis* tectonic vibration.

getas rigid.

gètèk I and **gèthèk** ferry.

gètèk II immodest (in conduct of woman).

getem.getem to express anger by gestures.

getir sour, acid, tart, harsh. **meng-kan** *hati* to embitter.

getok and **gethok** - *tular* from mouth to mouth, hearsay.

getol **ng-** to be keen on s.t.

getuk - *lindri* a delicacy made from cassava.

geulis (pron. eu as u in fur) pretty, beautiful (of woman).

gezak authority.

ghaib and **ghoib** 1 hidden, concealed, obscure. 2 occult, esoteric (only for the initiated); (s.) GAIB, also (coll.) *raib* and *raip*. -**lah ia** he vanished. *perkataan yg* - 'mysterious being,' spirits presiding over good and evil fortune, guardian angel, patron saint. *sembahyang* - prayer for the absent dead, as at a cenotaph.

Ghora Wira Madya Jala (in the naval fleet insignia) Stark Courage O'er the Seas.

gi (S.) PERGI.

giat ablaze, zealous.

gidik **ber-** 1 afraid. 2 to get excited. ~ *tengkuk* o's skin crawls, o's hair stands on end.

gigi ...**ber-** cog... -.- *berlubang* caries. - *buatan* prothesis, denture. -.- *(mesin)* clockwork. - *palsu* denture.

gigih grim. *perjuangan yg lebih* - a grimmer (,more intensive) struggle.

gigil - *(kedinginan)* cold shiver. -**an** 1 to shiver from cold. 2 shivers from cold.

gigit meng- *bibir saja* to look blank (,foolish).

gigrig *tdk* - *bulunya* he is not shedding his feathers.

gijuhèi (during the Jap. occupation) volunteer for mil. duty.

gila crazed. - *pd* to be crazy about. **ke-an** *kebangsaan* chauvinism. **ng-ni** causing loathing (,revulsion). **peng-** aficionado. ~ *burung* bird-lover. **ter-.-** *pd* to be crazed for. -.-**an** to act (like a) crazy (person). - *CIA* CIA-mania. - *hormat* full of self-importance. - *pangkat* job-hunter, office-seeker. - *turunan* proud of o's origin (,descent).

gilir *dua kelompok.-* two shifts. **ber-** *ke buritan* to be a henpecked husband. **ber-.-** to rotate. -**an:** ~ *gelap* blackout, outage. ~ *kerja* (work)shift. ~ *pemadaman (listrik mati)* blackout, outage. *pd* ~**nya** in (his) turn.

gimana (S.) BAGAIMANA. - *sih?* how's about it? *"G- sih, wartawan.wartawan ini kalau nulis?"* "Hey, what's with these reporters when they write?"

gimbal *(berambut)* - (with) tangled (hair).

ginékolog gynecologist.

ginékologi gynecology.

gini (S.) BEGINI. *kaya* - like this. **se-** as much as this. - *hari* 1 for this time of the day. 2 nowadays.

ginjal *ada batu dlm -nya* he suffers from kidney stones.

ginsèng 1 an herb with a thick, forked, aromatic root found in China, Korea, etc. 2 the root of this plant shaped like a man.

gip(s) plaster (of Paris). **di-** to be put in a cast.

giral *(uang)* - (bank) deposits.

girang peng- a cheerful person.

girap.girap to be startled. *membuatnya* - startled her.

giri mountain (in compounds, such as, *Inderagiri*).

girik 1 documentary evidence, document in support. 2 land tax assessment paper. **di-** to be assessed. - *bodong* a counterfeited *girik*.

girikan (in Banjarmasin) farm implement.

giris frightening. *angin bertiup* - the wind was blowing terrifyingly.

girlan [pinggir jalan] (in Bogor) sidewalk.

giro clearing, transfer of money. *uang* - money on deposit. -*bank* clearing house.

gita hymn. *G- Jaya* 'Song of Greater Jakarta,' name of the official hymn of the Greater Jakarta Capital Region. *G- Karya* name of a printing house in Jakarta (formerly: G. Kolff).

gitar meng- 1 curvaceous. 2 to play the guitar. - *pengiring* accompaniment guitar.

gitaris guitarist.

gites meng- to kill (lice) by pressing with the thumbnail.

gitok and **githok** 1 nape of the neck. 2 scruff of the neck. *membikin -nya mengkirig* it made his hair stand on end.

gitik meng- to fuck.

gitu (S.) BEGITU. *Jangan - dong!* Don't be like that! Don't say that! *kaya* - like that. **(be)-an** to fuck. **se-** as much as that. -**an** 1 shit 2 fucking. 3 reefer, marijuana cigarette. *film* ~ pornographic film. *penyakit* ~ venereal disease.

giur meng-kan exciting. **ter-** excited.

gizi nutrition. **ber-** nutritious.

gladi training. -**an** training, drill. - *militer* mil. training. *G- Berganda* (mil.) Joint Training (carried out by the Armed Forces Reserve Officers School of the Department of the Interior). - *bersih (,resik)* general (,dress) rehearsal.

gladiol gladiolus.

gladrah ng- unreliable.

glagah k.o. reedgrass in watery places.

glagepan to stammer (from stress).

glayung (in East Java) 4 kilograms.

glèdèg and **glèdhèg** -an hawker's cart; (s.) GELEDEK.

(glegar.)gleger to tremble (due to grenade explosion, etc.).

glègèk -an to belch.

glembug - *Sala* Solo sweet talk in order to tempt, deceive.

glendem ng- to speak unclearly, mumble thanks.

glenik soft words, empty promises. **ng-** to talk confidentially in order to deceive.

glidhig to work as a laborer, usually in sugar factories or sugarcane fields.

glondong spool.

glukosa glucose.

GMNI [Gerakan Mahasiswa Nasional Indonesia] Indonesian National College Students Movement.

GMNI-wati a female member of the *GMNI.*

go five.

gobang *film kelas tiga* - lower-class film.

gobèk areca nut pounder.

gobèt nge- to cut (,grate) in very thin slices.

gobog an ancient Chinese copper coin with a square hole in the middle.

gocap fifty (rupiahs).

goda -an 1 (mental) torment, worry. 2 annoyance, nuisance, teasing.

godam sledge(hammer).

godog, godhog and **godok meng-** 1 (mil.) to train. 2 to hatch, plan (a set of laws or regulations). **peng-an** intensive (mil.) training.

godot to fleece a person (to the last penny).

gogo (s.) GAGA.

gogoh *kena* - to be grabbed (,snatched).

gogrog 1 to fall (off). 2 to lose. *SOKSI semakin -!* SOKSI is losing more and more members!

gojèk ber- to romp.

gojlok meng- to haze. **peng-an** hazing (in a rough way in colleges).

go.kart go-cart.

gokdor [disogok lalu dor] "loaded and then 'bang' "; (s.) DORGOK. *pistol* - a muzzle-loader pistol.

gol to succeed. *mencetak* - to make (,score) a goal.

golak.gejolak flaring up.

golef (s.) GOLF. *padang* - golf course (,links).

golèk - *jènggèl* tumbler (an easily tipped, self-righting toy).

golèr ber-.- to lie around (in o's bed, etc.).

golf golf. **pe-** golfer.

golfer golfer.

Golkar [Golongan Karya] the government-backed quasi-party which is a coalition of functional groups uniting labor, youth, cooperatives and other organizations which are not affiliated with the traditional political parties. **keg-an** *Golkar* affairs.

Golkarisasi 'Golkarization,' i.e. the efforts to cause people to become members or, at least, sympathizers of *Golkar.*

golong peng-an alignment. -an: ~ *A, B, C* the three different classes of prisoners arrested after the uprising of 1965. ~ *darah* blood group. ~ *harapan bangsa dan nusa (,negara)* the hope of the nation, the younger generation. ~ *keras* (in politics) the hawks. ~ *lunak* (in politics) the doves. ~ *masyarakat* the social classes. ~ *menak* the feudal class. ~ *menengah* the middle class. ~ *minoritas (,minoritet)* minority group. ~ *ningrat* the aristocracy. ~ *pertengahan* 1 the middle class. 2 tradespeople, trading class(es), small-sized industry and craftsmen. ~ *PGPN* the government employees. *G~ Putih* 'White Group,' i.e. a loosely-knit grouping critical of the New Order's methods, such as the election of *Golkar*, the government supporters

and the army. ~ *sayap kiri* the left
wing. ~ *siluman* the whisperers.
~ *ultra.kanan* ultra-rightist group.

golput (s.) GOLONGAN (PUTIH).

gombal rag(ged clothing). *bagaikan -
mereka bergulung di bawah jembatan*
they huddled under the bridge like
sacks of potatoes.

gombenis and **gombunis** commie
(derisively).

gombrong too big (clothing).

gombyok bunch. *se- kunci* a bunch of
keys.

gompèl damaged. *pisau cukurnya sdh -*
his razor was damaged.

goncang -.*goncing* 1 to fluctuate. 2 fluctuation. - *otak* brain concussion.

goncèng peng- person who sits on the
(rear) carrier of a bicycle or motorbike.

gondas.gandes sexy.

gondok 1 angry, furious. 2 annoyed.
rasa - feeling of discontent. *menimbulkan rasa -* to bring about a feeling of
discontent. - *nadi* aneurism.

gondol meng-: ~ *gelar* to acquire a
degree. ~ *medali* to win a medal.

gondorukem a gum resin used for soldering (L. Pinus merkusil).

gondrong long and bushy (of hair).
rambut - acak.acakan sebatas pundak
shoulder-length, long and ill-kept
hair. *si Empat G-* The Beatles.
meng-kan *rambutnya* to make o's
hair grow long and bushy. **per-an** long-
hairedness.

gong I nge-(i) 1 (originally) to beat the
gong. 2 to say yes and amen to everything (in order to be through with it).

gong II -.-.-*!!* woof, woof, woof!!

gonggo spider. *sarang -* cobweb.

gongli [bagong lieur] 'dizzy pig,' i.e. a
teenage girl prostituting herself for
fun without receiving any money,
easy lay. **per-an** prostitution.

gongsèng I to dry-fry; (s.) KELAPA
(GONGSENG).

gongsèng II the string of bells tied
around the ankles of a *topeng* dancer.

gonio goniometry.

gonjang.ganjing to tremble.

gonjing in imminent danger of collapse.

gonjlang.ganjling (s.) GONJANG. GAN-
JING.

gono.gini husband and wife's joint
property acquired during marriage.

gontok to punch. -.-**an** 1 violence.
tanpa ~ without violence. 2 brawling.
3 to be at e.o.'s throat, come to
blows. *Jangan* ~! Don't get into e.o.'s
hair!

gopèk five hundred (rupiahs).

gordin *ruangannya* **ber-** the room had
drapes.

gorès meng-kan *geretan* to light a match.
ter-: ~ *di hati* unforgettable. *yg*
~ *dlm hatinya* what is in his mind.

gori unripened jackfruit (used in cooking).

gorila gorilla.

gorilya thief. - *kayu* lumber thief.

gorok peng-an slaughter.

gorong -.- culvert.

gosip gossip. **di-kan** to be gossiped
about.

gosok (**peng**)-**an** attrition.

go.to.hell **meng-kan** to send to hell.

gotong ber-.royong cooperative. **ke-.
royongan** mutual cooperation, collectivism.

gotuhèl (s.) GO.TO.HELL.

gotun five rupiahs.

goyang - *kaki* 1 to live an easy life.
2 to refrain from hard work. - *kepala
kita melihat...* we were surprised to
see... *tdk mudah - pendiriannya* to
be steadfast. **ber-:** ~ *iman* 1 to fall
promptly in love. 2 to revise o's views,
lose o's head morally. ~ *kaki* 1 to live
an easy life. 2 to refrain from hard
work. ~ *lidah* it whets o's appetite.
meng-kan *lidah* to lick o's lips.

grabadan a small farmer.

grabah ceramics.

graduil in degree, gradual.

grafika graphic arts.

grafikawan graphic artist.

gragas ng- 1 gluttonous. 2 acquisitive.

gragot(in) to pick at, gnaw, nibble,
munch.

graha (s.) GRHA. *G- Purna Yudha* Veteran's Building (in Jakarta).

grajèn sawdust, wood filings.

grambyang ng- to stray, wander (of thoughts).

Granadha [(Gedung) Graha Purna Yudha] (s.) GRHA (PURNA YUDHA).

granit granite.

grapak.grupuk hasty, hurried.

grapyak conversational.

grasi clemency.

gratak (little kids) cannot leave anything alone. **di-in** to be ramshackled, wrecked.

gratifikasi bonus (to personnel).

gratis gratis, free (of charge). *dia mau -* he wants it for nothing. **di-kan** *menginap di hotel perdeo* (euph.) to be imprisoned. **meng-kan** to give away for free. *film* **-an** a film shown free of charge.

G.R.Ay. [Gusti Raden Ayu] title for a married princess.

Grebeg Maulud (s.) GAREBEG.

grebek (s.) GEREBEKAN.

grècok to bother, trouble.

greget eager, disposed, inclined. **meng-kan** to infuriate (a person). **-an** 1 angry. 2 to become angry, fly into a passion, lose o's temper.

gréhon greyhound.

gremet di-i to be infiltrated. **ng-** to go very slowly.

grempel -an clod, lump, nugget (of gold), morsel.

grèndèl latch, bolt (of door, window).

grendeng meng- to grumble.

grengseng zest, spirit, enthusiasm. **ng-** *dgn usul.usulnya* enthusiastic with suggestions.

grènjèng (s.) KERTAS (GRENJENG).

grès *anyar -* brand new.

grèsèk.grèsèk used articles. *jago -* collector of used articles.

grha house. *G- Purna Yudha* Veterans Building (in Jakarta). *G- Wiyata Yudha* Army Command and General Staff College (in Bandung).

gringging -an to fall asleep (of arm or leg).

gringsing k.o. batik design, the so-called "flaming cloth."

gripfrut grapefruit.

griya (pron. griyo) house; (s.) GRHA. *G- Wartawan* 'Newsreporter Houses,' the name for the housing complex for newsreporters at Cipinang Muara, Jakarta.

grogi groggy.

grogot (s.) GEROGOT. **ng-i** to undermine (by gnawing).

grompol group, gathering. **meng-** to gather, form a crowd.

gronjong k.o. bamboo basket.

gropyok -an drive; (fig.) roundup.

grub (s.) GRUP.

grujug and **grujuk di-** to be poured (onto). *~ bom* to be bombarded. *~ roket* to be bombarded by rockets. **meng-(i)** to pour down on (of rain).

grumbul underbrush.

grundel meng-kan to grumble about. **ng-** to grumble (not daring to complain openly). **(peng)-an** grumbling, complaining.

grup (mostly in *PKI*-circles, an assembly of artists, etc.) group. **peng-an** grouping.

grupukan *hidup -* to be in a constant state of agitation.

grusa.grusu reckless, rash, hurried. *mengambil keputusan -* to jump to conclusions.

gruwung without a nose. *hidung -* a nose which has been eaten away by leprosy.

Gst [Gusti] (s.) GUSTI, e.g. *I Gst Putu Raka.*

GTM [Gerakan Tutup Mulut] Keep-Lips-Zippered Movement (of the *PKI*). **ber-** to refuse to speak.

G to G (maintain the English pron.) *secara -* from Government to Government.

Gub appellation for Gubernur. *Pak -* (in Jakarta) the appellation for Governor Ali Sadikin.

Gubernur -an Governor's residence.

gubis (S.) KUBIS.

gubris -an attention.

gubug and **gubuk** 1 (improvised) cottage, hovel. 2 (market) stall. 3 bungalow. *G- Penceng* Southern Cross.

guci *terbuka - rahasia (,wasiat)nya* his secret has been revealed. *- wasiat* (fig.) soil corrector (used in agriculture to improve soil conditions).

gudang godown. *- bawah lantai* cellar. *- laut (,eerste linie)* deep-sea godown (along the quays). *- pendingin(an)* cold storage. *- penyimpanan barang.barang* warehouse. *- senjata* armory, arsenal.

gudeg and **gudheg** soup consisting of young jack fruit, chicken and eggs cooked in *santan.*

gudèl 1 young of the *kerbau.* 2 calf.

gugah meng- *semangat* to encourage, stir up. **ter-** aroused.

gugat meng- to impeach, charge. **peng-** plaintiff. **ter-** defendant. *- balik* recompense.

guguk ng- uncontrolled, unrestrained. *nangis* ~ to cry uncontrolledly.

gugur killed in action. *menjadi -* to cease to operate (,have effect). **ber-an** to be pensioned off (plural). **ke-an** abortion. **peng-an** *kehamilan* induced abortion. *Lagu G- Bunga* 'Song of the Fallen Flowers (of the Nation),' i.e. a melody played every November 10 in honor of the fallen heroes. *- gunung* forced, compulsory, unpaid labor during exceptional events, disasters, etc., levee en masse. *- imannya* he was led astray (,away from the right course). *- salju* avalanche. *- sekolah* dropout (from school).

gugus -an: ~ *bintang* galaxy. *segenap* ~ *pulau Indonesia* the entire Indonesian archipelago. ~ *pulau.pulau* archipelago. *G- depan* a formation of the *Pramuka* Boy Scout Movement. *- sekoci* boat (,landing) wave. *- tugas* task force.

guha (S.) GUA.

Guiana Inggris British Guiana.

gula *- dlm mulut* an easy job. *ada - ada semut* bees flock to honey. *tablet* **ber-** sugar-coated tablet. *-.-* mistress. *- coklat* heroin mixed with 30% caffein. *- darah* bloodsugar. *- kelapa* brown coconut sugar. *- merah* brown sugar. *- pasir* (in Ujungpandang) code word for gunpowder, used for fishing purposes.

gulai *- ayam* chicken curry. *- babat* tripe with coconut milk. *- kambing* goat (,lamb) curry.

gulawentah (pron. gulowentah) (s.) GULOWENTAH. **peng-an** 1 care, attendance. 2 close supervision.

guling I per-an *th* turn of the year.

guling II peng- (in Sumatra and Malaysia) (scaly) anteater, pangolin.

gulma weeds.

gulowentah ng- to bring up, rear.

gulu neck (also of inanimate objects). *-menjing* Adam's apple.

guludan garden bed, ridge (of sugarcane field).

gulung meng- to stamp out, suppress, round up, render harmless, break up (a gang). ~ *lengan bajunya* to roll up o's sleeves and get down to work. ~ *tikar* to go bankrupt. *- transformator* (on signboards) transformer winding.

gumal ber- to meet up with. ~ *dgn kekurangan kertas* to encounter a paper shortage.

gumampang to take too light (,optimistic) a view of.

gumatok and **gumathok** fixed, invariable (giving assurance).

gumbaan (in Banjarmasin) farm implement.

gumelar -an revelation.

gumpal *awan gelap* **ber-**.- *datang dr timur* billowing dark clouds came from the east. **meng-** to congeal. *Gagasan ini* ~ *menjadi tekad,* This idea congealed to become determination. **peng-an** and **per-an** agglutination.

gumuk hillock, mound.

gumul ber- *(bersama)* and **meng-i** to fuck.

guna I *membalas -* to show o's gratitude. **ber-** 1 suitable, appropriate. 2 influential, beneficial. 3 to avail. **di-kan** to be put into action. **peng-an** *bahasa* (gramm.) production.

guna II meng-.-i to use black magic on
s.o.

guncang meng-.- *bahunya* shaking (with
laughter).

gundah - *gulana* apathetic.

gundal helper, associate, partner in crime.

gundar meng- to brush.

gundil and **gundhil** 1 hairless paddy.
2 (Jav. in) Arabic script without
vocalic marks; (s.) HURUF (ARAB
GUNDUL).

gundukan *se- manusia penganggur* a
bunch of unemployed human beings.

gundul peng-an *hutan* defoliation. - *pacul*
as bald as a coot (,billiard-ball).

gung liwang.liwung dense (of jungle).
Di Sumatera hutannya masih -, In
Sumatra the jungles are still dense.

guni jute gunny sack.

gunjing memper-kan to gossip maliciously
about. **-an** malicious gossip. *(men)jadi*
bahan ~ *orang* to be the talk of the
town.

gunolugu pragmatism.

Gunsèikanbu (during the Jap. occupation)
the office of the Military Administrator
of Java.

Gunsirèikan (during the Jap. occupation)
the 16th Army Headquarters.

guntai *secara* - (to own land) in absentee.

gunting meng- *dlm lipatan* to play unno-
ticed dishonest tricks on friends.
peng- *dlm lipatan* deceiver, cheat,
impostor (among o's own family or
friends). **peng-an** *dlm lipatan* deceit,
deception, imposture (among o's own
family or friends).

gunung *takkan lari - dikejar (hilang kabut*
tampaklah dia) and *tak lari - dikejar*
(biar lambat asal selamat) to make
haste slowly; haste makes waste.
pe-an (adj.) mountainous. *daerah* ~
a mountainous region. ~ *Alpen* the
Alps. ~ *Dafonsoro* the former Cyclops
Mountains in Irian Jaya. ~ *Pirenea*
Pyrenees. **-an** 1 (in the *wayang* play) a
symbolic triangle figure placed in the

middle of the screen. 2 the food-
mountain in the *Sekaten* ceremony.
G- Jati name of the Jakarta-Cirebon
fast train. *G- Srandil* Mount Srandil in
Cilacap (Central Java), considered to
be the center of the Island of Java.
G- Tidar Mount Tidar, south of Magelang (Central Java), considered to be
the nail that fastens the Island of Java
to the earth. -*.ganang* (many) mountains. -*.gemunung* mountain range.

gupermèntal governmental.

gurem 1 chicken flea. 2 insignificant.
partai - a small, ill-defined (political)
party,

guring *tempat* - (in Banjarmasin) hotel,
inn.

guru *(kalau)* - *kencing berdiri, murid*
kencing berlari pupils are apt to carry
the results of their teaching to
extremes. **ke-an** (adj.) teacher. *Institut*
K~ dan Ilmu Pendidikan Institute of
Teacher Training and Pedagogy.
ke- besaran professorship. **per-an**
educational institution. *P~ Tinggi*
1 Graduate School. 2 Academy.
P~ Tinggi Kedokteran School of
Medicine. - *agama* person who teaches
the Islamic religion in government
or private schools. *honorary - agama* a
guru agama paid by the government to
teach the Islamic religion to adults.
- *besar tamu* visiting professor.
- *(me)ngaji* person who teaches the
elementary principles of Islam in a
mosque, *musholla,* or village. - *sulih*
substitute (,intermittent) instructor.

gus (s.) BAGUS (title before names).

gusar *mengambil* - to take s.t. ill (,amiss),
resent.

gusel -.-an 1 to pet. 2 petting.

gusrek meng-.- *(alas meja)* to move
(o's hand) over (a table top) repeatedly.

Gusti (in Bali) name element placed
before personal names, such as, *Gusti*
Ngurah Rai, I Gusti Kompiang Raka.

gusur to drag away. *kena - haknya* had
their rights trampled on. *terkena* - to

be leveled (,torn down). **meng-** to
evict (squatters). **peng-an** 1 sweeping
away, wiping out. 2 evicting (squatters).
ter- 1 swept away, wiped out. 2 person
whose land has been confiscated.
gutuk worthwhile.
guyon 1 object of laughter; a laughing-

stock. 2 to kid around. *bahasa Indo* -
the amusing, joking Eurasian language
(a mixture of Dutch and Indonesian).
film - comedy. **-an** jokingly.
guyub friendly, helpful.
guyur to pour, water s.t. **meng-(kan)**
to pour water on.

H

haai high (on drugs); (s.) NGEHAI.
haas (pron. has) (S.) DAGING (HAS).
habat ber- half o's children are male and
half female.
Habiburrahman God, the Merciful,
Loving One.
Habil (the Biblical character) Abel.
habis 1 depleted. 2 (at beginning of
sentence) well, what can I say, then.
H- mesti bagaimana? Well, what do I
have to do then? *H- di Jakarta!* Well,
that's the way it is in Jakarta! *Tak - di
situ,* The matter didn't end there.
Uangnya - ke baju saja, He puts all
his money into clothes. *bahan* -
expendable equipment (such as,
filter paper, etc.). *- + a verb* after
…-ing. *H- makan, bagaimana kalau
kita nonton bioskop?* After eating,
how about us going to the movies?
- dr to have visited (,been to). *"Gue
dengar lu - dr Bali, Ridzal…"* "I
heard that you have been to Bali,
Ridzal…" *- diborong oleh* (the tickets
were all) bought up by (ticket scalpers).
- dipesan fully booked up (of hotel
accommodation). *Visanya dinyatakan
- masa waktunya,* Her visa was declared
expired. *- terjual* sold out. *tdk -
mengerti* cannot possibly understand
(, figure out). **ke-an:** *tak pernah* ~
inexhaustible. ~ *darah*
loss of blood (due to accident).
~ *ikhtiar* to be at o's wit's end. ~ *jawab*
to be at a loss for an answer. *kami
~ stok* we have run out of stock.
~ *tempat* sold out (seats). ~ *tenaga*

exhausted. **meng-kan** to spend (time).
*Hari.hari Minggu biasanya kami -kan
utk jalan.jalan di Balboa Park,* We
usually spent Sundays by taking a
walk in Balboa Park. ~ *waktu* to
spend time. *utk* ~ *waktu* in order to
kill time. *dgn se-.- kekuatan* with all
o's might. *usaha -.-an* all-out efforts.
- kalas exhausted.
hablur peng-an crystallization.
hacing! ah, choo!
hadap di-kan *pd satu di antara dua* to be
faced with a dilemma. **meng-** to appear
(in Court). **ter-** of. *Pengakuan* ~
Singapura, The recognition of Singapore. *di -an* in the presence of, before.
hadiah 1 bonus, premium. 2 award.
3 bribe. - *Nobel* Nobel prize. - *setia*
consolation prize.
hadir to appear, present o.s. *tak* - to be
absent. *memberikan keputusan tdk -*
to condemn (,sentence) by default.
Ia dihukum dgn tak -nya, He was
condemned in his absence.
hadirin and **hadlirin** *para* - the audience,
those who attend(ed).
hafal - *di luar kepala* to know by heart.
hai I hey there!
hai II high. **nge-** to become high (on
drugs).
haisom sea slug (,cucumber).
haiya interjection, expressing discontent:
Good Lord, gosh, gee.
haj Moslem pilgrimage to Mecca.
hajad [hari jadi] 1 anniversary of founding (a city). 2 birthday.
hajat I 1 the occasion for a celebration.

2 want, need. **ber-** to defecate. - *hidup* necessities of life. - *kecil* to urinate.

hajat II (s.) SEDEKAH.

haji the title for a man who has made the *haj*; this title is retained for life and precedes the name, e.g. *H(aji) Moh. Natsir. bln* - the 12th month of the Jav. (lunar) month. *kapal* - vessel used for the transportation of pilgrims to Mecca. **ber-** (S.) NAIK (HAJI). - *akbar* a full-fledged pilgrim; (opp.) - *kecil* a so-called 'tourist' pilgrim who makes the *haj* to Mecca off season and usually visits only certain places. - *laut* aspirant *haji* who uses a ship to make the required trip to Mecca. *H- Peking* the nickname given to Dr. Soebandrio, Prime Minister under President Soekarno, during the abortive communist coup. - *udara* aspirant *haji* who uses a plane to make the required trip to Mecca. - *umrah (,umroh)* (s.) HAJI (KECIL).

hajib concierge.

hajjah woman who has made the pilgrimage to Mecca.

hak *mempunyai - utk* to have a right to, be entitled to. *orang yg mendapat -* successor in title. *menjalankan - atas* to exercise rights over. - *al.yakin* absolute truth. - *azasi* fundamental rights. - *azasi manusia* human rights. - *berkumpul dan berapat* right of association and assembly. - *erpah (,erfpacht)* (col.) long lease right. - *erpah kecil* (col.) shorter lease right. - *gadai* (right of) lien. - *guna bangunan* building rights. - *guna usaha* long lease right. - *ikut menentukan* right of say. - *kebendaan* real property right. - *mendahulu* preferential right. - *mendarat* landing rights. - *mengadakan perobahan* right to move an amendment. - *mengajukan pertanyaan* right of interrogation. - *menjalankan regres* power of recourse. - *menuntut (ber)balik* power of recourse. - *opstal* (col.) building right.

- *pakai* usufruct. - *pendahuluan* priority, privilege. - *penentukan (,pertuanan)* right of disposition over. - *sewa* right to lease. - *suara* franchise. *-ulyakin* and *-.kul.yakin* absolute truth. - *usaha* right to use (land).

hakim arbitrator. *main - sendiri* to play God.

hal *dlm -* in case of. *dlm - ini* in this instance. *dlm - ini juga* here again. *dlm - itu* in that case. *dlm segala -* in every respect. *mengenai - itu* pertinent, to that effect. *mengenai - tersebut* (in letters) in reference to. **-nya**: *demikian ~ dgn* this was also the case with. *sebagaimana ~ dgn* as is the case with.

halal 1 lawful, legitimate. 2 permissible according to divine law, e.g. of food.

halal.bihalal asking forgiveness for mistakes and sins committed, to older people and superiors on *Lebaran* day. *pertemuan -* post-fasting informal get-together for the above purpose. **ber-** to pay o's compliments in order to ask forgiveness for mistakes and sins committed.

halang ber-an to be unable to come. *Jika Ketua Panitia ~ utk memimpin rapat, maka rapat dipimpin oleh seorang anggota*, When the Chairman of the Committee is unavoidably absent to lead the meeting, the meeting shall be led by a member. **peng-** obstructor. **peng-an** obstruction.

halkum Adam's apple.

hallo and **halloooo** hello! (in telephoning and as a greeting). *ya -* hello (on the telephone to s.o. who has been waiting on the line).

halma Chinese checkers.

halo (s.) HALLO.

halpbèk (in soccer) halfback. - *kanan (,kiri)* right (,left) halfback.

halte bus stop.

haluan ber-: *mereka yg ~ kanan* the rightist-oriented persons. *~ ke buritan* to be a henpecked husband. *~ maju* to

be progressive. ~ *melar* to have an
expansionist policy. *kaum* ~ *keras*
hardliners. **se-** in agreement.
halu.lasung (in Banjarmasin) farm
implement.
halus 1 a term used to describe the most
refined cultural traits in real life as
well as in characters in the *wayang*
play; all gestures, judgements, behavior
or temperaments which are refined,
smooth, gracious, pure, polite, noble,
subtle, civilized, sophisticated,
exquisite. 2 acute (of intellect). **ke-an**
subtilty. **meng-kan** *jalan* to grade a
road. - *makannya* working impercep-
tibly.
halusinasi hallucination.
ham I ham (meat).
HAM II [Hak.Hak Azasi Manusia]
Human Rights.
hama 1 the natural enemies of a crop.
2 plague. - *kelapa* squirrel. - *mentek*
rot in the roots of the rice plant
(according to folk belief eaten up by
setan.setan kerdil). - *sexava* disease of
the coconut tree.
Hamal *(Burjamal)* - Aries.
hamba - *penurut* slave. - *wet* the police.
hambat -an bottleneck. - *glotal* glottal
stop.
hamburger hamburger. *kedai* - hamburger
joint.
Hamengku Buwana and **Hamengku-
buwono** name of each Sultan of
Yogyakarta.
hamil ke-an pregnancy. **meng-i** to make
(a woman) pregnant. - *muda* pregnant
for less than six months. - *tua* pregnant
for more than six months.
hampa - *guna* useless, no good.
hampar meng- to spread out. **se-** a spread
out area of.
hampir -.- almost (expected to but
didn't). ~ *tdk* almost didn't (expected
not to but did).
hamud - *amino* amino acid.
hamzah the glottal stop.
hanacaraka the Jav. alphabet.
hancur - *hati* brokenhearted.

handai I associate.
handai II ber-.- to talk.
handal well-known.
handelmaatschappij trading company.
handil drainage canal, outlet.
hangat recent, topical, current. *sedang -
diperbincangkan* is much talked about.
masih - dlm benak kita is still fresh
(,present) in our minds. *Sekarang
sedang -.-nya orang membicarakan
(ttg) soal...,* Nowadays people are
busily discussing the matter of...
hangèk -.- *cirik ayam* (s.) ANGEK.
ANGEK (TAHI AYAM) and PANAS.
PANAS (TAHI AYAM).
hanggregetaké intolerable, unbearable.
Hankam [Pertahanan dan Keamanan]
Defense and Security.
Hanoman (s.) ANOMAN.
hansip [pertahanan sipil] 1 civil defense
corps. 2 member of the civil defense
corps. **ke-an** (adj.) civil defense.
hantam ber-.-an to come to blows.
di-.kromokan 1 perfunctory. 2 to be
over-generalized. **-an** *ombak* beating of
the waves, wash. - *kromo* to strike out
blindly. - *kromo!* attack! *main - kromo*
to take a strong line, take strong
action. **-.meng-** to come to blows with.
hantar peng- *makan* appetizer.
hantu 1 apparition. *takutkan - pelokkan
bangkai* and *takut di -, terpeluk ke
bangkai* from the frying pan into the
fire. 2 - + *a noun* to be a fiend for, be
addicted to. - *laut* sobriquet for the
navy amphibious tank.
hanyakrawarti hambaudenda to dominate
the world forcefully.
hanyut - *dibawa untung* to go where the
winds of fortune take o.
hapal *Inggris* -an memorized (phrases of)
English.
hapermot 1 rolled oats. 2 oatmeal
porridge.
hapus peng- *kaca* windshield wiper.
haqqul.yakin (s.) HAK(ULYAKIN).
harafiah (s.) HURUFIAH.
harakiri harakiri, suicide. **ber-** to commit
harakiri (,suicide).

haram peng-an prohibition, ban.
harap *berbesar* - to have high hopes.
dgn penuh **peng-an** hopefully. **-an**:
memberikan ~.~ besar promising.
itu memberi ~ baik that augers well.
memenuhi ~ to come up to expectations. *menyatakan (,menyampaikan)*
~ spy… to express the hope that…
harga *dgn - murah* at a low price. *dgn -*
Rp. 100,- at Rp. 100.00. *tdk* **ber-**
useless, worthless. *se- Rp. 300,-* at
Rp. 300.00. **-nya**… selling for…
- *ancer.ancer* suggested retail price.
- *bantingan* slashed prices, a bargain.
- *barang* commodity price. - *berdamai*
price to be arranged (,agreed upon).
- *bersaing* competitive price. - *di*
luaran the unofficial (,blackmarket)
price. - *diri* self-respect, self-esteem.
- *eceran* retail price. - *EZ* [*EZ* stands
for the Dutch: *Economische Zaken*
Department of Economic Affairs;
(pron) é-sèt] the official price. - *grosir*
wholesale (,trade) price. - *langit*
ceiling price. - *mati* 1 fixed price.
2 very lowest (rock-bottom) price.
- *miring* competitive price. - *pas*
fixed price. - *patokan* check price.
- *pembelian* cost price. - *pengangkutan*
freight rate. - *pokok* first cost. - *puncak*
ceiling price. - *setengah mati* bargaining
price. - *terendah* floor price. - *tertinggi*
ceiling price.
hari day (both the day of twenty-four
hours and the daylight hours alone).
pd - (yg se-) itu juga that very day.
pd tengah - at midday. *sampai pd - itu*
to date. *dlm satu dua - ini* o. of these
days, some day soon. *-.- belakangan ini*
these days. *saban -nya* day in and day
out. **ber-**: *~ jadi* to celebrate o's anniversary. *~ Minggu di…* to spend
Sunday in … *~ Natal* to celebrate
Christmas. **kese-an** 1 daily. *barang.*
barang keperluan hidup ~ the daily necessities of life. 2 daily life. *dipraktek-*
kan dlm ~ to put into effect in daily
life. **se-**: *dr ~ ke ~* day after day.
~ semalam around the clock. *~ sontok*

(S.) SEHARI (SUNTUK). **se-**.- 1 daily.
tugas ~nya his daily assignment.
2 colloquial. **sese-** every day, daily.
-an *pagi (,sore)* morning (,evening)
paper. *H- Aksara Internasional* and
H- Aksarawan Sedunia International
Literacy Day (September 8). *H- Armada*
Fleet Day (December 5). *H- Artileri*
Artillery Day (December 4). *H- Arwah*
All Souls' (Day). *H- Asadha* Asadha
Day; this day is celebrated every year
as the first day of the dissemination of
the teachings of Buddha. *H- Bayangkara*
(s.) HARI BHAYANGKARA. - *bayaran*
payday. *H- B(h)akti AURI* Devotion
Day of the Air Force (July 29).
H- Bank Bank Day (July 5). *H- Bea &*
Cukai Customs & Excise Day (Novem-
ber 1). *H- Berkabung Nasional* National
Mourning Day (October 1). *H- Berka-*
bung Nasional Korban 40.000 Jiwa
Sulawesi Selatan National Mourning
Day for the 40,000 Victims of the
Southern Celebes (December 11).
H- Bersyukur Thanksgiving Day.
H- Bhayangkara (s.) HARI
KEPOLISIAN. *H- Brimob* Mobile
Brigade Day (November 14). *H- Buku*
Book Day (May 21). *H- Dharma*
Samudera Ocean Duties Day (June
22). *H- Direktorat Jenderal Perguruan*
Tinggi Higher Education Directorate
General Day (April 14). *H- Film*
Nasional National Film Day (March
30). - *gajian* payday. *H- Ganefo* Games
of the New Emerging Forces Day
(November 25). *H- H D-* Day.
H- Industri (National) Industrial Day
(July 13). *H- Infanteri* Infantry
Day (December 15). - *jadi* 1 (lower
case) anniversary. 2 (upper case)
Christmas. *H- Kanak.Kanak Nasional*
National Children's Day (June 6).
H- Kanak.Kanak Sedunia International
Children's Day (June 1). *H- Kartini*
Kartini Day (April 21). *H- Kebangkitan*
Nasional National Awakening Day
(May 20). *H- Kejadian* Christmas.
H- Kejaksaan Public Prosecutors Day

(July 22). - *kelahiran* birthday. *H- (Kemenangan) Buruh* Labor (Victory) Day (May 1). *H- Kemerdekaan* Independence Day (August 17). *H- Kenaikan Isa Almaseh* Ascension Day (Christian). *H- Kepolisian* Police Day (July 1). *H- Kereta Api* Railway Day (September 28). - *kerja* weekday. *H- Kesehatan Nasional* National Health Day (November 12). *H- Keuangan* Finance Day (November 15). *H- Kewaspadaan Nasional* National Vigilance Day (September 30). - *kiamat* the great (,last) account *H- Lahirnya Pancasila* Anniversary of the *Pancasila*. - *libur bank* bank holiday. *H- Miraj Nabi Muhammad S.A.W.* Ascension Day (Moslem). *H- Nasional Bahari* National Seamen's Day (September 23). *H- Natal* Christmas. *Mengucapkan selamat H- Natal dan Tahun Baru*, Merry Christmas and a Happy New Year. *merayakan H- Natal* to celebrate Christmas. *H- Pahlawan* Heroes' Day (November 10). *H- Pattimura* Pattimura Day (May 15). *H- Payung (,Sayap ,Terjun)* Wing Day. *H- PBB* United Nations Day (October 24). *H- Pemasyarakatan* Penitentiary Day (April 27). *H- Pembasmian Malaria* Malaria Eradication Day. *H- Pemberantasan Buta Huruf Internasional* International Illiteracy Combat Day (September 6). *H- Pendidikan Nasional* National Education Day (May 2). *H- Penentuan* D-Day. *H- Penerbangan* Aviation Day (April 9). *H- Penggelaran* (Army) Inauguration Day, Commencement Day. *H- Perhotelan* Hotel Business Day (July 25). *H- Perhubungan Nasional* National Communications Day (the day is also known as: *H- Transport & Komunikasi Nasional*) (September 17). *H- (Peringatan) Kesaktian Pancasila* (Commemoration) Day of the Sanctification of the *Pancasila* (September 30-October 1). *H- Peringatan Pahlawan Nasional Raja Sisingamangaraja XII* Commemoration

Day of the National Hero Raja Sisingamangaraja XII (June 17). *H- Perkebunan* Plantation Day (January 31). *H- Postel* Post Office and Telecommunications Day (October 8). *H- Radio* Radio Day (September 11). *H- Raya Orang Kudus* All Saints' Day. *H- Robo* the last Wednesday in the month of *Syafar*. *H- Sandang Nasional* National Clothing Day (September 16). *H- Sarjana* Graduation Day. *H- Tani* Peasants Day (September 24). *H- Ulang Tahun AIRUD* Police Sea and Air Corps Anniversary Day (December 1). *H- Ulang Tahun Divisi Siliwangi* Siliwangi Division Anniversary (May 20). *H- Ulang Tahun Golkar* Golkar Anniversary Day (October 20). *H- Ulang Tahun IHRA (, Indonesian Hotels & Restaurants Association)* Hotel Day (February 9). *H- Ulang Tahun Kodam VIII/Brawijaya* Anniversary Day of *Kodam VIII/Brawijaya* (December 17). *H- Ulang Tahun Kodam XVII/Cenderawasih* Anniversary Day of *Kodam XVII/Cenderawasih* (May 17). *H- Ulang Tahun KOSTRAD* Army Strategic Command Anniversary Day (March 6). *H- Ulang Tahun Kota Jakarta* Jakarta City Anniversary Day (January 5). *H- Ulang Tahun Pertamina* Pertamina Anniversary Day (December 10). *H- Ulang Tahun Persatuan Isteri TNI-AD (Jalasenastri)* Armed Services-Navy Women's Association Anniversary Day (August 27). *H- Ulang Tahun PGRI* Republic of Indonesia Teachers Association Anniversary Day (November 26). *H- Ulang Tahun PEWARTA* Indonesian Radio and Television Reporters Association Anniversary Day (December 5). *H- Ulang Tahun POMAD* Army Military Police Anniversary Day (June 22). *H- Veteran Nasional* National Veterans Day (September 23). *H- Wartawan Afrika.Asia* Afro-Asian Journalists Day (April 21). *H- Wisuda Sarjana* Graduation Day (in university).

harim wife.

harimau (also, *rimau*) tiger. *terlepas dr mulut buaya masuk ke mulut* - between Scylla and Charybdis (the devil and the deep blue sea). *(sdh) masuk ke dlm mulut* - irretrievably lost. - *ditakuti sebab giginya* authoritative persons are feared for their powerful influence. - *mengaum takkan menangkap* barking dogs seldom bite. *anak* - *takkan jadi anak kambing* like father, like son. - *Jawa* the Java tiger (L. Panthera Tigris). - *kertas* paper tiger. - *loreng Sumatera* the striped royal tiger. - *sancang* the variety of tiger found in West Java (L. Felis Tigris). - *tutul* panther.

harlah [hari lahir] anniversary. **ber-** to celebrate an anniversary.

harmonika - *mulut* mouth harmonica.

harta *mengumpulkan* - *karun* treasure hunt.

hartawan millionaire. *para* - the rich.

harum 1 aromatic. - *manis* (often pron. arumanis) cotton candy. - *menghilangkan bau* legitimizing a questionable undertaking by implying direct association with another activity, person, or institution which is above reproach. 2 well-known. - *namanya* he is famous.

Harun (the Biblical character) Aaron.

harus 1 permitted by (Moslem) religion but not meritorious. 2 necessarily (resulting from s.t.). 3 to need, be obliged. *Saya* - *menilpon,* I need to make a phone call. *tdk* - do(es) not have to. *tdk* **di-kan** optional.

Hasan - *dan Hamzah* Hansel and Gretel.

hashis *daun* - hashish.

hasiat (S.) KHASIAT.

hasil proceeds. *tak membawa* - in vain, fruitlessly, without avail. **ber-:** *saudara akan* ~ you'll make it. *tdk* ~ can't make it. ~ + *a verb* to be able to. *Kini mereka* ~ *memperbaiki rumah. rumahnya,* Now they are able to renovate their homes. *Usaha mereka* ~ *digagalkan oleh Angkatan Darat*

Yaman, Their efforts could be thwarted by the Yemeni Army. **ber-.guna** useful. **keber-an** success. **peng-** producing. *sebuah negara Arab* ~ *minyak* an Arab oil-producing country. **peng-an** earnings. ~ *negara* national income. *Gaji dan* ~ *lain para anggota Direksi ditetapkan oleh Menteri,* The salary and other emoluments of the members of the Management shall be determined by the Minister. *orang.orang yg tinggi* ~*nya* those in the higher-income brackets. ~ *sekali banyak* mass production. -.- *air* marine products. - *alam* natural produce. - *bagi pemilihan* electoral quotient. - *kalori* caloric effect. - *kerja* 1 output. 2 working (,labor) efficiency. - *pendapatan karcis masuk* box-office (,gate) receipts. *H- Perdagangan Negara* State Trading Earnings. -.- *ternak* pastoral products.

hasrat - *belajar* eagerness to learn.

hastakarya handicrafts.

Hasyemit Hashemite.

hasyi hashish.

hati I mind, mood, disposition. - *saya tak ke situ* I'm not in the mood for it. - *sdh tak sedap lagi* 1 peevishly, crustily, testily. 2 uneasy. *bakar* - to make s.o. angry, mortify. *dpt* - to get o's wish (,will ,way). *dr* - *ke* - personal (talk, etc.). *lembut* - 1 soft-hearted, gentle, meek. 2 pliant, submissive. *makan* - to brood. *senang* - contented, satisfied. *senang* - *memandanginya* he has a pleasant personality, he is a pleasant-looking person. *dgn segala senang* - 1 with open arms, with the greatest pleasure. 2 I shall be delighted. *dgn sepenuh* - with full attention. *dgn setengah* - *saja* 1 reluctantly, unwillingly, grudgingly, with an ill will. 2 to like it halfway. *jauh di mata jauh di* - out of sight, out of mind. *jauh di mata dekat di* - absence makes the heart grow fonder. *membaca di dlm* - to read to o.s. *selalu dekat di* - keeping in touch. **ber-** to have the heart to. *tdk* ~ *(berjantung)* 1 insensi-

ble, hard, foolish. 2 shameless,
unashamed. *orang tua yg ~ muda* the
young at heart. **ber-.**- 1 to pay attention,
take care. 2 attentively, carefully.
3 accurate, exact. 4 (to listen to a
suspect) with ample reservation.
berse- unanimous, harmonious. *dgn*
memper-kan in consideration of.
per-an: *dgn penuh ~* with full attention. *utk ~* for the attention of. **pemer-**
(political) observer. **-nya:** *dlm ~*
(to say) to o.s. *kurang enak ~* resentful,
rancorous. *membaiki ~* to make it up
again with him. *timbul dlm ~ akan*
1 inclined, disposed to. 2 to take a
fancy to it. *dgn setulus.tulus ~* with
perfect singlemindedness. *sampai*
ke -.-nya to the core, throughout,
through and through, to the bottom
of o's heart. -.- (s.) BERHATI.HATI
di (,dlm) - kecil deep down in o's
heart of hearts. *- sanubarinya* his
inner nature (,self). *- terbuka* frank,
straightforward. *- terlonjak* to be
overjoyed. *- yg susah* a feeling of
depression.
hati II heart (in card games).
hawa I *sdh serasi dgn -* to be acclimatized.
ber- *dingin (,sejuk)* airconditioned.
hawa II *- harta* craving for wealth.
- nafsu passions, emotions, concupi-
scence, carnal lust.
hawa III *si H-* the woman. *Siti H-* Eve.
kaum H- the fair (,weaker) sex, women.
hawé **meng-.**- to wave.
hawermot (s.) HAPERMOT.
hayat *selama - dikandung badan* as long
as I live. **meng-i** to live to see,
experience. **peng-an** experiences.
hayo (S.) AYO.
hayoo (s.) HAYO. *Siapa - yg jadi suami*
saya dulu? Come on, who will be the
first to marry me?
hayu (s.) AYU. **meng-** *bagyo* to endorse.
H.C.S. [Hollands Chinese School]
Dutch-Chinese School, i.e. the Dutch
elementary school for Chinese which
covered the first seven grades.

hé hey (there)!
hébat *- nampaknya* looks grand. *Wah -*
lho! Great! Good for you!
héboh **ke-an** fuss, ado.
he'e(h) m-hm, uh-huh (informal 'yes').
heerendiensten (col.) corvée services.
hèiho non-Jap. conscriptee.
hèk 1 gate (usually made of iron).
2 fence.
hèktar hectare (= 2.471 acres).
hélat artifice.
hèlem (s.) HELM.
hélicak [helikopter becak] a motorized
becak, using a Lambretta scooter
motor; the passengers, who sit in front
of the driver, are in a closed dome-like
compartment. *super -* (s.) HELICAK,
but using a 125-cc Lawiel car engine.
hélikoptèr helicopter. *- yg diperlengkapi*
dgn meriam helicopter gunship.
hèlm helmet (of army man, motorcyclist,
etc.). *- penyelamat* crash helmet (used
by motorcyclist).
hèm *- kutungan* a short-sleeve shirt.
- strip a striped shirt. *- yg berlengan*
panjang a long-sleeve shirt.
hémar zebra.
hémat **peng-an** retrenchment, cut (in
wages), curtailment. *utk ~ tempat*
for the sake of saving space.
hembat di- carelessly.
hendak *(yg) tdk* **dike-i** undesirable. **ke-:**
atas ~ sendiri of o's own accord, on
o's own initiative. *~ alam* the ordinary
course of events. **menge-i** (S.) MENG-
HENDAKI. **seke-** *hatinya* arbitrary, to
o's heart's content.
hèndel **meng-** to handle.
hèngkang to run away, flee.
hening clear (of intentions). *- sunyi*
deathly still, a dead silence.
hènsel (S.) ENGSEL.
hentak **peng-** *botol* drunkard.
hentam **meng-kan** *kaki* to stamp o's
feet.
henti ber- to resign. *~!* avast! *(hendak) ~*
(dulu) to take a rest. **meng-kan** *penat*
to take a rest. **pember-an** dismissal,

removal from office. ~ *atas permintaan sendiri* dismissal at o's own request. ~ *bis yg beratap* bus shelter. ~ *dgn mendapat hak pensiun* dismissal with pension rights. ~ *seketika* immediate dismissal. ~ *sementara* suspension (of an employee). ~ *tdk dgn hormat* dishonorable discharge (military). **peng-an** cessation. ~ *permusuhan* armistice. **per-an** cessation. ~ *perjalanan sebelum mencapai tujuannya* stopover. *tak -.-nya* incessantly, unceasingly.

henyak ter- to be pressed hard.

hèr- a Dutch prefix meaning re-, in compounds, such as, *herorientasi, herregistrasi,* etc; (s.) UJIAN (HER).

héran surprised, astonished. - *kpd (,melihat ,memikirkan)* to be astonished at. *tdk - kalau (,bila)* no wonder that, it is not surprising that. **ter-.-** stupefied. - *bin ajaib* by a miracle, it was a miracle that, wonder of wonders, that is the limit, that beats everything.

hèrba weeds.

hèrder German shepherd dog.

hèrèng ter- slanted.

hèrmétis hermetic(ally).

héroik heroic.

héroin heroin.

hèrordening replanning.

hèrorièntasi reorientation.

hèrrégistrasi re-registration.

hèrscholing refresher training (,course).

hévéa a common variety of rubber tree.

héwan -.- *mammalia (,menyusui)* mammalia. - *qurban* sacrifice, sacrificial animal.

hias meng- to make-up, dress, garnish. **peng-** *etalase* window dresser. **per-an** *Natal* Christmas decorations.

hibur peng- 1 consoler, comforter. 2 entertainer. *utk* ~ *hati* 1 to console. 2 for relaxation.

hidang -an: ~ *kilat* fast food. *restoran* ~ *kilat* fast food restaurant. ~ *laut* sea food.

hidrat - *arang (,karbon)* carbohydrate.

hidrogén hydrogen.

hidrogéologiawan hydrogeologist.

hidrografi hydrography.

hidrolis hydraulic.

hidrologi hydrology.

hidung *H-nya tertarik oleh wangi sate yg dibakar,* The smell of barbecued *sate* tickled his nostrils. *potong - rusak muka* it's an ill bird that fouls its own nest; don't cut off your nose to spite your face. **ber-** *kapur (,putih)* 1 to seduce women. 2 to have o. love affair after another. - *belang* Don Juan, playboy. *sepasang merpati - belang* a couple of lovebirds. *di muka - mata* under a person's very nose. - *(mancung.) melengkung* an aquiline nose. - *pesek melebar* saddle nose. - *yg menjungkat* a turned-up nose, pug nose.

hidup - *sama -, mati sama mati* at o., in harmony, of o. mind, unanimous. *H- segan matipun tak mau,* 'Tired of living, but feared of dying.' *antara - dgn mati (,napas satu dua)* to hover between life and death, be at death's door. **ke-an** 1 sustenance. 2 mode of living. 3 coexistence. *bidang* ~ walk of life. ~ *berdampingan secara damai* peaceful coexistence. ~ *bermasyarakat* social life. ~ *keakademian* academic life. ~ *keluarga yg berantakan* broken homes. ~ *malam* night life. **peng-an** *malam (,spirituil)* night (,spiritual) life. **-nya** *dpt dihitung dgn zaman* his days are numbered. -.- alive. *ditangkap* ~ to be caught alive (a person). - *berdemokrasi* democratic life. - *bersama* (s.) SAMENLEVEN. - *dgn segala genap* to live the good life, live in clover. - *di bawah tangan orang* subordinate to others, dependent on others. - *morat.marit* to lead (,maintain) a precarious existence. - *rukun.damai* to live in harmony (,concord). - *terus* to continue to exist, endure, subsist, survive.

hijah to move.

hijau *baju -* (adj.) army. *berpakaian - to*

be an army man. **peng-an** 1 militarism.
2 militarization. 3 the green revolution.
4 reforestation. - *daun* chlorophyll.
- *gadung* light green. - *tanaman* chlorophyll.

hijrah 1 the hegira, Mohammad's flight
from Mecca to Medina, marking the
beginning of the Moslem calendar (in
about 622 A.D.). *th* - A.H., the
Moslem era which commenced in the
year 622 A.D. 2 the evacuation of
Indonesian Republican troops from
pockets in Dutch-occupied areas of
West Java to Republican-held territory
based on the Renville Agreement.
Tentara H- the regiment of the Siliwangi Division in West Java (under the
then Lieutenant-Colonel Sadikin)
which in 1947-48 evacuated to Solo
from pockets in West Java. 3 to move
(to another place). *perjalanan* - the
long march (1947-48) of the above
regiment. **-nya** *para sarjana* brain
drain.

hikayat chronicle in Malay (relating the
adventures of the national heroes of
the Malayan kingdoms or containing
chronicles of the relevant princely
houses).

hikmah and **hikmat** *dipimpin oleh -
kebijaksanaan* to be led by wise
guidance. *sbg* **di-** as if by magic.
- *(kebijaksanaan) musyawarah* (a
phrase in notarial instruments on
foundations, etc.) wisdom born of
consultation.

hikwan k.o. small pieces of food put in
soup.

hilang *tunggang* - *tak* - fortune favors the
bold. **ke-an:** ~ *kontrol* out of control.
~ *nyawanya* lost o's life. ~ *pedoman*
to be lost, not knowing what to do.
meng-kan: ~ *baunya* to deodorize.
~ *cape* to relax. ~ *lapar* to appease
o's hunger. ~ *nyawa* to kill, take
s.o.'s life. *utk* ~ *rasa sunyi* to dispel
loneliness. **peng-an** *bau* deodorizing.
- *ingatan* amnesia. - *keberanian* cowardly. - *kesabarannya* to lose patience.

- *kikis* entirely lost (,vanished ,disap-
peared ,faded away). - *lenyap tak
berbekas* and - *lenyap tak ketentuan
rimbanya lagi* vanished into thin air,
disappeared without (leaving) a trace.
- *muka* to lose o's prestige, lose
face. - *napas* apnea, breathlessness.
- *pikiran* to be at a loss of words.
- *suara* aphonic.

hilir *Kita mulai omong.omong ke - ke
mudik,* We began to chat about all
sorts of things. **berse-.semudik** *dgn* to
go through thick and thin with.
meng-.mudiki to go back and forth
over. **meng-.mudikkan** can make or
break. -.*mudik* to and fro, back and
forth. *tak tentu* -.*mudiknya* he cannot
make head or tail of it, he can make no
sense of it. *blm tentu* -.*mudiknya*
it's not yet sure how things will
develop (,turn out).

himbau *siamang* - howling-monkey,
howler. **meng-** to appeal. **-an** appeal.

himmah *tinggi* - full of ambition (,aspira-
tions).

hina 1 miserable, worthless. 2 despicable,
vile. **ke-an** abasement, humiliation.
peng-an abasement.

hinayana a Buddhist sect.

hindar **peng-an** abstention. *tak* **ter-kan**
unavoidable.

Hindu - *Dharma* (the new name for
agama Hindu Bali) Hindu-Bali religion.

hingkang (s.) HENGKANG.

hio joss stick.

hiperaktip hyperactive.

hipertènsi hypertension.

hipnotisir hypnotist.

hipnotisme hypnotism.

hipokrit hypocrite.

hipotésa hypothesis.

hippies hippies. **meng-kan** to transform
s.o. into a hippie.

hirarki hierarchy. *garis* - *yg bercabang
dua* dual command.

hiruk **ke-an** commotion.

hirup **peng-an** breathing.

H.I.S. [Hollands Inlandse School]
Dutch-Native School, i.e. the Dutch

elementary school for natives which
covered the first seven grades.

hisap meng- to inhale (cigarette). **peng-an**
1 extortion. 2 exploitation.

Hisbullah 'Legion of Allah,' i.e. the
former *Masyumi* youth given paramili-
tary training.

Hisbul Wathan 'Legion of the Fatherland,'
i.e. the name of the *Muhammadiah*
Boy Scout Movement.

hisit shark's fin.

histéri(a) hysteria.

histéris hysterical.

histologi histology.

hlstopatologi histopathology.

histori history.

historis historical.

hitam code word for various k.o. drugs.
- *arang* carbon black. - *di atas putih*
in black and white. - *jengat* pitch
black. - *manis* dark brown complexion
(used as a compliment).

hitung ber-: ~ *angka* calculations.
~ *mencongak* to perform mental
arithmetic. **berper-an** to be calculating.
sdh **di-** *pasti, kau bakal datang* we're
relying on you to come. **diper-kan**
to be compensated. **meng-** *surat suara*
to count the ballots. **peng-** counter.
per-an (bookkeeping) account.
~ *antar-bank* clearing. ~ *habis* final
settlement. ~ *harga pokok* cost
accounting. **ter-** *mulai* commencing
on. **-an:** *masuk* ~ to count for s.t.
tdk masuk ~ to receive no consideration. ~ *menurun* countdown. - *dagang*
commercial (,business) arithmetic.

hiu (speaking of an important corruptor
caught by the police, etc.) a big fish.

hiyang god.

hiyu (S.) HIU.

Hizbullah (s.) HISBULLAH.

Hizbul Wathon (s.) HISBUL WATHAN.

hla (s.) LHA.

hm(m) (particle used when thinking s.t.
over) hm'm. *"Es kopyor…?" "Hmm…
boleh."* "Kopyor ice…?" "Hm'm…
O.K."

Hoakiau the overseas Chinese.

hobi hobby. **ber-** to have (as) a hobby.

hockey hockey. - *di atas es* ice hockey.

hofmèstèr steward (on board a ship).

hoki(e) and **hok.kie** luck. *Rupanya -
blm ada pd almarhum*, It seems that
the deceased had no luck yet.

hokok - *kpd* to report (in the Jap. way,
by bowing or saluting to a higherup).

holomini (in Irian Jaya) penis-sheath.

homogén homogeneous.

homosèks(uil) homosexual.

honai (in Irian Jaya) house.

Honda I brand name of a Jap. motorbike.
berh- to ride a Honda motorbike.
Perampok ~ *menyikat TV dan radio*,
A bandit on a Honda motorbike stole
a television and radio set. - *bako*
a Honda motorbike purchased from
the receipts of a tobacco harvest.
- *bebek* the 70-cc Honda motorbike
(resembling a duck).

Honda II [Honorer (,honorair) Pemda
(,Pemerintah Daerah)] an honorary
worker (,teacher ,etc.) hired by a
regional (,local) government.
mengh-kan to hire such a worker
(,teacher ,etc.) and pay him a regional
honorarium.

Hondawan Honda driver.

hondayung (jokingly) bicycle; the
term comes from *Honda I* and
dayung (to pedal).

honé (s.) HONAI.

honeymoon honeymoon. **ber-** to
honeymoon.

hong I culvert, sewer.

hong II (s.) BURUNG (HONG).

hongerloon starvation wages.

hongeroedeem (pron. hongerudém) and
hongerudim hunger oedema.

hongi a heavily armed fleet of proas at
the time of the Dutch East India
Company (1602-1800) used during a
project to destroy nutmeg trees
where they were growing in abundance
(to keep the market price of nutmegs
at a high level). *pelayaran* - an expedition with such a fleet.

hong kew husband to be.

hongsip rheumatism.

honor (s.) HONORARIUM.

honorair (s.) HONORER.

honorarium honorarium.

honorèr honorary.

honyok ter- *pd* slammed against.

hoop (pron. oo as o in hope) head overseer (in sugarcane field).

hoopèng, hooping and **hoping** friend.

horde horde, wandering tribe.

hordèng curtain.

horé hurrah.

horèg meng-kan to shake the foundations of.

hormat - *dan salam* (in letters) yours faithfully (,truly). - *dan salam dr* with the compliments of. - *(dan) takzim (,taklim)* (in letters) yours faithfully (,truly). *memberi - pd panji* to salute the flag. *merasa - to* feel honored. *orang yg ter-* persona grata.

hormon hormone. - *kelaki.lakian* androgen. - *kewanitaan* estrogen.

hortikultura horticulture.

hoskut housecoat.

hospital hospital. **di-kan** to be hospitalized.

hostèl hostel.

hostès 1 hostess. 2 (in Indonesian the word has a pejorative meaning) whore.

hosti host, wafer.

hot hot. *lagu.lagu* - hot songs. **di-kan** to be jazzed up.

hotèl meng-kan (euph.) to imprison. **per-an** hotel business. - *kelas kresek* flea-bag hotel. - *mercusuar* luxury hotel. - *prodeo* (euph.) prison.

hotèlir hotel keeper.

hot pants hot pants. **ber-** to wear hot pants.

H.R. honorarium.

Hua.Hué (s.) HWA HWEE.

huap 1 a bite. 2 mouthful. - *lingkup* an old custom in which newlyweds put a ball of rice in e.o.'s mouth.

hubaya -.-! warning! take heed! ~ *jangan* absolutely may not.

hubbu love. -*l watani minal imani* and -*l wathon minal iman* (a saying often quoted in newspapers) love of o's native land is part of the Faith, chauvinism is part of the Faith.

Hubmas [Hubungan Masyarakat] (s.) HUMAS.

hubung ber- 1 since, seeing that. ~ *terlibat dlm gerakan separatis di sana* since he was involved in a separatist movement there. 2 because of, due to. ~ *naiknya harga kertas dan ongkos cetak* because of the increase in the price of paper and printing costs. ~ *dgn* in consequence of, as a result of. in pursuance of, pursuant to, on the strength of, in connection with, in view of. ~ *dgn surat Tuan tertanggal 7 Juni* with reference to (or, referring to) your letter of June 7. **ber-an:** *Harap ~ dgn...* Please contact... ~ *rapat dgn* inherent to. **keter-an** connectedness. **meng-i** *pembicaraan kita kemarin* referring to our talk of yesterday. **per-an:** ~ *keluarga semenda* affinity. ~ *majikan.buruh* labor relations. *memegang ~ yg baik dgn* to be on good terms with. **se-an** *dgn* 1 with regard to. 2 owing to. **-an** contact. ~ *antar.kepulauan* interinsular communications. ~ *dagang* trade relations. ~ *famili* family relationship, kinship. ~ *gelap* illicit relations. ~ *kelamin* sexual relations. ~ *keluarga* family relations. *Setiap pegawai yg mempunyai ~ kerja tetap dgn peserta...,* Every employee in the permanent employment of the participant... ~ *masyarakat* public relations. ~ *seks di luar perkawinan* extra marital sex relations. ~ *singkat* short circuit (in electricity). ~ *timbal.balik* 1 correlation. 2 (fig.) two-way traffic. *dlm ~ kelompok* in groups. *lebih mempererat ~ dgn* to draw closer ties (,bonds) with. *tdk ada ~ persaudaraan antara kita* there are no ties of blood between us.

hujah(an) (malicious) slander.

hujan *kagak - kagak angin* out of the clear blue sky. - *emas di negeri orang, - batu di negeri sendiri, baik juga di negeri sendiri* east or west, home is best. *sedia payung sebelum -* prevention is better than cure. - *berbalik ke langit* and *terbalik - ke langit* the world upside down. *bagai - jatuh ke pasir* it is like pouring water into a sieve. - *sdh agak menipis* it has almost stopped raining. *ada - ada panas, ada hari boleh balas* there's always an opportunity to take revenge (or, to return a favor). *mereka* **ber-.berpanas** *hrs mengantar surat.surat* rain or shine, they have to deliver letters. **di-i** *pertanyaan* to be bombarded with questions. **di-.anginkan** weather-beaten. **peng-** rainy (season). - *angin* a heavy shower, storm with rain, torrential rains. - *belerang* rain of sulphur (from volcano). - *deras* and - *lebat* a heavy shower, torrential rains. *tiba.tiba turun - lebat sekali* all of a sudden it rained cats and dogs. - *peluru* a shower (,rain) of bullets.

hujjaj the plural form of *haji. Jamiyatul H- Indonesia* Indonesian Hajis Association.

hukum I *mewakili di dlm dan di luar -* (in notarial instruments) to represent in and out of Court, represent in legal and other proceedings. **-an:** ~ *dlm sel* solitary confinement. *dikenakan* ~ *kurungan* condemned (,sentenced) to imprisonment. *dpt di- dgn* ~ *penjara* liable to imprisonment. ~ *penjara seumur hidup* imprisonment for life, life (long) imprisonment. ~ *perjanjian* suspended sentence. ~ *tutupan* custody, detention. - *antar. golongan* interpersonal law. - *asasi* basic law. - *dagang* commercial law. - *fiskal* fiscal law. - *gereja Katolik* (Catholic) canon law. - *intergentil* interpersonal law. - *kanonik* (Catholic) canon law. - *kewarisan* law of inheritance. - *niaga* commercial law. - *perjanjian* law of contract

(,obligations). - *pernikahan* marriage (,matrimonial) law, law of marriage. - *pidana* criminal law. - *rimba* jungle law. - *sipil* civil law. - *syarak (,syariat)* (Moslem) canon law. - *tantra* military law. - *tatanegara* constitutional law.

hukum II *H- yg Sepuluh* The Ten Commandments.

hukum III - *besar* (in the Minahasa, North Celebes) district head. - *kedua* (ditto) subdistrict head. - *tua* (ditto) village head.

hukumiah legal.

hulu *ke- ke hilir* (s.) (KE) HILIR (KE MUDIK). **kepeng-an** (in Riau) village.

hulubalang **ke-an** leadership.

humaniora the humanities.

humanis humanist.

Humas [Hubungan Masyarakat] Public Relations. *seorang h-* a public relations man.

humor humor. *suka* **ber-.-** to have a sense of humor.

hungkué, hungkwé and **hunkwé** 1 *(tepung -)* flour made from mung beans. 2 gelatinous pudding made with the above flour.

huni *tdk* **berpeng-** uninhabited (of a house). **berpeng-kan** to be populated by. **di-.kontrak** (the house) was occupied and leased. **peng-:** ~ *gua* cavemen. ~ *hotel prodeo* (euph.) prisoner.

hup, hup (command of bus passenger to driver) hold on, don't start yet!

huruf - *Arab gundul* Arabic characters used in writing Indonesian but omitting the vowel points. - *ikat* monogram. - *panggilan* call letters (of a ship). - *togé* musical note.

hurufiah literal.

husarenslah Russian salad.

Husni Thamrin a street in Jakarta named after Mohammad Husni Thamrin, a well-known nationalist, native of Jakarta. *Memberi bantuan utk memperkeras jalan itu sekaligus* **meng-.kan** *lingkungannya,* To grant aid in order to harden the roads and at the same

time improve the shantytowns in the
surroundings; (s.) PROYEK (MHT).
husnudh.dhon good prejudice.
hust hush!
HUT I [Hari Ulang Tahun] 1 birthday.
ber.- and *merayakan -nya* to celebrate
o's birthday. 2 anniversary, commemoration.
Hut II Pisces.
huta a Tòba-Batak settlement, i.e. a
very small cluster of houses standing
like an island in the midst of a rice
field; many Toba-Batak names have
this *huta* as their initial element:
Hutabarat, Hutagalung, Hutapea,
Hutauruk, etc.
hutan meng- to turn to forest.
hutang ber-: ~ *kiri kanan* and
~ *selilit pinggang* to be heavily in
debt. *si* ~ the debtor.
huwayu beautiful (of women). - *manyala*
of rare beauty.
Hwa Hwéé a popular Chinese gambling
game based on combinations of
pictures and riddles.
hwamèi *(burung)* - spectacled laughing
thrush (L. Carrulax canorus).
Hwéé *Tionghoa Siang* - Chinese Trade
Association.

I

I I (retain the English pron.) I (personal
pronoun).
I II (in Bali) k.o. article to indicate a
male person, placed in front of the
proper name, e.g. *I Darta, I Gusti
Bagus.*
ia (and *dia*) it; the word no longer ex-
clusively refers to animate nouns.
*Amerika Serikat menyatakan, - tak
akan membiarkan keseimbangan
kekuatan di Timur Tengah berobah,*
The U.S. stated that it will not allow
the balance of power in the Middle
East to change. *Tokio agak tersinggung
bhw keputusan Nixon utk mengunjungi
Peking tak terlebih dahulu diperbincangkan dgn d-,* Tokyo is somewhat
offended that Nixon's decision to visit
Peking was not discussed earlier with
her.
ibadah *melakukan (,menjalankan)*
-.- *keagamaannya* to carry out o's
religious duties.
ibarat *dgn* - figuratively.
ibing ng- to dance with a *doger* without
touching her.
iblik k.o. dance peculiar to the Dieng
plateau area (Central Java).
ibni and **ibnu** 1 son of. *Umar ibnu
Hathab* Omar the son of Hathab.
2 the first element of many personal
names, such as, *Dr. Ibnu Sutowo.*
Ibrahim Abraham.
ibtidaiy(y)ah (s.) SEKOLAH [IBTIDAIY-
(Y)AH].
ibu 1 housewife. 2 maternal. 3 spouse.
Menpen H. Ali Budiardjo bersama -,
Information Minister Haji Ali Budiardjo
and spouse. **ber.-kota** to have as its
capital. *Republik Demokrasi Kongo
yg ~ Kinshasha,* The Democratic
Republic of the Congo with its capital
Kinshasha. **ber-negerikan** *Payakumbuh*
to have Payakumbuh as its capital
city. **meng-kotakan** *Samarinda* to
make Samarinda the capital city (of
the East Kalimantan Province). *I-
Agung* Supreme Mother, i.e. Fatmawati
Soekarno. *I- Dharma Pertiwi* the
poetic epithet for an Armed Forces
member's wife. - *gede* 1 grandmother.
2 parent's older sister. *I- Korps Taruna
Akmil* Mother of the Military Academy
Cadet Corps, i.e. Mrs. Tien Soeharto.
-.*kos* landlady. *I- Kota Kedua RI* the
town of Bogor. - *mentua (,mertua)*
mother-in-law. *I- Negara* First Lady.
I- Pertiwi 1 Mother Earth. 2 Mother-
land. - *rumah tangga* housewife. *I-
Utama* Eminent Mother, i.e. the mother

of the late Hero of the Revolution
General Ahmad Yani: Ibu Wongsoredja.

Id feast day. *-ul Adha, -uladha* and
-ulkorban feast of the pilgrimage
to Mecca (an animal is slaughtered,
usually a goat or lamb). *-ul Fit(h)ri*
and *-ulfitri* the so-called Jav. New
Year.

Ida (in Bali) - *Ayu* title of the female
members of the Brahmanic caste.
- *Bagus* title of the male members of
the Brahmanic caste. - *Sang Hiang
Widhi Wase* and - *Sangyang Widi
Wassa* The One God.

idam ng- 1 to crave for special k.o. food
(of a pregnant woman). 2 to become
pregnant, conceive.

idap meng- *obat bius* to contract the
drug habit. **peng-** *narkotik* drug
addict.

idéal ideal. **meng-kan** to idealize.

idéalis idealist.

idem ditto. - *dito* stronger than ditto.

idèntifisir meng- to identify.

idèntik identical. - *dgn* identical with.
ke-an identity. **meng-kan** to identify.

idèntitas identity.

ider.ider to walk about, roam.

Idhata the female workers and employees'
wives association of the Department
of Education and Culture.

idih (usually dragged out: idiiiih)
(coll.) wow!

idiil ideal.

idu spittle. - *abang* (s.) DUBANG.

Ied (s.) ID. *sembahyang* - mass prayer
in the open on *Idul Fitri.*

IGGI [Inter-Governmental Group on
Indonesia] an international aid coordinating body composed of Japan,
Australia and Western developed
countries.

ih bah!

ihdom property.

ihram devotional, sacred.

ihsan kindness.

ihtifal party, social gathering.

ijabat the granting of prayer.

ijab.kabul signing the marriage contract

and accepting the bride.

ijasah and **ijazah ber-:** ~ *Sarjana
Muda* to have a B.A. degree. *tak* ~
unlicensed.

ijin concession.

ijma consensus of opinion, (esp.) on a
religious point.

ijo (S.) HIJAU. *sistim* **-n** 'ijon system,'
i.e. the system by which a peasant
mortgages his crop before the harvest
for money. **meng-n** *mahasiswa* to
recruit college students before they
have completed their studies by
granting them a 1-year scholarship.
peng-n purchaser of paddy while it is
still green (,growing in the field).
- *royo.royo* fresh green, green as
grass.

ijon (s.) IJO.

ijtihad conclusion formed after careful
study of evidence, conviction so
formed.

ikal ber- curled (of hair).

ikan 1 any meat dish accompanying rice:
- *ayam* chicken meat. - *babi* pork.
- *sapi* beef. 2 a generic name for fish:
- *anso* anchovy. - *bawal* pomfret
(L. Stromateus sp.). - *benter* k.o.
carp. - *cakalang* skipjack. - *duyung*
dugong, a large, whalelike mammal
found in tropical seas, sea cow. - *glodok*
mud skipper (L. Periophtalmus Spp.).
- *hias* ornamental aquarium fish.
- *kacang.kacangan* barracuda. - *kalengan*
canned fish. - *karper* carp. - *mas*
golden freshwater carp. - *pari* ray,
thornback. - *suji* swordfish. - *tembakul*
mud skipper (L. Periophtalmus Spp.).
- *tombro* blue or green goldfish.
- *yu* shark.

ikat woven fabric found in parts of the
Lesser Sundas. **ber-an** *dinas* to have a
service contract. **keter-an** tie, bond.
meng-: *bantuan itu tdk* ~ there are no
strings attached to that aid. ~ *dinas* to
enter into a service contract. ~ *persahabatan* to strike up a friendship.
meng-kan: ~ *ke leher* to wrap around
the throat. ~ *diri* to commit o.s. (to

s.t.). **ter-** tangled (of wire, rope).
~ *oleh* to be addicted to. **-an** club,
organization. *tanpa* ~.~ without
strings. - *kepala* batik headcloth.
ikhlas wholehearted. **peng-** devotee.
ikhtisar 1 effort, attempt, exertion.
2 estimation, opinion. 3 resources,
means. 4 option.
ikhwal meng-kan to give an explanation.
ikhwan brothers.
ikhwani brotherly, fraternal.
ikhwanun *kullul.muslimin* - all Moslems
are brothers.
I.K.I.P. [(pron.) i-kip; Institut Keguruan
dan Ilmu Pendidikan] Institute of
Teacher Training and Pedagogy.
ikke I (personal pronoun).
iklan peng- advertiser. **peng-an** advertising.
- *berlampu neon* neon sign advertising.
iklim - *panas* tropical climate. - *politik
yg baik* a favorable political climate.
- *sedang* subtropical climate.
ikrab (gramm.) declension.
ikrar pledge, attestation. - *bersama*
collective vow.
ikut ber- including. ~ *makan dan cuci*
including board and laundry. **ber-nya**
the following (,next). *hari* ~ the next
day. *th.th* ~ the following years.
di-.sertakan to be referred to.
kedua instansi ~ the matter was
referred to both bodies. **ke-sertaan**
participation. **meng-i:** ~ *arah jalan
jarum jam* clockwise. ~ *jejak* to trace
s.o. ~ *konperensi* to take part in a
conference. ~ *kuliah* to attend lectures.
~ *perintah* to obey an order. **meng-.**
sertakan to make... participate, include. **peng-.serta** participant. **peng-.**
sertaan participation. **-.-an** to keep up
with the Joneses. - *angin* (fig.) to trim
o's sails according to the wind, set
o's sails to every wind. - *berdukacita*
to condole, convey condolences.
tdk - *campur* to stay out of the picture.
- *dlm* to participate in. *mereka yg* -
dlm percobaan kup Gestapu/PKI
those who participated in the
attempted coup of the *Gestapu/PKI*.

- *gembira* to share s.o.'s happiness.
- *latah* 1 to reflect, echo. 2 also.
- *numpang orang* to get a ride. - *rasa
binasa* to give way to o's passions is
destruction. - *serta dlm* to participate,
take part in, join (a game, etc.). *Adam
Malik pd th 1937* - *serta dlm memben-
tuk Kantor.berita "Antara,"* Adam
Malik participated in founding the
"Antara" Newsagency in 1937.
- *suami* (in biographies, passports,
etc.) housewife. - *tua* to grow up.
ilaha God.
ilahat Godhead.
ilahi 1 my God. 2 Oh God!
ilahiyah divinity.
ilalang *laksana batang* - *terhembus angin*
irresolute, wavering, hesitant.
ilang (S.) HILANG.
ilapat omen (in reality or in dream).
ilat tongue. - *ngingel* mouth-watering.
- *ujar* speech defect.
iler ng- to crave for; (subject's) mouth
waters.
ilmiahwan and **ilmiyawan** scientist.
ilmu ke- pastian mathematical. - *aero-
notika* aeronautics. - *agronomi*
agronomics. - *alam* natural science,
physics. - *alam inti* nuclear physics.
- *angka* numerology. - *arti kata.kata*
semantics. - *astronotika* astronautics.
- *atom* atomic theory. - *bahan*
knowledge of commodities. - *bahari*
navigation, seamanship. - *bahasa
terapan* applied linguistics. - *barang.
barang kuno* antiquarianism. - *batin*
1 esoteric learning, mysticism.
2 the art of hypnotizing. - *bedah
syaraf* neurosurgery. - *belanja* (a
university subject) corporation finance.
- *berat* theory of gravity. - *bercocok.
tanam* and - *bertanam* plant breeding,
cultivation of plants. -.- *budaya* (the
arts and) humanities. - *bumi alam*
physical geography. - *bumi perekono-
mian* economic geography. - *bumi
sosial.ekonomi* socio-economic geography. - *cendawan* mycology. - *dagang*
commercial science. - *dakwah* the

Islamic version of the doctrine of the gospel. - *diagnostik klinis* clinical diagnostics. - *eksakta* mathematics, the physical and technological sciences. - *falak* 1 astronomy (usually confined to the calculation of the first day of the lunar month, eclipses, etc.). 2 astrology. - *fisik atom* atomic physics. - *gaya* mechanics. - *gejala penyakit* semiotic, symptomatology. - *geodesi* geodesy. - *hisab (,hitung)* arithmetic. - *iklim* climatology. - *inti (,teras)* nuclear physics. - *istilah* terminology. - *Jawi* Jav. philosophical mysticism. - *jiwa analitis (,urai)* analytical psychology. - *jiwa perusahaan* industrial psychology. - *jiwa tingkah.laku* behaviorism. - *kampung halaman* local lore. - *karang.mengarang* the art of writing. - *kebatinan* mystical philosophy. - *kedokteran hukum (,kehakiman)* forensic medicine, medical jurisprudence. - *kejahatan* criminology. - *kenegaraan* political science. - *kesaktian* occultism. - *kesehatan masyarakat (,umum)* public health. - *kesejahteraan keluarga* home economics. - *ketatanegaraan* public administration. - *keturunan* genetics. - *kewarganegaraan (,kewargaan negara)* civics. - *kewartawanan* journalism. - *kewedukan* the art of making o.s. invulnerable. - *kewiraan* military science. - *kimia anorganik* inorganic chemistry. - *kimia fisik* physical chemistry. - *kimia organik* organic chemistry. - *logam (elektro)* (electro) metallurgy. -*l.yakin* conviction based on knowledge. - *manusia* anthropology. - *mengenal barang* knowledge of commodities. - *murni* pure science. - *negara* political science. - *nujum* astrology. - *optik* optics. *contohlah - padi, kian berisi kian tunduk* (a saying) remain modest. - *parasit* parasitology. - *patirasa* immunology. - *pemasyarakatan* penology. - *pemerintahan* public administration (the term is used in the Gadjah Mada State University). -.- *pengetahuan*

kemasyarakatan social sciences. -.- *pengetahuan terpakai* applied sciences. - *pengobatan radang usus dan perut* gastroenterology. - *penyakit gigi dan mulut* oralogy. - *penyakit kanak.kanak* pediatrics. - *penyakit tua* gerontology. - *penyangga gigi* periodontology. - *penyutradaraan* play-directing. - *peran* acting, i.e. the act of performing on the stage. - *perbintangan* 1 astronomy. 2 astrology. - *perkamusan* lexicography. - *perkebunan* horticulture. - *peroketan* rocketry. - *pertambangan* mining engineering. - *pesawat* mechanics. - *peta* cartography. - *petilasan* archaeology. - *pidato* rhetoric. - *psikiatri* (also, *psikiatri*) psychiatry. - *ramalan bintang* astrology. - *serangga* entomology. - *serologi* serology. - *sihir* 1 hypnosis. 2 shamanism. -.- *sosial* social sciences. - *susila* ethics. - *syirik* polytheism. - *tanah pertanian* agrogeology. - *tata lingkungan* ecology. - *tata personalia* personnel management. - *tatarias* cosmetology. - *teater* dramaturgy. - *teknik* technology. - *teknologi dirgantara* aerospace science and technology. - *terpakai* applied science. - *toksikologi* toxicology. - *tulisan rahasia* cryptography, cryptology. - *ukur analitika (,analitis)* analytic geometry. - *ukur melukis* descriptive geometry. - *ukur tanah* surveying. - *usaha negara* public administration (the term is used in the Gadjah Mada State University). - *watak* characterology.

ilmuwan scientist.
ilung water hyacinth.
ilusi illusion. **ber-** to harbor illusions.
imajinèr imaginary.
imalat joining two sounds in pron., coalescence.
imamal leadership.
imbal I askew, lop-sided.
imbal II -an honorarium, pay. *dlm* ~ *sebenarnya* actually. ~ *jasa* bribe. *utk* ~**nya** for compensation.

imbang match, equal. *- yg tdk sepadan* an unequal, stronger opponent. **ber-** *dgn* in line with. **ber-an** *dgn* commensurate with. **kese-an** balance. **mense-kan** to balance. **per-an** *kekuatan* balance of power. **se-** 1 proportionate, adequate. 2 equivalent. ~ *dgn* proportionate with, commensurate with. **-an** counterweight. *dlm* ~ *sebenarnya* actually.

imigran immigrant. *- gelap* illegal immigrant.

imigrasi ber- to immigrate. **ke-an** 1 immigration. 2 immigrational.

imigrasiwan immigration officer.

iming meng-.- to tempt, entice, seduce. **peng-**.- temptation -.-an lure. -.- temptation (to evil).

imkolis [imperialis-kolonialis] *pihak -* the imperialists and colonialists.

Imlèk ber- to celebrate Imlek (,Chinese New Year).

Impala *- Udin* (in Bandung) a horse-drawn cart.

impas balanced, leaving no balance of debt on either side, square, even *mencapai titik -* to reach a break-even point.

impèk impact.

impi di-kan to be dreamt, be dreamed. **meng-kan** to have a dream about. **ng-** to dream.

implemèntasi implementation. **meng-kan** to implement. **peng-an** implementation.

implikasi implication.

importir -.- *aktentas* 'briefcase importers,' i.e. Indonesians whose sole office was their briefcase and sole function the obtaining of import licenses and foreign-exchange permits while their Chinese silent partners continued to manage the real business; (s.) ALIBABA and BABA.ALI. -.- *Benteng* 'Bulwark importers,' i.e. a group of smaller local importers who have been encouraged by the Indonesian government to form a 'bulwark' against foreign competition and for whom the government has received

the right to deal in special categories of goods.

improvisasi improvision. **ber-** to improvise.

imtihan examination, proof, test, trial.

imun *- thd* to be immune to. *Siapa saja tdk - thd bahaya itu,* Nobody is immune to that danger.

imunologi immunology.

in absèntia in absence; although not present. *mengadili -* to put s.o. on trial in his absence.

inang.inang Batak businesswoman plying between Belawan and Tanjung Pinang and/or Singapore and Tanjung Priok using the M.V. "Tampomas" of the Djakarta Lloyd.

inap di-kan to be provided with a place of temporary residence. **meng-** to stay for a period of time in (,at). ~ *semalam* to spend the night. **peng-an** hostel.

inaugurasi inauguration.

inayat assistance, aid.

incang awry.

incar -an 1 focus of attention. 2 watchful eye. 3 target. *gadis ~nya* the girl he has in mind.

inceng di- *di* seen from the point of view of. **ng-** to take a peep at.

incer (s.) INCAR.

indah *- tak -* indifferent. **peng-an** appreciation.

Indamardi [Industri, Dagang, Maritim dan Pendidikan] Industry, Commerce, Maritime (Affairs) and Education. *Kota -* The Industrial, Commercial, Maritime and Educational City (of Surabaya).

indehoy, in de hoy, indehoj and **in de hooi** illicit sexual relations, make out (,love). **ber-** to have illicit sexual relations.

indekos(t) and **in de kos(t)** board (i.e. to receive meals, or room and meals, regularly for pay). *rumah -* boarding-house. *Rumahku* **di-i** *anak dua,* There are two children taking room and board at my house. **di-kan** to be put out to board, be boarded out. **-an** (adj.) boarding; (s.) KOS(T).

indèn order for goods and partial payment of a deposit on these goods.

indèntor person who orders on the basis of an indent order.

indépèndèn independent. *mahasiswa -* an independent (i.e. non-affiliated) college student.

indera peng-an *jauh* remote sensing. *- keenam* a sixth sense.

India *kelas -* low-class.

Indian American Indian. **meng.-kan** to Indianize, i.e. to provide Indonesians (particularly, Jakartans) with accomodation (in the Condet area in Jakarta).

indigo Jav. blue dye for *batik.*

indikasi indication. **ber-** to show indications of.

indisiplinèr *kelakuan -* conduct contrary to discipline.

indo ke-an Eurasianship, i.e. the quality, condition or state of being an Indo (,Eurasian).

indoktrinasi meng-kan to indoctrinate. **peng-an** indoctrination.

indolèn indolent. *bangsa yg -* an indolent nation.

indolènsi indolence.

Indonésia -nya: *Apakah ~?* What is it in Indonesian? *~ ialah...* in Indonesian it is... *- Raya* 1 Greater Indonesia. 2 name of the Indonesian national anthem.

indonésiawi (adj.) Indonesian. *maksud tdk -* a non-Indonesian purpose.

indraloka 1 fairyland. 2 heaven.

induk 1 central organization. 2 (adj.) master. **ber-** to be under (a parent organization). **per-an** unit in the *Pramuka* Boy Scout Movement. *- kalimat* head clause. *- kesatuan* (mil.) parent unit.

induksi induction.

indung *- mutiara* pearl oyster.

industri ber- industrial. **per-an** *rumah tangga* home industry. *- berat* heavy industry. *- metal* metal(lurgical) industry. *- pariwisata* tourist industry. *- pembikinan barang-barang jadi* manufacturing industry. *- ringan* light industry.

industrialis industrialist. *kaum - besar* captains of industry.

industriawan industrialist. *- minyak* oil tycoon.

infarkt (heart) infarct.

infiltran infiltrator.

influènsa influenza, flu.

info info(rmation). *mendapatkan - dr tangan pertama* to obtain first hand information. *akibat salah -* as a result of misinformation. **meng-kan** to inquire after.

informasi *mendapat -* to have been informed. *Mereka sdh mendapat - bhw...,* They had (already) been informed that...

informil ke-an informality.

infra infra.

infrastruktur infrastructure.

infus to be fed intravenously. *dia terpaksa di-* he had to be fed intravenously.

ing of, for.

ingat *- akan (,kpd)* to think of. *- akan dirinya* to regain consciousness. *antara - dgn tdk* to remember (,recall) vaguely. **memper-kan** to draw o's attention to. **meng-kan** to recall (to mind). *~ akan* to be reminiscent of. *R.* **ter-** *bhw...,* It occurred to R. that ... *-.***memper-kan** to warn e.o. *(saling) -.***meng-kan** to think of e.o. **-an:** *Segera kutarik ~ku ke sana,* I immediately directed my attention to that matter. *~nya hilang* he doesn't know what to say or do, at a loss for words. *sepanjang ~ saya* as far as I remember. *sedikit terlintas ~ itu di benakku* I remembered that vaguely.

inger ng-kan to change the direction (of s.t.). *Peking berhasil ~ arah pandom politik luar negeri RI ke arahnya,* Peking was successful in changing the direction of the needle of Indonesia's foreign policy in her direction.

inggih yes. *-.- ora kepanggih* to give empty promises. *tukang -* yes man.

Inggris ke.-.-an Anglicism. **peng-an**

Englishification, Anglicization.

ingin *sangat - sekali utk mengetahui*
eager to know. *tdk* **di-i** to be undesirable. **ke-an:** ~ *berbelanja* shopping
spree. ~ *tahu* and **ke-tahuan** curiosity.
meng-kan to desire, long for. -.-**an** and
- *tahu* anxious, inquisitive.

Ingkang The Honorable. *(Sampeyan*
Dalem) - Sinuhun His Highness.
- *Wicaksana* His Excellency.

ingkar - *drpd janjinya* to break o's promise.
- *kpd* to set against, be opposed to,
be hostile to.

ingku (from: & Co.) joint venture;
(cp.) ENGKO.

ingsut ber- 1 to move. 2 to shift. *tak* ~
mundur satu milipun not yield even
an inch of ground. **meng-kan** *pinggul-*
nya to move over.

ingus *membuang* - to blow o's nose. -**an**
wet behind the ears, young and naive.
Penjudi yg masih ~ *pasti kalah,*
Gamblers who are still green must
lose. *anak (,bocah)* ~ whipper-snapper.

ini *bln - dan itu* this month and the
other.

inisiatif and **inisiatip** initiative. *atas -*
on the initiative of. *atas - sendiri* on
o's own initiative. **peng-** initiator.

inisiator initiator.

injak meng-: ~ *bumi Amerika* to set foot
on American soil. ~ *ke tingkat* ... to be
in the ...grade. -**an** *hidup* livelihood.

injèksi a shot (given by a physician).

inkaso collection. *bank* - collecting
banker.

inklaring Customs clearance.

inklusip inclusive.

inkonstitusionil unconstitutional.

inlander native, now used in a denigrating
way for Indonesian; (cp.) MELAYU.

Inmas [Intensifikasi Masal Swa Sembada
Bahan Makanan] Mass Intensification
for Self-Sufficiency in Food, i.e. an
agricultural development program
operated in conjunction with *BIMAS.*

inna lillahi wa inna ilaihi rajiun (,rojiun)
dust thou art and unto dust shalt
thou return.

inokulasi inoculation.

inovasi innovation.

inplinsa influenza.

INPRES [Instruksi Presiden] Presidential
Instruction. **mengI-kan** to subject...
to a Presidential Instruction.

inrèyen running in (time of car), road-
testing (of a repaired car).

insaf 1 strong belief. 2 consciousness,
notion. 3 cognizant, mindful. - *akan*
to be aware of, realize. **ke-an** awareness.
- **se-.-nya** to be firmly convinced.

insam root of a certain herb used medi-
cinally by the Chinese, Koreans,
etc., ginseng.

insèktisida insecticides.

inséminasi insemination.

insèntip incentive.

insinuasi insinuation, innuendo.

insinye badge.

insinyur (abbrev. *Ir.*) engineering degree
in Indonesian universities, comparable
to M.Sc. in... Engineering. - *ilmu alam*
physical engineer. - *kepala* chief engineer. - *pertambangan* mining engineer.
- *pertanian* agricultural engineer.

inspèksi *I- Gajah* 'Jumbo Inspection,' i.e.
the everyday name for the Income Tax
Inspection Office located at Jalan Budi
Utomo in Jakarta. *I- Keuangan* Finance
Inspection.

inspèktur *I- Jenderal Polisi* Police Inspec-
tor General. *I- Polisi (Tingkat) I*
Police Inspector First Class. *I- Upacara*
Master of Ceremonies.

inspirasi ter-kan to be inspired.

instalasi - *pemanas pusat* central heating
installation. - *penjernihan air* water
purification installation.

instalatur installer.

insting instinct.

institut institute. *I- Teknologi* Institute
of Technology.

instruksi meng-kan to instruct.
- *pengapalan* shipping instruction.

instruktur instructor.

instrumèntal instrumental.

instrumèntalia instrumental (gamelan)
music.

instrumèntasi instrumentation.

insubordinasi insubordination.

Insulinde the Indonesian archipelago.

insulin(e) insulin.

intai peng-an surveillance.

intan - *jambun* a bluish-colored diamond (found in southern Kalimantan).

integral 1 integral. *pembayaran* - payment in full. 2 integral calculus.

integrasi integration. **meng-kan** to integrate. **peng-an** consolidation. **ter-** integrated.

integrasionis integrationist.

integritas integrity.

intèl intelligence. *seorang* - 1 an (intelligence) agent. 2 a spy. **ber-** 1 to be an (intelligence) agent. 2 to be a spy.

intèléjènsia intelligentsia.

intelèk *kaum* - intellectuals, intelligentsia.

intelèktuil *kaum* - intellectuals, intelligentsia.

intèlijèn intelligence. - *yg berlaku* current intelligence.

intendans quartermaster. *Corps I-* Quartermaster Corps.

intènsifikasi intensification.

intènsip peng-an intensification.

intènsitèt intensity.

interaksi interaction.

interdépartemèntal interdepartmental.

intèren local (not national) examination.

interim interim.

intériur interior (decoration).

interlokal long-distance telephone call. **meng-** to make a long-distance telephone call.

internasional di.-kan to be upgraded to international standards (of swimming pool, etc.).

interogasi interrogation. *mengadakan* - to interrogate. **di-** to be interrogated.

interogatif interrogative. **ke-an** (adj.) interrogative.

interogator interrogator.

interpelator interpellator, questioner.

intervènsi intervention.

inti (adj.) nuclear. **ber-kan** to have s.t. as a nucleus. *neo-Barisan Soekarno yg* ~ *sisa.sisa G.30.S/PKI* the neo-

Soekarno Front the nucleus of which consists of remnants of the G.30.S/PKI. - *atom* atomic nucleus. -.*sari* digest. - *sel* (cell) nucleus.

intim *(utk lebih)* **meng-kan** *(pembicaraan)* to make (the conversation more) intimate.

intimidasi intimidation. **meng-** to intimidate.

intip ng-: ~ *studio* behind the scenes. *tukang* ~ peeping Tom.

intraunivèrsitèr student group organized on basis of school or subject, e.g. group of medical students.

intrik intrigue. **meng-** to intrigue, plot. *RRC sdh langsung mencoba* ~ *pihak tentara,* The PRC has directly tried to intrigue with the army.

intro introduction.

introduksi introduction. **meng-kan** to introduce.

introspèksi introspection. **ber-** to practice introspection.

intuitif intuitive.

invèntarisasi stock-taking. **meng-kan** to take inventory (,stock). **peng-an** inventory-(,stock-)taking.

invèntarisir meng- (s.) MENGINVEN-TARISASIKAN.

invèstasi ber- *ke* to invest in.

invèstor investor.

invoerpas (pron. oe as oe in shoe) entry for home use (i.e. a customs document).

IPA [Ilmu Pengetahuan Alam] (the) physics (department of a Senior High School).

ipar per-an relationship by marriage. -.**ber-** *satu sama lain* to be related by marriage. - *laki.laki* brother-in-law.

Ipéda and **IPEDA** [Iuran Pembangunan Daerah] Regional Development Revenues; a tax on land and income producing crops on land, collected in cooperation with the central government. The first 10% is taken by the province, an additional 10% is for collection expenses and the balance is allotted to *kabupatens.*

iprit I **ng-** to run (away).

iprit II *Mereka adalah korban* **ng-!** They have become the victims of their efforts to become rich overnight by surrendering their soul (,life) to all k.o. spirits and invisible creatures.

IPS [Ilmu Pengetahuan Sosial] (the) social sciences (department of a Senior High School).

ipuh poison from *tuba batang* tree roots.

iqra read!

iradat 1 will. 2 the will of God.

irah.irahan accessories to dance (hat, hair, etc.).

Iréda and IRÉDA [Iuran Rehabilitasi Daerah] Regional Rehabilitation Revenues, i.e. a property tax on commercial objects, such as commercial businesses, industries and markets as well as housing, agriculture and fish ponds. These revenues have developed from the former *Pajak Hasil Bumi* (Tax on Agricultural Produce) and are known in the regions by the term *Ipeda* and in Jakarta by the term *Ireda*.

Irian - *Barat* West Irian. - *Jaya* 'Victorious Irian,' i.e. the new name conferred upon *Irian Barat*.

iring dise-kan to be attended by, be accompanied by. **peng-** chaperon. **ter-** *salam utk* greetings also for. **-an** *musik* musical accompaniment. **-.-an** convoy. ~ *mobil* motorcade.

irit meng-kan to make cheaper.

Irja [Irian Jaya] (s.) IRIAN (JAYA).

irup (S.) HIRUP *se-* a sip.

isa I (S.) BISA.

Isa II Jesus.

isak.isak asthma.

isap **ng-** 1 to smoke. 2 to suck. 3 to inhale. ~ *morfin* to take morphine. **peng-** *ganja* pothead.

iseng -(.-) 1 to do s.t. out of sheer boredom. 2 to be bored. 3 to trouble, annoy, bother. *jangan -!* don't bother! *pria yg -* a man who fools around with girls and wants just to make love without any serious intentions (usually already married). *wanita -* prostitute.

sbg (,utk) - as a pastime.

isep (S.) ISAP.

isi table of contents. *memberi* - to conjure up powerful spirits in order to have them nestle in a *keris*. **ber-** pregnant. *sepucuk pistol* ~ *peluru* a loaded gun. *cangkir* ~ *teh* a cup of tea. ~ *kapur* calcareous. ~ *padat* heavy-set. ~ *zat arang* carboniferous. **di-** *suara* to be dubbed (in motion pictures). **-.meng-** supplementary, complementary. **peng-an** filling in (of forms). ~ *formulir* the completion (,filling in) of a form. ~ *suara* dubbing. **se-** *rumah(nya)* and everyone in the (,his) house. *Sampaikanlah salam saya kpd* **se-** *rumah*, Give my regards to the whole family. *surat* **-an** form.

isim 1 name; God's name (such as, *Yang Maha Kuasa*, etc.). 2 a Koran verse or text used as talisman.

Iskandar Alexander. - *Zulkarnain* Alexander the Great.

Iskandariah Alexandria.

islah to appoint s.o. to steer a middle course in a dispute between two persons.

Islam peng-an Islamization.

isobar isobar.

isolasi keter-an isolation. meng-kan to isolate.

isolasionisme isolationism.

isolir ter- isolated.

isolemèn isolation. *terlepas dr -nya* liberated from its isolation (an area, place, etc.).

isotop isotope.

Israèl Israel.

Israèli Israeli.

Israk - *dan Miraj* Mohammad's miraculous flight from Mecca to Jerusalem and his ascension to heaven.

issue issue. meng-kan to make an issue of s.t.

Istambul Constantinople.

istan 1 frivolous. 2 to take part in s.t.

Istana The Presidential Palace in Jakarta is actually composed of two separate buildings, back to back, separated by

a large garden: (a) The - *Merdeka*
('Freedom Palace') looks south onto
Jalan Merdeka Utara and Merdeka
Square and (b) the - *Negara* ('State
Palace') looks north onto Jalan Veteran,
formerly Jalan Segara. - *Bima Sakti*
name of President Soekarno's home
located on Jalan Batu Tulis, Bogor.
- *Mersela* [Istana Merdeka Selatan]
(s.) ISTANA (MERDEKA).

istaz Mr.

istazah Mrs. or M(is)s.

isteri ber- *dua* bigamy. **ber-kan** to take
s.o. to wife. **per-an** *tunggal* monogamy.
- *muda* the younger wife. - *tua* the
first (and usually older) wife.

istig(h)far ber- to ask pardon (from God).

istikharah *sembahyang (,shalat)* - and
ber- to pray for right guidance.

istikhlaf the appointment of a representative before the person concerned
dies.

istilah di-i to be named, be called by the
term. -.- *sopan* euphemisms.

istiméwa (of dishes of food) containing
more than the usual number or amount
of ingredients. **ter-** *utk hal ini* ad hoc.

istinja ablutions prescribed by Moslem
custom, consisting of the ceremonial
washing of buttocks after defecation.

istiqlal liberty, freedom, independence.

istirahat ber- to retire (from active
service). *balai* **per-an** vacation home.

istislam acceptance of the Moslem faith.

istiwa parallel.

Isyhadu bianna Muslimin (slogan used
during the 1977 general elections by
the Moslem groups) Testify that
we are Moslems.

is(y)u 1 issue. 2 rumor. **meng-kan** 1 to
make an issue of s.t. 2 to spread
rumors about.

itarad to critize, stand out against.

itaraf to recognize (a government, etc.).

item (S.) HITAM. - *legit* a darkbrown
complexion for a girl.

itibar 1 example, model. 2 contemplation,
consideration. 3 instruction, learning,
lesson.

itifak concord, agreement.

itik meng-.- *air liur* to make o's mouth
water.

itikad - *baik* good faith. - *jelek* ill-will.

ittifak (s.) ITIFAK.

itu - *saja* that's all. *Tdk - saja!* The
matter doesn't end there! -nya genitals,
the external sex organs. -.- *(juga)* and
- *ke* - *(juga)* (always) the same (person,
matter, etc.). *yg melakukan demon-
strasi orangnya* -.- *(juga)* those who
have demonstrated are always the same
persons. *orangnya - ke - juga yg muncul*
it's always the same person who
shows up. *Bukan soal bosan, tapi
kenapa hrs punya pacar -.- terus?* It
isn't a matter of being bored, but
why should o. keep on having the
same boy friend?

iudisasi the introduction of IUDs in
Family Planning.

iuran - *pensiun* contribution to the
pension fund.

iwadl compensation, indemnification.

iya yes (Stronger than *ya*. Indicates that
the speaker strongly agrees with the
previous statement or that the answer
is 'yes' in spite of the negative
assumption of the question. More
strongly confirming or disagreeing).
Isterinya adalah tipe **peng-**, His wife
is of an accomodating (,obliging)
nature. *yg* -.- sexual intercourse.

Iyayat u santi (s.) MANGUNI I.

izin concession. - *bertempat tinggal*
residence permit. - *bertolak ganda*
multiple exit permit. - *ekspor* export
license (,permit). - *kekaryaan penata
minuman* bartender license. - *keluar*
exit permit. - *masuk* entry permit,
admittance. - *masuk kembali* re-entry
permit. - *menetap* permit to stay,
resident's permit. - *meninggalkan
Indonesia* exit permit. - *penempatan*
occupancy permit (of house). - *utk
mendarat* disembarkation permit.
- *usaha* business license.

J

Jabal Tarik 'Tarik's Mountain,' i.e. Gibraltar.

jabang - *bayi* 1 placenta. 2 newborn baby.

jabar I **pen-an** curtailment.

jabar II **men-kan** to explain s.t.

jabat **di.pe- sementarakan** to be made a caretaker. **kepe-an** caretakership. **pe-** 1 officer. ~ *hubungan masyarakat* public relations officer. 2 acting. *P* ~ *Presiden* Acting President. ~ *negara* state official; based on the explanation to Article 11 of *Undang.Undang No. 8 Tahun 1974 tentang Pokok.Pokok Kepegawaian* state officials shall include: (a) the President and Vice-President, (b) Members of the People's Consultative Council *(MPR)* and Members of Parliament *(DPR)*, (c) Members of the Fiscal Control Board *(BPK)*, (d) the Chairman, Deputy Chairman, and Judges of the Supreme Court, (e) Members of the Supreme Advisory Council *(DPA)*, (f) Ministers, (g) Chiefs of Mission abroad with the status of Ambassador Extraordinary and Plenipotentiary, (h) Governors/Heads of Region, (i) Regents/Heads of Region, Mayors/Heads of Region, (j) Other officials set out in detail in a legislative regulation. ~ *sementara* caretaker. ~ *teras* key (,senior ,top) official. **-an** occupation, profession. ~ *guru besar* professorship. ~ *ketua* chairmanship. ~ .~ *lain yg tdk mungkin dirangkap* incompatibilities, i.e. positions that cannot be held at o. time by the same person. *pd waktu menerima* ~*nya* on his taking office, on taking up his duties. *karena* ~ officially, ex officio.

jablès sound of s.t. knocking against s.t. hard. **di-.-kan** to be knocked against.

jadah (s.) ZADAH.

jadam a black, bitter laxative from aloeswood.

Jadayat Capricorn.

jadi I will do, is all right. *seekor burung yg sdh* - a bird which has been trained (to talk, sing, etc.). *Mereka hanya mau terima* -, They only want to receive the results. *Potretnya - tdk?* Did the picture turn out well? *Cacar saya tdk* -, My vaccination didn't take. *tdk* - cancelled. *tdk bisa* - impossible. *tdk - soal* perfectly all right. *potlotpun* - a pencil will do too. *kerja apapun* - any kind of job will do. *ke mana sajapun* - no matter where to. *-lah!* all right! it's O.K.! *40 rupiah -lah* you can have it for 40 rupiahs. *-lah (dahulu)* enough (for today, etc.); (for the kampung) that may pass, it is pretty good. *- tak -(nya)* 1 anyway (you have to pay). 2 (it is still unknown) whether it will succeed or not, etc.... *-, tdkpun -* (if you...) it's O.K., (if you) don't (do it), it's also O.K. *sedikit* -, *banyak apatah lagi* a little bit is welcome, but a lot is of course better. **men-** 1 to assume the role of. *Siapa yg* ~ *Janaka?* Who played the part of Janaka? *kalau saya* ~ *saudara* If I were you. 2 as, so as to become. *dipilih* ~*presiden* to be elected president. ~ *kaya* to make money. *Penjudian di sana bukan main* **-nya**, Gambling is rampant there. ~ *tahu* to come to know, find out. *jangan sampai* **ter-** in order to prevent. *harimau* **-.-an** a ghost in the shape of a tiger. *- arang* carbonizing. *- sakit* to get sick.

Jadi II Capricorn.

jadwal **di-kan** to be scheduled. *- penerbangan* flight schedule. *- perjalanan* itinerary.

jaga 1 watchful, vigilant, careful, wary, attentive, cautious. 2 watch it! look out! **men-:** ~ *jangan sampai* to be careful not to, prevent. ~ *spy* to make sure that (,to). ~ *hati (,perasaan) orang* to consider o's feelings. ~ *langkahnya*

(,sikapnya ,kesopanan diri) to watch o's step. ~ *perkataan (,mulut)* to watch o's words. **pen-** caretaker. ~ *gawang* goalie. ~ *kamar* room attendant. *P~ Marine* Marine Guard. ~ *pantai* coast guard. ~ *(parkir) mobil* parking lot attendant. ~ *ruangan* (in the navy) quarters orderly. ~ *stand* stand attendant (in fancy fair, etc.). ~ *telepon* telephone operator.

jagad (S.) JAGAT. *politik* **-an** global policy.

jagapati bodyguard for VIP.

jagaraga bodyguard.

jago *si - merah* fire (personified), the red cock. **nge-** cocky. -.- *Betawi* Batavian (,Jakarta) folk-heroes, such as, Si Pitung, Si Djampang, Si Sabeni and others. - *debat* champion debater. - *kepruk* strong-arm man.

Jagorawi [Jakarta-Bogor-Ciawi] the highway connecting Jakarta, Bogor and Ciawi.

jagrak easel.

jagung I *setahun (,seumur)* - (fig.) three months. *Umurnya setahun -,* He is very young. *blm seumur -* not long ago, recently. - *beledug* popcorn. - *bose* crushed corn, eaten with coconut cream or milk. - *brondong* popcorn. - *cantel* a sorghum variety (L. Sorghum vulgare). - *pipilan* husked corn, with kernels stripped off. - *rote* (in Eastern Lesser Sundas) sorghum.

Jagung II [Jaksa Agung] Attorney General.

jagur *si J-* 'The clenched Fist,' i.e. the name of the sacred 'male' cannon once located at Kota Inten, now Sunda Kelapa, Jakarta, a place of pilgrimage for sterile women. The cannon's breechblock has the shape of a clenched fist with the thumb placed between the index and middle finger; in Indonesia this type of fist is symbolic of the male sexual organ. The cannon has now been removed to the Museum on Merdeka Barat in Jakarta.

jahanam **men-i** to curse.

jahat **ke-an** felony. ~ *anak.anak* juvenile delinquency. ~ *penipuan* fraud.

jahil evil-minded, malevolent. *tangan. tangan -* theft, thievery. **men-i** to steal.

jahiliah paganism.

jahit *tak ber-* unsewn. *mencari* **pen-** *dlm rumput* look for a needle in a haystack. **-an** (surgical) stitch, suture.

jailangkung (s.) JALANGKUNG.

jaja **men-kan** *diri* to prostitute o.s. **pen-:** *gadis* ~ salesgirl. ~ *koran* newspaper boy.

jajag (s.) JAJAK. *studi* **pen-an** *kemungkinan* feasibility study.

jajah I - *desa milang kori* 'to visit villages house by house,' i.e. to go from o. place to another, roam about the world. - *desa milang putri* to go from o. girl to another.

jajah II **pen-an** colonization. **-an** *kemahkotaan* crown colony (such as, Hongkong).

jajak **men-i** to ferret out, explore. ~ *kemungkinan.kemungkinan* to explore the possibilities. **pen-** *perdamaian* peacefeeler. **pen-an** exploration.

jajal -.- to try, make an effort.

jajan to eat secretly from s.t. which has been forbidden, in particular, of married men who like to play around with other women.

jajar I **ber-** *sepuluh* ten abreast. **di-kan** to be put on the same level (as), be compared favorably (with). *Sebuah hotel yg kamarnya dpt ~ dgn kamar hotel. hotel kelas setaraf,* A hotel with rooms that can be compared favorably with the rooms of equivalent hotels. **kese-an** parallel. **se-** *dgn* abreast of. *termasuk di antara* **-an** *nama.nama* ... ranking with ...

jajar II - *pasar* a common person (having nothing special over others).

jaka young man, youth. - *tingting* a 'pure' (,confirmed) bachelor. **per-** 1 young man. 2 bachelor.

Jakaria Zachariah.

Jakarta **dike-kan** to be sent to Jakarta. **men-kan** to make s.o. feel a true

citizen of Jakarta (or, at home in
Jakarta). - *Bebas* (coll.) Jakarta By-Pass.
- *Per* (coll.) Jakarta Fair.

jaksa District Attorney. **ke-an** office of
District Attorney. ~ *agung* office of
attorney general. ~ *tinggi* office of
high prosecutor. *J- Pembantu* (s.)
PEMBANTU (JAKSA). *J- Tentara*
Auditor in Court Martial, Judge-
Advocate. *J- Tinggi* High Prosecutor.

jakum and **jakun** Adam's apple.

jala.jala - *seret* dragnet, trawl. - *udara*
air system.

jalak k.o. starling which sits on the
back of the water buffalo to eat insects.
(burung) - *suren* pied starling (L.
Sturnus contra jalla).

jalan alley. *tak dpt* - out of commission
(bus, tram, etc.). *sdh* - *5 bln* well
over 5 months. *Dia baru berumur 20
th, - th ini,* Just this year he will be 20
years old. *Umur saya - 50 th,* I'm not
yet 50, I'm going on 50. *Hanya 10
menit - kaki dr sini,* It's only a 10-
minute walk from here. *berada pd - yg
tepat* to be on the right track. *Banyak
- kalau hendak pergi ke langgar,* All
roads lead to Rome. **ber-**: ~ *kaki* afoot.
~ *ke sana ke sini* back and forth.
~ *lambat spt keong* to go at a snail's
pace. ~ *melonjak.lonjak* to walk
affectedly (,arrogantly). *orang yg*
~ *kaki* pedestrian. ~ *terus* to proceed.
kese-an convergence, convergency.
men-.buntukan to have (discussions)
result in a deadlock. **men-i**: ~ *hukuman*
to serve a sentence. ~ *liburan* to go on
a vacation. ~ *operasi kecil* to undergo
a minor operation. **men-kan**: ~ *agama*
to fulfill (,perform) o's religious
(,church) duties. ~ *hak.hak atas* to
exercise rights over. ~ *jabatannya* to
take up o's duties. ~ *mobil* to start a
car. ~ *paksa thd* to bring pressure to
bear on. ~ *pimpinan thd* to direct,
control. **per-an**: *(selama) dlm* ~ and
di tengah ~ en route. ~ *balik (,kembali
,pulang)* homeward journey. ~ *bln
madu* honeymoon. ~ *jemaah haji*

pilgrimage. ~ *keliling* circle tour.
~ *olang.alik* commuter service. ~ *perdana* maiden voyage. ~ *pulang.pergi*
roundtrip. **se-** analog(ue). - *angin* air
passage. - *bebas hambatan* and - *tanpa
hambatan* freeway. - *belantan* corduroy
road. - *bentuk melingkar* ring road.
-.- *berlubang* potholed roads. - *cagak
tiga* three-forked road. - *cukai* toll
road. - *dlm* short cut. -.- *jerawatan*
potholed roads. - *Ho Chi Minh* Ho Chi
Minh trail. *dgn* - *kaki* afoot, on foot.
- *keluar* way out. - *kereta api kabel*
aerial railway, telpher line. -.*layang*
overpass. - *lingkar (lalu.lintas)* 1 circuit.
2 ring road. - *lingkar.luar* outer ring
road. - *lingkungan* secondary road.
- *lintas cabang* feeder line. - *lintas
layang* overpass. - *masuk* access. - *mati*
cul-de-sac. - *melereng* a sloping road.
- *melingkar* ring road. - *memotong*
short cut. - *menurun* a descent, way
down. - *naik* ascent. - *nengnong* (in
Medan) grade crossing. - *pelayaran*
maritime route. - *penerbangan* air line.
- *penghubung* feeder road. -.*pintas*
1 short cut. 2 by-pass. - *potong* short
cut. -.- *protokol* the streets in Jakarta
usually traveled by foreign dignitaries
beginning from Medan Merdeka Barat
in front of the *Istana Merdeka* as far
as Halim International Airport (these
streets receive special maintenance out
of respect for these dignitaries).
- *pungutan* toll road. - *raya berjalur
empat* a four-lane highway. *J- Raya
Lintas Sumatera* Trans-Sumatran
Highway. - *sepeda* bicycle path (,track).
- *serong* cunning ways. - *simpang* side
street. - *simpang empat* intersection,
crossroads (of four streets). - *simpang
tiga* T-intersection, three-corner.
- *tembus* 1 through street. 2 (fig.)
breakthrough. - *temu.gelang* beltway.
- *tengah* 1 middle course. 2 (fig.) compromise, mean. - *tol* toll road. - *yg
lengkung* roundabout way, detour.

jalang *perempuan* - whore. -.*Kedah* (in
Medan) gold digger.

jalangkung puppet derived from Chinese culture used to conjure up the spirits of the dead, k.o. ouiji board.

jalari [jantan luar negeri] (in the Asahan Regency, North Sumatra) a foreign-raised rooster.

Jalaséna Naraya Naval Award for Merit.

Jalasénastri name of the Navy Women's Association.

Jalésu Bhumyanca (,Bumyam Ca) Jaya Mahé (slogan in the Marines' standard) Even on the Seas and on Land are we Victorious and Great.

Jalèsvéva Jayamahé (motto of the Navy stated in its coat of arms) It is on the Seas that we are Glorious.

jali I plant with pea-like fruits (L. Coix agrestis Lour.). *bubur -.-* porridge made of *jali*-fruits (a very popular dish in Jakarta).

jali II -.- a popular Jakarta melody played on the *gambang kromong.*

jalin ke-an tying together. **men-***keakraban dgn* to take up with (a girl). -.**men-** *dgn* to be interwoven with.

jalla illustrious (of God).

jalma human being, man. - *budaya* a civilized (,cultured) man.

jalur I 1 trail. 2 belt. **ber-** *empat* four-lane (highway). - *bowling* bowling alley. - *cepat (,kendaraan)* roadway, gutter. - *hijau* green belt. - *Ho Chi Minh* Ho Chi Minh trail (in Vietnam). - *kiri* left lane. *menggunakan - kiri* to keep left. - *lambat (,jalan kaki)* sidewalk. - *pemisah* median (i.e. a strip of land between opposing lanes of a highway). - *pendaratan* runway. - *terbang* 1 runway. 2 airline, air-route.

jalur II (in Taluk Kuantan, Riau) a very long and slender racing proa.

jam time. *J- gini kok masih kerja!* Still working at this time (of day)? *taksi itu hrs dibayar -.-an* the taxicab has to be paid by the hour. -.- *berangkat/ pulang kerja* rush hours. - *bicara* consultation hours (of doctor). *J- D* H-Hour. - *kantor* office hours. - *karet* 'rubber time' (not being on time for

appointments, events starting late, etc.). - *kukuk* cuckoo clock. -.- *puncak* peak hours. - *wesminster* grandfather clock. -.- *yg ramai (,sibuk)* rush hours.

Jama Aries.

jamah di- *aspal* to be paved with an asphalt layer.

jaman *akhir* - the end of time. *nabi akhir* - the prophet of the end of time, i.e. Mohammad. **men-** to be out of date. - *atom* atomic age. - *bahari* time immemorial. - *batu.madya* mesolithic era. - *batu.muda* neolithic era. - *Buda* the pre-Moslem era in Jav. history. *J- Edan* The Age of Madness (in which we are living now), modern times. - *normal* the Dutch col. period. - *paleolitikum* paleolithic era.

jamang diadem.

jambak -.**men-** to pull e.o.'s hair, fight.

jambal k.o. sheathfish.

jambé areca nut.

jambon *berwarna* - carmine, crimson.

jambrèt *kena* - to be swiped, be lifted. **pen-** snatcher.

jambrong *Chevrolet J-* the 1946-Chevrolet truck.

jambu jambu (fruit) (L. Eugenia; many varieties). - *air* 1 mountain apple. 2 rosy, pink. - *bol* Malay rose apple. - *kelutuk* guava. - *mente* cashew.

jambul crest. **ber-** crested.

Jamer [Jawa Merauke] a descendant of Javanese people living in Merauke (Irian Jaya); (cp.) JATON.

jamhur - *dunia* world figure.

jami *mesjid* - principal mosque (used for collective prayers on Fridays).

jamin -**an:** *Dia dibebaskan dgn uang* ~, He was released on bail. ~ *(wesel)* guarantee, guaranty, backing. ~ *benda* collateral security. ~ *sosial* social security.

jamiyatul and **jamiyyatul** association, club, union.

jamu I di- to be entertained (with), be treated (to). *Di sana kami* ~ *dgn makanan ala Jawa dan Padang,* There

we were entertained with food prepared
in the Jav. and Padang way. -an:
~ *koktil* cocktail party. ~ *makan
malam kenegaraan* State banquet.
~ *makan perdana* gala dinner. ~ *santap
malam* a formal dinner (in the evening).
~ *teh* tea party.

jamu II all-purpose herbal preparation
which apparently cures most ailments
known to man. *pedagang - gendong*
woman streetvendor who sells *jamu*
in a basket carried on her back in a
sash. - *kuat* 1 tonic. 2 aphrodisiac.
- *lempuyang* a traditional internal
medicine prepared from a ginger
species, used by women to have a
rich lactation (when feeding a baby).
- *(galian) singset* reducer, reducing
remedy. - *temulawak* tonic prepared
from a certain k.o. curcuma (L.
Curcuma xanthorrhiza).

jamur men- to mushroom, appear suddenly in large numbers. - *kuping* thin
ear-shaped tree-bark fungus used for
sayurs. - *laut* anemone. - *merang*
straw-mushroom.

janda men- to live as a divorcee. - *bengsrat*
childless widow. - *kandel* a rich widow.

jangan -*pun* not even, let alone. *Kita
tdk takut apa.apa! J-pun gonggongan
anjing!* We don't shrink from anything!
Let alone the barking of dogs! - *harap*
to have no chance at all, forget about
it! not a hope!

Janggala name of an old Jav. kingdom in
East Java.

janggelan (sentenced) conditionally
(by judge).

janggo appellation for the marksman of
the Greater Jakarta Vth Military Area
Command.

janggolan (in the Banyumas area) a
certain percentage of the yield of
people's agricultural produce given to
a *lurah* as a compensation for services
rendered to the community.

janggrung (s.) LEDEK I.

janggut (S.) JENGGOT. *si J- Biru*
Bluebeard.

jangka - *pelunasan* repayment period.
- *waktu* term, period. *selama - waktu
30 th* for a 30-year term. - *waktu
pembayaran cicilan* amortization
period. - *waktu utk menghilangkan
ketegangan* cooling-off period. *utk -
waktu tdk terbatas* indefinitely.

jangkar *tali yg* **di-kan** an anchored rope.

jangkat a shallow, shoal.

jangkau *dr lereng bukit itu orang bisa*
men- *seluruh kota* from the mountain
slope you can overlook the entire
town. *biaya yg* **ter-** *oleh* expenses
within reach of. **se-an** *mata memandang*
as far as the eye can see. **-an** scope.
mempunyai ~ yg lebih jauh to have a
wider scope, be further reaching.
dlm ~ daya beli mereka within their
buying power.

jangkit ber- 1 to spread to, attack (the
adjacent buildings). 2 to break out
again. ~ *sakit influensa* flu is going
around.

jangkrik cricket. *Chevrolet J-* the 1942-
Chevrolet truck.

jangol nge- to prostitute.

janji ber- (,**men-**) *sama (,dgn) dirinya* to
resolve, determine, make up o's mind
(to...). *negara yg blm* **berper-an**
ekstradisi a country not yet having an
extradition agreement. **per-an:** ~ *carter*
charterparty. ~ *lebih.pihak* multilateral
agreement. ~ *lintas.batas* border-
crossing agreement. *P~ Non.Proliferasi
Senjata.Senjata Nuklir* Treaty on the
Non-Proliferation of Nuclear Weapons.
~ *sama.tengah* compromise. ~ *sewa
beli* hire purchase. ~ *sewa guna*
leasing. ~ *sewa.menyewa* contract of
hire, lease. ~ *tdk serang.menyerang*
nonaggression pact. - *jabatan* pledge
of office.

janma men-kan to anthropomorphize.

jantan *perasaan kejayaan* **ke-an** male
chauvinism. *sapi* **pe-** breeding bull.

jantuk curved. *jidatnya yg* - his curved
(,domed) forehead. **-an** to have a
curved (,domed) forehead.

jantung (corn) ear. *si - hati* the sweetheart,

darling. - *cangkokan (,pindahan)* a
transplanted heart. - *pisang* the white
flowers from inside the purple red
banana flower.

janturan in *wayang* performance: the
dalang's own words for historical
explanation, accompanied by soft
music.

janur green young coconut leaves,
frequently used for decorations
(,ceremonial ribbons). - *kuning*
ceremonial ribbons.

japin (S.) JOGET. **ber-** (S.) BERJOGET.

japit -**an** tongs (,pincers) for picking
through trash. - *dasi* tiepin.

jarak - *langit* as the crow flies. - *tembak*
range (of a gun).

jaran horse. *J- Goyang* 'Prancing Horse,'
i.e. a popular dance in Banyuwangi.
- *kepang* (S.) KUDA (KEPANG).

jarang *tdk* - *terjadi* it's no infrequent
occurrence. **men-kan** *kelahiran*
to extend the time between births,
practice birth control. **pen-an** *kelahiran*
birth control. -.- far apart, sparce.

jariah *amal* - good deeds.

jarig (pron. yarikh) a year old(er), today
(it's his, her) birthday; (s.) YARIG.

jaring *kena* - rounded up (by police).
ter- walked into a trap (set by security
officers). -**an**: ~ *kereta.api* railway
system, network of railways. *dlm* ~
otot intramuscular. *dlm* ~.~ *plastik*
in moth balls. ~ *spionase* espionage
network. ~ *telepon (otomatis)*
(automatic) telephone system. -.- *jalan*
a highway network. - *dorong* push net.
- *payang* seine net. - *perawi* long line
(in fishery). - *slerek* purse seine.

jaro (in Tanggerang) *R.W.-* chairperson.

jarotan old and tough.

jarum *menjalankan* - *(halus)nya* and
*melakukan (,memainkan ,memasukkan
,menusukkan)* - *halusnya ke dlm* 1 to
intrigue and cheat slyly. 2 to carry
through o's plans in a sly manner.
- *pedoman* compass needle. - *pentol* pin.

jas *setelan* - *berbuntut* a dress coat.

jasa - *sekretaris* secretarial service.

-.- *yg tak kelihatan* invisibles, i.e.
services, tourist travel or spending,
etc., not normally recorded in foreign-
trade statistics.

jasad -.- *renik* microbes, microorganism.

jasmani carnal, corporeal.

jaswadi condom.

jatah bribe.

jatilan and **jathilan** k.o. *kuda kepang*
performance peculiar to the Magelang
Regency (Central Java).

jatmika modest, unpretentious.

Jaton [Jawa Tondano] a descendant of
Javanese people living in Tondano
(Northern Celebes), usually of mixed
Jav. -Minahasan blood; (cp.) JAMER.

jatuh to crash (of aircraft). **ke-an** *hadiah
lotere* to hit the lottery. **men-kan**
pilihannya pd to settle (,fix ,decide)
on, choose, select. **pen-an** *talaq thd*
repudiation of (a wife). -**an**: ~ *debu
radio.aktif* radioactive fallout. ~ *udara*
air-drop. -**nya** its fit, cut (of clothing).
- *di atas tilam* to be kicked upstairs, be
removed from office but given a fat
sinecure as a consolation prize. - *di
pasir* and - *ke (padang) pasir* to find
no hearing, speak to deaf ears. - *di
(,ke) tangan seorang bukan warganegara
Indonesia asli* to get into the hands of
a non-native (born) Indonesian citizen.
- *hati melihat* and - *kasihan* to feel
sorry (for). - *ke atas* to have (a run of)
luck, be lucky. - *ke kasur* to be kicked
upstairs, be removed from office but
given a fat sinecure as a consolation
prize. - *ke laut* to splashdown (of
space craft). - *melarat (,meleset)*
to fall upon evil days. - *palit* (in notarial
instruments) to go (,fall) into bankruptcy. - *simpati* to feel sympathy for,
be in sympathy with (a person).
- *tempo(h)* to expire (a letter of credit,
agreement, etc.). - *tertangkup (,terte-
lungkup ,tertiarap)* fall(en) forward
(,on o's face ,headlong ,head first).

jatukrama marriage partner.

jauh *dr* -**(an)** from afar (,a distance).
tak - *beda dgn* not very different from.

- *di mata - di hati* long absent (or, seldom seen), soon forgotten. - *lainnya dr biasa* quite different from the ordinary. - *lebih baik dr* far better than. - *sebelum itu* long in advance, a long time ahead. - *terbesar* by far the biggest. *tdk* **ber-an** *dr* not far from. **ke-an** remoteness. *dr* ~ from afar. **men-kan** *diri* standoffish. **pen-an** *diri dr perbuatan.perbuatan agresi* refraining from acts of aggression. **se-**: ~ *yg saya ketahui* to my knowledge. ~ *masih ada...* as long as there is still... *sampai* ~ *mana* to what extent, as to how far. **se-**.- *mata memandang* as far as the eye can see. -.-: ~ *hari* (at an) early (hour). *dr* ~ *hari sebelumnya hari bayaran* already days before payday. *dr* ~ long in advance, a long time ahead. - *dekat* far and wide (,near).

Jawa *bahasa* - the Jav. language. *orang* - the Jav. - *Barat* (abbrev. *Jabar*) West Java. - *Tengah* (abbrev. *Jateng*) Central Java. - *Timur* (abbrev. *Jatim*) East Java.

jawab *bak kata* **ber-** *gayung bersambut* in the usual way (,manner).

Jawanisasi Javanization.

jawil **men-** 1 to touch slightly (to attract attention). 2 to bring to the attention of s.o.

jaya *Dia hidup -,* He prospers. - *bumi* ground superiority. -*jala* sea superiority. - *laga* combat victory. - *ntara* air superiority. - *raga* bodyguard. - *sara* arms superiority. - *yuda* war superiority.

jebol 1 broken, gone to pieces. 2 worn out (of chairs, etc.). **men-** to destroy. **pen-an** destruction, breaking through. **-an**: alumnus. ~ *sekolah* dropout. *Dia hanya* ~ *S.D. klas III,* He has only completed third grade.

jebor roof-tile factory.

jeda pause, interval. - *napas* breathing space. - *perang* armistice, truce.

jèdi **di-** to be indoctrinated.

jégal **men-** 1 to trip s.o. 2 to hamper. ~ *kelancaran...* to hamper the smooth

running of ... **-.men-** and **-.-an** to trip s.o. deliberately.

jeglek **nge-** to show up suddenly.

jeglèk click (a slight, sharp sound). *Aku suruh bawahanku* **men-kan** *kartuku sebelum jam delapan,* I instructed my subordinate to clock in my timecard before eight o'clock.

jeglong **-an** pothole.

jejak - *bumi* take-off (of aircraft). *melakukan - bumi* to take off (of aircraft).

jejaka - *bulukan* a confirmed bachelor.

jejal **ber-**.- 1 to crowd. 2 chock-a-block.

jejas 1 damage, injury, harm. 2 abrasion (of skin). 3 a slight collision.

jejel (S.) JEJAL. - *riyel* 1 crammed, packed. 2 to swarm (of people).

jèjèr *artileri tlh* **ber-** *wayang* (fig.) (our) artillery is (already) in combat readiness.

jejer major scenes of *wayang*-play.

jèkèt (S.) JAKET.

jelajah **pen-an** exploration.

jelalat restless. **se-** in a jiffy, in the twinkling of an eye. **-an**: *dgn mata* ~ with rolling, wandering eyes. *Tdk spt gadis sekarang, matanya* ~ *bila lihat laki.laki,* It is not like modern girls; when they see a man they cast wild glances at him.

jelamp(e)rang the flower of the wild gardenia. *hem motif* - shirt with such a motif. *kain* - a gaily colored sarong.

jelang **men-** 1 just (,shortly) before, on the eve of. 2 awaiting, looking forward to. ~ *akhir th 1961* late in 1961. ~ *th baru* New Year's Eve. *karena umurnya yg tlh* ~ *tua itu* owing to his advanced age. ~ *itu* before, formerly.

jelas *sdh* - no question about it. **-nya** i.e., that is to say. *hendak mengetahui* ~ (he) wants to know the ins and outs of it. ~ *begini* it is like this, it is this way.

jelata *si J-* the man of the masses.

jelèk **men-**.-**kan** to bad-mouth.

jeli (s.) MATA (JELI).

jelimet 1 fastidious, intricate. 2 sophisticated. **n-** fastidious.

jelita - *juita* beautiful.

jelma *ular* -**an** a ghost in the shape of a snake.

jelungan *bermain* - to play hide-and-seek.

jelutung a glutinous rubber-like substance obtained from spp. of Dyera (chiefly D. costulata) and Alstonia.

jemari toe. *hingga ujung.ujung* -*ku* to the tips of my toes.

jembatan ter-i bridged. - *air* aquaduct. - *daun semanggi* the cloverleaf bridge in Jakarta. - *jongkong* pontoon bridge. - *lengkung* arched bridge. - *lintas* interchange (place on a freeway where traffic can enter or depart). - *pelam-pung (,ponton)* pontoon bridge. - *penghubung dermaga* pier. - *penye-berangan* skywalk, pedestrian overpass. - *timbang* weighbridge.

jèmbèl ke-an poverty.

jembut pubic hair.

jempo (s.) JOMPO.

jempol *lulus* -**an** to graduate cum laude (from). - *kaki* toe.

jemput I se-: ~ *orang* a very few persons. ~ *saran* a tiny suggestion.

jemput II men- to greet, welcome. **pen**-person who meets s.o. -**an**: *Di Pracimantoro ada* ~ *mobil ke Wonogiri,* At Pracimantoro we were picked up by a car going to Wonogiri. *menunggu* ~ to wait for a pick up. *laki.laki* ~ a 'purchased man,' i.e. a man of good standing and o. (frequently) asked for in marriage.

jemu *sampai* men-kan *pikiran* over and over again, ad nauseam. *dgn tiada* -.-**nya** untiring. - *(drpd) hidup* world-weary.

jemur ber- *badan,* men- *dirinya* and **men**-*diri di bawah sinar matahari* to sunbathe.

jenak I moment.

jenak II -**an** name.

jenang ship's cook.

jenasah (S.) JENAZAH

jèndral I *jabatan.jabatan sipil* **di-kan** civilian posts have been occupied by (army) generals. - *bintang tiga (,empat)*

three (,four)-star general; (s.) BERBIN-TANG. *J- Polisi* Police General.

jèndral II general (pertaining to the whole). - *repetisi* general (,dress) rehearsal.

jenèwer 1 (Holland) gin. 2 (in the village of Bekonang, east of Solo) k.o. brandy extracted from fermented cassava (*,tapé*).

jeng (form of address to young girl) younger sister. *J-, hendak ke mana?* Where are you going?

jèngèk businesswoman plying between Ulee Lheue and Sabang; (cp.) INANG. INANG.

jènggèr young rooster.

jènggot *(Cina) kebakaran* - to cry bloody murder.

jengker stiff (of a dead body). **nge**- to sit proudly. *di tiang.tiang listriknya* ~ *lampu.lampu neon* neon lamps are sitting proudly on the electric lamp posts.

jengkerik (S.) JANGKERIK.

jèngki yankee; (s.) SERDADU (JENGKI). *celana* - blue jeans.

jèngkol *kacamata* - huge, mod sunglasses.

jenguk men- *orang mati* to pay a condolence call.

jeni genious.

jenis 1 species. 2 (gramm.) gender. **ber-**.-assorted. *dan lain.lain* se-nya and all that sort of thing.

jenjam (to sit) quietly.

jenjang 1 steps (of a ladder). *Gadis itu sdh pernah menaiki* - *mahligai rumah tangga,* The girl has been married before. 2 ranking. *pendidikan tak* **ber**-non-degree education. - *konstitusionil* constitutional hierarchy.

jèn.man (pron. jèn-mèn) a general's yes man.

jentat.jentit standing upright of squirrel's tail (during mating).

jèntelmèn gentleman.

jentera - *gigi* cog-wheel.

jepa k.o. nutritional food made from cassava.

jepit pincers (of a shrimp). **pen**- *kertas*

paperclip. **-an** clothespin. ~ *dasi* tiepin. ~ *mata ayam* grommet. - *uang* moneyclip.

jeprat.jeprèt to snap photos.

jeprèt men- to take a snapshot of. **-an** snapshot. *membikin* ~ to take pictures.

jeput *sehari* - (S.) SEJEPUT (HARI).

jer basuki mawa béya (pron. jer basuki mowo béyo) in order to find happiness (and well-being) you have to pay the price.

jera *tiada juga* **-nya** incorrigible.

jerangan cooking pot.

jerangkong skeleton (of human being).

jerawat(an) pimples, pustules, rash.

jerawut (s.) JRAWUT.

jèrigèn and **jèrikèn** jerrycan.

jermal k.o. offshore house built on a bamboo platform which has been placed on top of long and thick poles driven in the water.

Jerman *orang* - (in West Sumatra) any westerner.

jeruk citrus. - *Bali* pomelo. - *Garut* tangerine. - *gripfrut* grapefruit. - *keprok* tangerine. - *kingkit* (s.) KINGKIT. - *limau* smallest citrus. - *manalagi* similar to - *Bali*. - *manis* orange. - *nipis* (s.) NIPIS. - *pandan* similar to - *Bali*. - *pecel* lime. - *peras* tangelo. - *purut* dark green citrus (L. Citrus hystrise). - *Siam* (,*siyem*) tangerine. - *sinasapel* imported orange. - *sitrun* lemon.

jèsbèn jazzband.

jètisasi the introduction of jet aircraft.

jeungjing k.o. tree (L. Albizzia falcata).

ji two.

jibaku suicide attack. **ber-** to throw o.s. at the enemy (in the Jap. way).

jibun ber- a lot, lots, heaps (of money, etc.). *Cucu.cucunya sdh* ~ , He has a lot of grandchildren.

jicap twenty (rupiahs).

jicapgo twenty-five (rupiahs).

jigong tartar.

jihad the spread of Islam by force of arms. **ber-** 'striving for the Faith' (peacefully). *J- Akbar* Great War, i.e. the war against passions that fre-

quently is tempting mankind to deviate from the right track. - *fisabilillah* a struggle in God's cause.

jijik loathsome, detestable.

jika - *tdk* unless, if not.

jilat *Api* - *toko di Senen,* A fire has spread to stores in the Senen area. **men-** *air liurnya (,ludahnya)* to eat o's words.

jilatisme qualities characteristic of bootlicking.

jilid - *kawan* companion volume (of book).

jimpit **-an** pinch (of rice kernels collected o. by o., using the thumb and two fingers).

jin *tempat* - *buang anak* a haunted site.

jinak men-kan: ~ *api di sumur gas* to contain the fire in a gas well. ~ *bom* to defuse (,dismantle) a bomb. **pen-**: ~ *singa* lion tamer. *team (,tim)* ~ *bom* ordnance disposal team. **pen-an** (euph.) imprisonment.

jinem ke-an privacy.

jineman watchman in sugar cane plantation.

jingg(e)ring with high heels (of shoe). *gelas* - a long-stemmed glass. *sepatu* - high-heeled shoes.

jingkat walking on tiptoe. -.*langkah*. *lompat* hop, skip, and jump.

jingkrak ber- *kegirangan* to leap (,jump) for joy.

jinjit to stand on tiptoe. *sepatu* - high-heeled shoes.

jintan cumin seed. ground cumin.

jinten (s.) JINTAN.

jipang delicacy made from puffed rice and caramel or thick syrup.

jiplakan (s.) BUKU (JIPLAKAN).

jiran *negara* - neighboring state.

jirolu (s.) SIJI (LORO TELU).

ji.sam.su and **jisamsu** 'two-three-four,' i.e. a brandname of a *kretek* cigarette.

jisim -.*penangkis* antibody.

jitu definite, precise (answer). **ke-an** exactness.

jiwa *hutang* - *bayar* - an eye for an eye and a tooth for a tooth. - *tergantung*

pd seutas benang life hangs on a thread.
ber- 1 soulful. 2 active, existent. **pen-i**
inspirer. - *(dan) raga* body and soul
(,mind). - *gotong.royong* collectivism.
- *kecua* 1 coward. 2 worthless individual.
jiwani spiritual.
jiwasraya life insurance.
jiwit di- *dadi kulit, dicetot dadi otot*
constant dripping wears away a stone.
jlegur explosion.
jlèntrèh explanation, clarification.
　men-kan to explain lucidly, expound,
　to set forth, state, express in words.
　pen-an explanation, clarification.
jlomprong men-kan to trap.
jodoh intended (,meant) for s.o., i.e. the
　right o. (in love). **ber-** *dgn* to be married
　to. **per-an** *yg sumbang* mésalliance. **se-**
　to be well matched. **-an** (s.) SAMEN-
　LEVEN. **-nya** *tlh habis* to be divorced.
jog.jogan gratuities, handouts.
joglo (mountain) chalet, bungalow.
jogoboyo (s.) JAGABAYA.
jogotirto village irrigation officer
　(assistant to *lurah*).
jogrog nge- to appear suddenly. **-an**
　figure, silhouette.
Johan Budiman Till Eulenspiegel.
Johobu (during the Jap. occupation)
　Intelligence Agency.
jojing (s.) AJOJING.
joki jockey. **per-an** (adj.) jockeys'
Joko Kaha k.o. *adat* ceremony of the
　northern Moluccas.
joli se- *dgn* to be in cahoots with.
jolok men- *perhatian (,pikiran)* to
　sound s.o.
jomblang (s.) MAK (JOMBLANG).
jomplang nge- to lean back (in a chair).
　-an railroad crossing.
jompo (old-)aged and crippled.
jongga (in the Southern Celebes) a small
　deer.
jongko (roadside) stall (in market).
jongos (col.) (male) domestic servant.
jonjot flake, flock (of wool). - *salju*
　snowflake.
jon.towèl riffraff.
jor.joran competition.

jorong (in Sumatra) hamlet.
Jos (pron. yos) a naval cadet.
josua joss stick.
jrambah elevation (of floor).
jrawut shaggy. *rambutnya* - her hair
　was shaggy.
jrèng 1 strumming noise. *irama (musik)*
　-.- a certain rhythm characterizing a
　type of heavy rock music. 2 clinking
　of coins. *membayar* - to pay cash.
jual *orang yg* **ber-.beli** *uang* money-
　changer. **ber-an** *nasi* to sell (,deal in)
　rice. **di-:** ~ *murah* (in ads) bargain.
　dpt ~ marketable. **men-:** ~ *jamu*
　(fig.) to be a quack doctor. ~ *mentah.*
　mentah to bamboozle, cheat. ~ *muka*
　to show off. ~ *nama orang* to abuse o's
　name. ~ *suara* to be a professional
　vocalist. ~ *tegak.tegak* to bamboozle,
　cheat. **pen-:** ~ *bakmi dorongan* street-
　vendor using a pushcart to sell *bakmi.*
　~ *barang.barang kuno* antiquarian.
　~ *ganja* drug trafficker. ~ *kecap* (fig.)
　charlatan; (s.) KECAP. ~ *kepala*
　mercenary. **pen-an** *di muka* advance
　sale. **pen-.belian** trading. - *beli* to
　conduct (,carry on) trade, buy and
　sell. - *kawin* tie-in sale, 2-for-1 sale.
　- *koyo(k)* 1 to talk rubbish (,stuff and
　nonsense). 2 to tell lies. - *mahal*
　(speaking of girls) to play hard to get.
　- *muka* to show off. - *tampang* to put
　on airs.
juang per-an: ~ *golongan* class struggle.
　~ *mati.matian* fight to the death.
juara - *renang* swimming champion.
　- *samber jam tangan* professional
　pincher of wrist watches.
jubel (S.) JUBAL. - *kaya semut* to swarm
　like ants. *kereta.api* **di-i** *anak.anak*
　the train was packed with children.
judas and **judes** 1 sharp-tongued,
　malicious. 2 grouchy. 3 insulting.
judo judo. **pe-** judo player.
juga 1 even, likewise, further. 2 anyhow,
　anyway (after phrases with *biarpun,*
　meskipun, etc.). 3 very (after names of
　time periods). *pd hari itu* - that very
　day. *orang itu* - *yg...* it was the same

person who... *usul itu.itu* - it was always the same proposal. *tahu* - to know quite well. *Rupanya ibuku tahu - maksudku utk...*, It seems that my mother knows quite well my intention to... *tdk* - still not, not still. *Bila kedua surat itu ternyata tdk - dibalasnya...*, If it turns out that the two letters are still not answered by her...

juhi dried squid.

juita 1 charming. 2 highly esteemed, precious.

Juja Gemini.

jujat pen- backbiter.

jujur candid.

juk ukulele.

jukcong junior high school.

jukut - *laut* seaweed.

jula.jula (s.) ARISAN.

julig sly, cunning.

jumantara in the air. *angkutan* - air transportation.

Jum'at and **Jumat ber-** to attend mosque (on Friday). - *Agung* Good Friday (Protestant). - *Suci* Good Friday (Catholic).

jumbai bunch. *se- kunci* a bunch of keys.

jumbuh men-kan *dgn* to decide whether s.t. is similar to s.t. else.

jumeneng I -an entrance into office, inauguration (of prince).

jumeneng II acting (*bupati,* etc.).

jumlah ber- to the amount of. - *bulat (tanpa perincian)* lump sum. - *yg diasuransikan* the sum insured.

jumpa ber- *muka dgn* to meet personally. **ter-i** to be found. *J- Pers* Meet the Press.

jumpalitan 1 breakneck leap, somersault. 2 to fall down. *harga - ke bawah* prices have tumbled.

junggang -*(,jungkang ,jungkat) jungkit* to wobble, seesaw, bob up and down.

jungkal men-kan to turn over, turn upside down.

jungkat *hidung yg* **men-** a turned-up nose.

jungkir - *balik* to turn upside down. *Dua bis - balik,* Two buses turned upside down. **pen- balikan** overturning.

junjung men-*uban (di dlm kebesarannya)* seasoned.

juntrung orderliness, methodical. *tdk -* without method, disorderly set up. **-an** order, rule. *dgn tdk (tahu) ~nya* without any method, in a disorderly manner (,fashion).

juragan fisherman-employer (who has *pendegas* working for him and who provides seine nets).

jurai village head (in the Batang Hari River delta, Palembang).

jurang - *pemisah* gap.

juri member of a jury. **pen-an** serving on a jury, judging (a contest).

jurik bogey, spook.

juring -**an** slice (of cut off fruit).

jurit (in Kawi or Old Javanese) war, battle; the word is no longer used by itself, but usually in combination with the prefixes *pra-* or *per-*, to become *prajurit* or *perjurit* respectively.

jurnal logbook.

jurnalis - *plonco* a newcomer in the journalistic field.

juru ke- rawatan nursing. **men- bicarai** to be the spokesman for, reflect (the thoughts of). **mer- kamerai** to film. - *anggar* fencer. - *api* stoker, fireman. - *bayar* paymaster, cashier. - *cacar* vaccinator. - *gambar* draftsman. - *gudang* storekeeper. - *kampanye* campaigner. - *khitan* circumciser. - *kunci* cemetery caretaker. - *latih* trainer. - *layan (wanita)* steward(ess). - *lomba* racer. - *masak* professional cook. - *(tembak) meriam* artillerist, artilleryman, gunner. - *minyak* oiler. - *motor* motor driver. - *muat* loading clerk. - *parkir* parking lot attendant. - *peledak* blaster (in salvage). - *pemba-has* commentator. *J- Penerang Agung* Supreme Information Officer (i.e. o. of the titles given to President Soekarno). - *perbekalan* purveyor. - *periksa* interrogator. - *pijat* masseur. - *runding* negotiator. - *sita* confiscator. - *supit* circumciser. - *taksir* appraiser.

- *tera* gauger. - *terbang* airman. - *topografi* topographer. - *tunjuk* informant.
jurus I **-an** 1 track. *menuju ke ~ yg tepat* to be on the right track. *kereta.api ~ Bandung* the train for Bandung, the Bandung train. 2 a department of a *fakultas*. *~ kering* a department of

a *fakultas* attended by very few students.
jurus II certain stances in the national self-defense *pencak.silat* sport.
jus juice.
justa *mengarang cerita* - to fabricate a lie, make up a story.
juz o. of the 30 parts of the Koran.

K

KA [Kereta Api] train. **per.-.an** railway system.
Kaabah 1 Caaba, i.e. the cube-like building in the center of the mosque in Mecca. 2 the election symbol used by the Moslem-backed *Partai Persatuan Pembangunan* (abbrev. *PPP*) Development Unity Party, in the May 1977 general elections.
Kabag [Kepala Bagian] Section Head.
kabang.kabang spider's web, cobweb.
kabar account, notice. *tdk - tdk cerita* never utter a word. *tdk -kan dirinya* unconscious. **-nya** *blm terang* the ins-and-outs of the affair are not yet clear. - *burung (,tersiar)* 1 rumors. 2 gossip. - *cecek.bocek* scandal.
kabarèt cabaret.
kabaya (S.) KEBAYA.
kabé and **Ka.Bé** (from *KB: Keluarga Berencana)* family planning. **berk-** to practice birth control by using condoms.
kabèh all, everything.
kabel cable. - *tegangan tinggi* high-tension cable.
Kabil (the Biblical) Cain.
Kabilah the Kabyle (tribe).
kabin cabin. - *bertekanan* pressurized cabin.
kabinèt - *ahli* business cabinet. - *bayangan* shadow cabinet. - *demisioner* outgoing cabinet. - *karya (,kerja)* business cabinet. - *koalisi* coalition cabinet. - *nasional* national cabinet. - *parlementer* parliamentary cabinet. - *presidensiil (,kepresi-*

denan) presidential cabinet. - *yg disempurnakan* revamped cabinet.
kabir [kapitalis birokrat] bureaucratic capitalist, i.e. the term used by the *PKI* in attacking mil. officers managing state companies in early 1960's. **ke-an** capitalist bureaucracy.
kabisat (s.) TAHUN (KABISAT).
kablatur (s.) KARBURATOR.
kabriolèt cabriolet.
kabul - *akan* to consent to, grant (a request).
kabuli *nasi* - rice cooked with meat or fish, oil or butter, sweet stuff, etc.
kabung I the sugar palm [L. Arenga pinata (saccharifera)].
kabung II a white mourning head-band.
kabung III measure (for woven textiles) of 4 cubits.
kabung IV piece, portion.
kabur 1 foggy, filmy. 2 feeble, faint. 3 faded. *matanya sdh* - 1 he sees stars. 2 he is near-sighted (due to old age). *tulisannya* - his handwriting is illegible. *membawa* - *uang tunai* to abscond with the funds. **ke-an** 1 haze, fog. 2 blurring, dimming. - *pikiran* to be a bit weak in o's head.
kabus *hilang* -, *teduh hujan* after rain comes sunshine.
kabut faded, blurred. *hilang* -, *teduh hujan* after rain comes sunshine. **meng-i** to cover, shroud. - *basah* humid fog. - *malam* evening mist. - *minyak* oil spray.
kaca *stand -mata* (in soccer) the score 0

to O, draw. *mobil* **ber-** *gelap* a car with tinted-glass windshield. - *bakar* burning glass. - *bening [,tembus.pandang (,yg tembus.penglihatan) dr dua arah]* clear-glass windshield (of car). - *gelap [,tembus.pandang (,yg tembus.penglihatan) dr satu arah]* tinted-glass windshield (of car). *dr -mata* ... from the viewpoint of ... *-mata jepit* pince-nez. *-mata matahari* sunglasses. *-mata putih* (ordinary) glasses. *-mata yg berbingkai bulat lebar* mod glasses. - *mobil* windshield. - *rias* vanity, dressing table. - *spion* outside mirror (of car). - *teropong* periscope.

kacamatan (S.) KECAMATAN.

kacang I (esp. in Holland) a derogatory epithet for Indonesia-born Eurasians. - *mana buang lanjaran*, - *nggak buang lanjaran* and - *mongso ninggalo lanjaran* like father, like son. *panas hari, lupa* - *akan kulitnya* 1 the man who is rich now forgets his poor friends. 2 ungrateful. - *bendi* (in Malaysia) okra (L. Hibiscus esculentus L.). - *dodok* kidney beans. - *hijau* mung beans. - *kapri muda* snow peas. - *mede (,mente)* cashew nut. - *tojin* roasted peanuts with garlic. - *tunggak* small, round beans with black eye.

kacang II *ini baru* -.-**nya** this is just the beginning.

kacang III *ikan* -.- the barracuda.

kacapuri mausoleum.

kacau complicated, mixed up. *pikirannya* - he is worried. **ke-an** 1 agitation. 2 rebellion. **meng-.balaukan** to confuse, mess up.

kacèk 1 to differ. 2 different.

kacer *(burung)* - magpie robin (L. Copsychus saularis).

kaco (S.) KACAU **ng-** 1 out of order. 2 to gas, jaw. ~ *bélo* to talk nonsense. ~ *kerjanya* malfunctioning.

kacoa and **kacua** cockroach.

kada I 1 decree. 2 to make up for the neglected fast.

kada II to comply with, fulfill. - *hajat*

besar to defecate. - *hajat kecil* to urinate.

kadal scabies. *muka licin, ekor* - all is not gold that glitters.

kadam I sole of foot. *di bawah* - below the sole of the (sovereign's) foot.

kadam II slave, servant; (s.) KHADAM.

kadam III betel box.

kadang sibling. - *kadeyan* relatives.

Kadapol [Kepala Daerah Kepolisian] Chief of Police Region.

kadar 1 God's will, destiny. 2 nature, predisposition. 3 norm, rule. 4 about, approximately. 5 only, merely. 6 limit. *tetap* - equally. - *air* water content. - *hajat* pretty fair. - *lengas* humidity.

kadas(.kudus) and **kadhas(.kudhus)** ringworm, k.o. skin rash.

kade quay, wharf.

Kadé (s.) MADE.

kader **pengk-an** (s.) KADER(N)ISASI.

kader(n)isasi cadre formation. *tempat* - *bajingan* gangster training site.

kaderschool army cadre training school.

kades seaweed.

kadèt I 1 pickpocket. 2 robber.

kadèt II *(roti)* - (bread) roll.

kadim I relative.

kadim II future. **ke-an** eternity.

Kadin [Kamar Dagang dan Industri] Chamber of Commerce and Industry.

kadipatèn the area of an *Adipati*.

kadok *Pak K-* sucker, jerk.

kadung to miss o's aim, fall short in. *sdh* - (gone) too far, rash.

kaf name of the Arabic letter k; in Indonesian it often represents a glottal stop.

kafé cafe.

kaféin caffein.

kafétaria cafetaria.

kafilah (mil.) train.

kaftar hyena.

kagak **se-.-nyè** (S.) SETIDAK.TIDAKNYA.

kagok 1 (of speech) accented, dialectal. 2 (to feel) awkward, disagreeable. 3 unaccustomed, unusual. 4 difficult or becoming an obstacle to perform s.t. *katanya dgn bahasa Indonesia* - he said in halting Indonesian.

kagum meng-kan amazing, awe-inspiring.

-kah whether it is. *Semua warganegara, Jawa- ia, Sunda- ia,* ... All citizens, be they Javanese, Sundanese, ...

kahak phlegm.

kahar 1 despotic. 2 unavoidable.

kahat famine.

kahin soothsayer.

Kahira(h) Cairo.

kahrab amber.

kahwa coffee.

kaifiat manner, way, mode. - *da'wah* the way of preaching (the Islamic religion).

kaimat quantity.

Kain Cain.

kain - *basah kering di pinggang* as poor as a church mouse. - *jadi basahan* departed glory. - *dlm lipatan* designing female. - *alas bayi* baby linen. - *cinde* (esp. red-) patterned dyed Jav. fabric. - *hapus* cotton waste. - *has* gauze. - *jarik* linen. - *kadut* coarse sacking. - *kampuh* garment or blanket (of *kains* sewn together). - *kepar* twilled cloth. - *kulit* leather cloth. - *layar* oil cloth. - *lenan* linen. - *lintang* banner. - *mreki* American imported fabric. - *mori* white calico. - *pajangan* banner. - *pampasan* reparation cloth (from Japan). - *panas* flannels. - *panjang* a sarong. - *pel* mop. - *pembebat* bandage. - *pintu* door curtain. - *popok* baby linen. - *rahab* (S.) KAIN(RAHAP). - *rentang* banner. - *saringan* filter cloth. - *sarskin* sharkskin.

kaing ter-.- to yelp.

Kairo Cairo.

kaison caisson.

kait ber- coherent, connected. **ber-an** *dgn* to be linked to. **ber-.-an** to be linked together. **di-kan** to be implicated. *Ia meminta agar CSA tdk ~ dgn perbuatan Kosek,* He requested that the CSA not be implicated in Kosek's acts. **keter-an** coherence. **mengk-kan** to connect (s.t. with s.t.). *yg ada* **-annya** *dgn* which has a connection with. **-.ber-** to be inter-

woven. -. *kelingking* Malaysian custom in which the bride and groom descend the bridal dais with their little fingers hooked together.

kajang awning, waterproof matting. *lipat* - folded in two.

kajangan k.o. fish (L. Zenarchopterus dispar).

kaji *itu sdh - yg kedua* that's of secondary importance. **meng-** 1 to read the Koran. 2 to teach recitation of formulae. **mengk-** to examine (carefully), study. **ng-** *pumpung* to give in to o's passions. **peng-an** the simplest form of teaching the Islamic religion, found in every Moslem village. People learn the most elementary practices of Islam, such as, the 5-times a-day service, *fikh,* Koran reading, and the like, mostly taking place in the mosque, *musholla,* or in the house of an Islamic teacher. **pengk-an** (careful) examination, study. ~ *Indonesia* Indonesian studies. ~ *keterlaksanaan* feasibility study. *tiada* **ter-** inscrutable. **-an** consideration, studies.

kakafoni cacophony.

kakah *suara* **ng-***nya* the roaring sound of his laughter.

kakak I - *anak* placenta. - *misan* second cousin of older lineage.

kakak II ng- to laugh noisely, guffaw.

kakang - *adi* elder sibling-younger sibling relation.

kakao 1 cacao. 2 cocoa.

kakap 1 giant perch. 2 (criminal term) big fish (,shot). - *merah* red snapper.

kakau (s.) KAKAO 1.

kakawin old Jav. poetic work.

kakèk - *moyang* grand (and great-grand) parents.

kakèn (being) an old man; (s.) NINEN. *Semoga rukun.rukun selalu sampai -.- ninen.ninen,* May your marriage last through your old age.

kakerlak cockroach.

kaki I 1 base, pedestal. 2 classifier for objects with stems. *lima - payung* five umbrellas. *-nya dipalang dr belakang* he was tripped. *cepat -, ringan tangan* ready to help. *berjalan peliharakan -, berkata peliharakan lidah* look before you leap. *- untut dipakaikan gelang* it is like a blacksmith with a white silk apron. **ber-** *ayam* to be bare footed. **per-.limaan** system of sidewalks. *- bersilang* cross-legged. *- dinding* plinth. *- pendek* (euph.) 1 pig. 2 pork. *- telanjang* unshoed.

kaki II grandfather.

kakrupukan 1 alarmed, nervous. 2 panic; (s.) KEKRUPUKAN.

kaktus cactus.

kaku 1 hardened. 2 not (feeling) at home. *- ati* angry. *- beku* stiffened, no longer flexible. *- mulut* lockjaw.

kakung husband. *pengantin -* groom. *-.putri* husband and wife.

kala I *-.-* sea anchor.

kala II snare.

kala III scorpion. *K-* Scorpio.

kala IV **ke-an** periodicity. *tiada* **-nya** continuously.

kalah 1 inferior, not sufficient. 2 to fail (an exam). *- dgn* to rank below. *- membeli menang memakai* cheap goods are most expensive in the long run, quality costs (money). *-(dan) menang* chance(s). *tdk - dgn* no less, not less (than). *tak - menang* undecided (fight; equally strong). *tak mau - dgn* was not to be outdone by. **meng-** *mempersilakan yg lain jalan dulu* to yield the right of way to the other o. (,driver). *tak* **terkan** unconquerable, unbeatable. *yg* **-an** the underdogs. *- angka* to be held in not too high esteem. *- hati* downhearted. *- hawa (,pengaruh)* to be no match for. *- pintar oleh* to be beaten by ... in knowledge. **-.meng-** 1 to give and take; lenient. 2 (in traffic) to yield to e.o.

kalaidoskop kaleidoscope.

kalaidoskopik kaleidoscopic.

kalakemarin the day before yesterday.

kalang I *yg* **ter-** *di hatinya (,matanya)* what o. has on o's mind.

kalang II **-an**: ~ *atas* the upper echelons. ~ *mass.media* publishers. ~ *penjahat*

the underworld. ~ *resmi* official sources.

kalang III log raft.

kalap *- karena cemburuan* crazy with jealousy.

kalau I that; (S.) BAHWA. *- ... maka ...* whereas ..., (in contrast) ...

kalau II *-.-* lest. *takut* ~ ... to be afraid that ...

Kaledong (coll.) New Caledonia.

Kaledonia Baru New Caledonia.

kalem calm. *berbuat -* to keep calm (,quiet).

kalènder calendar. *- polos* pin-up calendar.

kali **didua.-lipatkan** to be doubled. **se-**: *banyak* ~ a lot. ~ *jalan* 1 (all) at once. 2 one way (trip). ~ *jalan dgn* along with. ~ *lihat* at first sight. ~ *main* short time (with prostitute). ~ *pandang saja* at first sight. ~ *pukul* at o. blow. *dgn* ~ *dayung* with o. pull. *dgn* ~ *guris* with a stroke. *dgn* ~ *lompat* in a single leap. *hanya tenaga,* ~ *lagi tenaga* sheer force and nothing but force. ~ *tempo (,waktu)* some day, o. day. *Kalau* ~ *waktu anda jadi penumpang kapal ...,* If o. day you are a passenger on a ship ... *dua hari* ~ every other day. ~*gus* without delay. *blm* ~*pun* on no occasion, never. ~ *dua* ... once or twice ... **se-.-** exceedingly.

Kalifornia California.

kaliber caliber. *orang* **ber-** *besar* a man of great caliber.

kalibut commotion.

kaligrafi calligraphy. *ahli -* calligrapher.

kalijoga fourth and worst period of the world.

kaliki papaya.

kalimaya glowworm.

KA Limex Sriwijaya [Kereta Api Limited Express Sriwijaya] the fast train between Batu Raja and Kertapati Palembang.

kalingan hidden, concealed.

kalkulasi **mengk-kan** to calculate.

kalm (s.) KALEM. *berbuat -* to keep calm (,cool).

kalong *(puasa)* **ng-** (in Jav. mysticism) to eat only fruits.

kalongwéwé vampire.
kalor - *listrik* electrothermal.
kalorimèter calorimeter.
kalowatan babirusa (L. Sus babirusa).
kalsit calcite.
kalsium calcium. - *fluorida* fluorite.
Kaltim [Kalimantan Timur] East Kalimantan.
kalus callus.
kam I bridge (of violin).
kam II camp. - *latihan* training camp.
kama 1 sperm. 2 love.
Kamajaya *(Batara)* - Cupid.
kamar I 1 cabin. 2 apartment. 3 gun chamber. *sebuah hotel* **ber-** *30* a 30-room hotel. **ng-** 1 to room in, live in (of a servant). 2 to rent a room for sexual purposes. 3 to go to a room for sexual purposes. - *bakar* combustion chamber. - *balut* first-aid room. - *bicara* telephone booth. *K- Dagang dan Industri* Chamber of Commerce and Industry. - *dingin* cold storage chamber. - *es* ice house. - *kasak, kusuk* lobby. - *laras* magazine (of fire arm). - *mayat* mortuary, the morgue. - *mesin* engine room (in ship). - *niaga* chamber of commerce. - *obat* pharmacy, dispensary. - *operasi* operating room (in hospital). - *penginapan* guest room. - *perban* first-aid room. - *perum* sounding room (in ship). - *peta* chartroom. - *sejuk* cold storage chamber. - *singel* a single room (in hotel, etc.). - *(tempat) mengepas* fitting room (in tailor's). - *urai* dissecting room. - *wartawan* press room.
kamar II moon.
kamariah 1 lunar. *th* - lunar year. 2 woman's name.
kamas term of address for older brother.
kambang floating. **peng-an** *Sterling* the floating of the (British) Sterling.
kambi rib, frame for wallpanels.
kambing *kelas* - very low class (prostitute). *bagai menghitung bulu* - to carry coals to Newcastle. *bagai* - *dlm biduk* extremely afraid. **peng-** follower, participant. - *biri. biri* sheep. - *perahan* milch-

goat. - *randuk* a rank old he-goat. *si - hitam* the scapegoat, fall guy.
kamboja tree with sweet-scented blossoms, often cultivated in cemeteries, frangipanni (L. Plumiera acutifolia).
kambuh - *kembali* to relapse. *penjahat* **-an** habitual criminal, recidivist.
kambut an open-mouthed plaited bag for rice.
kamekmek (s.) KEMEKMEK.
kaméra - *televisi* television camera.
kaméraman cameraman.
Kamerun Cameroon.
kamerwak orderly (the person).
kamfer camphor.
kamil 1 perfect, finished. - *mukamil* most perfect. 2 thorough. *insan* - a thorough man.
kamisosolen to stammer.
kamp - *kerja. paksa* a strict regime labor camp. - *konsentrasi* concentration camp; (s.) KAM II.
kampanye di-kan to be campaigned about. **mengk-kan** to campaign. - *pemilihan umum* (general) election campaign.
kampanyewan campaigner (for political party).
kampas canvass.
kamper (s.) KAMFER.
kampil -an broad sword.
kampse (euph.) hick, boorish; (S.) KAMPUNGAN.
kampuh ceremonial batik wraparound.
kampung shantytown. **ke-an** unsophistication. **per-an** village cluster. ~ *kaum nudis* nudist colony. ~ *Negro* Negro ghetto. *orang* **se-** fellow villager. *bahasa Inggeris* **-an** broken English. - *halaman- isme* provincialism. -.- *melarat* slum areas.
kampus campus.
kamsèn commission (payment).
kamsia and **kamsya** thank you.
kamtib [keamanan dan ketertiban] security and order.
kamu - *sekalian* you all.
kamuflase camouflage. **ber-** camouflaged. *dgn jalan* ~ under the cloak of, under (the) cover of. **di-** to be camouflaged.

kamus per-an lexicography.

kan the speaker is stating that the truth of the statement in which this particle occurs is or should be known to the hearer. Can translate as: isn't it, (don't) you know?

kana *gelang* - gold armlets.

Kanaan *(negeri)* - Canaan.

kanaat satisfaction.

Kanada 1 Canada. 2 Canadian.

kanal canal.

kanan - *kirinya* about, approximately.

kanari (S.) KENARI.

Kanbèra Canberra.

kanca friend. - *dolan* playmate. - *mitra* bosom friend, crony.

kancah - *dapur tukang besi* forge. - *kehinaan (,kenerakaan)* slough of despair. - *keributan* scene of disturbances. - *penderitaan* slough of despair. - *pertikaian* scene of disturbances.

kancil 1 the chevrotain, i.e. a miniature-sized deer, well-known for its slyness; when captured or driven into a corner it feigns death; due to its small size it can easily escape predators; for Indonesians the chevrotain is the symbol of slyness; scores of *kancil* stories exist in Indonesian society; in those fables all large animals are made to look the fool; among the *kancil* stories there are some which originate from the Indian *Panca Tantra* but many more are original; the most famous *kancil* story is the *Pelanduk Jenaka* (The Funny Chevrotain) in which the animal is frequently referred to as *Sang Kancil. si K-* sobriquet for Foreign Minister Adam Malik. 2 freshman.

kancing bolt. - *lengan kemeja* cuff link. - *tarik* zipper. - *tekan* 1 snap fasteners. 2 push button. - *tutup tarik* (s.) KANCING (TARIK).

kanda tradition, legend.

kandang *Dia pulang (,kembali) ke -nya,* He returned to his old stamping grounds. *di luar* - banned, ostracized. *masuk - kambing mengembik, masuk - kerbau menguak* in Rome do as the Romans

do. - *bibit* studfarm. - *lokomotip* locomotive shed.

kandas ter- aground.

kandi I -.- purse, satchel.

kandi II *bunga - putih* the white pitcher-plant.

kandidat 1 candidate. 2 bachelor (university degree).

kandil - *gantung* chandelier.

kandung ng- pregnant. **ter-** *maksud* to cherish the aim. -*annya sdh berumur empat bln* she is four months pregnant.

Kanèkès the area encompassed by the hamlets Cibeo, Cikertawa and Cikeusik (southern Banten, West Java).

kangen 1 - *(dgn ,akan)* to long for. 2 to be homesick. **ke-an** nostalgia.

kangguru (S.) KANGURU.

Kangjeng title for Jav. princely and high-noble persons and for high-ranking government officials. - *Lider* a *Bupati* upon whom the Dutch decoration: *Ridder* (= Lider) *in de Orde van Oranje Nassau,* meaning: Knight in the Order of Orange Nassau, has been conferred.

kangkang meng-i 1 to control, hold sway over. 2 (fig.) to appropriate. ~ *uang pungli itu sendirian* to appropriate *pungli* for o's own benefit. **ter-** astride, straddling.

kangkung I *spt - di ulak jamban* to breed quickly.

kangkung II *film* - pornographic film.

kangtau(w) 1 a windfall, an unexpected good fortune. 2 object which can yield a profit.

kanibal cannibal.

kanibalisme cannibalism.

kanigara sunflower (L. Helianthus annuus).

kanina canine.

kanisah 1 synagogue. 2 temple. *K-Rakyat* The People's Temple (in San Francisco).

kanjang perseverance.

kanker - *darah* leuc(a)emia. - *payudara* breast cancer.

kano canoe.

kanon 1 (music) catch. 2 round.

kans chance.

kanselaria chancellary.

kanselir embassy first secretary.

kanstof and **kanstop** lace (fabric).

kantata cantata.

kantin canteen, i.e. a place where refreshment and entertainment are provided.

kantonemèn cantonment.

kantong *mereka yg* **ber-** *tipis* the poor. **meng-i** *Rp. 500 setiap hari* to make Rp. 500.00 a day. - *kempes* broke, penniless. - *nasi* stomach. - *punggung* backpack. - *sampah* trash bag. - *tebal* well off. - *tipis* poor.

kantor bureau, agency. **ng-** to go to the office. **per-an** (adj.) office. **se-** *dgn* to work in the same office as. - *berita* news agency. - *bom (,bum)* Customs office. *K- Catatan Sipil* Registry of Births, Deaths and Marriages. - *dagang* business office. - *depan* front office. - *pembantu* branch office. - *pemilihan* polling place. - *penempatan tenaga* employment bureau. - *perjalanan* travel agency, tourist office. - *perjodohan* matchmaker (the office). *K- Pusat Perbendaharaan* Central Accounting Office. - *redaksi* office of the editorial staff (of a publication). - *stor* (in M.O. forms) office of payment.

kantuk ng- to be sleepy. *Mungkin -nya blm lepas,* Probably he has not yet slept his fill.

kanun laws, rules (civil).

kanvas canvas.

kanwil [kantor wilayah] regional office.

Kanya Virgo.

kaok ber-.- *setinggi langit* to scream at the top of o's voice.

kaos (s.) KAUS.

kap I *tali* - ship's cable.

kap II - *rambut* hairdressing.

kap III - *mesin* bonnet (of automobile), hood. *di atas - mesin mobil Rolls Royce* 'on top of the hood of a Rolls Royce,' i.e. with a Rolls Royce as a gift.

kapabel capable.

kapak *sbg - naik pemidangan (,peminang-*

an) utterly irrelevant.

kapal - *satu nakhoda dua* two captains on a ship. *besar - besar gelombang* high winds blow on high hills. **ber-.-** *diangkut ke Eropa* to be transported in shiploads to Europe. **peng-** shipper. **peng-an** shipment. - *(air) bersayap* hydrofoil (boat). - *angkasa* spaceship. - *angkasa berawak (,bermanusia)* manned spacecraft. - *api baling.baling* propeller ship. - *apiso* aviso, dispatch boat. - *bantuan* support ship. - *barang* freighter. - *barang curahan* bulk carrier. - *bargas* launch. - *batubara* collier. - *bendera* flagship. - *bengkel* repair ship. - *berbaling.baling* screw steamer. - *bijih besi* iron ore carrier. - *bor hisap* cutter suction-dredger. - *bulan* moonship. - *cadik* outrigger proa. - *cepat (peluru kendali)* speedboat (carrying guided missiles). - *curahan* bulk carrier. - *dagang (bertenaga nuklir)* (nuclear-powered) merchant vessel. - *depot utk - selam* submarine tender. - *derek apung* floating crane. -.- *dlm perjalanan pulang* homeward-bound vessels. - *es* ice boat. - *hewan* cattle boat. - *hidrofoil* hydrofoil (boat). - *hidrografi* hydrographic survey ship. - *hisap lumpur* suction-dredger. - *ilmiah* oceanographic ship. - *induk - selam* submarine tender. - *intel(ijen)* intelligence collecting ship. - *jentera* paddle wheeler. - *karantina* quarantine ship. - *keduk* dredger. - *kincir* paddle wheeler. - *kontiner* containership. - *laksamana (perang)* flagship. - *liar* tramp steamer. - *lin* liner. - *Maru* a vessel of the Jap. Tokyo Senpaku Kabushiki Kaisha (= Tokyo Shipping Company). - *mata.mata* spy-ship. - *mel* mail boat. - *minyak* (oil) tanker, oiler. - *monitor* gunboat. - *moring* mooring boat, i.e. a small boat which moors another ship by using cables, etc. - *motor torpedo* motor torpedo boat, MTB. - *niaga* merchantman. - *nuklir* nuclear ship. - *orang sakit* hospital ship. - *pabrik ikan* fish factory ship. - *pameran terapung* floating fair.

- *pantai* coaster. - *pasasir* passenger steamer. - *patroli* patrol boat. - *pelatih* training ship. - *pembajak* pirate ship. - *pembantu* support ship. - *pembersih alur* desnagging boat. - *pembor minyak lepas.pantai* off-shore oil drilling vessel. - *pemburu* - *selam* submarine chaser. - *pemburu torpedo* destroyer. - *pemecah es* icebreaker. - *pemimpin* flagship. - *pemukat* trawler. - *penangkap ikan paus* whaler. - *penarik* tug(boat). - *pencari muatan* tramp steamer. - *pendarat bulan* lunar module, moon-landing vehicle. - *pendarat tank* LST. - *pendingin* refrigerated ship. - *penempur berat* battle cruiser. - *pengangkut kayu* log-carrier. - *pengangkut lumpur* hopper barge. - *pengangkut pesawat (terbang)* aircraft carrier. - *pengangkut tentara* troopship. - *pengejar* - *selam* submarine chaser. - *pengembara* tramp ship. - *penggempur* battleship. - *pengukur* survey vessel. - *penjelajah peluncur peluru kendali* guided missile cruiser. - *penolong* lifeboat. - *penyebar ranjau* mine-layer. - *penyeberangan* ferry (-boat). - *penyelamat* salvage ship. - *penyelidik alam* oceanographic ship. - *penyelundup* smuggler (a ship). - *penyeret* tug(boat). - *penyusur pantai* coaster. - *perbekalan* supply ship. - *peremuk es* icebreaker. - *peronda* patrol boat. - *pesisir* cruise ship. - *prah* freighter. - *pukat* trawler. - *putih* a *K.P.M.*-steamer. - *radar* paddle boat. - *rambu* beaconing ship. - *riset ilmiah* scientific research vessel. - *ruang angkasa* spaceship. - *(rumah) sakit* hospital ship. - *samudera* ocean-going vessel. - *selam bermisil (,berpeluru kendali)* missile (,guided-missile)-carrying submarine. - *selam bertenaga atom (,nuklir)* atomic (,nuclear)-powered submarine. - *selam pembawa misil balistik* submarine carrying ballistic missiles. - *suar (pandu)* (pilot) lightship. - *tamasya* pleasure boat. - *tambang* ferry(-boat). - *tambangan ruang angkasa* space shuttle. - *tambat* tug(boat). - *tangker* tanker.

- *tangki raksasa* supertanker. - *tenda* awning-decker. - *tender* headquarter-ship. - *teng(ker)* tanker. - *tengah dua tiang* schooner. - *terbang becak* the DC-3 aircraft of the Garuda Indonesian Airways. - *tiang dua* barque. - *trol* patrol boat. *K- Tujuh* The Royal Dutch Navy cruiser "Zeven Provinciën." - *tunda* tug(boat). - *utk pelayaran tetap* liner. - *wisata* cruise ship. - *yg bertonase (,berukuran ,berbobot mati) 10.000 ton* a 10.000-tonner, 10,000-ton vessel, a ship of 10,000 dwt.

kapan I *th-?* (in) what year? -.- sometime, anytime. *Nantilah ~ saya datang*, Later, as soon as is convenient. I'll drop by. *K- saya bisa ketemu saudara? K~ saja.* When can I see you? Anytime. *~pun tdk* never (will). *sampai ~ suka* as long as (he) likes.

kapan II is not it, has not he, etc.; (s.) KAN. *lu tau - duluan* you knew it before, didn't you? - *itu sdh kau ambil* you have taken it, haven't you?

kapanèwon subdistrict (an administrative unit).

kapang *bln* -an eclipse of the moon.

kaparat expiatory sacrifice, peace-offering.

kaparinyo a Malayan dance. **ber-** to dance.

kapas *spt (,bagai)* - *dibusur* pure white. **per-an** (adj.) cotton. -.- *salju* snowflakes.

kapasitans capacitance.

kapcao (s.) KAPSAO.

kapèl chapel.

kapeling (s.) KAPLING.

kaper *(ikan)* - carp.

kapilaritas and **kapilaritèt** capillarity.

kapilèr capillary.

kapiran to result in a disappointment, be disappointed, be of no avail, go wrong. *Hidupnya ternyata tdk -,* It turned out that his life was not a failure.

kapita *per* - per capita.

kapital capital (money).

kapitalis - *birokrat* capitalist bureaucrat (a term used by the outlawed *PKI* to attack army officers directing state enterprises).

kapitalisme capitalism.

kapitalistis capitalistic.

kapitan headman of an ethnic division of the population in the eastern part of Indonesia.

kapi telaat gate crasher.

Kapitol Capitol (in the U.S.A.).

kapitulasi capitulation. **ber-** to capitulate.

kaplar(e)s boots.

kapling lot, parcel (of land). **meng(k)-kan** to lot (out), parcel (out). **peng(k)-an** lotting (out), parcelling (out).

kaplok - *dada* to strike o's breast.

kapocé condom.

kapok to be taught a good lesson. *biar mereka* - let them be taught a good lesson. *tdk* -.**-nya** never learned a lesson. - *lombok* to be taught a very good lesson, but keep on making the same mistakes.

Kapolri [Kepala Kepolisian Republik Indonesia] Chief, Republic of Indonesia (State) Police.

kaprah common, general, customary. *tdk* - extraordinary, uncommon. **kesalah.** **-an** *penerangan* mis-information. *salah.* **-an** established mistake.

kapri *kacang* - marrowfat (peas).

kapsalon hairdresser's.

kapsao coffee(,tea)pot.

kapsel hairdo, coiffure.

kapsul - *komando* command capsule (of space ship).

kaptèn di-i to be captained (of a ship).

kapulaga cardamom.

kapung ter-.- to float.

kapur ber- calcareous. **di-** *putih* to be whitewashed. **se-** *sirih* 1 a brief prefatory note. 2 in a nutshell. 3 a few words.

kapurancang ng- to clasp the hands with fingers intertwined and thumbtips touching.

karaba method of pisciculture in the Semarang regency using bamboo traps in which the fish can multiply and grow.

karabat (S.) KERABAT.

karabèn carbine.

karaf carafe.

Karakata (s.) KARKATA.

karakteristik characteristic.

karam to capsize. *tlh* - *maka bertimba* to lock the stable door after the horse is stolen. *spt Cina* - a pandemonium. - *kapal* ship wreck. *orang* - *kapal* a shipwrecked person.

karambol (in billiards) carom.

karamèl caramel.

karang I kepeng-an authorship. **peng-.serta** co-author. **-an** *acuan* bibliographical references.

karang II - *abang* burning ground. *tdk sedikit proyek militer yg menjadi* - *abang* not a few mil. projects were devastated.

karang III pe-an compound (of house).

karang IV - *emas* blood coral.

karangkitri fruit trees and coconut palms.

karantina di-kan to be quarantined. **pengk-an** quarantining. *ketentuan* ~ quarantine stipulations. - *politik* political quarantine.

karap weaver's comb.

karapan sapi (Madurese) bull race.

karat *dimakan* - rusty. **ber-** 1 to corrode. 2 corrodable. 3 corroded. *tdk* ~ non-corrodable. ~ *di hati* malice. **-an** 1 corrosion. 2 scrap iron.

karaté karate.

Karatsyi Karachi.

Karawang the new spelling for the place name Kerawang (located in West Java).

karawitan (Jav. *gamelan*) music.

karbit meng- to calculate, count.

karbohidrat carbohydrate.

karbol air force cadet.

karbon carbon.

karbonaci(s) *daging* - pork chop.

karburator carburetor.

karcis ber- which uses tickets. **di-kan** tickets are being issued for s.t. - *parkir* parking ticket. - *peron* platform ticket. - *sepur* train ticket. - *terusan* season ticket. - *undangan* complimentary ticket.

kardinal cardinal (the man).

kardiol (in the Karo area) gladiolus.

kardiolog cardiologist.

kardiologi cardiology.

karena for the sake of. *(oleh) - itu* that's why. **di-kan** caused by. **-nya** therefore, that's why, because of it. - *Allah* 1 for God's sake. 2 free of charge. - *apa?* why? - *dibawa* due to.

karèsèh.pèsèh (s.) KRESEH.PESEH.

karésidènan (s.) KERESIDENAN.

karèt 1 caoutchouc. 2 condom. **di-** to be postponed. *Pesta itu* ~, The party was postponed. **ke-an** postponement. **ng-** 1 to postpone. 2 to be late. *Dia selalu 'on time,' tak pernah* ~, He is always on time and never late. **per-an** (adj.) rubber. - *alam* latex. - *bongkah* crumb rubber. - *perkebunan* estate rubber. - *rakyat* smallholder's rubber. - *remah* crumb rubber. - *sintetis* synthetic rubber.

kari I (s.) QARI(AH).

kari II stay(ed) behind.

Karibia Caribbean (Sea).

karibu riding whip.

karièr (S.) KARIERE.

karisma (s.) KHARISMA.

Karkata Cancer.

karma *(hukum)* - the Jav. philosophical concept that o's fate is decided by o's deeds and that good breeds good just as evil breeds evil; the inexorable application of the law of cause and effect.

karmenaji (s.) KARBONACI.

karnivor carnivore.

karosèl merry-go-round.

karoseri (automobile) body.

karpèt carpet.

kartèl cartel.

kartéring charting, surveying.

karti act(ivity), action.

kartika 1 Pleiades. 2 (film)star. *K- Chandra Kirana* name of the Army Wives Association.

Kartini Indonesia's first women's emancipationist. **-an** to commemorate *Hari Kartini.*

kartografi cartography.

karton carton.

kartonis cartoonist.

kartu greeting card. **ber-** ... to have a ... card. - *kuning* the 1977-voter registration card. - *tanda masuk* boarding pass for aircarft, etc.). - *tanda penduduk;* (s.) KTP.

Kartum Khartoum.

kartun cartoon.

kartunis cartoonist.

karuhun ancestors.

karung.karung caul.

karya **ber-** to work. **di-kan** 1 to be appointed. ~ *sbg Dubes Luar Biasa* to be appointed as Ambassador Extraordinary. 2 *tdk* ~ to be out of operation. *selama demmo itu tdk* ~ as long as that *demmo* is out of operation. 3 to be used for profit illegally (but officially tolerated); cp. NGOBYEK. **ke-an** 1 work. 2 profession. *fungsi* ~ the function as a sociopolitical force (of the Armed Forces), a nonmilitary function. **mengk-kan** 1 to use s.t. for o's own profit (illegal but tolerated). 2 to put s.o. to work. **pe-** (s.) KARYAWAN. **pengk-an** employment, assignment (to a position). - *baku* standard work. *K- Bhakti* Civic Action. - *desa* (in Central and East Java) village (compulsory, unpaid) labor. - *ilmiah* thesis, dissertation. - *mat kodak* photographs. *K- Satya* Indonesian award for a 25-year uninterrupted term of office with the government.

Karyantara the mass organization of the "Antara" News Agency workers.

karyasiswa a company employee studying abroad, trainee.

karyawan 1 white-collar (government) worker. 2 worker in steambaths, (hospital) nurse, etc. - *ABRI* a member of the Armed Forces assigned to non-defense work. - *bahari* seaman. - *bank* bank employee. - *bulanan* monthly wage earner. - *harian lepas* casual worker. - *intelektuil* intellectual worker. - *militer* a member of the Armed Forces assigned to non-defense work. - *pariwisata* tour operator. - *perusahaan* industrial worker. - *riset* research worker. - *tambang* mineworker.

karyawani and **karyawati** female worker.

karyawisata work tour (,trip). **ber-** to make a work tour.

kas - *partai* party funds.

kasak.kusuk lobbying (legislative).

kasam grudge, spite.

kasat door-mat.

kasatmata visual.

kasbuk cashbook.

kaselak just in time.

kasemat grudge, resentment, spite. **ber-** to conflict.

kasèp - *bln* 1 delayed menstruation. 2 missing menstruation. *kapsul* - *bln* capsule inducing menstruation.

kasèt cassette. **mengk-kan** to record on a cassette. **pengk-an** recording.

kasi I castration, gelding. *ayam* - capon. *lembu* - bullock.

kasi II [kepala seksi] section head.

kasian (S.) KASIHAN.

kasidah melody accompanied by a *gambus*. **-an** such a musical performance.

kasi(h) **di-** to be given. ∼ *gelombang* to be waved (of hair). ∼ *makan* to be fed. **meng-** to give. **ng-** *bumbu* to season (a dish). **peng-** *tahu* informant. **K-an!** Poor thing! - *muka* 1 indulgent. 2 to indulge.

kasih (s.) KASI(H). *tdk* -.**meng-ani** ruthless (battle). **meng-i** to love.

kasino casino.

kasintu partridge.

kaskada cascade.

kaskaya 1 power, capacity. 2 wealth, means.

kasmaran (S.) KESEMARAN.

kasno [bekas cino] Chinese who has taken Indonesian citizenship.

kaso I roof beam.

kaso II a tall reed.

Kaspia Caspian.

kasrah name of o. of the vowelpoints in Arabic script (e or i).

kasta caste.

kastanyèt castanets.

kastil castle.

kastrasi castration.

kasur *jatuh di (,ke)* - to be kicked upstairs. *tidur di* - (fig.) married to a rich wife.

kasus a (judicial) case.

kasut shoes, boots. - *getah* gum boots.

kaswari cassowary.

Kasymir Kashmir.

kata *dgn* - *lain* in other words. **ber-:** *tak* ∼ *sepatahpun* do not say a word. ∼ *benar* to tell the truth. ∼ *bohong* to lie. ∼ *yg bukan.bukan* to talk through o's hat. *jangan* **di-(kan)** *lagi* not to mention, say nothing of, let alone. -.*akhir* (s.) STEMMOTIVERING. - *awas* words of caution. - *bermula* preface. - *bersusun* derivative. - *bilangan pangkat* ordinal number. - *dua* ultimatum. - *ekasuku* a monosyllabic word. - *ganti* pronoun. - *ganti pemilik* possessive pronoun. - *ganti penghubung* relative pronoun. - *ingkar* breach of faith. -.- *istilah* terminology. - *kepala* (in dictionary) entry. - *kerja bantu* auxiliary verb. - *kerja bertujuan* transitive verb. - *kode* codeword. -.- *lelamisan* phrases. - *nama hissi* concrete noun. - *pancung* acronym. - *pasti* decisive answer. - *pembuka* opening speech. - *pembukaan* preface. - *pengganti* relative pronoun. - *pengganti kepunyaan* possessive pronoun. - *pengganti orang* personal pronoun. - *pengganti penunjuk* demonstrative pronoun. - *pengganti taktentu* indefinite pronoun. - *pengganti tanya* interrogative pronoun. - *penghantar* preface. - *pengumpul* collective numeral. - *penyusul* epilog. -.- *pujian* words of praise. - *pungut* loanword. -.- *seasal* cognate words. - *wicara* speech.

katabèlecé (s.) KATTEBELLETJE.

katafalk catafalque.

katagori category. **meng(k)-kan** to categorize.

katai *si* - the Japanese.

katak I - *hendak jadi lembu* pride goes before a fall. - *ditimpa kemarau* to make a great noise. **peng-** frogman.

katak II short. *meriam* - mortar.

katalisator catalyst.

katalogès catalog. - *induk* union catalog.

katarak cataract.

katawi verbatim, word-by-word.

katédral cathedral.

katégori mengk-kan to categorize.

katekése catechesis.

kateketik and **katekismus** catechism.

katekis catechist.

katekisasi catechization.

katépé [from *KTP:* Kartu Tanda Penduduk] resident's card. **ber-** 1 to be in possession of a resident's card. 2 to reside at(,in), live at(,in). ~ *Bandung* to live in Bandung.

katholik (S.) KATOLIK. *K-Roma* Roman Catholic.

katimbang (s.) TIMBANG II.

katineung (pron. eu as u in fur) affection, attachment.

katode cathode.

katolik *K-Roma* Roman Catholic.

katrol mengk- to raise, lift, improve. **peng(k)-an** raising.

kattebelletje (pron. katebèlecé) short note to s.o. asking a favor for the bearer.

katu k.o. shrub with edible leaves and with berries.

katul a by-product from the milling of rice, consisting of the outer bran layers of the kernel with part of the germ, sometimes referred to as *katul dedek.*

katup closed. - *keamanan* safety valve.

kaucuk caoutchouc.

Kaukasus *orang* - Caucasian.

kaum I se- allied, related. - *Adam* men. - *agama* religious persons. - *bakulan* retailers. - *bendoro* the nobility. - *Boer* the Boers. - *dahriah* atheists. - *gelandangan* 1 the unemployed. 2 the homeless. 3 the hooligans. - *haus.duit* the money-grubbers. - *Hawa (yg lemah)* women. - *intelek(tuil)* intellectuals. - *kanan* rightwingers. - *kapitalis* capitalists. - *kepalabatu* diehards. - *kiri* leftwingers. - *lanjut usia* senior citizens. - *melarat* the under-privileged. - *menengah* 1 the middle class. 2 the small-sized industry and craftsmen. - *ningrat* 1 the nobility, aristocracy. 2 the well-to-do. - *Packard* the rich. - *pelawan* the members of the resistance. - *pemilih*

the electorate. - *pendeta* the clergy - *penentang* the opposition (party). - *pengkhianat* the quislings. - *pertengahan* 1 the small-sized industry and craftsmen. 2 tradespeople. - *plin.plan* those who play both sides. - *plintat. plintut* those lacking firm loyalties. - *pria* menfolk. - *pro.raja* royalists. - *punya* the haves. - *putar negeri* revolutionaries. - *samurai* the (Jap.) military. - *sedang* the moderates. - *Sekutu* the Allied Powers. - *tak punya* the have-nots. - *tangan panjang* thieves. - *tani* peasants. - *tengah* middle roaders. - *terkemuka* prominent people. - *tinggi* the higher-ups. - *tua* old people. - *vestin (,vested interest)* those with vested interests.

kaum II a religious official who cleans and takes care of the mosque. **-an** quarter of pious people in the vicinity of a mosque.

kaung (s.) KAWUNG I.

kaupui (in Jambi) middleman in the field of smallholders' rubber.

kaus (s.) KAOS. *di bawah* - below the sovereign's foot. - *kutang* undershirt. - *oblong* T-shirt. - *tubuh* body suit.

kavaleri 1 cavalry. 2 armored vehicles.

kaveling (s.) KAPLING.

kaver (s.) KOVER. **mengk-** (s.) MENGKOVER.

kaviar caviar.

kawah the hell of the Buddhists. *K-Candradimuka (,Condrodimuko)* 1 a cauldron shaped like a cow into which according to Buddhist teaching a man was thrown to be 'boiled' in scalding water for supernatural powers and strength. 2 Spartan training. 3 the Armed Forces Academy in Magelang. - *granat* shell crater.

kawakan dyed-in-the-wool, out-and-out.

kawal peng- chaperon(e). ~ *kehormatan* honor guard.

kawan - *dan lawan* friend and foe. **ber-dgn** to associate with. **ber-.-** to be (,have) allies. **perse-an** partnership. *dgn* -.-**nya** 1 with (o's) friends (,associates ,etc.). 2 with affiliates. - *berdansa* dancing partner. - *main* gambling friend. - *minuman* what o. eats or offers with drinks. - *nasi* side dish accompanying the *rijsttafel*. - *sederajat* equal partner. - *segabungan* associate. - *seimbang* equal partner. - *sekamar* roommate. - *semarga* clan-mate. - *semufakat* likeminded person. - *senasib* fellow-sufferer. - *sepaham* likeminded person. - *separtai* political associate. - *sepenerbangan* traveling companion (in aircraft). - *sepermainan* playmate. - *seperut* clan-mate. - *sesekolah* schoolmate. - *setawanan* fellow prisoner.

kawanisme cronyism.

Kawanua *masyarakat* - the Minahasan community (North Celebes).

kawasan 1 district, region, sphere. - *hawa panas* tropics. 2 estate. - *industri* industrial estate.

kawat - *jepret* staple (of stapler, the machine). - *spring* steel wire.

kawet di-kan to be tied up between the legs (of a sarong).

kawi supernatural. *adat yg* - time-honored customs.

kawin *blm* - (in advertisements) unmarried. *sdh* - *atau blm* (in application forms, etc.) marital status. **di-.suntik** to be artificially inseminated. **meng-.silang-kan** to crossbreed. **peng-.suntikan** artificial insemination. **per-an**: *di luar* ~ extra-marital. *sebelum* ~ premarital. *Gadis itu tlh menginjak jenjang* ~, The girl has reached a marriageable age. ~ *silang* crossing (of plants). - *berpamili* inbreeding. - *kontrak* cohabitation between (married) Filipinos working in the lumber business in eastern Kalimantan and Dayak women. - *dgn kopiah* to marry by proxy. - *gantung* officially married but not announced to the public, i.e. no wedding reception. - *miskin* wedding performed without levying fees from those concerned. - *sedarah (,sepamili)* inbreeding. - *silang* crossbreeding. - *suntik* artificial insemination.

kawiryan (adj.) military.

Kaw Puik (in Jambi, Sumatra; Chinese for) nine-eight; by saying *Kaw Puik,* in concluding a transaction in the rubber trade, the broker will receive 2% commission; (s.) KAUPUI.

kawruh knowledge. - *jiwo* psychology. - *padhuwungan* (s.) KERISOLOGI.

kawuk a giant *biawak* or 'mini dinosaur' found on the island of Nusakambangan.

kawula subject. - *Belanda* Dutch subject.

kawung I (dried sugar) palm leaf; (s.) ROKOK (KAWUNG).

kawung II classic pattern in batik from Solo and Yogya (originally developed for the royal palaces).

kaya I - *(h)utang* to be deeply in debt. - *melangit* very rich. - *muda* rich overnight.

kaya II and **kayak** as if. - *apa?* how? - *gini (,gitu)* like this (,that).

kayan I cut off.

Kayan II (in Bali) name element placed before personal names to indicate the first born child.

kayangan *dewi dr* - a pretty girl.

kayap destroyed.

kayek khang (from Dutch: ga je gang!) do as you please!

kayu tree. -.- planking. -.-**an** timbers of different kinds. - *api* white fir wood. - *beuk* beechwood. - *bulat (,bundar ,gelondongan)* logs. - *gelam* k.o. *kayu putih,* found throughout Indonesia (L. Melaleuca leucadendron). - *gergajian* sawn timber. - *gubalan* squared timber. - *hanyutan* drift wood. - *jati grajèn* sawn logs (of teak wood). -. *kayan* timbers of different kinds. - *kuda.kuda* (in Kalimantan) logs transported/pulled by humans considered to be pack horses. - *lapis(an)* plywood. - *lara* (in the Celebes) ironwood (L. Metrosideros petiolata Kds.). - *merbau* (in Irian Jaya) ironwood (L. Intsia bijuga O. Ktze.). - *pemadat* dunnage. - *pinus* pinewood. - *putih* cajuput (L. Eucalyptus alba) found only in the dry areas of the eastern part of Indonesia, esp. Timor. - *ulin* (in Kalimantan) ironwood (L. Eusider-oxylon zwageri T. et B.).

kayuh *segan - perahu hanyut* to miss o's chance.

KB [Keluarga Berencana] (s.) KABE. *karet -* (birth control) condom.

ke (S.) KEPADA. *Semua mata tertuju - dia,* All eyes were directed to her.

kebabal young jack fruit.

kebah (the fever) is gone.

kebaji black magic to alienate husband and wife.

kebal armored. *kereta -* a mil. tank. - *bakar* fireproof.

kebambam a mango species (L. Mangifera odorata).

kebat I (waist)band.

kebat II - *kebit* 1 to beat (of heart). 2 uneasy, restless (with beating heart).

kebayan *nenek -* (old) woman carrying out the duties of intermediary between two lovers.

kebelet to have to go to the bathroom immediately (it can't be postponed any longer).

kebelinger (s.) KEBLINGER.

kebiri capon. **di-** to be shortchanged (i.e. getting less than is due, such as, gas in gas station). **peng(k)-an** *uang* currency reform.

keblangsak *orang -* orphans, bums, people without regular family life; indigents.

keblinger tricked, fooled.

kebluk **ng-** to beat, whip (dough).

kebo 1 water buffalo. 2 (sl.) policeman. - *nusu gudel* 1 the old learn from the young. 2 the children support the parents.

kebréwonggor *daun -* leaf used as a contraceptive in *Irian Jaya.*

kebul **ng-** 1 to rise and disperse (as fog, smoke). 2 to smoke (a cigarette).

kebun **di-** **tebukan** to be converted into sugar cane plantations. **per-an**: *P.N. P~* Government Estate Enterprise. *~(buah buahan)apel* apple orchard. *~ budidaya* (rubber, tea) estate. *~ padi* rice estate.

keburu previously; (S.) BURU. *tdk - lagi* there is no time left. *Saya - menikah,* I married too early (,quickly).

kebut **di-** to be sped up. **meng-kan** to race (a car, etc.) recklessly. **ng-** 1 to drive recklessly. 2 (for government employees) to come to the office early to sign the attendance sheet and then to leave the office right away. 3 (for businessmen) to make profits by speculating, manipulating, bribing, etc. 4 (for stewardesses) to buy luxury items abroad and sell them in Indonesia. 5 to push ahead. 6 to compete fiercely. **peng-** reckless driver. **perng-an** racing recklessly. **-.-an** reckless driving, to race with e.o.

Kebyar Balinese squat dance; a conventionalized solo dance.

kecah (S.) KECUH.KECAH.

kècak Balinese monkey dance from the *Ramayana* story.

kecam **-an** critique.

kècap **-!** empty talk! nonsense! **meng-kan** to babble about s.t. **ng-** to brag, talk high-sounding nonsense. - *manis* Indonesian sweet soy sauce. - *No. 1* (fig.) empty talk.

kecapi I a boat-shaped, four-string plucked zither of West Java.

kecapi II yellow, hand ball-sized fruit with slightly downy thick skin, delicious white meat in segments with strawberry-like fragrance.

kècèk I - *tinggi* to talk big, brag.

kècèk II *main -* a game played with coins.

kecelé to look blank. **meng-i** to fool, trick.

kecelik (s.) KECELE.

kècèng with o. eye closed.

kecèwa frustrated.

kecil *dr - mula* from childhood. *soal.soal - trivia. sungguhpun -, tetapi lada kutu, cabe (,cabai) rawit, -.- lada api (,kutu)* and *-.- kutu* small but plucky (said of a person). - *teranja.anja, besar terbawa. bawa, sdh tua terubah tdk* once a use, ever a custom. *sampai yg -.meng-* down to the minutest details. **di-.-kan** to be counted for little. **diper-** to be reduced. **meng-kan** to reduce, turn down, lower (the volume of TV, etc.). - *hati* hurt in o's feelings. - *mungil* petite. - *takber-hingga* infinitesimally small.

kecimplung (s.) KECIMPUNG.

kecimpring (s.) OPAK.

kecimpung ber- to deal (,be active) in.

kecipir 1 leguminous plant. 2 the fruit of that plant.

kecoak cockroach.

kècoh cheating at cards, swindling by giving false weight. **ter-** tricked, fooled.

kecrèk pieces of metal strung on rope and clacked by the *dalang* to announce arrivals and departures of puppets or to accentuate their movements.

kecua (s.) KECOAK.

kecuali unless. *tanpa* **peng-an** without reserve. *dlm hal.hal yg* **ter-** in exceptional cases.

kecubung *batu* - amethyst.

kecundang conquered.

kecut peng- cowardly.

kedai *lemari* **-an** showcase (in store).

kedap peng- *suara* silencer (for gun). - *bom dan granat* shellproof. - *suara* soundproof.

kedap.kedip to blink.

kedar se- 1 according to. 2 as far as (I remember). ~ *maksudnya* as regards the purpose. ~ *pidato* a short address (,speech). **se-nya** somewhat, a little (bit).

kedas.keridas k.o. very itchy scabies.

kedaung *pokok* - a large tree (L. Parkia Roxburghii).

kedebong - *pisang* trunk of banana tree.

kedekak.kedekuk *Ia hidup* ~, He lives in poverty.

kedemat (S.) KHIDMAT.

kedemplung tobacco pouch made of *mengkuang* leaf.

kedengkik *tanah* - impoverished land.

kedep afraid.

kèdi caddy.

kedidi berse- to tap o's fingers.

kedok *dgn mengambil* - under the guise of. - *gas* gas mask.

kedondong Spanish plum, green when young, yellow brown when ripe, oval, egg size, sharp taste.

Kedubes [Kedutaan Besar] Embassy.

keduduk a generic name for some plants (L. Melastoma polyanthum and allied species).

keduk meng- to rake up. ~ *banyak duit* (fig.) to bring grist to the mill.

keduten a (nervous) twitch in eyelid; (S.) KEDUTAN.

keham river rapids.

Kèibitai (during the Jap. occupation) Garrison Guards.

Kèibodan (during the Jap. occupation) Vigilance Corps.

keja to make, cause. - *ketawa* to keep s.o. laughing. - *marah* to make angry.

kejai resilient, elastic.

kejam - *berbalas* - an eye for an eye, a tooth for a tooth. **ke-an** atrocity.

kejang *mati* - to drop dead. **ke-an** *sesudah mati* rigor mortis. - *jantung* angina (pectoris). - *mulut* lockjaw. - *terkejut* (to stand) stock-still.

kejap *dlm* **se-(an)** *mata* overnight, in a jiffy.

kejar di- to be superseded. *Berita ini kemudian* ~ *oleh suatu berita heboh lagi,* This news was later superseded (,overtaken) by another (recent) sensational news item. **di-.-** *waktu* to be late, rushed for time. **meng-:** ~ *kereta.api* to catch the train. ~ *waktu yg hilang* to make up for wasted time. -.**meng-** pursuit. **peng-** *pangkat* jobhunter, office-seeker. *dlm* **peng-an** under pursuit.

kejawèn Jav. philosophical mysticism.

kejelog 1 to break (of rope). 2 to shake, bump.

kejèn *besi* - pig iron.

keji disgraceful, infamous. **ke-an** abjection.

kejoan little green pigeon.

kejolak to flare up, increase.

kejora (s.) BINTANG (KEJORA).

kéju an abusive term for a full-blooded Dutchman.

kejungjun charmed, enchanted.

kejur 1 inflexible. 2 rigid.

kejut shock. **keter-an** start, a sudden, brief shock. **se-** touch-me-not (a plant). **-an** shock. ~ *budaya* culture shock. ~ *rohani*

psychic shock. *rumput* -.- touch-me-not
(a plant).

kèk I (final k pron.) cake.

kèk II 1 grandfather. 2 old man.

kèk III 1 (after each possibility or suggestion in a list) *apapun namanya: perploncoan -, perkenalan -, pembayatan
-, kebaktian -,* ... whatever the name:
whether it is called perploncoan, or
perkenalan, or pembayatan, or kebaktian ... (all words meaning 'initiation').
2 you should have just ..., why don't
you just ... (in commands and questions).

kèk IV (hand)loom.

kekabu (S.) KABU.KABU.

kékah offering at a death, 1,000 days
after a death, etc., usually consisting
of a sheep or 10 pigeons.

kekang curb, restraint. *tanpa* - unrestrained, uncontrollable.

kekar solid, substantial, stout, strong.

kekawin poetic epic written in Old Javanese *(Kawi)*.

kéké (in Manado) girl.

kékéyan peg top (a child's spinning toy).

kekiprah (s.) KIPRAH.

kekitir land tax assessment paper; (s.)
GIRIK.

kèkol bribe, illicit commission.

kekrupukan to be at o's wits' end.

kekucah favor(s).

kelabakan 1 to sprawl. 2 to feel desperate,
flounder around.

kelabang plait(ed), braid(ed) hair. *si - dua*
the girl with the two braids.

kelabu I ber-an grayish. *putih* - off-white.

kelabu II peng-an deception. **ter-i** be
fooled.

keladi aroid, calladium.

kelahi *pe- sapi* bullfighter. **per-an** *sangkur*
bayonet charge.

kelak *akhir* **-nya** finally.

kelakar di-i to be made ridiculous (,fun
of).

kelak.kelik to flicker.

kelam meng- to become dark.

kelambai k.o. ghost, such as, *langsuir*.

kelamin ke-an sex.

kelamun overwhelmed. **peng-** sentimen-
talist. **peng-an** whim.

kelana ber- *dunia naik mobil* to travel
widely about the world by car. **peng-**
tourist. - *yg hina.papa* a miserable wandering wretch.

kelangkang perineum. *tulang* - sacrum.

kelapa - *genjah* Malayan Yellow Dwarf,
i.e. a coconut species. - *gonseng* coconut flakes fried without oil. - *hijau*
green coconut. - *parut* grated coconut.

kelap.kelip to flicker.

kelar 1 finished. 2 O.K., let's go (conductor to bus driver when passengers have
finished getting on or off and the bus
can start again).

kelas - *berat* high-class. - *buruh* the working class. - *embun* low-class. - *India* low-
class. - *lele* big shot. - *ningrat* the aristocracy. - *penguasa (,yg meraja)* the ruling class.

kelasa 1 a hard, protuberant mass of
flesh. 2 muscular tissue.

kelasi a long-nosed primate (L. Hylobates
Leuciseus).

kelawar club (suit of cards).

kelèbat *dilihat* **se-** *mata* considered superficially. *dgn* **se-an** *saja bisa dilihat* it is
obvious at a glance.

kelebon Cino gundulan to be cheated.

kelecé di-i to be cheated.

kelèdar defensive measures or preparations. *topi* - safety helmet (for motor-
ists).

kelelegen (s.) KLELEGEN.

kelelesa chameleon.

kelembak k.o. tree (L. Aquilaria malac-
censis).

kelèncèr ng- to go on a spree.

kelengar and **kelenger** to faint, become
unconscious, stunned.

kelenjar - *ludah.perut* pancreas.

kelenteng cotton seed.

kelèpèt turned down.

kelepir testicles.

kelepon *[kue(h)]* - bite-sized, green balls
made of sticky rice flour; containing

liquid brown sugar (which leaks all over, if bitten carelessly) and rolled in grated coconut.

keles ng-in to approach, keep an eye on.

kelètah 1 affected. 2 coquet, to try to attract attention or admiration (usually said of women).

kelèwat too; (s.) LEWAT.

keli *ikan* - an edible river catfish (L. Clarias majur). - *dua selobang* two lovers of o. woman.

kèli carried along by the stream. **ng-** to have o.s. carried along by the stream.

keliang (in the Central Lombok Regency) village head.

kelibat se- (s.) SEKELEBAT. **se-an** cursory.

kelikat *sdh tahu bagaimana* **-nya** he knows his customers.

keliki(h) papaya.

keliling ber- *dunia* to travel around the world. **se-** around. - *bumi* circumference of the earth.

kelimis (s.) KLIMIS.

kelimpungan 1 to be at a loss. 2 embarrassed, confused.

kelinci - *percobaan* (fig.) guinea pig.

keling k.o. boat.

kelip to blink, flash.

kelipuk (in Palembang) (s.) ECENG.

kelitik ng- to knock, pound. *Fiat Sdr. kurang efisien* ~, Your Fiat pounds inefficiently.

keliyengan (s.) KLIYENGAN.

kelojotan anger.

kèlok -an *jalan* street curve.

kelola peng- director. *kurang* **ter-** undermanaged.

kelompok meng- to assemble. **peng-an** *kembali* regrouping. *K- 19* the 19-nation group representing the South in the *Dialog Utara.Selatan. K-77* the group representing the developing nations or Third World, the raw-material exporting countries. - *elang* (in politics) the hawks. *K- Kembang Sepatu* 'Hibiscus Group,' i.e. the sobriquet for the *Malari*-detainees connected with the Indonesian

National Party. - *kepentingan* interest group. - *kerja* working group. - *merpati* (in politics) the doves. - *pendesak* (*,penekan*) pressure group. - *pengkaji bersama* joint study group. - *perundingan* negotiating group. - *pulau* archipelago. - *suara* voting bloc.

kelonèng ding-dong.

kèlong (in the Riau archipelago) k.o. fish trap on poles.

kelontang a noisy clapper scarecrow.

kelontong 1 wooden cattle bell. 2 hawker's rattle.

kelop (s.) KLOP. *kurang* - unsuitable.

kèlor *dunia tdk sedaun* - and *dunia tak selebar daun* - 1 with time comes counsel. 2 there's more than o. fish in the sea.

kelotok I *kapal (,perahu)* - (s.) KLOTOK.

kelotok II ng- to peel off, scale off, come off (of paint from wall).

keloyor ng- to stagger around.

Kèlta Celt(ic).

kelu ke-an aphasia.

keluak *buah* - nut of the *kepayang* tree (L. Pangium edule).

keluan *menjilat* - *bagai kerbau* to make a long face.

keluang *bagai* - *bebar petang* in throngs.

keluar 1 to be spent. 2 to have an ejaculation. **meng-kan** to take out, remove, pull out, extract. ~ *cek (kosong)* to write a (bad) check. ~ *dekrit* to issue a decree. ~ *pendapatnya* to air o's views. ~ *suaranya* to cast o's vote. **meng-jawakan** to relocate outside of Java. **peng-an** expenditure. ~ *barang dr pelabuhan* Customs clearance. ~ *tak terduga* unforeseen expenses. ~ *obligasi* the issuance of debentures.

keluarga 1 society. *K- Mahasiswa Seni Rupa Institut Teknologi Bandung* Bandung Institute of Technology Fine Arts Students Society. 2 - *besar* community. *K- Besar Universitas Krisnadwipajana* Krisnadwipajana University Community. **ber-** to be married. ~ *semenda* to be allied (by marriage). **ke-an** 1 family.

2 brotherhood. 3 commonwealth (of nations). **per-an** *semenda* affinity. **se-** and family. *kami* ~ I and my family. - *berencana* family planning. - *retak* broken home.

keluat (s.) KHALWAT.

keluli steel.

kelumit **se-** a corner of the veil.

kelunak *ubi* - tubers.

kelupas **ter-** peeled off (skin, paint).

kelurut whitlow (on finger).

keluyu pandrong (in Lombok) the man-eating shark.

kémah **Per-an** *Wirakarya* (Boy Scouts) Community Service Camp.

kemak **di-.kemikkan** to be repeated again and again.

kemala talisman.

kemampang to take things too lightly.

kemandang (S.) KUMANDANG.

kemang evil spirit affecting new-born children.

kemangi basil.

kemantèn and **kemantin** (S.) PENGAN-TIN.

kemarau drought.

kemarin last, the other day, recently, a few days ago. *minggu (,bln ,th)* - last week (,month ,year). *pagi* - and - *pagi* yesterday morning. *Dia bukan anak -,* He was not born yesterday. *di hari* - in the past. -.- earlier.

kemas *kotak (,peti)* - (large-sized) container. **peng-an** *kembali* repacking. **-an** packing (for medicines, etc.).

kematu (s.) KEMBATU.

kematus tuberculosis.

kemayu to act cute and coquettish.

kembali back, again. *membayar* - to pay back. *hidup* - to come to life again. - *kpd* to come back to (the subject). - *ke rahmat Allah* to die. *Ada -?* Do you have some change? **peng-an** *bea. masuk* drawback (i.e. a refund of import duties when the taxed commodities are later exported). **-nya** the change. *Ambillah ~!* (Said to a waiter in a restaurant, etc.) Keep the change! *tdk*

-.- *lagi* never come back again. - *pulang* to return home.

kembang I **ber-** *hati* cheerful, bright.

kembang II **meng-.biakkan** to spread the cultivation (of a crop). **peng-an** augmentation.

kembang III code name for *daun ganja*. - *malam* prostitute.

kembang IV - *bopong (,sekar)* (in Java) (s.) ECENG.

kembar - *dampit* Siamese twins.

kembatu corn (on skin).

kemben breastcover used by women.

kemboja (s.) KAMBOJA.

kemèkmèk 1 frightened. 2 disconcerted. 3 confused.

kemelut crucial.

kemèmèk (s.) KEMEKMEK.

kemendalu mistletoe.

kemendikai watermelon.

kemendit (s.) KENDIT.

kemendur 1 commander. 2 - *laut* harbor master. 3 (S.) KONTE(R)LIR. 4 (S.) MANDUR.

kemeniran a shrub used as a medicine (L. Phyllanthus niruri L.).

kemenjaya (s.) KAMAJAYA.

kementam booming, thundering.

kemenyan benzoin. *membakar* - *spy godaan jauh* to burn incense (on Thursday evenings) to ward off evil spirits. *kayu* - the tree producing the benzoin (L. Styrax benzoin). - *arab* myrrh. - *hantu* (euph.) flatus.

kemi *ikan* - the sucking fish.

kemidi - *bedès* traveling monkey show.

kemik *hidung* - a snub nose.

kemil I *jato* - to be in luck, come at the right moment. **-an** food, things to eat.

kemil II tucked in.

kemiri - *jatuh ke pangkalnya* to return to o's native place.

kemirisasi encouragement to plant *kemiri* (,macademia nut) trees.

kemis 1 five. 2 fifth.

kemlandingan (s.) LAMTORO.

kemocèng (feather) duster, brush.

kemong gong.

kemongkrong (in Purbalingga, Central Java) person skilled in catching wild boars.

Kèmpai (s.) KEMPEITAI.

Kèmpèitai the dreaded Jap. mil. police during the Jap. occupation.

kempèng (s.) EMPENG. **di-** (the child was) kept quiet with the breast.

kempès *harapannya* - his expectations vanished into thin air.

kempos (S.) KEMPES.

kempunan calamity.

kemput entirely, through. *tlh dibaca -* (your letter) has been read through.

kemrekes feverish.

kemrungsung to get excited, worry, trouble o.s.

kemudi ber- *ke buritan* to be henpecked.

kemudian - *drpd itu* after that. *kereta.api -nya* the next (,following) train.

kemudu (s.) KUDU.

kemungkus addled.

kemuning name of a tree with yellow wood, bearing fragrant white flowers.

kemunting the rose myrtle (L. Rhodomyrtus tomentosa). - *Cina* a pink or white periwinkle (L. Vinca rosea).

Kèn (archaic) His (,Her) Honor, e.g. - *Arok* the first king of Singasari (1222-92).

kena 1 *K-!* Bull's eye! Done! 2 exact, accurate, precise. *tdk -* 1 evasive. 2 not applicable. *K- apa … ?* What's the reason that …? What's the matter? *yg -* the injured party. *yg - wajib …* those who are required to … *yg - wajib militer* the enlistee(s). **di-kan:** ~ *tahanan kota (,rumah)* to be put under city (,house) arrest. ~ *thd* to be applied to. ~ *wajib* to be obliged. *Berapa harga yg* ~ *utk satu … ?* How much do you charge for one … ? **meng-kan** 1 to impose. 2 to put on, wear. ~ *hukuman* to condemn. ~ *tahanan kpd* to jail. **peng-an** assessment. **ter-:** ~ *getahnya* to get the bad results of s.o. else's acts. ~ *kesukaran* to get into trouble. - *air* come into contact with water. - *bogem*

mentah get a punch. - *bom* be hit by a bomb. - *bubu* get netted (in a raid). - *gaet* get tricked. - *garuk* get pulled in (by police). - *gebuk* get beaten up. - *gempa* destroyed by an earthquake. - *gogoh* get snatched. - *gusur* be trampled on (by), dumped on (by). - *hama* infected, contaminated. - *hantam* get hit. - *hujan dan panas* weather-beaten. - *jaring* be rounded up (by police). - *kecek* be taken in. - *kepotong* to cut o.s. - *keserempet* be grazed. - *kili* get worked up, stimulated. - *lotere* to hit the lottery. - *pajak* taxable. - *panas* exposed to heat. - *penyakit* to fall ill. - *razia* be rounded up (by police). *Dia - rongrongan bininya,* He was bled dry by his wife. - *sapu* get pulled in (by police). - *semprot* (S.) KENA (SEMPERET). - *sensor* censored. - *serangan jantung* to have a heart attack. - *skors* get suspended. - *tembak* (fig.) be cheated. - *tembakan meriam* hit by gunfire. - *todong* be held up.

kenal - *akan (,dgn ,kpd ,pd ,sama)* 1 to know. 2 to be acquainted with. *tdk - capai* untiring. *tak - tak sayang* and *karena tak - maka tak sayang (,cinta)* unknown, unloved. *tak - takut* intrepid. *engsel pintu yg tak pernah - minyak pelumas* a doorhinge that never has been greased. *belajar - dgn* to get acquainted with s.o. **ber-an** *dgn* 1 to get acquainted with s.o. 2 to get to know. **ber-an** *pribadi dgn dia* to know him personally. **di-:** ~ *dgn nama …* to go by the name of … *yg lebih* ~ *dgn nama …* more widely known as … **keter-an** reputation, fame. **memper-kan** to introduce o.s. *"Per-kan dulu, saya Parman."* "Let me first introduce myself, I'm Parman." **meng-** to be familiar with. *tak* ~ to spare no (pains). *tak* ~ *kasihan* pitiless, merciless, ruthless. *tak* ~ *kompromi* uncompromising. *tak* ~ *mata huruf* illiterate, uneducated. *tak* ~ *menyerah* unconquerable. **meng-kan** *dirinya* to introduce o.s. **peng-an**

identification, distinction, discernment. **ter-:** ~ *akan* to be known for. ~ *jahatnya* notorious. -.-**an** circle of acquaintances.

kencana - *wingka* always standing up for o's child (,darling ,etc.).

kencang I meng-kan *tali.kursi* to fasten the seat belt (in aircraft).

kencang.kencung to jingle.

kencit (s.) TUYUL.

kencrang.kencring jingle-jangle.

kencur *masih* - still wet behind o's ears.

kendali peng-an: ~ *diri* self-restraint. ~ *huru.hara* riot control. *tdk* **ter-kan** *(lagi)* uncontrollable, impracticable.

kendan *batu* - obsidian.

kendara 3½ *jam dgn* **ber-an** *mobil* 3½ hours by car. **peng-:** ~ *beca(k)* pedicab driver. ~ *mobil* motorist. ~ *sepeda (motor)* (motor)cyclist. -**an:** ~ *hantu* vehicles, such as, *Colts, oplets,* trucks, etc. driving after sunset without switching on headlights. ~ *tahanan* paddy (,patrol) wagon.

kendat ng- to commit suicide.

kendel - *kandel, jerih ketindih* fortune favors the bold.

kendil pot for boiling rice.

kendiri (S.) SENDIRI.

kendit a narrow belt, often of coins. - *bumi* equator.

kendo loose (not tight), slack, relaxed. *stèl* - to relax.

kèndo Jap. stylized form of fencing, somewhat like judo with bamboo poles.

kendor 1 lax, flabby. 2 listless. 3 too late, slow (of watch). - *lima menit* five minutes slow. 4 to slacken. *mulai - semangatnya* his enthusiasm began to slacken. **ber-.-** 1 to slacken. 2 to relax. **ke-an** slackness. **meng-** to slacken (v.i.). **meng-kan** *urat.urat* to relax the nerves. **peng-an** relaxation. ~ *ketegangan* detente.

kèngkang bowlegged.

kèngsel *kena* - cancelled.

Kènia Kenya.

kenikir similar to big-leafed parsley, sharp taste, a little like turnip greens.

kènsel di- to be cancelled (out). *Penumpang tdk pernah* ~, Passengers are never cancelled out (,bumped).

kental 1 condensed (milk). 2 strong (of coffee, tea), solidified.

kentang - *goreng* potato chips. - *ongklok* broken boiled potatoes.

kentara *tak* - disguised.

kentut meng-i to fart upon. 2 (fig.) to fool, cheat, deceive.

kenut (S.) KENUP.

kenya virgin, girl.

Kènya Kenya.

kenyal ke-an elasticity.

kenyang *tak* -.-*nya* insatiable.

kenyit spasmodic, of movement of the lips or eyelids, hence, 'summer lightning.'

kenyut sucking movement.

kèp crest (of rooster).

kepai *udang* - a dirty white shrimp.

kepal a coagulated mass (of cooked rice).

kepala 1 first digit in a lottery number. 2 caption. *(arah) ke* - cranial. *tlh dua* -*nya* diplopia due to drunkenness. *ular* - *dua* hypocritical. *menjual - ke dlm kompeni* to join the army, enlist. *garuk. garuk* - to scratch o's head. **ke- batuan** stubbornness. - *angin* frivolous. - *bagian* section head. - *biarawan* abbot. - *biarawati* abbess. *K- Burung* the Bird's Head, i.e. an area in Irian Jaya. - *dingin* calm. - *dua* to make the best of both worlds. - *gudang* warehouse keeper. - *kamar mesin* (in ship) chief engineer. - *karangan* title (of newspaper article). - *kodian* the best (of a parcel of clothes). - *negeri* (in West Sumatra) head, about a district head (in Java). - *perahu* stem (of a proa). - *pulau* the highest part of an island. - *raja* (obsolete) stamp (with Queen of the Netherlands' image on it). - *ringan* intelligent. - *setasiun* station master. - *staf* chief of staff. - *wanua* (in the southern Celebes) village head.

kepalang *tdk* - *tanggung* 1 unreasonable. 2 going all the way.

keparat in misery.

kepaya (S.) PEPAYA.

kepayang a tree (L. Pangium edule); its fruit is pretty but dangerous to eat.

kepèk I notes for cheating on a test. **ng-** to cheat on a test, do schoolwork dishonestly by using a crib.

kepèk II betel pouch.

kepénak (s.) ENAK.KEPENAK.

képer twill, jeans.

kèpèt and **ng-** not cleaning with water after defecation; a term of abuse.

kepiat waste matter, refuse (coconut).

kepincut (s.) PINCUT.

keping coin (to pay bus fare). *se- hari ini, seonggok utk nanti* a stitch in time saves nine.

kepingin - *muntah* to feel nauseated.

kepiting mangrove crab. *sbg - batu* miserly. *-.kelapa* coconut crab (L. Birgus latro), climbs in coconut trees to pick the fruits, peel and eat them; the crab, which can reach a length of about 30 centimeters, is found in Ternate (Eastern Indonesia).

keplak meng- to slap in the face.

keplok -an applause.

kepodang black-naped oriole.

Kepprès [Keputusan Presiden] Presidential Directive. **di.-kan** to be created by a Presidential Directive.

keprak castanets, clacks.

kèprèt to sprinkle.

kèpsen (newspaper term) caption.

kepuk round rice-bin of bark.

kepul I closely packed, clotted, thick (as smoke). *kopi yg* **meng-** *panas* steaming-hot coffee.

kepul II peng- numbers runner.

kepung di- *wakul binaya (,buaya) mangap* to be in danger. **peng-** besieger. **-an** encirclement.

kepurun broth made from sago-meal.

kera - *menjadi monyet* and *spt - dgn monyet* it is quite the same. *sbg - dpt canggung* to cling to s.o. (in distress). *sbg (,spt) - kena belacan* to be very restless. *- dpt bunga* to cast pearls before swine. *- menegurkan tahinya* to wash o's dirty linen in public.

kerabat ber- to be allied.

kerabik and **kerabit** picking (,plucking) to pieces.

kerabu I a fish (,prawn) salad.

kerabu II (gold) ear stud.

kerah *juru* - (S.) PENGERAH.

kerahi and **kerai** k.o. small gherkin (L. Cucumis melo).

kerak - *besi* iron slag. - *gendar* rice *kripik.*

kerakap old dry sirih leaves (symbol of a hard life). *hidup spt - di atas batu* and *macam - tumbuh di batu* 'like a *kerakap* plant growing on a rock,' i.e. a hard life.

kerakeling cracknel.

kerak.keruk *bersumpah* - to swear by all that's holy.

keram cramp(-iron).

keramas *bedak* - a rice-flour cosmetic.

keramat *ditimpa* - slain by unseen powers for sacrilege at a sacred spot. *minta -* to ask for a blessing. *tempat yg -* a holy site. **mengk-kan** to treat s.t. as holy.

keramunting the rose-myrtle (L. Rhodomyrtus tomentosa).

keran crane. - *terapung* floating crane (in harbors).

kerang *batu* - (coral) rock. - *mutiara* pearl-oyster.

kerangka draft, blueprint, outline. - *hidup* a living wreck. - *jenazah* mortal remains. - *kekuatan* power structure.

kerangkai a tree (L. Quercus rajah Hauce).

kerangkèng (Customs) quarantine. **meng-** to limit. **meng-kan** and *memasukkan ke dlm* - to quarantine (goods).

keranjang - *kotoran* waste basket.

keranji a generic name for a number of trees (L. Dialuim sp.).

keranta k.o. louse.

kerantung bamboo tocsin.

kerap ke-an frequency.

kerapu grouper.

keras 1 heavy (work, rain). 2 close (guard). 3 drastic (measure). 4 violent. 5 pungent, caustic. 6 firm (conviction). 7 vigorous, determined. - *dugaanku (,sangkaku)* I'm perfectly sure. - *dijaga* closely guarded. *paling* - if worst comes

to worst. **ber-** *batang leher* to stand
firm, insist that. **ber-.-** to have a tug of
war. **ber-.-an** *mulut* to wrangle, **bersi-**
to hold firmly (to a belief). **ke-an**
assault, violence. *dgn (jalan)* ~ forcibly.
tanpa ~ non-violent. ~ *hati* determination. **ke-.kepalaan** stubbornness. **peng-:**
~ *rambut* hairspray. ~ *suara tanpa kabel*
wireless loudspeaker. **peng-an** *pembu-*
luh darah arteriosclerosis. -.- aloud.
- *kerak* not permanently hard. - *batang*
leher obstinate. - *hati* willful, energetic.
- *hidung* want to have the last say
(,word).
kerat rust.
keratabahasa folk etymology.
kerawat *makan* - as poor as a church-
mouse.
kerawit *cacing* - threadworm.
kerawitan 1 fine arts. 2 a *gamelan* melody.
3 overture.
kerbat a leather (water)bag.
kerbau numbskull, blockhead. *membeli* -
bertuntun to buy a pig in a poke. *bagai*
- *dicocok hidung* to be tied to o's wife's
apron-strings. *bagai* - *runcing tanduk*
to give a dog a bad name and hang him.
- *punya susu, sapi punya nama* desert
and reward seldom keep company.
- *besi* reference to a tractor (for rice
paddy). - *bulai (,bulé)* the Dutchman.
- *dungkul* 1 buffalo with horns bent
downwards. 2 madman.
kercap(-kercip) (,-kercup) 1 smacking.
2 noise of splashing.
kercut 1 a common sedge used in mat-
making and for sails (L. Scirpus mucro-
natus). 2 a sack of that sedge.
kerdam resonance. -.*kerdum* thudding.
kerdan *aras* - fritters.
kerdil **meng-kan** to dwarf (e.g. a tree).
kerdum resonance. -.*kerdam* continuous
thumping.
kéré *(orang)* - beggar, bum. - *dandan* (in
Semarang) female hobo who in the
evening dresses up to become a prostitute.
kerèdong a sarong sewn together in which
o. wraps the upper part of the body.

kèrèk - *majemuk* tackle.
kerèkot shrivelled up into a coil.
kereman fatted (calf).
keremi pinworm; (s.) KERMI.
keremot puckered, creased.
kerèmpèng emaciated, thin (of figure).
kerempung abdomen.
kerenggamunggu cardamom.
kerengkiang rice granary with four posts.
kerèpès *di ruang* - to be buried alive.
kererangga (large) red ant.
kereseng to dawdle.
Kerèsmis Christmas.
kerèta 1 gun-carriage, (gun) mount. 2
bobbin. **per-.apian** railway system.
- *api barang* goods train. - *api berlapis*
baja armored train. - *api bumel* local
train. - *api istimewa* special train. - *api*
ketelan train with tankcars.- *api langsam*
local train. - *api listrik* electric train.
- *api malam* night train. - *api monorel*
monorail train. - *api olang.alik* commuter train. - *api Purbaya* the Purwo-
kerto-Surabaya express. - *api senja*
night train. - *api sombong* fast train.
- *api t(e)rutuk* local train. - *dorong*
pushcart. - *gandengan* trailer. - *jenazah*
(funeral) hearse. - *kebal* armored vehicle. - *kecil* a mini car. - *siram* sprinkler. - *tambangan* carriage for rent.
- *udara* skylift.
keretot deformed.
keri ticklish.
keria *kuih* - a sweetmeat of yams and
sugar.
keriang-(,keriat-)keriut creaking (of row-
locks or of a door).
kerical *pacal.*- lowest of the low.
keridik mole cricket.
kerih laboriously.
kerik shaving of the front hair.
kerikil obstacle. *Masih ada banyak* - *yg*
mengganjel hubungan itu, There are
still many obstacles hampering those
relations.
kerinan oversleep.
kering poorly paid (work, job). - *dr* running low on (supplies of a liquid). *beri.*
beri - scurvy (without swellings). *latihan*

SAR yg bersifat - Search and Rescue maneuvers without troop mobilization. *tanah* - uncultivated land. - *kerontang (,kontang ,lekah ,lekang ,melenting ,mersik ,rendang ,ringkai ,terik)* bone dry. - *tempe* soybean cake.

keringat *Dia basah* **ber-**, He swam in his own sweat. - *dingin* cold sweat.

keriningan (bicycle-)bell.

keris kris, creese, a wavy bladed dagger, simultaneously a weapon, an ornament, a cult object (said to have magic powers); it is said that the responsibilities a kris owner has to bear are commensurate with the number of *luks* (waves) his kris has; the more waves it has the more responsibilities.

kerisi *ikan* - a sea bream (L. Synagris sp).

kerisologi knowledge of the kris.

keriting peng-an *rambut* permanent wave.

keriwil freewheel (device in the rear hub of a bicycle that permits the rear wheel to go on turning when the pedals are stopped).

kerja **be-**: ~ *lembur* to work overtime. ~ *penuh* to have a full-time job. *bisa (,dpt)* ~ *sendiri* capable of acting upon o's own initiative, independent. **-in** to fuck s.o. **mempe-.paksakan** and **meng-.paksakan** to draft for forced labor. **meng-.samakan** to have act together, make cooperate. **pe-**: *jumlah* ~ *dikalikan hari* - man-days. ~ *bangunan* construction worker. ~ *bulanan* monthly wage earner. ~ *kapal* longshoreman. ~ *lapangan* field-worker. ~ *pelabuhan* longshoreman. ~ *penuh* full-timer. ~ *riset* research worker. ~ *sambilan* part-timer. ~ *sosial* social worker. **pe-an**: *tdk mempunyai* ~ (in notarial instruments) of no occupation. ~ *bebas* liberal profession. ~ *dagang* (in notarial instruments) by occupation a merchant. ~ *gonta.ganti* interaction, interplay. ~ *persiapan* preparatory work. ~ *sambèn (,sambilan ,sampingan)* side job, part-time job. ~ *tuangan* castwork. ~ *tukang kayu* carpentry. ~ *tulis.menulis* administrative work. **pengk-.samaan**

concerted action, teamwork. **terpe-kan** employable. - *badan* physical work. - *duta* mission. - *kasar* manual labor. - *nyata* practical work (in laboratory, university). - *tempa* forging.

kerjang *emas* - (S.) EMAS (KERJANG).

kerkap.kerkup crunching.

kerkau claw-shaped.

kèrkop (European) graveyard.

kerlip flickering.

kermak a weed (L. Staurogyne setigera).

kermanici (s.) KARBONACI(S).

kermi *(cacing)* - maggot, pinworm. *(sakit)* **-an** suffering from pinworm, itch around the anus.

kernèk (S.) KORNET.

kernèli vanilla.

kernyau creaking, grating.

kéro *tempat tidur* - a steel bed with spring.

kerocok 1 a rattle. 2 to rattle.

kerodong ber- to screen, cover.

kerok ng-i to scrape the skin of a person with a coin until it becomes red, after it has been rubbed with oil, when he has caught a cold, has a headache, stiff neck, etc.

keroncong I rumbling, gnawing in o's stomach. **ber-an** to rumble (of an empty stomach). *perutnya* ~ he is famished (,starving). **-an** k.o. green manure with edible seeds (L. Grotalaria striata).

keroncong II ber-an to make *keroncong* music. **peng-** *keroncong* player.

keroncong III *gelang* - a large tinkling anklet.

keroncong IV bunt or inmost pocket of seine-net.

keroncor the male king-crab. *spt - dgn belangkas* indissolubly associated.

kèrong *(ikan)* - a small sea-perch (L. Sebastes stolizkoe).

kerong.kerang rattling.

kerontang very dry, bonedry. *kering* - extremely dry. *panas* - hot and dry.

kèrop (in Medan) care of.

keropak handwriting on palm leaves.

keropok spongy, woolly.

keropos hollow, spongy, not compact (of wood, stone, etc.); (s.) KROPOS.

ter- hollowed, not solid.

kerosi meng- to give s.o. a seat (in a representative body).

keroso (S.) TERASA.

kerosok *tembakau* - dried tobacco leaves.

kerotak *bising* **ber-** to creak.

kerpak the sound of crackling.

kerpas rustling sound.

kerpik sounds of cracking.

kerpis rustling sound.

kerpuk sounds of crackling.

kerpus provost (,punishment) cells.

kersai crisp, brittle. **ber-** crumbly. **ke-an** crispness.

kersak crackling, rustling.

Kersani *besi* - Khorassan iron, iron of proof.

kersang stiff and dry (of hair).

kersuk loud rustle.

kerta adinegara city planning.

kertak *be- giginya* to gnash o's teeth.

kertang *ikan* - a fish species (L. Epinephelus pantherinus).

kertap a sound such as that of a door being closed, slam.

kertas I -.**meng-** various k.o. paper. - *bernilai uang* valuable papers, securities. - *folio* legal-size paper. - *grenjeng* silver paper, tinfoil. - *karbon* carbon paper. - *karya* (,*kerja*) working paper. - *krèp* crêpe paper. - *kwarto* letter-size paper. - *lap* blotting paper. - *pak* mailing paper. - *pembungkus* wrapping paper. - *perbendaharaan* exchequer bills and treasury bills. - *stensil* stencil paper. - *telur* paper used for making kites. - *wangi pengusap muka* towellet. - *W.C.* toilet paper.

kertas II the rustle of crisp paper.

kerubung I **ng-** to gather around.

kerubung II a *padi* barn built of *pandan* leaves.

kerubut a plant with huge crimson flowers (L. Thottea grandiflora).

kerudung ber- (s.) BERKERODONG.

keruh I - *hati* 1 malicious. 2 dirty, corrupt.

keruh II - *bumi* linear measure (± 2 miles).

keruing a generic name for a number of trees yielding a special k.o. oil (L. Dipterocarpus sp.).

keruk peng-an dredging.

kerukut ber- curly.

kerul curl. *rambut* - trimmed (,barbered) hair.

kerumuk ber- to wrinkle, crumple, crease.

kerumun -an crowd.

kerun crown.

keruntang.pungkang entangled.

kerunting cow bell.

kerup munching noise.

kerupuk (s.) KRUPUK. - *legendar* crisp ground-rice chips. - *sermiyer* (usually red-colored) sago chips.

kerut meng- to shrivel. **peng-an** contraction. - *keningnya* his frowning.

kerutup cracking sound.

keruwek ng- disgruntled, displeased.

kès cash.

kesa first.

Kesada midnight ceremony of offerings by the Tenggerese people to the God of Fire who they believe lives in the crater of Mount Bromo (East Java).

kesal ke-an penitence. - *(hati)* 1 hurt, offended, to have a grudge, cannot stand. 2 discontented. 3 to be sorry, regret.

kesan *memberi* - to give the impression. *menanam* - *mendalam di* to make a deep impression on. **ber-** impressive, imposing, striking. **peng-an** *kandungan hati* expression of feeling. **ter-** *akan* to be impressed by.

kesang meng- to blow o's nose (using only o's fingers).

kesat 1 shaggy, hairy. 2 weather-beaten. 3 fade. 4 coarse, rude.

kesel 1 exhausted, tired. 2 to have had enough of, be tired of. 3 fidgety, nervous. 4 dejected.

keselak choke (on a piece of meat, etc.), to swallow the wrong way.

keseléo - *lidah* to make a slip of the tongue.

kesemek (S.) KES(E)MAK.

kesemsem to be keen on, be passionately

fond of, sexually excited.

kesengsem - *kpd* 1 enticed, eager for.
2 charmed, enchanted, fascinated; (s.)
KESEMSEM.

kèsèran cart, wagon.

keseser defeated.

kesiap ter- *(darah)* to be frightened.

kesik(.kesik) rustle.

kesimbukan k.o. climbing shrub (L.
Saprosma arboreum).

kesmaran ber- to be madly in love.

kesra [kesejahteraan rakyat] people's
welfare.

kèstul pistol.

kesu.kesi the sound of whispering.

kesuk.kesak the sound of whispering.

kesumba *merah* - fiery red.

ketak sound of rapping, tapping.

ketakar.ketèkèr and **kethakar.kethèkèr**
busy, occupied.

ketam *dgn gigi* **ber-** with clenched teeth.

ketanah k.o. tree.

ketang taut.

ketap stopcock.

ketar ber-.ketir *hati* to be afraid.

ketat tight, taut. **peng-an** tightening.

ketaton to get wounded. *spt banteng* - on
the rampage.

ketawa meng-kan to laugh at. - *gombal* to
laugh on the wrong side of o's mouth.

ketawan (S.) KETAHUAN.

kètèl - *angin* air chamber. - *uap* (steam)
boiler.

ketemu 1 to come across. 2 to see e.o.
minggu(,th) - *minggu(,th)* week (,year)
after week (,year). *tak* **ter-kan** could
not be found. - *akal* rational. - *batunya*
found his match.

ketia k.o. tree producing wood and oil.

ketiak *spt (,ba')* - *ular* wordy, tedious.
mengembang - *amis* wash o's dirty
linen in public. *Dia tdk mengeluarkan
pendapat itu semata.mata dr -,* He
wasn't speaking off the top of his head,
he wasn't talking through his hat. **ber-**
ular long-winded, tiresomely long.

ketial difficult to remove (as a cork from
the mouth of a bottle).

ketiap *perahu* - a houseboat used on rivers.

ketiau a large tree.

ketib (S.) KATIB.

ketimbang (s.) TIMBANG II.

ketimbul breadfruit.

ketinting a 2 HP-motorized proa used in
East Kalimantan; (s.) KLOTOK I.

ketlingsut and **ketlisut** mislaid.

ketok ng- to fool, deceive.

kétok moto (s.) KASATMATA.

ketoktular (s.) GETOKTULAR.

ketola a generic name for a number of
pumpkins (L. Lua cylindrica and
Trichosanthes anguina).

ketonggèng large, black (earth) scorpion.

ketopong ber- helmeted. *lahir* ~ to be
born with a caul.

ketoprak a dish consisting of beansprouts,
bean curd, red pepper and soysauce.

ketrucut (s.) TRUCUT.

ketua *K- Fakultas* Dean. - *pelaksana* 1
chief executor. 2 executive chairman.
- *umum* general chairman. - *wanita*
chairwoman.

ketuk meng- *meja* to knock on wood.
meng-.ketukkan to pound. ~ *jari.
jemarinya* to drum o's fingers. - *tilu*
name of a social dance popular in West
Java; dancers may not touch o.a. and
must remain at a distance of about o.
meter.

ketumbé - *tahi ayam* riff-raff, dregs.

ketumbi (s.) KETUMBE.

ketumbit a herb (L. Leucas seylanica).

ketup.ketap tapping noise.

ketus sharp(ly). .... *sahut Ibu Jamilah* -
... answered Mrs. Jamilah sharply.

Ketut (in Bali) name element placed
before personal names to indicate the
fourth born child, such as, *Ketut Lami;*
(s.) KTUT.

kewalahan 1 to be sick to death of it.
2 cannot hold out. 3 to be in a fix.

kèwes graceful, charming, pretty.

kéwuh meng-kan to embarrass.

khadam servant.

khalas the end.

khalwat ber- to go into retreat (,seclusion).

khamir yeast.

kharisma charisma.

khas typical, characteristic. **ke-an** peculiarity.

khasanah 1001 malam The 1001 Nights.

khat calligraphic writing.

khayal peng- fantaisiste, dreamer, visionary.

khianat treacherous, perfidious, traitorous.

khitan ber- to be circumcized.

khotibun nas biqodri uqulihim we have to address a person in accordance with his educational background.

khuldi (s.) BUAH (KHULDI).

khusuk mengk-kan *suasana* to solemnize the atmosphere.

khusunul khatimah happy end.

khusus mengkh- specialized. **mengkh-kan** to adapt for a particular purpose.

ki-yogo person who beats on a *gamelan*.

kial gesticulation, gesture.

kiam to stand erect during prayer.

kiamat fatal day. - *kita!* we are in a bad way! -*lah duniaku!* I won't survive! *sampai - dunia* till the end of time.

kiambang water lettuce, duck-weed (symbol of fleeting love). *biduk lalu - bertaut* said of relatives who make up again, after a short separation. *hidup spt -* to live an unstable life.

kian the more ... the more ...- *hari - nyata* clearer day by day. *berserak - kemari* knocked about all over the place. *mencari - kemari* to search high and low. **se-** *banyak* so many. *dlm jangka waktu* **seperse-** *detik* in a fraction of a second, in no time. - *saat* (changes) at any moment.

kiani royal.

kiap two pieces of wood propping up a mast.

kias I *mengambil -(an) drpd* to learn a lesson from, draw a moral from. **se-** analog(ue). *dgn* **-an** figuratively, metaphorically.

kias II *ilmu* - the art of preventing a disease or catastrophe by applying incantations.

kiat I sprained, dislocated.

kiat II 1 *ada* **-nya** there's a knack to it. 2 ruse. 3 hidden (meaning).

kiaupau inhabitant.

kibas *kambing* - a fat-tailed sheep. *Tanda start dilakukan dgn* **-an** *bendera,* The starting signal was given by waving the flag.

kibik (s.) KUBIK.

kiblat ber- oriented. ~ *ke Peking* Peking-oriented. **mengk-** *ke kota* urban-oriented.

kibrit ng- to run away.

kibul meng-i to kick in the ass. **ng-** *tdk* not fake, true. **peng-an** deceit.

kicau swindle.

ki cyak greedy for food, gluttonous.

kidobutai (during the Jap. occupation) shock troops.

kidul ng- to go south.

kidung 1 Old Jav. poetic work. 2 chant (lullaby).

kiekeboe (pron. kikebu) peekaboo.

kifayat *fardul* - collective religious (Moslem) obligations.

kihuru tree bark used for the manufacture of mosquito repellent.

kijang I *dpt - teruit* to get a windfall.

kijang II Police patrol car.

kik mengk- balik to kick back (money).

kikis scraping (the paint off wood). **meng-.habis(kan)** to root out, exterminate. **-an** 1 scrapings. 2 soil erosion. ~ *sungai* erosion.

kikitir assessment notice.

kilang peng-an mill site.

kilas *utk beberapa* - for a few moments.

kilat 1 fast delivery (of letters). 2 crash. *hari* - there's lightning. *pengumuman* - emergency announcement. *perkara* - summary process (in Court). *petir* - thunder and lightning. *program* - crash program. *sidang* - emergency meeting. *hilang - dlm kilau* to disappear in the crowd. **ter-** *di ingatan (,kepala) saya* it suddenly flashed into my mind. - *ber-*

api.api, - berdenyar, - bersinar(.sinar)
and - sabung.menyabung there's lightning.

kilau brilliance, radiance.

kili I female hermit (,recluse ,anchorite).

kili II -.-: *panjang* ~ a lot of pretexts.
~ *joran* (hose) reel.

kilik to fumble. **di-** to be incited. - *kucilik*
pretexts.

kilir ter- (s.) KESELEO.

kilo di-i to be sold by the kilogram.

kim I k.o. bingo.

KIM II [Kartu Izin Masuk] entry permit.

kima *siput* - a big marine shell.

kimblo k.o. Chinese vegetable soup.

kimbul 1 outboard platform at ship's
stern. 2 latrine (in a ship).

kimcam k.o. edible straw, o. of the ingredients for *kimblo.*

kimiawan chemist.

kimk(h)a kincob, gold brocade, damask.

kimono kimono. **ber-** to wear a kimono.

kimpa(l) welded, nugget. *emas* - native
gold.

kimplah(.kimplah) to ripple (of water).

KIMS [Kartu Izin Masuk Sementara]
Temporary Entry Permit Card (an
immigration document).

kina *pokok* - cinchona.

kinang betel chew (betel nut mixed with
leaves and lime). *tempat* **peng-an** small
carrying bag for betel requirements
made from woven bamboo with a black
and red painted *Dayak* mask motif on
it.

kinca sweet syrup of *gula Jawa.*

kinématika kinematics.

kinématis kinematic.

kinepung wakul, binasa mangap (s.)
KEPUNG.

kinétika kinetic.

kingkap kincob, gold brocade.

kingkit k.o. citrus with very small and
extremely sour fruit (L. Triphasia
aurantiola).

kingkong large logging truck.

kini modern (opp. *kuno*). - ... *nanti* ...
now (here) ... now (there); at o. time

..., at another time ... *Peranan Pertamina - dan nanti, Pertamina's* role today and tomorrow.

kinja *lompat* - to be mad, delirious (with
joy, etc.).

kinrohoshi (during the Jap. occupation)
compulsory labor service.

kintaka document, letter. **per-an** archives,
files, records.

kintal bullfrog.

kintil meng- *di ketiak* to be (largely) at
the mercy of, be practically left to the
mercy of.

kinyis.kinyis to look attractive (a woman).

kios 1 booth. - *tilpun* telephone booth,
pay phone. 2 kiosk, stand. - *buku* (in
railway stations) bookstand, bookstall.

kip (percussion) cap.

kipa 1 lame. 2 one-legged.

kipas.kipas pied fantail flycatcher.

kipat I di-kan to be shaken off, be hurled
away.

kipat II worm that attacks cashew plants.

kiprah 1 dance to break down and to
build up, simultaneously destructive
and constructive. 2 strut in victory.
3 to work together. **ber-** to strut in
victory. **ke-** whirl around. -.- wildly
and excitedly.

kipsiau Chinese earthenware teakettle.

kir examination, inspection. **mengk-** to
inspect (trucks, etc.).

kira 1 conjecture, supposition. 2 count
(ing). 3 (in questions, negatives) would
have thought. *Siapa yg - (bhw) dia
masih hidup!* Who'd have thought he'd
still be alive! **ber-.-** to make plans. **di-**
to be accused of. **diper-kan** supposedly.
dpt ~ 1 can be calculated. 2 can count
it on your fingers. **memper-kan** to esti-
mate. *tak* **ter-** immense, astronomical.
tdk **ter-(.-)** indescribable. -.-**an** calculation. **-nya** it seems that. *sudilah* ~ be
so kind as to. *diberkati Allah* ~ *adinda*
may God bless you. *di mana* ~ ...
where ever could ... be? *jikalau* ~
supposing that. -.-: 1 you wouldn't
mind! 2 budget. 3 presume, suspect.

4 possibly, maybe. *K~ masih jauh dr sini?* Would it still be far from here? *luar ~* cannot be relied on. *K~ dong!* Just think it over first! *K~ sedikit!* Mind your manners! *~ sendiri!* (pay) what you think is the right amount! (in bargaining).

kirab 1 to march out (of soldiers onto the battlefield). 2 parade. 3 procession.

kirah meng- *sayap* to stretch out o's wings.

kiri *-!* (passenger to busdriver) getting off here! *- depan!* (passenger to busdriver) getting off up ahead! *tak* **meng-.menganan** *lagi* point-blank, straight-out. *kaum -* the left wingers. *- cekar!* hard left! *- dlm* (in soccer) inside left. *- kapal* port (i.e. left side of ship). *- kemudi!* left rudder! *- luar* (in soccer) outside left. *- tengah* (in politics) left of center.

kirik puppy.

kirim di- *balik* to be returned (,sent back). **peng-** shipper. **peng-an** *uang* remittance.

kirmizi scarlet.

kisar ber- 1 to shift (wind). 2 to eddy (water). *~ antara 1.000 sampai 12.000 dolar* ranging from 1,000 to 12,000 dollars. *~ pd* (the story) is about.

kisas 1 retaliation. 2 blood revenge, vendetta. *hukum -* capital punishment (in retaliation).

kisat dry.

kisut ber- crumpled (up), rumpled, parched (of lips).

kit opium.

kita *-.- semua* all of us.

kitar se- approximately.

kiter (S.) KITAR. **ng-in** to be around (s.t.). *Mereka duduk ~ meja,* They sat around the table.

kiting di- to be pursued (,followed).

kitir letter (a written or typed message); (s.) KEKITIR.

kitri 1 fruit trees. 2 coconut tree seedlings.

kiya.kiya (s.) KYA.KYA.

kiyu nine.

KK [Kepala Keluarga] head of family.

klab club. *- malam* night club.

klaim claim. **mengk-** to claim.

klantung and **klanthung** to be out of work.

klaras a dry leaf (particularly, a banana leaf; in some areas maize).

klarinèt clarinet.

klasifikasi mengk-kan to classify (documents). **pengk-an** classification.

klasikal *secara -* class (teaching, etc.).

klausa clause.

klausul (S.) KLAUSULA.

Klein Ambtenaars Examen (col). Clerkship Examination. This examination was instituted in 1864 and held once a year. It covered the subjects: simple arithmetic, elementary principles of the Dutch language and clear handwriting. Those who had successfully taken this examination were eligible for the (lower) administrative functions.

klekap plankton.

klekek di- to be seized by the throat.

klelegen to choke (on).

klèm clamp. **ter-** clamped. *~ dgn plat logam* clamped with a metal plate.

klemak.klemèk slowly, sluggishly.

klembak (s.) ROKOK (KLEMBAK KEMENYAN).

klèmbrèh ng- to hang down, droop. *payudara itu ~* the breasts are drooping.

klenèngan informal *gamelan* concert.

klenger (s.) KELENGER. *jatuh -* to faint.

klèngkèng longan, laichi fruit (small, round, brown, dry-looking fruit; hard black seeds inside; very sweet).

klenik black magical practices inspired by the *hawa nepsu (,nafsu)* as opposed to the *batin.*

klentèng Chinese temple.

klenteng kapok seeds.

klèp valve.

klèptomania kleptomania.

klèrk clerk.

klès I vault, safe deposit.

klès II the so-called Dutch police actions (,clashes) (1947 and 1948).

klèsot -an to sit down comfortably.

kletak.kletik click-clack (sound).

klet(h)us di- 1 to be arrested. 2 to be

killed. **mengk-** *uang rakyat* to misuse the money of the people.

kletuk di- to be nabbed (a thief, etc.).

kléyar.kléyor adrift.

klian (in Bali) the leadership of a *banjar*.

klièn 1 client (of lawyer). 2 customer.

klik clique. **-.-an** cliques.

klimis clean(-shaven). *dicukur* - clean-shaven.

klinik - *berjalan (,mobil)* mobile clinic.

klinisi clinicians.

klintar.klinter to wander about.

klip (paper)clip.

kliping clipping (an item cut out of a newspaper, etc.). **mengk-** *koran.koran* to clip newspapers.

kliring clearing (in banking).

Kliwon the fifth day of the five-day week.

kliyengan 1 dizzy. 2 intoxicated.

klobot (s.) ROKOK (KLOBOT).

klolodan to choke, get s.t. stuck in the throat.

kloloten to choke, get s.t. stuck in the throat. *Dia - besi tua,* He was smothered in scrap iron.

klompen (Dutch) wooden shoes.

klop (s.) KELOP. *membikin* - to balance (a budget). *kurang* - not quite right. **mengk-kan** to square, balance.

klorofil chlorophyll.

klosèt toilet.

klosot *duduk* **ng-** to sit on the ground completely relaxed (without regard for o's surroundings).

klotok I a motorized proa in Banjarmasin (Kalimantan), water-taxi.

klotok II *dadu* - k.o. crap game.

kloyot ber-an epileptic.

klumpruk ng- to slump down.

kluntang.kluntung to loaf.

kluruk to crow. *jago* - a crowing rooster.

kluwak the seeds of the *pucung* fruit (used as a spice).

kluyar.kluyur to hang about.

kluyur (S.) KELUYUR. **ng-** to saunter, walk around the streets.

KMF [Kapal Motor Ferry] Ferry Motor Ship.

KNI [Kantorberita Nasional Indonesia] Indonesian National News Agency.

KNIL [Koninklijk Nederlandsch-Indisch Leger] Royal Netherlands Indies Army.

KNIP [Komite Nasional Indonesia Pusat] Central Indonesian National Committee; the functional equivalent of a Parliament in the Republican governmental system up to the formal transfer of sovereignty by the Dutch.

k.o. and **K.O.** [knock out] knock out. **meng-** (in boxing) to knock out.

koa k.o. Chinese card game.

koalisi coalition. **ber-** *dgn* to enter into a coalition with.

koar be- to speak loudly.

kobah kettle-drum.

kobakan wallow, (rain)pool, mudpool.

kobal(t) cobalt.

kobar ber-.- to be ablaze. **peng-** *perang* warmonger.

kobèr European, non-Moslem graveyard.

koboi mengk- to act wild. **-.-an** wild actions (of stealing, etc.).

kobol deficit.

kobongan little tent in which a circumcision takes place.

kobra I cobra.

kobra II great. *denda* - fine imposed on the village population due to a murder committed in their village by an unknown perpetrator. *Kiamat* - the Day of Judgment.

kocak I shaking, shock, concussion.

kocak II 1 egotistical. 2 *(gagah dan)* - smart, dashing.

kocar.kacir mengk-kan to scatter in disorder (an army).

kocèk - *negara* treasury.

koci chancre. - *lambung* stomach ulcer.

kocok meng- *perut* to make laugh. **peng-:** ~ *perut* clown, buffoon. ~ *telur* egg beater. **-an** pump (brakes). - *ulang* reshuffle.

kocor ng- to run (of water). *air leding tdk* ~ the tapwater doesn't run. **ng-i** to water (plants).

kocuk caoutchouc.

kodak I camera. *orang Mat K-* an amateur photographer.

Kodak II [Komando Daerah Kepolisian] Police Region Command -*propinsi* level.

Kodam [Komando Daerah Militer] Military Region Command.

kode - *daerah (,wilayah)* area code (of telephone).

Kodim [Komando Distrik Militer] Military District Command (i.e. the army area command intermediate between the *Korem* and *Koramil* — former *kabupaten* level; (s.) KODAM). **dik-kan** to be summoned to appear before a mil. district command authority.

kodok (s.) KATAK. *spt - ditimpa kemarau* raise the devil. *laksana - dpt bunga sekuntum* to cast pearls before swine. *berenang -* breast stroke. *mati -* to die for nothing. - *pohon* tree frog. -.*ulo* a gambling game played with dice on a revolving board.

kodrat I 1 power, ability. 2 almighty, omnipotent. 3 (for God's) sake. *tdk* **ber-** *lagi* powerless, impotent, effete. - *fitri* natural power.

kodrat II naturally, by nature, force of nature. *(letak) pd* **-nya** quite natural.

kodya [kotamadya] municipality. **se-** the entire municipality.

ko.édukasi co-education.

koèfisièn coefficient.

koèksistènsi coexistence. **ber-** to coexist.

Koeln Cologne.

koh (s.) ENGKOH.

kohési cohesion.

kohol (sipat mata) collyrium, black-eye salve.

koin coin.

koipuk middleman in the rubber trade.

koit and **ko'it** *mati -* to drop dead.

kojor *(mati)* - to drop dead. **-in** to kill, bump off.

kok particle or exclamation of surprise, often combined with irritation or wonder. *K- hujannya tdk henti.hentiya!* How come it never stops raining!

koka and **kokain(e)** cocaine.

kokas coke.

kokila mynah.

kokoh (S.) KUKUH. **peng-** stabilizer.

pengk-an (S.) PENGUKUHAN.

kokol signal block.

kokon cocoon.

kokonèta an Indonesian cocktail.

kokoro manggih mulud to make use of the opportunity.

kokorselan merry-go-round.

kokot bent (of hands through stiffness, etc.).

kokpit cockpit.

koktil cocktail.

kokus coccus.

kol I - *merah* red cabbage. - *umbi* Swedish turnip.

kol II *(pistol)* - a Colt (revolver).

kolaborasi **ber-** to collaborate (with the enemy).

kolam - *renang* swimming pool. - *tando* reservoir.

kolang.kaling 1 to and fro. 2 topsy-turvy, whirling helplessly.

kolase collage.

kolèktivisasi collectivization.

kolèktor commutator.

kolèna *pohon* - (s.) (POHON) GAMAL.

kolése college (a school).

kolèstrol cholesterol.

kolik the cuckoo (the female of the *tuhu*).

kolintang wooden xylophone of the Northern Celebes.

kolo sweet and sour (of Chinese dishes). - *bak* sweet and sour pork. - *kee* sweet and sour chicken.

koloid colloid. *spt -* colloidal.

koloidal colloidal.

kolokium doktum colloquium doctum.

Kolombia Columbia.

Kolombo Colombo. *Panca Negara -* the five Colombo countries: Sri Lanka, India, Pakistan, Burma and Indonesia. *Rencana -* the Colombo Plan.

kolomnis columnist.

kolone column. - *kelima* fifth column.

kolong hollow (under a table, bridge, etc.). *tidur di - jembatan* sleeping under a bridge. *di - meja* under the table. *tdk ada barang baru di - langit* there is nothing new under the sun. *rakyat di mana.mana di bawah - langit ini* people everywhere under the sun.

koloni - *pengemis* tramp colony.

kolonial colonial.

kolonjono an alfalfa-like grass used as cattle fodder.

kolor I with a drawstring. - *anget* hot pants.

kolor II **ng-** to curry favor.

kolportase hawking (goods).

koma coma.

koma.koma saffron.

komak.kamek (s.) KOMAT.KAMIT.

koman common.

komandan **di-i** *oleh Kapten A* under the commanding officer Captain A. **mengk-i** to be in command of.

komandemèn commandment (of Police Force).

komando **meng-i** *kapal* to be in command of a ship. **peng-an** commanding.

Koman(g) (in Bali) name element placed before personal names to indicate the third born child, e.g. *Dayu Koman Watika.*

komaran ceremony performed by fishermen from Cilacap, on the island of Majeti, near Nusakambangan; offerings are traditionally presented to *Nyai Loro Kidul.*

komat.kamit **ber-** to mumble, mutter.

kombanwa condom.

kombinasi **mengk-kan** to combine.

komèng I small, dwarfish.

komèng II congenitally impotent (of the male).

komèntar **ber-** to comment (upon).

komèntator commentator.

komèrsialis commercialist.

komèrsialisasi commercialization. **di-kan** to be commercialized. - *jabatan* 'job commercialization,' i.e. abuse of office (1976).

komèrsialisme commercialism.

komèrsiil commercial. **mengk-kan** to commercialize.

komèrsil **mengk-kan** *jabatan* to abuse a job.

komèt comet.

komet **meng-kan** to make dizzy.

komfor (S.) KOMPOR.

komidi - *bicara* 'talking theater,' i.e. the *Volksraad* (col.). - *ketek (,monyet)* a dance performed by monkies dressed as human beings imitating people; (s.). KEMIDI BEDES.

komik a comic (cartoon, strip, book).

Kominform Cominform, Communist Information Bureau.

Komintèrn Comintern, Communist International, the international organization of Communist parties.

komisaris **ke-an** commissariat. - *amanat* managing director. *K- Besar Polisi* Police Senior Commissioner. *K- Jenderal Polisi* Police Commissioner General.

komisi I board.

komisi II kickback.

komité committee. *K- Nasional Indonesia Pusat* Central Indonesian National Committee, i.e. the functional equivalent of a Parliament in the Republican governmental system up to the formal transfer of sovereignty. - *tetap* standing committee.

komitmèn commitment.

komoditi commodity.

komodo komodo dragon, a giant lizard found on an island near Sumbawa in the Lesser Sundas.

kompa pump.

kompak harmonious, with strong esprit de corps. **ke-an** harmony.

kompanyon partner. **ber-** *dgn* in partnership with.

kompartemèn and **kompartimèn** compartment, i.e. k.o. department under President Soekarno.

kompas I **meng-** to blackmail. **peng-an** blackmail.

kompas II **di-** entire contents removed.

kompatriot compatriot.

kompènsasi compensation.

komperènsi (S.) KONPERENSI.

kompès 1 to cross-examine. 2 to intimidate. **-an** interrogation (by police).

kompetèn competent. *sumber.sumber yg sangat* **ber-** highly competent sources.

kompetènsi competence.
kompetisi (in sports) competition. **ber-** to play a league match.
kompi (mil.) company. - *berdiri sendiri* separate company.
kompilasi compilation.
kompit (in the Northern Celebes) motor-proa.
komplèks - *gedung.gedung* a block of buildings. - *masalah.masalah* a complex of problems. - *toko.toko* a block of stores. - *rendah diri* inferiority complex.
komplikasi complication.
komplit with all the trimmings. *bistik -* steak dinner.
komplot conspiracy.
kompoi (S.) KONPOI.
kompon compound.
kompong *si* - eunuch.
komporisasi the introduction of furnaces in brickyards.
kompos compost.
komprador 1 supercargo. 2 comprador.
komprang (s.) CELANA (KOMPRANG).
kompréhènsif comprehensive.
komprèsi compression.
komprèsor compressor.
kompromis compromise.
komputerisasi computerization.
komputor and **kompyuter** computor.
komsat [komunikasi satelit] communication satellite.
komun(e) commune. - *rakyat* people's commune.
komuni - *suci* Holy Communion.
komunikasi communication. **ber-** to communicate (v.i.). **mengk-kan** to communicate (v.t.). - *satelit* communication satellite.
komuniké communique. - *bersama* joint communique.
komunis **mengk-kan** to communize. **pengk-an** communization.
komunisto.phobi communisto-phobia.
komuniti community.
konang -**an** caught, detected.
konco 1 comrade, crony. 2 confederate. 3 accomplice, satellite.

konco.isme cronyism.
kondangan 1 guest, invitee. 2 to visit a festival.
kondé *si - licin* the woman.
kondènsasi condensation.
kondènsat condensate.
kondènsor condensor.
kondom condom. **pengk-an** the utilization of condoms.
kondominium condominium.
kondomisasi 'condomization,' i.e. the popularizing of the use of condoms within the framework of birth control.
konduite efficiency report.
konèksi connection (a business associate, acquaintance, esp. an influential person).
konèngbesar zedoary (L. Curcuma zedoaria), used in medicines.
konféderasi confederation.
konfidènsi(i)l confidential.
konfigurasi configuration.
konfirmasi confirmation. **di-kan** to be confirmed.
konfrontasi Indonesian hostile confrontation against formation of Malaysia, involving mil. action, mostly along the East Malaysia borders, from 1963 through 1965. **mengk-kan** to confront.
kong (S.) ENGKONG.
kongèsti congestion.
Konggo (s.) KONGO.
Kong Hu Tju Confucius.
kongkalikong 1 intrigue. 2 jobbery. *(main)* - 1 to practice corruption. 2 to intrigue, plot. **ber-** 1 to fool a person. 2 to (plot and) scheme. 3 to swindle, cheat.
kongko (s.) KONGKOW.KONGKOW.
kongkol intrigue, scheme, plot, cabal.
kongkong 1 fetters. 2 foot irons. **ter-** *pd tempat tidurnya* bedridden.
kongkow.kongkow lobbying.
konglomerat conglomerate.
Kongo Congo. - *(B)* Congo (Brazzaville). - *(L)* Congo (Leopoldville).
kongrèsis conferee.
kongsi partner. **ber-** to be in collusion with *(dgn)*. **per-an** 1 partnership. 2 alli-

ance. - *dlm bisnis* business partner.

koni okra.

konis conical.

konita [mahkota wanita] (s.) RAMBUT KONITA.

konkrit (S.) KON(G)KRET. **di-kan** to be given concrete form.

konkurs competition, contest.

konokan (in Jember, East Java) 1 help, assistance. 2 reference to mice and rats (in superstitious awe and veneration).

konon 1 - *(kabarnya)* and *kabarnya* - (a) it is said. (b) the story goes. 2 (the reason of it, etc.) is ostensibly. *cantiklah dia* - she thinks that she is good-looking. 3 *tapi* - (under the guise of) but actually ... 4 *-lah, - lagi (,pula)* and *betapa* - (a) so much the more. (b) let alone ..., to say nothing of ... 5 *apa* - whatever. *siapa - yg* ... who would ... *cukuplah* - ... (the reader) should confine (himself) (to ...).

konotasi connotation.

konperènsi di-kan to be discussed in a conference.

konperènsisten *para* - the conferees.

konsekrasi consecration.

konsel(l)or counsel(l)or.

konsèntrasi meng-kan to concentrate. **ter-** concentrated.

konsèntris concentric.

konsèntrisitèt concentricity.

konsèp rough draft. **meng-** to make a rough draft.

konsèpsi concept for reconstruction presented by President Soekarno on February 21, 1957, which was later to be known as *demokrasi terpimpin* or as Soekarno described it "democracy with leadership."

konsèr - *gesek* string concert. - *vokalia* vocal concert.

konsèrvator (s.) PENYITAAN (KONSERVATOR).

konsèrvatorium and **konsèrvatori** conservatory, school of music.

konsiderans (legal) preamble.

konsinyasi 1 (commercial) consignment.

2 (mil.) restriction to base. **di-kan** to be consigned.

konsinyatir consignor.

konsinyir mengk- to confine to barracks (of army troops).

konsistènsi consistency.

konsistori consistory. - *rahasia* secret consistory.

konsol 1 the Ford Consul. 2 representative of *Muhammadiah's* Executive Board. **ke-an** consular.

konsolidasi consolidation. **ber-** to consolidate (v.i.). **mengk-kan** to consolidate (v.t.).

konsonan consonant. - *awal* initial consonant.

konsorsium consortium.

konspirasi conspiracy.

konspiratif conspirative.

konstatasi di- to be ascertained, be affirmed.

konstatir mengk- to mention.

konstèlasi 1 constellation. 2 configuration. - *politik* political alignment.

konstipasi constipation.

konstitusi *tdk menurut* - unconstitutional.

konstitusionil constitutional.

konstruktif constructive.

konsulat ke-an consulate.

konsulèn consultant. - *pajak* tax consultant.

konsulèr consular.

konsultasi *mengadakan* - to call into consultation. **ber-** to consult. - *perjodohan* marriage counseling.

konsultatif consultative.

konsumsi victuals. **mengk-kan** to consume.

kontak 1 ignition switch. 2 lightswitch. 3 to get an electric shock. 4 - *dr* to pick up a habit from. *Dia kena - listrik,* He got an electric shock. - *senjata* fire fight.

kontaminasi contamination.

kontan flatly (deny s.t.). - *keras* 1 hard cash. 2 on the spot, instantly.

kontang.kanting dangling and swaying.

konté *potlot* - conté (a hard, black-colored crayon of graphite and clay).

kontèks context.
kontèmporèr contemporary.
konténerisasi the use of containers.
kontès contest. **di-kan** to be contested.
  - *(adu) kecantikan* beauty contest.
kontèstan contestant.
kontèt small, stunted. *si K-* 'The Dwarf,'
  i.e. a rice variety.
kontinèn continent. - *Tiongkok* the
  Chinese continent.
kontingèn contingent.
kontinu continuous. *secara* - continuously.
kontinuitas continuity.
kontinyu continuous.
kontinyuitas continuity.
kontol I 1 scrotum. 2 penis.
kontol II short, stumpy and pendulous.
kontra I to collide with. - *dgn* to be hit
  by (a car).
kontra II counter-. *argumen* - counter-
  argument.
kontrabas double bass.
kontra.démonstrasi counterdemonstra-
  tion.
kontradiksi contradiction.
kontra.intèl(ijèn) counterintelligence.
kontrak di-kan to be leased. *perusahaan.
  perusahaan minyak yg* **di-karyakan** oil
  companies operating under a *kontrak
  karya.* **meng-** to lease. **peng-** concessionaire, contractee. **-an** leased. *menjadi* ~ to be(come) a contract laborer.
  - *karya* a contract in which the contractor is to conduct all stages of operation on behalf of the Indonesian government. The contractor pays the government for land rents and royalties,
  and in exchange receives a share of the
  profits. - *penyerahan* delivery contract.
  - *sewa.beli* hire-purchase contract.
kontra.opènsip counteroffensive.
kontra.révolusi counterrevolution.
kontra.révolusionèr counter-revolution-
  ary. **ke-an** counter-revolutionism.
kontras 1 contrast. 2 conflict.
kontrasèptif contraceptive.
kontra.spionase counterespionage.
kontribusi contribution (usually, in
  money).

kontrol check (on), inspection (of tickets).
  peng-an check (on), control. **ter-** to be
  controlled.
kontrolir 1 controller, comptroller,
  checker. 2 ticket inspector. **mengk-** to
  control.
kontur contour. - *lagu* tonal contour.
konus cone.
konvèks convex.
konvèksi ready-made clothing.
konvènsionil conventional.
konvergèn convergent.
konvèrsi conversion. **pengk-an** converti-
  bility.
konyak cognac.
konyugasi conjugation. **di-kan** to be con-
  jugated.
kookplaat (pron. kokplat) hot plate.
kooperatif (adj.) cooperative.
koor (pron. kor) choir. - *gereja* church
  choir.
koordinasi ter-kan coordinated.
koordinat coordinate.
koordinator coordinator.
kop 1 dome. 2 (letter)head. 3 head (in
  tape recorder). **ber-** domed. **mengk-** (in
  soccer) to hit the ball with o's head.
  - *surat* letterhead. - *telepon* earphones,
  headphones.
kopah mass, lump, quantity.
kopal copal.
kopel (s.) RUMAH (BENTUK KOPEL).
koperasi I ber- to co-operate. **per-an** system of co-operation. - *among tani* farmers co-operative. *K- Simpan Pinjam*
  (abbrev. *Kosipi*) Savings & Loan Co-
  operative.
koperasi II ke-an co-operative system.
koperasiawan a member of a co-operative
  organization.
kopi I 1 coffee (the bean). 2 coffee (the
  drink). **ng-** to drink coffee. **peng-** coffee
  hound. - *Arab* (in the Celebes) okra (L.
  Hibiscus esculentus L). - *encer* weak
  (,diluted) coffee. - *hitam (,pahit)* black
  coffee without sugar and milk. - *Jawa
  (,susu)* (in Java) okra (L. Hibiscus esculentus L). *mendapat - pahit (,keras)*
  to get a scolding. - *keras* strong coffee.

- *luak* coffee beans discharged in the excrement of civet cats; this type of coffee is considered excellent. - *tubruk* 'Turkish' coffee, i.e. extra strong coffee made by pouring hot water over coffee grounds.

kopi II copy, imitation, reproduction. **mengk-** to copy, reproduce.

kopilot copilot.

kopiok *telur itu* **di-** the eggs are whipped (from a recipe).

koplak - *bis* bus stop.

Kopra I [Kotapraja] Municipality.

kopra II - *asap* kilndried copra. - *jemur* sundried copra. - *dan bungkil* - copra and copra cakes.

kopral - *(tingkat) dua* corporal 2nd class. - *(tingkat) satu* corporal 1st class. - *kepala* master corporal. - *taruna* cadet corporal.

koprok *dadu.* - a gambling game like crapshooting.

koprol *main* - roll over.

kopter helicopter.

Koptik Coptic.

kopur denomination (money).

kopyor the soft, spongy meat of a coconut species *(kelapa puan)* from which a cold beverage is made, served with syrup.

koq (s.) KOK.

korak criminal who pilfers goods from a truck. [We were told that *korak* is the acronym of Komando Perak (Perak Command), since these criminals started to operate in the Perak port area of Surabaya].

Koramil [Komando Rayon Militer] Military Precinct Command (i.e. the smallest army area command) - *kecamatan* level.

koran *orang* - (newspaper) reporter. -.-**an** a trashy newspaper. - *"A"* newspaper for the religious groups. - *dinding* wallposter. -.- *got* the yellow press. - *Wong Li Cik PKI's* daily newspaper "Harian Rakyat" (name given by opponents).

korana (in Irian Jaya) village head.

Korawa (s.) KURAWA.

korban alms. *banyak makan* - to take many victims. *menjadi* - to fall a victim to. *Dia dijadikan -,* He was made the fall guy. *para* - casualties. - *empuk* a soft touch. - *penculikan* a kidnap victim. -.- *tempur* battle casualties.

kordinasi (S.) KOORDINASI. **mengk-(kan)** to coordinate. **pengk-an** *harga* price coordination.

kordinat coordinate.

kordinir mengk- to coordinate.

kordon cordon. - *saniter* cordon sanitaire.

Koréa Korea. - *Selatan (,Utara)* South (,North) Korea. *Republik Rakyat Demokrasi* - Democratic People's Republic of Korea.

korèk I matches. **meng-** *keterangan dr* to elicit information from. - *api Ronson* a "Ronson" lighter. - *kuping* ear swab.

korèk II correct. *bersifat* - *sekali* to assume a most correct attitude.

korèksi peng(k)-an correction.

Korèm [Komando Resort Militer] Military Area Command (i.e. the army command intermediate between *Kodam* and *Kodim* — former residency level).

koréografer choreographer.

koréografi choreography.

korèspondèn correspondent. - *keliling* roving correspondent.

korèt meng- to cut jungle grass (a tall coarse sharp-leaved weed) growing between cassava trees.

koro (s.) PENYAKIT (KORO).

koronèr coronary. *penyakit jantung* - coronary heart disease.

korosi corrosion.

korporasi corporation.

Korpri [Korps Pegawai Republik Indonesia] Republic of Indonesia (Government) Employees Corps, a constituent unit of *Golkar.* **peng.K-.an** *guru.guru* the incorporation of teachers into *Korpri.*

korps - *angkatan darat* army corps. - *diplomatik* diplomatic corps. *K-Komando (Angkatan Laut)* (Navy) Marine Corps. - *konsuler* consular corps. - *medis* medical corps. - *musik* (in armed forces) (brass) band. *K- Perda-maian* (U.S.) Peace Corps. - *wanita Angkatan Darat* WAC. - *zeni* corps of (mil.) engineers.

korpulènsi corpulence.

korsèl I merry-go-round.

Korsèl II [Korea Selatan] South Korea.

korsèt corset.

korslèting short circuit.

korting discount, price reduction. *harga yg tlh* **di-** the reduced price.

korup di- to be misappropriated.

Korut [Korea Utara] North Korea.

korvé and **korvee** fatigue duty.

korvèt corvette.

Kosak Cossack.

kosakata vocabulary.

kos 1 to board. 2 boarder. 3 boarding (house). *Seminggu yg lalu dia datang ke tempat -ku,* A week ago he arrived at my boardinghouse; (s.) INDEKOS(T).

kosbas lodging-house keeper.

kosèn ke-an gallantry.

kosièn quotient. - *pemilihan* electoral quotient.

kosmétika cosmetics.

kosmis cosmic.

kosmogéni cosmogony.

kosmonaut and **kosmonot** cosmonaut.

kosmos cosmos.

kosokbalèn and **kosokbali** opposite, contrary, reverse.

kosong 1 hungry (stomach). 2 unoccupied. 3 zero. 4 blank (paper). - *akan* without. *beromong.omong* - to chat. *dgn tangan* - (to return) without success. *tong - nyaring bunyinya* empty vessels make the most noise. - *melongpong* idle, empty. *Tempat ini -?* Anybody sitting here? **di-kan**: *daerah-daerah yg ~ dr militer* demilitarized zones. ~ *anginnya* to have (o's tires) go flat, be deflated. **peng-an** *angkasa (,atmosfir)* atmospheric discharge.

kost (s.) KOS.

koster coaster.

kostiksoda caustic soda.

kostim and **kostum** 1 uniform, dress (for certain civil authorities). 2 costume for formal wear.

kota per-an (adj.) city. - *administratif* 'administrative' city (o. level lower than the *kotamadya*). - *atas* uptown. - *bawah* downtown. - *besar* city (with more than 250,000 inhabitants). - *dunia* metropolis. - *kecil* city (with less than 250,000 inhabitants). - *kelahiran* native (,home) town. - *kembar* the twin-city of Telukbetung and Tanjungkarang (in South Sumatra). -*madya* (abbrev. *kodya*) municipality. -*pelabuhan* port(town). - *peristirahatan* resort. *K- Vatikan* Vatican City.

The following cities are named for some characteristic:
K- "4711" Cologne. *K- Amoi* Singkawang. *K- Anging Mammiri* Ujungpandang. *K- Api* Banjarmasin. *K- Asia Afrika* Bandung. *K- Asin* Banjarmasin. *K- Bandeng* Semarang. *K- Batik* Pekalongan. *K- Bawang* Tegal. *K- Bengawan* Sala. *K- Beras* Karawang. *K- Brambang* Brebes. *K- Buaya* Surabaya. *K- Budaya* Yogyakarta. *K- Bunga* Wonosobo. *K-Dingin* Bandung. *K- Empek.Empek* Palembang. *K- Gaplek* Wonogiri. *K-Gerbong Maut* Bondowoso. *K- Getuk Goreng* Purwokerto. *K- Gudeg* Yogyakarta. *K- Hijrah Revolusi* Yogyakarta. *K- Hujan* Bogor. *K- Indah* Singkawang. *K- Indekosan* Yogyakarta. *K- Jam Gadang* Bukittinggi. *K- Kartini* Jepara. *K- Kembang* Bandung. *K- Kretek* Kudus. *K- Kripik* Purwokerto. *K-Krupuk* Sidoarjo. *K- Lumpia* Semarang. *K- Mojang Parahiyangan (,Priyangan ,Priangan)* Bandung. *K- Musi* Palembang. *K- Nyiur* Palu. *K- Pahlawan* Surabaya. *K- Pata Cengke* Ambon. *K-Pelajar* Salatiga. *K- Pelajar (dan Mahasiswa)* Yogyakarta. *K- Pendidikan* Jakarta. *K- Pensiunan* Salatiga. *K-Perjuangan* Yogyakarta. *K- Proklamasi* Jakarta. *K- Resik* Tasikmalaya. *K-Revolusi* 1 Surabaya. 2 Yogyakarta.

K- Romantis Bandung. *K- Sejahtera* Ujungpandang. *K- Sepeda* Yogyakarta. *K- Sriwijaya* Palembang. *K- Tahu Pong* Semarang. *K- Taman* Bogor. *K- Tauco* Cianjur. *K- Turis* Yogyakarta. *K- Udang* Cirebon. *K- Ukir* Jepara. *K- yg tak pernah tidur* Sala.

kotak I gun housing. *masuk* - 1 (in sports) on the bench. 2 to be out of the picture, be shelved (of plans). 3 to be a mere cipher. **mengk-.k-kan** 1 to box in. 2 to compartmentalize. **pengk-an** sectioning, zoning. *- kecantikan* beauty case. *- makan siang* lunchbox. *- penyimpan* (in bank) safe-deposit box. *- suara* ballot box. *- uang* coin box (of telephone). *tilpon - uang* pay phone.

kotak II and **kothak** wooden chest in which *wayang* puppets are kept; also used to designate a set of puppets.

kotangèn(s) cotangent.

kotapraja municipality (replaced by *kotamadya*).

kotèk kotex (a brand name), sanitary napkin.

kotekelema(h) sperm whale.

kotès se- a pinch, very small quantity.

kotipa [kolera-tipus-paratipus] *vaksin -* cholera, typhus and paratyphoid vaccine.

kotok I *celana* - shorts.

kotok II blind. *- ayam* 1 twilight blindness. 2 chicken droppings.

kotokelemèh sperm whale.

kotong 1 short (of shorts). 2 sleeveless (of coat). *baju -* a jacket with short sleeves or no sleeves.

kotor *bercakap* - to talk smut. *datang* - to menstruate. **meng-i** and **meng-kan** to pollute. **peng-an** pollution, contamination. **-an** 1 refuse. 2 faeces.

kover (s.) COVER. **mengk-** to cover (a conference, etc.; in journalism).

kowak - *maling* black crown night heron.

KOWAL [Korps Wanita Angkatan Laut] Women Naval Corps.

kowar *jalan* - unattended road.

kowé di-.- to be talked down to, be scolded.

koyak disperse!

koyam *bubur* - broth made from *pulut* rice.

koyo(k) I nonsense, rubbish. *jual* - 1 to talk nonsense. 2 to tell lies.

koyo(k) II a (Chinese) penetrative medical plaster, such as, Salon Pas.

koyo(k) III (s.) KAYA(K).

K.P.M. [Koninklijke Paketvaart Maatschappij] Royal Mail Steam Packet Company.

Kraèng a Bugis (Ujungpandang) royal title.

Krakatau Krakatoa.

kram cramp.

kramantara (pron. kromantoro) style of Jav. language which is basically *krama* with *ngoko* references.

kranjing meng-kan to obsess.

krapu grouper.

krat crate.

kraton (S.) KERATON.

Krawang (s.) KARAWANG.

kréasi ber- to be creative.

krècèk dried (buffalo) hide, cut in pieces and baked.

krèdibilitas credibility.

krédit *debet dan* - debit and credit. **per-an** credit system. *- berputar* revolving credit. *- jangka panjang (,pendek)* long-(,short-)term credit. *- hipotek* mortgage credit. *- investasi* investment credit. *- macet* bad debt(s). *- tanpa bunga* non-interest bearing credit. *- verban* credit lien.

kréditir and **kréditur** creditor.

krèm cream(-colored).

krémasi cremation. **di-kan** to be cremated.

krématorium crematory.

kremes I k.o. sweet-tasting cassava cake.

kremes II *-(.kremes)* to crumble.

krèmpèng (s.) KEREMPENG.

kremus munched (up), crunched, to eat bones and all.

krenèk and **krenèt** (S.) KORNET 1.

krenteg longing, desire.
krenyes to crackle.
krèpot sunken (cheeks).
krèsèh.pèsèh to talk Dutch continually.
krèsèk *kelas* - flea-bag (hotel).
Kréta *Pulau* - Crete.
krètèk (s.) ROKOK (KRETEK).
kreton cretonne.
KRI [Kapal Republik Indonesia] Republic of Indonesia Ship.
kribo 1 curly. 2 kinky. *Rambutnya* -, He has curly hair. **di-** to be curled.
kricak broken stones, rubble.
Kricika Scorpio.
krida 1 activity, action. 2 (in schools) extracurricular activities. **di-kan** to be put to work, be given a job. *Tahanan. tahanan G-30-S/PKI ~ utk mencukupi pangan mereka sendiri,* The September 30 Movement and *PKI* detainees were given jobs to provide their own food. - *lumahing asta* (and *krido lumahing asto*) (euph.) to beg. - *wisata* study tour.
kridanirmala epidemic control.
kridit (buy) on time; (s.) KREDIT. *tukang* - and **pengr-** man who sells small items on time.
Krido Bekso Wiromo the classical dance and stage in Yogyakarta.
kriiing ringing (of telephone).
kriir di- to be created.
krim cream. - *antiseptik* antiseptic cream.
Krimia the Crimea.
kriminalitas and **kriminalitèt** criminality.
kriminil *tindak* - a criminal act. **mengk-kan** to make a criminal case (from a civil case).
krincing (s.) GONGSENG II.
krio (in Palembang) village head.
kripik - *gendar* rice chips. - *jagung* corn flakes. - *kentang* potato chips. - *puli (,putih)* rice chips.
kripto crypto. - *Muslim* crypto-Moslem.
kriptografi cryptography.
krisis **mengk-kan** to cause a crisis. ~ *kabinet* to cause a cabinet crisis. - *akhlak* moral crisis. - *ketenagaan* energy crises.

Krismes Christmas. **-an** Christmas celebration.
kristal crystal. **pengk-an** crystallization.
kristalisasi (fig.) crystallization.
Kristen Christian. **mengk-kan** to Christianize. **pengk-an** Christianization. *orang* - Christian (in Indonesia usually referring to 'Protestants' only).
kristenisasi christianization.
Kristus Christ.
kritérium criterion.
kritik critique. **mengk-** and **mengr-** (s.) MENGERITIK. - *yg membangun* constructive criticism.
kritikus critic.
kriting club (in card games).
kritisi critics.
kriuk -.-**an** rumbling (of stomach from hunger).
kriwikan brooklet. - *dadi grojogan* little strokes fell great oaks.
kriyep.kriyep half closed (of eyes).
kriyip (s.) KRIYEP.KRIYEP.
krobongan inner room (in Jav. house).
kroco 1 small crustacean. 2 low-class Eurasian. 3 low-echelon; (s.) KRUCUK. -.- low-ranking, worthless people.
krokèt croquette.
krokot k.o. purslane.
krol di- to be waved (of hair).
kromat - *seng* zinc chromate.
kromium chromium.
kromo 1 style in Jav. language used when speaking to a person of a higher status, a person of an older age, a person with whom o. is not well-acquainted. 2 *si* - the small (,little) man. -.*inggil* references to possessions, body-parts and actions of addressee or of a higher and/or older third person.
kromosom chromosome.
krompyang crash! *terdengar suara* - a crashing sound was heard.
Krona (Danish, Swedish money) (Scandinavian) Krone.
kroncong (S.) KERONCONG. **ng-** to make *keroncong* music.
kronik chronicle.

kronomèter chronometer. *jam tangan merek Rolex* **ber-** a Rolex wrist watch with chronometer.

kropok 1 mouldy, rotten. 2 spongy. 3 weak.

kropos hollow, to have a deteriorated internal part; (s.) KEROPOS. **ke-an** hollowing out.

krosboi male juvenile delinquent; (s.) CROSSBOY(S). - *ingusan* a good-for-nothing male juvenile delinquent.

kros.boy (s.) KROSBOI. *Jangan* **ngros. boy!** Don't behave like a crossboy!

krosgir(e)l female juvenile delinquent; (s.) CROSSGIRL(S).

kroto red ant eggs (used as food for certain bird species).

krucuk (s.) KROCO. *petugas* - lower-echelon functionary.

krukat crew cut.

kruntel di- (her hair) has been rolled. *Rambutnya ~ palsu,* She rolled her hair, intermingling it with an artificial bun.

krupuk generic word for many k.o. *krupuk* each with its own flavor, made from various k.o. flour with a variety of seasonings, for instance, tapioca flour with prawn flavor *(krupuk udang),* nuts *(krupuk emping),* tubers *(krupuk kentang),* beef skin *(krupuk kulit);* (s.) KERUPUK. - *putih* rice chips.

KTP [Kartu Tanda Penduduk] Resident's Card.

Ktut (in Bali) name element placed before personal names to indicate the fourth born child, such as, *Ktut Chandra;* (s.) KETUT.

kuala ber- it has its estuary (in).

kualahan (s.) KUWALAHAN.

kualon step-. *anak* - stepchild.

kuang *mati - karena bunyi* pride goes before a fall.

kuangwung coconut beetle (L. Oryctes Rhinoceros).

kuasa I ber- authoritative. **di-i** *oleh isteri* to be henpecked. **ke-an:** *~ bertumpuk. tumpuk* accumulated powers. *~ ekse-* *kutif* executive powers. *K~ Hitam* (in the U.S.) Black Power. *~ ke-4* 'the fourth estate,' i.e. the press. *~ kehakiman* judiciary. *~ legislatif* legislative powers. *~ penggentar* reign of terror. *~ penuh* carte blanche. *~ penyelenggara* executive powers. *~ perundang.undangan* legislature. *~ tiada terbatas* absolutism. *~ yudikatif* judicial powers. **peng-** authority. *~ tunggal* sole authority (this term refers to the regional heads: the governor, *bupati* and mayor in the Ujungpandang area). **peng-an** authorization. *~ (bersifat) mutlak* absolutism. - *di bawah tangan* private power of attorney. - *gaib* supernatural power(s). - *hukum* jurisdiction, judicial powers. - *kehakiman* judiciary. - *luas* broad powers. - *orang tua* parental power.

kuasa II *K- Usaha Sementara* Chargé d'Affairs ad interim. *K- Usaha Tetap* Chargé d'Affairs en pied.

kuat - *jua* to know better. - *tahan payah* to have stamina. *sdh - kembali* to have recuperated. *yg - keuangannya* backed by sufficient capital. -*kanlah hatimu!* take care of yourself! cheerio! **berke-an** to have the strength of. *dipisi.dipisi yg ~ kl. 12.000 orang* (army) divisions about 12,000 strong. **ke-an:** *~ beli* purchasing power. *~ lekat* adhesive force. *~ mobil* mobile force. *~ pemukul* striking force. *~ surat atau ~ saksi* evidence in writing or by parole. *~ tarik* drawing power. *~ tekan* pressure capacity. *~ yg beruntun* battle array. **peng-** *syahwat* aphrodisiac. **peng-an** *tandatangan* countersign. **se-.-** *tulangnya* with all o's might. -.- firmly, loudly, hard (adverb). - *beli* with purchasing power.

kuatir apprehensive, fearful. **meng(k)-kan** 1 causing worry (,apprehension). 2 to worry about.

kuau (Argus-)pheasant.

kubah dome, cupola. - *makam* a domed grave.

kubik cubic. *sentimeter* - cubic centimeter. *per* - per cubic.

kubisme cubism.
kubra(h) to liquidate. **peng-an** winding-up (of enterprise).
kubur ter- *hidup.hidup* buried alive. - *kalang* grave dating back to the neolithic era, found at Bojonegoro (Java). Based on legends the *orang kalang* had tails, in this case, extended spines.
kucai Chinese chives.
kucam pale. **ke-an** paleness, pallor.
kucel tousled, crumpled, disheveled.
kucica magpie robin.
kucil meng-kan to isolate. **ter-** isolated.
kucing *ikan gantung, - tunggu* tantalizing, torment. *bagai - kehilangan anak* to lose o's bearings. *spt - dibawakan lidi* 1 shy. 2 mortally afraid. *membeli - (di) dlm karung* to buy a pig in a poke. *bagai - dgn panggang* to set the fox to watch the geese. *kalau - bertanduk* tomorrow never comes. *main -.-an* to play cat and mouse. -.- the triceps muscle. - *hutan* the leopard cat (L. Felis bengalensis). - *jalang* a name sometimes given to the flat-headed cat (L. Felis planiceps) and sometimes to domestic cats that have run wild. - *tua* an old hand.
kuco (during the Jap. occupation, mostly in Java) village head.
kucur meng-kan to spend (money). **ng-** to spurt forth (liquid). **-an** spending, outlay.
kucut conical.
kuda I the knight in chess. *naik - hijau* to see pink elephants. *zaman - gigit besi* the dim past. - *anjing* a miniature two-hoofed horse, about the size of a dog (found on the Island of Sumbawa). - *beraksa* Pegasus. - *bibit* broodmare. - *kebiri* gelding. - *laut* hippocampus, sea horse. - *lomba* race horse. - *loreng* zebra. - *lumping* 1 a leather horse. 2 (S.) KUDA (KEPANG). 3 accomplice, lackey. - *pacu(an)* race horse. - *pacu jarak jauh* stayer. - *pusing* merry-go-round. - *putih* (fig.) a European prostitute. - *semberani* Pegasus. - *Troya*

(*,Troye*) Trojan horse. - *tunggangan* the (human) means by which s.o. else gains his ends. - *unggul (,yg berketurunan murni)* thoroughbred.
kuda II term for the Police ambulance cars.
kudéta - *tak berdarah* bloodless coup.
kudi.kudi in the rear, behind.
kudu *kemudu.*- to feel obliged to. **-nya** actually, strictly speaking.
kué(h) - *basah* generic term for pastries using rice flour and coconut or water. Some have to be eaten with *kinca* and some are filled with *uli.* Anyway, they are wet, such as, - *lapis*, - *pisang*. - *Cina (,keranjang);* (S.) KUE (RANJANG). - *kering* (opp.) - *basah*. - *pengantin* wedding cake.- *pisang* a slice of banana surrounded by a gelatin made of green bean flour; colored pink, brown or white. - *spekulas* (s.) SPEKULA(A)S. - *talam* cookie made of sweet potato flour or rice flour mixed with coconut milk and tapioca; two layers: brown and green, yellow and white, green and white or brown and white. - *terang bulan* and - *Tiong Ciu Phia* cake made to welcome the Mid-Autumn Festival which falls on the 15th of the 8th lunar month; it is stuffed with pork, chocolate, *durian, cempedak* (,k.o. jackfruit), milk, cashew nuts, etc. - *ulangtahunnya* his (,her) birthday cake.
kuil - *suci drpd jiwa* temple of the soul.
kuini the wild mango (L. Mangifera foetida).
kuit jerky movement of hand (,tail).
kujang 1 chopping knife. 2 name given to a battalion belonging to the West Java-based *Siliwangi* Division.
kukeruyuk cock-a-doodle-doo.
kuku *mereka itu bagai - dan (,dgn) daging* they are inseparable friends. *ibarat - jari tangan* and *ibarat - yg sulit dibrantas* ineradicable. *tdk ber-lagi* impotent, powerless. - *macan* 1 tiger claw. 2 (fig.) staple remover.
kukuh bersi- do not back away from.

peng-an consolidation.

kukul (fig.) potholes (in street).

kukup alluvial deposit, silt.

kulak to buy for resale, buy at wholesale. **-an** bought for resale, buying for resale.

kulakasar luggage.

kulasentana family of prince.

kulawangsa family.

kuli - *cemplong* worker charged with sugar cane planting. - *klenthek* worker charged with the gathering and cleaning of dried sugar cane leaves. - *kontrak(an)* contract laborer. - *mocok* 1 casual laborer. 2 substitute worker. - *sirat* worker charged with watering sugar cane.

kuliah 1 college course. 2 to follow lectures, attend classes. *ruangan* - lecture room. *th* - academic year. *uang* - lecture fee. **peng-** lecturer. **per-an** curricular.

kulina attached or addicted to s.t. due to habit.

kulino (s.) KULINA. -.*meneng* silence.

kulit *hanya di - saja* and *hanya yg nampak pd* - for the sake of appearances. *si - bundar* (soccer-)ball. *si - merah* the redskin. *si - putih* the white man. - *kayu manis* cassia vera, cinnamon stick. *Badannya tinggal - pemalut tulang,* He was all skin and bones.

kulkas refrigerator, icebox.

kulminasi meng- to culminate.

kulonuwun "anybody in? " (said when entering a home and seeing nobody).

kultur culture, civilization.

kultural (S.) KULTURIL.

kultus cult. **mengk-kan** to deify. **mengk-individukan** *raja.raja* to elevate (,raise) kings to the stature of gods. - *individu (,perorangan)* cult of personality.

kultuswan cultured man.

kulub heart.

kulum *menjawab dgn suara napas* **di-** to answer with bated breath. **meng-** under o's breath.

Kulunafsin zaikatulmaut everyone is mortal.

kulur bread-fruit tree (L. Artocarpus communis).

kumai carving, framework.

kumal slightly soiled.

kuman - *di seberang lautan tampak, gajah di pelupuk mata tiada tampak* see the mote in the eye of others, but not the beam in o's own.

kumango *barang* - sundries (dishes, glass, etc.).

Kumba Aquarius.

kumbang - *tdk seekor* there's more than o. fish in the sea. - *nyiur* coconut beetle.

kumico (during the Jap. occupation) head of a neighborhood association.

kuminter pedantic.

kumis - *kucing* a herb with medicinal leaves for renal calculus (L. Orthosiphon grandiflorus).

kumpai bulrush.

kumpal ber- to coagulate, clot. *bahan* **peng-** coagulant. -. *kampil* impoverished.

kumpul peng- *uang* 1 fund raiser. 2 numismatist. **peng-an** *uang* fund raising. **per-an:** ~ *amal* charitable society. ~ *dagang* chamber of commerce. ~ *gelap* an illegal organization. ~ *menabung* savings association. - *kebo* living together without being married.

kumulatif cumulative.

kumulus cumulus (clouds).

kunang *air* **ber-** glittering water.

Kunchantang Communist China.

kunci meng- to end, wind up. -*an bayonet* bayonet joint. - *gabungan* combination lock. - *ganda (,induk)* master key. - *ingatan* aid to memory. - *kontak* ignition key.

kuncung ber- crested.

kundak [*kunjungan mendadak*] a sudden, unexpected visit. *mengadakan* - to make a sudden, unexpected visit.

kundur (wax) gourd, calabash. - *tdk melata pergi, labu tdk melata mari* o. hand will not clasp, every agreement must come from both parties.

kung 1 the sound of a small gong. 2 the sound of the *perkutut.*

kungkang k.o. large water frog. *spt* - shy. *agih.agih* - make yourself an ass and men will ride you.

kungkum (in Jav. mysticism) sitting for hours in a river at night in auspicious places; (s.) MANDI (KUNGKUM).

kuning *keluar keringat -nya* he broke out in a cold sweat. *putih* - cream(-colored). *sakit* - jaundice. *si K- Emas* the rice. - *gading* cream(-colored). - *jingga* orange. - *kepodang* bright yellow.

kunjung peng- visitor. **-an:** *dpt ~ melimpah* to draw a full house. *mendapatkan ~* to receive visitors. *~ kenegaraan* State visit. *~ pamitan* farewell visit. *~ perkenalan* introductory visit.

kuntianak (S.) KUNTILANAK.

kuntit meng- to run after, pursue, chase. **meng-i** to keep surveillance over. **ng-in** to pursue, chase, be in pursuit of. **peng-** pursuer. **peng-an** pursuit, chase.

kuntul egret. - *hitam* reef egret. - *kerbau* cattle egret.

Kuomintang Nationalist China.

kup coup (d'état). **mengk-** to overturn (coup). - *tak berdarah* a bloodless coup.

kupak meng- to break open.

kupat (S.) KETUPAT.

kuping ng- 1 to overhear. 2 to tap. 3 to monitor. 4 to listen in too. *~ sana.sini* 1 to overhear here and there. 2 to keep an ear to the ground.

kupnat dart (in sewing).

kupur (S.) KUFUR.

kur a cry for calling fowls and birds.

kura -.- *hendak memanjat kayu* and *spt* -.- *hendak memanjat pohon kayu* tomorrow never comes, it is impossible to reach (,get ,succeed).

kurai the damascening of a kris.

Kuraisy the tribe to which Muhammad belonged.

Kuran Koran.

kurang 1 inadequate, lacking, short. - *dr* less than. *Saya - tidur,* I didn't get enough sleep. *tdk -* in plentiful supply. *Makanan tdk -,* Food is abundant. *(Apa) tdk boleh -?* Can't you come down (in price)? *paling -* at the least. *Saudara - apa? Tdk - (satu) apa.apa.*

What ails you? I'm fine. *tanpa - suatu apa* safe and sound. 2 with (a certain amount of time) still to go. *Masih - tiga minggu lagi,* There are still three weeks to go. **ber-** to abate. **ke-an:** *bernilai ~* undervalued. *~ darah* anemia. *~ (akan) personil* understaffing. *~ zat makan* malnutrition. *tdk ~ suatu apa* to be O.K. **ke-.beruntungan** lack of success. **ke-.hati.hatian** imprudence. **ke-.mampuan** lack of ability (to pay). **ke-.telitian** lack of care. **meng-.nilaikan** to undervalue. *dgn tdk* **meng-i** ... regardless of ... **peng-an:** *~ anggaran belanja* budget cut. *~ hukuman* remission of sin(s). **se-.-nya** in any case. **-nya:** *Apa ~ ... ?* What's wrong with ... ? *~ banyak* there's nowhere near enough. -.- ... *lebih.lebih* ... the less ... the more ... - *ajar!* and (funnier) - *ekor!* for heaven's sake! oh, hell! - *asin* tasteless (of food). - *pencahayaan* underexposed. - *pikir* rash, thoughtless. - *pikiran* stupid, unwise. - *sedikit* a little bit short.

kuras 1 to rinse, wash out. 2 to squander (money). *obat -* laxative. **di-** 1 to be stolen. *Uang setoran bus Rp. 12.000 ~,* The money which the bus had to deposit in the amount of Rp. 12,000.00 was stolen. 2 to be cleaned out. *Orang yg kantongnya mau ~ hrs disenang. senangkan dulu,* People whose pockets o. wants to clean out must first be pleased. **meng-** to clean out, drain off. **pengk-an** *otak* brainwashing.

Kurasao Curaçao.

kuratif curative.

kurator 1 (university) regent. 2 (banking term) trustee.

Kurawa the 100 brothers in the *Mahab-(h)arata.*

kurawal brace ({ }).

kurda furious, in a towering rage.

kurikulum curriculum. **ber-** *lama* to use the old curriculum (in a school).

kuring *kelihatan -nya* then the cloven hoof showed itself.

Kuripan an old kingdom in East Java.

kurir courier.

kuris (S.) KUDIS.

kuro threadfin.

kurs di- *ke(,dgn)uang Indonesia* to be converted into Indonesian currency. - *pari* parity rate. - *tetap* fixed rate. - *unjuk* sight rate (of exchange). - *wesel* exchange rate.

kursi - *bertali plastik* tubular plastic cord chair, chair with vinyl tubing. - *dorong* wheelchair. - *lipat* folding chair. - *listerik* electric chair. - *loncat (,lontar)* ejection seat. - *pangkas* hairdresser's chair. - *tengadah* reclining seat (,chair). *di - terdakwa* in the prisoner's dock.

kursis person taking a course (of study).

kurung di- in parentheses. *kata.kata yg ~* words in parentheses. *~ banjir* floodbound. **ter-** to be shut in. *~ salju* snowbound. **-an** detention.

kurus unprofitable (of a transportation line). *yg - keuangannya* backed by insufficient capital.

kus puss! puss!

kusa *rumput* - fodder grass.

kusam dim, cloudy. *pucat* - deathly pale.

kusat -*(.kusau)* and -*.mesat* completely confused.

Kusno a *PKI* name for President Soekarno.

kusruk *jatuh* **ng-** to fall forward, overturn.

kustawan male leper.

kustawati female leper.

kusuma 1 beautiful. 2 beautiful woman; (S.) KESUMA. *parang* - name of a batik pattern. - *wicitra* anthology.

kusut depressed. **ke-an** corruption, irregularities.

kuta (Karo Batak) usually larger than a *huta* consisting of inhabitants who have originated from various different clans.

kutak.kutik mengk- to tamper with.

kutang - *kebal peluru* armor vest.

kutat.kutet (S.) KUTAT.KUTIT.

kutèk(s) cutex (a brand name), nail polish.

kutet ber-an 1 to fight hard. 2 to be uncompromising, refuse to give in.

kuti.kuti fault finding.

kutik *tdk bisa* **ber-** couldn't do a thing. **mengk-.k-** (S.) MENGUTIK.NGUTIK.

kutil pickpocket. **ng-** to pickpocket.

kutilang *(burung)* - magpie robin (L. Copsychus saularis).

kutip peng- *pungli pungli* collector.

kutu scum, rabble. - *dlm selimut* an enemy in disguise. **-nya:** *mati ~!* his number is up! *sdh mati ~* hopeless. - *air* mycosis. - *bayur* 1 crab-louse. 2 rotter, baddy. - *buku* (fig.) bookworm. - *busuk* rabble, scum.

kutub center, axis, **ber-** *dua* bipolar. - *magnit* magnetic pole. - *positif* anode.

kutut *burung* - (S.) PERKUTUT.

kuud sitting (during *salat*).

kuwaci (s.) KWACI.

kuwajiban (S.) KEWAJIBAN.

kuwalahan (S.) KEWALAHAN.

kuwalat a sort of cosmic force that seeks retribution for disrespectful behavior toward elders; (s.) KUALAT.

kuwali (s.) KUALI.

kuwangwung (s.) KUANGWUNG.

kuwel di-.- to be crumpled up.

kuwu (mostly in Java) village head.

kuwuk *kucing* - wild cat.

kwa qua, as.

kwaci salted watermelon seeds.

kwadran quadrant.

kwadrat square. *tiga meter* - three meters square.

kwali (S.) KUALI.

kwalitatif qualitative.

kwangwung (s.) KUANGWUNG.

kwantitatif quantitative.

kwantum quantity.

kwarsa *pasir* - quartz.

kwartèr (geol.) quaternary.

kwartèt quartet. - *gesek* string quartet.

kwartir (mil.) quarters.

kwas paintbrush.

kwis quiz.

kwota quota, share.

kya.kya to have a good time.

L

la (s.) LHA.

laadbrief (pron. latbrif) consignment note.

laba I ber- advantageous.

laba II [lapis baja] 1 armor plate. 2 armor-plated.

laberang and tali - (in shipping) shrouds.

labil labile, unstable. ke-an lability, instability.

laboratorium laboratory. - bahasa language lab. - riset research laboratory. - ruang angkasa skylab.

labres dicukur - completely defeated.

labu I squash. - air bland squash (large, light green). - merah pumpkin. - siam summer squash.

labu II - holiem penis-sheath (in Irian Jaya).

labuh kelebihan hari ber- (shipping term) demurrage day, day on demurrage. di-i to be called at, touched at (a port). Pelabuhan kecil itu tdk banyak ~ kapal, Ships do not frequently call at that small port. pe-an: ~ antar.pulau coaster harbor. ~ karantina quarantine port. ~ pasang tidal harbor. ~ pembongkaran port of discharge. ~ pengapalan port of loading. ~ punggah port of shipment. ~ tujuan port of destination.

Labuhan a ceremony starting from the kraton in Yogyakarta to accompany offerings and submit clothes to Nyai Loro Kidul.

lacak trail, track. me- to trail (follow surreptitiously), trace.

lacur I Apa -? What can o. do? - betul what bad luck. nasib - an unlucky fate. orang pe-an an unlucky fellow.

lacur II lewd, lascivious. perempuan - and orang pe-an prostitute.

lada siapa makan - ialah berasa pedas as you make your bed, so you must lie on it.

ladang minta - yg berpunya wanting to have a married woman. ber- to culti-

vate, till. per-an liar shifting cultivation. - minyak oil field. - sapi ranch.

ladu (volcanic) mudstream carried along by rivers over land, lava.

lafal ada -nya pepatah dan ada maknanya a proverb has a literal and a figurative meaning. L- Sumpah Dokter Hippocratic oath.

lagak airs. ber-.- to attitudinize. me-(.-) 1 to put on airs. 2 to nag, tease. - bahasa dialect.

lagi ... - on top of it all, to boot. duanya - the other two (persons). -.- (once) again, once more, anew. ~ penjahat lolos once again criminals escaped. -an besides, moreover.

lagu 1 anthem. - kebangsaan national anthem. 2 carol. - Natal Christmas carol. - cengeng whine. - kesukaan favorite tune. - pemakaman (,sedih) dirge. - pop pop music. - rantau sailors' songs. - yg lama the same old song.

laguh.lagah to rumble (of cart).

lah just let him be! (s.) LA.

lahap covetous. me- to annex. Semarang yg kini sdh berstatus "kota raya" nantinya akan ~ bekas.bekas ibukota dan bandar Raden Patah – Demak dan Jepara, Semarang, which now has the status of a "greater city," will later annex the former capital and port of Raden Patah – Demak and Jepara. pe- cormorant.

lahir dr mula - from o's childhood. Kalau tak dpt dgn - dgn batin, If it does not work overtly, then do it covertly (,in a sneaky way). - (dan) batin 1 altogether, completely, entirely, all, everything. 2 (honest) to the core. 3 for good and all, definitely. 4 fully. 5 material and spiritual (support). 6 in body and soul, physically and mentally. - dr perkawinan yg sah (in birth certificates) born in wedlock. - di luar perkawinan yg sah (in birth certificates) born out of wed-

lock. *sejak -(nya)* since (his) birth.
bayi.bayi yg **ber-an** babies who are
born o. after the other. **me-kan** *suaranya* to cast o's vote. **ter-** née, born; used
to introduce the maiden name of a
married woman.

laici (s.) LECI.

laik (S.) LAYAK. **ke-an:** ~ *laut* seaworthiness. *studi* ~ *usaha* feasibility study.
- *laut* seaworthy. - *udara* airworthy.

la ilaha 1 there is no God but Allah. 2
exclamation of dismay, despair. *la
Ilaha Illallah(u)* and *la ilaha illa Allah*
there is no God but Allah.

**lailat al.kadar, lailat.ul.kadar, Lailatul
Kadar** and **lailatulkadar** Night of
Revelation, i.e. o. of the odd numbered nights of the last ten days of
Ramadan when the Koran was sent
down to the Prophet. *mendapat malam
lailatulkadar* to earn money hand over
fist.

lain I - *kali* 1 next time. 2 in future. *L-
lagi!* O, it's different! - *lagi (,pula)* not
including (,counting) (the remainder),
exclusive of (the remainder).- *X - Y*
X and Y are different. - *dr yg -* 1 special,
peculiar. 2 different from others, gen-
ius. - *perkara kalau* ... that is (quite)
another thing, if ...; that is quite a
different story, if ... - *dulu - sekarang*
other times, other manners. - *di mulut,
- di hati, (- lafaz, - itikad)* he says o.
thing but means another, insincere.
- *di muka, - di belakang* to play the
hypocrite. *Tdk ada yg - dpt saya lakukan, kecuali* ... There was nothing for
me to do but ... - *soal - jawabnya* that
is neither here nor there, utterly irrelevant. - *tdk (hanyalah* ... *)* and *tak -
(dan) tak bukan (ialah* ... *)* only, nothing else but ... *tak - karena* be only
because. *jauh* **ber-an** *dgn* to differ as
night from day. **ke-an** irregularity, peculiarity. ~ *kelamin* transsex. **se-** *drpd*
besides, in addition to. **se-nya** 1 the
rest. 2 besides. **-nya:** *L~?* (to customer) Anything else? *Apa ~?* What's

the difference? *Dan yg dua ~,* And the
other two. *jauh ~ dr biasa* most special
(,particular). -.-: ~ *katanya* and ~ *saja
jawabnya* shuffling excuses.

lain II - *porem* (coll.) land reform.

lajang pe-an celibacy.

Lajnah Tanfiziyah Executive Board (of
the former *PSII*).

laju 1 swiftly, speedy, rapid. 2 rate (of
inflation, etc.). **me-** to move fast.

lajurwan columnist.

lakcang Chinese sausages.

laken felt. *topi -* felt hat.

laki ber-.bini to be husband and wife.
ke-.-an mannish. -. *bini* husband and
wife.

laknat (ac)cursed, anathema.

lakon an episode from the Javanized
Ramayana or *Mahab(h)arata,* serving
as the plot for a single night's *wayang*
performance; *memegang (,memainkan)
-nya* to play o's role. **ng-i** to follow an
ascetic regimen. **pe-** *watak* character
actor. - *pertama* the first act. - *sandiwara* (stage-)play, drama, dramatic
piece. - *tampang* line-up operation (of
police).

laksa crunchy rice sticks served with a
combination of diced chicken, eggs
and shrimps.

Laksamana Admiral. - *Madya* Vice Admiral. - *Muda* Rear Admiral. - *Pertama*
Commander.

laksana *tdk dpt* **di-kan** impracticable,
infeasible, impossible of achievement.
keter-an feasibility. *laporan tlh* ~ feasibility report. *studi* ~ feasibility study.
pe-: ~ *bangunan* building contractor.
P~ Kuasa Perang War Administrator.
pe-an: *dlm taraf* ~ under way, in progress, in the implementation stage.
ketentuan.ketentuan ~ executory
provisions.

laktosa lactose.

laku 1 acceptable, generally accepted. 2
to be in favor, be favorite, be popular,
be in vogue. 3 to find a market (,sale),
find an outlet. 4 to be accepted, find

(‚meet with) favor. 5 to meet with a favorable reception, be well received, be warmly welcomed. 6 to yield (a certain sum of money). 7 to hold (good). - *keras* to be in demand. - *spt kue (‚goreng pisang)* and - *sbg goreng pisang* to sell like hot cakes. **ber-** current. *harga.harga yg ~ sekarang* prevailing prices. *sedang ~* afoot. *kenaikan gaji yg ~ utk semuanya* an across-the-board pay increase. *~ serong* to commit adultery. *~ surut sampai* to be retroactive to. *tdk ~* in abeyance. *dinyatakan ~* (of stipulations, etc.) to be declared effective. *dinyatakan tdk ~* to be declared (to be) void (‚invalid). *~nya kembali Undang. Undang Dasar 1945* the re-imposition of the 1945-Constitution. *waktu ~nya* term of validity **berke-an** *baik* to behave well. **diber-kan** to be imposed. *keadaan darurat yg tlh ~ hari Jumat yg lalu* emergency powers imposed last Friday. *~ kembali (‚surut)* to be made retroactive, be imposed retroactively. **keber-an** validity. **me-kan:** *~ desersi* to desert. *~ hubungan seks* to have sexual relations. *~ kesukaan* to take pleasure in. *~ ketrampilan* to display o's skill. **member-kan** to put (regulations) into effect. **pe-** agent, perpetrator. - *jantera hidup* cycle of life. - *lampah* conduct, life, behavior.

lalai off-handed, casual. **me-kan** *pikiran* to unwind, relax.

lalang elephant grass.

lalap 1 relish. 2 vegetables as a side dish. **di-** 1 to be overcome. 2 to be held up. *(habis) ~ api* to be burned down. **me-** 1 to defeat, beat (in sports). 2 to rape. *~ duit* to embezzle money. **pe-** *mode* clotheshorse, fancy dresser.

lalu **ber-.lalang** to pass by again and again. *jalan.jalan yg dpt* **di-i** *kendaraan bermotor* roads passable for motor vehicles. **keter-an:** *Adalah ~,* It is outrageous. *berlaku ~* to exceed all bounds. **me-i** by way of. *~ radio* over the radio. **pe-an** *angin topan* typhoon belt. *Itu*

ter-! That's the limit! That's going too far! -*.lintas dwimarga* two-way traffic. -*.lintas ekamarga* one-way traffic. -*.lintas giro* (banking term) transfer business. -*.lintas giro dan clearing* (banking term) transfer and clearing operations. -*.lintas kaki* pedestrian traffic. -*.lintas pembayaran dgn luar negeri* (banking term) transfer of international payments. -*.lintas penumpang* passage, way, thoroughfare. -*.lintas udara* air traffic.

lama 1 (of periodicals) back (number). 2 former, previous. 3 old-established. *blm - (ini)* recently. *paling -* not to exceed (length of prison term). *sejak - 1* long ago, long before this. 2 (it is) a long time since. *tak - antaranya (‚kemudian)* not long afterwards. **se-** for (time period). *~ 5 jam* for 5 hours. **se-.-nya** not to exceed. **-nya:** *utk berapa ~* for some time. *tiada berapa th ~* a few years ago. -*.-* gradually, in the long run, finally. -*.ke-an* at last, eventually.

lamak (s.) GALUNGAN.

lamar **ng-** to propose to.

lambai **me-(kan** *tangannya)* 1 to wave (o's hand). 2 to beckon.

lambang 1 heraldic arms (‚crest), coat-of-arms. 2 decal. - *gengsi* status symbol (a car, in Indonesia). *L- Negara* State coat-of-arms. **per-** symbolism.

lambat *paling -* at the latest (‚utmost). *biar - asal selamat* slow but sure; better late than never. **di-kan** *dr aturan* more sluggish than usual. **peng-an** slowdown. **ter-:** *berita ~* a belated news item. *lebih baik ~ drpd samasekali tdk* better late than never. *~ bln* late in menstruating.

lambé 1 lip(s). 2 mouth. 3 words, talk.

lambung a bounce. **me-** *ke atas* to skyrocket.

lamin (among the Dayak people of Kalimantan) longhouse.

lamis 1 (to speak) softly, coaxingly, nicely. 2 lipservice.

lampau ago. *enam bln -* six months ago. *tdk dpt* **di-i** insurmountable, insuperable. **me-i** to cap. ~ *baris* to exceed the bounds. **ter-** surpassed. ~ *pagi* premature. *blm (,tdk) akan* ~ *waktunya* still has the time to. **ter-i** surpassed.

lampias me-kan *hawa nafsunya* to give full rein to o's passions.

lampir me-kan to annex. **ter-** attached, enclosed.

lampu per-an lighting. - *abang.ijo* (coll). traffic light. - *anti.nyamuk dan anti. lalat* a (Philips) insect repellent lamp. - *belakang* rearlight. - *dim* parking lights. - *hijau* green light (authorization to proceed with some undertaking). - *hijau.merah* (coll.) traffic light. - *jalanan* street light. - *kerdip* turn signal flasher. - *kilat (pd kamera)* flash bulb. - *kontrol* control light (of bus or truck). - *muka* headlight, headlamp (of automobile). - *nomer plat* license plate light. - *(pengatur) lalu. lintas* traffic light. - *penyeberangan jalan* pedestrian light. - *petromak(s)* a pressurized gasoline lamp, Coleman-type lamp. - *rem* brake light (of automobile). - *stromking (,Stromking , Strongking)* and -. *tekan* a pressurized gasoline lamp, Coleman-type lamp. - *wasiat* Aladdin's lamp.

lampung pe- *penyelamat* life buoy.

lamtoro k.o. tree with edible seed pods (L. Parkia speciosa Hassk.).

lamtoronisasi the encouragement to plant *lamtoro* trees.

lamun -an idle, fancy. - *kosong* wishful thinking.

Lan shortening of the masculine proper names *Aslan, Dahlan, Ramelan,* etc.

lanai patio facing the ocean (used in Hawaii).

lanang 1 male. 2 virile, manly.

lancang 1 fearless. 2 rapid, rash. 3 insistent. 4 disrespectful.

lancar berse- surfing (on surfboard). -.*licin* smooth and easy.

lancip *sdh* - acute angle.

landa di- to be overrun by, stricken by, hit by, destroyed by.

landas ber-an anvilled. **ber-kan** based on.

me- to land (of aircraft). **-an** foundation, basis. ~ *heli* helipad. ~ *kontinen* continental shelf. ~.*menggelinding* taxiway. ~.*pacu* runway. ~ *pesawat terbang* airstrip, runway. - *kontinen* continental shelf.

landing landing (of aircraft).

landréform land reform.

landschap (pron. lanskap) the word was mostly used in the outer islands as the abbrev. for 'zelfbesturend landschap' (= selfgoverning area), 'zelfbesturend rijk' (= selfgoverning state), i.e. an Indonesian area under the suzerainty of the Netherlands.

Landstorm Landsturm; in the Netherlands Indies a force composed of all men liable to service not already in the army, navy or reserve.

lang *di tempat tiada -, kata belalang, akulah* - in the kingdom of the blind the o.-eyed man is king.

langendriyan Yogyakarta and Surakarta versions of opera (the stories are taken from the tales of the Red Knight *Menak Jinggo,* whose warlike acts occurred in East Java).

langen(h)arjan jacket the front part of which resembles that of an open jacket with lapels and a necktie, worn by Jav. men at ceremonies.

langgam - *bahasa (,kata)* 1 accent. 2 expression. 3 style.

langgan me-i to subscribe to. **me-ankan** to take out a subscription for s.o. **pe-** subscriber. **-an:** *menjadi* ~ to subscribe to. *para* ~ clientele. ~ *bui (,penjara)* jailbird, habitual lawbreaker.

langgar di- *pelor* to be hit by a bullet. **me-** *ranjau* to hit a mine. **pe-:** ~ *hukum* lawbreaker. ~ *lalu.lintas* traffic violator. **pe-an** misdemeanor. ~ *kriminil (,pidana)* criminal offense. *melakukan* ~ *hukum pidana* to break criminal law.

langgat ng-i to comply with.

langgeng me-kan to make eternal.

langguk arrogant.

langit me- to soar, skyrocket. **se-** (sl.) 1 swell, terrific. 2 to reach a peak.

ketidakpuasan sdh ~ dissatisfaction has reached a peak (or, has soared). 3 skyhigh. *tarif yg* ~ skyhigh rates.

langka scarce, scanty. *devisa yg* - scarce foreign exchange. *waktu* - grace period. **ke-an** scarcity.

langkah **me-** *maju* to proceed (of negotiations). **me-kan** *kakinya* to stride. - *kanan* very lucky. - *lanjutan* followup. - *pembuka* opening speech. - *penutup* closing word. - *pertama* 1 initiative. 2 first step. - *seribu* 'thousand steps.' *mengangkat (,membawakan, ,membuat ,melepas ,menarik)* - *seribu* to run away.

langkong *karyawan* - (in Belitung) daily worker.

langkuas galingale.

langsam slow.

langsat, langseb and **langsep** k.o. tasty fruit, yellow-white colored, like a *duku* (L. Lansium domesticum). *kulit* - (said of a woman) a yellow-white colored skin (well liked in Indonesia).

langsung *L-!* (bus conductor to driver) Go on! (there aren't any passengers who want to get off). **ber-** to be afoot, come off, happen. *demi* **ke-an** *hidupnya* for o's continued existence. **me-** *terus. menerus* to be durable. *Semuanya tlh* **ter-** It's too late to do anything about it.

lanjak *tlh* **me-** *usia yg tinggi* has reached (,attained) a great age.

lanjur *barang sdh* **te(r)-** it's too late to do anything about it.

lanjut *orang* - *usia* senior citizen. **ber-** 1 continuative. 2 continuous. **berke-an** to continue. *akan* **di-kan** to be continued. **ke-an** 1 follow-up. 2 continuity. **keber-an** continuativeness. **pe-** 1 continuer. 2 continuator. **-an** advanced. - *ke sebalik* please turn over (at the end of the page). *tlh* - *kemajuannya* far advanced.

Lanka Ceylon.

lanreporem land reform.

lanskap landscape.

lantah **me-** to pick up and take away.

lantai floor, story. **ber-** *dua* two-story. **pe-** dancer. - *atap* top floor. - *bawah tanah* basement. - *dasar* ground floor. - *dua (,tiga)* second (,third) floor. - *karet* rubber floor matting. - *satu* ground floor. - *terbawah* basement.

lantar **diter-kan** not cared for. **ter-** 1 unfinished. 2 unsuccessful. 3 in trouble. 4 became a victim. 5 virgin (forest).

lantas *tak* - *angan* absurd. **me-kan** *dendam* to take revenge. **pe-an** permeability.

lanting I **pe-** *pesawat terbang (,udara)* airplane catapult.

lanting II floating house.

lantoro (s.) LAMTORO.

lantung **pe-an** loafer, vagabond, hobo; (s.) LUNTANG.LANTUNG.

lantung.lantang *bunyi* - clamorous, tumultuous, noisy.

lanud 1 [pangkalan udara] air base. 2 [landasan udara] airstrip, runway.

laos galingale, a gingery root (used as a medicine and in cooking).

lap - *kesehatan* tampon, sanitary napkin.

lapak kiosk (in market).

lapang - *pula rasa dadanya* he breathed easy (or, was relieved). **-an** (shopping) plaza. ~ *berbatasan* adjoining ground. ~ *golf* golf course. ~ *kerja* scope (,sphere) of activities (,employment). ~ *kuda* race track. *L*~ *Merah* Red Square (in Moscow). ~ *minyak* oil field. ~ *ranjau* minefield. ~ *tembak* artillery-range, practice-ground. ~ *terbang* airfield, aerodrome. ~ *terbang kecil* airstrip. ~ *usaha* sphere of action.

lapar **ke-an** 1 to be starving. 2 from (,of) starvation. - *gizi* undernourished. - *uang* greedy for money.

lapat.lapat vaguely. - *ia memperoleh tau dr orang.orang kanan.kiri* he vaguely found out from people here and there.

lapis *sampai tujuh* - *anak buahnya* as far as the seventh generation. **ber-** *baja (,waja)* ironclad. *parkir* **ber-.**- double parking. **ber-kan** *aspal* with an asphalt layer. **me-** *dgn besi* to armor. **-an** (of minerals) deposit. ~ *aspal* asphalt layer. ~ *atas(an)* upper (,top) layer, superstratum. *segala ~ bangsa* all classes, all strata of the people (,nation), *segala ~ manusia* all strata of society. *~ paling bawah masyarakat* grass roots. *~ pelindung* protective coating. *~ tanah atas* topsoil. - *baja* 1 armored. 2 armor (plate).

lapor me-kan *diri pd* to register with. **me-.matakan** to give an eyewitness account. **-an:** *~.* *~ berpihak* tendentious (,biased) reports. *~ intelijen* intelligence report(s). *~ kecakapan* personnel performance record. *~ kemajuan (pekerjaan)* progress report. *~ (pandangan) mata* eyewitness account. *~ peninjauan* survey report. *~ pers* press report. *~ survey (,survai)* survey report.

lapud [lapang udara] airfield.

lapuk antiquated. *paham yg* - obsolete ideas. *sdh* - behind the times. *tak* - *di (,oleh) hujan, tak lekang di (,oleh) panas* and *tdk* - *dek hujan, tak lakang dek paneh* 1 not felled by wind or rain. 2 undying. 3 indestructible.

larang di-: *D~ berjualan di sini!* (signpost) No selling (,trading) here! *D~ kencing!* (signpost) No urinating! *~ keras* strictly forbidden. *D~ mangkal di sini!* (signpost) Prohibited to trade here! *D~ (masuk) bagi tentara (,militer)!* (signpost) Off limits! Out of bounds! *D~ masuk utk kendaraan!* (signpost) No thoroughfare! *D~ membuang sampah di sini!* (signpost) No littering here! **pe-** prohibitor. **pe-an** ban, embargo. *~ thd ekspor ternak* an embargo on the export of cattle. *bagian.bagian* ter- private parts. **-an:** *~ perangkapan jabatan* incompatibility of functions.

larap -an (s.) PENGETAHUAN (LARAP-AN).

laras kese-an harmony. *tdk se-* lagi out of date, old-fashioned.

larat I a species of orchid (L. Melodorum spp.).

larat II me-*jepat* as poor as a church-mouse.

lari ber-*terpontang.panting* to flee head over heels. **di-.malamkan** to be carried

away secretly (in the dead of night). **me-** to move to another place. **me-kan** *diri* 1 to desert. 2 at large. **pe-** deserter. *~ bugil* streaker. *~ jarak pendek* sprinter. *~ skat* skater. *~ telanjang* streaker. **pe-an** refugee. *di dlm ~* in exile. *pemerintah ~* government in exile. *Ke mana -nya ...?* Where did ... disappear to? *-.- kecil* to trip. - *bertemperasan* to flee in disorder. - *bugil* streaking (run naked in public). - *karung* sack race. - *kawin* to elope. - *ke barang* to rush into goods. - *ketakutan* to flee from fear. - *lintas gawang* hurdle-race. - *sekolah* to cut class, play hooky.

larik -an furrow.

laris - *spt goreng pisang* selling like hot cakes. **ke-an** to be all sold out.

laron (jokingly) people, populace (esp. when they flock together).

lars *sepatu* - boots.

Larte II (among members of the Army Search and Rescue Group) emergency rations, i.e. an allotment of food and provisions.

larung me- and **ng-** to throw (a *sesaji,* corpse, etc.) in the water (,river ,etc.). **pe(ng)-an** the throwing (of a *sesaji,* corpse, etc.) in the water (,river ,etc.).

larut I pe- solvent.

larut II - *malam* late-night (show).

las penge-an welding.

Lasam a place in Java celebrated for its painted cottons: *Batik* -.

laskar and **lasykar** partisans, irregulars. - *rakyat* local militia unit organized as an auxiliary force, partisans.

las.lasan (in) the teens. *Kata "bung" sdh ada sejak zamannya Indische Partij, jadi di th* -, The word "bung" has already been in existence since the period of the Indische Partij, hence since the 1910's.

latah suffering from k.o. hysteria, i.e. a state in which a person, usually a woman, always imitates another person's actions or carries out another person's instructions. *ikut* - *+ verb (,adjective)* also ... *Rupanya si suami* *tak mau ikut - patah semangat,* Apparently, the husband didn't want to also be brokenhearted.

latar setting. **ber-**: ~ *belakang biru tua* with a dark blue background. ~ *belakang politis* to have a political background. **ber-kan** with a ... background. **di-** belakangi with a backdrop of. **mebelakangi** to constitute a background for. **pe-an** platform. ~ *parkir* parking lot. ~ *perkemahan* campground. - *depan* foreground.

latih **-an**: ~ *jasmani* bodily exercise. ~ *kemiliteran* (mil.) drill. ~ *lapangan* field training. ~ *perang.perangan* (mil.) maneuvers. ~ *pertempuran dgn menggunakan peluru tajam* (mil.) live fire exercise. ~ *pola kalimat* sentence-pattern drill. ~ *sambil bekerja* on-the-job training. ~ *terjun payung* jumping course. ~ *widya yudha* tactical field training.

lauk food cooked for eating with rice. *-.pauk* all k.o. food (other than rice).

laundri laundry.

laut *di - dan di darat* on land and on sea. **kepe-an** navigation, seamanship. **me-** to splash down (of spacecraft). **-an** sea. *L~ Adriatik* Adriatic (Sea). *L~ Atlantik* Atlantic Ocean. *L~ Baltik* Baltic (Sea). *L~ (H)india* Ind(ones)ian Ocean. *L~ Kaspia* Caspian Sea. *L- Cina Selatan* South China Sea. *L- Egea* Aegean Sea. *L- Hitam* Black Sea. *L- Mati* Dead Sea. *L- Natuna (,Tiongkok Selatan)* South China Sea.

lawalata (*Lawalata* is the name of an Indonesian who traveled widely about the world on foot). **ber-** and **ng-** to go on foot, hike.

lawan **ber-** *cakap dgn* to converse with. **ber-an**: ~ *arah jalan jarum jam* counter-clockwise. *(datang)* ~ *arah* oncoming (car). *kendaraan yg* ~ *arah* oncoming cars. *dr arah* ~ from the opposite direction. **me-** to antagonize. *(~ dgn) ingkar* rebellious. ~ *kantuk* to fight sleep, keep awake. **nge-** to oppose. **pe-** *radang* antiphlogistic. *mengadakan* **per-an** *thd* to

offer resistance to. - *(angin) pasat* antitrades. - *berbicara* person with whom o. is conversing. - *debat* opponent in debate. - *jenis* person of the opposite sex. - *kerja* counterpart. - *radang* antiphlogistic. - *rakitik* antirachitic. - *skorbut* antiscorbutic.

lawang **pe-an** grade-crossing.

lawar **-an** ruthless(ly), merciless(ly).

lawas long (in duration).

lawat **pe-** caller, i.e. a person who makes a short visit. **-an** visit.

lawèt *(burung)* - k.o. swallow (bird).

lawon white cotton textile (esp. Jav. handwoven, for shrouds).

layah **me-** *rendah* and **me-.-** to fly low (of aircraft).

layak 1 worthy. 2 marginal. *dr sumber yg - dipercaya* from unimpeachable sources. *sertifikat - laut* certificate of seaworthiness. **ke-an** *laut* seaworthiness. *orang.orang yg bukan* **-nya** inefficient people (occupying positions of authority).

layan **me-i** *resep dokter* to fill a doctor's prescription. **pe-**: ~ *kabin* cabin boy. ~ *kantor* office janitor. ~ *meriam* gunner. ~ *serabutan* general utility man, i.e. an unskilled laborer who does odd jobs. ~ *telepon* switchboard operator. **pe-an**: ~ *di darat* groundhandling (of aircraft). ~ *di kamar* room service (in hotel). ~ *lepas jual* aftersales service. ~ *masyarakat* a public service. ~ *memuat/membongkar muatan* (re aircraft) ramp handling service. ~ *penuangan anggur* wine serving (in hotel). ~ *purna jual* aftersales service. **-an**: *tdk mendapat* ~ (love) remains unrequited. ~ *(jarak) jauh* remote control.

layang I **pe-an** ferry boat. **se-** *pandang (,terbang ,tinjau)* 1 cursory. 2 superficially. 3 roughly. *matanya* **ter-** he dozed off.

layang II **-.-** the white-breasted wood swallow. - *peluncur* hang glider.

layang III sea fish resembling the herring.

layap **nge-** to go out and wander around

(particularly in the evening).

layar *di belakang* - behind the curtain, in the background. **ber-:** ~ *ke pulau kapuk (,kasur)* to doze off, hit the sack. ~ *mengelilingi* to circumnavigate. **di-.** **perakkan** to be filmed, be made a motion picture of. **di-.TV.kan** and **di-tévékan** to be televised. *Sandiwara ini di-tevekan di saluran enam,* This play (,drama) was shown on TV on channel six. **me-.putihkan** to make a motion picture of. **pe-an:** ~ *bebas* free passage. ~ *niaga* merchant shipping. ~ *pertama (,percobaan)* shakedown cruise. ~ *wisata keliling dunia* around-the-world cruise. - *perak* silver screen, i.e. the screen on which pictures are projected in theaters. - *radar* radar screen. *dgn* - *terkembang* in (,under) full sail, with all sails set (,spread). - *teve* TV-screen.

layat di- has been paid a visit of condolence. **ng-** to pay a person a visit, call upon a person (due to sickness, a loss suffered), pay a condolence call.

layon corpse, dead body.

layu(h) - *kedua kaki* paraplegia. - *perasaannya* he is feeling down, depressed.

layung - *langit* afterglow, sunset (,evening) glow.

lé boy (vocative); (s.) TOLE.

lèak (in Bali) witch or the spirit of a living person practicing the art of black magic.

lebah - *betina* worker (a bee). - *jantan* drone (a male honeybee). - *pekerja* worker (bee). - *ratu* queen (in a colony of bees).

lèbar per-an widening. - *telinga* good at picking up rumors.

Lebaran - *Haji,* also called - *Besar, Idul Adha* and *Idul Kurban,* falls on 10 *Zulhijah,* marking the day on which the pilgrimage to Mecca is observed as the most important holiday in Arab and other Moslem countries. - *Idulfitri* falls on 1 *Syawal,* often referred to as *Lebaran.*

lebat *hujan turun* **me-** it is raining cats and dogs.

lèbat seke- *mata* superficially.

lebé a village religious official, registrar of records; (S.) LEBAI.

lebih - *baik* better, preferable. - *baik kamu* ... you had better ..., it would be best if you ... - *dr 12.000 orang* more than 12,000 persons. *seratus* - more than a hundred or so. - *kurang* about, approximately. *persetujuan* - *dahulu* prior approval (,agreement). **berke-an:** *merasa* ~ *dr* to have an advantage over. *kiranya tidaklah* ~ *bila* ... though perhaps superfluous, we would like to point out ... **ke-an** superiority, lead. *bernilai* ~ overvalued. **me-.** **nilaikan** to overvalue. - *berat badan* overweight (of person).

lebur peng-an 1 solution. 2 dissolving s.t. in a liquid. **ter-** *ke dlm* merged with.

lècèh lacking orderliness, depraved. **pe-** adulator, flatterer.

lècèk worn-out.

lècèt me- to chafe.

léci leechee.

ledak me- *tertawa* to burst out laughing. **pe-** burster. **pe-an** *penduduk* population explosion. - *di udara* air burst.

lèdèk I 1 female dancer in *kampungs* who, now and then, also seduces men. 2 a dance peculiar to villages in Central and East Java; shows are given in the evening and are performed by two or three young women.

lèdèk II di-(in) to be teased, be nagged, be baited (in order to stimulate s.o. to do s.t.). **menge-** to tease. **nge-(in)** to irritate, make angry, annoy. *Jangan* ~ *saya, ya!* Don't make me angry, will you! Don't irritate me, will you!

légal legal. **me-kan** to legalize.

légalisasi legalization. **me-kan** to legalize.

legènda legend. **di-kan** to be turned into a legend.

Legi the first day of the five-day week.

Légiun - *Asing* Foreign Legion. - *Pembebas Irian Barat* West Irian Liberation Legion.

lègo me- to sell s.t. to raise cash. **ter-** sold, disposed of.

Lègong Balinese dance performed by three young girls.

leha [lelaki hawa] gay, homosexual.

lèha.lèha to do s.t. at o's leisure (or, effortlessly). *Maka jangan dikira mereka akan dpt lenggang.kangkung - saja,* Don't think that they will be able to just stroll over (Indonesian territory).

lèhèr - *angsa* gooseneck (i.e. any of various mechanical devices shaped like a goose's neck). *kemeja yg punya - lidah lebar* a shirt with a broad collar.

lejit me- to jump up.

lekak.liku (s.) LIKA.LIKU.

lekang *takkan - dr hati* unforgettable, memorable, never to be forgotten.

lekas swift(ly).

lekat pe-an *benda* accession. **-an** attachment.

lèk.lèkan to stay awake (,up) (usually because o. has made a vow, has to guard a dead body, has to fulfill night duty, etc.).

lèksikon lexicon.

lèkton [kelek katon] the armpit is visible.

lèktur - *hiburan* light reading.

lelah *membuang* - to take a break (,rest), rest. *sesudah hilang -nya* after he has rested.

lèlang pe- auctioneer. **ter-** auctioned.

lelap me-kan *mata* to close o's eyes (for a sleep).

lelaunan slow, lingering. *bermain secara - to* protract (,spin out) the time.

lélé name of a fish species (L. Clarias batrachus) with long, sharp tentacles on the fins near the head; the species lives in ponds and rivers, on edges of the water, in mud or in holes, k.o. catfish. *kelas -* big fish (,shot), bigwig.

lèlèh to calm down. *Darah sang murid tak mau -,* The pupil did not want to calm down.

lèlèr ke- to be neglected.

lelet slow(ly).

lélété and **Lé Lé Té** facetious pron. of *RRT* (= *Republik Rakyat Tiongkok* People's Republic of China).

lelonobroto and **lelono.broto** 1 to go from place to place seeking inspiration in God's words. 2 the journey made to gain distance from all earthly things.

lelucon - *April* April Fool's joke.

leluhur ancestry.

lèm - *plastik* Scotch tape.

lemah berse- compliant. ~ *tak patah* 1 apparently accommodating (,compliant). 2 to adopt a go-slow policy. - *ingatan* mentally retarded. - *ketuaan* senility.- *pikiran* mentally deficient. - *semangat* 1 ailing. 2 weak (of morals). 3 - *syahwat* impotent.

lemak ber- greasy. - *ikan* fish oil.

lemang glutinous rice cooked with coconut milk in a green bamboo lined with banana leaf. *menyandang - hangat orang* pull the chestnuts out of the fire for s.o.

lemari cabinet (a piece of furniture). - *baterai* battery case. - *kodok* (in stores) showcase. - *obat* medicine cabinet.

lemas 1 drowning, gasping for breath. 2 obliging. **me-kan** 1 to purify. 2 to smother, stifle. ~ *rambut* to cream-rinse o's hair.

lembab pe- moisturizer.

lembaga me- to become customary, be institutionalized. *L- Administrasi Negara* National Institute of (Public) Administration. *L- Alkitab Indonesia* Indonesian Bible Society. - *pemasyarakatan* penitentiary, correctional institution. *L- Penelitian Penduduk* Demographic Research Institute.- *pendidikan* educational (,teaching) institution (,establishment). *L- Tenaga Atom* Atomic Energy Institute. *L- Tunanetra* Home for the Blind.

lembar -an *kuning* yellow pages (in telephone directory).

lembèk - *ingatan (,pikiran)* mentally retarded (,deficient).

lèmbèng (to act) resembling a woman.

lembir pe- s.t. to make a car run faster.

lembu - *kebiri* ox.

lembur ng- to work overtime.

lembut *warna* - a soft color. - *hati (,pe-rangai)* 1 soft-hearted, gentle, meek. 2 pliant, submissive.

lèmèk k.o. underlayer. - *kasur* under-mattress protective mat. - *kursi* seat cover.

lemes (S.) LEMAS. **Ng-in** *kaki!* Let's dance!

lèmpar me- to throw away. **me-(kan)** *senyum pd* to give s.o. a smile. **me-kan** *tanggungjawab dr bahunya* to rid o.s. of the responsibility. **pe-** *bom* 1 bomber (an aircraft). 2 bomb thrower. *daerah* **pe-an** *produksinya* outlet (,market) for o's products. - *lembing* javelin throwing. - *melayang* to skim (stones over the water).

lèmpèng a sod (of turf). **-(an)** *rumput* a piece of turf, a (turf-)sod.

lempit -an fold.

lempuyang a ginger (L. Zingiber cassu-munaar).

lemukut broken grains of husked rice.

lemu(ng)sir fillet of beef.

lemuru k.o. sardine.

lencam *(ikan)* - sea bream.

lenceng me- to veer.

lèncèr nge- to get a breath of fresh air.

lèncong me- to deviate, swerve.

léndé and **léndhé -an** to lean (against). *Dia - di tiang listerik,* He leaned against an electric lamp pole.

lèndot and **lèndhot ber-an** *di* to lean on, hang onto. **ng(e)-** to lean, recline (against).

lèngah *akan* **me-.-kan** *hati* for amusement, as a pastime. *utk* **pe-.-** *pikiran (,waktu)* for amusement.

lengang 1 empty, vacant. 2 uninhabited.

lènggang to wobble (to and fro) (swing-ing the arms, etc.). *tak berasak - dr ketiak* and *tdk akan jauh - dr ketiak* always the same. -. *kangkung* 1 (lit.) the swaying of the white or pink flow-ered convolvulus (L. Ipomea aquatica) when touched by a soft breeze. 2 (fig.) at a snail's pace, sluggish. -. *lenggok* swaying the hips (of a girl).

lènggotbawa swaying the hips (of a girl).

lenggut nge- very sleepy.

lengkap pe- 1 complement. 2 comple-mentary. **per-an** *ski* ski gear. - *bersen-jata (,persenjataannya)* armed to the teeth, equipped with modern material. *masih - berpakaian* and - *baju dan celananya* to be (still) well clothed.

lèngkèng (s.) KLENGKENG.

lèngkok me- to curve.

lengkung hole, hollow. *hidung* **me-** an aquiline nose. **-an:** ~ *bln* crescent. ~ *bumi* horizon.

lèngos me- to feel offended.

Léninis Leninist.

Léninisme Leninism.

lènong open-air folk play of the *pinggiran Betawi*-populace.

lènsa - *putih* (uncolored) eyeglass lens.

lènso (in the Moluccas and the Celebes) handkerchief.

lentuk ke-an flexibility.

lenyap - *tanpa bekas* vanished into thin air. **pe-:** *minuman* ~ *dahaga* thirst quencher. ~ *kesukaran. kesukaran* trouble-shooter.

léo male lion.

lèpa.lèpa proa from the Moluccas made of hollowed tree trunks provided with outriggers.

lepas ago. *Pd tgl 8 Mei 18 th yg tlh - ...,* On May 8, 18 years ago ... - *tengah.hari* after midday. *(seorang)* - *(seorang)* (o.) by (o.). - *demam* free from fever. - *dr pensensoran* passed by censor. *tdk ada sesuatu yg - dr perhatiannya* there is nothing that escapes his attention. **bersi-** *diri dr tanggung.jawabnya* to dis-claim its responsibilities. *Presiden* **di-** *dgn menggeloranya semangat massa,* The President was seen off while the masses' enthusiasm was reaching its peak. **keter-an** *mengatakan* to blurt out, blab. **me-** to say farewell to. ~ *jenazah* to render the last honors to a person. ~ *kangen* to reunite. ~. *landas* (s.) LEPAS (LANDAS). ~ *langkah seribu* to run away. ~ *th yg lama* to see the old year out, see the new year in. ~ *tinja* to defecate. **me-kan:** ~ *air*

matanya to weep. ~ *anak ikan* to set
fish. ~ *hampir 100.000 buruh* to lay
off almost 100,000 workers. ~ *dahaga*
to quench o's thirst. ~ *diri(nya) dr*
sekolah to drop out of school. ~ *hajat*
to go to the bathroom. ~ *hak atas* to
abandon the right over. ~ *kehendak*
1 obliging, indulgent. 2 to do what o.
wants. ~ *kepalan* to give a blow with
the fist. ~ *lapar* to appease o's hunger.
~ *marah* to give vent to o's anger. ~
masa membujangnya to give up o's
bachelor's days. ~ *mata* to look about
(for fun). ~ *napas yg terakhir* to die.
~ *pandang (,pemandangan)* to look
about (for fun). ~ *penat* to (take a)
rest. ~ *penerjun payung* to drop para-
chutists. ~ *pukulan* to strike (,deal) a
blow. ~ *rindu* to enjoy o.s. (in seeing
o's native region again). ~ *sesaknya* to
get out of an awkward predicament. ~
tangisnya to weep. ~ *tendangan* to
give a kick. ~ *tikaman* to stab (with a
dagger, etc.). ~ *tinju* to give a blow
with the fist. **pe-:** *suatu kesenangan*
~ *lelah sehabis kerja* a pastime. *sbg* ~
iseng (,keisengan) as a pastime. **pe-an**
hak (in notarial instruments) the re-
nunciation of rights (and titles). **peng-
an** release, freeing. **se-** after. ~ *dilantik*
Rektor after having been installed by
the President (of the university). *dgn*
se-.- *suara* at the top of o's voice. **ter-**
dr aside from. **-an** alumnus. ~ *tentara*
demobilee, ex-soldier. - *gudang* ex
warehouse. - *landas* to take off (aircraft). *(secara)* - *lelah* relaxed. - *pabrik*
ex factory, free factory. - *pantai* off-
shore (drilling).
lèpèr *kaki* - flat feet.
léperansir (S.) LEVERANSIR.
lèpot ber-an to be of low repute, notorious.
lepu *ikan* - scorpion fish.
lépya to think no longer of (,about).
lerai pe-an disengagement (of troops).
lèrèng (in Medan) bicycle. **ber-** to cycle.
lèrèt (S.) DERET. **se-** *dgn* in o. line with,
parallel with, on the same side of the
street as.

lèrok me- to steal a look at.
lès - *privat* private lesson.
lesap vanished.
lèsèh *duduk* **-an** to sit on the floor.
lèsèt me- 1 to slip away. 2 to miss. 3
won't do. ~ *besar* and *dugaan* ~ quite
wrong. ~ *dr rel* to derail. *jauh* ~ *dr* to
deviate much from (what another
says).
leslesan to be drowsy.
lèsot to fall apart.
lestari ke-an continuance. ~ *alam* environmental protection. **pe-an:** ~ *alam* ecology, conservation. ~ *satwa* wildlife
conservation.
lesu breathless, out of breath.
lesus 1 whirlwind. 2 gust (of wind).
letak *para* **pe-** *dasar Republik Indonesia*
the founders (,founding fathers) of the
Republic of Indonesia. **per-an:** ~ *lunas*
keel-laying (of ship). ~ *senjata* cease
fire.
lètèr be- to bleat.
lètersèter typesetter.
letih breathless, out of breath. *membuang*
- to take a break, rest. **me-.-** *tulang saja*
to knock o.s. out for nothing. -.*lesu*
breathless, out of breath.
lètoi and **letoi** tired, exhausted.
letong pe-an garbage pail.
lètoy and **letoy** (s.) LETOI.
letterlijk (pron. lèterlèk) literal(ly).
letus *ban sebelah kiri pesawat itu* **me-**
the aircraft's left tire blew up. **me-kan**
to blow up.
léver liver. *penyakit* - hepatitis.
lèvis (s.) CELANA (LEVIS).
lèwat ke- *pagi* premature. **ke-an** passed
(by). *dgn tdk* **me-kan** *tempo* immediately. - *darat* overland. - *telpon* by
(,over the) telephone. *Dia membunuh*
diri dgn makan Aspirin - ukuran, He
committed suicide by taking an overdose of Aspirin.
lèyak (s.) LEAK.
lèyèh ber-.- to lie around. **-an** and -.- to
lie down leisurely. *duduk* -.- to sit
leaning back, recline.
lha 1 look here (at this); used to get

hearer's attention. 2 here it is. *L-, kangkung saja sekarang seikat sdh Rp. 50,-,* Look here (or, Well), o. bunch of *kangkung* nowadays costs Rp. 50.00. 3 well, so (transition to next sentence). *L- iya!* That's it! That's right!

lhèdhèk - *khethek* (s.) KOMIDI (KETEK).

lho 1 exclamation of surprise: the speaker has learned or discovered s.t. which surprises him or her. 2 deictic: the speaker is pointing s.t. out to the hearer. *Sini -!* Right here! *gitu* - like that, that's the way it is (,was).

liangliong Chinese dragon manipulated by several persons.

liar disorderly, irregular. *taksi* - gypsy cab. **me-** to grow wild. **me-kan** to free domesticated animals in the jungle in order to increase the jungle population.

liat ng-in *aja* to stare after, eye s.o. **nge-** to see.

Libanon Lebanon.

libat keter-an involvement. **seke-** *mata* superficially. **ter-** *dgn* to be involved in.

liberalisasi liberalization.

Libéria Liberia.

libur ber- *akhir.minggu* to weekend, spend the weekend. **L-an** *di Musim Salju* Holiday on Ice.

licik crafty.

licin smooth. - *spt ular* slippery as a snake. *jalannya - betul* (said of a car) road-tested. *nasi - saja* just plain rice without any sidedishes. **berse-** *lidah* to debate, discuss. **me-kan** *jalan* to pave the way.

licurai welcoming dance of Timor Timur (former Portuguese Timor).

lidah - *(memang) tdk bertulang* 1 to allege s.t. without foundation, promise without further ado; also, said of an unreliable person. 2 to be careful with your words, it is easy for you to talk. 3 unreliable, empty talker. 4 to use double-talk. -*nya masin* he has influence (with them). -*nya seakan.akan terkalang* as if his lips were sealed. - *bercabang*

hypocritical, sanctimonious. - *buaya* aloe.

liga *L- Anti Komunis Rakyat Asia* Asian People Anti-Communist League. *L- Anti Komunis Sedunia* World Anti-Communist League. *L- Demokrasi* Democratic League.

ligyat clever and naughty.

lihat - *halaman sebelah* please turn over, P.T.O. **di-:** ~ *orang dgn sebelah mata* to be looked askance at (with disapproval). *blm* ~ *sdh terpaham* a word to the wise is sufficient. *tlh* **diper-kan** *dan terdaftar* (in notarial instruments) attested. **ke-annya** apparently. **me-:** ~ *ke depan* to predict. ~ *televisi (,TV ,tivi ,teve)* to watch television. *dgn tdk* ~ irrespective of. **me-.-** *etalase* to windowshop.

lika.liku ins-and-outs, details.

likir liqueur.

liku ber-.- intricate. **-.ber-** complicated. **ke-an** curvature.

likwidasi pe- liquidator.

likwidatur liquidator.

likwide liquid (capital).

likwiditèt liquidity.

lilin *lampu Petromaks (,Petromax) yg nyala dgn 100 - itu* the 100 candle-power Petromax lamp. *lampu Seterongking yg berukuran 300 -* a 300 candle-power Stormking lamp. - *lebah* beeswax. - *tanah* ozokerit(e). - *tawon* beeswax.

lilipur di- to be comforted, be consoled, be solaced.

lilit me- to wind around. *Hutang Sarinah sdh* ~ *pinggang sebesar 1,25 milyar,* The debts of (the Department Store) "Sarinah" have reached the strangulation point of 1.25 billion.

limbah cesspool.

limbat an edible catfish.

limbung confused, bewildered.

limosin limousine.

limpah ke-an affluence. **me-kan** *gelar Dr HC kpd* to confer the title of Honorary Doctor upon. **me-.-kan** to increase, enlarge. **me-(.ruah)** to overflow, run over.

bangunan **pe-** spillway (a passageway to carry off excess water, as from a reservoir). **pe-an** *kewenangan* delegation of authority. - *mewah* in abundance, in profusion. - *ruah* chock-a-block, crammed.

limpung ke-an to go back and forth.

lin (of tramcar) route. - *4* No. 4 route. - *gemuk* (in shipping and aviation circles) profitable (dollar-earning) routes (,lines) abroad. - *kurus* (in shipping and aviation circles) domestic non-profitable routes (,lines) which are only maintained for reasons of prestige and politics. - *penerbangan* airline.

linang -an *airmata* tears, weeping.

lincah 1·fluctuating, shifting, unreliable. 2 fidgety, restless. **ke-an** agility.

lincak low bamboo bench.

lindap shade. *di bawah - pohon kurma* under the shade of a date tree. **me-** 1 to decrease. 2 to disappear slowly.

lindi alkaline.

lindung I di-i *oleh* under the aegis of. **pe-** *terik matahari* sun visor. **per-an:** *di bawah* ~ under the aegis of. ~ *udara* air umbrella. - *tinjau* concealment.

lindung II *ikan* - eel.

lindur to be overcome with sleep and hence completely confused.

linggi the covered (,decked) portions at the prow and stern of a boat. - *muka* cutwater.

lingguis linguist.

lingguistik linguistics. *Lembaga L-* Institute of Linguistics.

lingguistis linguistic.

lingkar me- to go round and round. *di se-* in the surroundings. **-an** coil. ~ *arus* circuit. ~ *gila* vicious circle. *L*~ *Kutub Selatan* Antarctic Circle. *L*~ *Kutub Utara* Arctic Circle. ~ *mimang [,setan ,tak berujung (ber)pangkal ,yg jahat]* vicious circle.

lingkung -an 1 circumference, perimeter. 2 (in Lombok) (S.) DESA. ~ *hidup* 'Lebensraum,' living space. ~ *peruntukan* zoning. *di dlm* ~ *umur di antara 17 th hingga 24 th* in the age bracket

of 17 to 24 years. ~ *yg mengetahui* well-informed circles.

lingkup scope. **me-i** to overlap.

linglung abstracted, preoccupied.

lini 1 (all along the) line. 2 run (aircraft). - *Manado.Jakarta* the Manado-Jakarta run.

linjang ber-an and **se-** 1 to flirt. 2 to court, try to get the love of.

lintah me- *darat* to profiteer.

lintang *(secara)* **me-.pukang** (S.) LIN-TANG.PUKANG.

lintas me-i: ~ *udara* by air. "headline" *yg* ~ a banner headline. **pe-** *batas* border-crosser. **-an** *jalan kereta-api* grade crossing. - *batas* border-crossing. - *bebas* free passage. - *cabang* feeder line. - *damai* (navigation term) innocent passage. - *laut* seaborne. - *lewat* overpass. - *medan* cross-country. - *raya* overpass. - *tapal batas* border-crossing. - *utama* trunk line. - *wahana* transient visitor. - *sebra (,zebra)* zebra crossing.

linting me- to roll (a cigarette).

linuhung lofty, exalted.

lipat me- *uang kampanye* to embezzle (,peculate) campaign money. **me-duakan** to double. **me- tigakan** to triple. - *kajang* folded in two.

lipen, lippenstip and **lipstik** lipstick.

lipur *tak dpt kita - saja* cannot be ignored. **me-kan** to entertain. *utk* ~ *hati* for relaxation. **pe-:** *memberi* ~ *hati* to bring relief, ease the strain. *pembacaan* ~ light reading.

liput di-i: ~ *ketakutan* to be stricken by fear. ~ *ombak* awash. *masyarakat yg* ~ *suasana korupsi* a corruption-ridden society. **-an** coverage (in journalism). *mendapat* ~ covered (of event, etc.).

lir like. - *angkasa kang angemu dahana* like the sky burning with fire. - *gabah den interi* 'like paddy grains winnowed,' i.e. scattered.

lirih low, soft (of sound). *katanya* - (he) said softly. *tertawa* - laughed softly.

lirik I me-(.-)kan *ke* to look eagerly at. **-an** stealthy look.

lirik II lyric.

lis I - *karet kaca mobil* weatherstripping (of car). - *lukisan* picture frame.

lis II list.

Lisabon Lisbon.

lisan *dgn* - by word of mouth.

lisani oral.

list(e)rik ber- to have electric power. pe(r)-an 1 electricity. 2 electrical.

lisut 1 atrophic. 2 atrophy.

literèr literary.

litnan (S.) LETNAN.

liturgi liturgy.

liuk me-.- to flicker.

liwet ng(e)- to cook (not steam) (rice) in water.

liyak (S.) LIHAT.

lo (s.) LHO.

loa(k) me-kan *pakaian* to sell used clothes. *di* -an at the flea market.

loba eager, covetous, ravenous, avaricious. - *(akan) uang* money-grubbing.

lobak - *asin* salted, white radish.

lobi 1 lobby (a hall). 2 lobby (a group of lobbyists). me- to lobby.

locor ng- to fuck.

loda [lotto daerah] regional lottery.

logam - *hitam* ferrous metals. - *tdk berkarat* non-corrodable metal. - *warna* non-ferrous metals.

logat 1 word. 2 pronunciation.

logis reasonable.

logistik logistics.

loh - *jinawi* richly endowed with streams (of rivers). - *jinawi, subur kang sarwa (,sarwo) tinandur, murah kang sarwa (,sarwo) tinuku* flowing with milk and honey.

lok locomotive. - *adhesi* adhesion locomotive.- *bergigi* cog locomotive.- *lansir* shunting engine.- *uap* steam locomotive.

lokakarya workshop. ber- to hold a workshop. me-kan to hold a workshop about.

Lokal 1 Local, i.e. an army captain may have a *Lokal* rank of major when he occupies a post to which this rank is assigned; he loses the rank when reassigned. 2 stated after a university degree it means that the degreeholder has not yet taken the State examination for his field of study, such as, *Sarjana Muda Lokal* B.A. Local.

lokalisasi and peng-an localization.

lokasi ber- to be located.

lokcan Jakarta men's belt.

lokomotif (s.) LOK.

lokro too loose (of button, rope, etc.). ng- without hope. *katanya dgn hati* ~ he said hopelessly.

loksèk ruined, destroyed, bankrupt, insolvent.

lokuttara supramundane.

lola (S.) KELOLA.

loli(pop) lollipop.

loloh - *balik* feedback.

lolong -an *anjing* a dog's howling.

lolos - *dr lubang (,lobang) jarum* to have a narrow escape. *(tlh)* - *dr maut* escaped from death. - *sensor* passed the censor.

lomba per-an: ~ *bersambung* relay race. ~ *perahu layar* yacht race. ~ *persenjataan (,senjata)* arms race. ~ *ruang angkasa* space race. - *dayung* rowboat race. - *ketahanan* endurance race (for car racing).

lomban tradition observed on every *bada kupat* at *Kartini* Beach, Jepara (Central Java), in the hope that fishermen will get a good catch and survive safely on the seas.

lombong chasm, cleft.

lompat -.*langkah.berjingkat* and *jingkat. langkah.*- (in sports) a hop, a skip and a jump. me- *keluar* to bail out (from aircraft). pe- *jangkit* steeplechaser, person taking part in a steeplechase. *omongnya* -.- he skips from o. subject to another.

lompong *janji* me- an empty promise.

loncat pe- *tinggi* high jumper. L-an *Jauh Ke Depan* The Great Leap Forward.

loncèng - *kematian* death-(,funeral ,passing-)bell, death-(,funeral) knell.

londo Dutch. *di jaman* - during the Dutch era. - *durung jowo wurung* said when speaking about an Indo or Eurasian, meaning lit. 'not yet a Dutchman and failed in being a Javanese (read: Indonesian).' *wong* - westerner.

londoisme favoring western tourists over Indonesian tourists.

longak.longok to look around.

longgar me-kan to relax (restrictions or rules).

longgok pe-an accumulation.

longké (s.) TARI (LONGKE).

longkong chance. *Banyak biji - olehnya dibuang percuma,* He let many chances slip by in vain.

longok me- *(pandang)* to have (,take) a look at. **me-kan** *kepala* to crane o's neck in order to see s.t.

longsèr a Cirebon folk art.

longsoran soil erosion.

lonjak jump. *si* - kangaroo.

lonjong - *telor* egg-shaped, oval.

lonjor (S.) LUNJUR. *Dia duduk santai* **berse-** *kaki,* He sat in a relaxed way with his legs extended. *Kedua kakinya* **dise-kan** *ke atas meja,* He sprawled out with both his legs on the table. **se-** *sabun* a bar of soap.

lontar *gagasan yg* **di-kan** *Adam Malik* an idea raised (,brought up) by Adam Malik. **me-kan** *diri dgn alat otomatis* to eject (from an aircraft). **pe-** *roket* rocket launcher. - *martil* throwing the hammer (sport).

lonté - *lanang* gigolo.

loper messenger, delivery man. - *koran* paperboy. - *susu* milkman.

lorèng ber-.- camouflaged (fatigues).

lori lorry (a flat wagon without sides, fitted to run on rails).

Loro Jonggrang name of the main temple of the *Prambanan* complex on the road from Yogyakarta to Solo.

loro.loroning atunggal two in o. (esp. in mysticism).

lorong (navigation term) corridor. *L- Ho Chi Minh* Ho Chi Minh Trail.

Lorosaé the suggested new name for Timor Timur (ex Portuguese Timor).

loro setu lavender, k.o. fragrant grass.

lorot *suhu* **me-** the temperature dropped. **meme-kan** to dry up.

los 1 not divided up into rooms. 2 still free, not yet caught. **-.-an** to play rough, no holds barred.

losmèn hostel, cheap hotel.

lotong (s.) LUTUNG.

lotré (S.) LOTERE.

lowa fig (L. Ficus glomerata Roxb.).

loya (in West Kalimantan) k.o. *dukun* and soothsayer.

loyalita(s) loyalty.

loyo 1 lethergic, inert, lazy. 2 tired, fatigued, exhausted. *Dgn - ia menjatuhkan dirinya di kursi,* Completely exhausted he plumped himself down on a chair.

LP [Long Play] **di-.-kan** to be recorded, be made into a (Long Play) record. *Lagu.lagu pop* ~, Pop tunes have been made into (Long Play) records.

LS (s.) ELS.

lu *siapa - siapa gua* and *-.- gua.gua* 1 to live individualistically, selfishly. 2 every man for himself.

luang pe- 1 chance. 2 lull. 3 leisure. 4 occasion. 5 uncovered part of the body (in *silat*). *dlm waktu* **-nya** in o's spare time.

luar *di* - on the free (,black) market. *di - batas.batas kesusilaan* immoral. *dr - kota dan gunung.gunung* from far and wide. **ke-an** peculiarity. - *biasa* anomalous, abnormal. - *kanan (,kiri)* (in soccer) right (,left) wing.

luas capacious. **per-an** *arti* (gramm.) generalization. - *hutan* woodland area.

lubang (in moonlighting terminology) buyer, purchaser. *gali - tutup* - rob Peter to pay Paul. *barangsiapa menggali -, ia juga terperosok ke dlmnya,* he who digs a pit for others may fall into it himself. - *pantat* anus. - *penjebak teng* antitank trap, tankpit.

lubèr pe-an overflowing (of liquid), spill(age).

lubuk - *akal, tepian ilmu* an all-round man.

lucu me- to crack jokes. - *menggigit* satirical and funny.

ludah *sdh* **di-** *dijilat balik* to eat o's words, take o's words back. **me-** to spit. ~ *ke langit (muka juga yg basah)* to attempt to do the impossible. **pe(r)-an** cuspidor.

ludes and **ludhes** all finished, kaputt.

ludruk folk drama of East Java.

lugas 1 simple, unadored. 2 to the point. 3 businesslike. *berdasarkan hubungan - buruh.majikan* based on a business-like employee-employer relationship. **ke-an** businesslike character, matter-of-factness. **me-kan** to simplify.

lugu 1 true, the plain truth. 2 genuine, pure. 3 real.

luk curve (on kris).

luka *si* - the wounded. **me-.parahkan** to injure s.o. seriously. *-.- berat* trauma. *- di kantung nasi* stomach (,gastric) ulcer.

lukèk be-an to vomit, throw up.

luks luxury.

Luksemburg Luxembourg.

lukut 1 duckweed and, in general, all the fine verdure which grows in water or along the waterside on rocks. 2 moss.

lulo name of a social dance in the south-eastern part of the Celebes.

luluh (gramm.) assimilated.

lulur (beef) tenderloin.

lulus *- dr* to graduate from. **-an** alumnus.

lumas pe- lubricant.

lumayan 1 equitable. 2 substantial. *perbedaan yg - juga* a substantial difference. *Suatu jarak yg - juga,* A good distance. This is just far enough. 3 not bad.

lumba.lumba flipper. *- air tawar* (s.) PESUT.

lumer (to feel) fine and smooth.

lumping (made of) leather. *kuda -* 1 k.o. leather hobbyhorse. 2 (S.) KUDA (KEPANG).

lumpuh me-kan *bom* to disarm a bomb.

lumut algae. **ber-** mouldy. **-an** for a long time, for ages and ages.

lunas pe-an: *jangka ~* term of redemption. *~ bea ekspor* clearance out. *~ bea impor* Customs clearance. *~ dan pemindah-bukuan* redemption and transfer.

luncu lunch.

luncur di-kan to be sent aloft (of space-ship). **me-** to rush past. *~ gantung*

hanggliding. **pe-** *torpedo* torpedo tube. **pe-an** blastoff (of spaceship).

lungkrah 1 exhausted, weary. 2 inability, powerlessness.

lunglai *(lemah)* - feeble, limp (powerless). *lemas* - 1 (with) dragging steps, with leaden feet. 2 (to feel) powerless (,drugged).

lunglit [balung kulit] emaciated, abnormally lean. *bangsa* - a nation of skin and bones.

lunjak ng- to jump up.

luntang.lantung to knock about the streets, loaf.

luntur 1 to lose color, discolor (of laundry). 2 to fade (away). *namanya* - he has a bad reputation. *niatnya itu* - his intention faded away. *sdh - tembaganya* (his bad character) has come to light. **me-kan** *kepercayaan rakyat kpd* to shake the people's confidence in.

lunuk (in Palangka Raya) *pohon* - banyan tree.

lup barrel (of rifle). *- senjata* rifle barrel.

lupa *sifat* **pe-** aptness to forget, forgetfulness. *detik.detik yg tak* **ter-kan** unforgettable moments. *lakunya sdh -.- ingat* to suffer from weakness of memory. *- daratan* rash, reckless.

luput *- dr kematian* to escape from death. *- drpd kejahatan* escaping from evil. *tdk - dr ingatan* unforgotten. *tdk (pernah) - dr* to keep (on) ...-ing, continue ...-ing, continue to ... *tdk pernah - menuduh* to keep on accusing.

lurah ke-an village. *~ kota* administrative area in city. *~ pinggiran* administrative area on edge of city. *- polisi* assistant for security matters.

lurik hand-woven cotton from Yogya (the name is derived from the original striped designs).

lurug ng- 1 to fight, be up in arms. 2 to make an expedition, a trip. **-an** (to go on an) expedition.

lurup -an *mayat* winding sheet, shroud.

lurus literal, word-by-word. *terjemahan yg* - a literal (,verbatim) translation. *- hati* candid.

lusa *besok (atau)* - 1 one day (in the future). 2 before long, shortly. *pd hari Minggu* - on Sunday two days from now. *pd* -**nya** two days later.

lutung a long-haired black monkey. *L-*

Kasarung a Sund. literary work.

luweng cavern, cave.

luwes 1 elegant, stylish. 2 supple, flexible. **ke-an** flexibility.

M

maaf (said to a beggar to whom o. doesn't want to give a thing) sorry (don't bother me now)! **pe-** forgiving, inclined to forgive. -.**me-kan** *dan melupakan* to forgive and forget.

maag (s.) MAG.

maarif education.

MAB [Memayu Ayuning Buwana] (s.) MAMAYU HAYUNING BUWONO.

mabuk **di:** ~ *angan.angan* to be lost in thought. ~ *cinta* to be head over heels in love. ~ *kenangan* to be lost in thought. ~ *kekuasaan* craving for power. ~ *nasib yg malang* to be in trouble, be troubled. ~ *sayang* to be love sick. *Kedua insan yg sedang* ~ *sayang itu...*, The two love-sick human beings... - *cinta* to be madly in love. - *akan darah* bloodthirsty. - *ganja* high, stoned. - *harta* materialistic. - *kebesaran* to suffer from megalomania. - *kecubung* intoxicated by datura poisoning. - *kemenangan* with the flush of victory. - *kendaraan* motion sickness. - *keriangan* elated. - *perbuatan* audacious(ly). - *(dgn) pikiran* lost in thought. - *rasa* ecstacy. - *selasih* (slightly) intoxicated. - *uang* money hungry.

Mac (s.) MEK.

macam **ber-.-** assorted. *dan* **se-nya** and the like.

macan *membangunkan* - *turu* to awaken sleeping dogs. - *makan tuan* it backfires. - *hitam* the black panther. - *kertas* paper tiger. - *loreng* camouflage (clothing). - *sima* (in Central and East Java) the striped royal tiger.

macapat metre, verse.

macat (s.) MACET.

macet **ke-an** 1 deadlock. 2 stalemate. 3 stagnation. 4 stoppage. ~ *lalu.lintas* traffic jam. *di mana letak* -**nya** where the shoe pinches.

machtsaanwending (s.) PENGGUNAAN (KEKUASAAN).

machtsvorming (s.) PENYUSUNAN (KEKUASAAN).

macok k.o. mahjong.

Madagaskar Madagascar.

madaliun locket.

madat battlements, scaffolding.

Madé (in Bali) name element placed before personal names to indicate the second born child, such as, *Madé Geria, Madé Pugeg.*

madon to be mad about, be infatuated with, fool around with women.

Madrali [Madura.Australi] crossbreed between a MADurese and austRALIan cow.

madrasah Islamic teaching in this institution of learning is four-staged: *ibtidaiyyah, tsanawiyah, aliyah* and university.

madul.madul. (s.) RAMBUT (MADUL. MADUL).

madya intermediate.

maem (children's language) to eat.

maèn - *cap keliling* to goof off; (S.) MAIN.

maèngkèt a typical Minahasan dance.

mafia - *jati* mafia-type elements operating in the field of teakwood sales on the island of Muna (Southeast Celebes).

mafiaisme mafia practices carried out by

gangs who extort money from hotels and night clubs.

mag stomach. *sakit -* stomach (,gastric) pains.

magersari tiller, farmer, cultivator.

Magistèr Pendidikan the new master's degree conferred by *IKIP*-Jakarta, M.Ed.

Magrib Morocco.

Magribi Moroccan.

mah a stress indicator which is placed following the word, part of sentence or the sentence it refers to. *Itu - peraturan!* That's what you call a regulation!

Mahab(h)arata 'Great Epic of the Bharatas,' the second of the two great Hindu epics in Sanskrit adapted by the Javanese. It is believed to be based on a war between two families of the Bharata clan, the *Pandawas* and the *Kurawas,* in the 13th or 14th century, B.C.

mahajana a great man.

mahakuasa ke-an almightiness.

Mahamèru the World-Mountain which reaches from Heaven to Earth. At its peak the gods have their abode. The Javanese identify it with the *Gunung Semeru,* Mount Semeru, in East Java, whereas the Sumatrans are of the opinion that the mountain was supposed to have been located in Sumatra.

mahasiswa ke-an (adj.) student. *- abadi* eternal college student (derogatory epithet given to a student who has been in the same level for some time). *- pendengar* auditor. *- tingkat I (,Satu)* freshman. *- tingkat II (,Dua)* sophomore. *- tingkat III (,Tiga)* junior. *- tingkat IV (,Empat)* senior.

Mahawas Mahaya Swajama Parajama the motto of the Immigration Directorate, meaning: Protect and Supervise Citizens and Aliens.

mahir ke-an knowhow.

mahkamah court, tribunal. *M- Kehakiman Internasional* International Court of Justice. *M- Militer* Court Martial. *M-*

Militer Luar Biasa Extraordinary Military Tribunal. *M- Militer Tinggi* High Military Court. *M- Tentara* Court Martial.

mahkota *putera -* prince royal. **ke-an** (adj.) crown. *jajahan ~* crown colony (Hongkong). *- kejayaan* crown of glory.

mahligai *- cita.cita* castles in the air.

Mahmilti [Mahkamah Militer Tinggi] High Military Court.

Mahmilub [Mahkamah Militer Luar Biasa] Extraordinary Military Tribunal. **di.- kan** to be brought before the Extraordinary Military Tribunal.

mahoni to have nothing to do.

mahraj point of articulation.

mahsul *hasil -* yield, produce, products (of a field, country).

mahs(y)ar *hari -* Day of Resurrection. *padang -* Place of Resurrection.

mahu (S.) MAU.

maido (s.) PAIDO.

maimun lucky, fortunate.

main 1 to visit. *Silahkan - ke rumah saya,* Please, come and see me. 2 to play (,screw) around. *Kedua orang itu sdh biasa - di daerah hitam Kramat Tunggak itu,* The two guys were accustomed to fuck around in the Kramat Tunggak red-light district. 3 corruption, dishonest practices. 4 [followed by certain (verbal) root words — mostly accompanied by *saja* — forms a phrase meaning 'at random, without careful plan, unjustifiably, to make a practice of (doing s.t. deplorable)]. *- atur* not follow regulations (,rules), break the rules. *- bak.bak.kur* (s.) BERWOK-WOK (KETEKUR). *- beslah saja* to seize (smuggled goods) without reason. *- bom* to bomb recklessly. *- gelap.gelap-an* to act in an illegal way. *- hutang* to borrow money left and right. *- karet* to be delayed. *- kasar* to act like a boor. *- menang.menangan omong* to be a matter of winning a war of words. *- nrimo saja* to be a fatalist. *- pukul* to lash out with the hand. *- salip.salipan* to pass e.o. unnecessarily (in cars).

- *telpon* to engage in telephoning without any reason. - *tunjuk saja* to appoint (people) without careful choice. **ber-:** ~ *akrobatik* to perform acrobatics. ~ *tdk bersih* to sabotage. **me-kan** *lakonnya (,rolnya)* to play o's role. **memper-kan** to manipulate, victimize. **pe-:** ~ *belakang* (in soccer) back. ~ *biola* violinist. ~ *bola basket* basketball player. ~ *cadangan* (in soccer) reservist. ~ *drama* dramatist. ~ *gitar* guitarist. ~ *klarinet* clarinetist. ~ *musik rock* rock player. ~ *rugby prof* professional rugby player. ~ *selo* cellist. ~ *sepak.bola* soccer player. ~ *tenis* tennis player. ~ *tunggal* soloist. ~ *wanita* actress. ~ *watak* character actor. **per-an:** ~ *kucing.kucingan* game of cat and mouse. ~ *pat.gulipat* manipulations (in the bad sense). ~ *petak.sembunyi* hide-and-seek. ~ *sabun* a fixed game. *perusahaan* **-an** a phony company. -.-: ~ *saja* to pass the time. *Ia datang ke rumah saya utk* ~ *saja,* He came to my house just to pass the time. - *bola gulir* to play golf. - *bola gelinding* to bowl. - *domino* to play dominoes. - *duit* 1 to bribe. 2 to accept a bribe. 3 to misappropriate government funds. - *gampang.gampangan* and - *gampang saja* to take it easy, play it the easy way. - *(be)gituan* to fuck. - *hakim sendiri* to play god. - *kartu* to play cards. - *kayu* to play rough (,dirty). - *kejar.kejaran* to play tag. - *kongkalikong* 1 to fool a person. 2 to intrigue. 3 to swindle. 4 to be in league (with). - *petak.sembunyi* to play hide-and-seek. - *renggang* to maintain distant relationship. - *sabun* to fix (a game). - *sandiwara* (fig.) to put on an act. - *serampangan* to play for all or nothing. - *silap mata* to do conjuring tricks. - *sip* to play it safe. - *ski* to ski. - *tatakrama* to pull rank. - *tembak* to bribe (explained as '*ntar saya kasih* I'll give you s.t. later). - *tinggi* to have influence with the higher-ups. - *tonjok* to punch, thrust a blow with the fist, box. - *umpet.*

umpetan to play hide-and-seek.
maja a generic name for a number of *kemiri*-like plants. *M-pahit* Hindu-Jav. kingdom in East Java which held power over much of Indonesia from 1292–1398.
majas 1 figuratively. 2 figure of speech.
majelis *M- Luhur Taman Siswa Taman Siswa* Supreme Council.
majir ke-an sterility.
maju di-kan *ke dlm* to be indented. - *loncat katak* to advance by bounds. -.*mundurnya* the ups and downs. *M-terus, pantang mundur!* Onward, no retreat! *M-lah Singapura!* name of Singapore's national anthem.
Majuj (the giant) Magog.
mak - *jomblang* procuress, matchmaker. - *nyai* effiminate.
maka -nya *hujan* no wonder it rained. *M-itu!* That's just it! That's the reason!
makalah working paper.
makam pe-an *ulang* reburial. *M- Pahlawan* National Cemetery.
makan *membunuh diri dgn - aspirin lewat ukuran* to commit suicide by taking an overdose of aspirin. *banyak - uang* it comes expensive, it runs into a lot of money. - *sepuas perut* to eat o's fill. - *tanah seluas ...* to occupy an area of ... **di-** to be consumed, be hit, be affected by. *Uang itu ~nya sendiri,* He has used the money for his own benefit, he has corrupted away the money. *Sebuah kapal minyak Inggeris* ~ *api,* A British oil tanker caught fire. ~ *berdua* (money) enough to feed two people. *tak* ~ *besi (,senjata)* to be invulnerable. ~ *hari* to be weather-beaten. ~ *karat* to be rusty. ~ *keparat* 1 to be cursed. 2 to be hit by a disaster (due to marrying a *janda raja,* sacrilege, etc.). ~ *masa (,umur ,usia ,zaman)* timeworn, to be out of date. *dipagari dinding bambu berlobang.lobang* ~ *umur* (the garden) was fenced by a timeworn, perforated bamboo wall. *dia* ~ *pakaian* he is a clothes-horse. ~ *(cahaya) panas* to be weather-beaten. ~ *tikus* (fig.) to be

stolen. **me-**: ~ *tempo (,waktu) empat jam* to take four hours. *Ini ~ tenaga dan fikiran tdk sedikit,* This puts a great strain on o's energy and mind. **pe-**: ~ *bawang* hothead. ~ *daging* carnivore. ~ *daun.daunan* herbivore. ~ *gaji* wage earner. ~ *nabatah* vegetarian. ~ *orang* man-eater, cannibal. **ter-**: *Jangan ~ isyu!* Don't become the victim of rumors! *Banyak kendaraan yg mogok ~ lumpur,* Many cars stalled swallowed up by the mud. ~ *propaganda (,propokasi)* to fall a victim to propaganda (,provocation). **-an**: *menjadi ~* to fall a victim to. ~ *cepat (,ekspres)* light lunch(eon) meal, snack. ~ *cuci mulut* dessert. ~ *empuk* object much sought after (by thieves). *Skuter Vespa merupakan ~ empuk,* Vespa scooters are much sought after (by thieves). ~ *kecil* snacks. ~ *pencuci mulut* dessert. ~ *ringan* snacks. ~ *ternak* cattle fodder. ~ *utama* main dish. *- angin* to set well in a breeze (of sails). *- cepat (,ekspres)* to take a light lunch(eon). *- gaji buta* to have a soft job. *- modal (,pokok)* to eat into o's capital. *banyak - ongkos* expensive, costly. *sdh - 8 orang* (this gun) has already killed 8 persons. *- tempo tiga minggu* to take three weeks. *- tenaga* to cost much trouble. *tdk - tua* ageless. *Kapal itu -nya dlm air 20 meter,* The ship draws 20 meters.

makantar.kantar to blaze up.

Makao (s.) MAKAU.

makao.po Chinese prostitute.

makar stratagem, scheme, plan (to topple a head of state, etc.), revolt. *berbuat -* to scheme, plot, mutiny.

Makara Capricorn. **berm-** cancerous.

makarya practical.

makasih (S.) TERIMA KASIH.

Makau Macao.

makelar *- rumah (,tanah)* real estate broker, realtor.

makèt a (scale) model, mock-up.

maki *- (dan) nista* abuse. **pe-** reviler.

makin *- ... tambah ...* the more ..., the more ... **se-**: ~ *hari ~ bertambah* day

by day on the increase. ~ *th* increasingly over the years.

makmun to follow the *imam* (,Moslem priest) in an obligatory prayer.

makmur ke-an 1 luxury. 2 abundance.

maknit ber- magnetic.

makrifat (perfect, mystical) knowledge.

makruh 1 offensive. 2 blameworthy. 3 objectionable.

maksi big, large.

maksiat immorality, sin. **ke-an** vice, sin, wickedness.

maksimum me-kan to maximize.

maksud *utk - khusus ini* ad hoc. *dikandung -* it is our intention to ... **di-**: *ketentuan ~ dlm pasal 7* the provision referred to in (or, coming under) article 7. *yg ~ dgn penghasilan bersih adalah (,ialah) ...* by net income is understood ... *yg* **di-kan** *dgn X ialah ...* by X is understood.

maktab college.

makua k.o. African gorilla.

mal property.

malaikat and **malaèkat** *- pembalas* avenging angel. *- penolong* angel of mercy.

Malagasi Malagasy.

malakamo (S.) MALAKAMA. *buah si - a* proverbial fruit, fatal whether o. eats it or not. *spt (,bagai) makan buah si -, dimakan bapak mati, tdk dimakan ibu mati* and *spt (,bagai) makan buah si -, dimakan mati ibu, tak dimakan mati bapak* damned if you do, damned if you don't.

malam the night (including the evening) preceding a given day and included in that day, eve. *- Minggu* Saturday evening. *di - hari* in the evening, at night. *sampai jauh -* until the early hours of the morning, far into the small hours. *setiap - jam 03.00* every morning at 03:00 hours. *hari -lah* night is falling. **ber-**: ~ *Minggu* to spend the weekend. ~ *pertama* to spend o's wedding night. **se-**: *tak bisa merubah dlm ~* cannot be changed overnight. *Jenazahnya akan diber-kan ~,* The mortal remains will lie in state for o. night. ~ *(ini)* tonight.

se-an the whole evening (,night). *(pd)*
-nya and - *harinya* in the evening (of
that day). - *amal* charity show. - *mat.*
matan a social (,pleasant ,relaxing)
evening. *M- Natal* Christmas Eve.
- *silaturrahmi* a social evening. *M- Sunyi,*
M- Kudus Silent Night, Holy Night. *M- Th*
Baru New Year's Eve. - *tirakatan*
vigil.

malan painfully surprised, upset.

malang -nya! what bad luck! -.*migung*
criss-cross.

malangkerik both arms akimbo.

Malari [Malapetaka 15 Januari] The 15
January Disaster, i.e. the anti-Japanese
riots on 15 January 1974 in Jakarta
during Prime Minister Tanaka's visit.

malaria malaria. *kena* - to get malaria.
- *hitam* blackwater fever.

malarindu tropikangen (student sl.)
brokenhearted (pun on 'malaria
tropicana').

malas ber- *diri* to loaf. - *berbicara* to be
silent.

mal(a)un cursed.

maléan and malé'an k.o. *karapan sapi* on
the island of Lombok.

malem M-an *selamatan* held on the five
odd nights in the fasting month of
Ramadan starting with the 21st.

malèse (trade industrial) depression,
slump.

malet back pay.

ma.lima (s.) MO.LIMO.

Malindo [Malaysia.Indonesia] Malaysia-
Indonesian.

maling - *(ber)teriak* - the pot calls the
kettle black. - *amatiran* amateur thief.
- *hujan* a thief who operates during the
rainy season. - *prof* professional thief.

malu I - *bertanya sesat di jalan* o. should
not be embarrassed to ask advice from
others. Ber-*lah sedikit!* Behave yourself a bit! ke-.-an slightly timid. *tdk*
-.-*nya, tdk* -.- *lagi, dgn tdk tahu* - and
tdk kenal - shameless. *tdk usah* -.- there
is no sense in being embarrassed.
Jangan -.-! Don't be shy!

Malu II [Mantri Kehutanan dan Lurah]
the official in charge of forestry and
the village head.

mama mother.

mamang I absent-minded.

mamang II uncle (younger brother of
father or mother).

Mamayu Hayuning Buwono to adorn the
world (mysticism).

mambang - *kuning* ominous yellowish
red evening sky.

mambeg stagnant, dead (water). *rawa yg*
berair - backwater.

mambruk crown pigeon.

mami I aunt.

mami II madam (of house of prostitution).

mampat pe-an compression.

mampet clogged (of ditches, etc.), stuffed-
up (nose); (s.) MAMPAT.

mampir di-i to be visited. ke-an a brief
visit.

mampu berke-an *pancar sejauh ... kilo-*
meter to have a(n) ...-kilometer broadcast range. ke-an: ~ *berdwibahasa* bilingual ability. ~ *bertanggung.jawab*
culpability. ~ *(akan) membayar*
solvency. ~ *utk tetap hidup* survival.

mampus *boleh* -! and - *lu!* drop dead!

mamut mammoth.

mana I and besides. - ... *lagi* and ... besides (,as well). - *dpt, -kan boleh jadi*
and -*kan bisa?* how could? how is it
possible? - *suka* optional. - *tahu* who
knows. *"M- saya tahu? "* "How could
I know it? " *"Ini dr -? "* (over the telephone) "Who's calling? " *M- saya*
mampu beli mobil semacam ini! How
the hell could I afford to buy a car
like this! *M- sendirian, lagi.* On top of
it all, I was alone. *Di - saja dicarinya pul-*
pen itu? Where in the world did he
look for the fountainpen? -... -... ...
as well as..., not only... but also...
- *panas* - *berdesak.desak* it was warm
as well as crowded. -.- *yg bersekolah*
all the schoolchildren.

mana II (S.) BAGAIMANA. - *mungkin?*
how is it possible?

Manado the new spelling for the place

name Menado (located in North Celebes).

managemèn(t) and **manajemèn** management. -*perkantoran* office management.

manajèr manager. - *umum* general manager.

manasik ceremony. - *haji* ceremonies related to the pilgrimage to Mecca.

mancanegara a foreign country, abroad. *sapi* - imported cattle.

manda 1 unresisting. 2 to bear o's fate.

mandah to flee, run away. *Kabarnya seorang amoy yg berparas aduhai, terpaksa - ke Medan utk melakukan abortus, akibat hubungan gelapnya dgn orang yg penting,* It is said that a pretty Chinese girl had to flee to Medan to have an abortion performed, as a result of her illicit relationship with a very important person.

mandala I scene of operations. *M- Wisata* Tourist Information Center. *M- Yudha* Command, i.e. a military district under s.o.'s authority (during the 1945-revolution).

mandala II a magic circle or shrine built for meditation. Thus, the Borobudur, for example, is a *mandala.* O. of the smaller, army-run Indonesian airlines takes its name from the term.

mandana hysterical.

Mandarin Chinese; in *bahasa (,irama ,lagu pop) -.*

mandat authorization.

mandataris mandatory (person to whom a mandate has been given).

mandi ber-kan: ~ *air mata* to drown in tears. ~ *darah* to swim in o's blood. *tempat* **pe-an** bathing place. - *ala koboi* (to take a) splash bath. - *barat* to wash o's face. - *berendam* (to take a) tub (,sit-down) bath (opp. shower bath). - *bersiram* (to take a) shower bath. - *burung* (to take a) splash bath. - *junub* ablutions (after coitus). - *keringat* soaked with sweat, bathed in sweat. - *kungkum (,rendam)* (to take a) tub bath. - *sauna (,Turki)* (to take a) sauna bath. - *uap* Turkish bath.

mandireng - *pribadi* self-governing area.

mandiri independent, self-sufficient. **ke-an** 1 independence, self-sufficiency. 2 sovereignty. - *pribadi* self-resilience and self-reliance.

Mandrax k.o. imported barbiturate containing derivatives of quinazolone and diphenhydramine.

mandul ke-an sterility, infertility. **pe-an** sterilization.

mandur - *jalan* 1 superintendent of roads. 2 (fig.) vagabond, loiterer.

manekin mannequin, model.

manfaat ber- to avail, gain advantage. - *(dan) mudarat* 1 pro and con. 2 joys and sorrows.

mang 1 (s.) MAMANG II. 2 term of address for Sundanese men. *M- Ihin* the affectionate term of address for the former West Java Governor *Solihin G(autama) P(oerwanegara).*

mangan I S. MANGGAN.

mangan II - *ora* - *kumpul* whether we are eating or not, the main thing is we are together.

mangga various types of mangos are: - *arumanis* medium size, very sweet. - *daging* small mango variety. - *gedong* medium small, distinctive odor. - *golek* long mango. - *harumanis* (s.) MANGGA (ARUMANIS). - *Indramayu* large, roundish, sweet. - *kuèni* green, roundish, strong taste. - *madu* medium small, roundish, coarse texture. - *si manalagi* large and sweet variety.

Manggala Commandant of the Yogyakarta Palace Guards.

manggung to sing (of birds, esp. the *perkutut*).

manggut to nod with assent. -.- to nod o's head.

mangkal (s.) PANGKAL.

mangkanya (s.) MAKANYA.

Mangkasara (S.) MAKAS(S)AR.

mangkel resentful.

mangku (s.) PANGKU.

mangro.tingal 1 two faced. 2 to serve two masters, divide o's loyalties.

Manguni I a mystical bird in the coat-of-arms of the Minahasa area.

Manguni II a dissident organization which attacked the cavalry center in Bandung and the Presidential Palace in Jakarta (March 30, 1960).

mangut I **ter-** confused.

mangut II - *ikan* fish cooked in coconut milk.

manifès manifest (of a ship, etc.).

manifèst manifesto.

manifèstasi manifestation. **me-kan** to manifest, demonstrate.

manifèsto manifesto.

manikam 1 essence. 2 embryo. *jauhar juga yg mengenal* - it takes a jeweller to judge a gem. - *sdh menjadi sekam* to have lost o's value.

Manikebu [Manifesto Kebudayaan] Cultural Manifesto.

Manikebuis supporter of the *Manikebu.*

Manikebuisme the philosophy of the *Manikebu.*

manikur manicure. **ber-** to manicure (v.i.).

Manipolis supporter of Manipol. - *munafik* fake (,hypocritical) supporter of *Manipol.*

manipulasi graft. **me-kan** *uang rakyat* to embezzle money of the people.

manis honey, sweety. *Selamat malam, -!* Good evening, honey! *si M-* sugar. - *jangan segera ditelan, pahit jangan segera dimuntahkan* take with a grain of salt. *berhenti dgn* - to stop smoothly (of car). **ber-**.- *kpd* to kow-tow to. *sekedar* **pe-** *kalimat (,tutur) saja* to say s.t. just out of politeness.

manisé how beautiful.

manja ber- to coax, cajole.

mantab (s.) MANTAP.

mantap 1 stable, constant, firm. 2 well adjusted. **pe-an** *harga* price stabilization.

mantel - *bulu* fur coat

manteri (s.) MANTRI.

mantik logic.

mantiki logical. *penalaran* - logical reasoning.

mantol (s.) MANTEL. *organisasi* - undercover organization.

mantri (subordinate) government official. - *air* irrigation official. - *belasting* tax official. - *garam* official of salt monopoly. - *gudang* warehouse keeper. - *guru* headmaster. - *hutan* forester. - *jaga* warder, jailer. - *jalan* loafer, idler. - *kabupaten* first clerk of a *bupati.* - *lanbau* foreman of the agricultural information service. - *pajak* tax official. - *polisi* 1 instruction official (of the field police). 2 detective officer. - *ulu* water distribution overseer.

mantu (to hold) a wedding for o's child (or, by extension, somebody else's child).

manunggal 1 to become o. with *gusti* (the master) or *Allah* (God). 2 to integrate. 3 integrated. *-ing kawula.gusti* and *-ing kawula lan gusti* the unity of the subjects and the king, i.e. the president can do no wrong. **me-kan** to unite (with). **panunggalan** becoming o. with *gusti* or *Allah.* - *ajur.ajer* to become completely o. with.

manusia - *katak* frogman. - *mesin* apathetic person. - *purba* prehistoric man. *M- Salju* The Abominable Snowman. - *3 jaman* a person who experienced the Dutch colonial period, the period of the Jap. occupation and the present period of independence.

manusiawi *tdk* - inhuman.

manuswantara anthropomorphic. *paham serba* - anthropocentrism.

manut -(an) and - *lutut* obedient, docile.

manuver and **manuvre** manoeuver.

manyala -*(Bob)* groovy, terrific, fantastic (good or bad).

manyung *(ikan)* - k.o. sheath-fish.

mapan 1 established. 2 to fit, find its place; (s.) PAPAN.

maparon (s.) MARON.

mapatih chief minister (of the *Majapahit* empire).

Maperma [Masa Perkenalan Mahasiswa] college student initiation period.

mapitu (s.) MO.PITU.

Mapram [Masa Prabakti Mahasiswa] (s.) MAPERMA.

marah - *akan (,kpd)* to be angry at. - *yg tiada sampai* angry of short duration.

marak *namanya naik* - his esteem is growing.

maraton marathon. *berjalan* - marathon race.

marbodat (in Tapanuli) person who raises a monkey trained to pick coconuts for a certain fee.

marbot (S.) MARBUT.

marca(pada) (on) earth.

marem satisfied.

marèng transition period between the end of the rainy season and the beginning of the dry season, about March, April, May. -an (s.) MUSIM (MARENGAN).

marga road.

margasatwa - *besar* big game.

marge (pron. marse) - *keuntungan* profit margin.

marhumah (followed by a woman's name) the late.

mari *M-! (M-!)* a politeness formula used in inviting s.o. to do s.t., in leave-taking (after a visit or at the end of a conversation), in agreeing to a price after bargaining. **dike-kan** to be brought here.

marifat - *putus* (mystical) concentration of thoughts (to obtain s.t.). *berjumpa dlm* - to call s.o. to mind.

marinir marine (the person).

markas pe-an quartering (of soldiers).

markisa passion fruit (L. Passiflora quadrangularis).

markonigram marconigram

Marksisme Marxism.

marmer (S.) MARMAR.

marmut (S.) MARMOT.

maro(n) (s.) PARO.

marquisa (s.) MARKISA.

mars 1 marching tune. 2 a march.

Marsekal Chief Air Marshal. - *Madya* Air Marshal. - *Muda* Air Vice Marshal. - *Pertama* Air Commander.

martabat ber- 1 worthy. 2 dignified.

martani I to notify.

martani II bringing salvation, consolation.

martelaar and **martir** martyr.

maruf (S.) MA'RUF.

marwata.suka to be overjoyed (due to happiness).

Marxisme Marxism.

Maryam (The Virgin) Mary.

masa I *dr - ke* - from time to time. -nya: *ada* ~ sometimes. *dpt* ~ to take place. *Kalau sdh dpt* ~ ..., If I see my chance to ... - *azali* time immemorial. - *bebas bayar (,bunga)* grace period. - *belajar* study period. - *berhentinya haid* menopause. - *birahi* mating season. - *datang* future. *pd - depan yg dekat ini* in the (very) near future. - *jabatan* term of office. - *kecil* childhood. - *kini* the present time, nowadays, contemporary. *Lukisan - kini,* A contemporary painting. - *lampau* the past. - *mulai pembayaran cicilan* grace period. - *prabakti mahasiswa* college student initiation period. - *silam* the past. - *tenggang (waktu) pembayaran* grace period.

masa II - *iya?* 1 is that so? are you kidding? 2 oh, no. *ah, -!* that's impossible! *bersikap - bodoh* don't care o. way or another. ke- **bodohan** indifference.

masa III (s.) MASSA. - *mengambang* the floating mass.

masak I *paham yg sdh* - a foregone conclusion. me- *air* to boil water. ke-an maturity. -an *bungkus* carry-out food. -.*ma(ng)sai* dyed-in-the-wool. - *sekolahnya* he has had sufficient schooling.

masak II (s.) MASA II. -! come on, are you kidding!

masalah memper-kan to discuss, argue about.

masalora (Central Celebes) custom whereby a guest must not refuse to partake of what is offered to him or bad results may occur.

masam ke-an acidity.

masing -.-an everybody stays to himself, doesn't know his neighbors.

masjid house specially built for people to say their daily prayers and also the Friday prayer; mostly situated in a larger area; (cp.) MUSHOLLA.

maskapai - *anak* subsidiary (company).

maskara mascara.

masker face-guard.

maslahat advantage, profit. **ber-** to gain advantage.

masmédia mass media. **di-kan** to be put in the mass media.

masrum mushroom.

massa the masses, the people. - *apung (,mengambang)* the floating mass. - *ontslah (,ontslag)* mass layoff.

massal mass (unemployment, etc.). *kuburan* - mass-grave.

mastautin ber- to reside, live, maintain a permanent residence.

masturbasi masturbation.

masuk (in hotel) check-in. *tak - nasihat* pig-headed. **me-i** ... *th* to enter o's ... year. **me-kan:** ~ *kembali Irian Barat dlm wilayah RI* to re-annex West Irian. ~ *prepentip* to keep s.o. in custody. **-an** input. - *asuransi* to insure o.s. - *asuransi jiwa* to buy life insurance. - *bekerja* to take up office. - *daftar hitam* to be blacklisted. - *kelambu* to go to bed. - *kotak* 1 (in sports) on the bench. 2 to be out of the picture. 3 to be a mere cipher. - *milisi (,militer)* to enlist. - *perangkap* to walk into a trap. - *televisi* to be on television. - *tentara* to enlist.

masyaf handwritten sections of the Quran.

masyarakat inhabitant. *ribuan - ibukota* thousands of inhabitants of the capital. *kesehatan* - public health. **me-** to become common. **me-kan** to return to society (of prisoners, etc.). ~ *diri* to go public. - *gotong.royong* a communal society. - *pedesaan* a rural community. - *tanpa uang tunai* a cashless society. - *yg bersifat (,serba) jamak* a pluralistic society. - *yg bersifat tunggal* a monolithic society. - *yg majemuk* a pluralistic society.

mas(y)hur ter-: ~ *berani* to be generally known as brave. ~ *jahatnya* he is a notorious villain.

Masyumi [Majelis Syuro Muslimin Indonesia] Consultative Council of Indonesian Moslems.

mat *(berbuat)* -.-**an** to sit around and enjoy life.

mata - *ganti* -, *gigi ganti gigi* an eye for an eye and a tooth for a tooth. *-mu!* are you crazy! *dgn - tdk sedap* with regret. *melihat dgn sebelah* - to look at s.t. with disdain. *di bawah empat* - privately. - *ditutup dgn kain* blindfolded. *tdk kelihatan - hidungnya* he was nowhere to be seen. *titik* - public eye. **ber-:** ~ *awas* to be sharp-eyed, observant. ~ *sipit* slanty eyed. **se-** *wayang* only o. -.-: ~ *rangkap* double agent. ~ *ulung* master spy. - *acara iklan* (TV) commercials (i.e. announcements advertising or promoting an article). - *bugil* the naked eye. - *ijo* green with envy. - *ikan* corn on the toe. - *itik* buttonhole. - *jeli* 1 alluring eyes. 2 All-Seeing Eye, The Big Eye. - *kucing* the magic (green-colored) eye (in some older radio sets) indicating that the radio has warmed up and is ready for use. - *mobil* headlights (of a car). - *perang nuklir* nuclear warhead. - *pintal* spindle. - *pulpen* the nib of a fountainpen. *M- Rumah Oranye* The House of Orange (in the Netherlands). - *sapi balik* fried egg over. - *uang* currency. - *yuyu* tending to cry easily. *si - biru* the European.

matabelo k.o. herring.

mataliur (S.) MITRALYUR.

matan firm. *janji* - a firm pledge.

matang 1 definite, certain. 2 finished. *mebel* - finished furniture. **pe-an** ripening, maturing.

matématika mathematics.

matématikawan mathematician.

matéri (subject) matter.

mati expired. *Banyak di antara mereka itu masih memegang paspor Belanda yg sdh lama* -, Many among them are still holding Dutch passports which expired a long time ago. - *kutumu!* you're finished! *karet itu sdh* -

the rubber has lost its elasticity.
- *oleh kekerasan* a violent death. *takkan
-.-* immortal. - *anjing* to die like a dog,
die for nothing. *penyakit - bujang*
"Sumatran disease," i.e. a disease
affecting clove plants, esp. in West
Sumatra. - *disambar listrik* to be
electrocuted. - *hanyut* to be drowned.
- *jalan* hopeless. - *kaget* to die of
fright. - *kelaparan* to starve. - *lemas*
to be drowned. - *napas* apnea. - *raga*
deep in meditation. - *separuh* semi-
paralyzed. - *suri* apparent death.
- *teraniaya* cruelly slain.

maton reasonable.

matra (gramm.) meter. **ber-** and **ke-an**
dimensional. - *lengkap* acatalectic.

matrikulasi matriculation.

matur nuwun thank you very much.

mau - *hujan* it looks like rain. *dua hari -
Lebaran* in two days we'll have *Lebaran.
- mati* at the brink of death. *-mu!*
(coll.) I bet you'd like it! *Jangan -
memperkenalkan mereka,* You should
refuse to introduce them. *Kalau orang
itu mengajak saudara, jangan -,* If that
man invites you, don't accept. - *tahu
saja* nosy. - *sama* - by mutual agreement, without coercion. **ke-an:** *kalau
ada ~ ada jalan* where there is a will
there is a way. *~nya pulang.pergi* he
has no firm will. *~ baik* goodwill. *atas
~ sendiri* of o's own accord (,free will).
-in to be after (my money). **se-** *gue* at
my (own) discretion, as I think fit,
just as o. pleases. **se-nya** whatever o.
would like (to). **se-.-nya** arbitrary. **-nya**
wanted to (but didn't). *"M~ siapa? "*
(over the telephone) "Whom do you
want to talk to?" *banyak ~* hard to
please.

Maulud -an to celebrate *Maulud.*

maung - *lodaya* (in West Java) the striped
royal tiger.

maupun and also.

maut (sl.) terrific! great!

mawas introspect(ion) **(me)-** *diri* to
introspect. - *pribadi* introspection.

mawut turned upside down.

maya ber- illusory.

Mayang Virgo.

mayonès mayonnaise.

mayor - *genderang* drum major.

mayorèt - *genderang* drum majorette.

mayoritas - *bungkam* the silent majority.

mbah I appellation for old people.

mbah II (taboo word) term of address
used when meeting a tiger in the
jungle.

mbak term of address for young woman.
- *ayu* 1 older sister. 2 (in some regions)
middle-aged woman. - *ayu bakul jamu*
door-to-door female seller of traditional (Jav.) medicinal herbs.

mbarep.lanang the eldest (first-born male).

mbé tit very profitable.

mbé twi loss.

mbok I 1 mother. 2 appellation for adult
woman of lower and middle classes.
ayam mB- Brèk Jav. chicken in a basket; the chicken is simmered in spiced
coconut milk before being fried.

mbok II do (emphatically). - *iya!* please
do! *-.-* well, well! (surprised, astonished). - *sdh (,wis) jangan menangis!*
do stop crying!

MCK [Mandi, Cuci dan Kakus] public
bath, wash and toilet.

mdleming to talk to o.s.

Mébéa.Bingo a three-wheeled passenger
car using a 50 cc-motor.

mébelèr furniture.

médan - *bhakti* battle field. - *dharma*
field of honor. - *yg berat* a rough
terrain. - *yudha* battle field.

médebewind the power of a local government to perform duties delegated
to it by the central government or by
a higher level of local government.

média media. - *massa* mass media.

mèdik medic.

mèdikal medical.

médio mid-. *pd - Januari* (in) mid-January.

médis medical.

medit and **medhit** stingy.

méditasi meditation.

Méditèrania Mediterranean.

médium (spirit) medium.

meerwinst excess profit.

mégal.mégol to wiggle o's hips prova-
tively.

mégalomania megalomania.

megap.megap to be in bad straits. - *kepedasan* (mouth) is on fire.

mégaton megaton.

megeg.megeg to be firmly in the saddle.

megibung (in Bali) a Hindu-Bali religious
ceremony consisting of a joint meal;
the food is placed in a *dulang*.

mègrèk sickly.

mèh pulse.

méhé flat(-nosed).

mèhèk ter-.- out of breath.

Mehfil.E.Qirat Koran reading contest.

méja di- hijaukan to be summoned to
appear in court. - *cuci muka* wash-
stand. - *dgn laci* chest of drawers.
- *kedaian* counter (in bar). - *kursi*
furniture. - *perundingan* conference
table.

mèk Mac, buddy, man. *Hebat, -!* Great,
man!

mekangkang *duduk* - to sit straddling.

mékanik mechanic.

mékanika mechanics. - *teknik* structural
mechanics. - *teoretis* theoretical mechanics. - *terpakai* applied mechanics.

mekar me-kan to expand. **pe-an** expansion, development. ~ *kota Jakarta* the
growth of Jakarta.

mèkasi (S.) TERIMA KASIH.

mekepung (in Bali) water buffalo racing.

mèl 1 to report. 2 illegal highway toll.
bayar - to pay tax to illegal posts.

Mélanésia Melanesia.

melar *karet itu tak bisa* - the rubber has
lost its elasticity.

melayu (lower-case) a derogatory term
used by Indonesians in reference to
themselves.

Melayu.Polinésia Malayo-Polynesian.

melèk *menjadikan masyarakat - obat*
to make the community (,society)
medicine-minded. **-.-an** to stay up

(late at night), burn the midnight
oil.

melèng with all o's attention concentrated
on.

melèngken (S.) MELAINKAN.

mèlèr to keep running (of nose). *hidung*
- a running nose.

melesek to collapse.

meliat (S.) MELIHAT.

mélik - *nggéndong lali* (improper) desire
frequently inveigled into neglect.

Melindo [Melayu.Indonesia] Malay-
Indonesian, in *Ejaan* - the Malay-
Indonesian Spelling (1959).

meling absent-minded.

melinjo (s.) MLINJO.

melit *tanya dgn* - wanting to know the
ins and outs of it.

meliwis (s.) MLIWIS.

mélodi ber- melodious, tuneful.

mélodigitar melody guitar.

melukut rice-dust, broken rice. *spt - di
tepi gantang* of little importance.

mèmang se-nya by nature, naturally.
M-nya Do you think that...? What
do you think, ...? (Slightly angry).

memelas (s.) WELAS.

mémoar memoir.

mempan 1 to penetrate into (of bullet,
knife, etc.). 2 to catch fire. 3 to understand. 4 *tdk* - (a) impenetrable (of
tank). (b) (the propaganda) found no
response. (c) no good purpose can be
served by. (d) to be unaffected (,un-
touched) by.

Mènag [Menteri Agama] Minister of
Religious Affairs.

mènagemènt management.

Ménak stories about the Islamic hero
Amir Ambyah, depicted in *wayang
golèk* dramas.

menang - *asal* - victory at any cost. **di-kan**
to be won. **ke-an** *melimpah* landslide,
an overwhelming victory. **pe-** *hadiah
Nobel* Nobel Laureate (,prize winner).
- *derajat* to be held in high esteem. -
mapan to have the advantage (over).
- *pangkat* to be held in high esteem.

- *pengaruh* to predominate (over).
- *sendiri* self-serving.

menara - *pemboran minyak* oil rig. - *pengawas* control tower.

méncla.ménclé unreliable, inconsistent.

Mèndagkop [Menteri Perdagangan dan Koperasi] Minister of Commerce and Cooperatives.

Mèndagri [Menteri Dalam Negeri] Minister of the Interior.

mendak I to stoop (while walking past, out of politeness).

mendak II (s.) PENDAK.

mendam intoxicated. - *berahi* to be madly in love.

mendek (s.) MENDAK I. -.- 1 crawl stooped over. 2 to throw o.s. at a person's feet, sit on the floor (,ground) in a humble posture in front of s.o.

mendem (s.) MENDAM.

mendingan it would be better to.

mendung *setelah - jalipun tiba* after rain comes sunshine.

menéér (in Manado) form of address for teachers, etc.

mènejemèn (s.) MANAJEMEN.

menejer (s.) MANAJER.

menep to keep quiet.

mengelèdèk (s.) LEDEK I.

mengerti *saya tdk (,blm)* - 1 I don't get it. 2 I don't know (Java, polite). *sdh* - tamed, domesticated. - *tak* - to understand only half of it. **Se-** *saya nama itu salah ditulis,* If I'm not mistaken (or, If I have got it right) that name has been misspelled. - *sendiri* bribe.

menggah se-.-*nya* only child.

Menggala Bengal.

menggerip (s.) MAGRIB.

mengkali (S.) BARANGKALI.

mengkerut (S.) MENGKERET.

mengkilap **me-kan** to shine s.t.

mengkirig and **mengkirik** hair-raising, terrifying.

mengkuang the screwpine (L. Pandanus atrocarpus) and other species of Pandanus.

mengolkol and **mengolkon** to cough.

mèngong crazy.

mèngsol awry, askew, slanting. - *otaknya* he is insane.

mengudung swollen (of rice ears).

Mènhankam [Menteri Pertahanan dan Keamanan] Minister of Defense and Security.

Mènhub [Menteri Perhubungan] Minister of Communications.

meninjo (s.) MELINJO.

meniran and **meniren** tired (due to speaking too long).

Mènkes [Menteri Kesehatan] Minister of Health.

Mèn Kesra and **Mènkesra** [Menteri Kesejahteraan Rakyat] Minister of People's Welfare.

Mènko [Menteri Ko(o)rdinator] Coordinating Minister (under President Soekarno). *Kompartimen Maritim ini* **di.-i** *oleh Mayor Jenderal Ali Sadikin,* The Coordinating Minister of this Maritime Compartment is Major General Ali Sadikin. - *Polkam* [Menteri Ko(o)dinator bidang Politik dan Keamanan] (under President Soeharto) Coordinating Minister for the Political and Security Sector.

Mènmud [Menteri Muda] Deputy Minister.

menor brilliant, glorious.

mènor shapely.

Mènpan [Menteri Negara Penertiban Aparatur Negara] State Minister for the Control of the Machinery of the State.

Mènpen [Menteri Penerangan] Minister of Information.

Mènperbu [Menteri Purburuhan] Minister of Labor.

Mènperdag [Menteri Perdagangan] Minister of Commerce.

Mènperhub [Menteri Perhubungan] Minister of Communications.

Mènristèk [Menteri Riset dan Teknologi] Minister of Research and Technology.

mèns to have o's period.

Mènsèknèg (s.) MENSESNEG.

Mènsèsnèg [Menteri Sekretaris Negara] Minister/Secretary of State.

Mènsos [Menteri Sosial] Minister of Social Affairs.

mentah semifinished. *mebel* - semifinished furniture.

mental to be launched (of missile).

Mèntan [Menteri Pertanian] Minister of Agriculture.

mentas to graduate.

mentèk and menthèk a disease that attacks the roots of rice plants.

mentèrèng dignified, formal. ke-an gorgeousness, pomp.

menteri *M- Tenaga Kerja* Minister of Manpower.

mèntog, mènthog and mèntok (s.) ENTOG.

mèntol menthol.

mentolo to stand s.t.

mèntor mentor.

Mèntranskop [Menteri Transmigrasi dan Koperasi] Minister of Resettlement and Cooperatives.

menu menu.

menung *duduk* ter- to be lost in thought.

Menur Putih Snowwhite.

mèong - *gede* (in West Java) the striped royal tiger.

mèpèt small profit.

merabu *(burung)* - k.o. heron (L. Leptoptilus javanicus).

mèrah di-.hijaukan to be provided with a traffic light. pe- *pipi* rouge. - *gincu* carmine. - *menyala* fiery red.

merak hati sweet, winsome, attractive (of appearance).

meranti 1 large tree (L.Shorea albida) with timber in great demand for boards, etc. 2 a mahogany-like wood.

mercu - *minyak* oil rig.

Mèrcy the Mercedes automobile.

Merdèka -*!* Freedom! Greeting from the time of the 1945 Revolution, used by republicans when meeting o.a., at the opening and closing of letters, speeches, etc.

meréka -.- people, folks.

mèri to be envious.

meriam - *air* water cannon. - *gunung* mountain artillery. - *katak (,kodok)* mortar. - *sapu jagat* heavy guns. - *tanpa. tolak.belakang* recoilless gun.

mèrjer merger.

mèrkuri mercury. *lampu* - mercury lamp.

merongos (s.) MRONGOS.

merosot ke-an 1 drop, setback. 2 degradation, deterioration. ~ *akhlak* degeneration.

merpati - *laut* seagull. - *pos* carrier pigeon.

mèrsi (s.) MERCY.

mertamu to visit, call at.

mertéga (S.) MENTEGA.

mertelon to divide into three. *sistim* - system whereby the crop is divided as follows: two parts for the landowner and o. part for the tiller.

mertua parents-in-law. *bapak* - father-in-law. *ibu* - mother-in-law.

mès (mil.) mess.

Mesa Aries.

mesin per-an (adj.) engineering. - *absensi karyawan (,pegawai)* attendance time recorder, time clock. - *cacah* perforating machine. - *cetak tangan* hand printing press. - *dikte* dictaphone. - *gilas (,giling) jalan* roadroller. - *hitung* calculator. - *jahit kaki* treadle sewing machine. - *kembar* twin engine. - *pelapis plastik* laminator. - *pemancang* pile driver. - *pembeli rokok otomatis* cigarette machine. - *pemusnah sampah kertas* paper shredder. - *pencuci piring* dishwasher. - *pengering rambut pakai listrik* electric hair dryer. - *penggilas jalan* roadroller. - *perontok padi* paddy thresher. - *pons* punching machine. - *pontong kertas* paper cutting machine. - *pontong rumput* lawn mower. - *reken* calculator. - *tempel* outboard motor.

mesiu gunpowder.

meski - *begitu* although that's the case, even so.

mésolitikum mesolithicum.

mesra ke-an 1 intimacy. 2 closeness. -.-an romantic.

mesti inevitable, invariable, predictable. *tdk - sama dgn* need not always be the

same as ... *orang - mati* man is mortal.
*setidak. tidaknya pesan Bapak - saya
sampaikan* at least, I'll leave no stone
unturned in conveying your message.
Tdk - perut ini kemasukan nasi, We
were not sure when we could eat rice.
tdk **di-kan** to be optional. **se-nya** 1
appropriate, as it should be, fitting,
proper. 2 properly speaking, naturally.
sdh ~ naturally, as was to be expected.
-nya as a natural consequence of (the
foregoing). ~ *tdk usah demikian* this
should not be the case. - *hrs* to have
to, must (emphatic).
métalurgi metallurgy.
metenteng tense (of feelings); (s.) MET-
(H)ENTENG.
météor meteor.
météorologi meteorology.
mèter di-kan to be converted to meters.
-an *taksi* taximeter. - *parkir* parking
meter.
meterai ber- sealed (of a document).
metet(h)et tight. *celana* - (a pair of) tights
(as used by crossboys in Central Java).
met(h)enteng to take a (firm) stand.
métil alkohol methyl alcohol.
métodelogi and **métodik** methodology.
metri me- to honor, respect, venerate,
revere.
métrik metric. - *ton* metric ton.
Mètro a variety of corn first grown in
South Sumatra.
métrologi metrology.
métropolitan me-kan *Medan* to make
Medan a metropolis (,capital city).
métropolitanisasi incorporating certain
areas into the Jakarta metropolis.
meubel (S.) MEBEL.
meubilair furniture; (s.) MEBELER.
mèwah smart, stylish.
mèwèk 1 pursing up the mouth to cry.
2 pouting.
mi - *godok* parboiled egg noodles. - *goreng*
pan-fried noodles. - *kering* dried noodles. - *kuah* noodles in broth.
miang *tdk takut barang* **se-** to be not a
bit afraid.
micara 1 articulated. 2 to speak in a

deliberately attractive (,provocative)
way.
middenstand 1 middle classes. 2 tradespeople, petit bourgeois.
midi *hasil* - a mediocre (,moderate)
income.
mid-nait-so (s.) MITNAITSYO.
midodarèni the night before a wedding
(for the bride to be).
migas [*(departemen)* minyak dan gas
(bumi)] (department of) oil and
(natural) gas.
migran migrant.
migrasi migration. **ber-** to migrate.
mijah pe-an spawning.
Mikaèl the Archangel Michael.
Mikimus and **Miki Tikus** Mickey Mouse.
Mikraj -an the commemoration of Mohammed's ascension to Heaven.
mikro micro. *gelombang* - microwave.
mikroba microbes.
mikrofilm microfilm.
mikrofon (S.) MIKROPON. **ber-** *ganda*
to have a dual microphone system.
Mikronésia Micronesia.
mikroorganisma microorganism.
mikroskop microscope.
milangkori 1 to make house-to house
visits. 2 to travel widely.
milat (s.) ATMIL.
milik ber- propertied. **kepe-an** ownership.
pe: ~ *jasa angkutan laut* shipowner.
~ *tanah secara guntai* absentee landlord.
militan militant.
militansi militancy.
militèr *kaum* - the military clique. **di-kan**
to be militarized. - *atase* military attaché. - *sukarela(wan)* volunteer. -
wajib conscript.
militèrisme militarism.
mil.milan snacks. *jajan* - to eat snacks.
milo (s.) MULO.
milyard -an in the billions.
milyardèr billionaire.
milyonèr millionaire.
mimang *akar* - aboveground intertwined
roots, usually of the banyan, to which
superstition is attached, k.o. magic

roots; (s.) LINGKARAN (MIMANG).

mimi king-crab. *kaya (,spt) - dan mintuna* inseparable (of lovers); (s.) MINTUNA.

mimik I mimics.

mimik II to drink (child's word).

mimpi ber- *berjalan* sleepwalking. **pe-** 1 dreamer. 2 sleepwalker. - *basah* a wet dream (dream accompanied by an ejaculation).

Mina Pisces.

Minah (s.) PERTAMINA. *si* - petroleum.

minalaidin walfaizin 'from those who have celebrated their victory for keeping the fast,' i.e. the congratulation expressed on *Lebaran* day for successfully keeping the fast.

Minang Minangkabau.

minat *tdk ada - utk bekerja* don't feel like working. *menjadi - dunia* to be of worldwide fame.

mindah (S.) PINDAH.

minder *merasa -* to feel inferior. *rasa -* submissiveness, subservience.

minderhèidsnota minority report (in *M.P.R.*).

mineur somber, not very cheerful, depressed.

minggat to escape.

minggir *M-!* Move to the side! Get out of the way! **di-kan** to be pushed aside.

minggu - *Palma* Palm Sunday. - *tenang* cooling-off week (i.e. the week in which the contesting political parties during the general elections were not allowed to campaign—April 25–May 1, 1977).

mingser (s.) PINGSER.

mini 1 small. 2 miniskirt. **ber-** and **ber. rok -** to wear a miniskirt. *gadis.gadis ber-* miniskirted girls. *M- Ekspres* (in West Sumatra) the Honda pickup (car).

Minicar a jitney-like, 3-wheeled vehicle propelled by a 4-stroke Honda S-110 engine.

mini.skirt miniskirt; (s.) MINI.

minoritèt di-kan to be counted as a minority (group).

minsua temple guard.

minta *M- bicara dgn ...* (on the telephone)

May I speak with ...? **me-:** *tanah Mekah* ~ he wants to die in Mecca. ~ *keluar* to tender o's resignation. ~ *korban* to claim some victims. **per-an** application. ~ *kredit* application for credit. *mengajukan* ~ *palisemennya* to file o's petition. ~ *suaka* request for asylum. *pendek (,singkat)* ~ (will) die soon. *atas* ~ *sendiri* at o's own request. -.-: -*lah* let's hope that ... ~ *saja* ...let's hope that ... will happen (but it probably won't). - *adik* he (,she) is asking to have a younger sibling (said of a crying child). - *ampun!* O, my God! Unbelievable! - *banding* to lodge an appeal. - *lepas* to resign (o's position). - *perkara* to lodge an appeal.

mintak (S.) MINTA.

mintakad and **mintakat** zone. - *tropika* tropical zone.

mintaku'lburuj the Zodiac.

mintuna 1 female sea crab; (s.) MIMI. 2 the Twins (Zodiac); (s.) MINTAKU'L-BURUJ. *M-* Gemini.

minum *M-nya (apa)?* (waiter to customer) And what will you have to drink? **di-nya** *sekali teguk habis* he drank it in one gulp. **pe-** drunkard. ~ *candu* opium smoker. **-an:** ~ *campuran* mixed drinks. ~ *lembut (,lunak)* soft drink. ~ *meruap* aerated waters. ~ *pelenyap dahaga* thirst quencher.

minus *kabupaten - beras* a regency suffering from a rice shortage.

minyak ber- *air dgn* 1 toady. 2 to flatter, cajole, wheedle. **per-an** (adj.) oil. *politik* ~ oil policy. - *akar wangi Jawa* Java vetiver oil. - *atsiri* volatile oil. - *bijan* sesame oil. - *bumi* mineral oil. - *diesel* k.o. diesel fuel for low r.p.m. engines. - *eteris* etherical oil. - *gelap* black oil: industrial diesel oil, IDO. - *gerek* drilling oil. - *jagung* corn oil (like Mazola). - *karbol* carbolic oil. - *kasar* crude oil. - *kruing* oil from a Dipterocarpaceae. - *lampu* kerosene. - *lobak* rapeseed oil. - *macan* a liniment (Tiger Balm). - *makan* edible oil. - *mawar* rose oil.

- *mesin* engine oil. - *mineral* mineral
oil. - *nilam* patchouli oil. - *pala* nutmeg oil. - *palem* palm oil. - *pelikan*
mineral oil. - *pelincir* (fig.) bribes.
- *permen (,pepermin)* peppermint
oil. - *poko* a peppermint oil which
is used to dispel pain. - *putih* petroleum, premium, supergrade gasoline,
etc. - *rambut* brilliantine. - *rapa* rapeseed oil. - *samin* fat prepared from
goat suet in cooking. - *sereh* citronella
oil. - *silinder* cylinder oil. - *singa laut*
an aphrodisiac. - *solar* solar oil, i.e. k.o.
diesel fuel for high r.p.m. engines. - *ter*
tar oil. - *terbang* volatile oil. - *tesala* a
panacea against all k.o. diseases. - *tum-
buh.tumbuhan* vegetable oil.

Miraj Nabi Mohammad Mohammed's
ascension to Heaven.

Miriam (s.) MARYAM.

miring - *otaknya* he is crazy.

miroso tasty.

Miryam (s.) MARYAM.

mis miss. *pemilihan* -.-*an* contest for Miss
this and Miss that.

misai ber- mustached.

misal di-kan assuming that, supposing
that.

misbar [kalau gerimis penonton bubar]
'when it drizzles, the moviegoers disperse;' (s.) BIOSKOP (MISBAR).

misi (s.) MISSI.

misih and **misik** (S.) MASIH.

misil missile. - *anti.balistik* antiballistic
missile. - *balistik jarak menengah* medium range ballistic missile.

miskin - *ruh* poor in spirit.

miskram miscarriage.

missi mission. *sekolah* - Catholic mission
school. - *muhibah* goodwill mission.
- *pencari fakta, - penjajagan* and - *siasat
hakikat* fact-finding mission. - *perdagangan* trade mission. - *suci* sacred
mission. - *tempur* combat mission.

mis(s)ionaris missionary.

mistéri mystery.

mistérius mysterious. **ke-an** mystery.

mistik 1 mysticism. 2 system for predict-

ing lottery winners.

misuh to use abusive langauge.

mit mid-. *ujian* - *semester* midsemester
examination.

mitnaitsyo midnight show. **di-kan** to be
given as a midnight show.

mitologi mythology.

mitoni ceremony held for a woman in
the seventh month of pregnancy;
(s.) SELAMATAN (MITONI).

mitos myth. **pe-an** cult.

mitra friend. *M- Wisata* a doorless automobile manufactured in Indonesia by
P.T. Garuda Mataram Motor Company
for short-distance transportation of
tourists.

mitralyur me- to machinegun.

miyang to make a living at sea (for
fishermen).

miyar.miyur undecided, wavering, hesitant.

miyosi to commemorate o's birthday
falling on *Sabtu.Pahing.*

Mizan Libra.

mlaka.mlaku to keep walking back and
forth.

mlinjo k.o. tree with edible seeds. - *muda*
small clusters of these seeds, look like
immature dates; colored red, yellow,
green; non-descript taste, a little bitter.
(*Emping* is made from the meat of the
seed of the mature *mlinjo* or *mlinjo
tua*).

mliwis mallard.

moa (s.) MUA.

mobat.mabit to exhaust o.s.

mobèt (in Jakarta) k.o. motorized *becak.*

mobil mobile. **ber-** to drive. **per-an** 1 auto-
motive. 2 car business (,matters). -
acuan racing car. - *ambulans* ambulance. - *ban baja bergigi* caterpillar
tractor.- *barang* motor truck. - *berp(e)-
lat hitam (,merah)* a privately (,gov-
ernment)-owned car. - *brengsek* jalopy.
- *derek* tow truck. - *keran* crane truck.
- *panser* armored car. - *pembersih*
cleaning truck. - *pengangkut personil
lapis baja* armored personnel carrier.

- *pengangkutan* motor truck. - *pengintai* police van. - *penumpang* passenger (,private) car. - *penyelamat* rescue car. - *penyerkap* paddy wagon. - *perecik* sprinkler. - *person* passenger (,private) car. - *sakit* ambulance. - *sewa* (taxi)cab. - *siram* sprinkler. - *tahanan* paddy wagon. - *tangga* ladder-truck (of fire department). - *yg separuh pakai* and - *yg sdh dipakai* a used car.

mobilèr (s.) MEBELER.

mobilèt a moped of the 'Mobylette' trade mark.

mobilisasi pe-an mobilization.

mobilita mobility.

moblong cloudless, clear.

mobyor (dressed) sparklingly.

mocok to substitute a person temporarily in a job. -.- casual (laborer).

modal ber- *kuat* financially strong. **berkan** ... with ... as capital. *dgn - dengkul* (without capital of o's own) making money by way of receiving goods for sale on a commission basis (using only o's knees, *dengkul,* for walking, getting a *becak,* etc. in looking for prospective buyers). - *domestik asing* 'foreign domestic capital,' i.e. the term referring to capital originating from indigenous foreign groups, particularly Chinese. - *kursi* money acquired through graft and favors connected to o's position. - *pemula* initial capital. - *statuter* authorized capital.

modar to kick the bucket, die.

modèl fashion. *sekarang ini sedang -* that's now in fashion.

moderasi moderation.

moderat moderate.

moderator moderator. **di-i** to be moderated (by).

modifikasi me-kan to modify.

modiste dressmaker.

modol and **modhol** messy. *jorok -* a (big) dirty fellow.

modong k.o. black magic. **di-** to be put the hex on. *tukang -* black-magic practitioner.

modul module.

modulasi modulation.

mogok - *lapar* hunger strike. **pe-an** *liar* wildcat strike.

mogol 1 immature, uncooked. 2 to fail. 3 unsuccessful. *murid -* a dropout.

mogor to whore. **Pe-** Bluebeard, Don Juan. **pe-an** prostitution.

moh don't want, (I) don't want to! - *tumbuh* won't grow.

Mohamad Mohammed. - *Rasul(l)ol(l)ah* Mohammed the prophet of Allah.

mohon per-an application. ~ *kredit* application for credit. **ter-** petitionee.

mojang - *Priangan* a beauty from the Preanger region (West Java).

Mojopahit (S.) MAJAPAHIT.

mokaha not worth while.

mokal impossible. *asal anda percaya pd yg -.-* provided you believe in impossible things.

mokoyong k.o. *soto* made of dog meat.

molèk pe-an *jalan.jalan* the beautification of streets.

molèr whore, prostitute.

mo.limo the five sins, starting with *mo* (Jav. script for *m*): *madat* (opium addiction, opiumism), *minum* (boozing), *main* (dissipation), *madon* (promiscuity) and *maling* (stealing).

molor to hit the sack, go to bed.

momong -an child to be taken care of. - *anak* to raise a child.

momot di-i *sayuran* (a) vegetable-laden (cart, truck, etc.).

Monako Monaco.

monarki monarchy.

Monas [Monumen Nasional] National Monument.

monat.manut to obey.

mondar.mandir to go back and forth, shuttle between ... and ...; (S.) MUNDAR.MANDIR.

mondong to carry (away) o's bride in the arms, symbolizing that she is a prize being carried off.

mong nge- to take care of.

Monggo (response to *Kulo Nuwun:* phrase for announcing o's presence as a visitor at the door of s.o.'s home)

Come in! Hello!

mongki bisnis (coll.) monkey business.

mongkog and **mongkok** to feel flattered, delighted.

Mongol Mongolian.

monitor monitor. **me-** to monitor. **pe-an** monitoring.

monografi monograph.

monokultur monoculture.

monopoli pe-an monopolization.

mono.rèl monorail.

monoton monotonous.

monsinyur monseigneur.

montase assembly. - *mobil* automobile assembly.

montit plantation railway.

montok shapely, with large breasts. *Perempuan itu memang - banget!* That woman is indeed a sex-bomb! **ke(penuh)-an** shapeliness.

montong don't.

monumèn monument.

monyèt a term of abuse. - *keluar dr lengan baju* then he showed the cloven hoof.

monyong.dowèr protruding. *bacotnya -* his mouth is protruding.

mo.pitu *mo.limo* plus gluttony and false witness.

morat.marit *hidup -* to lead a precarious existence.

moré (in Irian Jaya) woman's loincloth.

morfém morpheme.

morfologi morphology.

morfin (s.) MORPIN.

morfinis (s.) MORPINIS.

moril *rusak -nya* he is demoralized.

morotin (s.) POROT.

morpin morphine.

morpinis morphine addict.

mortalitèt mortality.

Mosambik Mozambique.

mosin crazy.

Moskou (S.) MOSKWA.

mosok exclamation of skepticism; (s.) MASA II.

motèl motel.

motif ber- to have a motive.

motivasi ter-kan motivated.

motong (S.) POTONG. - *(jalan)* to take a short cut.

motor impetus behind s.t. - 2 *tak* two-stroke engine. - *bakar* internal combustion engine. - *balap* speedboat - *duduk* inboard motor. - *tempel* outboard motor.

motorisasi motorization.

mpok (older) sister.

MPS [(Sistim) Menghitung, Menetapkan dan Menyetor Pajak Sendiri] Self-Assessment (System) (in taxes).

mpu 1 master craftsman. 2 armorer. 3 a form of address for those who have attained high distinction in literature, philosophy, etc. 4 honorary degree conferred by the *Universitas Nasional* (National University) in Jakarta upon professors who have reached the age of 60.

mrèngkal unwilling to cooperate.

mrongos with (too) large, protruding teeth (mouth cannot be closed).

MS [Magister Sains] Master of Science, M.S(c).

mua *ikan -* eel.

muasal (s.) ASAL(.MUASAL).

muat pe-an loading (of ship, etc.).

mubaligh religious foreman, local religious teacher who actively teaches the Islamic religion to adults by giving lectures in offices; (S.) MUBALLIG.

mubalighat female instructor at religious schools.

mubarak *Id -!* Happy *Id!*

mubazir 1 redundant, extravagant, overly generous. 2 to waste. **ke-an** 1 a waste. 2 redundancy. **me-kan** to waste.

mucikari (s.) MUNCIKARI.

muda - *di hati* young at heart. **ke-an** early age. **kepe-an** (adj.) youth. **pe-** chap. ~ *belasan th* a teenage boy. *P~ Peuyeumbol* 'Yeast-Sweetened Cassava-Bun Youth,' i.e. the derogatory epithet given to the youth in Bandung as they were unsuccessful in making a stand against the advancing Jap. troops. ~ *putus.sekolah* a dropout. *P~ Rakyat* People's Youth, i.e. the youth arm of

the *PKI.* ~ *teruna* adolescent. *(pe)-.(pe)-
mudi* young people - *belia* in the prime
of life, in the flower of o's age. - *mentah* very young. - *teruna* youthful (and
still unmarried).

mudah ke-an facilities. - *saja se- berdiang*
nothing could be simpler. *utk* **-nya** for
convenience sake. - *bergaul* easy to get
along with. - *di mulut* easily said. -
meledak (,meletup) explosive.

mudi I berke- *di haluan* to be under the
thumb of, be henpecked. *tdk dpt* **dike-
kan** not under command. **ke-** steering
wheel.

mudi II *muda.-* young men and women.
pe- young girl. ~ *belasan th* a teenage
girl. ~ *teruna* adolescent.

mudik to repatriate. **me-kan** to navigate
(a boat) upstream.

mudun.leumah a joint (religious) meal in
commemoration of a child's seven-
month birthday.

Muhammadiyah a modernist, orthodox
but reformist Moslem movement.

muhasabah introspection.

muhibah ber- to be on a goodwill mission.

mujahid fighter (for Islam).

mujahidin the plural of *mujahid.*

mujaib [mujarab dan ajaib] effective and
wonderful (of medicine).

mujair (in moonlighter's jargon) small,
minor, less lucrative. *obyek.obyek* -
less lucrative objects.

mujarad abstract. **pe-an** abstraction.

mujarap (S.) MUJARAB.

mujidat and **mujizat ber-** miraculous.

mujur *ia* **pe-** *benar* he is a lucky bird.

muka *cari* - to flatter. *membuang* - *kpd
orang tua* to disregard o's parents.
mengambil (,membuat) - to wheedle.
lain di -, *lain di belakang* hypocritical.
ber-: ~ *dua* hypocritical, untrustworthy.
~ *tembok* impudent, insolent. **pe-**
foreman (in charge of a group of
prisoners). **per-an:** ~ *bumi* earth surface. ~ *jalan* (road) surface. ~ *laut*
sea level. - *dua* hypocrisy, two-faced.
dgn - *yg tebal* bare-faced, impudent.

mukadin assistant of the *imam.*

mukah pe- fornicator.

mukena the white veil a woman wears in
performing the *salat.* **ber-** to wear a
mukena.

mukhtasyam 1 sublime, majestic. 2 respectable.

mukim to stay in Mecca for longer than
the single visit as a *haji.* **pe-an** *(kembali)*
(re)settlement. **per-an** residence, living.

mukimin inhabitants, residents.

muktamirin conferees.

mukti to be well off.

mula -i *dgn (+ noun)* to begin with. **pe-**
apprentice. **per-an** early days. *dr* ~
sampai penghabisan from beginning
to end. *dr* **(se)-** *jadi, sejak* **se-** and *dr* -
lahir from childhood. *dr se-* a priori.

mulat - *sarira* to carry out an introspection, self-correction.

mulia pe-an *tebu* (sugar)cane breeding.
pe- *biakan ternak* animal breeding.

Mulo and **M.U.L.O.** [Meer Uitgebreid
Lager Onderwijs] Junior High School
grades 8, 9 and 10 for Dutch and native
children.

multi *proses* **ke-bahasaan** multilingual
process. *-kompleks* multicomplex.
-nasional multinational. *perusahaan
-nasional* multinational corporation,
MNC. *-rasial* multiracial.

multijutawan multimillionaire.

multijutawati female multimillionaire.

Muludan *selamatan* for the birthday of
the Prophet.

mulur to be extended (of time).

mulus undamaged condition. *dlm keadaan*
- (in advertisements selling cars) in
good running condition. **ke-an** perfec-
tion.

mulut - *terlanjut emas tentangannya* in
for a penny, in for a pound. *lepas dr* -
harimau jatuh ke - *buaya* out of the
frying pan into the fire. *merasa sedikit
gatal dlm* - to have an aversion (to certain food). *lain di* - *lain di hati* saying
o. thing and doing another. *di* - *rakyat*
in popular parlance. *gula dlm* - an easy
job. *tiada lepas drpd* - to have a lot to

say about. - *jalan* road entrance.

mumbang the young green coconut.
menanam - to undertake a hopeless
affair. - *jatuh kelapa jatuh* death keeps
no calendar.

mumet confused.

mumpung 1 while. *"Minumlah kopimu.
M- masih hangat!"* "Drink your coffee,
while it's still hot!" - *ada kesempatan*
when the opportunity arises. 2 oppor-
tunistic.

mumpungisme opportunism.

mumpuni highly skilled.

munajat private devotions.

munas [musyawarah nasional] national
conference.

munasabah to fit, be suited.

muncang.mancing to walk up and down.

muncar *ikan* - whale.

munci 1 concubine. 2 prostitute.

muncikari madam (woman in charge of
a brothel).

muncrat to spurt up (,out).

muncul ber-an to appear (plural subject).
Kursus.kursus Inggeris ~ *bak kedai
dan restoran*, English language courses
are mushrooming. pe-an début.

munding *(ber)turut* - to follow blindly.

mundur ke-an 1 retreat. 2 setback. me-
kan to set back (the clock, etc.); (S.)
MENGUNDURKAN.*(bersikap)-.maju*
(constantly) vacillating, hesitating.

mungkin *tdk* - 1 out of the question. 2
no way. *bukan tdk* - not impossible,
not out of the question. ke-an even-
tuality. me-kan feasible.

mungkret to shrink, contract. di-kan to
be folded up (of bicycle).

mungsret too short.

munjuk atur to report, notify.

Mun.Mèn [Muntah dan Mencret] 'vomiting and having diarrhea,' gastroenteritis.

muntabèr [muntah dan berak] 'vomiting
and defecating,' gastroenteritis.

muntah *Gunung Semeru* - *api*, Mount
Semeru is spitting fire. di-kan spewed
forth. - *bocor* (s.) MUNTABER.

muntaha (mysticism) end, final stage.

muntap very angry. pe-an *unek.unek*
venting o's gall (,spleen).

muntir (S.) MONTIR.

muntup to appear, be visible.

murah - *di mulut mahal di timbangan*
quick to promise, slow to perform. ke-
an *belanja* to live cheaply owing to
low price levels. - *rejeki* plentiful of
luck. - *tangan* liberal. - *tawa* to laugh
readily.

murai *(burung)* - *batu* the white-rumped
shama (L. Copsychus malabaricus).

murak to eat, consume.

murbé and murbéi mulberry.

murbi proletarian woman.

murca to vanish in a mysterious way.

murid - *mogol* dropout.

muring grumbling, irritable.

Murjangkung (the Dutch Governor General) Jan Pieterszoon Coen (1611–
1629).

murni unadulterated, genuine. ke-an
cleanliness.

mursid male guide.

mursidah female guide.

murtad di-kan to be excommunicated.

murung ke-an hypochondria. pe- melan-
choliac.

musabaqoh competition between Koran
readers.

musalla (s.) MUSHOLLA.

musang - *berbulu ayam* a wolf in sheep's
clothing.

muséum museum. me-kan to put in a
museum. per-an (adj.) museum.

mushaf (S.) MASYAF.

musholla prayer house, place where
people can say their prayers; not used
for Friday prayers; found in any small
area, for example, in a residential
area of about 500 houses and in offices.

musibah and musibat calamity, disaster.

musik pe- musician. - *kamar* chamber
music. - *klasik* classical music. - *lembut*
soft music. - *lutut megal.megol* the
twist (dance). - *ngak.ngik.nguk* rock-'n-
roll. - *pop* pop music. - *remaja* teenage
music. - *rok* rock music. - *tiup* wind
music.

musikal musical.

musikalisasi putting s.t. to music.
musikan musician.
musikolog musicologist.
musikologi musicology.
musikus musician.
musim *sdh* -nya ... it's the time to ...
- *angin gombal* the lean season for the fishermen's community (from August through December). - *barat* west monsoon. - *berpengantin* honeymoon. - *giling* (sugarcane) harvest season. - *haji* the time of year when pilgrims go to Mecca. - *marengan* the end of the rainy season. - *perjodohan* mating season. - *ramai* peak season. - *rendengan* rainy season. - *salju* winter.
musisi musicians.
Muslimin Moslems. - *mazhab Hanafi* the Hanafi Moslems, Hanafis.
musnah me-.hamakan to sterilize. pe-an annihilation. ~ *hama* antisepsis. ~ *masal* genocide.
muson monsoon.
Muspida and MUSPIDA [Musyawarah Pimpinan Daerah] Regional Executive Council; formed August 1, 1967 to replace the *Pancatunggal* (under President Soekarno) and created as a new advisory body to assist the *kepala daerah* (local executive chief) at the provincial *(Muspida tingkat I),* regency *(Muspida tingkat II)* and subdistrict *(Muspida tingkat Kecamatan)* levels. Chaired by the *kepala daerah,* the council meets whenever there are pressing problems connected with the maintenance of peace and security. Its members include local mil. commanders, the local prosecutor, the local judge and the chief of police. The *Muspidas* at the various levels are sometimes, for convenience, referred to as *Muspida Daerah* and *Muspida Setempat* 'the regional authorities' and 'the local authorities' respectively.
Mus(s)abaqah Til(l)awatul Qur'an Koran Reading Contest.

mustahak important.
mustahaq person entitled to receive the *zakat.*
mustahil ke-an absurdity, impossibility.
mustaid 1 in working order, ready for use. 2 ready.
mustika - *delima* a bezoar, magic jewel used as a remedy and giving its owner a certain rank and function in society.
musuh (sl.) purchaser. - *dlm selimut* a wolf in sheep's clothing. ber-an hostile. ~ *dgn* to be at odds with di-i to be hated, have enemies. per-an *kebuyutan* hereditary enmity. - *bebuyutan* hereditary enemy. - *negara* State (,public) enemy. - *nomor satu* archenemy.
musyala (s.) MUSHOLLA.
musyawarah - *kerja* workshop.
musyawarat (S.) MUSYAWARAH. pe-negotiator.
musykil delicate.
musyollah (s.) MUSALLA.
mutahir (s.) MUTAKHIR.
mutakhir up to date, latest.
mu'tamad final.
mutasi transfer (of government employee, etc.). di-kan to be transferred (of government employee, etc.). pe-an transfer (of a top-ranking army man, diplomat, etc.) to a new post.
mutawif (s.) MUTHOWIF.
muthaqqafin intellectuals.
muthowif licensed guide for Moslem pilgrims when visiting Medina (the Prophet's grave).
Mutiara express train which shuttles between Jakarta Kota Station (via Cirebon and Semarang) and Surabaya.
mutlak a must. *Pelajaran agama - di Perguruan Tinggi,* Religious instruction is a must in colleges. *syarat* - conditio sine qua non. - *perlu* prerequisite.
mut.mutan to suck and chew (candy; like children or older toothless people).
mutu ber- *rendah* inferior.
mutung to sulk, pout, nurse a grievance.
muyeg action-filled.

muzakarah exchange of thoughts (,views
,ideas).
muzawir escort for Moslem pilgrims.

N

n - *gelung* ŋ. - *tilde* ñ.
na - *lu, - lu!* (children's language) I had
you there!
nabatah (s.) ALAM (NABATAH).
nabi - *Zulkifli* Ezekiel.
nabrak.nabrak to look for money here
and there.
nada pe-an intonation. - *menaik* rising
pitch. - *menurun* falling pitch.
nafas ber-kan to be infused with.
nafsu ber- to be eager to. - *alami* natural
instinct. - *besar, tenaga kecil (,kurang)*
the spirit is willing, but the flesh is
weak. - *makan bertambah kurang* to
have no appetite. - *merusak* spirit of
destruction, vandalism. - *yg tak*
tertahan unbridled (,unrestrained)
passion.
naga *rakyat - merah* 'red dragon people,'
i.e. the PRC Chinese.
nagari Minangkabau village community;
(S.) NEGERI.
nah lu serves you right!
nahas inauspicious, foredoomed to
misfortune.
Nahdijjin and **Nahdlijjèn** *ummat (,warga)*
- the members of the *NU* party.
nahi abstinence.
naib (Moslem) government religious
official empowered to legitimize
and register marriages.
naif *cita.cita yg* **di-kan** ideals which
could not possibly be reached.
naik - *melompat turun terjun* pride goes
before a fall. *Pesawat Concorde itu*
di-i *oleh anggota.anggota MEE menuju*
Eropa, The Concorde was boarded by
members of the European Economic
Community bound for Europe. **me-**.
turunkan to load and unload. **pe-:** ~

bis bus passenger. ~ *mobil* motorist.
~ *sepeda* cyclist. ~ *sepedamotor*
motorcyclist. - *banding* to lodge an
appeal. - *cetak* to go to press (newspaper). - *dok* to go into drydock, be
(dry)docked. - *kaki* on foot. - *kapal*
to board (a ship). - *nilai* agio, premium.
- *omprengan* to hire a car collectively
for economy. - *pan* to get angry. -
perkara to lodge an appeal. - *pesawat*
(terbang) to board a plane, enplane.
- *pitam* to get angry, fly into a rage.
- *suara* to raise o's voice. - *takhta* to
mount (,ascend) the throne. - *tinggi*
to fly (in drug world). - *turun* 1 to
fluctuate. 2 *kepalanya - turun* he
nodded.
naitklab night club.
najik diamond (in card games).
nakal ke-an delinquency. ~ *remaja*
juvenile delinquency.
nak(h)oda di-i to be captained by.
nalar 1 consideration, reason(ing power).
2 idea, notion. 3 (common) sense.
4 matter, issue. **pe-an** reasoning.
-.*wajar* common sense.
Nalo [Nasional Lotere] National Lottery;
a full ticket consists of six or seven
digits and can be bought officially;
(cp.) BUNTUT.
naloka [betina lokal] (in the Asahan
Regency, northern Sumatra) a domes-
tically raised chicken.
naluriah instinctive.
nama me-kan *diri(nya)* so-called, self-
styled. -.*akhir* last name. *Sophia*
Scicolone yg kemudian merubah
-.*akhirnya jadi Loren...,* Sophia
Scicolone who later changed her last
name to Loren... - *besar* (in the

when circumambulating the *Kaabah.*
MX [Mandrax] (s.) MANDRAX.

Minahasa) family (,last) name. - *kaum* family name. - *muka* first (,Christian) name. - *sepuh* adult name. - *tje.tje.an* Dutch diminutive names, such as, Mientje, Saartje, etc. - *turunan* family name, surname.

nambor 1 (of towns, cities, etc.) name-sign. 2 (affixed to door) name- (,door-) plate.

namnam fruit tree (L. Cynometra cauliflora) the fruit of which grows on the stem and which when stewed, tastes like stewed pears.

nampak to appear, come into sight. -*nya* apparently, evidently. ~ *tdk ada*... it looks like there is no...

namun - *begitu* nevertheless.

nanak.nunuk to walk to and fro like a blind person looking and groping for s.t.; also, for instance, to find a way out.

nanar 1 bewildered. 2 dazed.

nanas - *belanda (,seberang ,tali)* agave.

nangka *orang makan -, awak kena getahnya* pull the chestnuts out of the fire for another.

nangkring 1 to be a wallflower. 2 to sit, squat.

nang.ning.nong (,.nung) *bahasa* - the Indonesian language. *masyarakat* - the Indonesian community.

nanti 1 later (in the day). *Bagaimana -?* Let's see how things are a little closer to the time. - *malam* and *malam* - (later) this evening, tonight. - *petang (,sore)* and *petang (,sore)* - (later) this afternoon. *bulan Nopember* - next November. *Itu perkara (,urusan) -,* That's a matter for later concern. *Sampai -(lah),* Till later, OK? *di hari* - and -.- later, in the future. 2 or else, otherwise. *Awas - jatuh!* Take care or else you'll fall! *N- dulu, blm ada tempo!* O. moment please, I've no time yet! *tak* - will never. *Pasukan Itali tak - mampu utk membendung invasi Sekutu,* The Italian forces would never be able to dam up the Allied invasion. *pd suatu waktu* -

(referring to the future) o. day. -*nya* afterwards, later.

nanting to sound out a person, approach a person (with a view to his accepting the office).

Nanyang Southern Sea, i.e. the South China Sea.

napak (s.) TAPAK.

napal edible marl. *batu* - k.o. hard marl. - *kapur* lime marl.

napas *kasi dia - dulu!* (coll.) give him a little breathing space (,time) first! *menarik - (panjang)* to breathe deeply. - *(tinggal) satu.satu, - tinggal separo. separo* and -*nya satu dua* to be dying, be at death's door. **ber-*lega*** relieved.

napi [nara pidana] convict.

Napoli Naples.

nara man, person, human being. - *praja* government official.

narkotika narcotics, drugs.

narwastu (spike)nard oil.

nas text.

nasabah customer, client. - *bank* bank customer (,depositor).

Nasakom di.-kan to be 'Nasakom'-ized.

Nasakomis supporter of the *Nasakom*.

Nasakomisasi 'Nasakom'-ization.

Nasakom.phobi *Nasakom*-phobia.

nasi I - *sdh (men) jadi bubur* what is done cannot be undone; it is no use crying over spilt milk. - *dan lauk. pauknya* the Indonesian *rijsttafel.* - *gudeg* rice, young jackfruit prepared with coconut milk and served with chicken curry. - *liwet* 1 rice cooked until it has absorbed all the water placed in the pan with it. 2 (outside Central Java) rice cooked in coconut milk. - *putih* plain (,white ,steamed) rice. - *uduk* rice cooked with coconut cream.

nasi II nation.

nasib ber- *baik* to have good luck. **se-.sepenanggungan** sharing o.a.'s trials. -.-*an* haphazardly. -*nya sedang terang* he has luck.

nasihat *tak masuk* - to be pigheaded, be

opinionated. *memberi* - to advise. **pe-**advisory. ~ *politik* political adviser. ~ *perkawinan* marriage counselor.

nasion nation.

naskah - *pilem* scenario.

Natal pertaining to the birth of Jesus Christ. *pd hari* - at Christmas. **ber.-(an)** to celebrate Christmas. **-an** 1 to celebrate Christmas. 2 Christmas celebration.

natijah 1 alternative. 2 conclusion. 3 results, consequences, aftermath.

natirlek of course.

natura (in) kind. *pembayaran dlm* - payment in kind.

naudu billahi, naudzubillah, na'uzu billahi and **nauzu billahi (min zalik)** we ask protection from God (against that matter), i.e. an expression uttered on seeing s.t. horrible. *bau durian yg naudzubillah harumnya* the smell of the *durian* fruit which is damned fragrant.

naung ber- *di bawah* to be affiliated with. **me-i** to overshadow.... *di bawah* **-nya** and its affiliated...

nautika *Dinas N-* Nautical Service.

navigator navigator (of Air Force).

nawala.patra 1 letter, writing. 2 deed, instrument.

Nawalapradata name of a book of laws in the Jav. Sultanates of Yogyakarta and Surakarta.

nayaga player in *debus* performance.

nayaka councillor (of the State).

N.B. [nota bene] note well, take notice.

ndak (s.) ENDAK.

ndara (s.) NDORO. - *mas* appellation used for a son of the Sultan of Yogyakarta from o. of the *garwas*.

ndhuk girl (vocative).

nDolalak art form peculiar to the Purworejo regency.

ndoro 1 Mr., Sir. 2 Mrs., Madam. - *kang-jeng* the *bupati*.

ndoro.isme obedience, submissiveness.

ndremilnil (s.) DERMIMIL.

né mother.

nèbèng 1 to hitchhike, freeload. 2 to live at the expense of others.

nebus weteng a joint (religious) meal in commemoration of the fact that an expectant mother is 7 months pregnant.

nèces (S.) NECIS.

Néderlan(d) Holland, the Netherlands.

Néfo(s) [New Emerging Force(s)] The New Emerging Forces.

negara 'The State' in the sense of 'the government of a country.' - *adalah saya* l'état c'est moi, I'm the State. *wanita.* *wanita* **se-nya** her (fellow-) country-women. *N-.- As* the Axis Powers (during World War II). - *asal* country of origin. - *bebek* satellite state. - *beriklim tropis* a tropical country. *N- Gajah Putih* Thailand. - *gundal* satellite state. - *hukum* a constitutional state. *N- Indonesia Timur* the State of East Indonesia; this entity was established by the Dutch in 1946 and eventually constituted as a state of the United States of Indonesia (1949-1950). - *kepulauan* archipelagic state, island country. *N- Kesatuan Kalimantan Utara* the Unitary State of North Kalimantan, i.e. Sabah (under President Soekarno). *N- Kesatuan Republik Indonesia* the Unitary Republic of Indonesia. - *konco* satellite state. -.- *Nefo(s)* the Newly Emerging Nations. -.- *non.blok* the non-aligned countries. -.- *Oldefo(s)* the Old Established Nations. - *palu.arit* a communist country. - *penampung pertama* first-asylum country (i.e. a nation which initially receives Indochinese refugees; the first-asylum countries are: Thailand, Malaysia, Indonesia, Singapore, the Philippines and Japan). - *pengekor* satellite state. -.- *Poros* the Axis Powers (during World War II). -.- *raksasa* the super powers. - *republik apartheid* Verwoerd's South Africa. - *sakura* Japan. - *satelit* satellite state. - *sejahtera* welfare state. - *serikat* confederated state (Geneva). -.- *Skandinavia* the Scandinavian countries. - *Stars and Stripes* the United States of America.

- *suapan* satellite state. - *super* super
state. -.- *ter(ke)belakang* underdeveloped countries. - *terkunci daratan* and
- *tdk (,tak) berpantai laut* a landlocked
country. -.- *Timur Tengah* the Middle
East countries. - *tirai bambu* the Peoples Republic of China. - *tirai batik*
the Republic of Indonesia. - *tirai besi*
Soviet Union. - *tujuan* country of
destination. -.- *yg baru tumbuh* the
newly emerging countries. -.- *yg cinta
damai* peace-loving nations. -.- *yg
kurang maju* the underdeveloped
countries. -.- *yg sedang berkembang
(,tumbuh)* the developing countries.
-.- *yg sdh maju* the developed nations.
- *yg suka berperang* a warlike country.
- *yg terkunci dan tdk berpantai* a landlocked country.

negeri the village community of the
Minangkabau, i.e. a cluster of *kampungs. di - awak* in o's own country.
di - orang abroad, in a foreign country.
pergi ke - to leave for the Netherlands
(referring to Dutchmen). - *Belanda* the
Netherlands, Holland. - *di atas angin*
1 (originally) Arabia, Persia and India.
2 (extended meaning) Europe. - *dingin
(,kincir)* the Netherlands, Holland.
- *Hang Tuah* Malaysia. - *Kuda Semberani* North Korea. - *leluhur* country of
origin (of a person). - *Mabuhai* Philippines. - *Sakura (,matahari terbit)*
Japan. - *Sirikit* Thailand.

négosi negotiation. **di-kan** to be
negotiated.

nek 1 sickening, nauseating, disgusting.
2 sick, queasy. *rasa -* vertigo, dizziness,
nausea.

nèkad 1 desperate, (act) of despair. 2 bold,
indifferent, careless, cool, confident.
3 obstinate, determined. 4 with
contempt for death. 5 irreconcilable,
implacable. 6 radical, drastic. 7 self-
willed, wayward, wilful. 8 naughty,
mischievous. *sdh - dan hilang malunya*
he is capable of anything, he will
stop at nothing.

néko -.- 1 various. 2 at will, as o. likes.

bertindak ~ to act at will.

Nékolim [Neokolonialis(me), Kolonia-
lis(me) dan Imperialis(me)] Neocolo-
nialist/m, Colonialist/m and Imperial-
ist/m.

nelayan ke-an fisherman's.

nelongso *serba -* deplorable, regrettable.

nèm young.

nem shortening of various female
names, such as, *Parsinem.*

nènèk 1 old woman. 2 granny, old thing.
ber- moyangkan to have...as o's
ancestors. - *kebayan* (in fairy tales)
chaperon. *si - loreng* (euph.) tiger.

nènèr young (freshly caught) bandeng
(L. Chanos chanos).

Nengah (in Bali) name element placed
before personal names to indicate
the second born child, such as, *I
Nengah Wedja;* (s.) MADE.

nèngnong bell.

néo. neo-.

néolitikum neolithic period.

néon *lampu -* neon light. **me-kan** to
neon-light.

népotisme nepotism.

neraca *membuat -* to draw up the balance
sheet. - *dagang aktif* a favorable trade
balance. - *pembayaran* payments
balance, balance of payment. - *percobaan* trial balance. - *perdagangan*
trade balance, balance of trade.

nerak sarak against the regulations.

nerimo (s.) NRIMO.

nétra eye (in compounds); (s.) TUNA
(NETRA).

nètral unaligned.

nètralis neutralist. *golongan -* the neutral-
ists (in Vietnam).

nètralisasi neutralization. - *Vietnam
Selatan* the neutralization of South
Vietnam.

nètron neutron. *bom -* neutron bomb.

Ngabè(h)i title for: (1) a middle-grade
official; (2) a man of lower nobility;
(3) a chief of police (in the rural areas).

Ngabektèn the occasion of showing
respect to older people by kissing the
knee at *Lebaran* day (in the *kraton*).

Ngabekti to show respect to older people by kissing the knee at *Lebaran* day (in the *kraton*).

ngabuburit to wait to break the fast.

ngadulag (s.) DULAG.

ngak.ngik.ngok *kebudayaan* - imperialist (,colonialist) culture. *musik* - rock-'n-roll music.

ngalong (s.) KALONG.

ngalor to go north. -.*ngidul* 1 (to differ) widely, immensely. 2 wild (stories). *sambil cerita* -.*ngidul* while telling wild stories, stories you can make neither head nor tail of.

ngana you.

ngandung (S.) MENGANDUNG.

ngangrang (S.) RANGRANG.

ngap.ngap(an) 1 tired, panting. 2 to gasp for breath.

ngarsa (pron. ngarso) in front; (s.) ARSO. *N- Dalem* His Highness (the Sultan of Yogyakarta).

ngawèsi (in Purwakarta) a cooperative system between a worker in a rice paddy and its landlord.

ngayap (s.) (NGE)LAYAP.

ngayau (in Kalimantan) headhunting.

ngebet 1 to hurt, ache, smart (of a wound). *bisul* - the abscess (,tumor) was aching. *Hati bang Kojan sdh empot. empotan* -, Kojan's heart was beating fiercely (so that it) hurt. 2 to long for. - *sama* to hanker after. *kalau cewek* - *sama cowok* if a girl hankers after a boy. *Banyak priya* - *ingin menemani saya*, Many men are keen on accompanying me. 3 horny, to be sexually frustrated. 4 tired of waiting. - *menyedot duit* to be out to hoard up money.

ngebluk to beat, whip (dough).

ngeboat and **ngebo'at** (s.) BOAT.

ngecoprak (s.) COPRAK.

ngeden to strain (during bowel movement), exert abdominal pressure.

Ngèksigondo (the former kingdom of) Mataram.

ngelangut far off, remote, desolate.

ngelentuk to nod, be very sleepy.

ngèlmu knowledge, usually esoteric. - *kadigdayan* knowledge of magical power (,supernatural invulnerability).

ngelonèng to get some fresh air.

ngemot to suck (,nibble) on. - *bombon karet* to hold a piece of chewing gum in o's mouth, suck (,nibble) on a piece of chewing gum.

ngenes 1 dejected, downcast, downhearted. 2 to pine, waste away (through grief). **me-kan** pitiable, sad.

ngèngèr 1 to serve (as a servant). 2 to live in with.

ngenggenjot (s.) GENJOT.

ngèngkèl to fight, quarrel.

ngenjot (s.) GENJOT.

ngèntot to fuck, screw; (s.) ENTOT.

ngenyèk to mock, ridicule, deride.

ngèpèt *babi* - a sneak thief (esp. at night).

ngepla 1 too much. 2 overdo.

ngepiah and **ngepie** sincere, open, upright.

ngèpot 1 to walk quickly looking straight ahead. 2 to screech around the corner (of car, motorcycle, etc.).

ngeran annoyed.

ngeres 1 annoying feeling in the eye. 2 to feel sad (,distressed). *bikin* - to sadden.

ngersa (pron. ngerso) (s.) NGARSA.

nges 1 sensitive, impressionable. 2 moved. 3 emotional. *kurang* - apathetic, stolid.

ngeslong not hold (of a car's brakes).

ngètngot accordion.

ngga(k) **yg** -.- 1 nonsense. 2 unmotivated (accusations). 3 impossible, foolish.

nggo cyak greedy for sex.

nggreges shivering. - *akibat suntikan* shivering due to an injection.

ngibing (teenage jargon heard in the Tanjung Priok port area in Jakarta) to look for goods which have fallen off trucks.

ngibrit (s.) KIBRIT.

ngikèu (in Bangka) outdated, antique (automobiles) (it comes from Chinese '29', referring to the outdated 1929-Chevrolet which is still running on the island).

ngikngik to languish, be ailing.

ngirab the last Wednesday in the month of *Safar;* (s.) RABU(WEKASAN).

ngiung.ngiung sound of motor.

ngkali (S.) BARANGKALI.

nglangut in the distance, far off.

nglomprot sloppy, untidy.

nglosot (s.) KLOSOT.

nglunjak insolent, impertinent.

ngluyur (s.) KLUYUR.

ngo I (personal pronoun).

ngok to collide.

ngoko the Jav. language level used towards friends, family and persons of lower social status.

ngongso.ongso *ia tdk ada rasa* - he is not ambitious.

ngorok *penyakit* - k.o. septicaemia, i.e. a cattle disease.

ngos.ngosan to breathe deeply, pant, gasp, be out of breath. *hidupnya* - he can't make ends meet.

ngot.ngotan irregularly.

ngowos to boast.

ngoyo to take the trouble to (do s.t.). -.- to go to a lot of trouble. *tdk usah* ~ you don't have to...

ngoyoworo to stray, get off the (beaten) track.

Ngr. [Ngurah] name element in Balinese names, such as, *I Gst. Ngr. Pinda.*

ngrèh (s.) REH.

ngremo welcoming dance.

ngrowa (s.) KAWIN (GANTUNG).

ngrowot (in Jav. mysticism) to eat only cassava all day.

ngubleg.ngubleg to meddle in. - *keamanan dlm negeri* to meddle in the internal security.

ngudang to speak to o's child while praising him and expressing hopes for a bright future.

ngukngik to be ailing.

ngulo (in South Sumatra) moonlighting.

nguncluk to walk fast without looking backward.

ngurek eel.

nguyung to walk with o's head bent (due to sorrows, fatigue, etc.).

Ni (in Bali) k.o. article to indicate a female person, precedes the proper name, e.g. *Ni Luh Putri, Ni Wayan Catri.*

nia she, a once proposed personal pronoun.

niaga ke-an (adj.) business. *bangsa* pe- a trading nation. *N- Ekasari* the women's association of the Department of Commerce and Cooperatives. -.*jasa* bureau. -.*Jasa perjalanan* travel bureau.

niagawan businessman.

niat - *hati* wish.

nifo (s.) NIVO.

nih 1 here (handing s.t. over, pointing at s.t., etc.). *Nyang manè, bang? N-, lu liat kagak?* Which o., buddy? Here, don't you see it? *Mau duit, nggak, -!* Here, do you want the money or not? 2 now. *Mau ke mana -?* Where are you going (now)?

nik term of address to young girl.

nikah - *bedol* wedding performed at home. - *gantung* (in advertisements) legally married but waiting for the appropriate opportunity to celebrate the marriage with the customary festivities.

Nikaragua Nicaragua.

nikel nickel. **per-an** (adj.) nickel.

nikmat pe- (art) lover. ~ *hidup* o. who enjoys life.

nikotin nicotine.

nilai pe- *(barang.barang modal)* appraiser. se- with a value of. - *ganti* replacement value.

ninèn (being) an old woman; (s.) KAKEN.

ningrat me-kan to ennoble, raise to the rank of nobleman, make s.o. a member of the nobility.

ninik.mamak village chief.

ninitowok and **ninitowong** female puppet (coconut shell head attached to a stick which is possessed).

nipis (s.) JERUK (NIPIS).

nir having no, free from, without. - *bentuk* amorphous. - *busana* without clothes. *orang - busana* nudist. - *gelar* nondegree. - *laba* nonprofit. *organisasi - laba* nonprofit organization. - *suara* voiceless.

Nirbaya place of detention for former government big shots and mil. brass who were involved in the communist-inspired September 30, 1965 Movement, located southwest of Jakarta, in the neighborhood of *Lubang Buaya.* Lately, political detainees accused of subversive activities were also held in this place.

nirlaka and **nirléka** prehistory.

nisan code name for marijuana.

nisbi ke-an relatively.

Nitya Cas Samapta (motto of the *AIR UD* Corps) Constantly Fully Prepared.

Niugini Papua-New Guinea, i.e. the eastern half of the island of New Guinea and the islands of New Britain, New Ireland, Manus and Bougainville.

nivo level.

niyaga the performers in a Jav. *gamelan* orchestra.

nJawani act like a Jav., in a Jav. manner.

njelèhi disgusting.

njlimet (to work, search) with the greatest attention; (s.) JELIMET.

njomplang imbalanced.

Nobèl *hadiah* - Nobel prize.

no cèng two thousand (rupiahs).

nodèk (in Medan) *tdk diambil* - not take notice of it, not heed it.

nok (vocative) young girl.

nol *murid kelas* - pupil of Kindergarten.

nominal nominal.

nomor ber- numbered. *kartu* ~ a numbered card. **me- duakan** to put in second place. **pe-an** numbering. - *atom* atomic number. - *bewès* licence number registration card. - *keluar* outside (telephone) line. - *kembar* two volumes of a magazine combined in o. volume. - *pemanggil* call number. - *perdana* premier issue (of a newly published magazine). - *tukar* (of a newspaper, magazine) exchange number. - *urut* serial number.

non I 1 non-. *kaum* - the non-cooperators, i.e. the so-called (Indonesian) republicans who did not work together with the Dutch during the Dutch-Indonesian clashes (between August 1945 and December 1949). **ber-kooperasi** to non-cooperate (with the Dutch). **me-.aktifkan** to put on inactive duty. **peng-.aktifan** inactivation. -.*agresi* nonaggression. -.*aktif* nonactive, i.e. not in active service. -.*intervensi asing* nonforeign intervention. -.*konvensionil* nonconventional. -.*kooperator* a non-cooperator; (s.) KAUM (NON). -.*kurikulèr* noncurricular. -.*militer* nonmilitary. -.*pemerintah* nongovernmental. -.*pri(bumi)* (s.) PRIBUMI. -.*reguler* irregular. *penerbangan* -.*reguler* irregular flights. -*stop* nonstop. -.*vaksentral* nonaffiliated (labor party). 2 (S.) BUKAN. *seorang* -.*mahasiswa* a person who is not a college student.

non II miss (to telephone operator).

nonè miss. *N- Jakartè* Miss Jakarta (in beauty contest).

nongkrong to lie idle; (s.) TONGKRONG.

nongol (s.) TONGOL.

noni 1 a Caucasian girl. 2 (loosely) a white girl. - *panggilan* call girl.

nonie - *Sulut* Miss North Celebes (in beauty contest); (cp.) NONE (JAKARTE).

nonok cunt.

nonton to watch (TV, movies, sports events, etc.). - *bioskop (,film)* to go to the movies. - *etalase toko* windowshopping.

nontoni a friendly meeting arranged in order that the future husband and wife can see e.o. and the two families can discuss particulars of the marriage.

nopèk two hundred (rupiahs).

norak hick, country-bumpkin.

norma -.- *hukum* legal norms (,standards).

normalisasi normalization. **me-kan** to normalize, standardize.

nostalgia nostalgia. **ber-** to be homesick.

not - *angka* numerical notations (in music). - *balok* staff, i.e. the five horizontal lines and four intermediate spaces on which music is written or printed.

nota - *beda pendapat* (s.) MINDER-
HEIDSNOTA.
nota béne note well, take notice.
notariat office of notary.
notaris - *perangkap* substitute notary
public.
notok -(an) corner.
notulen minutes (of a meeting, etc.),
minutes of proceedings. *membuat -*
to draw up the minutes.
notulis minute clerk.
nrawang (s.) TRAWANG.
nrecel dense (of population).
nrimo (s.) TRIMO.
nrimois adherent of the *nrimo* state of
mind.
nrocos (s.) CROCOS.
'ntar (s.) ENTAR.
NU [Nahdlatul.Ulama] 'Renascence of
Moslem Clergy,' i.e. the name of a
Moslem political party.
nuansa nuance.
nubuat prophecy. **ber-** to prophesy.
nuchter matter-of-fact.
nudis nudist. **ke-an** 1 nudism. 2 (adj.)
nudist. *masalah ~ di sepanjang pantai
Kuta* the nudist problem along Kuta
Beach (in Bali).
nugraha 1 mercy, favor. 2 gift (from o.
of higher position than the recipient).
nun - *jauh* (far) away.
nunak.nunuk (s.) NANAK.NUNUK.
nunut to freeload, get a lift (in a vehicle).
me-i to ask s.o. for a lift.
Nupiksa Yasa (a government) Research
Institute.
nusa *utk (,guna) - dan bangsa* for country
and nation. **me-kambangankan** to
deport s.o. to *Nusa Kambangan,* the
Indonesian Elba. *N- Ina* Ceram.
N- Kambangan name of an island off
Java's south coast, site of detainees
who participated in the abortive coup
of 1965.
Nusantara *bahasa.bahasa* - the regional
languages of the Republic of Indonesia.
nutfah 1 sperm, seed of life. 2 germ.
3 gene. *bank plasma* - germ plasm bank.

nutrisionis nutrionist.
nuwun - *sewu* 'thousandfold thanks.'
tanpa bilang - sewu without opening
o's mouth.
-nya 1 your. *Mobil- di mana?* Where's
your car? *Nama- siapa?* What's your
name? 2 how (exclamatory); (S.)
ALANGKAH . . . -NYA. *Bagus-!* How
nice! *Panas-!* How hot it is! 3 of.
panas- api the heat of the fire. 4 (ana-
phoric) the (aforementioned). *Sabun-
di mana?* Where's the soap? 5 the other
(of a pair or series) *yg satu- lagi* the
other (o.). *yg satu biru, satu- merah*
o. is blue, the other is red. 6 per, each,
a(n). *70 sen satu pon-* 70 cents a pound.
7 forms nouns out of verbs or adjec-
tives. *tinggi-* the height. *berat-* the
weight. *pergi-* (s.o.'s) going. *dilaksana-
kan-* the implementation (of it). 8 of
course, by all means. *Bisa- bisa, tapi
malas,* Of course he can do it; he is
just lazy. 9 the next following, the o.
that belongs to that day. *Minggu-* the
Sunday after, the following Sunday.
malam- the evening of that day.
nyadik addicted to.
nyadran I (s.) BERSIH (DESA).
nyadran II leading an ascetic religious
life denying o.s. food and sleep as a
self-sacrificial act in order that o's
desires be fulfilled.
nyah -lah! go away!
nyaho to know, be acquainted with,
understand. *Saya - bener,* I know for
sure.
nyai (older) woman of some social
standing. *N- Loro Kidul* the authority
controlling the Ind(ones)ian Ocean
around whom so many believe-it-or-not
stories are interwoven.
nyak (S.) IBU. *Babe dan N- Nolly* Mr.
and Mrs. Nolly (Tjokropranolo)
(Greater Jakarta's Governor).
nyala 1 in a blaze. 2 to be ablaze (of
house, etc.), be aflame. **ber-** alight,
ablaze. **ber-(.-)** 1 to inflame, kindle.
2 to catch fire. 3 to burn (with patriot-

ism). **me-kan** to turn on, switch on (the light, TV, etc.).

nyalang *matanya* - he has a sharp look.

nyalawadi mysterious. *orang yg* - a mysterious person.

nyalé a sea worm.

nyali ber- *besar* to be brave. *-nya gede* he is brave (,valiant). *- (nya) kecil* and *punya - kecil* to be afraid.

nyaman 1 agreeable. 2 pleasing. 3 comfortable. *Badannya kurang -,* He does not feel well. *bertambah -* to regain strength, recuperate (of a patient). *hati tak -* peevishly. *tdk - pikirannya* he is not in his right senses. **ke-an** comfort.

nyambi (s.) SAMBI.

nyamikan 1 snack, refreshments. 2 misstress.

nyamleng 1 enjoyable. 2 tasty.

nyampang.nyampang (just) in case, by chance.

nyamuk *- pers* newspaper reporter.

nyana *tdk di- tdk diduga* to be quite unexpected.

nyanyi pe-: ~ *jalan* street-singer. ~ *kabaret* cabaret singer. ~ *pop (,tenar)* pop singer. *-an* carol, chant. ~ *bersama* choir. ~ *fajar* aubade (opp. serenade). ~ *Natal* Christmas carol. ~ *rakyat* folksongs.

nyap.nyap 1 to talk confusedly. 2 to gripe (about), nag, scold. **ber-** to talk idly.

nyaring *dgn suara* - aloud.

nyata 1 (to attract attention) conspicuously. 2 heavy (losses, defeat, etc.). *keadaan yg* - the reality. *perhitungan yg* - real matter-of-fact plans, etc. *sebesar* - life-size. *aku dpt* **ke-an** I have noticed. **me-kan** 1 to indicate. 2 to notify, declare, display. 3 to reveal (in Christianity). 4 to express, state. 5 to say (thanks), show (respects). ~ *berlakunya jam malam* to impose a curfew. ~ *kembali* to reiterate. ~ *kesanggupannya* to promise. *Dia* ~ *kesanggupannya utk melaksanakan*

instruksi itu, He pledged himself to carry out the instruction. **per-an:** ~ *keadaan darurat perang* proclamation of martial law. ~ *pendapat* reasons given for o's vote (in politics). ~ *riwayat hidup* curriculum vitae. ~ *sarju (,simpati)* expression of sympathy. ~ *turut berdukacita* condolence. *-.-* 1 (to look at a person) keenly, (to look) straight (at). 2 obviously (influenced), publicly, openly. **ter-** it turned out that, turned out to.

nyawa *ada - ada rezeki* with time comes counsel; the future will look after itself. *hendak melepas -* to be dying. **ber-** animate. **takber-** inanimate. **berse-** to agree completely, see eye to eye.

nyawang (in Bali) cremation of effigy.

nyelekit to hurt o's feelings.

nyemek, nyemèk and **nyèmèk** *-.-* just right.

nyèntrik excentric. *kacamata* - excentric glasses.

nyenyep *tidur* - to be sound asleep, sleep soundly.

nyenyet still. *sepi* - deadly quiet.

Nyepi the Balinese New Year according to the *Saka* calendar (a day of absolute silence without light, work, traffic, etc.).

nyi (s.) NYAI.

nyilih 1 to borrow. 2 borrowing.

nyingnying the small, stinking housemouse.

nyinyir *orang tua* - an old bore.

nyok kiss. **di-** to be kissed.

nyolnyolan talkative.

Nyoman (in Bali) name element placed before personal names to indicate the third born child, such as, *Nyoman Sudi, Nyoman Munia.*

nyong I hi there!

nyong II *- Sulut* Mr. North Celebes (in beauty contest).

nyongsah *- ati* to tantalize s.o.

nyontèk to cheat on exams.

nyonya 1 wife (with reference to

Europeans and Chinese). 2 woman.
-*nya* his wife. *si* - 1 a type of *rambutan*.
2 reference to a goldfish species from

Cianjur (West Java).
nyungsung easily going into a trance.
nyureng to stare at.

O

o (s.) (E)NOL.
obat (teenager sl.) pot, marijuana. **ber-**:
~ *ke (,kpd) dokter* to be under a doctor's treatment, undergo medical treatment, call in (or, go to) a doctor.
~*lah hatinya* he was very pleased (to
hear or to see). **meng-kan** to send s.o.
for treatment. **peng-an**: ~ *ceplok*
treatment by cupping and sucking of a
cold or headache. ~ *dgn air kencing*
(in India) auto-urine therapy. ~ *(dgn)*
tusuk jarum and ~ *kyungkrak* accu-
puncture. *tdk* **ter-i** incurable. - *anti.*
biotika antibiotics. - *anti mabok kendaraan* anti-motion sickness pill. - *asah*
abrasive. - *aspirin* aspirin. - *cacing*
anthelmintic, deworming medicine.
- *demam* antipyretic. - *kejang* anti-
spasmodic. - *kuat* aphrodisiac. - *kuat*
badan restorative. - *lawan.asam* antacid.
- *mata* collyrium. - *nyamuk* mosquito
coil. - *pelawan serangga* insecticide.
-.- *pelindung tanaman* pesticides.
- *pemberantas hama* pesticide. - *pemusnah hama* antiseptic. - *penangkis*
prophylactic. - *pencahar* laxative,
aperient. - *pencegah kehamilan* contraceptive. - *pencuci perut* laxative,
aperient. - *penenang* tranquilizer.
- *pengelat* astringent. - *penghilang rasa
nyeri* sedative. - *penguat* corroborant.
- *penguat jantung* cardiac. - *penurun
demam (,panas)* antipyretic. - *perangsang* drug, dope. - *perangsang seks*
aphrodisiac. - *pereda nyeri* sedative.
- *sedingin* antipyretic. - *senapan*
ammunition. - *stimulansia* stimulants.
-.*telan kontraseptik* oral contraceptive.
- *tetes mata* eye lotion, collyrium.
obituari obituary.

oblok.oblok k.o. food made of leftovers.
obrak.abrik **meng-** to dismantle. **peng-an**
break-up.
obral *lebih murah dr* - dirt-cheap.
obras overcast, the sewing over an edge
with loose stitches so as to prevent
raveling. **meng-** to sew in such a way.
obrol **ding-kan** to be talked (,told) about.
tukang **ng-** chatterbox. **-an** bragging,
boasting.
obsèrvasi observation. **meng-** to observe.
obstétri obstetrics.
obyèk object for earning extra money
(by moonlighters). *Pembebasan film
Amerika kini banyak* **di-kan,** The
release of American films has currently
been made an object for earning extra
money (usually illegally). *Istana
Bogor* **di- pariwisatakan,** The Bogor
(Presidential) Palace has been made an
object for tourism (this is legal). **ng-**
1 to earn extra money by moonlighting
(usually, by acting as a middleman in a
sale). 2 to earn extra money by selling
at a profit o's own goods which were
bought at a bargain. 3 to commit
bureaucratic graft or corruption, e.g.
by renting out the house you are allowed
to live in because of your government
job. **(me)ng-kan** *arloji digital Sicura*
to sell a "Sicura" digital watch with the
idea to make a profit. **peng-an** using
s.t. to *'ngobyek.'* **-an** commercial
item s.o. sells as agent to earn extra
money. ~ *yg empuk* item which sells
readily in moonlighting.
ocèh *terlalu banyak* **ng-** *tapi sedikit yg
dikerjakan* much ado about nothing;
much cry and little wool.
odalan community prayer (by adherents

of the *Hindu Dharma* religion).

odeklonyo and **odekolonye** eau-de-cologne.

odènsi audience, a formal hearing.

oditif auditive.

oditur judge advocate. - *jenderal* judge advocate general. - *militer* mil. prosecutor. - *militer pengganti* alternate mil. prosecutor.

oditurat judge advocate's office.

odmilti [oditur militer tinggi] high mil. prosecutor.

odol toothpaste.

odolan retail.

odo.odo singing of the puppetmaster (in *wayang* performance).

ofisial an official (in sports).

ogah ke-an aversion. ~ *berubah* inertia.

ogé whore.

ojèk a bicycle (motorized or not) used as a *becak* by taking the passenger on the back seat. **peng-** an *ojek* driver.

ojèkwan (s.) PENGOJEK.

ojok.ojok to instigate, incite. **peng-** instigator.

OKB [Orang Kaya Baru] nouveau riche.

okol(.okolan) a wrestling match in which two opponents try to push e.o. back with outstretched arms.

oktan octane. **ber-:** *bensin yg ~ 94* 94-octane gas. *bahan bakar yg ~ tinggi* high-octane fuel.

oktroi charter.

okupasi occupation.

olah ber- capricious. **meng-.ulang** to recycle. **peng-an** processing, tilling. ~ *cerita* scenario. **-an.ulang** recycled (lubricants).

olahraga peng- sportsman.

olahwedar ber- *(dlm)* to be active (in).

olang.alik (adj.) commuter.

old and new **ber-** to celebrate New Year's Eve.

old-crack old hand at s.t.

Oldéfo(s) [Old Established Force(s)] Old Established Force(s).

olèh ber- to get, receive (implies passive reception by subject). **memper-** to get, acquire, obtain (implies active

effort on part of subject). **diper-** *dgn jalan tdk halal* ill-gotten. **per-an** acquisition, yield. -.- bribe.

oli(e) lubricating oil.

oli(e)man oiler.

oligarki oligarchy.

Olimpiade Olympics.

olrait all right.

om (s.) OOM.

oma 1 grandma. 2 old woman.

ombak - *yg kecil jangan diabaikan* a small leak will sink a big ship; small beginnings make great endings. **ber-** choppy. *Rambutnya ~ air,* His hair was waterwaved. *Rambutnya yg meng-lembut,* His softly wavy hair.

omong to speak (a language). *banyak -nya* he is talkative. *-nya lompat.lompat* he hops from twig to twig; he beats around the bush. **ber-.-** *kosong* to talk about o. thing and another. **meng-** to speak about s.t. **ng-.ng-** and -.- *(nih)* by the way, incidentally. **-an:** ~ *yg terloncat dr mulut begitu saja* a slip of the tongue. *jadi ~ orang* to be much talked of. *~nya ngaco* he blathered.

omprèng (thin) eating trough. **di-kan** 1 to be loaned out for illegal use (vehicles). *Bus kota itu ~ kpd supir lainnya,* The city buses have been loaned out to other drivers who were looking for extra income. 2 to be illegally used to carry paying passengers, freight. *Truk sampah ~ mengangkut kayu jati balokan,* A garbage truck was illegally used for the transporation of teak wood logs. **ng-** 1 to eat from a (tin) eating trough. 2 to taxi illicitly, i.e. drivers of both government and private cars transport passengers in cars they drive and keep the money they collect in fares. 3a to live like a parasite. 3b to benefit from s.t. without paying for it. **-an** passengers picked up clandestinely by a bus en route to a certain station. *truk ~* truck used to carry passengers illegally.

ompu highest honorary title for member

of Batak community.

omsèt and **omzèt** turnover, gross yield, the gross (in a business).

onani ber- to masturbate.

oncat to escape.

onclang di- to be fired (of office personnel).

oncom - *gejos oncom* mixed with shredded coconut from which the milk has been pressed.

oncor I bamboo torch.

oncor II -an irrigated. *bukan* ~ irregularly irrigated (rice paddies).

oncor III -.-an 1 to make a higher bid than, try to outbid. 2 competition, rivalry.

onderan (S.) KECAMATAN.

ondo k.o. sweet potato (sometimes poisonous).

onèng.onèng great-great-great grandchild.

onggrok di-kan to be left unattended to.

ongji 1 consent, permission. 2 passport.

ongkak timber truck without wheels.

ongkang.ongkang 1 to sit with the feet dangling. 2 (fig.) to take it easy, sitting and ordering people around.

ongklok (s.) KENTANG (ONGKLOK).

ongko (S.) ANGKA.

onkos - *administrasi* service charges, handling charges. - *eksplo(i)tasi* working expenses. - *inklaring* Customs fees.

onjèn fish(lure).

ontang.anting only (child).

ontong 1 maize crib. 2 counter for corn.

ontowacono dialogue.

ontran(.ontran) disturbances, riots.

ontslag (S.) ONSLAH.

oom (S.) OM.

opa grandpa.

opak cakes made from sticky rice flour.

opelèt the C-46 Dakota aircraft. - *kosong* (fig.) a girl who chases after men.

openkap mobil - a convertible (car).

oper meng-kan *bola* (in basketball) to pass the ball.

operasi 1 operation. **ber-** to operate. - *militer* mil. operation. 2 maneuver. - *politik* a political maneuver.

operasional operational.

operator operator. - *telepon* telephone operator.

operbelas overloaded, overcrowded (with passengers).

oplaag and **opla(a)h** 1 (of a book) number of copies printed. 2 (of periodical) circulation. **ber-** to have a circulation of (magazine, etc.).

oplèt (S.) OPELET.

opname hospitalization. **di-** *di rumah sakit* to be hospitalized, be sent to the hospital. **meng-** to take a picture (of).

opor chicken-and-coconut-milk preparation generally classified as a curry, but unlike most curries, *opor* comes out with a white sauce that clings to the meat without overwhelming the chicken taste.

oportunisme opportunism.

oposisi opposition.

Oppo (in the Minahasa, Northern Celebes) the ancestors of the Minahasan people.

opsèn surcharge, surtax.

opsèt di- to be stuffed (of animals).

Opstib [Operasi Tertib] Operation 'Order,' i.e. an anticorruption drive. **di.o-.kan** to be subjected to anticorruption measures taken in the framework of the above operation. **peng-.an** subjection to anticorruption measures taken in the framework of the above operation.

optimal and **optimum** optimum.

optimis ke-an optimism.

ora not. - *keduman* do not receive o's share. - *pantes* improper, undignified. - *tedas tapak paluné pandé* and - *tedas sisané gurindo* to be invulnerable to weapons.

orad [olah raga arus deras] shooting the rapids.

orang I 1 classifier. *tiga - perwira* three (army) officers. 2 people, they, we, you, o., a man. *dibuat - utk obat* made by people for medicine. 3 someone else's. *kucing -* a cat belonging to s.o., someone else's cat. *negeri -* not our country. 4 subordinate. *Mana -mu?* Where are your subordinates? *O- Pak*

Lurah blm datang, The village head's staff is not yet in. 5 (indicating an ethnic) - *Ambon (,Batak)* an Ambonese, a Batak. - *itu* 1 he. 2 they, those people. *menjadi* - to be(come) s.o., i.e. a person of consequence. *si* -, *bukan si mesin* reference to 'the man behind the gun.' **berse-** *diri* completely alone. **per-an** an individual. **perse-an** individualism. **se-**per head (,person). *tak ~ dua* (to have) more than two (children). *~ (pun) tak (ada yg), tdk ~ (pun), - tak ada ~ juga* and *tdk ~ juga* nobody, no o. *~ (saja)* 1 to be alone. 2 (to say to) o.s. *yg ~ lagi* the other o. **sese-** and **se-.-** 1 s.o. or other. 2 per head (,person). 3 individual. **sese-:** *~ dokter* 1 a doctor (speaker knows him, but hearer doesn't). 2 this doctor (coll. English). *~ yg bernama Jackson* a Mr. Jackson. **-nya** 1 the person in question (or, under consideration), he, she. *O~ cantik,* She was pretty. *O~ bagaimana? Gemuk pakai kacamata,* What's he like? He's fat and wears glasses. *O~ tdk ada,* 1 (on the telephone) He (,she ,the person in question) is not at home [(or,) is not in (the office ,etc.)] . 2 That (historical) character (,figure) has never really existed. *bukan ~* not the man for. *Apakah gadis ini memang ada ~? Memang ada.* Does this girl (i.e. the subject of a painting) really exist? Yes, indeed. *~ cuma se- juga* and *~ yg se- itu juga* (it's o. and) the same person. 2 the k.o. person to. *Saya ~ tdk mau percaya begitu saja,* I'm the k.o. person who doesn't easily believe things. *-.-an* scarecrow. - *baik.baik* respectable people. - *bumi* native. - *dalam* insider. - *dip* [displaced Indonesian person] o. who was taken out of Indonesia by the Jap. during World War II. - *gedongan* the well-to-do. *-hina.dina* humble, poor people. - *hulu* country bumpkin. - *kaya baru* (s.) OKB. - *kecil* the ordinary people. - *kelinci* bunny (of Playboy Club). - *kepercayaan* confidant. - *lama* old

timer. - *makan gaji* a wage earner. - *makhluk* genie, spirit. - *nomor 2* the second man. - *pidak pedarakan* the downtrodden. - *sangiang* (in Palangka Raya) *dukun* for spirits.

orang II (by analogy to Jav. *wong*) since (the reason is), because. *Mana dpt membayar, - blm gajian,* How can I pay, since I haven't received my salary yet.

orang III (implies surprise since you can't understand the situation) *O- sdh besar kok masih nangis!* You're already a big boy and yet you're still crying! *O- mobil begini kok bagus!* You call such a car a nice car?

Orba 1 [Orde Baru] the New Order. 2 [ora bayar] (he) doesn't pay (whispered by man-in-the-street when army man is not paying his fare on public means of transportation). **mengo-kan** to impose the New Order upon. **peng. -an** imposition of the New Order. *~ (,peng.Orde Baru.an) aparatur Departemen Dalam Negeri* the orchestration of the apparatus of the Department of the Interior with the New Order.

orbit ber- to be in orbit. **meng-** to orbit.

orde order. *O- Baru* the New Order (after September 1965). *O- Lama* the Old Order (before September 1965).

ordening planning, regulation.

ordonansi ordinance.

orèt sketch, design.

Organda [Organisasi Gabungan Angkutan Darat] Organization of Land Transportation Unions.

organisasi ke-an and **peng-an** organizational. **ter-** organized. - *mantel* front (,cover) organization. - *perjanjian* treaty organization. - *perusahaan sejenis* guild. - *seazas* subsidiary organization (of political party).

organisir *kejahatan yg* **ter-** organized crime.

orièntalis orientalist.

orièntasi - *pd program* program oriented. **ber-** to have an orientation. **ber-(kan)** *kpd* to be oriented towards.

orisinil ke-an originality.

orkès - *filharmoni* philharmonic orchestra. - *simfoni* symphony orchestra.
ormas [organisasi massa] mass organization. ke-an mass organization system.
ornitologi ornithology.
orok infant in arms.
oro.oro open space, meadow.
orsidé (s.) KEMBANG (ORSIDE).
Ortodoks Orthodox. *Gereja* - Orthodox
Church.
osaka (in South Tapanuli, Sumatra) a
4-wheel push cart, 2 meters long and
1 meter wide, with a steering gear at
the rear end.
oséanografi oceanography. *sarjana* -
oceanographer.
osing *orang* - a native of Balambangan
(Banyuwangi, East Java).
oskultasi auscultation.
otak - *udang lu!* you stupid! *memutar
(,memecahkan)* - to rack o's brains.
-an psychopath. - *(benak)* brain(s).
- *besar* cerebrum. - *kecil* cerebellum.
- *kera* monkey brains (considered by
Chinese to be an aphrodisiac).
oté.oté undressed.
otèng.otèng lady-bird.
otobiografi autobiography.
otogén autogenous.
otoklaf autoclave.
otokrasi autocracy.

otokritik self-criticism.
Otoman Ottoman.
otomat meng-kan to automatize.
- *minuman* vending machine for
beverages.
otomatik automatic.
otomatisasi meng-kan to automate.
otonom autonomous. ke-an autonomy.
otonomi ber- autonomous.
otorisasi authorization.
otorita authority.
otoritèt and otoritéit authority.
otot - *kawat balung wesi* and - *kawat
tulang besi* as strong as steel, hard as
nails. ng- *lawan* ng- to want to have the
last word.
overkompènsasi overcompensation.
overproduksi overproduction.
overste lieutenant colonel.
overzak to pour (Cibinong cement) from
its original bag into a (Gresik cement)
bag (in order to increase the selling
price; k.o. fraud); (S.) OPERSAK.
owé I.
oyan black Chinese painting powder.
oyo -.- (s.) NGOYO(.NGOYO).
oyod period in which the rice plant
ripens; about 6 months.
oyok ng-.ng- *waktu* to race against time.
oyot *kena* - *mimang* vexed by invisible
creatures.

P

pabila -*pun tdk* never.
pabrik mill, plant, works. di-kan to be
manufactured, be fabricated. *rumah yg
bahannya sdh* ~ *lebih dulu* a prefab
house. pem-an manufacturing. ~ *sabun*
soap manufacturing. - *cetak uang* (coll.)
The Mint. - *kertas koran* newsprint
factory. - *pemaduan* assembly plant.
- *pemasak minyak* oil refinery. - *pemasangan (mobil)* (automobile) assembly plant. - *tempat memasang (mesin)*
assembly plant.
pabrikan manufacturer.

pacal.kerical lowest of the low.
pacar *Dia memang tipe perempuan yg
pantas utk* di-i *semata.mata,* She's
indeed the type of woman suitable to
merely flirt with.
pacek ber- to mate (of male animal).
sapi pem- stud bull. pem-an mating.
paceklik *th.th* - the lean years.
pacu -an *kuda* horse racing. - *jantung*
pacemaker (for heart).
pada (marks plural subjects) (they)
all...
padah *(emas)* -an*nya* he had to pay

dear(ly) for it.

padam I putting out (a light, fire, etc.).
pem-an *[(aliran) listrik]* electric power
outage, blackout. -.-**nya**: *takkan* ~
will never extinguish. *usaha yg tak* ~
unwearyingly on the go.

padam II *merah* - fiery red (of face).

padan ber-an *dgn* commensurate with.

padang *lain* - *lain belalangnya, lain lubuk
lain ikannya* so many countries, so
many customs. - *peternakan* ranch.

padarakan (s.) PEDARAKAN.

padat ke-an *daya.tampung* congestion (in
harbors). **mem-i** to cram, pack s.t. (with
s.t.). ~ *ruangan dansa* to crowd the
dance hall. **mem-kan** *kantongnya* to
line o's pockets. - *berisi* plump. - *karya*
labor intensive. - *modal* capital intensive.

paderi *perang* - (1821-1837) the war
between the orthodox Moslems and
the upholders of *adat* law on Sumatra's
west coast (backed by the Dutch).

padi paddy, rice in the husk. - *segenggam
(dgn senang hati), lebih baik drpd -
selumbung (dgn bersusah hati)* a bird
in the hand is worth two in the bush.
-.-**an** cereals. - *basah* wet stalk paddy.
- *dalam* late-bearing paddy. - *genjah*
early-bearing paddy. - *jero* late-bearing
paddy. - *kering* dry stalk paddy.
- *ladang* stalk paddy from shifting
fire-farming. - *PB.5* and - *PB.8* so-
called miracle rice. - *rendeng(an)* rice
grown during the rainy season. - *sawah*
stalk paddy from wet cultivation.
P- Sentra Paddy Centers (established
in 1961).

Padjadjaran (the pre-1972 orthography is
retained here) a university in Bandung
(West Java).

padu *kalau cinta* **ber-** if love is recipro-
cated. **ke-an** firmness. **keter-an** unity.
mem- *kasih* to love and be loved. **pem-**
gambar (film) editor. **pem-an** *gambar*
(film) editing. **ter-** integrated. *pende-
katan* ~ integrated approach. -**an** 1 mixture, mixing, blending. 2 coordination.
3 combination. 4 alloy.

padudan 1 opiumpipe. 2 (any foreign-
made tobacco) pipe.

paduka *P- Tuan* His Excellency (past
title for governor, resident, etc.).

paès make-up.

pagar - *makan padi (,tanaman)* 1 to
nourish a viper in o's bosom. 2 the
expenses surpass the proceeds. **ber-**
betis cordoned off. *P- Ayu* 'Charming
Fence,' i.e. the name given by the
man-in-the-street to the charming
young girls who comprised the *Bhin-
neka Tunggal Ika* Front and had
protocol duties (under President
Soekarno). - *batas* demarcation fence.
- *dek* (ship's) deck railing. - *desa*
village guard (,militia). - *hidup* hedge
consisting of growing plants. - *tutup*
demarcation fence.

pagelaran (s.) GELAR II.

pagi *terlampau* - and **ke-an** (fig.)
premature. -.- (fig.) at the very outset,
early on.

pagon 1 unchanged. 2 lasting, durable.

pagupon dovecot.

paguyuban association, club, union,
party. - *kulawarga* family union.
P- Widiyani (,Widyani) Civitas Aca-
demica.

pahalawati heroine.

paham 1 (difference of) opinion. *menurut
(,pd)* - *saya* in my opinion. *angan lalu* -
tertumbuk 1 almost helpless. 2 when it
comes to the point nothing happens.
3 - *dlm* to be well-versed in (this
subject). *Dia* - *dlm bahasa Indonesia,*
He knows Indonesian. *Saya sendiri
tdk berapa* - *akan perkara itu,* I myself
do not understand this matter very
much. *kurang* - ignorance. *kurang* -
akan don't understand. 4 -ism.
- *demokrasi borjuis* liberalism. - *hidup
berdampingan secara damai* peaceful
coexistence. - *(serba) naskah* concep-
tualism.

pahang to smell offensive.

pahat pem- *(patung)* carver, sculptor.
- *alur* anvil (,bolt) chisel. - *gerek buntu*
blind plain chisel.

paheman organization, association.

Pahing the second day of the five-day week.

pahit I 1 black (coffee). 2 gin. - *getir* (to experience) the advantages and disadvantages (of s.t.), (to know) all the perils (of s.t.). *-nya modernisasi* the agonies of modernization. *-.manisnya* (s.) PAHIT(.GETIRNYA).

pahlawan mem-kan *mereka yg masih bernafas* to honor those still alive as heroes. *P- Islam dan Kemerdekaan* Hero of Islam and Independence, i.e. a title conferred upon President Soekarno by the Afro-Asian Islamic Conference (May 1964). - *kebenaran* martyr. - *tak.kenal.takut* the intrepid hero.

paido 1 fussy, quarrelsome. 2 hard to please.

pail -an famine.

pailit ke-an bankruptcy.

Paing (s.) PAHING.

Pajajaran the last medieval Hindu kingdom in West Java.

pajak ke-an fiscal system. - *bangsa asing* foreigners tax. - *candu* public opium den, opium farm. - *dividen dan tantieme* tax on dividends and bonuses. - *gadai* pawnshop. - *jalan* road tax (,toll). - *kepala* capitation tax. - *keuntungan perang* wartime profits tax. - *meterai* stamp duty. - *negeri* government tax. - *pendapatan* income tax. - *penggunaan jalan* road use tax, toll. - *peralihan* transitional tax. - *perponding* ground tax. - *perseorangan* capitation tax. - *perusahaan* enterprise tax. - *potong (hewan)* slaughter tax. - *rumah tangga* household property tax. - *tonggak* tax on electric poles. -.- *yg berdaftar* assessed taxes. -.- *yg tdk berdaftar* non-assessed taxes.

pajar - *buta* still pitchdark. - *menyingsing* day is breaking (,dawning). - *sidik* about 04:00 in the morning.

paju angle. ber- angular. *bintang* ~ *lima* 5-pointed star (,medal).

pak I -dé 1 grandfather. 2 'Big Daddy' (= President Soekarno).

pak II *uang - dan uang lisensi* leases and licenses (money).

pak III penge-an packing, wrapping, packaging.

pakai - *baju safari* wearing (,in) a short-sleeved dress jacket. - *apa?* 1 by what means of transportation? 2 what's in it? *tdk - gula* without sugar, unsweetened. *sekali* - single use. **ber-an**: ~ *hawa* nude. *polisi yg* ~ *preman* a plain-clothes policeman. **di-**: *tdk* ~ in abeyance. *tdk dpt* ~ *lagi* unusable, useless. **di-kan** to be dressed in s.t. (by s.o. else). *Ia* ~ *pakaian penganten,* He was dressed in groom's clothing. **mem-i** to dress s.o. **pem-**: ~ *jalan* road user. ~ *jasa angkutan laut* shipper. *spy* **ter-** serviceable. **-an** apparel, attire. ~*nya diseterika licin lagi rapi* he was dressed spick and span. ~ *atas* outer wear (,garments). ~ *bebas* casual dress. ~ *biasa* everyday dress. ~ *dinas harian* (mil.) daily uniform. ~ *dinas upacara* (mil.) dress uniform. ~*.jadi* ready-made clothes. ~ *korvé* fatigue uniform, fatigues. ~ *lapangan* (mil.) battle dress, green battle fatigues. ~ *lengkap* coat and tie. ~ *loreng* (mil.) camouflaged uniform. ~ *malam* evening dress. ~ *mandi* swim suit. ~ *preman* civilian clothes. -.*buang* dispensable.

pakar expert. - *bahasa* language expert.

pakaryan 1 (art)work. 2 (handi)craft.

pakat kese-an agreement.

Pakem [Pengawas Aliran dan Kepercayaan dalam Masyarakat] Committee for the Supervision of Trends and Beliefs in Society.

pakèt package. **di-kan** to be made into a (tour) package. - *dgn ketentuan harga tanggungan* insured parcel (in post office). *P- Kelistrikan Desa* Rural Electrification Package. - *turis* tour package.

pakéwuh (s.) EWUH.

pakihang (among some Kalimantan people) small bottles filled with a special k.o. oil that has previously been given magical power.

paking gasket. - *asbes* asbestos gasket.

pakis various k.o. ferns. - *aji* various k.o.
tree ferns.

pakpung I cigarette containing morphine.

Pak Pung II brand name of a well-known
peppermint oil against colds and other
diseases.

paksa *menjalankan - thd* to bring pressure
to bear upon. **keter-an** coercion.
terlalu. **mem-kan**.*diri* overstrain. **ter-**
has no choice but to, to be certain to.
*Dia ~ meninggal dunia setelah kepala-
nya ditembus peluru,* Death was inevitable since the bullet penetrated his skull.
-an *badan* (in notarial instruments)
imprisonment for debt.

Paksebali (s.) GALUNGAN.

paksi - *jangkar* capstan.

pakta - *militer* military pact. - *non.agresi*
nonaggression pact.

paku pip on army uniform (for rank
below second lieutenant). **ber-** *kpd* to
adhere to. - *Belanda* obstinate. *P-buana,
P-buwana* and *P- Buwana (,Buwono)*
name of each Sunan of Surakarta.
- *jembat* rivet. - *mati* a nail not to be
extracted. - *payung* thumbtack.

Pakuan center of the *Pajajaran* kingdom
in West Java at the beginning of the
16th century.

pakusarakan *semangat -* patriotism.

pala I nutmeg (L. Myristica fragrans).

pala II se-.- *mandi biar basah, se-.- basah,
biarlah mandi benar* and *se-.- berdawat
biar hitam* in for a penny, in for a
pound; may as well he hung for a
sheep as a lamb.

palagan battlefield.

palamarta merciful, good-natured, kind.

palang crossbeam joist. *Kakinya* **di-** *dr
belakang,* He was tripped. **ke-.merahan**
(adj.) Red Cross. -.- *jalan* 1 roadblock.
2 level-crossing barrier (of railroad).
P- Merah (Internasional) (International)
Red Cross. - *pintu* crossbar with which
in older Indonesian houses the doors
are reinforced from the inside during
the night. - *roda* wheel axle.

Palapa Indonesia's first communication
satellite (July 8, 1976).

palatal (in phonetics) palatal.

palawija (s.) POLOWIJO.

palé to work on s.t. to change it, transform. **di-** *menjadi* to be metamorphosed
into.

palélé (s.) PAPALELE.

palèn trade(r) in small wares. *toko -*
hardware store.

paléolitikum the paleolithic period.

paléontologi palaeontology.

palèt a (painter's) pallet.

paling I most, -est (used in superlatives).
- *kecil (,mahal)* smallest (,most expensive). - *kanan (,kiri)* far right (,left).
- *malam* not later than (in the evening).
- *sial* under the most adverse circumstances. - *tdk* 1 at least. 2 anyway,
anyhow. - *untung* at (the) best. **se-.-nya**
at most.

paling II **ber-**: ~ *dr* to abandon (o's
faith). ~ *haluan (,pendirian)* to switch
to another subject. ~ *tadah* to abandon
o's faith. **mem-kan** *percakapan
(,cakapnya)* to switch to another
subject.

Palma [(Ilmu) Pengetahuan Alam dan
Matematika] Natural Sciences and
Mathematics.

palsu **pem-** adulterator.

palung **-an** crib (of Jesus in the stable of
Bethlehem).

paméo adage.

pamèr **di-i** to be modelled (of clothing).
-an: ~ *busana* fashion show. ~ *kekuatan* show of force. ~ *makanan* food
festival. ~ *mode batik* batik fashion
show. ~ *(model) pakaian* fashion
show. ~ *sandang murah* inexpensive
clothing exhibit. ~ *tunggal* one-man
show.

pamis *(batu)* - pumice.

pamit - *pd,* **ber-an** *dgn (,kpd)* and **mem-i**
to say goodbye to.

pamong **ke.P-.Praja.an** (adj.) Civil Service.
- *desa* village officials, i.e. the executive
part of the village administration.

pamor 1 power, authority, influence.
2 glory, fame.

pampang **ter-** 1 striking, notable, 2 be

displayed, spread out.

pampas *kain* **-an** cloth sent to Indonesia as part of Japanese war reparations.

pamrih 1 ulterior motive. 2 self-seeking, selfish. *bekerja tanpa* - to work without ulterior motives. **ber-** to have the intention (,secondary motive).

pamungkas 1 latest, recent. 2 deadly, fatal. *senjata* - a lethal weapon.

pan- I comprising, embracing, or common to all or every, pan-. *P- Amerika* Pan-American. *P- Asia* Pan-Asian.

pan II (cooking) pan.

pan III indicates speaker's surprise that hearer doesn't know s.t.; (s.) KAPAN and KAN. *P- rumahnya di Jalan Madura?* His house is on Madura Street, isn't it?

pana ter- deeply moved.

panah ber- arrowy. **-an** archery. - *Amor* Cupid's arrows.

panakawan court-jesters.

Panama 1 Panama. 2 Panamanian.

panar 1 stunning, stupefying. 2 amazement, astonishment.

panas 1 enthusiastic, active. 2 tense (situation). *rumah* - (s.) RUMAH (ANGKER). *(sakit)* - (to have the) flu. **di-.embunkan** weather-beaten. **mem-.m-i** to instigate, incite. **pem-** *hati* hot-tempered, passionate. **pem-an** *(terlebih dahulu)* warming-up. -.- *tahi ayam* 'as hot as chicken droppings,' i.e. short-lived enthusiasm. - *berdenting (,men-denting ,terik)* broiling, sweltering. - *bumi* geothermal. - *dingin* 1 to be on pins and needles. 2 ups and downs. - *hati* angry, annoyed.

panasaran I disturbed, alarmed. 2 exasperated, annoyed.

panasaran II erroneous way, error.

panca *P- Azimat* (s.) (LIMA) AZIMAT. *P-Cinta* 'The Five Loves,' i.e. the educational policy adopted by the nonreligious and communist-oriented educational institutions (under President Soekarno). *P- Dharma Bhakti* 'The Five Devotional Missions' for university students. *P- Krida* 'The Five-

Point Working Program' of the First *Kabinet Pembangunan* (formed by President Soeharto on July 5, 1968). *-muka* multidimensional. *P-negara* the five nonaligned nations which sponsored the *Konperensi Afrika.Asia:* Indonesia, Ghana, India, the U.A.R. and Yugoslavia. *-rona* 1 of many colors. 2 gay, bright with colors. *P- Satya* 'The Five-Point Code of Honor' for government employees. **P-sila** and **P- Sila** 'The Five-Point Indonesian State Ideology,' comprising the following five principles: (1) *Ketu-hanan YME* Belief in the Only One God; (2) *Kemanusiaan yang adil dan beradab* Just and Civilized Humanitarianism; (3) *Persatuan Indonesia (Nasionalisme)* Indonesian Unity/Nationalism; (4) *Kerakyatan yang dipimpin oleh hikmah kebijaksanaan* Democracy led by wisdom born of consultation; (5) *Keadilan sosial bagi seluruh rakyat Indonesia* Social Justice for the entire Indonesian population. - *suara* cacophony (of sounds). *P-Tunggal* The Five-in-one Unit consisting of the five local-level leaders from the local government, the Army, Police, Public Prosecutor's Department and the National Front (1964). *P- Usaha* The Five Efforts,' i.e. a system used to provide agricultural guidance to the farmers at the initiative of the *Institut Pertanian Bogor. P- Wardhana* 'The Five Developments,' i.e. the educational system which laid down the five principles for primary education.

pancal mem- to press down on the pedal.

pancang *mesin* - pile driver. **pem-an** pile driving. *melakukan* ~ *tiang pertama* ground breaking. **-an:** ~ *kaki.pantai* beachhead. ~ *tonggak* 1 milestone. 2 landmark.

pancar di-kan *melalui televisi* to be televised. **-an** *mata* (bright) glance (,look) (of the eye). - *gas* jet (plane).

Pancasila (s.) PANCA SILA. **ber-** and **kep-an** Pancasila-based.

Pancasilais and **Pancasilawan** supporter of the *Pancasila.*

pancèn (in the Priangan area) (s.) JANGGOLAN.

pancing mem-: ~ *keheranan* to cause (,create) surprise. ~ *kesalahan* to split straws. ~ *minat* to arouse interest. **pem-** *ikan* angler, fisherman.

pandai specialist. **mem-kan** to make intelligent. - *bergaul* to have good manners. - *bersilat lidah* silver-tongued. - *hidup* 1 to know how to make both ends meet. 2 easy to get along with. - *membawa diri* and - *menegur orang* easy-going. - *pidato* eloquent. *segala* - *ia* and *ia* - *segala hal* he is well-rounded.

pandam I k.o. resin used for sticking a knife, etc. into its sheath.

pandam II - *pekuburan* cemetery.

pandam III a light.

pandang *keduanya saling tertumbuk* - their glances met. **ber-an**: *Mereka* ~. They looked at e.o. *pimpinan yg* ~ *jauh ke muka* a leadership with a far-sighted vision. **bersi-an** (s.) BERPAN-DANGAN. **di-** *kecil (,remeh ,tak penting)* count for little. **mem-:** ~ *bulu* to show partiality. ~ *enteng* to have a low opinion of. ~ *leceh* to think lightly of, belittle. ~ *rendah kpd* to look down upon. *tdk* ~ *lawan* to fear no o. **pem-an** *umum* (in Parliament) general debate. **-an**: *bangunan itu mempunyai* ~ *muka ke sebelah Utara* the building faces north. ~ *kemudian* afterthought. *jatuh cinta pd* ~ *pertama* to fall in love at first sight. ~ *tajam menusuk sumsum* a sharp, piercing (,penetrating) look. - *dengar* audiovisual.

Pandawa the five brothers of the *Mahab(h)arata* epic.

pandéga 1 master (in s.t.), adept. 2 a *Pramuka* of the age bracket 21-25 years.

pandir ber-.- *diri* to play ignorant, pretend ignorance.

Pandit Ratu the ideal Jav. ruler.

pandom 1 compass needle. 2 compass.

pandrong (s.) KELUYU PANDRONG.

pandu ke-an pilotage. *K*~ *Bahari* Sailing Directions. **mem-i** to guide. *Turis itu memisahkan diri dr rombongan yg* **di-i** *penduduk setempat,* The tourists detached themselves from the group guided by local inhabitants. **pem-** guide (the person). - *pariwisata [,wisata(wan)]* tourist guide. - *putri* girl scout. - *wreda* former scout (reference to older people).

panèl panel. *diskusi* - panel discussion.

panèlis panelist.

panembrana and **panembrono** 1 anthem. 2 choir.

panèn to be booming, be doing well financially. *cepat* - quick-yielding. **mem-** being harvested. **memp-i** to harvest. **-an** heyday, boom.

panèwu assistant district chief (in Yogyakarta and Surakarta).

pangèran - *pati* Crown Prince.

panggang barbecued. *jauh* - *dr api* completely off center, wrong. *terlampau* - *jadi angus* pride goes before a fall. *bagai kucing dgn* - set the cat to watch the cream. - *ayam* and *ayam* - barbecued chicken. - *kambing* and *kambing* - barbecued goat.

panggih mem-kan to confront (bride and groom).

panggil di- to be addressed. **mem-** *pulang* to recall (an ambassador, etc.). **pem-** caller. **pem-an** summons (to registration, etc.). ~ *dinas tentara* recruitment. *merasa* **ter-** *utk...* to feel called on to... **-an**: *tdk terima* ~ (on signboards in front of the residence of medical doctors) no house calls made. *sdh* ~ *darahnya* it is in o's blood. ~ *suci* sacred mission.

panggorga Batak carver.

panggul coxa. **mem-** 1 to bear, shoulder. ~ *senjata* to bear arms. 2 to accept (responsibilities).

panggung m- to appear on the stage.

pangkal ber-: ~ *pd* 1 to originate from, have its roots in. 2 founded on, based on. ~ *tolak dr* to have o's starting point at... *seorang perantara yg* **ber-kan** *Lon-*

don a London-based broker. **m-** to stay temporarily at a certain place to work, trade, harvest, wait for passengers, etc. **-an** (mil.) base. ~ *angkatan laut (,udara)* naval (,air) base. ~ *bambu* selling place for bamboo. ~ *dagang* site where o. or more persons carry out trade. ~ *kayu* timber depot. ~ *roket* rocket base. ~ *taksi* taxicab stand. - *fikiran (,pikiran)* underlying idea, fundamental supposition.

pangkat - *kapten (,nakhoda)* captaincy, captainship.

pangkèk to be lynched. **mem-** to lynch.

pangkèng (S.) PANGKING.

pangku *M- Negara* and *M-negara* title of a ruling Jav. prince with a special area *(Mangkunegaran)* independent of the *Susuhunan* of Surakarta. *m-* *temanten* taking the bride and groom on o's lap as part of the wedding ceremony. **pem-** *kehutanan* forest ranger. **pem-an** *jabatan* installation in an office.

panglima - *pangkalan* harbor master, port officer.

panglong lumber mill.

pangrèh (s.) REH. - *praja* civil servant.

pangrukti maintenance.

pangsi k.o. black silk.

pangur tooth file. **di-** to be evenly filed (of teeth).

panik 1 panic-stricken. 2 panicky.

paniki bat (the animal).

panitera Ke-an 1 Registrar's Office. 2 Record Office. *P- Fakultas* (of university department) Registrar. - *pengganti* alternate Court registrar.

paniterama (s.) PANITRAMA.

panitia di-i to be taken care of by a committee. *P- Angket* Committee (,Board) of Inquiry. - *bersama* joint committee. - *kerja* 1 working committee. 2 permanent committee. - *kecil* subcommittee. *P- Koordinasi Bantuan Luar Negeri* Coordinating Committee for Foreign Aid. - *pelaksana* executive committee. - *pembantu* relief committee. - *pengarah* steering committee.

P- Penyelidik Persiapan Kemerdekaan Independence Preparations Investigation Committee (March 1, 1945). - *penolong* relief committee. - *perumus* steering committee. *P- Sensor* Censorship Board.

panitrama [panit(e)ra utama] chief secretary.

panjak *gamelan* player, member of *lenong* folk-play.

panjang *hendak - terlalu patah* pride goes before a fall. *waktu lebih* - more time. - *tdk* - medium length. **ber-** *kalam* to expatiate. **ber-.-** too long, tedious. *tdk perlu* **diper-** *lagi* needs no further argument. **mem-kan:** ~ *leher* to crane. ~ *rambutnya* to let o's hair grow long. **mem-.m-kan** *tempo* to gain time. **se-** in so far as. ~ *hari* all day. ~ *hidupnya* all his life. ~ *masa (,waktu)* always, continually. ~ *umur zaman* for many years to come. -.- too long, long-winded, tedious. - *bulat* oblong. - *jalan* the distance (to be covered). - *mata* lewd, lascivious. - *tangan* 1 to finger everything, cannot let things alone. 2 like to steal.

panjat di- *kaya* to become rich overnight. **mem-kan** *syukur* to say a prayer of thanks.

panji I a title among the descendants of a sovereign, prince, etc.

Panji II name of the legendary prince of Janggala or Kahuripan.

panjunan I potterymaker.

panjunan II and **panjonan** brothel.

pankréas pancreas.

panorama panorama.

panser armored (troops).

pantai 1 coast. 2 coastal zone.

pantang ber-: ~ *dilawan [,(k)alah]* invincible. *Ia* ~ *kelintasan,* He is (the) cock of the walk. *sebelum ajal* ~ *mati* nobody dies before his time. ~ *patah di tengah* to persevere, press on, see it through. ~ *surut* adamant. *Itulah* **ke-an** *saya,* That's s.t. I never do. *tak pernah* **mem-** *lawan* to shrink from nobody. **mem-kan** to abstain from

(smoking, due to asthma, etc.). **-an**
makan diet, regimen. - *berubah* invariable, unchangeable. - *dibantah*
pigheaded, opinionated. - *kerendahan*
1 high-spirited. 2 do not want to be
surpassed. - *mengalah* heroic. - *patah
di tengah* persevering. - *surut* adamant.

pantar se-an *dgn* of the same age as.

pantas appropriate, adequate. **-(an)**! no
wonder!

pantat 1 ass. *angkat - dr sini* (coll.) to
get out of here. **mem-** *getah* (coll.)
to work o's ass off. 2 vulva. - *kuning*
1 miser, scrooge. 2 miserly, stingy.
- *mabuk* drunkard.

panti *P- Asuhan* Social Welfare Organization. - *cukur* barbershop. *-karya* workshop. - *pengetahuan umum* university
extension class(es). *P- Perwira* Officers
Mess. *P- Pijat* Massage Parlor. *P- Wreda
(,Werdha)* Senior Citizens Home, Old
Age Home.

panting particle which precedes a verb or
adjective and gives it a plural meaning.
*Anak.anak sdh - nguyek di tegalan
depan rumah Gatet,* The children were
swarming everywhere on the lawn of
Gatet's house.

pantok (to have reached) the end.
seorang pelajar yg blm - sekolahnya
a dropout.

pantomin pantomine.

pantul (s.) TEMBAKAN. **-an** backlash,
recoil.

pantun *Apa - tuan?* What is your rebuttal
(,rejoinder) (to the accusation)?
Keadaan perkara ini mesti balik -,
The plaintiff certainly will become the
accused.

panu skin disease causing light-colored
blemishes.

panunggalan (s.) MANUNGGAL.

panunggaling association, club, union.

panutan leader, guide.

panyecep present, gift (usually in the
form of money).

papa *P- Boot* sobriquet for President
Soeharto during his visit to Timor
Timur (ex Portuguese Timor) in

July 1978.

papacang fiancé(e).

papain papain, an enzyme found in
papaya.

papalélé (in the Southern Celebes)
middleman (in fish-collecting centers,
for cattle, etc.).

papan kem-an complacency. **m-** 1 to find
the right place, fit. 2 to occupy a place.
3 to take the attitude (,posture) of. 4
established. *kaum* ~ the establishment.
Ia jadi orang ~ *dgn keangkuhannya,*
He became a person self-complacent in
his arrogance. **pem-an** *(dgn)* adaptation
(to), fitting in (with). - *beroda* skateboard. - *dam* checkerboard. - *lapis* plywood. - *luncur* skateboard. - *mèrek*
signboard. - *nama* name (,door) plate.
- *pelancar* surf-board. - *penempelan*
billboard. - *pengumuman* bulletin
board. - *perkenaan* target (for rifle
practice). - *reklame* advertising board.
- *seterika* ironing board.

papas ber-an *dgn* to pass e.o. (going in
opp. directions). *Mobil kami* ~ *dgn
sebuah mobil lain,* Our car passed
another car.

papatong dragonfly. - *ageung* helicopter.

papaya - *semangka* a very tasty red fleshed
papaya.

papi daddy.

papirus papyrus.

papras di- to be cut off, made smaller.

para I 1 - *hadirin* the audience, those who
attended. - *Hemingway* the
Hemingways. *banyak - peternak* a
great many poultry-farmers. 2 also used
to indicate the plural of organizations.
- *organisasi parpol dan golkar* the political party organizations and functional
groups.

para II paratrooper. **ke-an** (adj.) paratroop.

parade parade. **ber-** (mil.) to parade,
assemble in mil. formation for review.
- *udara* fly-pass.

paradoksal paradoxical.

Parahiyangan 1 name of the express
train between Jakarta and Bandung.
2 the West Java region.

para.ilmu jiwa para-psychology.
paramarta good, noble. **ber-** (s.) AMBEG
[PARAMARTA (,PARAMA ARTA)].
paramasasterawan grammarian.
paramèdik paramedic.
parampara political adviser.
parang classic pattern in the batiks
from Solo and Yogya. - *baris* and
- *rusak* k.o. batik designs.
paranti ancestral custom or institution.
paraplégia paraplegia.
parapsikologi parapsychology.
paras ber- *lumayan* good-looking.
parasitolog parasitologist.
parasitologi parasitology.
parasut parachute.
paré bitter melon (L. Momordica
charantia Linn.).
parèwa troublemaker.
pari I par value (of stocks). **ke-an** parity.
pari II *ikan* - ray, thornback.
pari III first word in compounds for
various k.o. rice.
Parijs (pron. ij as éy) Paris. - *van Java* the
city of Bandung (West Java).
parikan streetsong.
paring a gift from a higher in status to a
lower. *kemerdekaan* -*an* given
(,granted) independence.
paripurna 1 plenary (session). 2 finished.
3 corrected.
Paris Paris. -*nya Jawa* (s.) PARIJS (VAN
JAVA). -*nya Timur Tengah* Beirut.
Paris Club Group of Indonesia's main
noncommunist creditors who held
talks in Paris following the fall of
Soekarno about the handling of Indonesia's debts.
parit pem-an entrenchment. - *laut* sea
mine, depth charge. - *pengalir* drain.
- *pertahanan* defense trench.
paritèt parity.
pariwisata *obyek* - tourist attraction. **ber-**
to make a tour. **ke-an** 1 tourism. 2 (adj.)
tourist. **mengobyek.-kan** to make s.t.
into a tourist attraction.
parkir *juru* - parking lot attendant. *tempat*
- *(umum)* (public) parking lot (,space).
per-an (adj.) parking. *keadaan* ~ park-

ing conditions. **ter-** parked. *masalah*
-.**mem-** parking problem(s).
parkit parakeet.
parlemèn -.-**an** would-be parliament.
parmitu (in Medan) boozer.
paro half. **m-** 1 to divide into two. 2 to
cultivate (a field) based on métayage.
m-n sharecropped (field). *sistim* ~
system whereby the crop is divided
into two: o. portion for the landowner
and the other for the tiller. **menye-kan**
to divide in two (farm produce).
paron share cropping, métayage.
parpol [partai politik] political party.
ke-an party system.
parsiil partial. *integrasi* - partial integration.
partai I parcel, lot. *dlm* - *besar* in bulk.
partai II - *gurem* small party.
particuliere landerijen latifundia in possession of Chinese and Europeans.
partikel particle.
partikelir and **partikulir** (in notarial
instruments) private individual. **di-kan**
to be converted into a private enterprise (of State Trading Corporation,
etc.)
partisipan participant.
partisipasi participation. **ber-** to
participate.
parud (S.) PARUT. -**an** *kelapa* 1 coconut
grater. 2 grated coconut.
paruh se: ~ *harga* half price. ~ *umur*
middle-aged. **se-.-** *hati* halfhearted.
paruman *P- Agung* 1 Council of Balinese
Rulers. 2 the Balinese council consisting
of representatives from each *swapraja*.
P- Negara Advisory Council (in Bali).
pas I pass (document entitling o. to travel,
etc.). - *naik* boarding pass.
pas II it fits exactly, just (the) right
(amount). *harga* - fixed price. **memp-**
kan to equalize, put s.t. into line with
s.t. else. -.-**an** (to live) from hand to
mouth, on a shoestring.
pasah mem- to plane (wood, etc.).
pasak *besar* - *dr tiang* live beyond o's
income, have champaign tastes on a
beer budget.

pasal - *demi* - (in government regulations, etc.) article by article, clause by clause. *Itu lain* -, That's another question. *Apa - sampai Bandung ikut aturan Jakarta?* Why has it gotten to the point that Bandung is following Jakarta's regulations? *P-.- penutup* (in notarial instruments dealing with an Inc.) Closing articles.

pasang I ber-.- and se-.se- in couples.

pasang II di- 1 to be offered (for). *Sepeda perempuan ~ utk Rp. 25.000,* Lady's bicycles are offered for Rp. 25,000.00. 2 to be planted (of spies). **mem-:** *~ bicara ini.itu* to talk about nothing in particular. *~ geretan* to light a match. *~ harga tinggi* 1 to ask a high price. 2 to make great demands. *~ mata* 1 to make good use of o's eyes. 2 to watch, be on the watch. *Dia ~ warta berita pukul 23.00 di TV,* He turned on the 23:00 hour newscast on the television. **pem-**assembler. *~ adpertensi (,iklan)* advertiser. **pem-an** fitting. **-an:** *~ afiks* simulfix. *~ setarap* partnership. -.-**an** to place bets.

pasar se- o. Jav. five-day week. **-an** 1 market (usually fig.). *~ pembeli* buyer's market. 2 a day of the Jav. five-day week. - *induk* central distributing market for o. item. - *maling* thieves' market. - *serba ada* supermarket.

pasca post-. - *mati* post-mortem. - *panen* after-crop, after-harvest. - *sarjana* postgraduate.

paseran (in Yogya) dart.

pasfoto passport-size photograph.

pasièn - *jalan* out-patient.

pasif ke-an passivity.

pasih (S.) FASIH. **memper-kan** *lidah* to practice speaking (a language). **ke-an** *berkata.kata* eloquence.

pasin (S.) PASIEN.

pasinaon course (of study), institute of learning.

pasindèn (s.) SINDEN.

pasir *jatuh di (,ke) (padang)* - (his words) fall on deaf ears. **mem-** to silt up. **per-an**

(adj.) sand. - *awukir* hilly sand dune.

Pasisir the north coast of Java, esp. the area between Cirebon and Surabaya.

Pasopati 1 name of Arjuna's invincible magic arrow. 2 code name given by the *Gestapu/PKI* to the *Cakrabirawa* troops.

pasowan (in Yogyakarta and Surakarta) place of assembly, meeting place.

PasPal [(Ilmu) Pasti dan Pengetahuan Alam] the department of mathematics and natural sciences in a Senior High School.

paspor passport. - *dinas* service passport. - *diplomatik* diplomatic passport. - *konsuler* consular passport. - *non.pri (bumi)* (coll.) a passport belonging to a non-native-born Indonesian which needs screening by Immigration authorities. - *pri(bumi)* (coll.) a passport belonging to a native-born Indonesian which needs no screening by Immigration authorities.

pasrah - *bongkokan pd* to give in to.

pastèl I pastel, drawing chalk.

pastèl II a meat and vegetable pie.

pasti ke-an *hukum* legal security.

pastor and **pastur** Catholic priest (,minister). **ke-an** rectory, vicarage. **-an** (Roman Catholic) presbytery, priest's house.

pasukan unit in the *Pramuka* Boy Scout Movement consisting of four *regus:* 40 members. - *amfibi* amphibious troops. *P- Gerak Cepat Angkatan Udara* Air Commandos. - *jibaku* suicide squad. - *keamanan (setempat)* (local) security forces. - *kehormatan* honor guard. - *khusus* special forces. - *KKo* (also, - *KKO*) (Indonesian) marines. - *laba* armored troops. - *lintas udara* airborne troops. - *marinir A.S.* U.S. marines. - *payung (,para)* paratroops. - *pemeliharaan perdamaian* peace-keeping force. - *pemukul yg mobil* mobile striking forces. - *pendarat* landing troops. - *pengawal* guards. - *penyerbu* shock troops. - *perhubungan* signal troops. -.- *sekutu* allied forces. - *tempur* combat troops. - *terpilih* crack troops.

pasung a wooden block for a mentally retarded person, put on him in such a way that o. of his limbs, either leg or arm, is squeezed in it; this to prevent him from running away or damaging things. **mem-** 1 to put a mentally retarded person in a *pasung*. 2 to isolate. 3 to curb. **pem-an** 1 the putting of a mentally retarded person in a *pasung*. 2 isolation. 3 curb.

pat I (shortened form of *tempat*) - *tidur* bed.

pat II ber-.gulipat *dgn* to have an affair with. -(.-) *gulipat* 1 a children's game to which rhymes are sung. 2 corrupt conduct, fraudulent practices.

patah - *tumbuh hilang berganti* 'o. dies, another is born,' i.e. no o. is indispensable. *tak pernah - seterika celananya* his pants are never without pleats. **ber-** *arang* to break off with a person. -.- broken (use of a language). *Dia berkata dlm bahasa Inggeris* ~, He spoke in broken English. - *cinta (,hati)* brokenhearted. *tdk lekas-hati* adamant.

pataka banner, standard.

patang four.

patèn patent.

patfinder boy scout.

pathol (in Rembang, Central Java) a traditional fishermen's wrestling sport somewhat resembling Jap. sumo.

patih chief minister to a king.

patil antenna (of the *lele* fish, etc.).

pating particle which gives a plural effect to verbs: it precedes the verbal root which usually has an r or l in the second syllable or starts with o. of these letters: - *seliweran* cruising around (of many cars, etc.).

patirasa immune.

patner partner.

patok I 0.45 hectares.

patok II *harva* -**an** floor price. -.*tapal.batas* boundary marker, i.e. a pole to mark the frontier of a country.

patok III - *may* yellow-breasted sunbird. - *muda* brown-breasted sunbird.

patolog pathologist.

patologi pathology.

patorani a flying fish species (in the waters of eastern Indonesia).

patrap application. **pem-an** application.

patrasèli parsley.

patriot ke-an patriotism.

patriotisme patriotism.

patroli patrol. *P- Jalan Raya* Highway Patrol. *P- Lingkungan* (in Padang) Beat Patrol. - *penghubung* contact patrol.

patromak (s.) PETROMAK.

patron - *kosong* blank shells.

patuh loyal, dutiful. - *kpd undang.undang* law-abiding. **ber-** *kpd* to be loyal to. - *kebenaran* faithfully.

Patundu name of a South Celebes dance.

patung effigy. *membakar - Presiden* to burn the President in effigy. **mem-** like a statue. - *salib* crucifix.

patungan to do s.t. collectively and for that purpose each makes a contribution. *Para wartawan tlh - utk memberikan buket kpd Ibu Tien,* The journalists have put their money together to give a bouquet to Mrs. Tien (Soeharto).

patut suitable, appropriate. *tdk* - unfair, improper. *orang* -.- proper society. - *dipuji* praiseworthy.

pauhi abalone.

paut ber- *kpd* to hang onto a person's every word. *hatinya (,cintanya)* **ter-** *kpd* to be in love with.

pawai - *alegoris* allegorical procession. - *kesenjataan* show of force. - *mobil berhias* flower-bedecked parade (using floats).

pawang - *anjing* dog handler. - *hujan* k.o. sorcerer who claims to have the power to stop rain. - *hutan* bushranger.

pawiyatan 1 educational institution; (cp.) WIYATA. 2 school for shadow-play performances.

payah 1 severe (illness). 2 overworked. *tdk* -.-**nya** indefatigable.

payang seine net. **m-** to fish with a seine net.

payudara (woman's) breast. - *subalan* falsies.

payung *(ber)sedia - sebelum hujan* and *ber- sebelumnya hujan* prevention is better than cure. - *kekuatan nuklir* nuclear umbrella. - *pradan* the gilt umbrella (in the kraton of Yogyakarta).

(**padi**) **PB-5 dan PB-8** [(padi) Peta Baru 5 dan Peta Baru 8] high-yielding rice varieties known abroad as 'miracle rice;' they are crossbreds of Indonesia's *Peta* rice, Philippines' *tangkai rotan* and Taiwan's *Dee-geo-woo-gen*.

PBB di.-.kan to be brought up for discussion in the United Nations.

P.D. II [Perang Dunia II] World War II.

pecah *plastik yg tak bisa* - unbreakable plastic. - *sbg ratna* to be killed (in action). *mengalami - ban* to have a flat tire. **di-** *(menjadi) tiga* to be divided into three parts. **mem-**: ~ *kesunyian* to break the silence. ~ *masalah* problem solving. ~ *sepi* to break the silence. **pem-**: ~ *aksi mogok* strikebreaker. ~ *belah* the fissiparous tendency. ~ *masalah* problem solver. **pem-an** *atom* atom smashing. **per-an** a split. **ter-kan** solvable. **-an** denomination. ~.~ *Rp. 1, -- dan Rp. 2,50* denominations of Rp. 1.00 and Rp. 2.50. - *berderai* broken in scatters. - *kulit* husked rice. - *riak* breakers, surf.

pecak crossnet.

pecat pem-an: ~ *atas permintaan sendiri* dismissal at o's own request. ~ *dgn mendapat hak pensiun* dismissal with pension rights. ~ *dgn tdk hormat* dishonorable discharge. ~ *seketika* immediate dismissal.

Pecinan (s.) CINA.

pecuk I the common Eurasian, the Eurasian in the street.

pecuk II little black cormorant. - *padi* pygmy cormorant. - *ular* darter.

pecundang di-i (in sports) to be defeated.

peda salted and dry-smoked seafish: *kembung* or *layang* (a side dish).

pedanda (in Bali) a Hindu priest of the highest caste.

pedang - *pendek* cutlass.

pedarakan (s.) PIDAK (PEDARAKAN).

pedas acrid, acrimonious.

pedèt and **pedhèt** calf.

pedhotan pause in singing (by *waranggana*).

pédiatri pediatrics.

pedoman di-i to be guided by.

pedot broken (rope, etc.). -.- frequently broken off. *penerbitannya* ~ the publication was spasmodic.

peduli *saya tdk* - I'm indifferent, I don't care. - *amat* (s.o.) doesn't give a damn.

pé-èr (s.) P.R.

pegal ke-an stiffness.

pegang and **pègang** (coll.) **ber-**: ~ *(k)pd* to rely fully on, cling to. ~ *kpd haknya* to assert o's rights. ~ *teguh pd* to cling desperately (,firmly) to. **mem-** *setir* to drive (a car). **pem-**: ~ *arsip* archivist. ~ *hak manfaat* usufructuary. ~ *izin (,konsesi)* concessionaire. ~ *peluru* cartridge holder, clip. ~ *saham* stockholder. ~ *stir* driver. ~ *surat mandat* mandatory. **pem-an** *jabatan* tenure (of office). **buku -an** directory. - *batang* to be a full-fledged driver. - *pesawat* to fly a plane.

pegat -an *dgn* blocked off from.

pegawai clerk. **ke-an** (adj.) personnel. - *administrasi* clerical officer. - *bulanan* monthly wage earner. - *catatan sipil* registrar (of births, deaths and marriages), registration officer. - *darat* (in the shipping business) shore staff. - *duane* customs officer. - *kotapraja* municipal employee (,officer). - *menengah* middle-grade (government) employee. - *negeri* government employee; based on the explanation to Article 2 of *Undang.Undang No. 8 Tahun 1974 tentang Pokok.Pokok Kepegawaian* government employees shall include: (1) Civilian Government Employees and (2) Members of the Armed Forces of the Republic of Indonesia. The Civilian Government Employees are further divided into:

(a) Civilian Government Employees of the Central Government, (b) Civilian Government Employees of the Regional Governments, and (c) Other Civilian Government Employees determined by Government Regulation. - *pendaftaran warga* (s.) PEGAWAI (CATATAN SIPIL). - *PGPN* government employees. - *rendah* lower-level (government) employee. - *teras* key (,senior ,top) employee.

pegimanè (S.) BAGAIMANA.

pèh ill (,bad) luck.

pejal massive.

pejam *kami sukar* **mem-kan** *mata* we couldn't sleep a wink.

Pejambon a street in Jakarta, the location of the Foreign Office.

pejera the sighting bead of a gun.

pèk (s.) EMPEK.

pèka 1 sensitive, touchy. 2 response. - *thd* allergic to. **ke-an** 1 allergy. 2 responsiveness.

pekak **ber-.-** *diri* to pretend not to hear or to be deaf.

pekan *P- Raya* (Industrial) Fair.

pekasam a strong-smelling preserve of fish (,meat ,vegetables, etc.).

pekat **ke-an** density.

pekéwuh (s.) PAKEWUH.

pèktai (s.) PENYAKIT (PEKTAI).

pèl **memp-** and **nge-** to mop.

pelabi trick, ruse.

pelaga cardamom.

pelan **mem-kan** to reduce speed. *Saya -kan mobil saya,* I reduced the speed of my car. *Langkahku sengaja ku-kan,* I slowed up on purpose. *distel -.-* turned down low (of a radio).

pelanduk the smaller chevrotain (L. Tragulus kanchil). *mata* - a small shrub (L. Ardisia crenata). *(se)bagai - di dlm cerang* like a fish out of water.

pelantaran *anak raja* - child of a concubine.

pelat 1 automobile license plate. - *hitam* the black-colored license plate (for privately-owned cars). - *merah* the

red-colored license plate (for government-owned cars). 2 disk. 3 sheet. - *èser* sheet iron.

pelatnas [pemusatan latihan nasional] national training center. *Mereka* **di.-.kan** *di bawah asuhan Suwardi Arland,* They will be put in the national training center under the leadership of Suwardi Arland.

pelatuk woodpecker.

pèlbak refuse-bin (for public use).

péléh to separate (two people fighting).

pèlek wheelrim. *tutup* - hub cap.

Pelèkat name of the town of Pulicat on the coast of Coromandel (India's east coast), the place of origin of the *kain (,sarung)* - which has striped and checkered motifs.

pelepah (mid)rib (of palm-leaf). - *bawah luruh, - atas jangan gelak* he is a happy man that takes warning from another man's mistakes.

pelesiran dalliance.

pelesit a spirit controlled by a sorcerer to suck the blood of a person or eat a child's corpse.

pèlèt k.o. black magic. *dukun* - sorcerer, magician (who is only after money). *ilmu* - 1 knowledge of how to attract women. 2 means of getting women. *minyak* - love-oil, containing tears of the *ikan duyung* or manatee (to rouse love), toadyism. *tukang* - person who persuades another. **mem-** to bewitch, enchant.

pelihara **mem-:** ~ *bahasa Inggerisnya* to keep up o's English. ~ *kumis* to wear a mustache. **mem-kan:** ~ *dr bahaya* to save, rescue. ~ *dirinya* to mind o's p's and q's. ~ *hati* to respect, consider (s.o.'s feelings). ~ *nyawa* to save, rescue. ~ *pangkat* to live up to o's rank. ~ *perasaan* to respect, consider (s.o.'s feelings). **pem-** *lebah* apiarist. **pem-an:** ~ *khewan* animal husbandry. ~ *pohon* arboriculture.

pelik **ke-an** curiosity.

pelikan *(burung)* - pelican.

pelintat.pelintut devious.

pelipir - *jalan* sidewalk.
pelisir (S.) PELESIR. **-an** *ke* to take a trip to.
pelit ke-an stinginess. **-.-an** to pinch pennies. *Dia ~ spy dpt memborong oleh.oleh*, He is pinching pennies so that he can buy as many gifts as possible.
pelonco mem- to haze, initiate.
pelong bike fender.
pelopor ke-an (adj.) pioneer. *~ ABRI* ABRI's spearheading. **mem-i** to be a pioneer in.
pèlor - *melempem* a dud.
pélotaris hai-lai player.
peluang ber- to have an opportunity.
pelud [pelabuhan udara] airport.
peluh - *berpancaran* to be bathed in perspiration.
peluk ber-: ~ *lutut (,tubuh)* to do nothing, laze about. ~ *tangan* 1 with folded arms. 2 to do nothing. **mem-** *dada saja* to do nothing. **mem-kan (,mem-per-kan)** *(kedua belah) tangannya* to fold o's arms. - *dengkul* to do nothing. *tinggal - tangan saja* not willing to lift a finger.
pelupuk *tdk berani menegakkan - mata* afraid of turning up o's eyes.
pelur -an mortar.
peluru - *garis pertama* first-line ammunition. - *kendali antar.benua* intercontinental guided missile. - *kendali anti.balistik (,anti.peluru kendali)* antiballistic missile. - *kendali berbedorkan nuklir* nuclear warhead guided missile. - *kendali bumi.ke.udara* ground-to-air guided missile. - *kendali dr udara ke darat* air-to-ground guided missile. - *kendali nuklir* nuclear guided missile. - *kendali Polaris* Polaris guided missile. - *kendali udara.ke.udara* air-to-air guided missile. - *nyasar* a stray bullet. - *payar* cruise missile. - *suar* a flare. - *tajam* live ammunition.
pematang causeway.
Pembesrèv [Pemimpin Besar Revolusi] Great Leader of the Revolution (title conferred upon President Soekarno).

Pemda [Pemerintah Daerah] Regional Administration. **di.-kan** to be arranged by a Regional Administration.
Pemilu [Pemilihan Umum] General Elections.
péna - *isi* fountain pen. - *pemukul* firing pin. - *penyelamat* safety pin (of hand grenade).
penampan tray.
penat *membuang* - to take a break. *tak -.-nya* indefatigable.
penatu the laundry. **di-kan** to have s.t. laundered.
penca [penderita cacad] the physically handicapped.
pencak mem- *lidah* to debate, discuss. **(me)m-.m-** to jump on s.o., flare up at s.o.
pencar ber-(.-) to disperse.
pencèt mem- to squeeze. ~ *knop* to push a button.
pencil keter-an and **pem-an** isolation.
pèncong askant, awry.
péncut ke- *(k)pd* to fall in love with, be captivated (by), attracted (by).
pendak and **pendhak m-** to commemorate the first, second, etc. anniversary of a person's death. *memperingati ~ pisan* to commemorate the first anniversary of a person's death.
pendapa and **pendhapa** (pron. pendopo) open audience-hall at the front of the *Kabupaten*.
pendaringan a large bowl. - *kosong* broke, penniless.
Pendawa (s.) PANDAWA.
pendéga fisherman working for a *juragan*.
pèndèk - *kaji* in short. - *permintaan* will die soon.
pèndel shuttle.
Pendet (in Bali) the presentation of an offering in the form of a ritual dance.
pendéta *kaum* - the clergy. - *armada (,angkatan laut)* navy chaplain - *tentara* chaplain.
pending lady's belt.
Pendok [Penerimaan Dokumen] receipt of documents (in Customs office).
pengantèn ber- *baru* to honeymoon.

- *laki.laki* bridegroom. - *perempuan* bride. - *sunat* child who is to be circumcized.

pengap 1 airless. 2 tight in the chest, stifled.

pengaruh - *lingkungan* environmental influence. - *sampingan* side effects.

pèngèn to wish, desire.

penggulu second in age (of children).

penghulu 1 priest, in general. 2 title of head of mosque personnel. 3 government official appointed by the *bupati* to perform such duties as the supervision of marriages, divorces and inheritance. - *hakim* a *penghulu* acting as *wali* for marrying off women, in the absence of appropriate male nearest relatives. - *kawin* official uniting bride and groom in marriage. - *landrat* a *penghulu*, member of district joint court.

pengin (S.) KEPINGIN.

pengki a shallow, elliptically shaped bamboo basket with an open mouth used to carry dirt, sand, etc.

pèni code word among Jakarta bandits for *Tekab*-member.

peningset engagement present.

penisi Buginese proa with two mainmasts.

pénisilin penicillin.

penjuru ber- angular. ~ *lima* five-pointed.

pénologi penology.

pénoména phenomena. - *kebudayaan* cultural phenomena.

pènsiun *Ketika - turun, 25 th silam, tubuhnya masih kekar,* When he retired, 25 years ago, he was still sturdy. **mem-kan** to pension off. **pem-an** pensioning (off), retirement. - *janda* widow's pension.

pènstrèp penicillin-streptomycin.

pèntab [pendahuluan tahun ajaran baru] freshman orientation and hazing, college initiation.

pentang to bend, draw. - *gendéwa* to bend (,draw) the bow.

pentas theater. **pem-an** performance (on stage). ~ *hidup* live show.

penting berke-an: ~ *thd* to have an interest in. ~ *utk* to be interested in ...-ing. *Yg tdk ~ dilarang (,tdk boleh) masuk* (sign) Employees only; No unauthorized personnel. **ke-an:** ~ *kebendaan* material interest. ~ *yg tertanam* vested interest. *demi ~ umum* in the public interest.

pentolat.pentalit (s.) PLINTAT. PLINTUT.

pentung -an night stick, truncheon.

penuh charged (of battery). *sehari* - the whole day. - *dgn (,berisi ,oleh)* abound with. *berdiri* - *di belakang*... to stand fully behind... *berisi* - *dgn* fully loaded with. *disetor* - to be fully paid up, be paid up in full. *orang* - *naik turun* many people getting on and off (bus, train, etc.). *rakyat masih* - *di pekarangan* a dense crowd was still in the garden. *seorang apoteker yg bekerja* - a full-time pharmacist. **mem-i:** ~ *harapan* to come up to expectations. ~ *undangan* to accept an invitation. **mem-.sesaki** to pack to capacity. *dgn se- hati* with full attention. *dgn se-(.-) hati* heartily, with all o's heart, whole-heartedly. - *madet (,sarat)* chockfull.

penyang (in Kalimantan) little stones, pieces of wood, small bottles filled with magical oil, animal tusks, etc. worn around the waist or neck as a talisman.

pènyèt flattened (due to long use); (s.) PENCET.

pènyot dented, bashed in.

péot (s.) TUA (PEOT).

pepal coherence.

peparu lungs.

pepéling warning.

Peperda [Penguasa Perang Daerah] Regional Military Authority (composed of the Regional Head of the Civil Service, members of the Regional House of Representatives and the Regional Chief of Police, under the chairmanship of the regional commander).

pèpès - *ikan mas* gold fish roasted in

banana leaves; said to be an aphrodisiac.

pèpèt **ke-** broke, in a tight spot, in trouble, cornered, be pressed up against. *Orang yg ~ mau buang air hrs bersabar sampai ia tiba di rumahnya,* A person who is hard pressed (or, has to go to the bathroom) must be patient until he has come home. **m-** to be right on (top of).

pepètèk 1 a small seafish, salted and dried. 2 small-time. *pengusaha -* a small-time businessman (starting his business on sidewalks or by carrying his goods from house to house).

pèpton peptone.

pèr I fair, festival. *Jakarta P-* Jakarta Fair.

pèr II as of. *- 1 Juli* as of July 1.

per per, by. *satu - satu* one by one.

pera (s.) BERAS (PERA).

perabu (s.) PRABU.

perabut *- desa* village messenger.

peraga *Balai Pendidikan* **Ke-an** Teaching Aids Center. **pem-** mannequin, model.

peragawan male model.

peragawati **ke-an** (adj.) modeling. *soal ~* modeling matters.

perahu *menginjak dua -* to make the best of both worlds. *segan kayuh - hanyut* to miss o's chance. *- bandung* houseboat. *- golekan* medium-size sailboat. *- tarik* canal boat.

perai (S.) P(E)REI.

perak (s.) PERA.

peram **ber-** *di rumah (,dlm kamarnya)* to stay at home, stay in o's room. **mem-kan** *perasaannya* to hide o's feelings. **pem-an** fermentation.

perama (s.) RAMA.

peran role, part. **ber-** to play a role. *~ besar dlm* to play a great part in. **mem-i** to play a role. **pem-** player, actor. *~ utama* principal actor. **pem-an** acting. **-an:** *~ bertujuan* a purposeful role. *~ memimpin* a leading role. *~ utama* a principal role.

perang *P- tanpo Bala, Menang tanpo Ngasoraké* War without Troops, Victory without Defeat. **ber-** to wage war. *~ dingin* to wage a cold war. **pe-an** *kecil.*

kecilan hostilities. *- adu pintar* battle of wits. *- catur* war of words. *- dingin* cold war. *- meletihkan* war of attrition. *- panas* hot war. *- pijat knop* push-button war. *- sabil Allah* and *- fī sabilillahi* 1 Holy War. 2 the Aceh war against the Dutch. *- tanding artileri (,meriam)* artillery duel (,exchange). *- (urat) saraf* psywar.

perangah *duduk* **ter-** to sit in wonder.

perangai temperament. *lembut -* 1 softhearted, gentle. 2 pliant, submissive. **ber-** temperamental.

perangas.perongos quick to take offense, touchy.

perangko *tdk* **ber-** unstamped, postage due. *- berlangganan* prepaid postage.

peras **mem-:** *~ keringat* to toil. *~ otak* to rack o's brain. **pem-** blackmailer, extortionist. **pem-an** extortion, compression.

perasat (S.) FIRASAT and PIRASAT.

perawan inexperienced (of men, in the field of women). **di-i** 1 to be raped. 2 to be inaugurated. *- ting(ting)* a 'pure' virgin. *-.- tua* 'old virgins,' i.e. the three-wheeled motorized vehicles dating back to the years 1931-1933 and known by their brand names, such as, *Demmo, Masco* and *Masca.*

perbal a summons, subpoena; (s.) PROSES.PERBAL. **di-** to be ticketed (,tagged) (for a traffic violation).

percaya *boleh - tdkpun tak jadi apa* and *- boleh, tdk juga boleh* believe it or not. *- kpd diri sendiri* to rely on o.s. *lantas -, mudah - saja* and *main -* credulous(ly). **ke-an** creed. *~ (akan) diri sendiri* self-confidence. *orang ~* confidant. *memperoleh ~ yg tebal dr* to enjoy the full confidence of. **keter-an** reliability, credibility. **te-** bona fide. *tak ~* in bad faith.

percik **se-** *api* and **-an** *api* a spark. **-an** (fig.) a slice of the pie, a piece of the action.

percuma *tdk -* it is not for nothing that.

perdam.perdom **memp-** to curse roundly.

perdana maiden. *penerbangan* - maiden flight. *penerbitan* - first publication (of a book). *perjalanan* - maiden voyage. **di-kan** to be previewed (of a film). *- pertunjukan* gala performance, preview.

perdiping floor, story.

perdu base of tree-trunk. *pohon* - shrub. *tanaman* - shrubs, brushwood. **se-**clump.

perduli *Dia tdk - dgn saya,* He doesn't care for me. *tdk - thd* do not care for, pay no attention to. *tdk - apa(kah)* no matter whether. *tdk (meng)ambil -* to ignore, take no heed of. *- amat!* (I) could care less! (I) don't give a damn!

peréi I 1 free from service, school, work; off, on vacation. 2 set free.

peréi II broke, penniless.

peréi III (s.) PREI.

perèksa (S.) PERIKSA.

pèrèlèk grains of rice which have fallen out of holes in bags during transportation.

perempuan *- galak* an aggressive woman.

perenjak (s.) PRENJAK.

perètèl (s.) PRETEL.

peréwa adventurer.

pèrformansi performance.

pergandering meeting.

pergi 1 to go out, have gone out. 2 to pass away. *-!* go away! **ke-an***nya* his passing away. **mem-kan** to send away. *- berbelanja* to go shopping. *- ke darat* to go to Jakarta (used by inhabitants of nearby islands). *- kerja (,makan ,perang ,dll.)* to go to work (,eat ,war ,etc.). *- les* to take lessons (with, from). *- mandi* to go for a bath. *- mengikut* to go with, follow. *- menghindar* to run for safety, take to o's heels. *- ronda* to patrol (of police).

peri pem-an 1 description. 2 definition.

peria bitter melon (L. Momordica Charantia). *sdh tahu - pahit* to have learned from bitter experience.

perian *suaranya spt - pecah* he has a harsh (,grating) voice.

peridi prolific.

perihatin (s.) PRIHATIN.

perikeadilan justice. *citarasa* - sense of justice. *- pidana* criminal justice. *- politik* political justice. *- sosial* social justice.

perikemanusiaan *perbuatan di luar -* inhumane action. *tdk* **ber-** inhumane.

periksa *datang utk -* to come for a medical examination. *kurang -!* let me look into it! *Si anak itu sebaiknya* **di-kan** *pd seorang dokter anak.anak,* It's best that the child be examined by a pediatrician. **mem-kan** *(pd)* to send to s.o. to be examined. **pem-** auditor (for State finances). **pem-an**: *dlm* ~ under investigation. *guna menjalani* ~ in order to be investigated. ~ *buku.buku* audit. ~ *dgn sinar tembus* X-ray examination. ~ *pendahuluan* preliminary investigation. **ter-** the person under investigation, the investigated.

periksawan investigator, inspector.

perilaku behavior.

perimbon (s.) PRIMBON.

périmèter perimeter.

perimpèn well kept, put away carefully.

perinci m- to itemize, detail. **-an** *tugas* job description.

perintah to tell s.o. to do s.t. *atas* - by order of. **ke-an** (in the northern Celebes) government (as an institution). **pem-** the government, administration. *P~ Agung dan Badan.Badan P~ Tertinggi* Supreme Government and Highest Government Agencies. ~ *bayangan* shadow government. ~ *dlm pengasingan* government in exile. ~ *gotong.royong* 'mutual-aid government,' i.e. a national coalition government (as suggested by the now proscribed *PKI*). ~ *interim* caretaker government. ~ *konco* satellite government. ~ *mandiri* self-government. ~ *pelarian* government in exile. ~ *yg berkuasa di dlm negeri* home government. **pem-an** 1 government (as an institution). 2 the governmental system. *tokoh.tokoh di luar* ~ nongovernmental leaders (,figures).

- pembayar blanko a clean payment instruction. *- pembatalan* countermand. *- penegasan* confirmatory order. *- pengusiran* expulsion order. *- tembak di tempat* order to shoot on the spot.

perintis (referring to airlines) the flight schedule can be changed daily.

période pem-an periodization.

Periskatani, Periska Tani and **PERISKA TANI** [Persatuan Isteri Karyawan (Departemen) Pertanian] Association of the Department of Agriculture for Employees' Wives; the name means: To develop the welfare of farmer communities.

periuk *besar - besar keraknya* those that have plenty of butter can lay it on thick. *- mengumpat belanga* the pot calls the kettle black. *- api laut* sea mine. *- gandar* ball bearing.

Perjan [Perusahaan Negara Jawatan] Departmental Agency.

perjuta [perjuangan bersenjata] armed struggle.

perkakas 1 appliance(s). 2 materials. *- menulis* writing materials.

perkara affair, concern. *Ah, siapa bicara - mahal?* Ah, who's talking about expensive? *Habis -!* That's the end of it, no more problems! *dpt -* to become involved in a case. *Saya tahu duduknya -,* I know the ins and outs of the matter. *Letaknya - begini,* It's like this. **be-** *perdeo (,tanpa biaya)* to sue in forma pauperis, sue as a poor person. *kedua belah pihak yg* **ber-** the two litigating parties. *- bandingan* appeal case. *- dagang* business matter. *- pemerasan* extortion. *- sengketa* civil action.

perkasa brave and noble, high-spirited and daring. **ke-an** the might.

perkosa memp- to disgrace. **pem-** rapist. **-an** transgression.

perlu 1 compulsory, obligatory. 2 should. *P- kau ingat, bhw...,* You should remember that... 3 important. 4 it cannot be helped, it has got to be done. 5 urgently. *- akan (,dgn)* to require, need, want. *Beliau tdk -...,* He does

not have to ... *dan kalau -* and, if need be. *P- apa?* Why? *perabot rumah yg -.-* urgently needed furniture. **ke-an:** *guna (,utk) ~* ... in behalf of ..., for the sake of ... *~ bersama* common interest. *~ hidup (pokok)* (basic) necessities of life. *~ kantor* 1 stationery. 2 office equipment. *Saya ada ~ lain,* I have other things to attend to. **mem-kan** *datang ke...* to put o.s. to the trouble of coming to ... **-nya:** *tak ada ~* there is no point in that. *Apa ~?* Why? *dan benar. benar dirasakan ~, bhw* ... and the need is really felt that ... **se-nya** in as far as this is necessary. *yg* **se-.-nya** *saja* the most necessary, the barest necessities. *- ain* (in Islam) individual obligation. *- kifayah* (in Islam) collective obligation.

permadani *disambut dgn - merah* to be given the red carpet treatment. *- yg menutupi seluruh lantai (kamar)* wall-to-wall carpeting.

permak memp- sl. to fix, take care of. **pem-an** alteration (clothes).

pèrmanèn permanent. *Pasar Seni Rupa Ancol akan* **di-kan,** The Art Fair at Ancol will be given a permanent character.

permati critical.

permèn I *- karet* chewing gum. *- strong* strong peppermint.

Permèn II and **Per-Mèn** [Peraturan Menteri] Ministerial Regulation.

Permèsta [Perjuangan Semesta] Charter of Universal Struggle, signed by 51 local leaders of the Celebes demanding full autonomy for the four eastern provinces.

permil per mil.

permisi excuse me (for asking permission). *- dulu* good-bye now.

permosi 1 promotion. 2 salary increase.

pernah (family) relationship, kindred. **ke-** to be related to s.o. as (brother, nephew, etc.). *- paman* to be related to s.o. as nephew, have him as an uncle.

pèron platform (in railway station).

peropot (s.) PROPOT.

perosok memp-kan to plunge (into).

perponding (s.) PAJAK (PERPONDING).

Perpu [Peraturan Pemerintah Pengganti Undang.Undang] Government Regulation in lieu of Law (No. ...).

pèrs - *asing* the foreign press. - *delik* press offense. - *got* yellow press.

persada 1 platform, dais. 2 delightful place, beloved (fatherland). 3 center, rallying-point. *di* - on the altar of (the fatherland). - *tanah air* native country.

persasat 1 like, as. 2 as if, as though.

persekot di-in to have had sexual intercourse with s.o. before marriage. *Nonong sdh dia* **-in,** He has already had sexual intercourse with Nonong before being officially married.

persènan present.

persèntase percentage.

persèntasi (s.) PERSENTASE. *kalau dihitung secara* - proportionally.

Perséro [Perusahaan Negara Perseroan] Public/State Company.

Pèrsia Persia.

pèrsil premises.

Persit [Persatuan Isteri Tentara *(Kartika Chandra Kirana)*] Army Wive's Association.

persnèling *oper gigi* - to change gear. *pindah* - *ke rendah* to shift down. *tungket* - gear shift.

persona (S.) PESONA. **memp-** (S.) MEMPESONAKAN.

pèrsonalia 1 personnel. 2 personal notes.

pèrsona non grata and **pèrsona-non-grata** persona non grata. **memp-kan** to declare s.o. persona non grata.

pèrsonifikasi personification. **memp-kan** to personify.

pèrspèktif perspective.

pèrsuasi persuasion.

pertama *utk* - *kali(nya)* and (sometimes) *utk kali* - for the first time. **-.tama** above all. ∼ *di waktu pagi* first thing in the morning.

Pertamina [Perusahaan Negara Pertambangan Minyak dan Gas Bumi Nasional] National Oil Mining and Natural Gas Company, i.e. the State-owned oil company.

Pertiwi the women's association of the Department of the Interior.

perum I pem-an sounding.

Perum II [Perusahaan Negara Umum] Public Corporation. **mem.-.kan** to convert ... into a Public Corporation.

Perumisasi conversion into a *Perum*.

perut 1 abdomen. 2 middle (of the season). - *gembung* a swollen stomach (due to gas formation). - *kapal* a ship's hold. - *karet (,karung)* to be a glutton. - *memilin.milin* (to suffer from) gastric upset.

Perwalan [Persatuan Wanita Lembaga Administrasi Negara] Women's Association of the National Institute of Administration.

perwira ke-an 1 heroic. 2 officership. - *bawahan* junior officer (of merchant marine). - *bina rohani* chaplain. - *geladak* deck officer (of merchant marine). - *intelijen* intelligence officer. - *jabatan* professional officer. - *kamar mesin* engineroom officer (of merchant marine). - *kesehatan* medical officer. - *menengah* field-grade officer. - *penyerah perkara* officer who turns case over to Court when ready for trial. - *perbekalan* supply officer. - *pertama* first-grade officer. - *petugas* duty officer. - *piket* sergeant of the guard. - *provos* provost marshall. - *remaja* junior officer. - *satu* chief officer (of merchant marine). - *senior* senior officer. - *tinggi* general-grade officer.

pesan *habis* **di-** to be fully booked up (of hotel accommodation). **mem-** ... *agar* to instruct s.o. to ... **mem-kan** *hotel* to make hotel reservations. **pem-** booker (of film). *mengadakan* **pem-an** *60 kamar* to make a reservation for 60 rooms. **ter-** *habis* fully booked up, reserved.

pesangon severance, dismissal. *uang* - severance pay.

pesantrèn educational institution with a Moslem background where the students

live together in a compound of boarding houses; there are thousands of such
institutions in Indonesia, particularly
on the island of Java.

pesawat 1 appliance. 2 airplane. - *250*
extension 250. - *ambulan* ambulance
plane. - *amfibi* amphibious plane.
- *angkasa (luar)* spaceship. - *antariksa
yg bersenjata (,tak berawak)* armed
(,unmanned) space vehicle. - *becak* the
DC-3 aircraft. - *berbadan lebar* wide-
bodied plane. - *bermesin dua (,satu
,turbo.prop)* twin-engined (,single-
engined ,turboprop) aircraft. - *bermotor empat* four-engined aircraft.
- *bolak.balik antariksa* space shuttle.
- *cabang* extension (the device).
- *Capung* the Beachcraft (airplane).
- *capung dom* helicopter. - *darat air*
amphibious plane. - *foto* camera.
- *induk* command module. - *intai*
reconnaissance plane. - *jet* jet plane.
- *langsung* (of telephone) main
number. - *layang gantung* hangglider.
- *pelatih* training plane. - *pelempar
bom penyelundup* dive bomber.
- *pembom berawak (,selundup ,super-
sonik antarbenua ,tempur)* manned
(,dive ,supersonic intercontinental
,fighter) bomber. - *pencegat* intercep-
tor. - *pendarat* landing vehicle. - *pendarat di bln* lunar module, LEM.
- *pengintai* reconnaissance plane.
- *pengintai tanpa pengemudi* a pilot-
less reconnaissance aircraft. - *pengisap
debu* vacuum cleaner. - *penumpang
komersiil* commercial airliner. - *ruang
angkasa bolak.balik* space shuttle.
- *sayap putar* helicopter. - *sayap tunggal*
monoplane. - *Stol* Short take-off and
landing aircraft. - *supersonik serbaguna*
all-purpose supersonic aircraft. - *tak
berpilot* drone. - *telepon* telephone
(the instrument). - *televisi* television
set. - *tempur yg berpangkalan di
daratan* land-based fighter (plane).
- *terbang air* seaplane. - *terbang bermesin dobel* twin-engined aircraft.
- *terbang bersayap putar (,tetap)* rotary

(,fixed) winged aircraft. - *terbang
carter(an) (,pengangkut AS bermesin
4 ,pengintai ,penumpang)* charter
(,four-engined U.S. transport ,recon-
naissance ,passenger) plane. - *terbang
supersonik* supersonic aircraft. - *tilpon
pencètan* push-button telephone.
- *turbo.prop bermesin dua Antonov.24
buatan Uni Sovyet* a Russian-built
twin-engined Antonov 24 turboprop
plane.

pesemendan bridesmaids.

pèsèr *tdk se-* *buta* penniless.

pesing *bau* - smelling of urine.

pesisir beach.

pèsok sagging (of woman's breasts).

pèsta - *kawin* wedding party. - *pora*
bacchanal, orgy. - *taman* garden party.

pèstipal festival.

pèstisida pesticides.

pèstlubi [pesta luarbiasa] extraordinary
party.

pesut k.o. fresh water dolphin (found
in the Mahakam River of Eastern
Kalimantan; can also be trained like
the American dolphin) (L. Orcaella
brevirostris).

pet the lights all of a sudden failed; (cp.)
BYAR. -.-*an* (it becomes) dark (before
o's eyes).

peta and **pèta** *mem-* to map. **pem-** cartographer. - *buta* outline map. - *kadaster
(,pendaftaran tanah)* cadastral map.

petai a smelly, edible bean (L. Parkia
speciosa Hassk.). - *cina* (s.) LAMTORO.

petak *main* - *asin (,sembunyi ,umpat
,umpet)* to play hide-and-seek.

pètak *per-an* 1 lotting (out), parceling
out. 2 lot, parcel (of land).

pétan to hunt lice in s.o.'s hair (often
done by village women, sitting in line,
with each working on the hair of the
woman in front of her). *perempuan
yg -an* a woman who is hunting lice.

petang 1 afternoon. *Jum'at - jam 16.45*
Friday afternoon at 16:45. 2 late
afternoon. *Hari sdh pukul 7 - ketika
kami tiba di San Diego,* It was 7 p.m.
when we arrived in San Diego.

3 evening, night. *Sejak jam 22.30 -*,
Since 22:30. *hari semakin - juga* it's
nearing twilight. **ke-an**: *ilmu* ~ the
science of making o.s. invisible. *orang* ~
policeman in charge of the night watch.
petangtang.petingting to walk excitedly
back and forth.
peté (s.) PETAI.
pé.té [from *PT:* Perseroan Terbatas]
incorporated.
péterséli parsley.
peti mem(p)-.eskan to be put aside (,in
the deep freeze) (a matter). **pem-.esan**
shelving, putting on ice. *- balut* ambulance box. *- jenazah* coffin. *- kemas*
container (in shipping). *P- Perjanjian*
Ark of the Covenant.
petik I mem- *sebuah bunga* (fig.) to find
o's life partner. **pem-** player of a
stringed instrument.
Petik II *- Laut* traditional ceremonial
event in fishermen's communities to
thank God for bestowing marine
fortunes on the sea.
petilan and **pethilan** fragment (of *wayang*
play).
petinggi village head.
petir *bagai - di siang bolong* and *bagaikan
- di terik matahari* like a bolt from the
blue, like a bombshell.
pétrokimia petrochemical.
Pétromak pressurized kerosene lamp,
like a Coleman lamp.
Pétruk a character in the *wayang* play
with a tall, long nose who serves the
Pandawas. mBah - Mount Merapi (in
Central Java). *- menjadi Raja* to go
hog-wild.
petuk piece of evidence (dealing with
land tenure).
peusing anteater.
PEWARTA [Perhimpunan Wartawan
(Radio dan Televisi Indonesia)] Indonesian Radio and Television Reporters
Association.
pèyèk (s.) REMPEYEK. *- kacang* peanuts
fried in spiced batter.
PGPN [Peraturan Gaji Pegawai Negeri]
Government Employees Pay Rates.

PGRI [Persatuan Guru Republik Indo-
nesia] Republic of Indonesia Teachers
Association.
ph [(pron. pé-ha) piringan hitam] phono-
graph record. **di-kan** to be recorded,
be made into a record.
Philindo [Philippines-Indonesia] reference to the joint Filipino-Indonesian
naval maneuvers.
phisik (s.) FISIK.
phobia phobia.
PIA "Ardhya Garini" the Air Force Wives
Association.
piagam *- kekaryaan* certificate of achievement.
piala *- berganti (,bergilir ,berkisar ,bertu-
kar)* challenge cup. *P- Thomas* Thomas
Cup.
pialang broker. *perusahaan -* brokerage
firm.
pianis pianist. **ke-an** piano virtuosity.
pianswie (s.) PENYAKIT (PIANSWIE).
piau commission agent (in Pontianak).
piawai *orang -* expert.
picek (s.) PECAK.
picing se- *(pun) tdk tertidur* could not
sleep a wink. *matanya tiada* **ter-** *sedikit
juapun* he could not sleep a wink.
pidak pedarakan of the lowest social
level. *orang.orang -* the downtrodden,
ignorant.
pidana penalty (for criminal offense).
dijatuhi - penjara to be sentenced to
prison. *dpt* **di-kan** to be punishable. **di-
mati** to be sentenced to death. **ke-an**
criminal, penal. **mem-kan** to convict.
ter- a convict. *- mati* death penalty.
- penjara imprisonment.
pidanawan offender, wrongdoer.
pidari (s.) PADERI.
pidato *- kenegaraan* state-of-the-nation
address. *- mahkota* address from the
throne (esp. in the Netherlands: Royal
Speech). *- pengarah* briefing. *- perpisahan* farewell address. *- purnasantap*
after-dinner speech.
Piet Hitam Black Peter, i.e. the black
man who accompanies *Sinterklaas.*
pigimana (S.) BAGAIMANA.

pihak *dr - Pemerintah* on the part of the government. **ber-** tendentious. *laporan. laporan* ~ tendentious reports. ~ *kpd* to defect to (the enemy). *tak* **mem-** impartial. **pem-an** choosing sides. **se-** one-sided, unilateral. *- atas(an)* superiors. *dr - atas(an)* on the part of the authorities, from (,on the part of) the government, from a high quarter, on high authority. *- kedua* the party of the second part. *- ketiga* outsider(s). *- kolot* the old-fashioned people. *- lawan* the other party (,side), the opponents. *- pertama* the party of the first part. *mendapat persetujuan - ramai* to enjoy popular approval. *- sana* (col.) the Dutch (colonizers). *- sini* (col.) the Indonesians (nationalists). *- situ* (col.) the Indos, i.e. the Eurasians. *- teraniaya* the injured party. *- yg bersengketa* the disputants. *- yg berwenang* the competent authorities. -.- *yg mengadakan kontrak* the contracting parties.

piil *rendah -nya* inferior, immoral, having bad conduct.

pijat, pijet and **pijit** massage. **mem-:** ~ *bel (,knop ,tombol)* to ring the bell, press the button (,bell). ~ *klakson* to blow the horn. *- knop* push-button.

pijitwati massage girl, massage parlor hostess.

pikap and **pik.ap** pick-up (car).

pikat **pem-** allurement. **ter-** captivated. **-an** allurement.

piké *(kain) -* piqué.

pikèt picket, guard duty.

pikir *pd - saya* in my opinion. *- dahulu pendapatan, sesal kemudian tdk berguna* look before you leap. *tanpa -(.-) panjang* without thinking very long, without a moment's thought. **ber-:** *asyik* ~ abstracted. ~*(an) panjang* farseeing. ~ *secara mandiri* to think independently. *blm* **ke-an** *mau apa* I haven't yet thought about what I'm going to do. **pem-an** thought. ~ *kembali* rethinking. *Ini hendaknya menjadi* ~, This should be a matter to

think about. *pd* ~ *selanjutnya* on second thoughts. **-an:** *hilang* ~ to lose o's head, be confused. *Pakailah* ~*mu!* Use your brains! *sepanjang* ~ *saya* in my opinion. *Saya mendapat suatu* ~, The idea occurred to me. *Tapi satu hal yg menjadi* ~ *yaitu* ... , However, o. thing provided food for thought ... ~ *ini timbul dlm kepalanya* this thought crossed his mind.

pikul **mem-kan** 1 to load s.t. on (an animal). 2 to inflict (reparations) on (a defeated country). 3 to apportion (expenses) among. 4 to blame s.t. (on a person). **pem-** *kekuasaan (,prabawa. praja)* person in authority.

pikun 1 forgetful (of an old person). 2 senile. **ke-an** 1 senility, dotage. 2 old age.

pik.up (s.) PIKAP.

pil *- anti.disenteri* anti-dysentery pill. *- anti.hamil* and *- kontraseptif* birth-control pill. *- MX* a tranquilizer. *- pelangsing tubuh* diet pill. *- perangsang seks* sex pill. *- tidur* barbiturate, soporific.

pilek 1 a cold. 2 gonorrhea, the clap.

pilem (s.) FILM. **mem(p)-kan** to film. *- biru (,gituan)* blue (,porno) film. *- koboi* cowboy film.

pileuleuyan goodbye!

pilih *boleh - (,mem-)* optional. *banyak yg dpt* **di-** many to choose from. *Ia dpt* **di-** *kembali (,lagi),* He is eligible for re-election. **pem-:** *para* ~ constituency. ~.~*nya* the electorate. **pem-an** *pendahuluan* primary election (in the U.S.) **ter-** elected but not yet sworn in, ... elect. **-an** *karangan* selected works. *- kasih* favoritism.

pilot pilot. **di-i** to be piloted by.

pilu *- hati* melancholy.

pimpang (s.) PINGPONG.

pimpin **ber-** *tangan* to go hand in hand. **pem-:** *P*~ *Besar Revolusi* (abbrev. *Pembesrev*) Great Leader of the Revolution, i.e. President Soekarno. ~ *cilik* (fig.) a small wheel. ~ *gedé* (fig.) a big wheel. ~ *madya* middle-

level manager. ~ *paberik* factory
manager. ~ *rakyat* demagogue. ~ *tertinggi* topleader. -**an** directives, manual.
menjalankan ~ *thd* to direct, control.
pimping k.o. reed.
pinak (s.) (BER)ANAK.PINAK.
pinang - *sebatang* to be all alone in the
world. *(menyerupai) spt - dibelah dua*
to be as much alike as two peas in a
pod. *spt - pulang ke tampuk* 'as an
areca nut returning to its calyx,' i.e.
to be in high feather.
pincang ke-an *berpikir* faulty thinking.
pincuk a shell-shaped eating trough
made from a piece of banana leaf by
folding it down and fastening it
by means of a bamboo pin.
pincut ke- *pd* to be swept off o's feet by;
(s.) PENCUT.
pindah *dompet - tangan* the wallet was
snatched (,pickpocketed). **ber-**: ~ *dr
negeri yg fana ke negeri yg baka* to die.
~ *jenis* to change sex. *bersifat* **ber-.-
mobile. **di-** (to be) moved, transferred.
setasiun bumi yg dpt **di-.-** a mobile
earth station. **di-kan** (in bookkeeping)
carried forward. **di-.bahasakan** to be
translated. ~ *ke bahasa Sunda dan Jawa*
to be translated into Sundanese and
Javanese. **di-.tangankan** to be transferred (of ownership). *kendaraan bermotor yg* ~ motorvehicles which have
been transferred. **di-.tugaskan** to be
transferred (to another place, army
personnel). **di-.tukarkan** to be relocated
and replaced (by another o.). *Di Jakarta
banyak asrama tentara* ~, In Jakarta
many army barracks have been relocated
and replaced (by other ones). **mem-
bukukan** to transfer (to current account). **mem-.tanamkan** to transplant
(of heart, kidney, etc.). **m-** to change.
~ *gelombang* to change the wavelength
(of a radio). **pem-an**: ~ *air* water dis-
placement (of ship). ~ *hak* transfer of
ownership. ~ *jantung* heart transplant.
~ *pasukan* troop movement(s). ~ *tanah*
ground excavation (,sliding). ~ *tangan*

and **pem-.tanganan** transfer of ownership. **ter-kan** transferable. -**an** (in bookkeeping) brought forward. - *bekerja* to
change jobs. - *jalur* to change lanes (on
a road). - *tidur* to sleep every night in a
different place due to fear of being
kidnaped by government forces (during
the 1977 election campaign).
pindang and **pindhang** meat, usually
fish, cooked with a spicy sauce containing tamarind juice and other
ingredients. *spt - dlm kuali* like sardines
in a tin.
pinggir *P-!* (bus conductor's command to
driver) pull up (on the roadside)!
P- depan! (ditto) pull up ahead! **mem-**
to give right of way to (a passing car).
-**an**: ~ *Betawi* Jakarta's perimeter:
Pal Merah, Kebayoran Lama, Tanggerang, Kramat Pulo, Klender and
Pasar Rebo. ~ *kota* city limits. - *jalan*
sidewalk.
pingin (S.) INGIN.
pingit -**an** seclusion.
pingpong and **ping.pong** ping-pong. *Ia* **di-**
oleh pejabat.pejabat yg bersangkutan,
He was sent from pillar to post by the
officials concerned.
pingser **m-** to get out of place, shift.
pinisepuh 1 elder. 2 confidant.
pinisi the Buginese proa.
pinjam **di-.pakaikan** *kpd* to be given on
temporary loan to. **mem-** *telepon* to
make use of s.o.'s telephone. **pem-**
tangan perpetrator. -**an**: *mendapat*
~ *mobil penumpang* to obtain on loan
passenger cars (under the Soekarno
regime; the cars were used for the
transportation of dignitaries partici-
pating in mass demonstrations).
~ *jangka panjang (,pendek)* long
(,short)-term loan. ~ *lunak* soft loan.
~ *tdk berbunga* non-interest bearing
loan.
pinta a request; (S.) MINTA. **di-** to be
asked.
pintar *paling - dr yg lain.lain* to excel.
dia - bicara he has the gift of gab, he

speaks fluently.

pintu I - *angin* 1 swinging door (to protect against draft). 2 air sluice. - *gulung* roll-a-door. - *jalan ke* gateway to. *P- Kecil* the street of Chinese moneylenders and merchants in Jakarta, which has the same symbolic connotation as Wall Street had for the Populists in the U.S. - *lintas jalan* railway crossing. - *pabean* tollgate. - *pelintasan jalan kereta api* and - *perlintasan kereta api* railway crossing.

pintu II (in Pontianak) commission agent.

pinus pine-tree.

pinusisasi encouraging the planting of pine-trees.

pioh k.o. turtle.

pionir pioneer, a type of mil. engineer.

pioniria female pioneer.

pipa per-an (adj.) piping. - *(pabrik)* chimney. - *halus (,kapiler ,rambut)* capillary tube.

pipi *berdansa - lekat* - to dance cheek to cheek.

pipik mem- to become thin, thin out.

pipilan pulled (,torn) off (corn grains from the cob).

pipit *yg - sama -, yg enggang sama enggang juga* birds of a feather flock together.

pir I spring (of a watch, etc.).

pir II pear.

piramid(a) pyramid.

piranti device, tool, equipment.

piring di- hitamkan to be recorded. - *cangkir (,mangkuk)* dinner-set. - *kelung* deep plate. - *terbang* flying saucer.

Pirngon Pharao.

pirsa pem- *TV* televiewer.

pirsawan televiewer.

pirsidèr an electric refrigerator.

pis I to piss.

pis II piece (textile), bolt.

pisah keter-an 1 apartheid (the strict racial segregation in the Republic of South Africa). 2 separation. **pem-an** disengagement. ~ *diri* separatism. *dgn* **ter-** under separate cover. *bagian.*

bagian yg **ter-**.- knocked-down parts (of imported car). - *kebo* to separate legally. - *makan dan - tempat tidur* separation from bed and board. - *pasukan* troop disengagement.

pisan very, completely, at all. *di depan hidungnya* - under his very nose. *gedé* - very large. *nggak adè reramèan* - there is no party at all.

pisang - *goreng* and *goreng* - fried banana, banana fritters. *laku sbg - goreng* (or, *goreng* -) to sell like hot cakes. *tak akan dua kali - berbuah* once bitten twice shy. *mendapat - terbuka (,terkubak)* to obtain a windfall. - *mas di luar, onak di dalamnya* all is not gold that glitters. Various types of bananas are: - *Ambon* the Chiquita banana. - *Bali* pink peel type. - *batu* acid variety with green skin. - *hijau* (s.) PISANG (AMBON). - *kapas* squat, angular type. - *kapok* squarish type. - *klutuk* (s.) PISANG (BATU). - *Lampung* and - *mas* very small and sweet. - *nangka* large type. - *raja* red/yellow type. - *raja serai* short and thin, red/yellow. - *seribu* extremely small type. - *Siam* blotchy skin type. - *susu* short, fat, and sweet type. - *tanduk* long horn shaped type. - *uli* green when ripe.

pisau - *belati* small daggerlike knife. *bangsa - dua belah mata* a hypocrite.

pisik physical.

pispot piss-pot, chamber pot.

pistol and **pistul** - *air mata* tear-gas pistol. - *berperedam* pistol with a silencer. - *bius* tear-gas pistol. -.-*an* a toy pistol.

pisuh 1 to call names. 2 abusive word (,language). **di-i** to be scolded.

pisungsung present (,gift) of honor.

pit bicycle.

pita tape. **di-.suarakan** to be taped. *Pengakuan yg* ~ *oleh B. tlh diperdengarkan kembali olehnya,* The confession taped by B. was played back by him. - *cukai* tax stamp. - *magnetis* magnetic tape. - *penutup* poster stamp. - *rekaman (,suara)* recording

tape. - *rekaman bergambar* videotape.
Pitekantropus Pithecanthropus (erectus).
pites - *kutu* to pinch (,crush) a louse to
death with the fingernails of o's
thumbs.
piting -**an** stranglehold.
piton python (snake).
pitrun [to pit and run] U.S. Highway
Engineers in constructing the Jakarta
Bypass—now called Jalan Raya Jos
Sudarso—looked for soil and sand for
the roadbed at Citeureup (West Java);
they found a mixture of clay and sand
in the exact proportion wanted and
called the excavated material *pitrun*
meaning that o. has only to excavate
and 'run away' with the material.
pitulikur twenty seven. *hostess yg*
hayunya tumpuk - a very beautiful
hostess.
piutang *si* **ber-** the creditor.
Pj. [Pejabat] acting.
plafon ceiling.
plagiat **memp-** to plagiarize.
plagiatisme plagiarism.
plagiator plagiarist.
plakat poster.
plakèt plague.
plampang temporary bamboo or iron
platform with thatched roof of palm
leaves or canvas roofing added to a
building to function as a seating structure for spectators.
planétarium planetarium.
plang signpost, billboard.
Planit a red-light district in Jakarta.
plankton plankton. - *hewani* zooplankton.
- *nabati* phytoplankton.
plat (s.) PELAT.
plataran (S.) PELATARAN.
platform platform (of political party).
platnomor license plate.
plato plateau.
plébisit **di-kan** to be the subject of a
plebiscite.
plédoi plea, the address to the Court.
plegak.plegok (,**pleguk**) - *di depan yg*
hadir (to speak) stammeringly (,with

difficulty) in front of the audience.
Tapi kalau berbahasa Indonesia, masih -,
But, when he speaks Indonesian, he
still speaks haltingly.
plékat (s.) PELEKAT.
plengek **ke-** struck dumb.
plèngsèngan talus, slope.
pléno **di-kan** to be brought up in a
plenary session.
plèster -**an** plastering, stucco.
pletak sound of hard object hitting a
firm surface.
pléyat.pléyot 1 shaky, wobbly. 2 bent.
pliket sticky.
plin.plan (s.) PLINTAT.PLINTUT. *mata*
uang yen masih - the yen is still following a wait-and-see policy. *orang* - a
wishy-washy person. **ke-annya** his lack
of firm loyalties.
plinplanisme deviousness.
plintat.plintut not straightforward (in o's
dealings), devious.
plinteng and **plintheng** catapult; (s.)
PELINTENG.
plit (s.) FLIT.
plombir **memp-** to plug up (a leak). **ml-**
untu to fill a tooth.
plonco 1 novice, neophyte. 2 a first-year
college student who is undergoing
hazing. **per-an** hazing.
plong - *rasanya* and *merasa hatinya* - to
feel relieved.
plonga.plongo (to stare) with open
mouth, open-mouthed, gaping (as in
astonishment); (s.) (ME)LONGO.
plontos 1 bald. 2 (close-)shaven. 3 (close-)
shaven freshman of the Armed Forces
Academy at the Gunung Tidar, Magelang (Central Java). **di-** to be defeated
(in soccer). **ke-an** baldness, baldheaded-
ness. **memp-i** to shave bald.
plotot to open o's eyes wide.
plug shift (group of employees working
in relay with another).
pluh (s.) PLUG.
plung.lap 1 sound of s.t. falling into
water and then disappearing, plop.
2 (fig.) to defecate in a river.

pluntir memp- to twist.

plus 1 plus. 2 and. 3 with enough food to feed itself and still have some left over.

plutokrasi plutocracy.

plutokrat plutocrat.

P.M. [Pro Memorie] (in budgets, etc.) for remembrance. *mata anggaran* - pro forma entry.

P.N. **di-kan** to be converted into a State enterprise.

pnémonia pneumonia.

pnématik pneumatic.

poatang discovered, caught.

pocong -an a shrouded corpse; (s.) SUMPAH (POCONG).

podium podium.

podo (s.) PADA.

poen (pron. pun) (teenager sl.) marijuana.

pogrom pogrom.

pohon - *hayati* arbor vitae. - *jarum* conifer. - *kelapa* coconut tree. - *peneduh (,perindang)* shade tree. *P-* Terang Christmas Tree.

pojok **mem-kan** to corner. **ter-kan** cornered. **-an** corner.

pok (s.) (E)MPOK.

pokat (s.) BUAH (APOKAT).

pokèt (mil.) pocket (an isolated group of soldiers).

pokok *(terus) menuju* - to the point. **-nya** *ialah* ... the main thing is that ..., the primary consideration is that ... - *acara* item of agenda. -.- *ajaran agama* tenet, dogma. - *nama* family name, surname. - *perlawanan* pocket of resistance. - *persoalan* the gist of the matter. - *pikiran* basic idea.

pokrol **memp-.bambukan** to distort, twist. **per-an.bambu** hairsplitting. -.-an quibbling, dabbling.

pol I 1 full (of motorbus, etc.). *gaji* - gross salary. 2 paid, settled (of debt). *paling* - at the most.

pol II volt(age). *lengkap* -.-*nya* with complete electrical illumination.

pola blueprint. **memp-kan** *hidup sederhana* to fashion a simple life. - *bunyi*

phonology. - *induk* master plan.

polah way of acting.

polang.polèng painted in camouflage colors.

Polantas [Polisi Lalu.Lintas] Traffic Police.

polarisasi polarization.

polder polder.

polès mem- to make up (o's face, nails, etc.). - *muka* face cream.

poliandri polyandry.

poligami polygamy.

poliglot polyglot.

poligon polygon.

poliklini(e)k polyclinic. - *gigi* dental polyclinic.

Po Limo The Five P's (President Soekarno's pun on *Mo Limo*, 1959): *Perut, Pakaian, Perumahan, Pergaulan dan Pengetahuan* The Stomach, Clothing, Housing, Social Association and Knowledge.

Polinésia Polynesia.

polip polyp.

polis - *bersusut (,terbuka)* floating (,open) policy.

polisi - *anti.kerusuhan* riot police. - *berkuda* mounted police. - *kesusilaan* vice squad. *P- Militer* Military Police. - *pengendali huru.hara* riot (control) police. *P- Perairan dan Udara* Sea and Air Police. - *rahasia* detective. - *susila* vice squad.

Politbiro Politburo.

politéis polytheist.

politéisme polytheism.

politik *menjalankan* - 1 to participate (actively) in politics. 2 to pursue a (vigorous, etc.) policy. 3 to be in power. *orang* - politician. **ber-** to take part in politics. **memp-kan** to politicize. **per-an** 1 politicizing. 2 political. - *antropologi* anthropological politics. - *berdampingan secara damai* policy of peaceful co-existence. - *bermuka dua* double-faced policy. - *(ber)tetangga baik* good neighbor policy. - *dekat. mendekati* policy of rapprochement.

- *dua.Cina* 2-China policy. - *ekspansionis* expansionism. - *kepungan* policy of containment. - *keuangan ketat* tight-money policy. - *luar negeri yg aktif dan bebas* a non-aligned foreign policy (of the Republic of Indonesia). - *menentang* an aggressive policy. - *mengalah demi perdamaian* appeasement policy. - *pat.gulipat* a manipulating policy. - *Pemerintah* Government policy. - *pengepungan* policy of containment. - *pintu terbuka* open-door policy. *P- Putih Australia* White Australia Policy. - *satu.Cina* one-China policy. - *tempel.menempel* patchwork. - *tdk berpihak* non-aligned policy. - *uang* financial policy. - *uang seret* tight-money policy.

politikus politician.

politikawan politician.

politis politic(al).

politisir memp- (s.) MEMPOLITIKKAN.

politur polish. **mem-** to polish (furniture).

polo - *air* water polo.

polonès polonaise.

polong I *kacang* - pods, green peas.

polong II (forms of) hysteria (attributed to magic, witchcraft, sorcery, etc.). *spt - kena sembur* 1 submissive, docile. 2 to be off like a shot.

polong III **-an** *air* drain, sewer.

polonis (s.) POLONES.

polorogo illegal retribution on the transfer of lien on land, slaughter of cattle, transactions of houses, etc.

polos 1 simple, solid (of color), plain. *warna* - a solid color. *Pikiranku yg masih - tak membayangkan akan terjadi kejadian yg mengerikan itu,* Not being conscious of having done any wrong, I could not imagine that such a horrible event was going to happen. 2 uncovered. *payudaranya yg* - her uncovered breasts. *dlm keadaan* - and *telanjang* - stark-naked. 3 single, unmarried. 4 straightforward. *pengakuan.pengakuan* - *dr Dewi* the straightforward confessions of Dewi.

ber-.- uncovered, naked. **ke-an** naturalness.

polowijo nonstaple food crops, subsidiary or secondary to rice.

Poltas Swasta [Polisi Lalu.Lintas Swasta] 'Private Traffic Police.' Individuals pose as traffic police for personal gain (by pocketing fines, 'donations,' etc.).

polusi pollution.

Polwan [Polisi Wanita] Policewoman.

pom - *bensin* gas station.

POMAD [Polisi Militer Angkatan Darat] Army Military Police.

pompa di- *ke atas* to be jacked up. *Sekarang secara buatan harga kopra ~ ke atas,* Nowadays the price of copra has artificially been jacked up. **di-kan** *kpd* 1 to be pumped in. 2 to be crammed in. **mem-kan** *semangat* to inspire. - *angin* air pump.

pompanisasi introduction of pumping systems.

pompong I k.o. squid.

pompong II (S.) KEPOMPONG.

pompong III ke-an to be taken aback.

Pon the third day of the five-day week.

ponco poncho.

poncol a small market.

pondok I Moslem religious study center consisting of a teacher-leader, usually a *haji,* who is called *kiyayi,* and a group of male students, called *santris.*

pondok II m- to stay with s.o. temporarily. -an: *menerima ~ utk dua karyawati* to accept two female employees as boarders (,paying guests). *tempat ~* housing accommodation.

pongah arrogant. **ber-** to boast.

ponis *menjatuhkan* - to pass a verdict (on).

pons punch (instrument). *mesin* - punching machine.

pontang.panting ter- in a rush.

pontianak (S.) KUNTILANAK.

ponton pontoons.

pop of or pertaining to popular songs, such as, *lagu.lagu* - pop music, *penyanyi*

- pop singer, etc. **nge-** to sing pop music. *berpakaian* ~ to be dressed in mod fashion (wearing Levi's, jeans, etc.).

popi 1 doll. 2 puppet.

poplin poplin.

popok I swaddling clothes.

popok II ointment of powder mixed with water. **mem-kan** to apply such an ointment on.

popor - *senjata* rifle butt.

populasi population.

populèr widespread (of disease). **pem-an** popularization.

pora I liberal, generous, lavish. *berpesta -* to celebrate lavishly, indulge in orgies.

PORA II [Paspor Orang Asing] Passport for Foreigners.

porak.poranda (S.) PORAK.PERANDA. **di-kan** to be turned upside down, be made a mess out of.

pori ber-.- *dgn* to have pores filled with. **ke-an** porosity.

porlep [portir lepas] casual porter (at Kemayoran Airport, Jakarta).

pornès oven. - *gas (,listrik)* gas (,electric) oven.

porno 1 pornography. 2 pornographic. **ke-an** pornography.

porok fork.

poros ber-kan to be centered around. - *engkol* crankshaft. - *kardan* cardan shaft.

porot mem- to gnaw at. **m-in** to gnaw away at.

porsèn (S.) PERSEN.

porsi portion, order, serving. *satu - nasi goreng* one order of fried rice.

portal (iron) roadblock.

portefolio portfolio. *menteri tanpa -* minister without portfolio.

portir porter.

pos I *tdk dpt disampaikan -* undeliverable (by mailman). **menge-kan** *surat* to mail a letter. - *gombal* junk mail. - *tercatat* registered mail.

pos II -.- *peralihan* (in balance sheet) items running into the following year.

pos III *pulang ke -nya* to return to o's

(diplomatic) post. - *anjur* advance post. - *komando depan* advance command post. - *pendengar* listening post. - *penjagaan* sentry post. - *pertemuan rahasia* (intelligence term) safe haven. - *pertolongan* aid station. - *tinjau udara* aerial observation post.

pose pose (fixed position assumed in posing). **ber-** to pose, attitudinize, strike an attitude.

posisi - *depan* (mil.) advanced position. - *kunci* key position. - *tawar.menawar* bargaining position.

poskar postcard.

posma [pekan orientasi studi mahasiswa] college orientation week.

pospat phosphate.

postèl [pos dan telekomunikasi] postal and telecommunications (service).

poster poster.

poswèsel postal money order.

potènsi potential.

potlot - *alis* eyeliner. - *tinta* copying (-ink) pencil.

potong di- *25%* reduced 25%. **mem-:** ~ *angin* crosswind. *landasan yg* ~ *angin* crosswind runway. ~ *jalan* to take a short cut. ~ *karcis* to punch tickets. **pem-an** stoppage (of wages), deduction (of salary). ~ *gaji* deduction of salary. ~ *uang* currency reform, reorganization of the currency. **se-** *sabun* a cake of soap. **-an:** *dgn* ~ *waktu tahanannya* minus the time spent in custody. *Lihat dulu dong* ~ *orang,* You'd better look first at who's standing before you. - *kalimat* to interrupt. - *kompas* a short cut.

potrèt m- to take pictures. **-.mem-** photography.

poyokan *nama -* 1 pet name. 2 (fig.) trade-mark.

pp [peraturan pemerintah] government regulation.

P.R. [(pron. pé-èr) pekerjaan rumah] homework.

Pra-Adhyaksa Assistant Magistrate.

praakhir penultimate.

pra.anggapan prediction, projection.
  ber- 1 to prejudice. 2 prejudiced,
  biassed.
prabawa influence, prestige.
prabu 1 king, sovereign. 2 title for a
  king. ke-an 1 majesty. 2 empire.
  - anom 1 crown prince. 2 title for a
  crown prince.
pradésa home of certain ethnic groups
  living in isolation (the so-called
  masyarakat terasing).
pragawati mannequin. ke-an (adj.)
  modeling.
pragmatis pragmatic.
praja I 1 seat of the sovereign. 2 capital
  (city). P- Kejawèn (s.) VORSTEN-
  LANDEN.
praja II di- 1 to be defeated. 2 to be killed.
Pra.Jaksa (s.) PRA.ADHYAKSA.
Prajayud(h)a (s.) (OPERASI) SITARDA.
prajurit 1 (col.) designation for the
  indigenous soldiers who served for
  keeping peace and order, and who
  were placed under the direct command
  of the Civil Service. 2 (since independence, August 17, 1945) any soldier
  not engaged in colonialist and
  imperialist practices. ke-an (adj.)
  military. - dua private. - kepala master
  private. - Kraton Kraton soldiers;
  formerly the soldiers of the Yogyakarta
  palace constituted o. batallion, divided
  into several groups, such as, Wirabraja,
  Daeng, Patangpuluh, Jagakarya, Pra-
  wiratama, Nyutra, Ketanggung and
  Mantrijero wearing various uniforms
  and carrying different flags. - pena
  pressman, journalist. - satu private first
  class. - tak dikenal the unknown soldier.
  - udara dua airman second class.
  - udara satu airman first class.
prakala before, prior to. - Perang Dunia II
  prior to WW II.
prakarsa initiative. atas - on the initiative
  of. atas - sendiri on o's own initiative.
  mem(p)-i to take the initiative, initiate.
  pem- initiator, promotor, originator.
prakasa famous, well-known.
prakondisi prerequisite.

praktèk ber- to practice (of doctor).
  meletakkan -nya (speaking of a
  physician) to retire from practice.
  - umum general practice.
praktikan trainee.
praktikum practical course, laboratory
  work.
praktikus practician.
praktis ke-an practicability.
praktisi practicians.
pralambang profound simile.
prama [(Masa) Prabakti Mahasiswa]
  a male freshman.
pramana standard, norm.
prambos raspberry.
prami [(Masa) Prabakti Mahasiswi]
  female freshman.
pramubayi baby sitter.
pramub(h)akti roomboy. - pakaian valet.
pramugara - gereja male usher (in church).
pramugari - (angkasa) (airline) stewardess.
  - darat ground stewardess. - gereja
  female usher (in church). - laut hostess
  on board ferryboats plying between
  Surabaya and Kamal (Madura).
pramujasa insurance agent.
pramuka ke-an 1 (adj.) boy scout. 2 Boy
  Scout Movement. memajukan ~
  to promote the Boy Scout Movement.
  P- Bhayangkara Boy Scout in the
  Police Field. - putra boy scout. - putri
  girl scout. P- Saka Bahari Sea Scout.
  P- Wirabumi Rural Scout.
pramuniaga salesman. - wanita salesgirl.
pramupijat masseuse.
pramupintu concierge.
pramuria night club hostess.
pramusiwi baby sitter.
pramustand girl standing in a booth,
  stall or stand in a trade fair, etc.
pramutamu receptionist.
pramuwicara announcer, M.C.
pramuwidya museum guide.
pramuwisata (tourist) guide. ke-an (adj.)
  tourist guide.
pranata institution.
pranata mangsa Jav. solar year calendar
  (begins at the end of June, solstice).
prangko (S.) PERANGKO. - 50 rupiah

a fifty-rupiah stamp. **pemr-an** prepayment (of postage).

pra.Olimpiade pre-Olympics.

Prapatan 10 (in Jakarta) address where Indonesian groups met to decide to split from Menteng 31-group (because too leftist) on August 18, 1945.

prapendapat prejudice.

pra.perang prewar.

praperistiwa precedent.

prapupa cocoon.

prasaja 1 simple, not ornated. 2 modesty.

prasangka ber- 1 to prejudice. 2 prejudiced, biassed. - *bangsa* racism.

prasarana 1 infrastructure. 2 public utilities.

prasarjana undergraduate.

prasetya pledge of loyalty.

pratanda sign.

pratangkas [prajurit tangkas] skillful soldier.

pratidina every day.

pratisabda echo.

pratiwi (s.) PERTIWI.

prawacana introduction, preface.

prawan (S.) PERAWAN. **ke-an** maidenliness, virginity.

prayitna 1 vigilant. 2 cautious. **ke-an** 1 vigilance. 2 caution.

prayojana motives, grounds.

prédikat designation. **di-i** to be designated, be called.

préfèktur prefecture.

préferènsi preference.

préferènsiil preferential.

prèh *pohon* - k.o. banyan tree.

préi *(daun)* - chives, leek, spring onions.

prekéwuh 1 hindrance. 2 difficulty. 3 hindered. 4 to experience difficulties.

prékondisi prerequisite.

prèman (in Medan) (s.) CROSSBOY. *Seorang agen polisi yg berpakaian -,* A plain-clothes policeman.

prémi bonus.

prémièr première (first public film showing). **memp-kan** to première.

premisi (s.) PERMISI.

prenèsen 1 roguish, impish. 2 funny,

prenjak bar-winged wren-warbler.

préparat (blood) preparation.

prérogatif prerogative.

près I nge- 1 to press. 2 to be close up against. **penge-an** pressing (of clothes).

près II carton (of cigarettes).

prèsdir [presiden direktur] president director.

présedèn precedent.

présidèn ke-an 1 (adj.) presidential. 2 Presidential Palace. *P- Seumur Hidup* President For Life, Lifetime President. *P- terpilih* President elect.

Présidium Presidium.

prèstasi memp-kan to achieve. - *kerja* 1 output. 2 working efficiently.

prèstise prestige.

prètèl mem(p)-i to pluck, plunder, rob, strip, pull apart. *dlm bentuk -an* in a completely knocked down state (automobile). **P-in** (coll.) punning reference to the *Fretelin* political party in former Portuguese Timor (now the Indonesian province of Timor Timur).

prétènsi pretension.

prèthèl (s.) PRETEL. **mr-i** breaking and falling off (leaves, fruits, etc.).

prévèntif preventive.

préwangan (spirit) medium.

pri (s.) PRIBUMI.

pria *dunia* **ke-an** man's world.

priai (s.) PRIYAYI.

Priangan *(tanah)* - the interior plateau of West Java, heartland of the Sundanese.

pribadi memp- to be private, be personal.

pribumi earth, land. *(orang)* - 1 native, indigenous person. 2 (in some areas of South Sumatra which accommodate transmigrants from Java) the native of those areas. *(orang) non.-* 1 the non-native, i.e. the Indonesian of foreign (read: primarily Chinese) extraction. 2 (in the same areas of South Sumatra which accommodate transmigrants from Java) the transmigrants from Java who are considered by the local native residents to be favored by the Central government, because most of these transmigrants belong to the Armed Forces. **memp-kan** to nativize.

pribumisasi 'nativization,' i.e. the assimilation to Indonesian customs (of Catholic rites).

prigel ke-an *tangan* handicraft.

prihatin sad, depressed, dejected. **ber-thd** to be concerned at, be worried about. **ke-an** concern. **mem(p)-kan** to worry (, be concerned) about.

prilèns freelance.

primadona prima donna.

primat primate.

primbon handbook which contains predictions, calculations of unlucky days, etc.

primitif ke-an primitiveness.

primpen *disimpan di tempat yg -* safely stowed. **di-i** to be kept (,stored) safely, be in safe keeping.

primpèn di-i to appear to s.o. in a dream.

pringas.pringis to sneer, grin.

pringgitan space behind the *pendopo.*

prinjak (s.) PRENJAK.

prinsipiil of principle. *hal.hal yg -* matters of principle.

prioritas memp-kan to give priority to. **memp- pertamakan** to give top priority to. *- pertama (,utama)* first (,top) priority.

priskoran price list.

prisma prism. *- nama* desk marker, name plate (on desk).

prit (pron. pri:t) the sound of a traffic police whistle. **di-** to be stopped by police. *Banyak sekali mobil.mobil yg* ~, A great many cars were stopped by police (by giving a signal on their whistle). *- jigo* a manner of extorting bribes, exercised by some traffic policemen; (s.) JIGO.

privé private.

priwil freewheel; (s.) KERIWIL.

priyayi 1 the Jav. aristocratic elite. 2 (loosely) the upper classes.

pro pro. *- dan kontra* pros and cons.

Probanjir [Proyek (Pengendalian) Banjir] Flood Control Project.

problèm and **probléma** problem.

problématik problematic.

pro bono publico for the public good.

procot to be born.

prodéo gratis, free.

produksi *- pangan* food production. *- sekali banyak* mass production.

produktif ke-an productivity.

produser producer.

profèsional ke-an professionalism.

profèsionil professional.

profil profile.

prognose prognosis.

program ber- programmed. **di-kan** to be programmed. *- kesederhanaan* austerity program. *- pendidikan tanpa gelar* non-degree program. *- politik* platform (of political party).

programa program. **ber-** programmed.

programatis programmatic.

progrèsif ke-an 1 progressiveness. 2 progressivism.

proklamator proclamator (of Indonesia's independence).

prokurasi power of attorney.

proletar ke-an proletariat.

proletarisasi the introduction of a proletariat (as in Marxism).

proliferasi proliferation.

promès promissory note. *- perbendaharaan* treasury bill.

promosi 1 promotion, furtherance. *penjualan* sales promotion. 2 (becoming a doctor) graduation taking a doctoral degree. 3 (the ceremony) degree ceremony, commencement. *berhak menempuh -* to be entitled to take o's doctoral degree. **memp-kan** to promote, further the growth of. ~ *penggunaan bahan.bahan batik* to promote the use of batik materials.

promotor professor presenting the graduating student.

promovèndus candidate for doctor's degree.

prongkol lump *-an* in lumps.

prop cork material. *topi -* topee, a pith sun helmet.

Prop. [Propinsi] Province.

propagandis propagandist.

propèsi profession.

propokatip provocative.

proporsi proportion.

propot *mak* - procuress. *pak* - pimp.

prosès lawsuit. **pemr-** *data* person who processes data. **pemr-an** processing. ~ *data* data processing - *akulturasi* acculturation process. - *kemerosotan* drifting process. - *pem.Baratan* westernization process. - *pendemokrasian* democratization process.

prosès.perbal (,.**verbal**) (official) report, record, deposition.

prospèk prospect.

protal iron roadblock.

protèksionis protectionist.

protèstan *P- Angelsaksis Putih* White Anglo-Saxon Protestant, WASP.

protokol protocol. **ke-an** (adj.) protocol.

protokolèr (adj.) protocol.

protol and **prothol** to come off, break. **di-i** to be robbed, be held up. *Penumpang otobis* ~, The bus passengers were robbed.

provokasi **di-(kan)** to be provoked.

Provo(o)st Provost Marshall.

proyèk *P-.P- Mandataris (,Mercusuar)* The 'Mandatory (,Lighthouse) Projects,' i.e. the *Monumen Nasional* National Monument, *Jalan Silang Monas* National Monument Intersection, *Menara Ancol* Ancol Tower, *Mesjid Istiqlal* Istiqlal Mosque, etc. under President Soekarno. *P- MHT* [Proyek Moh. Husni Thamrin] the *kampung* improvement project in Jakarta. *kampung.kampung yg tlh* **di.-MHT.kan** shantytowns which have been improved in conformity with the *MHT* project. -.- *padat karya* development projects emphasizing the use of an unemployed and/or semi-unemployed labor force, labor-intensive projects. - *pelopor (,percobaan ,percontohan)* pilot project. - *perindustrian* industrial project. - *perintis* pilot project. -.- *prasarana* infrastructural projects.

proyèksi projection. **di-kan** *sbg* to be projected as.

proyèktil - *balistik antarbenua* intercontinental ballistic missile.

proyèktor projector.

psikiater psychiatrist.

psikiatri psychiatry.

psikiatris (s.) PSIKIATER.

psikologikal psychological.

psikose psychosis. - *ketakutan* psychosis of fear.

psiko.somatik psycho-somatic.

puak clan.

puan 1 a lady. 2 Mrs. 3 Miss. 4 Ms.

pua.pua casuarina tree.

puas **ber-** *hati* complacent. **ke-an:** ~ *hati* complacency. ~ *seksuil* sexual satisfaction. *tdk* **ter-kan** insatiable. **pem-** satisfier. *Wanita kita hanya berfungsi sbg bahan* ~ *nafsunya orang asing,* Our women only serve as objects to satisfy the passions of foreign nationals. *Anak .anaknya dpt -.- memutar lagu kesayangannya,* His children could play their favorite tunes to their heart's content.

puasa *hari mangkat* - the day before *Puasa.*

puber adolescent. *masa* - coming on age.

publikasi **memp-kan** 1 to publicize. 2 to publish. ~ *diri* to advertise o.s.

publikatif *secara* - through publication.

publisistik science of communications.

publisitèt publicity.

pucat **ke-an** paleness. **ke-.-an** palish, somewhat pale. - *benihan (,lesu ,bagai mayat)* deathly pale.

pucuk - *dicinta ulam tiba* 'a shoot is longed for, but raw vegetables are coming,' i.e. to get a windfall. *tak - di atas enau* conceited, cocky. *spt - eru* to trim o's sails according to the wind, set o's sails to every wind. *minta - pd alu* to cry for the moon. *bagai - dilancarkan* (to go off) like a shot, as swift as an arrow. **mem-**pimpinan to become a member of the governing board of ... - *lembing* spearhead. - *nuklir* warhead.

pucung a tree with intoxicating fruit (L. Pangium edule).

pudel *(anjing)* - poodle.

puguh naturally, of course.

puh exclamation of feeling hot.

puing mem- to become ruins.

puisiwan poet.

puitis poetical.

puitisasi turning into poetry.

puja pem- adorer. **pem-an** *nenek moyang* ancestral worship. **-an** idolized. ~ *hati* adored o.

pujangga - *keraton* court poet.

puji ter- commendable. *melemparkan* **-an** to trumpet forth praises, be loud in o's praises.

pukang k.o. small, tailless and very shy monkey the skin of which is used in black magic practices to give its owner great authority and prestige.

pukat - *harimau* trawl.

pukau *kena* - 1 absent-minded. 2 perplexed.

puki - *mai!* 'your mother's cunt,' kiss my ass!

pukul *sekali* - at o. blow, off-hand, straight away. **di-:** ~ *mundur* to be repulsed, be beaten back. *(kalau)* ~ *rata* on an (,the) average. **di.ratakan** on the whole, in the main. **mem-** *mati* to kill, beat to death. **pem-:** ~ *drum* drummer (of a band). ~ *lalat* fly swatter. **-an:** ~ *mati* deathblow. ~ *mematikan* (in boxing) a deadly blow. - *dan menghilang* to hit and run. - *terus!* continue! move ahead!

pul pool (cars, etc.). **menge-** to pool.

pulang to go back to (home, office, room, etc.). *Semuanya itu - kpd soal ...,* The whole thing boils down to ... **ber-** *(ke alam baka, ke rahmat Allah, ke asalnya)* to pass away. **ke-an** homecoming. **mem-kan:** ~ *keamanan* to restore order. ~ *kembali* to deport, expel s.o. from a country. ~ *pertanyaan kpd* to toss the question to. *Kisah orang Amerika di tanah Cina* **ter-** *jauh ke awal abad ini,* The story (,history) of Americans in China goes back as far as early this century. - *balik ke kantor* to come back to the office. - *girang* (for the Jakartan) to go to the countryside, i.e. Bogor, Sukabumi, etc. - *kandang* to return to o's residence. - *ke hulu (,udik)* to go (back) to the countryside. - *ke*

haribaan Tuhan to pass away. - *ke kampung* to return to o's village after having worked in the city for a rather long time. - *nama* to pass away. - *(negeri Belanda)* to go (back) to Holland, repatriate (for Dutch people). - *tambah* to give delicacies, etc. to a *dukun,* etc. after a successful treatment. - *tongsang* to go (back) to o's ancestral country, repatriate (for Chinese).

pulau di.P- *Seribukan* (of drug addicts) to be 'isolated' on *Pulau Seribu.* *P-Agama (,Dewata ,Hippies)* Bali. *P-Antah.Berantah* Fantasy Island. *P-Kerapan* Madura. *P-* *Panaitan* (the former) Prinsen Eiland, off Java's west coast. *P- Paska* Easter Island. *P-Seribu* and **Ke-an** *Seribu* a subdistrict in the Bay of Jakarta consisting of about 110 islands. *P- Wisatawan* Bali.

pulen thick, soft and smooth (of cooled cooked rice).

pules sound asleep.

pulkanisir - *ban* vulcanizing tires.

puluh the ten digit. *Berapa -?* How many tens? **ber-** *ceritera mengenai* dozens of tales about. **-an** 1 dozens. 2 the years of a particular decade. *lima* ~ the 50s.

pulung 1 lucky star. 2 luck. *kejatuhan* - luck has come o's way.

pumigasi fumigation.

pun (s.) POEN. **nge-** to shoot up, inject drugs.

punakawan 'attendant,' (in the *wayang* play) the small group of comic, male companions of the chief heroes.

punca - *kekuasaan* the reins of power. - *politik* prominent politicians. - *yg layak dipercaya* a reliable source.

puncak - *(kejadian)* highlight.

pundèn and **pundhèn** 1 holy site to worship the souls of o's ancestors, the guardian spirits of the village, etc. 2 site where village people make a vow.

pundi.pundi - *udara* air pocket.

punggawa (in Bali) district head.

punggung - *gunung* ridge of a mountain.

pungkah (in the immigration office at Balikpapan) k.o. bribe, not the same as *pungli,* but more resembling alms.

pungkas mem-i to bring to an end. **-an** conclusion, termination. *kesimpulan* ~ the final conclusion.

pungli [pungutan liar] illegal retributions (levied for car parking, without issuing parking tickets, etc.). **mem(p)-** and **m-** to subject s.o. to *pungli.* **per-an** illegal levying.

pungliwan *pungli* collector.

pungsa [pungutan paksa] illegal retributions accompanied by using force.

punguan association.

pungut mem- *penumpang* (city buses) to shovel in (as many) passengers (as possible). **pem-** 1 collector. ~ *bola golf* caddy. ~ *puntung rokok* collector of cigarette butts. 2 picker. ~ *hasil tanaman kapas* cotton picker. **pem-an** *anak* adoption of a child. **-an** revenues. ~ *tambahan* surcharge.

punjul ke-an excellence. *orang.orang yg punya* ~ *dlm bidang itu* those who are outstanding in that field.

punjung arbor.

Punt! (pron. u as Indonesian e) That's the end of it! Period!

punten (phrase for announcing o's presence as a visitor at the door of s.o.'s home) anybody in?

puntir (s.) PLUNTIR. *kabel* **-an** a twisted cable.

punuk hump, hunch on the back.

punya 1 to have, own. *Gua tdk - bapak lagi,* I don't have a father any more. *tinggal di sebuah rumah -nya sendiri* to live in his own house. 2 *ada yg -* to have a boy (,girl) friend, spoken for. 3 personal pronoun or noun + *punya* + noun characterizes a possessive relationship in the sense that the morpheme preceding *punya* indicates the possessor. *saya - bini* my wife. *mobil - ban* the car's tire. 4 qualitative + *punya* + synonymous qualitative expresses high degree of the quality. *ganjil - ajaib* extremely strange. 5 verb(al root)

+ *punya* + the same verb(al root) indicates the duration, intensity of the action: after long ...-ing. *bekerja - bekerja* after persistent efforts. *cari - cari* after long searching. *cerita - cerita* to make a long story short. *Tetapi hitung - hitung, uangnya tak mencukupi,* However, no matter how often he counted his money, it was insufficient. *ikut - ikut* ultimately, finally. *kongkow - kongkow* after long chatting. *ngomong - ngomong* finally, at last. *periksa - periksa* after interrogating back and forth. *putar - putar* after long shuffling. *selidik - selidik* after a thorough investigation. *tunggu - tunggu* after much waiting. *usut - usut* after a thorough investigation. **ber-:** *si* ~ the haves. *yg* ~ *dan yg tak* ~ the haves and the have-nots. *sdh* ~ already married (,engaged ,spoken for). *kursi.kursi yg sdh* ~ the occupied seats. **ke-an** ownership.

PUPN [Panitia Urusan Piutang Negara] State Debts and Claims Committee. **di-.-.kan** to be inspected by the *PUPN.*

pupiuk oto (in West Sumatra) horn (of automobile).

pupuk *bagi* **pem-an** *kas partai* for filling the party coffers. - *bawang* 1 (to be) a mere cipher. 2 figurehead. 3 boondoggle. *menjadi - bawang* to sit mum. - *hijau* compost. - *kandang* manure.

pupus I young leaf. *hijau -* leaf-green.

pupus II *Dan -lah sdh harapan,* And all hope has vanished into thin air.

puput I -an undaunted.

puput II - *puser* falling off of the umbilical cord.

puput III pem-an the blowing of smoke into a mouse hole to suffocate the mice.

pura I ber-.- hypocritical. *dgn ~ sbg* under cover of. *Jangan -.- alim!* Don't be hypocritical!

pura II city (in compounds, such as, *Singapura, Jayapura,* etc.).

purba ke-an ancientness.

purbakalawan archeologist.

purbasangka bias. ber- biased.
purbawisésa full power.
Purèk [Pembantu Rektor] Assistant to the President (of university, etc.); (s.) REKTOR.
purn. ret.; (s.) PURNAWIRAWAN.
purna karyawan a retired employee of a State enterprise.
purnakata 1 last words. 2 conclusion. 3 postscript.
purnasarjana doctor, Ph.D. *orang yg akan* di-kan Ph.D. candidate.
purnaungu ultra violet.
purnawirawan a retired mil. person. di-kan to be retired (,pensioned) (of an army man).
purser purser.
purwadaksina origin, descent.
purwakanti alliteration, assonance.
purwarupa prototype.
purwocèng an aphrodisiac.
pusaka di-kan *kpd* to be bequeathed to, be left to.
pusakawan male inheritor.
pusakawati female inheritor.
pusara bond, tie, link.
pusat *P-* the Central Government, Jakarta. se- concentric. ter- centrally positioned. - *gempabumi* epicenter. - *kesehatan* health center. *P- Pengkajian Masalah. Masalah Strategis dan Internasional* Center for Strategic and International Studies, CSIS (Indonesia's think tank). - *perbelanjaan* shopping center. - *perhatian* cynosure. - *pertokoan* shopping center.
puser 1 umbilical cord. 2 center. *Menurut beberapa dongeng orang Jawa menganggap Tanah Jawa sbg -ing bumi,* According to several legends the Javanese consider the Island of Java to be the pivot of the world.
pusing sexually aroused, horny. *tdk diambil (,mengambil) - kpd (,atas)* and *tdk* di-kan 1 do not mind, take no notice of, do not care about, pay no attention to. 2 do not get excited about, do not make a fuss about. *tdk* mem-kan not care about, pay no at-

tention to. -an centrifugal.
puskesmas [pusat kesehatan masyarakat] public health center; (coll.) medical clinic.
puso 1 parched, arid. *sawah yg -* dried-up rice paddies. 2 empty. *padi -* empty paddy.
pus.pus call for cats.
pustaka per-an *keliling* mobile library.
Pustaka.raja 'Book of the Kings,' i.e. the name of a voluminous, quasi-historical work of R. Ngabehi Ranggawarsita.
pustakawan 1 (male) librarian. 2 (male) bibliophile.
pustakawati 1 female librarian. 2 female bibliophile.
pusu I ant-hill.
pusu II confused.
pus(y)er pusher, tug boat.
putar ber-: ~ *dr kanan ke kiri* counterclockwise. *Angin sdh ~ dr kanan ke kiri,* The wind has backed. *~lah pikiranku* I changed my mind. ber-.- to drive about. ~ *(lidah)* to beat around the bush. mem-: ~ *kaset lagu.lagu Hawaii* to play cassettes of Hawaiian songs. ~ *saluran enam* 1 (when TV is not yet on) to turn on the TV to channel 6. 2 (when TV is already on) to switch to channel 6. ~ *sepedanya* to (bi)cycle. ~ *telepon* to phone. m-.m- to go around and around, wander around (without any fixed destination). peman *film (,pilem)* film showing. *dlm* -an *akhir* in the last round (in sports). -.- (s.) MUTAR.MUTAR. - *kayun* to tour, turn around.
puter I the wood pigeon.
puter II (s.) PUTAR.
putera - *remaja* adolescent.
puteri *P- Mawar* Princess of the Briar Rose Tale. *P- Salju* Snowwhite.
puthau not loyal to o's parents.
puti puttees.
putih gray (of hair). - *di luar kuning di dlm* appearances are deceiving. *P- Pak Harto, P- Rakyat,* (scribbled on the walls after the abortive communist coup) What is good for Pak Harto (i.e.

President Soeharto) is good for the People. *tdk membilang - maupun hitam* never utter a word. *lebih baik ber- tulang drpd ber- mata* death before dishonor. **ke-an** leucorrhoea. **m-** to eat small amounts of steamed (white) rice taken in the cupped hand without any side dishes, drink a few gulps of plain drinking water, stay awake, practice religious concentration and meditation for three days and three nights; a procedure o. has to go through before being able *memberi isi* to a kris. **mem-kan** to examine closely (foreign capital). 2 (fig.) to legalize. **pem-an** 1 close examination (of foreign capital). 2 the issuance of a building permit for buildings which previously were constructed without permit, k.o. legalization. **-an** pious people, i.e. who observe religious prescriptions. *- hati* sincere. *- mentereng (,salju)* snowwhite. *- susu* milkwhite.

Putri Hijau the special express train between Medan and Tanjung Balai (Sumatra's Eastcoast).
putri malu mimosa.
Putu I (in Bali) name element placed before personal names to indicate the first born child, such as, *Putu Setia.*
putu II rice flour cake filled with brown sugar.
putung 1 **m-** to grumble. 2 to give up.
putus *tdk* **berke-an** ceaselessly. **mem-kan:** ~ *segala pengharapan* to frustrate all hopes. ~ *sekolah* to drop out (of school). ~ *umur kabinet* to topple a cabinet. **pem-an** *hubungan* disengagement, severance of relations. **ter-** dissolved. *(dgn) tdk -.-nya* and *(dgn) tiada -.-* unceasingly, constantly, continually. *- harga* to agree on the price. *- hati* in despair. *sdh - kaji* settled. *- sekolah* dropped out (of school).
puun tribal chief of the *Baduis.*
puyunghai (s.) FUYUNGHAI.
PV [Personeel Verzorger (,Verzorgster)] Personnel Affairs Assistant (approved by immigration officers to look after personnel matters, so that persons concerned need not appear before immigration officers in person).
pwak gambling.
PWI [Persatuan Wartawan Indonesia] Indonesian Journalists Association.

Q

qari male Koran reader.
qariah female Koran reader.
qas (s.) KHAS.
qasidah (s.) KASIDAH. **ber-** to sing religious melodies in Arabic.
qori (s.) QARI.
qoriah (s.) QARIAH.

R

Raad van Justitie Court of Justice.
raba *tak tentu -* to be all at sea, confused.
rabat discount.
Rabbi *Ilahi -* the Lord God.
Rabbul.alamin the Lord of the worlds.
Rabbul.gafur the all-forgiving Lord.
Rabbul.izzati the Lord of all honor.
rabet **me-** to beat up.
Rabithah.al Alam.al Islami International Moslem League.
rabuk *spt - dgn api* don't set the fox to watch the geese.
rabun nearsighted, myopic. *(penyakit) - ayam* night blindness. *- dekat* nearsighted.
racun **ke-an:** ~ *jamur* mycotoxicosis. ~ *sendiri* auto-intoxication. ~ *zat arang* asphyxiation. *- api* extinguisher (sub-

stance). - *hama (,serangga)* insecticide.
- *tikus* arsenic.

rada -(.-) somewhat, fairly. - *miring* 1
somewhat slanting (,sloping). 2 (fig.)
somewhat crazy.

radang - *buah ginjal* nephritis. - *hati*
hepatitis, inflammation of the liver.
- *kandung empedu* cholecystitis. -
kura anthrax. - *tonsil* angina. - *umbai
cacing* appendicitis.

radar radar.

radèn - *adipati* title for vice-regent of
Yogyakarta and Sala. - *ngabehi* title
for married male or female aristocrat.
- *nganten* title for married woman of
medium-low status. - *rara (,roro)* title
for unmarried high-status girl. - *tumeng-
gung* title going with a certain office
held.

radi may (God) bestow favor; in the expression: - *Allah an-hu* and - *Allahuanhu*
may Allah be satisfied (,content) with
him.

radial radial (tire).

radiasi radiation. - *atom* atomic radiation.

radikal 1 drastic, sweeping. 2 fundamental.

radikalisme radicalism.

radio **di-kan** to be over the radio. - *amatir*
an amateur radio operator. - *canting
(,dengkul)* rumors. *Menurut siaran -
dengkul* ..., Rumors have it that ... -
gelombang pendek short-wave radio.
- *kaset* pretaped messages. *Bus kota
sdh diperlengkapi dgn - kaset,* The
city buses have already been equipped
with pretaped messages. *dgn - mulut*
by word of mouth. - *salon* console
(radio). - *transistor* portable (,transis-
tor) radio.

radioaktivitèt radioactivity.

radiogram radiogram.

radiograp radiograph.

radio.isotop radioisotope.

radiologi radiology.

radiologis radiologist.

radiotélegrafis radio telegraphist.

radli (s.) RADI.

rafaksi allowance (for damage or mois-
ture, in rice trade).

raf(f)lésia a giant flower without stalk
found in Sumatra and named after the
first and only British Governor-General
of Indonesia Sir Thomas Stamford
Raffles (1811–1816): an insectivorous
plant.

Rafidi and **Rafizi** 1 (lit.) 'forsakers' —
the name used by Sunnites for the
Shi'ah sect. 2 schismatic, heretic
(Moslem).

raga **pe-an** demonstration (practical showing of how s.t. works or is used), display. ~ *busana (,mode)* fashion show.

ragam I **berse-** uniformed (of army men,
etc.). **menye-kan** to uniform. **pe-an**
diversification.

ragam II (gramm.) voice. - *gramatikal*
grammatical voice.

ragawi physical. *antropologi* - physical
anthropology.

ragbol ceiling mop, a feather duster on a
long stick.

ragu *dgn tdk - lagi* undoubtedly, without
doubt, certainly. *membangkitkan* **ke-an**
to cause confusion.

rahab and **rahap** *kain* - shroud.

raharja and **raharjo** prosperous, successful,
lucky.

rahasia covert, crypto. - *dipegang teguh*
strict(est) privacy assured. *Bukan
menjadi - lagi bhw* ..., It is no longer a
secret that ... **ke-an** secrecy, privacy.

rahayu free from sorrows or catastrophes,
to escape danger.

rahmat - *tersembunyi (,tdk langsung)* a
blessing in disguise.

rahmatullahi *wa-* and God's mercy.

raiged(h)èg and **raigedèk** shameless,
impudent.

raih **me-:** ~ *dgn pemberian* to appease
with presents. ~ *hati* charming, en-
chanting. ~ *perhatian* to draw the
attention.

raimuna 1 (originally a word used by o.
of the ethnic groups in Irian Jaya)
traditional assembly of ethnic chiefs

to discuss community matters. 2 (now, also) jamboree, esp. for *penegaks* and *pandegas.*

rais president. *R- Jumhuriyah* The President of the Republic (of Indonesia).

raja I (in Ambon) village chief. *sang R-.di.R-* the Shah (of Iran). **be-** *di hati, bersultan di mata* monarch of all o. surveys. **me-** to rule. *- hutan* tiger. *- minyak* oil shiek. *- putra* prince. *- putri* princess.

raja II *- udang* white-colored kingfisher.

rajaberana treasures.

rajah *- tangan* the lines on the palm of the hand. *ahli - tangan* palmist.

rajaléla keme-an rampage (noun).

rajang pe- *kayu* wood chips.

rajapati murder.

rajin habitually. *Orang.orang yg - mengunjungi nite club,* People who habitually visit night clubs. **peng-** craftsman. *- kerja* industrious.

rajungan k.o. edible small black crab (L. Portunus spp.).

raka 1 older brother. 2 senior college student.

rakan *- hewan* livestock. *- lembu* cattle stock.

rakanita female senior college student.

Rakata the volcanic island of *Krakatau* (Krakatoa).

rakawati female senior college student.

rakawira male senior college student.

raker [rapat kerja] working meeting. **ber.-** to hold a working meeting.

rakerna [rapat kerja paripurna] plenary working meeting.

rakit I **be-.-** *ke hulu, berenang. renang ke tepian* after rain comes sunshine. *- penyeberangan* ferry (boat). *- penyelamat* life raft.

rakit II **me-** to assemble (cars). **pe(ng)-** assembler (of cars). **pe-an** assembling. *perusahaan* ~ assembling plant. *sedan* **-an** an assembled sedan *-.-an* spare parts.

rakit III **pe-** clerk (belonging to category C of the Government Employees Salary Scale). ~ *telekomunikasi penerbangan*

radio flight operator.

raksa *- bumi* member of village municipality, irrigation overseer.

rakus (adj.) cormorant.

rakyat smallholder, in compound words of the type: *karet (,kopi)* - smallholders' rubber (,coffee). *tdk* **me-** does not appeal to the people, does not strike (the imagination of) the people.

ralip *pd* **-nya** normally.

ralliwan participant in an automobile rally.

rama (s.) ROMO. **pe-** primate.

ramah hearty, cordial, affectionate. *-.tamah* affable, amiable, amicable, jovial. **be-.tamah** *dgn* to talk confidentially with. **ke-(.tamah)an** cordiality, affability, amicability, amiability. **pe-** 1 jovial, affable, genial, sporting. 2 hearty, cordial. 3 talkative, chatty, gossipy.

ramai *di mata -* in the eye of the public. *di muka (khalayak) -* in public. *jalan yg - dilalui kendaraan* a road with heavy traffic. *Ada apa -?* What's up? What's doing? What's the trouble? *jam.jam yg -* peak hours. **(be)-.-** 1 (attacked, mistreated, etc.) by many people together. *Sala Kabiran secara ~ tlh dianiayai oleh para awak kapal,* Sala Kabiran was mistreated by the entire body of the ship's crew. 2 with combined efforts, with forces combined. 3 jointly. 4 in great numbers. 5 to make merry, feast. **ke-an** *utk para pria* stag party. *-.pasien* busily frequented by patients (a doctor's office).

ramal pe- forecaster. **-an:** ~ *bintang* horoscope. ~ *cuaca* weather forecast.

Ramayana 1 Great Hindu epic, originally composed by the Indian poet Valmiki, narrating the life and adventures of Rama, Vishnu's seventh incarnation, and how his wife Sita is kidnaped by the demon Rawana and carried off to the island of Sri Lanka (Ceylon). Sita is rescued by Rama and his friend *Anoman,* the monkey king. 2 name of an Indonesian restaurant in New York City, opened on October 7, 1971.

rambatè - *ratè hayo* to carry a heavy burden in mutual cooperation.

rambu *bea* - beaconage. **pe-an** beaconing. - *suar* light beacon (,buoy).

rambung rubber.

rambut filament. *Ia tdk menduga seujung -pun,* He would not dream of, he has not the slightest intention of. - *sama hitam, hati masing.masing berlainan* so many countries, so many customs. *bagai - dibelah tujuh (,seribu)* a bit. *Jiwanya bergantung kpd (,di) - sehelai,* His life hangs in the balance. *si - pirang* the blonde. *seorang laki.laki* **ber**- *putih* a grey-haired man. - *buatan* a wig. - *dipotong pendek* crewcut. - *gondrong* bushy, long hair. - *hiasan* a wig. - *ikal* curly (,wavy) hair. - *jagung* auburn (,reddish brown) hair. - *keriting* curly (,wavy) hair. - *konita* a wig. - *madul. madul (,terurai)* dishevelled hair.

rambutan I a fruit with a hairy integument (L. Nephelium lappaceum), usually red, similar to leechee, in season November-February. - *cilebak* round, meat easily separated from seed, red color, sweet sour. - *lengkeng* sweet, dry, red, round, not much hair, small. - *si macan* oval, sweet, dark red. - *si nyonya* dark red, long hair, round, difficult to separate from seed, juicy, sweet sour, cheap. - *rapiah* short hair, small, green, very sweet, cheap, with a *kelengkeng* taste.

rambutan II - *laut* sea urchin.

Ramelan (S.) RAMADAN.

rames **ng-i** to examine (carefully).

rampah **me-** to generalize. **pe-an** generalization.

rampang -.*rempus* and *tdk dgn* -.-**nya** unsure, uncertain.

rampas **pe-an** *kekuasaan negara* coup d'état. **-an** *perang* spoils of war.

rampog and **rampok** **ng-** to rob, plunder, loot.

rampung *proyek yg diborongkan sampai* - turnkey project. **pe-an** finish, workmanship.

ramput **ng-** to lie to, trick.

rana atrophy.

rancah **pe-** *bor* drilling rig.

rancang **pe-** *mode* fashion designer. *masih berada dlm* **-an** (it) has still not come off, in the planning stage.

rancu **pe-an** confusion.

randa - *kembang* young childless widow.

randai a Minangkabau traditional theater.

randa.rondo to walk in a stooping position looking here and there (as if searching for s.t.).

randu (used by the *TNI.AL* for) 'Roger.'

rangah proud, haughty, supercilious.

rangda character in Balinese dance-play; looks like a witch and represents 'evil.'

rangga tine of antler. *rusa betina tdk* **be**- the female deer has no antlers. - *gunung* mountain crest (,ridge).

rangka *dlm* - *perjanjian ini* under (,in the framework of) this agreement. *Sdr. di Indonesia dlm* - *apa?* For what purpose are you in Indonesia? What are you doing in Indonesia?

rangkai *satu* **-an** *peluru mitralyur berisikan 150 butir peluru* a 150-bullet machine-gun cartridge belt.

rangkak **pe-** crawler.

rangkap *(dlm)* - *dua (,satu ,tiga)* in duplicate (,single copy ,triplicate). *tdk dpt* **di-** *dgn* to be incompatible with. **me-menjadi** concurrently.

rangking (world) ranking.

rangkul - *pukul* (*PKI* slogan) embrace and hit.

rangkung *nafas sdh di* **-an** to be dying.

rangsang *adegan yg* **me-** an erotic scene (in a film).

rangsek *bola* - volleyball. *main bola* - to play volleyball. **me-** to take hold of.

rangsum **pe-an** rationing.

ranjang - *lipat* folding bed. - *pengantin (,perkawinan)* marriage (,nuptial) bed.

ranjau *duduk meraut - tegak meninjau*

jarah to be continually at work, be always on o's guard. - *apung* floating mine.

ranji allotment, share.

ranjing ke-an ... -mania. ~ *main judi* gambling-crazy.

ransel knapsack.

rantai - *babi* k.o magical matter which, it is said, can make its owner invulnerable to the penetration of bullets in a war; it is allegedly found in the tusks of a wild boar which lives alone, since the animal in question is afraid that the power he possesses in his tusks might be seized by other boars; a very expensive commercial object. - *komando* chain of command.

rantang multiple-unit container, metal food carrier, stackable picnic pack. **nge-** to order o's meal from a restaurant or private person who specializes in preparing food for others; the meals are delivered in *rantangs. mengusahakan makanan* -**an** to run a business for catering food in *rantangs.* - *manggut* (s.) JAELANGKUNG.

rantau 1 secluded (of spot), isolated. 2 the areas not belonging to the (Minangkabau or Aceh) heartland, foreign countries. *di* - *(orang)* (to live) abroad, in foreign parts, in a foreign country. *sampai di segala pojok* - as far as the remotest regions. 3 colony, settlement. - *takluk, teluk (dan)* -, *daerah* -, - *daerah* and - *jajahan* 1 area, territory. 2 dependency. 3 bights and reaches. **me-** to out-migrate. **pe-an** out-migration.

ranté 1/25 of a hectare.

rapa *biji* - rapeseed.

rapai k.o. tambourine covered with goatskin.

rapat I ke-an *besar* congress, conference. - *akbar* mass meeting. *R- Komandan* Commander's Call. - *kerja* working meeting. *R- Kerja Panglima* Commander's Call. - *paripurna* plenary session. - *rutin* routine meeting. - *tahunan* annual meeting. *dlm* - *tertutup* in closed session. - *umum anggota* general (members') meeting. - *umum luarbiasa para pemegang saham (,andil)* extraordinary general meeting of stockholders. - *umum tahunan para ahli peserta* and - *umum tahunan para pemegang saham (,andil)* annual general meeting of stockholders.

rapat II close together. *daerah yg* - *penduduknya* a thickly populated area. **me-kan:** ~ *diri dgn (,kpd)* 1 to sit close to s.o. 2 to look for closer relations (in politics, etc.), make overtures (in politics, etc.). ~ *telinga ke* to keep o's ear against (the wall). -.- tightly. *menutup pintu* ~ to close a door tightly.

rapèl 1 reminder, esp. with respect to an obligation which so far has not yet been fulfilled due to negligence. 2 *uang* - arrears, outstanding debts.

rapiah (s.) RAMBUTAN (RAPIAH).

rapuh rigid.

ras 1 race. - *kuning* the yellow race. 2 pedigreed. *anjing* - a pedigreed dog.

rasa *tdk menimbang (,bertimbang)* - heartless. *dpt (,tahu) menimbang* - 1 sensitive, delicate. 2 helpful, ready to help. *timbang* - 1 flexibility, suppleness, elasticity. 2 (in Malaysia) sympathy. *tiada mengenal* - *tenggang. menenggang* inexorable, relentless. **be-** *segar* to feel fit. **nge-in** to taste. *Saya nggak pernah* ~ *sekolah*, I never went to school. **R-in** *lu!* Serves you right! **ng-ni** 1 to talk about s.o. 2 to gossip. 3 to have bad feelings toward s.o. **pe-an:** ~ *bersalah* guilty feelings. ~ *tdk puas yg makin meningkat* an ever-growing dissatisfaction. **se-** it feels as if. - *benci* feelings of hate (,resentment). - *gondok* feeling of discontent. *menimbulkan* - *gondok* to bring about a feeling of discontent. - *hati* mood. - *kasihan* commiseration. - *kejang.jantung* angina pectoris (i.e. angina of the chest). - *menyendiri* feeling of alien-

ation. -.**me-kan** tasting (of tea, etc.).
- *senasib.sepenanggungan* sense of belonging. - *sukur* gratitude, thankful-
ness. - *tanggung.jawab* sense of responsibility. - *terima kasih* gratitude, thank-
fulness.

rasalat apostleship.

rasam (s.) RESAM.

rasamala a huge forest tree producing
fine and lasting wood.

rasan -an cynosure. *menjadi* ~ to become
the topic of the day.

rasé civet cat.

raseksa monstrous giant.

rasi me- to calculate cabalistically whether
a boy and a girl are well matched (by
giving to the letters of their names certain values, etc.).

rasia (s.) RAZ(Z)IA.

rasialisme racism.

rasionalisasi reduction in force, rif. *Ia
kena -,* He was riffed.

rasuk di- *mimpi* to have a dream. *orang
ke-an* medium (the person).

rasul -an 1 (in general) a ceremony exalt-
ing Mohammed. 2 (in West Java) a
ceremony announcing an intended
marriage. 3 (in Central and East Java)
a post-harvest feast.

rata *sdh - mencari* to have searched all
over the place. **me-** even(ly). **meme-kan**
to distribute evenly. **pe(me)-an** equali-
zation, an even distribution. *di sedunia* all over the world. -.- average,
each and every. *kecepatan* ~ average
speed.

ratib continuous reciting of the words *la
ilaha illallah.*

ratifikasi ratification.

ratna (s.) PECAH (SBG RATNA).

ratu 1 prince. 2 princess. 3 'queen' in
beauty, fashion, etc. contest. *R- Batik*
Batik Queen. *R- Kecantikan* Beauty
Queen. *R- Kecantikan Sejagat* Miss
Universe Beauty Pageant. *R- Pariwisata*
Tourist Queen. *R- Sejagad* Miss Universe.

raun to make a tour of … (in a car).

raung -an *sirene* the roaring (,roar) of
sirens.

raut - *wajah* facial expression.

rawan I *(sayu)* - moved, affected; weak.
daerah - trouble spot. *memberi* - to
stir the emotions. **ke-an** concern. **me-
kan** *hati* moved, affected. - *hati* rap-
ture.

rawan II classifier for articles made of
cordage or string.

rawan III *takhta* - a vehicle mentioned
in romances.

rawat pe- *udara* flight nurse. **pe-an:** *Pusat
P~ Sepanjang Hari* Day Care Center. ~
gigi dental care. ~ *kaki* pedicure. ~
keluarga home nursing. ~ *kuku* manicure. ~ *kulit* skin care. ~ *lanjutan* after-
care. ~ *muka* 1 face massage. 2 make
up. ~ *rambut* hair care. ~ *sebelum kelahiran* prenatal care. ~ *tangan* manicure.

rawé.rawé rantas, malang.malang putung
(nationalist slogan) everything hampering us in our forward march will be
swept away.

rawon boiled beef prepared with *kluwak*
sauce.

rawuh ke-an trance.

raya pe-an festival.

Rayagung *bln* - (in West Java) the twelfth
month of the Moslem year.

rayah me-i *jalan raya siang.malam* to
raid the highways day and night.

rayan te-.(r)- between sleeping and walking.

rayap I termite. *spt* - packed like sardines
in a tin.

rayap II corruptor, embezzler.

rayon district; precinct; (s.) KORAMIL.
pe-an (s.) RAYONISASI.

rayonisasi districting, dividing into dis-
tricts (schools).

rayu me- to court.

razi (s.) RADI.

razzia *kena* - to be raided. *mengadakan
(,melakukan)* - *thd* to make a clean
sweep of.

réaksi be(r)- to react. - *berantai* chain
reaction.

réaktor reactor. - *atom* atomic reactor.

réalistis mengr-kan to make realistic.

réalita(s) and **réalitèt** reality.

réalpolitik political realism.

rebah - *tertiarap* fall(en) forward (,on o's face ,head first).

rébèn *kacamata* - Ray Ban sunglasses (considered a luxury).

rèbewès be- to possess a driver's licence.

Rebo - *pungkasan (,wekasan)* the last Wednesday in *Sapar*.

réboisasi regreening.

rebon *(udang)* - a very small species of rivershrimp.

rebung - *tdk jauh dr rumpunnya* like father, like son. *pucuk* - chevrons (as a design in art).

rebus *kacang (,telur ,ubi)* - and - *kacang (,telur ,ubi)* peanuts (,eggs ,sweet potatoes) boiled in water. *telur* - *setengah matang* a soft-boiled egg. **-an** decoction.

rebut be-: *bertengkar* ~ *mulut* to wrangle, quarrel. ~ *nama* said of ambitious persons. ~ *rezeki* to fight for o's existence. *senja* ~ *dgn malam, siang* ~ *dgn senja* and *di kala alam* ~ *senja* the transition from twilight to dark. **be-an** to scramble. ~ *kekuasaan* to seize power. **be-.-an** *kata* to wrangle, quarrel.

recall **me-** to recall (members of Parliament).

rècèt to burst out crying.

rèchtswége van - ipso jure, by operation of (the) law.

rècok -.- *di belakang* (unpleasant) aftermath (of a revolution).

reda ke-an *ketegangan* détente. **pe-an** quieting down.

redaksi di- *oleh* to be edited by. **ke-an** (adj.) editorial. *di bidang* ~ in the editorial field.

redaksionil (adj.) editorial.

redam pe-: ~ *bunyi* silencer (of a pistol). ~ *suara* muffler.

réduksi reduction.

redup 1 glassy (of eyes of dead body). 2a - *dan sejuk* (afternoon) coolness (after hot day). 2b the lee(side) of (a tree). 2c to subside, abate (of storm). 2d waning (glory). 3 to fade (away), grow dim(mer) (of light of setting sun),

dying (away) (of sound). 4 almost dying (of fire), vaguely burning (of lamp).

redut *hatinya* **me-** he felt hurt (,insulted).

ré.édukasi re-education.

ré.èkspor re-export. **me-** to re-export.

réferat 1 report, paper. 2 lecture.

réferènsi reference.- *bank* bank reference.

réformasi reformation.

réformulasi reformulation.

rega (S.) HARGA.

regang -.*kain* banner.

regèn ke-an regency.

régénérasi regeneration.

régim regime.

régional regional. *kerjasama* - regional cooperation (among southeast Asian countries).

régistrasi me- to register.

régol gate, door.

regu 1 smallest tactical unit of the *TNI* consisting of 12 to 14 men. 2 smallest unit in the *Pramuka* Boy Scout Movement consisting of *penggalangs* (membership maximum: 10). *R*- *Bela Diri* Self-Defense Squad of the now proscribed *PKI*. - *bunuh diri* suicide squad. - *penembak* firing squad. - *penolong* rescue squad.

reguk me- to gulp down.

régular and **régulèr** regular. **di-kan** to be regulated.

rèh ng- to govern.

réhabilitasi me-kan to rehabilitate.

réhat (in Malaysia) rest, break. **be-** to relax, take a break.

réindoktrinasi reindoctrination.

réinkarnasi reincarnation.

Rejeb name of the seventh Jav. month. *nyesel tujuh* - regret forever. *sampai tujuh* - even unto the seventh generation, forever and ever.

rejeki (s.) REZEKI. *kalau ada* - ... if fortune favors us ... - *saya ini* and *ada* - I'm lucky, luck is on my side. -*(nya) murah* he's doing well, things are going well for him. *kejatuhan* - to have (,receive) a windfall. - *jangan ditolak* you should not let the opportunity slip by. *membawa* - bringing good luck. *men-*

dapat - to get a cut, share.

rejeng me- to grab hold of.

réjim regime. - *totaliter* totalitarian regime.

rèk to bet on each number in a series (lottery).

réka -an coinage (of new words). -. *bentuk* design.

rekah *spt delima* **me-** said of beautiful lips.

rékalsitran recalcitrant.

rekam me- to tape (songs, speeches, etc.). **pe-an** taperecording. **-an** 1 copy. ~ *dikirimkan kpd* (under a letter, in Sumatra) c.c. 2 recording.

rekan colleague. *dgn* -.*-nya* 1 with his friends, companions, associates. 2 with affiliates. **pe-** supplier. **pe-an** *makanan* catering. - *sekelas* classmate. - *setahanan* fellow detainee. - *sewartawan* co-reporter, co-journalist.

rekanita female colleague.

rekat pe- *gigi palsu* denture adhesive.

réken be- to figure out.

rékening 1 receipt (a written acknowledgment of having received a specified amount of money), bill presented for payment. - *listrik (,gas ,air ,dll.)* the electric (,gas ,water ,etc.) bill. *Dia dikenakan - sebesar 2.500 dolar,* A bill in the amount of 2,500 dollars was presented to him. 2 (bank) account. *membuka - pd sebuah bank* to open an account with a bank. - *deposito* deposit account. - *koran* statement of account. - *penjualan* account sales. *R- Rupiah Bukan Penduduk* Nonresident's Rupiah Account. - *tabungan* savings account.

rekès application letter. *membuang -* to send (,write) application letters at random.

rekisitor (s.) REQUISITOIR.

réklame mengr-kan to advertise.

réklaséring discharged prisoner's aid, after-prison care.

rékomèndasi recommendation. *surat -* recommendation letter.

rékor *memecahkan -* to break a record. - *dunia* world record.

rékos review (o's studies).

rékréasi ber- to take some recreation.

rékrut draftee. **peng-an** drafting, recruitment.

rèkstok horizontal bar (gymnastics).

rèktor President (of university, *FKIP, FIPIA,* etc. and some academies).

rekurs to repeat a course.

rèl *keluar dr* - to derail, go off the rails.

réla ke-an aquiescence.

rélaks and **ber-** to relax.

rélasi depositor (in bank).

rélatif *dlm waktu yg - singkat* in a relatively short time.

rèlban railroad.

réligi religion.

réligius and **rélijius** religious.

relikwi relic.

rèm *menginjak -* to put on the brakes. *bekas* **-an** skid (,tire) mark. - *cakram* disc brake. - *torpedo* coaster (,back-pedalling) brake.

rèmah *karet* - crumb rubber.

remaja 1 teen-age. 2 nubile. 3 junior. *dlm usia - putra, sedang gadis -* and *muda -* at a marriageable age, in the prime of life. *golongan -* the teen-age set. **me-kan** to renovate, (urban) renew. **pe-an** renewal, renovation. ~ *kota* urban renewal.

remang (s.) REMENG. **ke-an** 1 twilight, dusk. 2 faint glow. -.- dim, dusky. *tampak* ~ vaguely visible in the dark.

remas me- *(kertas)* to rumple, crumple (paper).

rématik (s.) DEMAM (REMATIK).

rembang *sebelum - tengah hari* before noon. *hari sdh - tengah hari* it's getting on to noon.

rèmbèng be- *dgn* next to.

rembes me- *masuk* and **me-i** to infiltrate. **pe-** infiltrant.

rembug pe-an (S.) PEREMBUKAN. *R-Desa* legislative institution of village administration.

rembuk -an lobbying.

rèmburs C.O.D.

rèmèh di-kan to be considered unimportant, count for little.

remeng (S.) REMANG. -.- shady. *tokoh*
~ a shady character (,figure).

remi rummy (a card game).

remis I k.o. mussel.

remis II (s.) REMISE. *bermain* - to draw
(,tie).

remise a draw, tie.

remisi remission, pardon, forgiveness.

rempak kese-an *kerja* teamwork.

rempela gizzard.

rempèyèk (s.) PEYEK (KACANG).

renang be- *gaya dada* to crawl (in swimming).

rencana *tinggal dlm - saja* is not yet set in
motion, still in the planning stage.
secara **be-** *dan sengaja* premeditated,
of malice prepense, of (,with) malice
aforethought. **di-kan** *tiba* estimated
time of arrival. **pe-an:** ~ *keluarga*
family planning. ~ *kota* city planning.
- *induk* master plan. - *lima th* 5-year
plan. - *pekerjaan* scheme of activity,
work schedule. *R- Undang.Undang*
Draft Bill. - *urgensi* urgency program.
- *usul* draft proposal. - *waktu* time
schedule.

rendah ke-an: ~ *budi* immorality. ~ *hati*
and *ke-.hatian* modesty, humbleness.
me-.diri to humble o.s. - *hati* unassum-
ing, unobtrusive. - *pengawakan* small
of stature.

rendang and **rendhang** k.o. beefstew
cooked in chillies and coconut milk
until dry.

rèndemèn conversion rate; for example,
conversion of milled rice from stalk
paddy.

rendeng west monsoon, the rainy (,wet)
season.

rendet and **rendhet** slow.

rèng lath. - *kayu* a wooden lath.

rengak (S.) RENGAT.

rengas a generic name given to some trees
which yield fine timber (L. Gluta
rengas).

rengat me-kan to crack, split.

renggang me-kan *pertalian (,pertemuan
,hubungan)* to alienate (friends).

rengginang semi-cooked sticky rice patted

into small cakes; sundried and fried.

renggut me- to take away (by force). ~
nyawa to take (away) s.o.'s life. **me-
kan** *kaki hendak mati* to be in convulsions.

rengkah - *dua* broken in half [,two (parts)].

rèngkèt me- *(ketakutan)* to tremble with
fear.

rengkudah loaded down.

rengsa ke-an listlessness, apathy.

renjana be- emotional. **ke-an** emotional-
ity.

rénovasi renovation.

rentan allergic. *orang itu sangat* - that
person is hypersensitive. **ke-an** allergy.
- *hati* quick-tempered, irascible.

rentang *jembatan 5.* **-an** a five-span bridge.

rèntèng *Tanggung.jawab dr pendiri.pendiri
adalah secara -,* The liability of the
founders (of the corporation) is collective.

rèntenir 1 rentier, person of independent
means, person who has a fixed income
from real estate, bonds, etc. 2 loan
shark, moneylender.

rèntèt se-an *diplomat* a parade of diplo-
mats.

renung -an contemplation.

réog I a comic performance of a group of
5 to 6 comedians in special costumes,
each carrying a drum of a different
size tied to the waist by a sash and
dancing in a circle.

réog II [reorganisasi] reorganization.

réol sewer, drain.

réorganisasi me-(kan) to reorganize.

réot ramshackle, broken-down. *sebuah
gubuk* - a ramshackle bungalow.

réparasi me-(kan) to repair.

répatrian repatriate, i.e. a person who has
returned to his fatherland.

répatriasi repatriation. **di-(kan)** to be
repatriated.

Répelita [Rencana Pembangunan Lima
Tahun] Five-Year Development Plan.

répèrto(w)ar repertoire.

répetir *bedil* - repeating rifle.

répli(e)k reply by *jaksa*, counterplea (in
lawsuit).

répormir 'reformed,' i.e. Calvinist(ic).
Kristen - Calvinist.
réportase coverage, report covering,
reporting.
réporter (news)reporter.
rèpot ke-an 1 stir, bustle. 2 very busy.
-.-: *Jangan ~!* Don't go to any trouble!
Please, don't bother! *Mau minum apa?*
Ah, jangan ~! What would you like to
drink? Ah, don't go to any trouble!
répresèntatif (of receptionist, secretary,
etc.) good-looking and making a good
impression on people, presentable,
prepossessing.
réprèsif repressive.
réproduksi me-kan to reproduce.
rèptil reptile.
républik republic. *R- Demokrasi Jerman*
German Democratic Republic. *R-*
Demokrasi Rakyat Korea Democratic
Peoples Republic of Korea. *R- Demo-*
krasi Vietnam Democratic Republic
of Vietnam. *R- Dominika* Dominican
Republic. *R- Indonesia* Republic of
Indonesia. *-.pulau* island republic, i.e.
Singapore. *R- Rakyat Cina (,Tiongkok)*
People's Republic of China.
républikan republican. ke-an (adj.) republican.
républikéin (s.) REPUBLIKAN. - *bon-*
cengan (Indonesian) republican fellow-
traveler, i.e. a republican in name who
sympathized with the Dutch-created
federal system.
requisitoir summation, prosecutor's demand that accused be punished.
rerangka framework.
reresanan topic of the day, subject of
discussion.
reridu ng- to cause trouble.
rerongkong skeleton.
rerumputan lawn.
resah ke-an 1 restlessness. 2 frustration.
resam - *minyak ke minyak, - air ke air*
birds of a feather flock together.
resèpsi and résèpsi reception. be- to give
(,hold) a reception.
resèpsionis and résèpsionis receptionist.
resèrse investigation. *R- Kriminal* Crimi-

nal Investigation (Service).
resèrsir plain-clothes man.
résèrvasi reservation. *membikin* - to make
reservations.
resèrve reserve. *tanpa* - without reserve,
frankly, openly.
resès recess. be(r)- to be in recess (Parliament). di-kan to be recessed, sent on
recess.
résèsi recession.
resi religious ascetic and mystical teacher.
résidèn ke-an 1 office of a *residen.* 2 the
residence of a *residen.*
résidivis recidivist, repeated offender.
resiko ber.- risky. me-kan *dirinya* to take
a chance. - keamanan security risk.
résiprositèt - *diplomatik* diplomatic
reciprocity.
resisir (s.) RESERSIR.
résital recital (i.e. a musical program).
Rèskrim [Reserse Kriminil] Criminal
Investigation (Service).
resmi meng-kan to inaugurate, dedicate.
pe-an *pemutaran* (film) premiere.
rèsor(t) area; (s.) KOREM and RESSOR(T).
rèssor(t) district, (area of) jurisdiction,
police precinct.
rèstitusi reimbursement to government
employee for travel expenses, medical
expenditures, etc.
rèstoran pe-an restaurant business. - *kaki.*
lima roadside eating stall.
rèstorasi restoration. di- to be restored.
rèstriksi restriction. di- to be restricted.
réstrukturisasi restructuring.
rèt diamonds (in card game).
retak ke-an rift. *-nya rumah tangga* broken
homes. - *kepribadian* split personality.
retènsi the right to retain goods belonging to another until debts in connection with these goods have been settled.
rètètèt.tètèt *-nya senapan mesin* the
rattling of a machine gun.
retool di- to be brainwashed, down-
graded, retired, dismissed or jailed; (s.)
RITUL.
retooling the process by which civil servants of doubtful loyalty were replaced
by others who were more sympathetic

to the (Soekarno) regime.

rétribusi 1 repayment of money advanced for a specific purpose from the proceeds of that purpose. 2 payment for use of services or facilities owned by the government. 3 a duty collected by a government agency for the use of government goods or services; includes light and sewer bills.

réuni reunion.

ré.unipikasi reunification.

révaluasi revaluation. **me-(kan)** to revaluate.

revans revenge. *mengambil -* to take o's revenge.

révisionis revisionist.

révisionisme revisionism.

révisir (S.) MEREVISI.

révolusi R- (upper case) the Indonesian Revolution. **ber-** and **ber.R-** to revolt, bring about a revolution. *- dua babak* a two-stage revolution. *R- Fisik (,Phisik)* the Physical Revolution, i.e. that part of the Indonesian Revolution waged from 1945 through 1950. *- istana* palace revolution.

réwanda monkey.

réwang ng-i to help, be instrumental (in achieving s.t.).

rèwès *tdk* **(me)-** to ignore, pay no attention to.

réyog (s.) REOG.

rezeki (s.) REJEKI. *ada nyawa (,umur) ada -* with time comes counsel. *terbuka -nya* he stands a good chance. *banyak mendapat -* to earn a lot. *membagi -* to share the luck (obtained after having rendered a service to an importer, for instance, by granting him an import license, etc.). *- nonjok (,nomplok)* a windfall, an unexpected good fortune.

ri a cry for calling ducks (usually repeated: *ri, ri, ri, ri*).

ria arrogant, proud.

riah keme-an 1 solemnity. 2 grandeur.

riak be- *tanda tak dalam, berguncang tanda tak penuh* empty barrels make more noise. **be-.-** to heave (of water). *- yg berdebur.debur (,memecah) di*

(tepi) pantai breakers, surf.

rial real (a former coin, worth about 2 guilders). *jika tiada - di pinggang, saudara yg rapat menjadi renggang* a friend in need is a friend indeed.

riang be-.- to have a good time, enjoy o.s.

rias pe- make-up artist. *~ rambut* hairstylist. *- wajah* make-up. *tukang - wajah* make-up artist.

Riau *- Daratan* Mainland Riau, i.e. that part of the Riau Province located on the island of Sumatra with Pekanbaru as its capital as opposed to *Kepulauan Riau,* the Riau Archipelago located south of Malaysia and Singapore.

ribut noisy. **ke-an** 1 rioting. 2 agitation.

ridha, ri(d)la, ridza and **ridho** blessings. *- Tuhan* God's blessings.

rido (s.) RIDHA, etc. **di-i** to be blessed.

rijsttafel (pron. rèstafel) Indonesian smorgasbord, consisting of white rice with a large variety of side dishes.

rikuh *merasa* **di-kan** to feel embarrassed.

rilèks relax(ed), informal.

rim a ream (of paper).

rimba *- larangan* State forest.

rimbat gunwale (of boat).

rinci (S.) PERINCI.

rincu(h) confused. **ke-an** 1 confusion. 2 disorder. 3 a mess.

rindang ke-an shade. *di ~ pokok.pokok palem* in the shade of palm-trees.

rinding *bulu kudukku* **me-** my hair stood on end.

rindu *melepaskan -nya* to indulge o's fancies. *- dendam (,rawan)* head over heels in love. *- ke kampung, - kampung dan halamannya, - kembali ke desanya, - akan tanah airnya* and *nafsu - negeri* to be homesick, nostalgic.

ringan inexpensive. *dgn -* easily. *dgn harga - * at a moderate price. *- sama dijinjing berat sama dipikul* 'if it is light in weight it is carried in the hand jointly, if it is heavy it is carried on the shoulders jointly,' i.e. to share o's joys and sorrows. **me-kan** *langkah* to take the trouble to.

ringgit the Malaysian dollar.

ringkas -an 1 abstract. 2 abbreviation.
- *cerita* to make a long story short.
ringkih ke-an weakness.
ringkus me- to arrest. pe- captor.
rintang -an: ~ *bahasa* language barrier.
~ *kawat* entanglement. ~ *pohon* abatis.
tanpa ~ and *tdk* di-i unimpeded, un-
hampered.
rintis me-*jalan* to pave the way.
rio(o)l sewer(pipe).
Ripta.loka (in the *Bina Graha,* Jakarta)
Operations Room.
risafel reshuffle. di- to be reshuffled (of
Cabinet).
risau pe- troubleshooter.
risèt research. me- to do research work.
pe- researcher, research worker. - *atom*
atomic research. - *ilmiah* scientific research. - *terpakai* applied research.
risik I news. *blm ada -.-nya* there is still
no sign (,trace) of it (e.g. of the lost
money).
risik II to rustle (of paper, leaves, etc.).
ke-an rustling. -an the rustle.
risiko be- risky.
riskan risky.
riskir me- to risk.
riskol Jakarta batik headdress for men,
permanently sewn in shape.
risol rissole, i.e. minced meat mixed with
bread crumbs, egg, etc. enclosed in a
thin pastry and fried.
rispot Indonesian stew.
rit run (bus, truck), trip (made by busdriver).
ritme rhythm. - *biologis* biorhythm.
ritul me- (under President Soekarno) to
replace civil servants of doubtful loyalty by others who are more sympathetic
to the regime. pe-an (s.) RETOOLING.
riung mungpulung to be together (of
college students in West Java). *mengadakan acara* - to organize a get-together
program.
riwan a bad dream.
riwayat *habis -nya* it's all over with him,
he's done for. - *hidup (yg ditulis) sendiri* autobiography.
riweng and riwing to be at o's wits' end,

be at a loss what to do.
rizki and rizqi 1 livelihood. 2 luck; (s.)
REJEKI.
robah di- to be amended. *sebagaimana
tlh ~ dan ditambah* (i.e. a set phrase in
regulations, etc.) as has been amended
and supplemented. pe-an *kabinet* cabinet shakeup.
robot robot.
robur k.o. motorized pedicab.
Robusta a species of coffee.
roda -an (in the Karawang area, West
Java) a *padi* dealer who makes use of a
cow-drawn cart for selling *padi.* - *gendeng* flywheel. *motor Harley - tiga* a
Harley Davidson motorcycle with sidecar.
rodok I me- to fuck.
rodok II (S.) RADA.
rofel me- to put together into o.
roga (in Ujung Pandang, Southern Celebes) pedicab, tricycle.
roi *garis* - building line.
Rois Chairman.-*A(a)m* General Chairman
(of the *P.B. Syuriyah N.U.* or Executive Board for Legislative Affairs of
the *Nahdlatul Ulama* Party). - *Awal*
First Chairman. - *Tsani* Second Chairman. - *Salis* Third Chairman.
rojolélé a rice variety.
rok I - *ketat* straight (,tight) skirt. - *mini*
mini skirt. - *mini serba kelihatan* see-
thru mini skirt. - *span* straight (,tight)
skirt. - *terusan* a sheath dress.
rok II (s.) MUSIK (ROK).
rokèt missile. me- to skyrocket. me-kan
kariernya to make o's career shoot up.
pe-an rocketry, weapon system. - *dua
tingkat* two-stage rocket. - *terkendali*
guided missile.
rokhani(a)wan spiritual leader, (male)
ecclesiastic.
rokhaniwati female ecclesiastic.
rokok I me- *terus sambung.menyambung*
to be a chain smoker. ng(e)- to smoke
a cigarette. - *berfilter* a filter cigarette.
- *bermentol* a mentholated cigarette.
- *cengkeh* a clove-flavored cigarette.
- *jengking* a cigarette which uses as its

basic material cigarette butts collected by bums or loiterers who pick them up in the streets. - *kawung* a cigarette wrapped in dried sugarpalm leaves. - *klembak kemenyan* a cigarette filled with rhubarb and incense (popular among the people of Kedu and Banyumas). - *klobot* a cigarette wrapped in leaves of the cornhusk. - *lima.lima* the State Express 555 cigarette. - *putih* an ordinary cigarette.

rokok II (in Ujung Pandang, Southern Celebes) code word for a detonator, used for fishing purposes.

roko.roko the black ibis.

rol role, part (in film, theater, etc.). *memegang - jagoan* to play the leading part, be the leading man (,lady).

rolade scrambled egg rolled in slices of spiced fried beef.

rolèt roulette.

roman appearance. **se-** *dgn* to resemble. - *muka* features.

romantika romantics.

romantis ke-an romanticism.

rombak pe-an restructuring.

Romi Romeo.

Romli dan Zubaèdah Romeo and Juliet.

romo RC priest.

romok me- 1 to look poorly (,scrawny) (of chickens). 2 to look depressed (of persons).

romol.romol junk, mess.

romong large pepper (the fruit of a capsicum).

rompiok bundle. **be-** in bundles.

rompong (fish) lure.

romsus cream puff.

roncé me- and **nge-** to rob a person of s.t.

rondok me- (S.) MERUNDUK.

ronéo me- to mimeograph.

rongga antrum. - *insang* gill opening. - *perut* abdominal cavity.

rongrong -an depravations.

ronsen (s.) RONTGEN.

rontal (S.) LONTAR.

rontgen me- to X-ray.

rontok shot down (of aircraft). **me-kan** to shoot down (an aircraft).

roofbouw (pron. rofbaw) 1 (mines) wasteful exploitation, premature exhaustion. 2 (ground, also) exhaustive cultivation.

roréhé (in the eastern part of Indonesia) k.o. fishing-smack.

Roro Kidul (s.) NYAI (RORO KIDUL).

rosario Roman Catholic rosary.

rosèla plant belonging to the mallow family used as a vegetable and also for its fibers.

rosot (s.) MEROSOT.

rotan *tiada - akarpun berguna* 'if there is no rattan even a root is useful,' half a loaf is better than none.

Rotari *Perkumpulan -* Rotary Club.

roti - *bakar* (in Jakarta) (S.) ROTI (PANGGANG). - *blok.blokan* (s.) ROTI (SOBEK). - *gerobakan* bread sold on a pushcart. - *kukus* k.o. steamed cupcakes. - *mentega* bread-and-butter. - *sobek* bread cut in large cube-like portions wrapped in plastic bags; sometimes the bread is prepared with chocolate or pineapple jam.

rowa bulky.

royal -.-an 1 to dissipate, squander. 2 to indulge o's tastes frequently.

royemèn cancellation.

RPKAD [Resimen Para Komando Angkatan Darat] Army Para Commandos Regiment.

RRC [Republik Rakyat Cina] People's Republic of China, PRC.

RST [Rumah Sakit Tentara] Army Hospital.

ruah I chock-full, crammed, packed, (over)crowded, filled to overflowing. *tumpah -* poured out en masse.

ruah II souls. *bulan R-* the eighth month (of the Moslem year).

ruang -an ~ *jurubahasa* interpreter's booth. ~ *juruterbang* cockpit. ~ *konperensi* conference room. ~ *kuliah* lecture room (in university). ~ *operasi* operating room (in hospital). *R~ Pancasila* the area in the Foreign Office in Jakarta where the *Pancasila* was proclaimed (June 1, 1945). ~ *pemungutan* *suara* voting booth. ~ *sidang* assembly hall. *R~ Sidang Ampera* the *Ampera* Meeting Hall in the Department of Public Works and Electric Power. ~ *tempat duduk* seating accommodation (in bus). ~ *tunggu* waiting hall (in station, etc.). - *angkasa* outer space. - *bawah tanah* basement. - *berhias* dressing room. - *duduk* living room. - *hidup* Lebensraum. - *jinem* private chambers. - *kerja* office (in a building). - *konperensi* conference room. - *lingkup* scope. - *muat* cargo space, tonnage. *R- Niaga* Economy Class. -.*pamer(an)* showroom. *R- Pariwisata* Tourist Class. - *pembakaran* combustion chamber. - *pengeram telur* brood chamber. *R- Perawatan Khusus* (in hospitals) Intensive Care Unit. *R- Pertama* First Class. *R- Pola* Operations Room (in the *Balai Kota,* Jakarta). - *rekreasi* recreation room. - *sidang* meeting room, assembly hall. *R- Yudha* War Room (in Army Headquarters, Jakarta).

ruas segment. *bertemu - dgn buku* to be hand in glove. **se-** *tebu yg berulat* the scapegoat of the family.

ruba [rumah di bawah (tanah)] 1 underground tunnel built by communist fugitives, after the 1965 abortive coup, for their leaders. 2 -.- shack.

rubel ruble.

rubiah *orang -* a pious woman. a female *guru (me)ngaji.*

rubut **ke-an** a gang.

rudapaksa violence, force.

rudat Islamic-inspired folk play of the island of Lombok.

rudin 1 poor. 2 bankrupt. 3 without means.

rugi drawback. - *menentang laba, jerih menentang boleh* nothing ventured, nothing gained. *sdh* **be-**.- to have gone to great expense. **ke-an:** ~ *yg berwujud materi* material loss. ~ *laut* average (i.e. loss incurred by damage to a ship at sea or to its cargo). **-nya:** *Apa* ~? Do you mind? Have you any objection?

tak ada ~ it can do no harm, we may as well.

rujak - *cingur rujak* with slices of soft meat. - *gobet (,serut)* a *rujak* variety, the different k.o. fruit are grated and mixed with crunched peanuts.

rujuk to be in agreement, approve. **-an** reference. *buku* ~ reference book. - *kembali* to reconcile. - *masyarakat* social settlement (of conflict).

rukun I 1 - *agama* and *lima - Islam* The Five Pillars of Islam. 2 (fundamental, basic) principle, directive.

rukun II **ke-an** reconciliation. - *(dan) damai kpd* to associate nicely with. - *kerjasama* a co-op association. *R- Tetangga* (abbrev. *RT*) Neighborhood Association, composed of about 40 families. *R- Warga* (abbrev. *RW*) Citizens Association; formerly called *R- Kampung* (abbrev. *RK*).

rum rum.

rumah *dr - ke -* from door to door. *bagai - di tepi tebing* to live on a volcano. - *buruk disapu cat* an ostentatious person. **be-:** ~ *tangga* 1 married. 2 to marry. ~ *tinggal* to live, reside. **di-.sakitkan** to be sent to hospital, be hospitalized. **me-kan** (euph.) to place s.o. under house arrest. ~.*sementara* to temporarily keep s.o. at home (due to participation in a strike, etc.), k.o. layoff. **pe-an** 1 lodgings. 2 (euph.) house arrest. ~ *murah (,rakyat)* low-cost (,income) housing. *ia* **se-** *tangga* he and his family. **se-.-nya** the whole family. - *angker* a haunted house. - *asap* smokehouse (in processing rubber). - *bentuk kopel* duplex house. - *berloteng (,bertingkat)* [one- (,two- ,etc.)] storied building, highrise. - *bilyard* billiard lounge, poolroom. - *bongkar.pasang* a prefabricated house. - *buruh* laborer's house. - *dempet* duplex house. - *gedung* a brick (,concrete) building. - *ibadat* house of worship. - *induk* main building. - *judi* casino. - *kaca* greenhouse, hothouse. - *kematian* morgue. - *kemudi* wheelhouse. - *kenikmatan* house of pleasure. - *kosong* unoccupied house. - *liliput* lilliputian house, hut (occupied by bums). - *minim* low-cost housing. - *mode* fashion (,dressmaking) house, dress shop. - *panggung* [one- (,two- ,etc.)] storied building, highrise. - *pangsa* apartment building. - *pemasyarakatan* penitentiary. - *pemotongan hewan* slaughterhouse. - *percontohan* model home. - *peribadatan* church. - *pijat* massage parlor. - *sakit jiwa* lunatic asylum. - *sakit lepra* leprosarium. - *sakit petirahan* convalescent hospital. - *samping* annex. - *setan* 'devil's house,' i.e. the theosophical lodge. - *siput* 1 snail shell. 2 lilliputian house, hut (occupied by bums). *R- Tahanan Militer* Military House of Detention. - *tangga* family. - *tangga retak* broken home. - *Versluis* government official's house.

Rumania Romania.

rumbang.rombèng shabby.

rumpon (fish) lure.

rumpun *(ter)masuk [(dlm) bagian]* - and **se-** to belong to a (language) family, of the same race (,kind). - *kata* parts of speech (syntactic class). - *telinga* outer ear.

rumpung (s.) ROMPONG.

rumput *bicarakan - di halaman orang, di halaman sendiri - sampai ke kaki tangga* see the mote in the eye of others, but not the beam in their own. *mencari penjahit dlm* - look (,hunt) for a needle in a haystack. **me-** 1 to graze (of cattle). 2 to sod with grass. **-an** gramineae. - *laut* seaweed. - *setan* witchweed (L. Striga lutea).

rumuk (s.) ROMOK. **me-** huddled, curled up, crouched.

runcing mempe- to exacerbate. **pe-an** extremism.

runding *setelah* **di-kan** *dgn* upon consultation with. **pe-an:** ~ *pembatasan persenjataan strategis* strategic arms limitation talks, SALT. ~ *perdamaian* peace talk(s). ~ *segi tiga* tripartite conference.

rundung di-: ~ *bencana* to be struck by misfortune, bad luck. ~ *cinta* to be head over heels in love. ~ *kesulitan* to be careworn.

rundu.randa (s.) RANDA.RONDO.

rungguh -an pledge, item pawned. *rumah* ~ pawnshop.

rungsing 1 quarrelsome. 2 angry. **me-kan** to worry about. ~ *hati* to worry.

rungu audibility, hearing.

rungus me- to grumble.

rungut be-an to complain.

runsing (s.) RUNGSING.

runtih torn off. **me-** to tear off. **-an** tatter, shred.

runtuh me-kan to pull down, demolish (a house). ~ *hati* to capture (,win) the heart of. ~ *iman* tempting, alluring.

runtun *dua th* **be-** for (a period of) two years. **be-.-** successively, in succession. - *konsonan* alliteration. - *vokal* assonance.

rupa *mabuk* - to look only at the appearance. **be-.-** assorted. **se-** *dan sebangun* congruent. **-.-nya** evidently, apparently. - *rungu* 'sound slide,' i.e. a slide backed up by a cassette for the sound (used as an audiovisual aid).

rupiah me-kan to convert into rupiahs. ... **-an** a note worth Rp. ...

rusa - *di hutan, kancah sdh terjerang* sell the skin before the bear is caught. *spt* - *masuk kampung* like a fish out of water.

rusak *namanya* - he has a bad name (,reputation). **me-:** *bahan makanan yg mudah* ~ perishable foodstuffs. ~ *pandangan mata* unsightly. ~ *susila* to demoralize. **mengr-kan** (S.) MERUSAKKAN. **me-kan:** ~ *nama* to slander. ~ *pandangan mata* unsightly.

Ruslan Russia.

rustig (pron. as Indonesian resteh) calm, quiet.

rusuh ng-i to upset s.o.'s plans. **pe-** agitator.

rusuk - *bersayap* dovetail (carpentry).

rute route, way.

rutin routine.

ruwat I ng- vow to request reprieve from the pending *hukum karma.* -an feast in which a vow is made; it has the form of a shadow-play performance with leather puppets.

ruwat II ng-an exorcising.

ruwet - *renteng* difficulties, troubles. - *rentenging praja* a succession of State difficulties. pe-an complication.

ruyat sight, observation. - *al hilal* sight of new moon that fixes the beginning and end of the *Ramadan* Fast.

ruyatul.hilal to see the sickle moon in order to fix the beginning of the Fasting period.

RW [Rintek Wu'uk] dog meat (a Manadonese dish).

S

3.S [suka sama senang] 'like to be happy,' k.o. bribe.

saat time. *dr - ini ke atas* in future, henceforth. pen-an timing. *sdh sampai -nya* it's high time. - *genting (,yg memutuskan ,yg menentukan)* a crucial moment. - *terakhir utk memasukkan berita* deadline (of newspaper).

saba to frequent (restaurants, movie theaters, etc.).

sabana savannah.

Sabang *dr - sampai (,hingga) Merauke* 'from Sabang (off the northern tip of Sumatra) to Merauke (in the northern tip of Irian Jaya),' i.e. an expression of the territorial unity of the Republic of Indonesia including *Irian Jaya.*

sabar calm. *-lah dahulu!* and -kanlah *hatimu!* be patient! ber- *hati* to be patient.

sabatikal sabbatical; (s.) TAHUN (SABATIKAL).

sabet meny- to capture, grab, snatch away. -an slamming (of windows).

sabha (in Bali) congress, conference.

sabil way, road, course. *mati* - to fall in a Holy War. - *Allah, -lah, -ullah* and -illah I Allah's (,God's) cause.

Sabilillah II name of the *Masyumi* militia organization during the 1945 revolution.

sabit peny-an cutting of grass.

sableng nuts.

sabot peny- saboteur.

sab.sab masturbate using soap.

sabuk - *peluru* cartridge belt. - *pengaman* (,penyelamat) safety belt.

sabun ny- embezzling. - *beko* bar of soap. - *colek* cream.

sabung peny- *ayam* cockfighter.

sabut untung - timbul, untung batu tenggelam nobody can escape his destiny.

sad six (only in compounds). *S- Tunggal* The Six-in-one Unit consisting of the Regional Head, Chief of Police, Army Commander, Public Prosecutor, Judge and Chairman of the National Front (under President Soekarno).

sadap meny- to tap (a telephone). peny-an (wire) tapping. ~ *suara* bugging.

sadar - *dr tidur* awake(ned). *tdk - akan dirinya lagi* and *tdk -kan dirinya lagi* unconscious. - *akan dirinya,* - *dr pingsan* and -kan *diri* to recover consciousness. *menjadi - akan* to become aware of. *antara - dan tiada* half-conscious. berke-an *bank* bank-minded.

sadarusalam paradise on earth.

sadel saddle (of bicycle, etc.).

sadèrèk sibling.

sadhumuk bathuk sanyari bumi (soldiers' pledge) to defend each inch of the fatherland against the colonizer.

sadis ke-an sadism.

sadisme sadism.

sadran to bring offerings to graves or to go to a holy place for a vow praying for s.t. *tempat* -an offering place.

sadri celery.

sadurungé before, prior to. *ngerti (,weruh)* - *winarah* to be prophetic, foresee the future.

saé good.

saf row, line. *Penumpang berhadap.ha-dapan dlm dua -,* The passengers were facing e.o. in two rows. **ber-.-** in rows (,lines).

Safar the second month of the Moslem era. Tradition has it that this month is danger-ridden, an unlucky month, consequently on the last Monday of this month people ward off these dangers; (s.) SYAFAR.

safari travel. **ber-** to travel. *S- Golkar* itinerant troops of actors, singers, musicians, etc. delegated to certain areas by *Golkar* in the framework of the 1971 election campaign; (s.) BAJU (SAFARI).

sagu code name for narcotic powder.

saguèr and saguir k.o. palm wine (a Minahasan, North Celebes, drink).

sah authoritative, authentic. *tak -* 1 (in general) illegal, unlawful. 2 (of a child) illegitimate. **ke-an** legality, validity. **pen(ge)-an** authentication, legalization, confirmation, authorization.

sahabat **ber-** friendly, amicable. ~ *dgn* to associate with, go about with (a person), mix with (people), rub shoulders with. ~ *karib (,kental)* to be very friendly. *- pena* pen pal.

sahaja **ke(ber)-an** simplicity. **member-kan** to simplify.

saham stock (certificate). *- atas nama* registered stock. *- biasa* common stock. *- preferèn (kumulatip)* (cumulative) preferred stock. *- prioritas* preferred stock. *- tanpa nama* and *- tdk bernama* stock to bearer. *- utama timbun* cumulative preferred stock.

sahib master, owner of.

sahibulhikayat the (usually unknown) author of the story; the author's 'we.' *Kata - ...,* The story has it that ...

sahid witness.

sahih authentic, genuine.

sahnio 120-gram package in which morphine is clandestinely sold.

sahut **ber-.-an** answering, respondent. *tdk ada yg* **ny-** no answer (on the telephone).

said (s.) SAHID.

saidani the two lords Hasan and Husain.

Saidi *-, ya -!* O Lord!

saikéiréi to bow in honor of the Jap. Emperor; obligatory on all public occasions during the Jap. occupation in World War II.

Saikosikikan (during the Jap. occupation) Supreme Commander.

saing **per-an** *bebas* laissez faire. **ter-i** to be competed over.

sains science.

sa'ir lottery hunch.

sais coachman, cabby.

sa.iyek.sa.éka.praja and saiyeg.saékapraja unanimous, in harmony.

saja 1 instead [of some alternative]. *Saya takut, ayo pulang -!* I'm scared, come on, let's go home [instead of going ahead]! 2 (follows the lesser of two opposites, emphasizes or enlivens the preceding part) *Gampang -!* It's easy! *Begini -!* Like this! *Tentu -!* Sure! *Saya pergi -,* I just go. 3 (any ..., every ...) *Siapa - yg mau boleh ikut,* Anyone who wants can go along. *Apa - di dunia ini,* Anything (,everything) in the world. 4 (not) even. *menjelaskan - tdk bisa* he can't even explain. 5 (X and only X) *Sebutkan nama ikan sepuluh -,* Name ten kinds of fish (and only ten).

sajak as if, as it were, so to speak.

sajèn offering; (s.) SESAJI.

sak (S.) SE-. *Saya - keluarga,* I and (,together with) family.

Saka a year according to the (old) Jav. calendar (commencing 78 A.D.).

sakai dependants, retainers, subjects.

sak.a(m)breg.a(m)breg 1 lots of. 2 in great numbers.

sakar *- susu* lactose.

sakarin saccharine.

sakato alam (in the Minangkabau) consensus of the people.

sak.dek.sak.nyet instantly, all at once.

sakduk handkerchief.

Sakenan (s.) GALUNGAN.

sakharin (s.) SAKARIN.

sak.ini now.

sakit **berpeny-an** sickly, ailing. **ke-an** with pain. *Dia menjerit ~,* He screamed with pain. **peny-:** *~ Apollo* name of a disease consisting of the bleeding of the cornea caused by the Virus Entero-702, found among people in Africa, Europe and Asia. *~ batuk kering* tuberculosis. *~ beguk* struma, scrofula. *~ biduran* urticaria, hives. *~ budug* scabies. *~ busung lapar* malnutrition. *~ cacar teh* blister blight, i.e. a disease of teashrubs. *~ cacing tambang* ankylostomiasis, hookworm. *~ darah putih* leukemia. *~ dua bahasa* saying o. thing but meaning another. *~ eltor* k.o. cholera. *~ gatal. gatal "a go.go"* scabies. *~ gemuk* obesity. *~ GO* gonorrhea. *~ gudig* scabies. *~ jembrana* cattle plague. *~ jirian* spermatorrhea. *~ kaki gajah* elephantiasis. *~ kanker darah* leukemia. *~ kegemukan* obesity. *~ kekurangan vitamin* avitaminosis. *~ keputihan* discharge, leucorrhoea. *~ keturunan* a hereditary disease. *~ kolera* cholera. *~ koro* a temporary impotence caused by stress. *~ kronis* a chronic disease. *~ krumut* small pox. *~ lumpuh separoh* hemiplegia. *~ mulut dan kuku* hoof-and-mouth disease. *~ nikmat* venereal disease. *~ panggung* stage fright. *~ pektai* discharge, leucorrhoea. *~ pembuluh darah* arteriosclerosis. *~ pianswie* polio. *~ pitam* apoplexy, stroke. *~ psikosomatik* psychosomatic disease. *~ sendi* arthritis. *~ sentrap.sentrup* cold, catarrh. *~ sesak napas* asthma. *~ sikil gajah* elephantiasis. *~ tekanan darah tinggi* hypertension. *~ tidur* encephalitis. *~ tropis* tropical disease. *~ tua* infirmities of old age. *~ (dlm) tulang* arthritis. *~ usus buntu* appendicitis. *~ waham kebesaran* megalomania. *mencari ~* to look for trouble. **peny-an** to be sickly. *- asma* asthma. *orang yg - asma* asthmatic. *- hati* angry. *melepaskan - hati kpd* to take revenge on. *- kuning* hepatitis. *- lambung* gastralgia. *- pat(h)èk* yaws, framboesia. *- payah* seriously ill. *- pinggang dan pegal* lumbago. *- sangat* seriously ill.

- sinu 1 nervous, jumpy. 2 affliction of the nerves. *- teruk* seriously ill. *orang - a* sick person, patient. *-.-: dlm ~, ~ saja* and *sdh ~* sickly, ailing.

sakit II **pe-an** the accused, captive.

sak.madya moderate.

sakral *Pancasila perlu* **di-kan,** It's compulsory to sanctify the *Pancasila.*

sakramèn *menurut -* sacramental.

sakratulmaut (S.) SAKARATULMAUT.

saksang pork cooked with blood and spices.

saksi *menjadi (,naik) -* to appear as a witness, give evidence (in Court). *satu - bukan merupakan -* o. witness is no witness, 'unus testis nullus testis.' **ke-an** *di bawah sumpah* affidavit. **meny-kan** *pertunjukan TV* to watch a television show. *- baptisan* sponsor, godfather, godmother. *- bohong (,dusta ,palsu)* false witness. *- lelaki* (during wedding) bestman. *- pemberat (,yg memberatkan)* witness for the prosecution. *- perempuan* (during wedding) maid of honor. *- peringan (,yg meringankan)* witness for the defense. *-.- yg tlh didengar di bawah sumpah* (in legal judgments) the witnesses heard (,examined) on oath, the witnesses taken the sworn testimony of.

saku *- kempes* broke, penniless. *- pencernaan* digestive sac.

sal I hall.

sal II shawl.

Sala (S.) SOLO.

salah I *tak - lagi* certainly, surely, of course, take s.t. for granted. *kalau saya tak -* if I'm not mistaken. *tdk akan -* unfailing, infallible. *kasih - pd diri sendiri* to blame o.s. *S- sedikit ia tdk datang,* It is just a pity that he did not show up. **ber-.-an** *paham (,pendapat)* to disagree with o.a. *Dia tdk dpt* **diperkan** *atas ...,* He cannot be held responsible for .... *hrs* **di-kan** *kpd A* (this) has to be blamed on A, A has to be blamed for it. **di- interpretasikan** to be misinterpreted. **di- manfaatkan** (s.) DISALAH.GUNAKAN. **di- mengerti-**

kan to be misunderstood. **di- pakaikan**
(s.) DISALAH.GUNAKAN. **ke-an**
defect. *di luar ~nya sendiri* through no
fault of his own. **keber-an** guilt. **mens-.**
arahkan to misdirect. **meny- artikan**
and **meny- tafsirkan** to misinterpret,
misconstrue. **-nya:** *~ (sedikit)* it is
(just) a pity that. *tapi adalah ~, yakni*
bila ... but it also has its disadvantage(s),
namely when ... *Apa ~?* What does it
matter? What is there against it? *Tdk*
ada ~, kalau ... It doesn't matter if ...,
There's nothing wrong in ... *Maka Pak*
Tjokro minta maaf atas ~ itu, (Then)
Mr. Tjokro apologized for his mistake.
-.- 1 if you make the mistake of ...-ing.
S~ bersikap takut akan tertuduh pula,
If you make the mistake of showing
fear, you will be accused too. *S~ bisa*
konangan, You might be discovered.
2 although guilty. *S~ dibebaskan juga,*
Although guilty he was released anyway.
S~ anda bisa dirampok di jalan, If you're
off your guard you can be robbed in
the street.
In many compounds: in error, by mistake. *- alamat* to have come to the
wrong address (,place). *- anggapan* misunderstanding, misapprehension. *- duga*
mistake. *- jalan* to get lost. *- jam* the
wrong time. *- kaprah* 1 an improper
usage that has become customary. 2 to
use the wrong assumption. 3 misappre-
hend. *- kira* 1 misunderstanding. 2 to
take (s.o.'s remarks) amiss. *- langkah*
to make blunders. *- lidah* slip of the
tongue. *- lihat (,mata)* 1 to look at a
person of the opposite sex in an improper way. 2 to mistake ... for ...
- mengerti 1 misunderstanding. 2 to
take (s.o.'s remarks) amiss. *- ngomong*
to misspeak. *- nguping* to mishear.
- paham 1 misunderstanding. 2 to take
(my remarks) amiss. *- pengertian* misunderstanding. *- penggunaan* misuse.
utk menghindarkan - pengertian yg
berakibat - penggunaan to avoid misunderstanding resulting in misuse.
- perasaan to have an uncomfortable

(,unpleasant) feeling. *- pikiran* mistake
in thought. *- pukul* to misunderstand,
misconstrue. *- rasa* to have an uncomfortable (,unpleasant) feeling. *- rumah*
to be at the wrong address. *S- sambung!*
(telephone) Wrong number! *- tampa* 1
misunderstanding. 2 to take (my remarks) amiss. *- terjemahan* mistransla-
tion. *Akh, saya jadi malu dan - tingkah,*
Heck, I became embarrassed and didn't
know what to do next. *- tulis* 1 slip of
the pen. 2 misquoted. *- ucap* mispro-
nounced. *- urus* mismanagement. *-*
wesel to be wrong, miss the point.
-.meny-kan to accuse o.a.
salah II *- satu (,sebuah ,seorang)* 1 o.
(among two or more things, persons,
etc.). 2 s.t. (,s.o.) or other, o. or other
(of these books, of his friends). *- seorang*
dr mereka o. of them.
salai di- to be smoked (of *tengkawang*).
salak a plum-sized, oval fruit with a brown,
snake-skin exterior.
salam I *Sampaikanlah - saya kpdnya,*
Please send my regards to him; please
remember me to him. *teriring(,tertum-*
pang) - with kind(est) regards. **meny-**
to greet. *Letnan itu tdk ~ kembali,* The
lieutenant did not return the greeting.
meny-i to greet, shake hands with.
Tuan Wolcott ~ saya, Mr. Wolcott
greeted me. *- Natal* Christmas greetings.
- templek (,tempel) 'sticking-together
greeting,' k.o. bribe given by bus and
truck drivers to officials.
salam II salmon.
salang.surup a mix-up.
salar market excise levied from vendors
or shops located in markets.
salatri to be famished.
salè *S-.- katè maapin sajè,* If I have hurt
your feelings, please forgive me; forgive me for my past indiscretions (formula uttered on *Lebaran* day).
salé dried. *pisang -* and *- pisang* sun-dried
banana. *- tdk berapi* a pregnant, unmarried woman.
salin per- *selengkapnya* a suit of clothes,
an outfit.

saling to ... e.o. (,o.a.). *kedua orang itu - memukul* the two persons beat e.o. The word also may precede a reciprocal verb form: - *pukul.memukul* to hit e.o. - *kasih.mengasihi* to love o.a. - *bergantungan* interdependent. - *isi. mengisi* to be complementary to o.a. 2 mutual. - *pengertian* mutual understanding.

salip meny- to overtake, catch up to. **peny-an** overtaking. -.-**an** to overtake o.a.

salon - *kecantikan* beauty salon. - *politikus* armchair politician.

salur di-kan *(k)pd* to be distributed to. **meny-kan** *uang (k)pd* to funnel funds (,money) to. **peny-**: ~ *sandang.pangan* food-and-clothing distributor. ~ *tunggal* sole distributor. **peny-an** channeling. ~ *pegawai.pegawai* reduction in force, compulsory retirement. -**an**: ~ *hawa* airshaft. ~ *pencernaan makanan* alimentary (,food) canal.

salut I salute. *memberi - kpd Indonesia* to give Indonesia a salute.

salut II ber- *emas* gilded.

sama alike, resembling. - + *adj. (,verb)* all (referring to a plural subject). *Orang. orang desa itu - melarat,* The villagers are all poor. - *juga (,saja)* it does not matter. - *saja* exactly the same. - *sekali* at all, altogether, completely. - *sekali tdk* not at all. **ber-** communal. ~ *dgn* coupled (,together) with. **ber-.-** together, in concert. *baik* ~, *maupun masing. masing sendiri* (in notarial instruments) both collectively and individually. **keber-an** togetherness, (sense of) community. **di- artikan** *dgn* to be synonymous with. **meny- normakan** to normalize, standardize. **per-an** *kepentingan* community of interest. **se-** 1 fellow(-). *kita* ~ *anak Timur* we orientals. ~ *bangsa* fellow citizen. ~ *makhluk* fellow man. ~ *main* playmate. ~ *mereka* among themselves. ~ *negara komunis* fellow communist countries. *kita* ~ *perempuan (,wanita)* we girls. ~ *serikat* 1 ally. 2 mutual. ~ *menguntungkan* mutual

profit. ~ *hormat.menghormati* mutual respect. -.- 1 both. ~ *tdk* neither of them. 2 together, in concert. 3 o.a. ~ *salah mengerti* to misunderstand e.o. *dgn dasar* ~ on an equal basis. ~! (the) same to you! (as a reply to a congratulation). - *melekat* coherent. - *dan sebangun* (math.) congruent. - *tengah* neutral.

samanéra aspirant Buddhist monk.

samapta ready, prepared. *test - jasmani (ABRI)* squat jump.

samar secret, mysterious, unknown, covert. -**an** camouflage, mask.

samat peny-an *kerudung putih siswa perawat* capping day.

sambar peny- *sepeda* bicycle thief.

sambat -an cooperation.

sambet ke- suddenly sick (possessed by evil spirit).

sambi ny- 1 to do s.t. at the same time as s.t. else. 2 to have a side job.

sambil -an part-time. *mahasiswa* ~ part-time student. - *lalu* cursory.

sambung ber-: ~ *ke halaman IV* continued on page IV. ~ *keluarga dgn* to be related to. ~ *tangan* to lend a hand (in the work). **di-**: *(akan)* ~ (in a serial) (to be) continued. *minta* ~ *dgn* (over the telephone) please, connect me with. **meny-** 1 to resume (contacts). 2 to pass on (orders). 3 (in telephone conversation) to connect, put through. ~ *hidupnya (,nyawanya)* 1 to save a man's life. 2 to support o.s. ~ *hidup sehari.hari* to make ends meet. ~ *keturunan* to breed, propagate. **meny-kan** to plug (it) in. **peny-** *lidah* 'extension of the (people's) tongue,' i.e. spokesman, vox populi. -.**meny-** to extend (o's period of service), enter into (a new contract). -**an**: *penerbangan* ~ *dr Jakarta ke Singapura* a connecting flight from Jakarta to Singapore. ~ *turunan* propagation (of the race, etc). - *singkat* short circuit.

sambut ber-.- continually. *datang* **meny-** to (bid) welcome. -**an** 1 reaction (favorable and unfavorable). 2 ~ *baik* sym-

pathy. ~ *hangat* (to receive) much
attention. 3 *pidato* ~ commemorative
address (,oration), speech of the day
(,evening). 4 response, commentary
(on a newspaper article, etc.).

samenléven to live together as husband
and wife (without legally being married).

sami - *mawon* exactly the same, it's all
the same.

samir a colored ribbon round the neck
(of the bearers of royal and princely
insignia).

samijaga family toilet.

Sam Karya Nugraha a banner awarded to
army divisions for outstanding services
rendered in carrying out the tasks assigned to them by the government.

sampah meny- rot (of fallen leaves).

sampai go so far as to. - *dgn* up to and
including. - *di kuping (,telinga)* to
come to o's ears. - *ke mana?* to what
end (,extent)? *sdh* - arrived (of goods).
sdh - *besarnya* arrived at adulthood.
tdk - not quite, less than, in less than.
ny- to arrive. **se-nya** upon arrival. **-.-** be
forced (by circumstances) to, even.
- *akal* logical. - *hati* to bring o.s. to the
point of. - *kini* up to now.

sampak - *songo* a certain tempo in Jav.
gamelan music, towards the end of the
play, near its culminating point.

sampèk (S.) SAMPAI.

sampeu k.o. cassava.

sampéyan 1 foot. 2 you. 3 your (very
polite). *S- Dalem* His Highness (title
for Jav. prince).

sampi (s.) SAPI.

sampilik stingy.

samping *gang* - sideway (opp. main road).
menge-kan, mengeny-kan and **meny-
kan** to discard, sidetrack. **-an** side, not
main.

sampo shampoo.

sam sam sen [sama-sama senang] (in
Manado) to have fun together.

samsiti a salad prepared from salted
vegetables.

samsu I sun.

samsu II Chinese arrack (from sugar
cane).

samudera *ketujuh* - the seven seas. **ke-an**
oceanographic. *S- Indonesia* (Indonesian term for the) Indian Ocean.

samuderawi oceanic.

samudra (S.) SAMUDERA.

samudrawi (s.) SAMUDERAWI.

samurai samurai. *kaum* - the Jap. mil.
caste.

sanak ber-*(.saudara)* to be related. **kekeluargaan** (family) relationship.

sandal ber- jepit to wear thongs. - *jepit*
thongs.

sandang meny- *gelar BA* to bear the title
of Bachelor of Arts. **ter-** *di bahunya*
strapped over his shoulder.

sandar ber- *di dermaga* to be moored at
the quay (of a ship). **meny-kan** 1 to
lean s.t. against *(pd). (menumpang)* ~
nasib (,untung) kpd to rely (,depend)
upon. 2 to base on. 3 to set (o's hope)
on. **-an:** ~ *kepala* (in car seat) headrest.
~ *kepala yg dpt disetel* adjustable headrest. ~ *pendapat* (s.) STEMMOTIVE-
RING.

sandera di-kan to be made hostage.

sandi 1 secret. 2 concealed intention.
meny-kan to encode. **per-an** cryptography.

sandiasma cryptogram, concealment of
the author's name.

sandibonéka puppet show.

sandiman cryptographer.

sandisastra cryptology, secret language.

sandisuara (mil.) countersign.

sandiwara peny-an dramatization.- *boneka*
puppet show. - *radio* broadcast play.

sandra meny- to describe.

Sandya Kara Murti the women's association under the jurisdiction of the Department of Communication.

sang *S- Belang* the Tiger. *S- Hyang* and *S-
yang* alternative titles to *Batara* for
male deities. - *isteri* your honored wife.
S- Monyet (in fables) the Monkey. *S-
Penebus* the Redeemer (Jesus Christ).
S- Saka Merah Putih The Inherited
(and Venerated) Red-and-White Flag.

(Since 1968 this flag has no longer been hoisted, due to the fact that it is threadbare. It has been replaced by a replica made of Indonesian-manufactured silk). - *suami* your honored husband.

sangadi (in Bolaang Mongondow, North Celebes) village head.

sangga I the smallest unit in the *Pramuka* Boy Scout Movement consisting of *penegaks;* membership maximum 10.

sangga II - *baita* dry-dock.

sangga III - *buana* an old Jav. royal title.

sanggama meny-i to have sexual intercourse with. - *terputus* coitus interruptus.

sanggar - *kerja (,latihan)* workshop. - *teh* tea house.

sanggarunggi suspicious.

sanggat ter- run aground.

sanggup se- *tenaga* to the best of o's ability.

sangit (it has a) burnt (smell).

sangka imagination, assumption. *dgn tiada* **di-** accidentally. *si* **ter-** (jur.) the suspect.

sangkepan (in Bali) a meeting.

sangkut ber- *(paut) dgn* to be connected with, be tied up with, refer to, have a bearing on. **ter-** to be stuck. ~ *hati* lovingly attached.

sangsi 1 doubtful, suspicious. 2 suspect. *dgn tdk usah - lagi* undoubtedly. **di-kan:** *masih (dpt)* ~ it is still doubtful, that remains an open question. *masih sangat* ~ *kebenarannya* its accuracy is still very much in doubt. *tdk usah* ~ *lagi* it cannot be questioned any longer, it is not open to any doubt. *dgn tdk usah* ~ *lagi* undoubtedly, certainly, admittedly. *dgn tdk -.- lagi* unhesitatingly, without reserve.

sanitasi sanitation. *tenaga* - sanitarian.

sanjak rhyme.

sanjung peny- flatterer. **-an** adulation.

sans (in bridge) no-trump.

Sansibar Zanzibar.

santai I box, i.e. a short, newspaper article enclosed in borders.

santai II 1 relaxed. 2 relaxation. **ber-(.-)** to relax (v.i.). *tempat* **ber-** recreation site. **ke-an** relaxation. **meny-kan** to relax (v.t.). **pe-** vacationer.

santan (white-colored) coconut milk pressed from shredded coconut meat.

santap ber- *siang* to lunch. **-an** *laut* seafood. - *niaga* business lunch. - *siang* lunch.

santase blackmail.

santer 1 strong (of feelings). 2 loud (of rumors).

santèt k.o. of black magic. *tukang* - person who practices black magic. **di-** to be put the hex on. **per-an** putting the hex on.

santiaji indoctrination.

santiajiwan indoctrinator.

Santo and **Santu** Saint. - *Fransiskus Asisi* Saint Francis of Assisi.

santun 1 compassionate. 2 ready (,willing) to help (,assist). **meny-i** to take a close look at. **peny-** sympathizer. *dewan* ~ board of trustees. **peny-an** 1 rehabilitation. 2 insurance. **-an** compensation (paid by insurance company).

sanyo (during the Jap. occupation) informer.

saos to visit an exalted person. - *bekti* to pay o's respects to - *bekti ing Ngarso Dalem* to pay o's respect to His Majesty the Sultan of Yogyakarta.

Sapar (s.) SAFAR.

sapi - *anakan* calf. - *bibit* stud. - *Fries Holland* Holstein-Friesian. - *gadis* heifer. - *Grati* crossbreed between Holstein-Friesian and Java cow. - *kebiri* ox. - *kereman* fattened cow. - *Onggole* Brahman. - *paron* (in Timor) fattened cow. - *pelacak* stud. - *perahan* milch-cow. - *pontong* beef cattle.

sapih meny- to separate, disengage.

saprodi [sarana produksi padi] and **saprotan** [sarana produksi pertanian] rice (,agricultural) production facilities, i.e. fertilizers, first-quality seeds and insecticides.

sapu *spt - diikat dgn benang sutera* it is like a blacksmith with a white silk apron. **di-** *dek (,jagat)* and **di- bersihkan** to be swept clean, be annihilated, be wiped out. **peny-:** ~ *jalan* street sweeper, scavenger. ~ *kaca* windscreen wiper. **peny- bersihan** wiping out, getting rid of. - *duk (,ijuk)* broom made of black sugar-palm fibers. - *kaca mobil* windshield wiper. - *listrik* vacuum cleaner.

saput ter- *awan* socked in by clouds.

saradasi a suggested new word for *subversi.*

saran - *pribadi* autosuggestion.

sarana means, facilities, aid(s), (mass) media, services. - *komunikasi* means of communication. - *olahraga* sports facilities. - *pelayanan masyarakat* public utilities. - *pemerintah* government apparatus. - *pendidikan* educational aids. - *produksi* means of production. - *umum* public utilities.

sarang - *burung walet* (edible) swallow nest. - *Gestapu* a hotbed of the September 30 Movement. - *misil* missile site.

sarangan chestnut.

sarap ber-an to (eat) breakfast. **ny-** to eat s.t. for breakfast. **-an** *(pagi)* breakfast.

saraséhan 1 symposium. 2 discussion.

sarat *sedang* - (of animal) with young. - *air (,kapal)* draft (of ship).

Sarathan (s.) SARTAN.

sardèncis sardines.

saré pe-an 1 sleeping place, bed. 2 grave, graveyard.

saréan village head.

sarèh calm, quiet.

sarèn black pudding of coagulated blood.

sareukseuk (in the Bandung area) unpleasant to the eye.

sari I meny- to make juice. **meny-.patikan** to summarize (a story). - *buah(.buahan)* fruit juice. - *delé* [sari kedele] soybean powder. - *kopi* instant coffee. - *madu* royal jelly. - *nanas* pineapple juice. - *pati* core. - *teh* tea extract.

sari II (contraction of *sehari*) -.- every day, daily. *tdk spt* -.-**nya** different from others.

sariawan 1 sprue (usually manifested in o's lips), gingivitis, Indonesian sprue; also, scurvy. 2 name of a plant (L. Elaecarpus obtusa) the leaves of which are used for the preparation of *obat* - against the above sprue.

saring peny-an *minyak* oil refinery.

sarjana 1 scientist. 2 academician. 3 (the academic degree of) master. 4 (college) graduate. **ke-an** scholarship, i.e. the skills of a scholar. - *atom* atomic scientist. *S- Ekonomi* (abbrev. *S.E.*) M.Sc. in Econ. - *farmasi* pharmacist. - *geofisika* geophysicist. *S- Hukum* (abbrev. *S.H.*) Master of Laws, LL.M. - *kedokteran* (medical) doctor. *S- Madya* [in some colleges: *Universitas Gadjah Mada* (Yogya), *Universitas 17 Agustus* (Semarang)] a degree between *Sarjana Muda* and *Sarjana*. - *muda* undergraduate. *S- Muda dlm Tarbiyah* Bachelor of Education, B.E. - *nuklir* nuclear scientist. - *peneliti* research scientist. - *penuh* master's degree holder. - *sujana* top scientist. *S- Teknik Kimia* Chemical Engineer. *S- Teknik Listrik* Electrical Engineer. *S- Teknik Mesin* Mechanical Engineer. *S- Teknik Perminyakan* Petroleum Engineer. - *wisuda* degree candidate. - *wiyata* educationalist.

sarjanaisasi the turning out of *sarjanas* (,master's degree holders).

sarju sympathy.

sarkasme sarcasm.

sarkofagus sarcophagus.

sarkon [sarung kontol] condom.

sarli [sarung peli] condom.

sarmud [sarjana muda] Bachelor of Arts.

sarsaran to beat rapidly (of heart).

Sartan Cancer.

saru I peny- (intelligence) agent. ~ *as(e)li* genuine (,true) agent. ~ *bantuan* support agent. ~ *keliling* roving agent. ~ *menetap* resident agent. ~ *palsu* bogus agent. ~ *penindak* action agent. ~ *penunggu* dormant agent. ~ *rangkap* dual agent. ~ *tunggangan* double agent. ~ *utama* principal agent. **peny-an** (intelligence) cover. ~ *berlapis* cover within a cover. ~ *mendalam* deep cover. ~ *perorangan* personal cover. ~ *pertemuan* *bersama* group cover.

saru II ill-mannered, indecent, rude.

sarung *orang.orang* **-an** the Moslem community. - *karet* condom. - *pistol* holster. - *tinju* boxing gloves.

sarwa all.

sasak beehive (hairdo). *berambut* - with 'teased' hair.

sasakala at the time of.

sasana place, location. - *tinju* boxing arena.

sasar meny-i to target. **meny-kan** to misdirect **ny-** to get lost, (go a)stray. **-an:** ~ *mata* object of attention. *tdk pilih* ~ haphazardly.

sasat per- to do as if.

sasis chassis (of automobile).

sasmita warning, signal, hint.

sasrahan gift (from person in love with a girl to her parents).

sas.sus rumor(s). **di-kan** to be rumored.

sast(e)rakanta thesis.

sata 100. *dwi-warsa* bicentennial.

satai (s.) SATE.

saté pieces of goat, pork or chicken roasted on wooden skewers and customarily dipped in peanut sauce before being eaten. **ny-** to grill *sate*. - *babi manis* pork on skewers served with *kecap manis*.

satelit men(g)s-kan to make (a certain country) a satellite. **per-an** (adj.) satellite. - *antariksa* space satellite. - *buatan manusia* man-made satellite. - *bulan tak berawak* unmanned moon satellite. - *bumi tak berawak* unmanned earth satellite. - *cuaca* weather satellite. - *komunikasi* communications satellite.

satgas [satuan tugas] task force.

satir satyr.

sato (wild) animal.

satori (in Buddhism) enlightenment.

satria and **satrya** 1 a member of the second Hindu caste of rulers and warriors. 2 a knight. **ke-an** knightly.

satron di-in 1 to be the enemy of. 2 to be forced (an entrance) into, be raided (by the police).

satu - *dua th* several years. *dihadapinya pd* - *antara dua* he was faced with a dilemma. - *lagi* another. *"S- dua, dua tiga!"* yell of bus conductors to passengers already sitting in a bus to move up, in order to create more seating-accommodation. **ber-** coalesce. ~ *jalan* to go in the same direction. ~ *kembali* to reunite. ~ *kita kukuh bercerai kita rubuh* united we stand, divided we fall; union is strength. *Kaum Buruh seluruh Dunia, B~!* Workers of the World, Unite! **di- komandokan** to be placed under o. command. *Perdagangan* **di-tangankan**, Trade has been put (,placed) in o. (a single) hand. **ke-an** 1 integrity. *satu ~ yg tdk terpisahkan* o. integrated whole. 2 union. *K~ Aksi Mahasiswa Indonesia* (abbrev. *KAMI*) Union for Indonesian University Students' Action. **mens- tarafkan** to rank s.o. with. **pemer-** 1 unifier. 2 unifying. *alat* ~ unifying instrument. **pemer-an** unification. **peny-an** *keluarga* family reunion. **per-an** unity. *P~ Advokat* Bar Association. ~ *dan* **ke-an** unity and integrity. **-an:** ~ *korbankan diri* suicide squad. ~ *mata uang* monetary unit currency. *S~ Tugas* Task Force. **-.-nya** the only. ~ *jalan ialah* ... the only way is ... *kebun binatang* ~ the only zoo.

satwa (s.) SATO. *-liar* wild animals.

satyagraha nonviolent resistance.

saudara 1 sibling. 2 kinsman. *S-.S-* Ladies and Gentlemen. **berper-an** to have a sense of fraternity (,brotherhood). - *senasib* companion in distress.

Saudi Arabia Saudi Arabia.

sauk - *air mandikan diri* to stand on o's own two feet.

saus - *tomat* tomato catsup.

sawah meny-kan to turn into rice paddies. **pe-an** (S.) PERSAWAHAN. **per-an** *pasang.surut* tidal rice paddies. - *(ber)- bendar langit* rice field dependent on rainfall. - *bengkok* a *sawah* given to s.o. in usufruct. - *lebak* rice paddy in swampy areas. - *pasang.surut* a tidal ricefield. - *rumput* grassland. - *tadah hujan* ricefield dependent on rainfall.

sawan - *babi* convulsions.

sawat.sawat vague (of hope).

sawèr the ceremony following the *sembah.* The newlyweds having completed their rounds go outside the house to take their respective seats on a specially reserved chair under the protection of a large umbrella which is held behind them by o. of the relatives of the bride. An elderly woman then performs the *sawer,* i.e. throwing nickel coins and rice grains out of a bowl.

sawi - *hijau* celery cabbage (tasty salad greens). - *putih* Chinese cabbage.

sawo and **sawu** sapodilla (plum), sapote, zapote.

say feces.

sayagi service.

sayah a plaited tray. *dijual - dibeli tempurung* six of o. and half a dozen of the other.

sayang 1 it's a pity! too bad! *amat* **di-kan** to be most regrettable, be most deplorable. 2 honey, darling. *"Duduk sini -," pintaku halus, sambil menarik lengan Efra,* "Have a seat here, honey," I asked gently, while pulling Efra's arm. *anak* **ke-an** favorite child. **-nya** ... the trouble (,problem) is that ...

sayap - *pintu belakang* rear panel (of car).

sayeg saéko kapti working together with a mutual purpose.

sayembara quiz.

sayonara - *prints* Jap. many-colored tulle for ladies' blouses.

sayu pensive. *sedih.pedih dan -, pilu dan -* and - *rawan* sad. *suram lagi* - melancholy.

sayup.sayup - *mata memandang* and - *tampak* vaguely visible.

sayur ... *bisa* **di-** *asem* ... can be used to prepare *sayur asem.* - *asem (,asam)* k.o. vegetable soup using tamarind as its main ingredient. - *bendi* (in Malaysia) okra (L. Hibiscus esculentus L.), 'ladies fingers.'

SD Inpres [Sekolah Dasar Instruksi Presiden] an elementary school built with special funds earmarked by the President and allocated by a Presidential Instruction.

se - + *some verbs* after having... *-usai membaca Qur'an* after having finished reading the Koran. *-hilangnya* ... after the disappearance of ...

SE [Septichomia Epizootica] *penyakit -* k.o. cattle disease; (s.) (PENYAKIT) NGOROK.

sebab **di-kan** *[dr (,karena)]* due to, to be caused by. **peny-** cause, agent. ~ *kematian* cause of death. ~ *penyakit* pathogenic. ~ *perobahan* agent of change. - *musabab* the primary causes.

sebak *bermata -* and - *matanya* to have swollen eyes (due to weeping).

sebal I **meny-** to deviate.

sebal II **meny-kan** disgusting, nauseating. - *hati* sad.

sebambangan (in southern Sumatra) marriage by elopement.

sebar **di-.luaskan** to be propagated. **meny-.luas** to be widespread. **meny-.luaskan** to spread widely. **peny-** *penyakit* disease carrier. **peny-.luasan** dissemination. **peny-an** *seluas.luasnya* dispersion.

seberang foreign, abroad. *di - sana* on that side (further away). *tak berani aku memandang lelaki yg duduk di -ku itu* I was afraid to look at the man sitting in front of me. **ber-an** *dgn* across from. **meny-** (in a political sense) to defect (to the enemy). **peny-** 1 defector. 2 bordercrosser. **peny-an** 1 defection. 2 crossing (of a river, street, etc.). - *laut* oversea(s). *S- Perai* (the town of) Butterworth (in Malaysia).

sébra zebra.

sebrot **ny-** to pickpocket.

sebut *secara populer* **di-** popularly referred to as. **peny-an** denomination, name. *menjadi -.-an* to be much-discussed.

seconlèt manatee-oil (i.e. oil of the *ikan duyung*) used in order to be loved by a girl or woman.

sedap amused. *sedaapp!* terrific! *tdk - (di) hati* 1 peevishly. 2 uneasy. *tak - rasa badan* does not feel well. **peny-** *rasa* flavoring. *- hati* complacent. *- malam* (fig.) prostitute.

sedekah offerings for spirits. *Anak itupun* **di-i,** A religious meal was organized for that child. *- bumi* a sacrificial feast for the well-being of the village. *- desa (,deso)* the ceremony performed after the harvest in the form of a collective religious meal. *- laut* (s.) KOMARAN.

séder cedar.

sedia I original. *ada -* to have in stock. **di-kan** to be earmarked (in budget) **peny-an** *uang* monetary supply. **per-an:** *dlm ~* ready stock. *dpt dijual dr ~* deliverable from stock. *selama masih ada ~* while supplies last. *~ kami habis* we have run out of stock.

sedia II **-nya** 1 actually, as a matter of fact. 2 strictly speaking, could have. 3 according to the usual procedure. *~ ... tetapi ...* of course ... but ...

sedih peny- pessimistic, gloomy. **-nya** *ialah, bhw...* the tragedy (of it) is ...

sedikit *(dr) - ke -* and *- demi -* gradually, little by little *- hari lagi* and *dlm - waktu* in a short time, shortly. *- lagi!* o. moment, please! **-pun tdk** not at all, by no means. *tanpa kesulitan -pun* without the slightest difficulty. *- baik* slightly better. *tahu - bahasa Indonesia* to know a little Indonesian. *banyak* **-nya** more or less.

sédong an excavated site or excavation, a small cave.

sedot ke- tapped (of electricity). **meny-:** *~ hawa* to breathe in. *~ rokok* to smoke.

sedulur 1 sibling. 2 relatives. **per-an** 1 relationship. 2 friendship. 3 fraternity, brotherhood.

sé ès [from *c.s.:* cum suis] with o's friends (,companions ,associates). **-nya** and others.

séf (s.) SIP.

segala and other red-tape, and all that nonsense (,jazz ,stuff ,crap ,sort of thing). *Saudara kira itu cukong.cukong*

apa mau repot.repot dgn kantor pajak dan surat fiskal -? Do you think that those Chinese wheeler-dealers want to bother about the tax office, fiscal certificates and all the other bull shit? *Duilah cakapnya, pakai tahi lalat - di pipi!* Gosh, what a beauty, she has beauty marks and all that stuff on her cheek!

segan *- kpd, - dan hormat akan* and *- dan gentar kpd* to stand in awe of. *tak -* not dare to do. *-.-: tdk ~ lagi* not hesitate to. *dgn tak ~ lagi* unhesitatingly.

segar ke-an *jasmani* physical fitness. **meny-kan** *aki* to charge a battery.

sègel peny-an sealing (up).

segi *S-tiga Emas* The Golden Triangle (on mainland Southeast Asia).

sehèding ber- *(ke belakang)* with a part (to the back) (speaking of hair).

sèif (s.) SIP.

Sèinèndan (during the Jap. occupation) Youth Corps.

Sèinèndojo (during the Jap. occupation) Youth Training Center.

sèismik seismic.

sèismograf seismograph.

sejak *sdh -* as long ago as. *- dahulu (,dulu. dulu)* for quite a while, for a long time (from the past to the present), from ancient times.

sejarah *- (itu) berulang* history repeats itself. **ke-an** historical. *- kesenian* art history. *- kuno* ancient history. *- pertumbuhan* genesis.

sejara(h)wan historian.

sejuk peny-an cooling. *- hati* contented, tranquil.

sek *mak -* (killed) outright.

séka peny: *~ kaca* windshieldwiper. *~ muka* towelette.

sekakelar (S.) SAKLAR. *- (listrik)* cutout.

sekal chubby, hefty; (s.) SEKEL.

sekap di- (euph.) to be imprisoned. **meny-** to hold (as hostages). *matang -an* artificially ripened (of fruits).

sekar ny- to put flowers on a grave. *S-Kedaton* 'Flower of the Palace,' i.e. the special designation for the first born daughter, descendant of a princess of the *Kraton*.

sekarat death throes. *dlm keadaan* - to be at the point of death.

sékasé (Dutch pron. of *C.K.C.:* Centraal Kantoor voor de Comptabiliteit) Central Auditing Office.

sekat - *pemisah generasi* generation gap.

sekèdèng the part (of the hair); (s.) SEHEDING.

sekel 1 to form a solid lump (rice, etc.). 2 robust, strong (of person); (s.) SEKAL.

sèkèng 1 poor, indigent. 2 pauper.

sékertarès female secretary.

sekerup di- *mati* (the screw) was tightened firmly.

sekiram draft screen.

sèkjèn [sekretaris jenderal] secretary general.

séko (mil.) to reconnoitre.

sekoci - *pendarat* landing craft.

sekolah *mereka yg meninggalkan - sebelum waktunya* dropouts. **peny-an** 1 schooling. 2 sending to school. **per-an** school system. *S- Aliyah* Senior High School. - *anak.anak nakal* reformschool, reformatory. - *angka (,ongko) loro* 'two-figure school,' i.e. the lowest type of school entered by the Jav. village boy; the school levies a tuition ranging from two cents to two nickles. - *berasrama* boarding school. - *bina taat* reformatory. - *bruder* Catholic seminary school. - *dasar* elementary school. - *desa* village school. *S- Dokter Jawa* (coll.) School for the Training of Native Physicians [in 1926 it became a Medical College and in 1947 was renamed *Fakultas Kedokteran (Universitas Indonesia)]*. - *guru* teacher training school (High School level). - *guru agama* theological seminar. *S- Ibtidaiyah* Elementary School. *S- Komprehensif* Comprehensive School. - *liar* illegal school. *S- Menengah Ekonomi Atas* Economic Senior High School. - *mengemudikan mobil* driving school. - *menjahit* sewing school. - *negeri* public school. - *netral*

nondenominational school. - *pelayaran* nautical (training) school. *S- Pembangunan* Comprehensive School. - *pertukangan* junior vocational school. - *prebel* Kindergarten. *S- Staf Komando Angkatan Darat* Army Command and General Staff College. - *stir mobil* driving school. *S- Tsanawiyah* Junior High School.

sekongkol ber- *(dgn seorang lain)* aid and abet. **per-an** intrigues, conspiracy.

sekor mens- to suspend (from duty), fire. **pens-an** suspension, adjournment.

sekores (s.) SKORS.

sekoteng ginger syrup.

sèkpri [sekretaris pribadi] private secretary.

sekréning screening.

sékretarèsse and **sékretarisse** (s.) SEKERTARES.

sékretariat ke-an secretaryship, secretarial sciences. *S- Bersama* Joint Secretariat. *S- Negara* State Secretariat, i.e. the center of administration of the nondepartmental government agencies at the central government level.

sékretaris *ilmu* **ke-an** secretarial sciences. - *akonting* accounting secretary. - *eksekutif* executive secretary. - *(ke) satu* first secretary (in embassy). *S- Negara* State Secretary, i.e. the head of the *Sekretariat Negara*. - *perusahaan* business secretary. - *pribadi* private secretary.

sekrining screening; (s.) SEKRENING.

sekrit secret.

sèk(s) sex.

sèksi sexy. **ke-an** sexiness.

sèksofon saxophone.

Sèkspir (coll.) Shakespeare.

sèksualitas sexuality.

sèksuologi sexuology.

sèktaris sectarian.

sèktarisme sectarism.

sékularisme secularism.

sekuriti security.

sekutu ber- 1 allied, united. 2 to associate, unite. ~ *dgn* 1 to side with, be an ally of. 2 to make common cause with. *tlh*

(,turut) ~ *dgn* accessory to. **memper-
kan** to make divisible. - *yg bekerja*
active partner (in corporation). - *yg
beserta* silent partner (in corporation).

sékwen (in motion pictures) sequence (a
part of a film story treating an episode
without any interruption of continuity).

sé kya small child.

sèl - *bicara* telephone booth. -.- *komunis*
communist cells.

selada Boston (,bib) lettuce. - *air* water-
cress.

selah (s.) SLAH(RUM).

selai - *nanas* pineapple jam.

selaju ber- *di atas es* ice skating.

selak ny- to press, intrude (into). - *kemu-
dukudu* can hardly wait to. -.*seluk* to
infiltrate, penetrate.

selalap ke-an *duri* to choke on a (fish)-
bone.

selam meny-i *lebih dahulu* to suspect,
presume.

selamat *asal badan sendiri* - and *mau -
sendiri* bent on own safety. **di- datangi**
to be welcomed. **ke-an:** ~ *kerja* job
safety. ~/*kesejahteraan rakyat yg
tertinggi adalah hukum* salus populi
suprema lex esto, the security of the
people shall be the final law. **-an** ceremony which includes the custom of
giving away sacred food which will
give security to the host and his family.
~ *brokohan* ceremony given at child-
birth and in connection with the nam-
ing ceremony. ~ *jenang abang* ceremony
held after a circumcision. ~ *mitoni* ceremony held on the seventh month of
pregnancy. ~ *nyepasari* ceremony
held on the fifth day after birth. ~
puput puser ceremony held on the
occasion of the falling off of the umbilical cord. - *bekerja!* success with your
work! - *berjumpa!* how do you do?
- *berkongres!* success to the congress!
- *bermotor!* happy motoring! - *bertemu
lagi!* Hope to see you soon! - *berulang
tahun!* many happy returns of the day!
- *berusaha!* success in your efforts!
- *diterima* duly received (of a letter, in

commercial correspondence). - *hari
lahir!* happy birthday! *S- (Hari)
Lebaran!* Happy *Lebaran!* - *hari ulang
tahun!* 1 happy birthday! 2 happy
anniversary! - *maju!* success in your
progress! - *main!* good luck (with your
gambling)! - *minum!* to your health!
cheers! - *panjang umur!* 1 many happy
returns of the day! 2 talk of the devil,
and he will appear! *S- panjang umur,
semoga sejahtera selalu!* Long life to
you (and) may you always be prosperous! - *sampai* duly received (of a
letter, in commercial correspondence).

selampik handkerchief.

selang I 1 alternative. 2 periodicity. -
setengah jam every half hour. *blm -
berapa lama ini* recently. *tdk - berapa
lama* not long afterward. - *beberapa
waktu yg lalu* some time ago. **ber-** 1
varied. 2 intermittent. *blm lama* ~ *(ini)*
recently, lately. *tdk* ~ *lama* not long
ago. -.*seling* alternative, intermittent.

selang II tube hose, pipe.

selangkang(an) basement.

selapan - *hari* 35 days. **-an** *desa* village
meeting held every 35 days.

selaput - *bening mata* cornea. - *kegadisan*
hymen.

selasih basil (L. Ocimum basilicum).
ayam - chicken with black feathers,
bones and meat.

selat *S- Dardanella* Dardanelles. *S- Jabal.
al. Tarik* Straits of Gibraltar. *S- Sumatera* Straits of Malacca.

selatan ter- southernmost.

selèdèr inattentive.

séléksi mens- and **meny-** to select.

selempit ny- *di antara* ... to be slipped in
among ...

selenggara peny- *pembubaran* liquidator.

selèngkatan disorderly.

selenting -an rumors.

selepètan slingshot.

seléra *soal - memang tak dpt diperteng-
karkan* there is no accounting for
tastes. *masih pahit terasa -ku* doesn't
feel much. - *tajam* (to have) a great
appetite (,inclination). **ber-** 1 zestful.

2 appetizing. 3 (sensually) eager.
selesai following, after. *juru* **peny-** liquidator. **peny-an** accomplishment. **se-
nya** upon completion.
selesma coryza.
seletuk **ny-** to inadvertently let drop.
sèlfkorèksi self-correction.
sélibat celibacy.
selimpat arabesque. **ber-** arabesqued.
selimut **di-i** (fig.) to be covered with, be
blanketed in.
selinap **meny-:** ~ *ke (dlm)* hati (a desire
of …) comes over s.o. ~ *ke (dlm)
kalbunya (,hati sanubarinya)* (my
words) reach him. *tak selintaspun* ~
dlm pikiran kita it never entered our
head. **ter-** hidden.
selingkuh 1 insidious, insincere, unreliable. 2 secret, surreptitious.
selingkung **per-an** disagreement.
selip **ny-** to skid (of a car, etc.). **ter-**
keluar dr mulut to let slip, i.e. say s.t.
inadvertently.
selisih **ber-** to conflict. ~ *jalan dgn* to
cross. *Surat Tuan* ~ *jalan dgn surat
saya,* Your letter has crossed mine.
~ *lalu* to ride past, pass.
seliwer **ber-** to crisscross. **-an** to cruise
around.
sélofan cellophane.
selomot to burn, sear.
Sélon(g) Ceylon. **dis-** to be deported, ex-
pelled from a country (read: Indonesia)
(formerly to Ceylon, now Sri Lanka).
Dr. Tjipto Mangunkusumo yg ~ *ke
Nederland,* Dr. Tjipto Mangunkusumo
who was deported to the Netherlands.
selongsong - *peluru* casing (of bullet).
selonong **ny-** 1 to emerge (suddenly),
turn up (suddenly). 2 to slide (due to
its velocity, speaking about motorcars).
sélopan (s.) SELOFAN.
selubung *membuka* - to unveil (a monument, etc.). **ter-** disguised.
seluk.beluk the ins and outs, details.
sèlulèr cellular.
sèluloid celluloid.
sèlulosa cellulose.
selumbar splinter, piece (of broken glass).

selumbari the day before yesterday.
selundup **peny-** *alkohol* bootlegger.
selungsum **ny-i** to shed the skin (of snake).
-an slough (of snake).
seluruh *dlm* **ke-an***nya* in sum. *(yg)* **meny-**
1 integrated. 2 comprehensive. **meny-i**
to cover the entire … **meny-.lengkap**
comprehensive.
selusup **ny-** to infiltrate.
selusur **meny-i** to trace, follow (,exam-
ine) closely.
sèm crazy.
sema **ber-.-** catarrhous, having a cold.
sémah spouse.
semak *dr - ke belukar* from the frying
pan into the fire. **di-i** to be overgrown
with … weeds.
semanak friendly.
semangat *berbunga* **-nya** he was very
happy. *dgn - yg tinggi* high in spirit. *dgn
penuh* - enthusiastically. *sbg ditinggal-
kan* - as if unaware. **ber-** 1 pugnacious,
bellicose. 2 animated (reception). 3
eager, passionate. ~ *perang* warminded.
~ *tempe mlempem* disheartened. - *ber-
gelora* ardor. - *juang* dedication. - *kelas*
class feeling. - *kereguan* team spirit. -
menyimpan thriftiness. - *persatuan*
esprit de corps. - *puputan* an undaunted
spirit.
semaput 1 to faint. 2 half-dead.
semarak brilliant, glorious, excellent.
namanya jadi - he became famous.
ber- adorned. **ke-an** luster, splendor.
semat wealth, riches, prosperity.
semata.wayang only, sole. *mobil - yg ada
di kantornya* the only car found at his
office.
Semawisan (adj.) Semarang.
semayam **ber-** to abide. **meny-kan** to lie
in state. **per-an** abode.
sembah to hold the hands with the palms
together, finger tips upward, at the
height of the face, so that the thumbs
touch the nose, as a sign of honor or
homage shown to a superior. **peny-an**
high respect. - *berhala* idolatry. - *sungkem* the inferior kneels before the
superior, holds the superior's hands

and puts his forehead against the superior's knees.

sembahyang - *hajat* prayer for fulfillment of a wish; (collectively carried out) prayer meeting.

sembarang *bukan (,tdk)* - *orang* not just anyone. **di-i** (he) has been made a fool of. **-an:** *bertindak* ~ to act arbitrarily (,unfoundedly). *Ia bukan* ~ *orang* and *Ia bukan gadis* ~, She is not just anybody. *Bagi saya* ~ *saja!* It is all the same to me! *Jangan omong* ~*!* Don't talk nonsense!

sembelit meny-kan to constipate.

sembir(an) compass error.

sembuh peny- healer (the person). *tdk akan* -.*-nya* incurable (illness).

sembul ter- emerged.

sembunyi ber- *di balik alang.alang sehelai* (fig.) to clear o.s. of blame. **ter-** surreptitious.

sembur ber-an to splash. **peny-** *api* flame thrower.

semburit sodomy. *melakukan* - to commit sodomy.

semèdi ber- with religious concentration, to meditate.

semek (S.) DEMEK.

semekan breastcover (for women). **ber-** to wear a breastcover.

semèn meny- to cement. **peny-an** cementing. - *asbes* asbestos cement. - *biru* Portland cement.

sémen semen.

semenanjung *S- Iberia* Iberian Peninsula. *S- Krimia* Crimean Peninsula.

semenda ber- to be allied (by marriage).

semenjak from (o. point).

sementara I *utk (,buat)* - *(waktu)* for a while. - *blm* ... as long as ... not yet **ke-an** transitoriness.

sementara II some, several.

sementelah(an) 1 especially. 2 furthermore, moreover.

semeraut (s.) SEMRA(W)UT.

semèsta nationwide. - *alam* all over the world.

semèster semester.

Sem Gim (coll.) Asian Games.

sémi. semi-, half-. -.*pemerintah* semi-government.

séminar seminar. **ber-** to hold a seminar. **mens-kan** to discuss in a seminar.

séminari seminary.

semir peny- *sepatu* shoeshine boy. - *oli(e)* lubricating oil.

semor (s.) SEMUR.

sempang hyphen. **ber-** hyphenated. **meny-** to hyphenate.

sempat to succeed in ...-ing, manage (,contrive) to... *tdk* - to fail to. *7 orang* - *selamat* seven persons managed to save their skin. *ia* **berke-an** he could afford the time. **ke-an** occasion.

semperong glass lamp chimney. *kapal S-Biru* a ship of the Blue Funnel Line.

sempit *dlm waktu yg* - *ini* 1 in such a short time. 2 while we have so little time. **peny-an** de-escalation. ~ *arti* (gramm.) specialization.

semplah to hang off in pieces. - *hati* disheartened.

sempoyongan *dlm keadaan* - groggy, staggering.

semprit di- to be whistled at (by traffic police in order to stop traffic violators). **ny-** to whistle (by traffic police in order to stop traffic violators). *korban* **-an** a traffic violator.

semprong (s.) SEMPERONG.

semprot peny-*(tangan)* (hand) sprayer. **-an** criticism.

sempur name of a tree the wood of which has a tendency to petrify.

sempurna ke-an accomplishment. **meny-kan** to revamp. **ter-i** *oleh* to be completed by.

semra(w)ut disorderly, unruly. *keadaan yg paling* - chaos. **ke-an** *dlm perjalanan lalu.lintas kereta api* the dislocation of railway traffic.

semu I quasi, mock.

semu II facial expression.

semua the whole, entire. **ke-** all of. **ke-nya** *ini* all this. **-nya** all of it (,them). - *mereka* they all. - *serba ada* all sorts of things.

semur - *ati* braised liver. - *ayam* braised

chicken in soya sauce. - *daging* beef prepared as above.

semut *mati - karena gula* to be contented. **meny-i** to swarm over.

senam pe- gymnast.

senandung meny-kan *nyanyian* to hum a tune.

senang - *sekali* perfectly happy. - *pd* to be interested in. - *dgn buah* to like fruit. *sdh tdk* **di-i** *lagi* to be out of favor. **ke-an** fun. *Anak.anak itu* **-nya** *setengah mati,* Those children were delirious with joy.

senapan di- *mesin* to be machinegunned. - *lantak (,locok)* muzzle-loader.

senar string (stretched on a musical instrument).

senarai list. **meny-kan** to list. - *makalah* list of (newspaper) articles.

senda ber- *gurau* to crack a joke.

sendang (water)spring.

Sendangsono (in Central Java) the Indonesian 'Lourdes.'

sendat ber-.- intermittent. **ter-** choked up.

séndé *dijual* - to be sold with the right of repurchasing. **di-kan** to be rented. *Sawahnya* ~ *kpd seorang bermodal di kota,* His irrigated ricefields were rented to a capitalist in the city. *sistim* **ny-** rent system.

sènder transmitter.

sèndèr meny-kan to lean (s.t.).

sendi ABC's. **ber-kan** *kpd* based on, founded on. - *bahasa* the ABC's of language.

sendiri I in person, by oneself, alone. - *saja* all alone. *Saya masih -,* I'm still single. **ke-an** loneliness. **meny-** standoffish.

sendiri II the ultrasuperlative. *Inilah yg terbesar (,paling besar) -,* This is the very biggest. *Dia duduk di muka -,* He sits right in the front. *di atas* - right at the top.

sèndok meny- to shovel in. ~ *penumpang sebanyak.banyaknya* (city buses) stuff in as many passengers as possible. - *teh* teaspoon.

sendratari [seni drama tari] ballet. **di-kan**

to be dramatized. *Kisah Imam Bonjol* ~, The story of Imam Bonjol was dramatized. **meny-kan** to stage.

sendu depressed, dejected, melancholic; (s.) SEDU. **ke-an** depression of spirits, dejection, melancholy.

senduduk (s.) KEDUDUK.

senep 1 stomach discomfort. 2 desire to defecate (but unable to).

senerai (s.) SENARAI.

senèwan (s.) SENEWEN. **ke-** nervousness.

senèwen neurotic, emotionally disturbed.

sengaja *dgn tdk* - accidentally. **ke-an** intention.

sengal ter-.- gasping. - *tulang* rheumatism.

sengam peny-an corrosion.

sengangar flash of lightning. *panas* - blazing hot.

sengap di- (he) has received a crushing snub.

sengat -an *matahari* sunstroke.

senggak to interpose.

senggama (S.) SANGGAMA. **meny-i** to have sexual intercourse with.

senggar.senggur to snore.

sènggol ber- to come into contact with. *Maka saya pesanlah segala macam makanan yg selama ini tak pernah* **ber-** *an dgn lidah saya,* So I ordered all k.o. dishes I never tasted before. **di-** *mobil* to be sideswiped. **ke-** to come into contact with.

sengir ny- to turn up o's nose, pull faces. *mukanya* ~ he grinned. ~ *kuda* to turn up o's nose like a horse.

sèngkèdan terrace (flat platform of earth with sloping sides, rising o. above the other).

sengkeling meny- to cross the legs slightly by laying o. just over the other.

sengkèta per-an 1 (the matter in) dispute. 2 bone of contention. 3 conflict.

sèngon k.o. large tree.

sengsara ke-an calamity.

seni ny- artistic. *S- Balih.Balihan* (in Bali) secular (,profane) art. *S- Bebali* (in Bali) ceremonial art. - *drama tari* (abbrev. *sendratari*) ballet. - *peran* acting (in film). - *rupa* fine arts. - *suara* art of

singing. - *sungging* art of enameling.
S- Wali (in Bali) sacral art. - *yudha* art
of war.

seniman ke-an artistry. **ny-** to become an
artist.

sénior (university sl.) male sophomore
and higher.

séniorita (university sl.) female sophomore and higher.

senirupawan artist of plastic arts.

sènjang ke-an 1 asymmetry. 2 gap. 3
discrepancy.

senjata arm(s). **ber-**: ~ *sebelit pinggang*
and ~ *serba lengkap* armed to the teeth.
ber-kan to be armed with. ~ *lengkap*
armed to the teeth. **ke-an** arm (of mil.
forces). ~ *infanteri (,kavaleri)* the
infantry (,cavalry) arm. - *anti.tank*
antitank weapon. - *api gelap* illegal
firearms. - *bahu* rifles. - *dorgok* muzzle-
loader, zip gun. - *gelap* illegal weapons.
- *genggam* small arms, pistols and re-
volvers. - *inti* nuclear weapon. - *lawan
tank* antitank weapon. - *otomatik* automatic weapon. - *pemersatu fikiran* a
weapon to unify ideas. - *ringan* small
arms. - *tajam* pointed weapon. - *tanpa
(tolak) balik,* - *tanpa tolak belakang,* -
tdk berbalas and - *tdk bertolak* recoilless weapon. - *termonuklir* thermonuclear weapon.

Sénopati 1 commander of the army; (S.)
SENAPATI. 2 reference to *BAKIN*
[Badan Koordinasi Intelijen Negara]
headquartered at the entrance to *Jalan
Senopati* in Jakarta.

sènsasi sensation. *penuh* - sensational.

sènsasionil sensational.

sènsitif and **sènsitip** sensitive.

sènsor *tdk kena* - uncensored. **di-** to be
censored. **peny-an** censoring.

sènsuil sensual.

sènsus mens- to take census.

sèntak *satu* -**an** *udara* a puff of air.

sèntigram centigram.

sèntiliter centiliter.

sèntimèn *sebab bisa.bisa si murid* **di-i** *di*

sekolah because it is quite possible that
they will take it out on the student in
school.

sèntimèntil ke-an sentimentality.

sèntimèter centimeter.

sentiong Chinese grave.

sèntra centra. *Karet S-* (in Jambi, Sumatra) Rubber Centers.

sèntral 1 (of trade unions) federation.
2 power station.

sentrap.sentrup (s.) PENYAKIT (SEN-
TRAP.SENTRUP).

sèntrifugal centrifugal.

sèntripetal centripetal.

sentuh *tdk* **ber-an** *dgn* to leave out of
consideration, not take into consideration. **meny-** *luka lama* to reopen old
sores.

senut.senut to throb with pain.

senyawa pens-an alloying.

senyum *mahal* - does not smile readily.
murah - to smile readily. **meny-i** to
smile at. **ter-.**- *kering* with o's tongue
in o's cheek. *kaya dgn* -**an** to smile
readily. - *digumam* with o's tongue
in o's cheek. - *dikulum (,terkulum)* a
weak smile.

séok ter-.- *kakinya melangkah* she dragged
herself forward.

sép (s.) SIP.

sepah *habis manis* - *dibuang* to take advantage of s.o. (,s.t.) and then toss
him (,it) away.

sépak - *ke atas* to kick upstairs.

sepakat ke-an consensus, concord.

sépakbolawan soccer-player, footballer.

sepanduk (S.) SPANDUK.

sepatu ber- *roda* roller-skating. *S- Ajaib*
Puss in Boots. - *bot* boots. - *es* ice
skates. - *kayu* wooden shoes (of Holland). - *lapangan* (mil.) boots. - *larsa*
boots. - *perahu* platform shoes. - *roda*
roller-skates. - *ulek.ulek* stubby shoes.

sepéda ber- *motor* to motorcycle. - *balap*
racer. - *banci* sports cycle. - *biasa* road-
ster. - *mini* mini bike.

sepèkuk (s.) SPEKKOEK.

sepélé *barang* - trivia, trifles, unimportant matters. **meny-kan** to disparage, soft-pedal.

seperti - *di atas* ditto.

sepet I (to have) burning eyes. **ny-.ny-i** *mata* offensive (to the sight).

sepet II outer fiber (of coconut).

sepi losing popularity. *pekerjaan sedang -* there is no work at hand. *tak - duit* not lack for money. **ke-** pamrihan disinter-estedness. **ny-** to withdraw somewhere for solitude and meditation. - *mati* deserted. - *ing pamrih* 1 selfless. 2 without any ulterior purpose. 3 desireless. -.- *hangat* the calm before the storm.

sepion (s.) SPION. **meny-i** to spy on.

sepokat code name for morphine.

sepon sponge (soles).

sepuh I -(an) *rambut* hair-dye.

sepuh II old (of town, etc.).

sepuk humus.

sepur (S.) SEPOR. - *ejes.ejes (,klutuk)* slow local train. - *lempung* steam train. - *tumbuk* roadroller.

seput speed, haste.

serabi *kueh* - a thick pancake covered with a coconut milk and brown sugar sauce.

serabut I -an disorderly.

serabut II -an for everything and anything, all purpose.

seradak.seruduk 1 to swoop down, as a hawk on prey. 2 perfunctory, routine, hasty and superficial.

seragam **ke-an** uniformity.

serah **di-i** *tugas* to be entrusted with the task of. **di-** terimakan to be transferred. **meny-** *kalah* 1 to capitulate. 2 to concede (defeat). *terpaksa* **meny-kan** *mobil kpd penodong* forced to yield the car to a holdup artist. **peny-an:** ~ *hak* ceding (rights). ~ *kpd penanggung* abandonment. - *terima* transfer.

serakah **ke-an** stinginess.

serambi 1 lobby. 2 hall. *S- Mekah* 1 Aceh. 2 Banten.

serang **peny-an** onset, assault, aggression.

~ *secara frontal* frontal attack. **ter-** to be attacked (by a disease). ~ *kantuk* overcome by sleep. **-an** onset, onslaught. ~ *balasan* counterattack. - *sambar* strafing (by aircraft).

serap **meny-** *banyak tenaga.kerja* labor-intensive. **peny-** absorber. ~ *goncangan* shock absorber.

serasi **mens-kan** (S.) MENYERASIKAN.

serat book.

serba completely, very, well-, all-, purely. **ke-** gunaan multipurposeness. **ke-** rupaan heterogeneity. **ke-** samaan homogeneity. **ke-** sederhanaan austerity. **ke-** takutan psychosis of fear. **ke-** turisan everything for the tourist. - *acak.acakan* a whole mess. - *ada* well-supplied, well-provided. - *aksi* spick and span. *berpakaian* - *aksi* to be dressed spick and span. - *aku* 1 egoism. 2 egotistic. - *alat* mechanical. *dgn* - *alatnya* (to serve up a meal) on a complete dinner set. - *baja* all-steel. - *beres* in applepie order. - *canggung* poor, imperfect. - *dpt* all-round. - *ganteng* spick and span. - *geografi* purely geographical. - *guna* pragmatism. - *jenis* assorted. - *kalah* inferior. - *kebetulan saja* quite by accident. - *keblinger* wrongheaded. - *kedinginan* icy-cold. - *kekurangan* lacking everything. *rok mini* - *kelihatan* see-thru miniskirt. *semua* - *komputer* everything was computerized. - *kurang* in short supply. - *macam* assorted. - *majemuk* pluralism. - *menyenangkan* completely satisfying. - *mesin* technological. - *mewah* posh. - *miskin* poverty-stricken. - *modal* capitalism. - *modern* hypermodern. - *negara* étatism. - *neka* assorted. - *paksa* autocratic. - *pasaran* commercialized. *Seni kecak Bali menjadi - pasaran,* The Balinese monkey dance has been commercialized. - *prihatin* most distressing. - *purna* turnkey. - *putih* snowwhite. - *ramai* (a road with) heavy traffic. - *salah* caught in the middle. - *satiah* automatism. - *sedikit* a few things. - *susah*

screwed up. - *swagati* automatism. -
tahu to know the ins and outs of it.
- *tak punya* poverty-striken. - *tak resmi*
completely unofficial. - *terus* continuous. - *zat* materialism.

serbuk - *bunga* pollen. - *kelantang* bleach-
ing powder. - *mesiu* gunpowder.

serdadu (neocolonialist, colonialist and
imperialist) soldier. - *berpayung* para-
trooper. - *jengki* the G.I. - *sewaan* mercenary. - *ubel.ubel* Gurkha soldier. -
Yankee the G.I.

séréalia cereals.

sérémonial ceremonial.

serempak meny- to advance together.
meny-kan to synchronize.

serèmpèt meny-.ny- *bahaya* to pursue
brinkmanship, skirt danger. **ny-** to
sideswipe (usually of car). -.- *bahaya*
to skirt danger, live dangerously.

serentak *serangan* - simultaneous attack.

serep ny-.ny-in to penetrate thoroughly
into, inquire into a thing thoroughly.
~ *kabar* to ferret out information.

seresah mulch.

seret rigid, stiff, **ke-an** rigidity, stiffness.

sèrèt di- *ke muka pengadilan (,meja hijau)*
to stand trial.

sergap peny-an surprise attack.

sergep industrious.

sèri cherry.

séri *secara* - serially, as a series.

sérial di-kan to be serialized.

seriawan (s.) SARIAWAN.

serigala 1 fox. 2 wild dog. 3 wolf.

serikat ber- to associate, join. **ke-.kerjaan**
trade unionism. **per-an** *negara* confederation. **per-.buruhan** unionism. *S-
Bangsa.Bangsa* League of Nations. -
sekerja labor union.

serimpet ke- stumbled, caught o's foot
in. *hampir* ~ *berkat rok panjang* almost stumbled over the long dress.

serimpi a classical female dance performed
by a group of four principal dancers
representing the heroines of the *Menak*
romance.

serimpung meny- to curtail. **peny-** cur-
tailer.

seringai meny- 1 to grimace. 2 to move
(o's lips, from anger).

sérius serious. **ke-an** seriousness.

séro mempe-kan to convert (a State company) into a limited company. **pe-:** ~
komanditèr limited partner. ~ *pengurus*
active partner. **per-an:** ~ *dagang* trading
company. ~ *dgn (,di bawah) firma* open
partnership. ~ *induk* mother company.
~ *komanditèr* limited partnership. ~
tanggung.jiwa life insurance company.

serobok ber- *dgn* to run into, encounter
by chance.

serobot meny-: ~ *masuk* to enter illegally.
bicara dgn ~ to interrupt without further ado. **peny-** 1 sneak thief, pickpocket. 2 pilferer. 3 illegal occupier
(of land), squatter.

sérok scoop net.

serotan straw (for drinking).

sèrpis I dinner set.

sèrpis II sexual servicing of man by prostitute. **mens-** to service (cars, etc.).
pens-an servicing (cars, etc.).

sersan *S- Taruna* Cadet Sergeant.

serta be- *dgn* along with. **di-i** along with,
accompanied with. *tiada berarti buat*
di-kan to be of no account. **meny-kan**
1 to annex. 2 to enter (s.t. in a contest).
pe-: *utk* ~ *beregu* for group participants. ~ *kongres* congressee. ~ *pengurus* managing partner. ~ *sederajat*
equal partner. - *merta* spontaneous,
prompt, ready. - *tantra* (s.) MEDEBE-
WIND.

seru 1 fierce, exciting. 2 awfully. **meny-**
to urge. **meny-kan** to appeal to.

seruduk to collide with. *truk* - *sepeda* a
truck collided with a bicycle, a truck
hit a bicycle. *seradak.-* to push e.o.
meny- to collide.

serundèng shredded coconut, spiced and
fried.

seruntul ny- to go on without looking
left or right.

seruput meny- *kopi pagi hari* to sip the
early-morning coffee (audibly).

serutup meny- *kopinya* to sip o's coffee.

sèrvice (s.) SERVIS and SERPIS II. **mens-**

to service.

sèrvis service (of car). **mens-** (s.) MEN-SERVICE.

ses a hissing (,sibilant) sound. **nge-** to hiss, make a hissing sound.

sesah meny- to wash clothing.

sesaji offering, sacrifice.

sesak meny-.ny-_dada_ breath-taking. **meny-kan** _jalan_ to block a street (by double parking). - _dada (,napas)_ asthma. - _(padat)_ chockful.

sesal - _dahulu pendapatan,_ - _kemudian tdk berguna_ look before you leap. _terbit -nya_ he began to regret. **kemeny-an** repentance.

sesanti 1 prayer. 2 blessing.

sesapi laut brown-breasted bee eater.

sesat peny-an deceit, delusion. **ter-** _berbe-lit.belit_ to get into trouble.

sesel (S.) SESAL. **ny-** to regret.

sesenggokan and **sesenggukan** sobbingly.

sesepuh 1 elder. 2 chairman.

sèsèr peny- a _nener_ fisherman.

sèsi cession. **mens-kan** to cede.

Sèskoad [Sekolah Staf Komando Angkatan Darat] Army Staff and Command School. **di.-kan** to be sent to the _Seskoad._

Sèskowan (Army) Staff and Command School graduate.

sesowanan ceremony whereby the _Kraton_ family and all the officials pay a visit to the _Sultan_ (of Yogyakarta) to congratulate him on his birthday.

sèspan sidecar (of motorcycle). _sepeda motor -nya_ his motorcycle and sidecar.

sesuai similar, identical, appropriate. - _dgn_ in accordance with, in line with. - _dgn contoh_ to come up to sample. - _dgn hatiku_ after my own heart. **ber-an** to agree. **meny-kan**: ~ _diri dgn iklim_ to acclimatize. ~ _diri dgn kehendak zaman_ to keep pace with the times. **per-an** _kehendak (,paham)_ consensus. - _kaji_ agreed.

sèt (me)nge- (,mens-) _rambutnya_ to set o's hair. **nge-** to set type.

sètan spirit. _Memang - engkau ini!_ The devil is really in you! You're really like o. possessed! _senja kala perulangan_ - twilight is the time for haunting. _menonton gambar - berkejaran di layar tévé_ to watch an interfered with picture on the TV screen. - + _noun_ to be addicted to ... - _alas_ tormentor. - _gundul_ 1 'bald devils,' i.e. devils who have all their hair shaved off except for a topknot. 2 a member of the outlawed _PKI_ or o. of its mass organizations who must report to the Military District Command Headquarters. - _jalan_ speedhound. - _kerdil_ a very small devil. - _laut_ purchaser in fish-collecting centers.

setandar 1 flag or banner used as a symbol of a mil. unit. 2 bicycle or motorcycle standard attached at the hub of the rear wheel or other place, for holding the bicycle or motorcycle upright when not in use. 3 standard (of quality). 4 a stand. _Tarohlah TVnya di-,_ Set the television on the stand. **meny-kan** to put (a bike) on a stand.

setangan handkerchief.

setapsiun (S.) SETASIUN.

setater (s.) STARTER.

setèl _satu - cangkir.piring_ a place setting. _satu - kartu_ o. deck (of cards). **meny-** to tune (radio), change (stations on radio).

setèm peny-_piano_ piano tuner. **peny-an** _piano_ piano tuning.

sètèng o. on top of another.

setènggan stengun.

setènsil stencil. **meny-** to stencil.

seterum (s.) STRO(O)M and STRUM. **peny-an** charging (batteries).

setiakawan solidarity.

setoka _ikan (pari)_ - k.o. small ray.

Setomo (s.) JAGUR.

setop (s.) STOP. **-an** _abang.ijo_ (coll.) traffic light.

setopen [setoran penjinak] payola.

setopkontak (S.) STOPKONTAK.

setor di- _penuh_ paid up fully (,in full; of stocks). **meny-** _(uang)_ (taxicab, pedicab drivers) to turn in o's receipts (to owner). **peny-** depositor.

setra **meny-kan** to isolate.

Setra.Gand(h)amayu legendary forest where the goddess Durga dwells with hosts of demons.

setrat street.

setrèn foreland, foreshore.

setrika (S.) SETERIKA. - *bumi* (coll.) steam roller (for roads).

setrip (fig.) dotty, crazy.

setuju per-an: *P~ Buruh Kolektif* Collective Labor Agreement. *P~ Lintas Tapal Batas* Border-Crossing Agreement. *~ segi.tiga* tripartite agreement. *atas ~ kedua belah pihak* by joint consent.

séwa *apa yg* **di-kan** (in notarial instruments) the rented property. **meny-.beli** charter purchase. **meny-kontrakkan** to lease.

sèwot angry. **di-i** to be scolded.

sèwu thousand.

sexava *hama* - pest which attacks smallholders' coconut trees.

S.H. [Sarjana Hukum] Master of Laws, LL.M.

shalat (s.) SHOLAT. - *Ied* prayer meeting held at *(Hari Raya) Idul Fitri* and *(Hari Raya) Idul Adha*. - *sunah* an extra prayer other than the five obligatory prayers.

shè first of three (Chinese) names, surname.

shi (during the Jap. occupation) municipality.

shidokan (during the Jap. occupation) leader, guide.

shirèi (during the Jap. occupation) instruction, order, notice.

shirèibu (s.) SIREIBU.

shodancho (during the Jap. occupation; in *PETA* hierarchy) section commander.

sholat (s.) SHALAT. - *Jumat* the Friday prayer.

sholawat to cheer, raise a battle cry; (S.) SELAWAT.

Shonanto the Jap. name given to Singapore during WW II.

Shusangikai (during the Jap. occupation) Provincial Advisory Assembly.

si I four.

si II (s.) SIH.

si III (s.) SHI.

si IV [the particular o. (of a pair, group, etc.)] . - *abang* the older brother. - *hitam* asphalt. - *roda dua* the Vespa scooter. - *tangan jahil* the bad guy.

sia **mens-.-kan** to betray (a confidence).

siaga I - *penuh* full alert.

siaga II member of the *Pramuka* Boy Scout Movement between 8 and 11 years, cub.

siamang *bagai - kurang kayu* like a fish out of water.

siamsèng gangster.

siang I in the daytime, midday, late (in the morning, when the sun is practically at the zenith), i.e. from about 11 A.M. to 4 P.M. *jam dua belas* - 12 noon. *ada - ada malam, ada sial ada mujur* after rain comes sunshine. *berbeda sbg - dan malam* to be as different as day from night, differ as night from day. *Senen* - Monday, late in the afternoon. *tidur* - to take a(n afternoon) nap. *Datangnya* **ke-an,** 1 He got here too late (i.e. during midday rather than in the morning). 2 He got here too early (i.e. in the midday rather than late afternoon). *Sdr. bisa datang agak* **-an,** You may come a bit later in the day (between abt. 11 A.M. and 4 P.M.). **-nya** 1 in the afternoon (of that day). 2 later in the day.

siang II **mempe(r)-i** to remove the skin from (a snake).

Siang Hwee Chinese Trade Association.

sianide cyanide.

siankali cyanide of potassium.

siap *tetap* - stand by. **di-.siagakan** to be put on full alert. **ke-an**: *~ di udara* air alert. *~ tempur* combat readiness. **ke-.siagaan** readiness. - *muat* ready to load. *dlm keadaan -.siaga* to be confined to o's barracks. - *tanam* ready to plant. - *(utk) tempur* combat ready.

siapa *S- Apa?* Who's Who? *S- lu, - gua* every man for himself. *se- saja* whomever. *-.-: tdk ~* nobody. "*S- yg ada di*

rumah waktu itu?" "Tdk ada ~."
"Who was at home at that time?"
"Nobody."

siapuuuh 1 interjection in *kroncong*-songs (of approval). 2 would you ever! fancy! (used as an exclamation of mild surprise).

siar di-kan: *sedang* ~ to be on the air. *tdk* ~ to be off the air. *Ia minta agar soal ini jangan* **di-.-kan,** He asked that the matter not be broadcast (or, that the matter be hushed up). **meny-** to proselytize. *Setiap malam TV* **meny-kan** *kejahatan.kejahatan ngeri,* Every evening horrible crimes are shown on TV. **meny- luaskan** to disseminate. *ada kabar* **ter-** there is a report abroad. **-an** *pers* press release.

siasat peny- strategist.

sibak meny- to cleave through.

sibasol cibasol, i.e. a sulfa preparation.

Sibéria Siberia.

sibi (teenager sl.) 1 [sih biasa] as far as ... is concerned, it's common. 2 [sikap biasa] an ordinary attitude.

sicé a five-piece sitting-room set consisting of a table and four chairs.

sidang peny-an trial. - *puncak* summit meeting. - *ramai* the audience.

Sidarta o. of the names of Buddha.

sidat and **sidhat** *(ikan)* - a (river) eel.

sidi a full member of the Protestant Church.

sidik peny-an identification.

sido (coll.) eyeshadow.

sidokan (during the Jap. occupation) trainer.

sidomukti k.o. batik design.

Sièr(r)a Léoné Sierra Leone.

sifat character, nature. *-nya gampang marah* he's hot-tempered by nature. **ber-:** ~ *gado.gado* heterogeneous. ~ *keilmuan populer* popular scientific. ~ *maju* progressive, pushing. ~ *nasional* nationwide. ~ *penjajagan* explorative, exploratory. ~ *seni* artistic. ~ *subversif* subversive in nature. *tak* **ter-** *lagi* indescribable. - *dunia* that's life. - *pelupa* forgetfulness.

sift shift. - *pertama (,kedua)* the first (,second) shift.

sigar a cut piece. *terbelah* - *menjadi dua* split in two.

sih 1 (in questions, k.o. indirect question) I wonder ... *Dia kenapa* -? What's the matter with him? *Berapa* - *ini?* How much is this? How much would this be (if I were interested in buying it)? 2 (after the subject) as for. *Itu* -, *salah dirinya sendiri!* As to that, it's his own fault! 3 (at the end of a clause) because. *Habis, jauh* -, Well, because it's far. 4 (concessive, of the type: *X* - *X) Dpt* - *dpt, cuma kagak semua!* (It's) true I have gotten s.t., but not all! *Bagus* - *bagus, tapi mahal!* It's nice indeed, but expensive!

sihir peny- *ular* snake charmer.

siip (s.) SIP.

sigarèt cigarette; (s.) ROROK (PUTIH).

siji one.

sijil list. - *anak buah* crew list.

sikap general appearance, bearing. **ber-:** ~ *masa bodoh* to be apathetic. ~ *menjauhkan diri* to hold s.o. aloof. ~ *menentang* to assume the aggressive. ~ *menunggu* to sit on the fence, adopt a wait-and-see attitude. - *beri.terima* a give-and-take attitude. - *berlebih.lebihan* over(re)acting. - *gagah.gagahan* bravado. - *lunak* a lenient attitude. - *menunggu (,tunggu dan lihat)* a wait-and-see attitude. - *yg lurus.lilin* a posture as straight as an arrow. - *yg mencla.mencle* an ever-changing attitude.

sikat - *arang* carbon brush.

sikering fuse.

siklam mauve.

siklamat cyclamate.

sikloida cycloid.

siklon and **siklun** cyclone.

siklus cycle (period of time).

siksa peny-an torture, punishment. ~ *tingkat ke-3* third degree torture.

siksak zigzag.

siku peny- complement (math.).

sikukuh ber- (s.) KUKUH.

sila -*kan* help yourself (an invitation).

silabus syllabus.
silang ber- *tangan* to cross o's arms.
silap ter- by mistake, erroneously, mistakenly.
silat pe- devotee of silat. *cabang* **per-an** silat sport branch.
silèt 1 (originally) a Gillete razor blade. 2 (now) any razor blade. **di-** to be slashed. *Taskulitnya ~ oleh pencopet,* Her leather handbag was slashed by a pickpocket. **peny-an** *muka* cutting up a person's face with a razor blade.
silih ber- *ganti* 1 to alternate. 2 o. ... after another. **di-** to be altered. - *berganti* uncertain, precarious. *telepon yg berdering -.sambung* a continuously ringing telephone.
silinder cylinder.
silit ass. *S-!* You ass hole!
Siliwangi 1 *Prabu* - the founder of the Pajajaran kingdom. 2 the white tiger, symbol of *Pajajaran.* 3 name of the army division stationed in West Java.
siluman *perusahaan* - a phantom enterprise, i.e. an enterprise producing items sold without permit; (cp.) (PERUSA-HAAN) AKTENTAS.
SIM [Surat Izin Mengemudi] driver's license.
simak meny- to monitor.
simbah 1 grandfather. 2 grandmother. 3 predecessor.
simbiose symbiosis.
simbol and **simbul** symbol. **ber-** symbolic. **meny-kan** to symbolize.
simpan meny- (euph.) to imprison. **peny-an** 1 savings (in bank). 2 storing (of goods). **-an** mistress, kept woman.
simpang ber- *kata (,sebut)* to differ (in opinion). **ke- siuran** crisscrossing. **meny-** *dr peraturan.peraturan* (euph.) to commit corruption, etc. - *empat* crossroads. - *jalan ke* and *jalan - ke* a side street to. - *siur* 1 swing(ing compass needle). 2 *segala - siur penghidupan* all complications of life. - *tiga* T-intersection.
simpansé chimpanzee.

simpati ber- *kpd (,dgn)* to sympathize with.
simpatisan sympathizer.
simplifikasi simplification.
simposium symposium. **mengs-kan** to discuss at a symposium.
simpul ke-an *pungkasan* final conclusion.
sim.sulap.salabim sleight of hand.
sinagog synagogue.
sinambung and **ber-** continuous. *cerita yg* **berke-an** a serial.
sinar - *kosmis* cosmic rays. - *mengumpul* converging rays. - *merah.infra* infrared rays.
Sinca Chinese New Year.
sinder overseer.
sind(h)èn to sing to the accompaniment of *gamelan* music (of female singers). **pe-** female vocalist with *gamelan* accompaniment. **-an** dancing and singing.
sindikalisme syndicalism.
sindikat syndicate.
sindir peny- sneerer.
sindrom(a) syndrome. - *kemiskinan desa* rural poverty syndrome.
sinéas cinematographer.
sinéma cinema, movie, motion-picture theater.
sinématika cinematics.
sinématografi cinematography.
Singa Leo. *s-.laut* dolphin.
singahak ter- startled, surprised.
singangar (s.) SENGANGAR.
Singapurawan Singaporean.
Singasari name of the kingdom near Malang (East Java), preceding *Majapahit.*
singgah - *di (,ke ,kpd)* 1 to call at (a person's house, a port). 2 to stop (briefly) in (,at ,by).
singget *dinding* **-an** partition wall.
singgung *tdk bisa turut* **di-.-** (of an authority) to be inviolable. **ke-** *pernya* he felt offended. **keter-an** offensiveness, insult. **meny-.ny-:** *tdk ~* to leave out of account. *tdk ~ sedikitpun* 1 to snub. 2 does not mind at all. **per-an** contact. *~ bebas* free sex.

singit I to grumble. 2 to weep, cry.

singit II ter- 1 barely visible (of sun or moon on the horizon). 2 *rahasia itu baru sedikit ~ selimutnya* only a tip of the iceberg of the secret was visible.

singkang meny- to reject, disdain, scorn s.o.

singkat *paham (,pikiran)* - shortsighted. - *tdk terulas, panjang tdk terkerat* everybody dies when his time is up. **meny-** *waktu* to shorten the time. **-nya** all things considered …, in short, in a word. - *cerita* in short, to put it briefly, cut a long story short. - *kata* all things considered …, in short, in a word.

singkir meny-kan *jiwa* to kill. *orang* **ter-** displaced person. **ter-kan** deposed.

singkong - *gendruwo* bitter cassava, a cassava species thought effective against cancer (L. Manihot utilissima). - *pohung* (fermented) cassava.

singlèt singlet. *(kaos)* - a man's sleeveless undershirt.

singsal ke- disappeared.

singset tight, taut; (S.) SINGSAT. *jamu* - Jav. medicinal herbs for slimming. **men-kan** to make (a mother's stomach) tight (after having given birth).

sinkronisasi synchronization. **men(g)s-kan** to synchronize.

sinode synod.

sinologi sinology.

sinom locks of hair on the temples.

sinoman young people, youth (bound to carry out services in the village community).

sinsèi and **sinsyè** Chinese healer.

sinso chain-saw.

sintaksis syntax.

Sinterklaas Saint Nicholas, a white-bearded old man in a red suit, who makes toys for children and distributes gifts on December 5.

sintése synthesis.

Sinuhun (s.) INGKANG (SINUHUN).

sinyalemèn accusation, pointing out (s.t. bad).

sinyalir mens- to give a description of

(s.o. wanted by the police, etc.), detect, discover.

siomoy Chinese snack resembling *bakso*, but not using a sauce; it consists of a mixture of bean curd, potatoes and cabbage.

Sionisme Zionism.

sip safe, certain to succeed. - *deh!* it's all taken care of, no sweat!

sipat *garis* **-an** building line, alignment.

sipik ny- to commit graft or corruption in army Civic Mission circles.

sipil mens-kan to convert to civilian administration.

sipit *si mata* - the Chinese.

sipoa ny-in to add on an abacus.

Siprus Cyprus.

siput - *kema* clam.

sir to like.

siram ter- *hujan* wet from rain. *upacara* **-an** ritual bathing ceremony, (a) following a circumcision, (b) after first menstruation, (c) before the wedding (of a bride).

sirap ter- singing, ringing (of the blood in o's ears).

sirat I ter- implicit. *ancaman yg ~* a veiled threat. *yg ~ di hati* what is going on in o's mind.

sirat II -.- *gigi* space between the teeth.

siratul.mustakim the razor-edged bridge over which true believers pass into heaven.

sirèibu (during the Jap. occupation) (army) headquarters.

sirep anesthetic (k.o. magic formula to put s.o. asleep). *ilmu* - the skill to put s.o. asleep. **ny-** to put s.o. to sleep.

siring ditch. *ke* - to urinate.

sirk(u)it circuit. *televisi* **ber-** *tertutup* closed circuit television, CCTV. - *listrik* electrical circuit. - *singkat* short circuit.

sirkulasi ber- with a circulation of.

sirkwit (s.) SIRK(U)IT.

Sirnaning Jakso Katon Gapuraning Ratu motto of the Diponegoro army Division stationed in Central Java, meaning 'If

the Giant (,Demon) has disappeared
the Gate to the King is visible.'
sis (s.) ZUS.
sisi ber-.-an abreast. - *kapal* beam-ends.
sisih di-kan to be deposed.
sisik.melik clues. *memperoleh* - to obtain
evidence.
Sisilia Sicily.
Si Singa Mangaradja name of the last
Batak king defeated by the Dutch in
1906.
sistématisasi mens-kan to systematize.
sistim - *banyak partai* multi-party system.
*S- Bombardemen (,Pemboman) Orbit
Fraksionil* Fractional Orbital Bombardment System. - *demokrasi parlementer*
parliamentary democratic system. -
dwipartai (,dua partai) two-party system. - *gaduh* a system whereby financial aid is reimbursed in kind. - *multi
partai* multi-party system. - *partai
tunggal* mono-party system. - *pilih.bulu*
favoritism. - *tanpalogam* a-metallism.
siswa - *bidan* student midwife. - *tamu*
guest student.
siswi female college student.
sit (pron. i as ee in sheet) (stencil) sheet.
SIT [Surat Izin Terbit] Publication Permit.
sita di- *eksekusi* to be taken (,seized)
under an execution. **meny-** *seluruh
waktunya* to take up all o's time. **pens-**
and **peny-** confiscator. **pens-an (,peny-
an)** *sementara* attachment before judgment. - *jaminan* (jur.) garnishee.
Sitarda [Integrasi Taruna Wreda] Senior
Students Integration (with the People)
(of the Armed Forces Academy).
siter zither.
Sitiung an area in West Sumatra. **dis-kan**
to be relocated (,transmigrated) to the
Sitiung area.
situ lake.
situs situs, site of archeological find.
siu skimming push net.
sivilisasi mens-kan to civilize.
SK [Surat Keputusan] Decision Letter.
skak (in chess) check!
skakelar (electric) switch.

skalanisasi scaling.
Skalu [Sekretariat Kerjasama Antar Lima
Universitas] 1 Cooperating Secretariat
among Five Universities: *Universitas
Indonesia, Institut Teknologi Bandung,
Institut Pertanian Bogor, Universitas
Gadjah Mada* and *Universitas Airlangga.*
2 admittance test to any of the five
universities mentioned above.
skandal scandal.
Skandinavia Scandinavia.
skat skate.
SKB [Surat Keputusan Bersama] Joint
Decision Letter.
skéma scheme, sketch.
skématis schematic.
skénario scenario.
skèpter scepter.
skèptis sceptic(al).
skèptisisme scepticism.
skip target (in shooting). - *bergerak*
moving target.
SKKS [Sekolah Kesejahteraan Keluarga
Atas] Senior High School for Domestic Sciences.
skors pen(g)s-an temporary suspension,
adjournment.
skorsing (s.) PENSKORSAN.
Skot Scot. *orang bangsa* - Scotsman,
Scotchman, Scot.
Skotlandia Scotland.
skrining screening.
skripsi a scholarly paper.
SKUT [Surat Kir untuk Truck?] Inspection Booklet for Trucks.
skuter scooter.
skwadron squadron.
slagorde (pron. slakh-orde) order of
battle.
slah *blm tahu* -nya have not gotten the
hang (,knack) of it.
slahrum whipped cream.
slametan (s.) SELAMATAN.
slang (s.) SELANG II.
slèbor 1 a drinking spree. 2 boozer.
melakukan - to booze, be addicted
to liquor.
slèm (in bridge) slam. - *besar (,kecil)*
grand (,little) slam.

slèndang and slèndhang sling for carrying
children.

slèndro five-note *gamelan* scale.

slilit food particles between the teeth.
mencukil.cukil - to pick food particles
from between the teeth.

slingkuh (s.) SELINGKUH. *berlaku* - to
act in a secretive (,underhanded) manner.

slof 1 slipper. 2 carton (of cigarettes).

slong (s.) NGESLONG.

sloyar.sloyor to go adrift.

slundap.slundup to sneak in.

slundup (s.) SELUNDUP. nyl- *kerja* to
sneak into a job.

smokel (s.) SEMOKEL. per-an smuggling.

so (in Manado) (S.) SUDAH.

soak (s.) SWAK. *aki* - a weak (car) battery.

soal point in question. *tdk menjadi* - it
makes no difference. *itu bukan - saya*
that is no concern of mine. *bukan -
baru* it's not news. *itu - nanti* that is a
matter for later concern. per-an: *di
sini letak* ~ here lies the problem,
here's where the viper bites. ~ *cinta*
love affair. -nya: *Apa* ~? What's up?
What's the trouble? ~ *begini* ... the
point is that... - *hidup.mati* and - *mati.
hidup* a question of life and death. -
kecil.kecil trivia. - *peseran buta* trifle.

soa.soa k.o. iguana (L. Farannus indicus).

soba buckwheat.

sobèk -an scraps.

sodèt I spatula.

sodèt II meny- to carve (up), cut through.
peny-an carving up (of city). -an canal.

sodok *S- keluar si A!* Kick out A! di- to
be arrested. ~ *keluar* to be kicked out.
meny- to strike at the belly (in *silat*).
ny- (s.) NGOMPRENG I. -an a stab,
attack. -.-an to be at loggerheads.

Sodom dan Gomorah Sodom and
Gomorrah.

soen (pron. sun) a kiss; (s.) SUN. di- to
be kissed. mengs- and nge- to kiss.

sofbol softball.

Sofia Sofia.

sogili *(ikan)* - a large k.o. eel.

sogok meny- to prod, poke. - *upil* a Jav.

dress fashion consisting of a blouse
and finery.

sohun transparent bean thread; (S.)
SO'UN.

sok I ke-an pretension. - *aksi* to put on
airs. - *iseng* amuse o.s. by abusing o's
authority. - *keminter (,pintar)* pedant.

sok II -.- sometimes.

soklat 1 chocolate. 2 brown; (s.) COK(E)-
LAT. - *pucat* pale brown.

SOKSI [Sentral Organisasi Karyawan
Sosialis Indonesia] Central Organization of Indonesian Socialist Workers.

sol sole (of shoe). *sepatu yg* ber- *karet*
rubber-soled shoes. mengs- to sole
(shoes).

solar (s.) MINYAK (SOLAR).

solat (s.) SYALAT.

solist soloist.

solor -an gutter, ditch.

solot angry.

solvabilita solvency.

som I *perahu* - Siamese (,Thai) junk.

som II sum.

soma moon.

sombong ke-an *bangsa* 1 racism. 2 chauvinism.

somèl sawmill.

somoy (s.) SIOMOY.

somplok ke-an *dgn* to meet, come across.

somprèt *S- betul orang itu!* That son-of-a
gun!

sonebril dark glasses.

songar ke-an arrogance, pride.

songkèt *kain* - fabric woven by using
silver and gold thread ornamentation;
found in Palembang (Sumatra) and Bali.

songkro garbage truck.

songsong *dua mobil yg* ber- two oncoming cars. meny- to go to meet. ~ *pemilihan umum* to be on the eve of the
general elections. ~ *tamu* to go to meet
a guest.

sonji bet.

sonokeling tree, supplier of hardwood
(L. Dalbergia latifolia).

sonokembang *kayu* - sandalwood (L.
Pterocarpus indicus Willd.).

sontèk peny-an cheating, cribbing.

sontok *dunia sdh* - to be at o's wits' end, be at a loss what to do. *pikiran* - narrow-minded.

sop *daun* - celery, leek, and the like. - *buntut* oxtail soup. - *kaldu* broth.

sopir - *tembak* hustler at bus terminal who has obtained the 'confidence' of busdrivers to drive their bus and look for passengers, while the drivers have a rest at the terminal; these hustlers usually have no driver's license, but are controlled by a syndicate who can force the bus drivers in case they refuse to make their bus available to them.

sorangan alone, o. person. *S- waé?* All alone? (said to a girl sitting alone in a pedicab, etc.).

soré ke-an (depending on the reference time) 1 (too) late, i.e. in the *sore* rather than the next earlier time period *(siang).* 2 (too) early, i.e. in the *sore* rather than the next later time period *(malam).* -**nya** that (very) afternoon. -.- *hari* 1 afternoons. 2 late in the afternoon.

sori sorry. *minta* - to apologize, ask forgiveness.

sorog -**an** 1 artificially ripened. 2 poked off tree before ripe.

sorong ter- compelled.

sorot di- and *mendapat* -**an** to be spotlighted.

sociëteit (pron. sositèit) social club.

sos (s.) SOCIËTEIT.

Sosba [(Ilmu Pengetahuan) Sosial dan Bahasa] Social Sciences and Languages.

SosBud [Sosial dan Budaya] the department of social sciences and culture in a Senior High School.

sosial di-.kontroli to be social controlled. - *budaya* sociocultural.

sosialisasi pen-an socialization.

sosiatri (in Gadjah Mada University, Yogyakarta) sociology of deviant behavior.

sosiawan male social worker.

sosiawati female social worker.

sosio-kulturil socio-cultural.

sosiolog sociologist.

sositèt (s.) SOCIËTEIT.

sosok - *badan, suatu* -, *sebuah* - and *se-tubuh* (a) shape, form, figure. (**se**)-*mayat* (a) corpse.

sosor meny- to attack with the beak (like geese).

Sos.Pol [(Ilmu Pengetahuan) Sosial dan Politik] the sociopolitical department in a Senior High School.

soto a soup-like snack, or main course. - *Madura soto* with chicken entrails.

sotok peny- *nener nener* fisherman. -**an** *nener* catch.

sovinis chauvinist.

sovinisme chauvinism.

Sovyèt Rusia Soviet Russia.

Sovyètisasi Sovietization.

sowan di-i to be visited. -**an** custom of visiting older generation relatives.

S.P. [Sarjana Pendidikan] Master of Education, M.Ed.

Spaanse vlieg (pron. spanse vlih) Spanish fly.

spada (S.) SEPADA.

span tight (of skirt). - *rok* tight skirt.

spaneng (s.) SPANING. *naik* - to become angry.

spaning (sl.) wants to approach (a girl).

spèk bacon.

spèkkoek (pron. spèkuk) (spiced) layer cake.

spèktakulèr spectacular.

spékula(a)s *(kueh)* - spiced windmill cookies.

spékulasi speculation.

spèlrégels (pron. g as kh) rules of the game.

spési mortar. - *kapur* lime mortar.

spésial special. *bakmi goreng* - special fried noodles (i.e. with eggs).

spésialisasi mens- *diri* to specialize. **ter**-specialized.

spésifik specific.

spidol k.o. felt pen, marker.

spidomèter speedometer.

spiku (s.) SPEKULA(A)S.

spion spy; (s.) SEPION. - *bermuka dua* double agent. - *top* master spy.

spionase espionage.

spir muscle.

spiral (in family planning) IUD. di-kan (the village mothers) had a spiral inserted.

spiralisasi the introduction of IUDs in family planning.

spirituil spiritual. *kepentingan materiil dan* - material and spiritual interests.

spiritus (methylated) spirit, spirits. *kompor* - spirit stove. *lampu* - spirit lamp.

split di- to be divided (into two or more parts).

sponsor sponsor. mens-(i) to sponsor.

sponsorisasi sponsorship.

spontan ke-an spontaneity.

spontanitas spontaneity.

spoor (s.) SEPUR.

srakah (s.) SERAKAH.

srakat ke- to live in misery.

srama (s.) SROMO.

srati - *babi* swineherd.

sreg and srek adequate, fitting. *kurang* - not adequate enough. di-kan to be made adequately.

sregep industrious.

srèng *(mercon)* - fireworks. - *dor* rocket (fireworks) which explodes in the air.

sri 1 a personal name element. 2 title for royal personages. *S- Baginda* His (,Her) Majesty. *S- Paus* His Holiness Pope (So-and-So). *S- Ratu* (Her Majesty) The Queen. *S- Sultan* His Majesty the Sultan (of Yogyakarta). 3 goddess of rice, also *Dewi S-*. *S- Sedana* 1 the goddess of rice and her spouse Sedana. 2 symbol of prosperity.

sribombok white-breasted waterhen.

srigunting Jav. black drongo.

Srikandi *Dewi* - a *wayang* character who loved *Arjuna* from afar; the favorite character of modern Indonesian women. *kaum* - warlike women. - *Jamilah* Heroine Jamilah.

srimpet (s.) SERIMPET.

srimpung (s.) SERIMPUNG.

sripah a death. ke-an to suffer loss by death. *Sri Sultan* ~, His Majesty the Sultan (of Yogyakarta) suffered a loss by the death of ..., His Majesty the

Sultan lost ...

sri.panggung prima donna.

Sriwijaya name of a maritime empire in South Sumatra in the second half of the seventh century.

sromo k.o. sharecropping arrangement usually for three years in Central Java in which the peasant who takes care of the cultivation has to give some key money to the landowner in order to acquire his land for tillage. In addition, the peasant has to hand over 70% of his yield, so that the tiller himself receives only 30%.

srong *ikan* - whale.

sronggot di- *(lokomotip)* to be hit by (a locomotive).

SS-77 [Senjata Serbu - 77] an offensive weapon, manufactured by the *Pindad* (,*Pusat Industri Angkatan Darat:* Army Industrial Center) in Bandung. O. type has a rifle butt (980 millimeters in length) and the other a folding rifle butt (880 millimeters in length).

Ssst (an exclamation calling for silence) Sh! Shush!

Staatsblad (col.) Statute Book.

stabil stable. ke-an stability, stabilization. mens-kan to stabilize.

stabilisator stabilizer.

stadion per-an (adj.) stadium. - *balap anjing* dog track.

stal stable (for horses).

standar(d) standard; (s.) SETANDAR.

standardisasi mens-kan to standardize.

start start. *uang* - initial capital.

starter starter (of car).

stasion and stasiun - *komunikasi* communications base. - *penelacak bertenaga nuklir* nuclear-powered tracking station. - *pengendali* (at Cibinong, for communication satellites) telemetry, tracking and command station. - *penyambung* repeater station (in telecommunications).

statutèr statutory.

stèk cutting (of plant).

stèl a (matched) set; (s.) SETEL. ber-an *abu.abu* to wear a gray suit. -an 1 a (matched) set. 2 a suit (jacket and trousers). 3 uniform. ~ *Panglima AD Belanda* Dutch Army General's uniform.

stèlling (mil.) position; (S.) SETELING.

stèmbusaccoord ballot box accord.

stèmmotivéring account for o's vote (in M.P.R.).

stèmpel I (s.) SETEMPEL. **ber-kan** with a ... stamp. - *kering timbul* a seal.

stèmpel II (in Kalimantan) a long, narrow river craft powered by an outboard motor.

stèn I gun.

stèn II - *wedana* head of a subdistrict.

sténograf stenographer.

sténografia stenography. *S- Karundèng* the Karundeng stenographic system, i.e. the Standard Stenographic System for Indonesia.

stèpler stapler (the device).

stèrek strong. **di-** to be recharged (of a battery).

stéréo stereometry.

stérilisasi sterilization.

stérilisator - *desakan tinggi* autoclave.

stérilitas sterility.

stèsen stationwagon.

stétoskop stethoscope.

stévia k.o. shrub originating from Uruguay now cultivated in the village of Pekuncen (Banyumas); the plant contains sugar which could replace saccharine.

stiker sticker.

stil well-dressed.

stim.bat steam bath.

stimulir mens- to stimulate.

stip I (s.) SETIP.

stip II convulsion.

stir (s.) SETIR. - *kanan (,kiri)* right-(,left-)hand drive. -*stang* steering column.

stock stock. - *opname* stock taking.

stofbril sunglasses.

stok (s.) STOCK.

stone 1 code name for morphine. 2 to 'fly' (on drugs).

stop (s.) SETOP. **mens-** to stop. **-an** *bis* bus stop.

stopkran stopcock.

STOVIA [School tot Opleiding van Indische Artsen] School for the Training of Native Physicians (in Jakarta). [The oldest medical school still in existence in Southeast Asia; established in 1851; in 1926 it became a Medical College and in 1947 it was renamed *Fakultas Kedokteran (Universitas Indonesia)*].

strafoverplaatsing transfer to a remote station for punishment.

'strahat (mil.) at ease!

strap punishment. **di-** to be punished.

stratégi strategy.

stratégis strategic.

stratifikasi - *sosial* social stratification.

stratigrafi stratigraphy.

stratokumulus stratocumulus.

strip (S.) SETERIP. *bintara berpangkat - satu bengkok kuning* noncommissioned officer, sergeant second class.

striptis striptease.

Strodom k.o. LSD.

Strong.Pa trade-mark of medicinal capsule to increase men's sexual potency (extract from the *pasak bumi* root, found in Central Kalimantan along the Barito River).

stro(o)m electric current; (s.) STRUM. *kena - (listrik)* to get an electric shock. **di-** to be electrified (of barbed wire).

strum spiritual influence.

studi - *grup* study group. - *kasus* case study. -.*sesudah.sarjana* postgraduate study. - *trip* study trip (,tour).

studio studio. - *film* film studio.

stuip (s.) STIP II.

STUJ [Surat Tanda Uji Jalan (untuk kendaraan bermotor)] State Inspection Certificate (in U.S., sticker).

stumwals roadroller.

su (also written: **soe**) a personal name element originally with the meaning of 'beautiful, good,' such as, in *Sumantri, Soeharto, Soekarno,* etc.

sua ber- *kembali dgn* to see (,meet) again.

suai - *iklim* acclimatization.

suak to miss. *Blm pernah N yg - menje-*

lang pamannya, N hasn't missed visiting his uncle.

suaka - *politik* political asylum.

suami *kedua* - *isteri* the couple. **ber-.isteri** *yg bertanggung.jawab* responsible parenthood.

suaminda husband (respectful form of address).

suang *tak* -.-(nya) unceasingly, all the time.

suangi (in the eastern part of Indonesia) s.o. engaged in witchcraft (,sorcery).

suap *makan (uang)* - to accept bribes.

suara *kelebihan* - majority of votes. *memberi(kan) (,melahirkan ,mengeluarkan) -nya* to cast (,give) o's vote. *mengangkat* - to begin to speak, take the floor. *naik* - to raise o's voice. *dgn 20* - *mupakat dan 5* - *menyangkal* by twenty votes in favor and five against. *semua buruh yg berhak memberi* - all enfranchised employees. *apabila jumlah* - *yg setuju dan tdk setuju sama banyaknya, apabila* -.- *sama berat* and *dlm hal* -.- *sama banyaknya* in case of a tie vote. *dgn* - *yg terbanyak* by a majority vote. *tiga* - *jatuh atas* three votes were cast (,polled) for. -*nya spt perian pecah* he has a voice like a cracked violin. - *rakyat adalah* - *Tuhan* the voice of the people is the voice of God; vox populi, vox Dei. *tdk memberi* - to abstain from voting. *tak* **ber-** noiseless. **meny-i** to dub. - *blangko* abstention, an abstaining vote. *dgn* - *bulat* by acclamation, unanimously. -.- *burung menyebutkan* … rumors (,unconfirmed reports) have it that … - - *genta* ringing voice. - *menggelegar* rumbling (of volcano). - *rendah (wanita)* alto.

suarawati female singer.

suasana - *hati (,jiwa)* mood.

suatu - *pagi (,sore ,dll.)* o. morning (,afternoon ,etc.). - *apa juga* anything. -*pun tdk ada* nothing. *pd* - *ketika* at some point in time. **se-nya** necessities, o's needs.

sub sub-. -*kontinen India* the Indian sub-

continent. - *panitia* sub-committee. -*tropis* subtropical.

subal (inferior) material mixed with s.t. else (to make the latter seem heavier, appear to be more than it really is; fraudulent). *daun.daun utk* - *keranjang arang* leaves used to fill up a charcoal basket. **-an** (s.) PAYUDARA (SUBALAN).

subat **ber-**.- to beseech.

subbul khatimah bad at the end.

Suberban (S.) SUBURBAN.

subsidi subsidy, grant. **ber-** subsidized. **mens-** to subsidize.

substansi substance.

substantif **mens-kan** to substantize.

substitusi substitution.

subvèrsi subversion. **mens-** to subvert, overthrow.

subyèktivisme subjectivism.

suci **mens- hamakan** to sterilize. **mens-kan** *diri di bawah pohon* to purify o.s. under a tree (through meditation). - *hama* aseptic. - *hati* pure of motive. - *lamisan* hypocritical, sanctimonious.

sudah OK, we're here (said to *becak* driver when arriving at destination). *S-ya, saya hrs pergi,* OK, I've got to go (now). – + *time indicator* + *baru* + *verb* it won't, it didn't happen until. - *jam tiga baru kereta api berangkat* the train didn't leave until three. -*lah* 1 all right. 2 never mind, forget it. **ber-**.- *berfamili* to break (off) with o's family. **ter-i** finished, settled.

sudèt and **sudhèt** divert water. **peny-an** (drainage) canal.

Sudéten Sudeten.

Sudirman name of the first Commander-in-Chief of the Indonesian National Army who led the fighting against the Dutch. *lembaran* - *yg bernol empat* (coll.) a 10,000-rupiah bill (which has the Sudirman image on o. side). *selembar* - *dgn nol tiga* (coll.) a 1,000-rupiah bill.

sudut aspect. **ber-** angular. *bintang ~ lima* a 5-pointed star. **meny-** angular. **meny-kan** to push into an unimportant position. **meny- matakan** to look at s.o. out of the corner of o's eye. - *penyiku* (in mathematics) complement.

sugeng healthy, safe.

suh bond, tie, band (of plaited rattan round a broom).

suhu I *penurunan* - tapering off, cooling down. - *lebur* melting temperature.

suhu II teacher.

suiké (s.) SWIKE.

Suishintai (during the Jap. occupation) Promotion Corps, i.e. an activist auxiliary of the Jawa Hokokai whose members were given elementary training in drilling with wooden rifles and assigned various propaganda and civil defense tasks.

sujana intelligent, thoughtful.

sujèn (in Medan) a dimple (in cheek).

sujud ber- to prostrate o.s. in prayer. *Presiden ~ syukur,* The President prostrated himself in prayer as a token of thanks.

suka often, frequently, apt to. **be-an** to go steady with e.o. *lebih* **di-i** *yg blm berkeluarga* (in advertisements) preferably bachelors. **ke-an** 1 delight, enjoyment. 2 popular. 3 favorite. *makanan ~ saya* my favorite dish. **se-** *hati (saja)* to o's heart's content.- *berperang* warlike, bellicose. - *berusaha* enterprising. - *hati* to be in high spirits. - *lupa* forgetful. - *sabar* obliging, accommodating. - *sama* - between you and me. - *tak* - willy-nilly, whether (you) want to or not. *dlm* - *(dan) duka* in love and sorrow. *mana -mu* (do) as you please. -.- frequent, very often.

suket grass. - *gerinting* Bermuda grass.

suk nya bet.

suksès successful. *S- ya!* Good luck to you! - *medikal* medical success. **ke-an** success. **men(g)s-kan** and **meny-kan** to make s.t. successful. **pen(g)s-an** successful(ness).

suku 1 a half *rupiah;* originally 1/4 of a real, i.e. a former Spanish monetary unit. 2 rate (of interest). 3 *rasa* **ke-an** ethnic feelings. **ke-bangsaan** tribal.

peny-an *kata* syllabification. - *bunga* interest rate. - *cadang* spare part(s). - *dinas* service (branch of department). *orang yg punya nama (yg terdiri atas) tiga* - *kata* reference to a Chinese, since Chinese names usually consist of three elements. *orang yg punya nama (yg terdiri atas) dua* - *kata* reference to an Indonesian of lower social status, esp. in the rural areas, as their names usually consist of two syllables. - *kata praakhir* penultimate. *pengawas* - *peralatan* parts foreman.

sukuisme clanship, tribalism.

sukwan [sukarelawan] (mil.) volunteer.

sulam (s.) TAMBAL (SULAM).

sulap *spt* **di-** *saja layaknya* as (if) by magic, magically.

sulit **meny-kan** to impede, hamper, restrain.

Suliwatang a Buginese title.

sultan **ber-** (s.) BERAJA (DI HATI, BERSULTAN DI MATA).

sulur tendril, clasper (of *keladi* plant, etc.). *(batang)* -.-**an** climber, creeper.

sulut I **peny-** *sumbu* provocation.

Sulut II [Sulawesi Utara] North Celebes.

sumarah to comply with the wishes of s.o.

sumaré to be buried.

sumasi giant perch.

sumbang **peny-** *darah* blood donor.

sumber **ber-** *dr* to be derived from. -.- *alam* natural resources. - *daya* resource(s). - *(di) tepi jalan* tramp (woman). - *gempa* epicentrum (of earthquake). -.- *keuangan* financial resources. - *yg layak dipercaya* a reliable source. *dr* - *yg layak dipercayai* on good authority.

sumbu I axle. **ber-** *satu* with o. axle (of vehicles).

sumbu II burner (on stove). *kompor 10* - a 10-burner cooker.

sumèh (to smile) friendly (in serving a customer in a store).

sumek (s.) SEMEK and DEMEK.

sumpah *mengikrarkan* - to take (,swear) an oath. **ber-:** ~ *bohong* to commit perjury. ~ *kerak.keruk* to swear a solemn oath, swear by all that is holy. ~ *setia* to swear allegiance. **di-** *menjadi Presiden* to be sworn in to the Presidency. **ny-i** to curse (,swear at) s.o. - *bohong* perjury. - *jabatan* oath of office. - *kerak.keruk* a solemn oath. - *mimbar* an oath administered by a judge in a church. - *pocong* an oath administered by a judge in which the individual swearing the oath is wrapped in a funeral shroud, performed in a mosque. - *potong ayam* an oath administered by a judge in a Chinese temple.

sumpal *Mobil yg* **meny-** *Jalan Raya Massachussets ...*, Cars riding bumper-to-bumper on Massachussets Avenue ...

sumpama (S.) SEUMPAMA.

sumpek 1 crowded, jammed. 2 choked. - *berjubel* chock-full.

sumput ny- to hide, lie low.

sumringah cheerful, gay, in high spirits. **ber-** to look happily.

sumsum meny- *ke dada (,tulang)* (the cold) pierces you to the very marrow.

sumur - *tambang* shaft mine.

sun (s.) SOEN. **nge-** to kiss. - *ceplok* a smacking kiss.

sunat di- to be pilfered. **meny-** *uang* to reform currency (by halving banknotes or otherwise). **peny-an** shortening, curtailment (of *wayang* play).

Sunbulat Virgo.

Sunda ke-an (adj.) Sundanese. *unsur ~* Sundanese elements (in music).

Sunda Kelapa Pasar Ikan (Jakarta).

sundep noxious insects, esp. rice borers.

sungai *ke -* (euph.) to defecate.

sungguh ber-.- 1 serious. 2 attentively. **ke-an** intensity. **-an** the absolute truth.

sungkem (s.) SEMBAH (SUNGKEM).

sungkur ter- *termakan tanah* to bite the dust.

sungsang - *sumbel* somersault, head over heels. *hidup - sumbel* a hand-to-mouth existence.

sungsep ny- to crash.

sunsum (S.) SUMSUM.

sunti herb (L. Zingiber gramineum Bl.) used for folk medicine.

suntik di- *pes* to be vaccinated against the plague. **peny-an** *ulangan* revaccination. - *kebal* immunization.

sunting di- *oleh* to be edited by. **meny-kan** *belaian hatinya* to marry o's sweetheart.

sunukung monkey.

sunyi ke-.senyapan serenity.

supa general name for mushrooms. - *lember* Jew's ear fungus (L. Auricularia auricula-judae).

supel gets along with people easily.

super super-, instant. - *mi* instant noodles.

Super.98 code word in use at Tanjung Priok port area to refer to bribes.

superbèn a station wagon.

superfosfa(a)t superphosphate.

Superman code word in use at the Tanjung Priok port area for: a strong man, an official, or any backing that can be of help to quickly clear incoming goods through Customs.

supermarkèt supermarket.

Super Semar [Surat Perintah Sebelas Maret] 1 The 11 March Order Letter. 2 President Soeharto's nickname.

supidol (s.) SPIDOL.

suplai supply. **mens-** and **meny-** to supply. **pens-** supplier. **pens-an** and **peny-an** supply.

supradin stimulant containing multivitamins and minerals.

surat ter- explicit. *ada yg ~ ada yg tersirat* o. should read between the lines. *sesuai dgn apa yg ~ dan tersirat* in letter and in spirit. *tlh ~ sejak dahulu* predestined. **-an** *di atas* heading (of newspaper article). - *amanat Paus* encyclical (letter). - *andil* share certificate. - *asal.usul* family tree. - *baptisan* baptismal certificate. - *bebas ganti.rugi* letter of indemnity. - *berharga* (valuable) securities. *S- Berharga Bepergian* k.o. traveler's check (issued by *Bank Bumi Daya*). - *bom* letter bomb. - *budek* anonymous letter. - *bukti* voucher. -.- *bukti* (documentary) evidence. - *bukti kewar-*

ganegaraan Indonesia certificate of Indonesian nationality. - *buntu* undeliverable (,dead) letter. - *cacar* vaccination certificate. - *dagang* business letter. - *fiskal* fiscal statement, i.e. a document stating that s.o. has paid all his taxes (the document is required if s.o. wants to leave the country). *S- Gembala* Pastoral Letter. - *giro* giro form, transfer card. - *hutang* debenture. - *ikrar* affidavit. *S- Impor Valuta Asing* Foreign Exchange Import Permit. - *introduksi* letter of introduction. *S- Izin Mendarat* Landing Permit (for aircraft). *S- Izin Mengemudi* (abbrev. *SIM*) Driver's License. *S- Izin Penduduk* Permission to Take Up o's Residence. *S- Izin Terbit* (abbrev. *SIT*) Publication Permit. - *jalan* a letter that o. could be required to carry to present on demand to army, police, immigration or customs officials in the outer islands of Indonesia (Maluku, and in some areas of Irian Jaya, Nusa Tenggara and Kalimantan); obtainable from the local police station. - *jaminan* letter of indemnity. - *jawatan* official letter. - *kenal lahir* (s.) SURAT [KETERANGAN LAHIR (,KELAHIRAN)] . -.- *kepercayaan* credentials. - *keputusan* (from President) Executive Order. - *keterangan* 1 certificate. 2 written reference. 3 testimonial. 4 identity card. - *keterangan adat.istiadat* certificate of good character. - *keterangan asal barang* certificate of origin. - *keterangan atas sumpah* affidavit. - *keterangan bebas "Gestapu/PKI"* statement of non-involvement in or disassociation from *Gestapu/PKI*. - *keterangan blm pernah menikah* certificate of unmarried status. - *keterangan berbadan sehat* certificate of good health. - *keterangan (ber)kelakuan baik* certificate of good character. - *keterangan dokter* physician's certificate. - *keterangan hidup* life certificate. - *keterangan lahir (,kelahiran)* certificate of clarification of birth (different from a birth certificate). - *keterangan lolos.butuh* and -

keterangan tdk berkeberatan berhenti certificate of dispensability. -.- *kewarganegaraan* citizenship papers. - *kilat* express letter. - *kilat khusus* special delivery letter. - *kiriman* letters to the editor. - *kredit* letter of credit, L/C. - *kredit perjalanan* traveler's check (,letter of credit). - *kuasa di bawah tangan* private authorization. - *laut* (nautical term) certificate of registry. - *mengemudi kendaraan bermotor* driver's license. -.meny- 1 correspondence. 2 to correspond. - *pajak* income-tax form. - *pancang tanah* land survey document. - *pembaca* letters to the editor. - *pembelaan politik* apology. - *pemberitahuan pajak peralihan* transitional tax returns. - *pemberitahuan pemasukan barang* entry for home use. - *penduduk* resident's card. - *pengakuan lahir* (s.) SURAT (KETERANGAN LAHIR). - *perbendaharaan* exchequer bill. - *perintah penggeledahan* search warrant. - *pernyataan maksud* letter of intent. - *persaksian hidup* life certificate. - *pertanggungan jawab* statement of accountability. - *rekomendasi* letter of recommendation. -.- (in Court decisions, etc.) the official papers, documents. - *setangan* note, memo. - *skorsing* suspension order. -.- *tahunan* annual reports and accounts. *S- Tamat Belajar (Sekolah Rakyat)* (Elementary School) Certificate. - *tamu* appointment-request form. *S- Tanda Kebangsaan* (nautical term) Certificate of Registry. - *tanda setoran* (in bookkeeping) deposit slip. - *unjuk* bearer document(s). - *yg bersambung.sambung* a chain letter. -.- *di bawah No. A 568* (in advertisements) write Box A 568.

surèn tree (L. Toona sinensis or ureni) the wood of which is made into planks.

surgawi heavenly.

suri *pantas* **di-.tauladani** worthy of imitation, worthy to follow (an example).

surjan *(klambi)* - men's coat with high collar and wide flaps on front.

surogat surrogate, substitute.

suruh meny- to request, ask (s.o. to do s.t.).

suruk meny- to penetrate. *Perkampungan itu ~ jauh ke tengah rawa dan sawah,* The *kampung* complex deeply penetrates swamps and rice paddies. **ter-.-** all bent over.

surut 1 go back. *Ia - selangkah ke belakang,* He took a step backward. 2 decline. *-nya kekuasaan Majapahit* the decline of Majapahit's sway. **meny-kan** *ingatan ke* to take a retrospective view of.

survey mengs- to survey. **pens-an** surveying.

sus (s.) ZUS.

susah ber-.-: *jangan ~* take it easy. *tak usah ~* don't stand on ceremony. *- hati* sorrowful. **-.-** 1 to go to a lot of trouble. *Mereka tdk usah ~ masak,* They need not go to the trouble of cooking. 2 to work hard. *Ketika ditanya mengapa ia masih ~ mengusahakan toko kue.kue ia menjawab:* ... When asked why she is still putting all her efforts into running a pastry shop she answered: ... *tanpa ~* without going to any pains. *~ senang* it's not so bad as all that.

susila *- kedokteran* medical ethics.

suspènsi suspension.

susteran convent school.

susu I *rusak - sebelanga karena tuba setitik* o. rotten apple will decay a bushel. *- dibalas dgn tuba* the world's wages are ingratitude. *- beku* curdled milk. *- bubuk tanpa lemak* skim milk powder. *- skim* skim milk.

susu II [sumbangan sukarela] 'voluntary contribution,' k.o. bribe. *- tante* [sumbangan sukarela tanpa tekanan] 'voluntary contribution without pressure,' k.o. bribe.

Susuhunan The Venerated.

susuk I *- kondai (,kondé)* (hair) bun pin.

susuk II -an canal.

susun meny- *barisan* to close ranks. **peny-iklan** ad-writer. **peny-an** *kekuasaan* organization of power. **-an:** *~ bahasa* style. *~ berita* text. *~ kalimat* sentence structure. *~ mata pelajaran* curriculum. *~ tempur* battle array.

susup peny- penetrant.

susur meny-i *jejak* to track, trace, trail.

susut peny-an *harga* depreciation.

Sutan 1 (in the Minangkabau area) reference for adult children of the better classes. 2 in the coastal areas of the Minangkabau, such as, Padang, this title is hereditary from father to son and usually precedes the personal name, i.e. *S- Mohammad Zain, S- Takdir Alisjahbana,* whereas in the interior areas of Sumatra, the title usually follows the personal name, i.e. *Rustam S- Palindih, Abbas S- Pamuntjak nan Sati.*

sutradara ke-an stage management.

suudh.dhon bad prejudice.

su'un (S.) SO'UN.

suvenir souvenir.

suwargo *- nunut naroko (,neraka) katut* to share the good and the bad.

suwiké (s.) SWIKE.

suwita system of patron-client relationships traditionally extending throughout Jav. society.

suwung ke-an emptiness.

suwur di-kan to be made famous (,widely known).

Swabhuwana Paksa (motto of the Indonesian Air Force) With the Wings We are Masters in Our Own World (,Country).

swadaya men(g)s-kan to auto-activate.

swadèsi self-sufficient, self-supporting.

swa.disiplin self-discipline.

swagaya innate energy, potential, auto-activity.

swahara autotrophic.

swaharga self-respect.

swak weak, not feeling good.

swakarsa 1 spontaneous. 2 self-supporting.

swakarya self-activity.

swakerti self-activity.

swakritik self-criticism.

swanama proper name.

swanggi *daun* - a leaf used as a contraceptive in Irian Jaya.

swapraja autonomy, self-rule. *daerah -* self-governing principality.

Swa Prasidya Purna Rehabilitation Center for the Handicapped.

swarga (s.) SUWARGO.

swasambada and **swasembada** self-support-ing. **ber-** to be self-supporting in. ~ *pangan* to be self-supporting in food. *S- Beras* Self-supporting in Rice.

swasiswa self-taught.

swa.sraya self-service.

swasta di-kan to be converted into a pri-vate enterprise.

swastawan private person.

swatantra ke-an (adj.) regional autonomy.

swèmpak bathing suit.

swiké fried green frog's legs (a Chinese delicacy).

swing swing (music).

switer sweater. **ber-** to wear a sweater.

syablon stencil.

syafar (s.) SAFAR. **ber-** and **-an** to go (in throngs) to sacred places to ward off dangers.

syahwat *puncak* **ke-an** orgasm.

syal scarf.

syalat ied (s.) SHALAT or SHOLAT.

syankah possessing influential strength.

syanker chancre.

syarat *dgn -.- sbg berikut* on the follow-ing conditions. *dgn tiada memakai -*

unconditionally. *mempunyai - bertin-dak hukum* to have legal ability to make contracts. *tanpa - apapun* with-out any proviso whatsoever. *dgn tdk* **ber-** unconditionally. *- damai* condi-tions can be discussed, we can come to an agreement. *- hidup* living condi-tions. *-.- kerja* working conditions. *-.- mengadakan asuransi* insurance clauses. *-.- pembayaran* terms of payment. *-.- penerimaan* entrance requirements. *-.- perburuhan* working conditions. *- pokok* essential conditions.

syaria (S.) SYARIAT.

syariah (S.) SYARIAT.

syèh *- (haji)* and *- (jema'ah)* person who renders services to Moslem pilgrims by providing them with housing or camp-ing facilities and who escorts them to observe religious duties.

syooi (s.) ASYOOI.

syorgawi (s.) SURGAWI.

syuhada martyr.

syuhadaa plural of *syahid.*

syukuran thanksgiving.

syur 1 interesting. 2 appealing. *film.film yg paling -* most appealing films. 3 popular. *tarian -* a popular dance. *merasa -* to be in raptures about.

syuting shooting (of a film).

syuur (s.) SYUR.

T

ta (Jav. *tak-* first person with object-oriented forms: by me) I. *Tak ngaku, - suruh gebuk kamu!* If you don't con-fess, I'll have you beaten up!

taala most high. *Allah -* God Most High.

taaruf reception.

taasub dogmatic, bigoted.

taaziah ber- 1 to grieve with, condole. 2 to feel (,express) sympathy.

Tabanas [Tabungan Pembangunan Na-sional] Savings for National Develop-ments (which are not bound to a cer-tain length of time, exempt from prop-erty tax and which can be withdrawn

any time). **dit-kan** to be put in a savings account.

tabir *- kabut* air of secrecy.

tablèt tablet. *- bergula* dragee. *- hisap* lozenges. *- pencegah mabok perjalanan* anti-motion sickness pill.

tabrak pen- the person (,driver) who hit(s). **ter-** to be hit (by a vehicle). ~ *matinya seorang tukang beca oleh mobil* the fatal collision of a pedicab driver and a car. **-an:** ~ *beruntun* a chain(-reaction) collision. ~ *maut* a fatal collision. *- lari* hit and run. *-. tubruk* (various) collisions.

tabuan (in Palangka Raya, Kalimantan)

bee. *sarang* - beehive.

tabuh *akan dijadikan - singkat, akan dijadikan genderang berlebih* between hay and grass.

tabung - *gambar* picture tube. - *oksigen* oxygen cylinder.

tacik older sister.

tadarus alternate Koran reading (during the month of *Ramadan*).

tadi mentioned previously, referred to (earlier). *baru* - a moment ago. *orang* - the person referred to. *dr (,sejak)* - 1 a short while ago. 2 in advance. 3 for a long time. *malam* - and - *malam* 1 tonight. 2 last night. *pagi* - and - *pagi* this morning. *sore* - and - *sore* (just) this afternoon. *yg* - the o. we were just talking about, s.o. (,the o.) just had, the o. s.o. just had, the o. we know about just before. **T-nya** *rumah ini hanya dua jendelanya,* Originally this house had only two windows.

taèk (s.) TAHI. *T- sama mereka!* To hell with them!

tafahus men-(kan) 1 to investigate. 2 to frisk.

taferil scene, picture.

tafsir pent- commentator, annotator. **-an** *hurufiah* literal interpretation.

tagih pen- addict. ~ *alkohol* alcoholic. ~ *(h)utang* creditor. ~ *rekening* bill collector. **-an** *susulan* supplementary claim for payment (of a tax, etc.).

tagorub to approach God.

tahajud *sembahyang* - prayer at a time other than o. of the five daily Islamic prayer times (usually, for asking God to grant o. s.t.).

tahan *tdk* - *thd* allergic to. **ber-** to stand firm, hold o's own, hold (of luck). **ke-an** 1 viability, resilience. ~ *moral* moral defensibility. 2 survival. ~ *di hutan* jungle survival. **memper-kan** *hidupnya* to survive. **men-:** ~ *diri utk* to refrain from. *tdk dpt lagi* ~ *gelaknya* no longer being able to control o's laughter. ~ *banyak kesusahan* to endure many difficulties. ~ *sabar* to be patient. *tak dpt lagi* ~ *sabarnya* to lose o's patience.

tdk dpt lagi ~ *seleranya* no longer being able to control o's appetite. **pen-:** ~ *kejut* shock absorber. *simpanan* ~ *larat* a nest-egg, provision for a rainy day. **pen-an** captivity. **-an** captive, arrest. ~ *kata hati nurani* reference to a 'political detainee.' ~ *kota* city arrest. ~ *luar (,di rumah ,dlm rumah)* house arrest. ~ *muka* detention in custody. ~ *rumah* house arrest. - *cuci* (of colors) fast. - *debu* dustproof. - *getaran (,goncangan)* shockproof. - *karat* rustproof. - *kena api* fireproof (dish, etc.). - *magnit* antimagnetic. - *udara* airtight. - *uji* tried and true.

Tahdiriyah Kindergarten.

tahfidz knowing by heart.

tahi shit. - *banyak* - *minyaknya* many shuffling excuses. - *serutan* shavings. - *ayam* chicken droppings. - *kucing!* bull shit! - *kuping* earwax.

tahlilan gathering to recite the confession of faith: *la ilaha illallah* there is no God, but Allah, over and over again, to commemorate the seventh, hundredth and thousandth day after a person has died.

tahniah congratulation(s). *memberi* - *kpd* to congratulate.

tahu I (the 'h' is usually not pronounced) *tdk* - never. *Orang itu tdk - marah,* That person is never angry. *Dia sdh - keluar negeri,* He has been abroad. *Kamu -?* You know what? Guess what? *Mau - saja,* Just curious. *Saya tdk - pasti,* I'm not sure. (Utk menutup ketekoran yg) *siapa* - (terjadi, ada tambahan cadangan Rp. 20 juta), (For making up) any possible (deficits there is a supplemental 20 million rupiah reserve). - *benar dlm* to be thoroughly conversant with. - *ada saja,* - *beres (saja)* and - *beres deh!* leave it to me! it'll be all right! that will straighten itself out! *Dia - beres saja,* He does not trouble his head about it. *Saya - beres,* Do as you please. - *makan - simpan* to keep a secret carefully. - *senang saja, tak - apa. apa yg kurang* and *semangat yg hanya mau - sedia saja* do not bother about a thing. - *sama* - 1 you scratch my back and I'll scratch yours. 2 to connive through bribery or kickbacks. *tdk - di mata surat* illiterate, uneducated. *Saya tdk mau - ttg (,dgn) hal itu,* I take no notice of it. *macam orang tak - lagi* like a vacuous person. *spy - saja!* just for your information! *blm* - never (up to now). *Ia blm - minum wodka,* He has never drunk vodka. - *akan* to be aware of, be conscious of. *sdh - akan dirinya* to regain consciousness. *T-kah engkau akan orang tadi?* Do you know the o. we were just talking about? Are you acquainted with the person just referred to? *tdk - akan dirinya (lagi)* unconscious. *tdk - diri* impudent. *biar dia - diri sedikit* he needs a lesson. **ber-kan** to acquaint with, inform of, advise of. **berke-an** *dgn* to get acquainted with, get to k~ v. **dike-i** it's understood. *perlu ~, bhw ...* it should be known that ... *spy ~ saja!* just for your information! *utk ~* (in correspondence) for your attention. *utk ~ dan diperhatikan* and *spy ~ dan dijalankan* (in correspondence) for your guidance and information. *dgn tdk ~nya* unconsciously, unaware. **penge-an:** *~ eksakta* exact sciences. *~ kejuruan* professional skill. *~ larapan* applied sciences. *~ masyarakat* social sciences. *menurut (,sepanjang) ~ saya* to (the best of) my knowledge, for all I know. *banyak -nya* he has a lot of experience. -.- unsuspectingly. *tdk -.**men-** 1 to know nothing of, do not know anything about it. 2 do not care about o.a. 3 do not know e.o. *blm -.**men-** *ttg* to not have the faintest idea about (up to now).

tahu II bean curd. - *pong* bean curd cut into small pieces and baked until it pops up. - *tempe* a side dish of *tahu* and *tempe.*

tahun *dr - ke -* and - *demi* - year by year. - *berselisih musim berganti* in course of time. **se-** *dua* fly-by-night, short-lived. - *ajaran* school year. - *anggaran*

fiscal year. *T- Baru Hijrah (,Islam)* Moslem New Year (which falls on Muharram 1 or Suro 1). - *Jawa* a 210-day year made up of 30 *wukus.* - *kuliah* academic year. -.- *kurus* lean years. *T-Masehi* Anno Domini, A.D. - *pelajaran (,pengajaran)* scholastic year. - *sabatikal* sabbatical year.

tahwé walking over live coals.

taik (s.) TAEK. - *kotok* chicken droppings.

taiso drill, physical exercise. **ber-** to do physical exercises.

tajam memper- to aggravate. **men-** *kuping-nya* to strain o's ears.

tajao (in Banjarmasin) large earthen pitcher for storing rain water, etc.

tajuk editorial.

tajwid correct pronunciation of the Arabic of the Koran.

tak ke- berpihakan non-partisan. *-bernyawa* inanimate. *-masukakal* senseless. *-sama* unequal.

takar -an the instrument used to measure capacity. *~ penghidupan* standard of living.

takbir *-ul.ihram* the first *takbir* in the liturgical prayers. - *di pangkal lidah* to be at the point of death.

takdir *(tinggal) menunggu* - let things take their (own) course, let things slide.

take.off **ber-** to take off.

takokak name of a plant resembling the *terong* (,eggplant) the fruit of which is used for *lalap.*

takowah k.o. dish made from soybean-cakes with a sauce.

takraw and **takro** a woven rattan ball. *sepak* - a game using a *takraw* and a net, a combination of badminton and volleyball.

takrif definition. **ment-kan** to define.

taksir I pen- appraiser. estimator. *~ mutu* grader.

taksir II (me)n- to be after s.o. (sexually). *Emang, banyak lelaki pd n- samu lu,* Really, a lot of men are after you.

taksiun (railway) station.

taktik tactics.

taktok -.- *memainkan lidah dlm mulut* to

make a clicking noise with the tongue.

tak.umpet peekaboo.

takut - *tujuh keliling* to be deadly afraid. **pen-** cowardly. **-an** easily frightened. **-.-** scrupulous. ~ *segan* half reluctantly.

takwinul alam cosmogeny.

takwo *baju* - k.o. dark blue Yogyakarta jacket, closed with a broad lapel and button on the shoulder.

talang - *air* aqueduct.

talen **-an** chopping block.

tali **ber-** related (by blood or marriage), allied, joined, coherent. ~ *darah dgn* and ~**(an)** *keluarga dgn* to be related to. ~**an** *dgn* to be tied up with, refer to, bear upon. *tdk ada* **per-an** *keluarga antara kita* there are no ties of blood between us. - *bahu jabatan* (mil.) braid indicating rank. - *keselamatan* safety belt. - *komando* (gold) aiguillette (of army commanders). - *menali* rigging. - *paranti* tradition. - *persahabatan (,silaturahim)* ties of friendship. - *pinggang pengaman* safety lap belt. - *temali* intertwined with o.a.

taligrap telegraph.

talik -*(. talak)* the conditions under which a *talak* can be pronounced.

talimarga communication. *alat* - means of communication.

taliu (in Banda) a fruit having the taste of *kenari* and the shape of a very small cigar.

talu prelude.

tamah cozy.

taman **per-an** park. - *burung* aviary (in zoo). *T- Candra Wilwatikta* 'Garden of the Light of Majapahit,' i.e. the name of the site (in Pandaan, East Java) where the International *Ramayana* Festival was held in September 1970. - *hiburan* amusement park. - *margasatwa* zoo. *T- Pahlawan* Cemetery. - *parkir* parking lot. *T- Remaja* (Children's) Playground. - *ria* amusement park. *T- Siswa* name of a national privately owned school organization, consisting of the following types of schools: *T- Dewasa* Junior High School, *T- Guru*

Teacher's College, *T- Indria* Kindergarten, *T- Madya* Senior High School, *T- Muda* Elementary School and *T- Tani* Peasants School.

tamasyawan tourist, sightseer.

tamat - *belajar* to graduate.

tambah *T-!* Have some more, have another helping! **ber-** increasing, augmentative. ~ *(banyak)* to accrue. ~ *kuat* to regain (o's) strength, get stronger. ~ *kurang* to grow less continually. ~ *lama* ~ ... in the course of time ... ~*nya* increase, increment. **di-** and, plus. *dua* ~ *tiga jadi lima* two and (,plus) three makes five. ~ *dgn* to be eked out by. **men-kan** to add (a sentence while speaking). *"...," katanya* ~, "...," he added. **pen-an** addition. **per-an** *jiwa* increase in population. **-an** annex, addition. ~ *pembayaran* surcharge.

tambal *secara* - *sulam* in a makeshift way.

tambat **pen-an** mooring (of ship). **-an** *batin* shelter.

tambeng disobedient. - *macam gedek* opinionated and annoying.

tambo *membuka si* - *lama* to rake up old stories, dig up the past.

tamburin tambourin.

tamèng **ber-** to hide o.s. behind a shield.

tampa (S.) TANPA.

tampa kaya ceremony in which the groom gives money to the bride.

tampak to appear, come into sight. - *olehku* I saw. *tak* -.- *(lagi)* do not show up again.

tampan 1 figure. 2 handsome, good-looking. - *di badan* (the clothes) are becoming.

tampang I **pen-** *silang* cross section.

tampang II - *Afrika* Afro (k.o. hairdo).

tampar **-an** clapping.

tampek measles. - *Jerman* German measles, rubella.

tampil **berpen-an** to make o's début. **pen-mula** débutant.

tampuk 1 center (of power). 2 rudder (of the ship of State). 3 lever (of government machinery).

tampung **men-** to accommodate. *Hotel yg dpt* ~ *tamu.tamu luar kota,* A hotel capable of providing accommodation for out-of-town guests. ~ *bahaya (,keberatan.keberatan ,kesulitan)* to obviate (,remove) danger (,objections ,difficulties). **pen-an** collection, placement (of evacuees).

tamsil **ber-** 1 analogical. 2 allegorical. **pen(t)-** allegorist.

tamu **ber-** *ke (,di ,dgn)* to visit. **mer-** to be a guest of. - *(yg) tak diundang* an unwanted guest. - *menginap (,pembayar)* paying (,house) guest.

Tan I (s.) SUTAN.

tan II (in Jav. literary language) not. - *antara* not long thereafter.

tanah - *absentee* land situated outside the area where a government employee who owns it resides. - *bangunan* building site. - *dingin* Europe, in particular the Netherlands. - *erpah* lease hold land. - *gambut* fen-land. - *garapan* land for cultivation (,tillage). - *gogolan* (in Java) communal landownership. - *guntai* land situated outside the area where a government employee who owns it resides. *T- Hijau* Greenland. - *kersik* silica. - *longsor* soil erosion. *T- Merah* name of the site in Digul (Irian Jaya) where the Dutch, prior to World War II, interned their Indonesian political exiles. - *milik.bersama* communal landownership. - *napal* marly soil. - *pangonan* pasture(-land), meadow. - *pasini* (in the Celebes) privately-owned land. - *pelungguh* ap(p)-anage. *T- Perjanjian* Promised Land. - *perkotaan* urban land. *T- Rencong* the Aceh Special Area. *T- Sepi* West Sumatra. *T- Suci* The Holy Land, i.e. Arabia for the Moslems. - *terbis* soil erosion. - *tumpah darah* native soil. - *wakaf* land for religious purposes.

tanak **di-nya** *semua berasnya* his bolt is shot, he has fired his last shot.

tanam **ber-** to plant (a crop for a living). *Dia* ~ *padi,* He's a rice farmer. **di-i:** *dpt* ~ to be fit (,suitable) for cultiva-

tion. *tanah* ~ land under cultivation. **men-.akarkan** to instill, inculcate. **-an:** ~ *industri* industrial crop. ~ *keras* perennial plants (such as, rubber, coconut, cacao). ~ *makanan* food crops. ~ *menjalar* creeper, climber. ~ *muda* annual plants. ~ *pengganggu* weed. ~ *perdagangan* commercial crops. ~ *sela* intermediate crop (such as, corn, pepper, etc.). ~ *tumpangsari* catchcrop, i.e. a fast-growing crop planted as a substitute for a crop at a time when the ground would ordinarily lie fallow. ~ *yg merayap* creeper. *T- Paksa* (s.) CULTUURSTELSEL.

tancap and **tancep** **men-** *(,-) gas* to press (,step on) the accelerator. **ter-** vested (interests).

tanda 1 a mil. rank. 2 as a sign of (,that). **ber-** *tangan* to sign. *Saya, yg ber- tangan di bawah ini, Soekamto, dgn ini menerangkan, bhw...,* I the undersigned, Soekamto, do hereby declare that ... **pen-** (gramm.) marker. ~ *gramatika* grammatical device(s). ~ *tangan* signer. **pen- syahan** legalization. - *air* watermark. - *aman* all-clear signal. - *bahaya udara* air raid warning. - *baptisan yg kudus* certificate of the holy baptism. - *bekas reman* skid mark. - *buka.kata* (beginning) quotation marks.` - *diakritik* diacritical marks. - *dipiden* dividend coupon. - *gambar* election symbol. - *jadi* (commercial sl.) deposit. - *kehormatan* decoration. - *kenaldiri* identification card. - *kurung siku* brackets: [...]. - *lalu.lintas* traffic sign. - *nyatadiri* I.D. card. - *penerimaan setoran* receipt for payments made. - *pengenal* sign of recognition. - *pisah* dash. - *sah diri* I.D. card. - *sempang* hyphen. - *seru* exclamation point. - *setuju* (fig.) green light. - *terimakasih* bribe. - *tutup.kata* (end) quotation marks.

tandang **ber-** *ke (,pd)* to pay a visit to.

tanding **per-an:** ~ *kembar campuran* (in tennis) mixed doubles. ~ *persahabatan* friendly match. **-an:** *tak ada* ~*nya, sukar dicari* ~*nya* and *tdk akan bersua*

~*nya* incomparable.
tando (s.) KOLAM (TANDO).
tandon and **tandhon** *barang* - articles from stored stock (laid in).
tandu (s.) UANG (TANDU).
tanduk I *keluar -nya* he got angry. *macam - dgn gading* affinities. *runcing - (bengkak kening)* known all over the place. *menantikan kucing* **ber-** a futile hope. *T- Afrika* the Horn of Africa. - *rusa* antler.
tanduk II (coll.) front bumper (of car).
tandur - *alih jantung* heart transplant.
tanfiziah executive (council).
tangan - *mencencang bahu memikul* regret comes after the sin. *memegang kemudi - sebelah* to drive with o. hand. **men-i** to handle. ~ *kemacetan* to unscramble a (traffic) jam. **pen-an** handling, tackling. *menjalankan - besi* to take a strong (,drastic) action, take a strong (,firm) line (against, *thd*). - *dingin* a green thumb. - *kiri* the left hand, used for personal sanitary functions and therefore considered unclean; it's offensive to give or receive things, particularly food or money, with this hand. - *usil (,jahil ,kotor)* the bad guys, malevolent elements. *dr - pertama* straight from the horse's mouth. *keterangan (dr) - pertama* first-hand (,inside) information.
Tanganyika Tanganyika.
tangga - *berjalan* escalator. - *pesawat terbang* ramp of aircraft. - *putar* ramp.
tanggal I *jam tangan Seiko otomatis yg* **ber-** *serta berhari* a "Seiko" automatic day-date wrist watch. *arloji otomatis* **ber-an** an automatic calendar watch. **men-kan** *surut* to antedate. - *akhir. tenggang* date of expiration. - *kadalu-(w)arsa* the due date, expiration date. - *kelahiran* date of birth. - *muda* 1 the first quarter (of the moon). 2 early in the month. - *pemberangkatan* date of departure. - *terakhir* deadline. - *tua* 1 last quarter (of the moon). 2 late in the month.
tanggal II **men-kan** *kewarganegaraan* to repudiate citizenship. **pen-** repudiator (of citizenship). **pen-an** repudiation (of citizenship).
tanggap I (gramm.) passive. *katakerja* - a passive verb. -. *tanggon dan trengginas* bright, trustworthy and agile. **-an** response.
tanggap II **men-** to have (a dancer, etc.) perform for a payment.
tanggon trustworthy. **ke-an** reliability.
tanggor **ke-** 1 to run into, encounter by chance. 2 to meet o's match.
tangguh I **pen-an** adjournment, suspension.
tangguh II 1 steady, reliable. 2 protected by witchcraft, immune.
tangguk **men-** *di air keruh* 1 (lit.) to fish in troubled waters. 2 (fig.) to profit from a bad situation. **pen-** *di air keruh* profiteer.
tanggul causeway.
tanggulang **men-i** to oppose, cope with, overcome, combat, defend against, ward off, hold back. ~ *kesukaran* to back out of a difficulty. ~ *soal.soal ekonomi* to face up to economic problems. **pen-an** overcoming, surpassing.
tanggung *T- beres!* Leave it to me! **ber-:** ~ *jawab atas* answerable for. ~ *jawab (k)pd* to be responsible to. *dpt (,mampu)* ~ *jawab* culpable. *oknum.oknum yg tdk* ~ *jawab* irresponsible persons. **di-:** ~ *(deh)* sure, of course, absolutely. ~ *oleh Negara* to be borne (,payable) by the State. **pen-:** *P~ Jawab I* (of newspaper) Director-in-Chief. *P~ Jawab II* (of newspaper) Managing Editor. **per-an:** *memberikan* ~ *jawab atas* to render an account of. *utk dimintakan* ~ *.jawabnya* to account for. *pihak* **ter-** the insured, policy holders. *blm* **terper-.jawabkan** not yet accounted for. **-an** dependent. ~ *saya* 1 my dependents. 2 my responsibility. *atas* ~ *sendiri* and *dgn ~nya sendiri* at o's own risk. *menjadi* ~ ... are chargeable to ... *cuti di luar* ~ *Negara* leave not paid for by the State. *dgn tdk -.-* wholeheartedly. - *jawab* responsibility.

tan.gir and Tan.Gir (s.) TANTE (GIRANG).

tangis -. *berhiba.hiba* to weep bitterly. - *kegembiraan* weeping for joy.

tangkai -an by the (individual) flower.

tangkal - *bisa* antitoxin.

tangkap ke- *(basah)* (S.) TERTANGKAP (BASAH). men-: ~ *basah* to catch in the very act. ~ *percakapan* to overhear a conversation. *mata* ~ *seorang* to spot, catch sight of s.o. *Sekonyong.konyong mataku* ~ *seorang yg menuruni lereng Kali Krukut,* All of a sudden I spotted a person coming down the slope of the Krukut River bank. ter-: ~ *tangan* caught in the act. *kalau bicara hampir tak* ~ when he spoke he was almost inaudible.

tangkar pen- *benih* nursery.

tangkas ke-an *berkuda* equitation, horsemanship.

tangki - *penimbun* storage tank.

tangkis -. *balik* reply to *Jaksa,* counterplea.

Tangkiwood name derived from Kampung Tangkilio in downtown Jakarta, site where once film artists used to live; the name was coined by Soediro, o. of the first mayors of Jakarta, as a counterpart of Hollywood.

tangkup *tak* se- asymmetric(al). ter- *makan tanah* to bite the dust.

tangkur sea horse. - *buaya* an aphrodisiac.

tangkuwèh candied (orange, lemon) peel, succades.

tangsel wedge. - *perut* padding.

tani per-an *buah* orchard.

taniwan farmer. per-an farm. ~ *kolektif* collective farm.

taniwati farmer's wife.

tanker tanker. - *raksasa* supertanker.

tanpa ke- pamrihan disinterestedness. - *daksa* deformed, crippled. - *dipungut bayaran* gratis. - *krana* without reason. - *pamrih* without ulterior motives. - *persiapan* impromptu. - *reserve* unreservedly, frankly. - *wujud* spiritual.

tanpasta toothpaste.

tante aunt (either blood aunt or courtesy aunt; term commonly used among city dwellers and the middle and upper class). *T- Girang* 'Merry Aunt,' i.e. an amorous married woman from the upper classes who chases after men.

tanting (s.) NANTING. pen- K.P., kitchen police.

tantième dividends.

tantra (s.) HUKUM (TANTRA).

tanur - *kapur* limekiln.

tanwir advice.

tanya ber- to wonder. ~ *dlm hati* and ~ *pd diri sendiri* to ask o.s. ~ *jalan* to ask directions. men-i to interview.

tao (s.) KESUWUNGAN.

taodèk to steal.

tapa penance. - *brata* 1 ascetism. 2 initiation (period in university).

tapak I n- tilas *perjalanan Gatot Subroto* to traverse the route taken by Gatot Subroto. se-: ~ *pun tdk* not an inch. *jalan* ~ (path)way.

tapak II site. - *perindustrian* industrial site.

tapak III *cium - tangan, berbaukah atau tdk* to search o's own soul. - *Sulaiman* starfish.

tapak IV - *jalak* black-colored stone for a ring allegedly possessing the psychological property of giving its owner the strength of having an unshakable attitude.

tapal pen- *kuda* shoeing smith. pen- batasan frontier area.

tapé (S.) TAPAI. - *laos* remedy for infrequent pregnancy.

tapèk.o *ndak* - not so much.

taping foreman of prisoners.

tapir tapir (animal).

tapol [tahanan politik] political detainee (,prisoner).

taqwa (S.) TAKWA.

tara image.

taraf ber- prestigious. men-kan to upgrade. pen-an upgrading.

tarak pen- *alkohol* abstainer, teetotaler.

tarbiyah training, upbringing.

targèt target. di-kan to be targeted.

tari men-kan to dance (v.t.). pen-: ~ *agogo*

go-go dancer. ~ *balet laki.laki* ballerino.
~ *balet perempuan* ballerina. ~ *perut*
belly dancer. ~ *strip* stripteaser. -an:
~.~ *berirama* rhythmic dances. ~
pujaan ritual dance. - *lilin* candle dance.
- *longké* dance peculiar to the Cirebon
area. - *payung* umbrella dance. - *perut*
belly dance. - *rakyat* folkdance. - *selen-
dang* scarf dance (of Timor). - *topeng*
mask dance (of West Java).

tarik (bus conductor's command to driver)
OK, go ahead! **di-** (money) is collected.
Bir tambahan akan ~ *harganya,* You
pay for an extra beer. ~ *keluar* to be
pulled out (of troops). ~ *tambat* to be
pulled up by a rope. **men-** salient. ~
anggota baru to secure new members
(for a political party). ~ *seorang Dubes*
to recall an ambassador. ~ *keuntungan*
to profit by, take advantage of. ~
langkah seribu to run away. ~ *napas
panjang* to breathe a sigh of relief, feel
relieved. ~ *pajak* to levy taxes. ~ *pelatuk*
to cock the hammer. ~ *pulang perintah
(,perkataan)* to countermand an order
(,words). **n-** (in Jakarta) to drive (a
vehicle, usually *becak*). **pen-:** ~ *hati*
attraction. ~ *pajak* tax collector. ~
pemilih votegetter. **pen-an** collection.
~ *contoh* sampling. ~ *keluar* pullout.
~ *kembali* cancellation. **ter-:** ~ *dgn*
interested in. ~ *hati* moved, touched.
termen- most interesting. -.-**an** 1 tug
of war. 2 (drivers sl.) to overtake e.o.
- *leher* to hawk (goods, services) ver-
bally. - *muka duabelas* to make an
unhappy face, grimace. - *tambang* tug
of war. - *urat* to stick it out, hold out.

tarip - *bongkar* cost for unloading. - *muat*
cost for loading.

tarling [gitar dan suling] musical performance in which guitars and flutes
are the instruments most active during
the show.

taroh (s.) TARUH. -*lah* let's say.

tarok (in Tegal) (s.) PACAR.

Tartar Tartar.

tar.tar.tar sound of pistol shots.

taruf reception.

taruh -*lah empatpuluh!* (let's) say forty!
ber- *dlm pacuan kuda* to back a horse
in the race. **men-** *harga* to charge (an
amount of money), ask for. **pe-** backer.

taruna 1 (mil.) cadet. 2 (s.) PLONCO. 3
young people. - *wisata* youth hostel.
T- Wreda Senior Student of the Armed
Forces Academy.

taruni (s.) PLONCI.

tas attaché case. - *jinjing* handbag. - *pe-
siar* traveling bag. - *samsonite* Samsonite attaché case.

tasamuh tolerance.

tasa(w)wuf mysticism.

tasbih *menghitung buah* - to count (,tell
,say) o's beads.

tasiun (S.) SETASIUN.

taswir speech, address.

tasyakuran to prostrate o.s. in prayer.

Tasykèn Tashkent.

tasyrih (S.) ILMU (TASYRIH).

tata *negara mawa -, desa mawa cara* 'the
cities have their own customs and the
villages their own traditions,' i.e. the
principle of observing ethical codes in
communication. **ke-** laksanaan *personil*
1 personnel management. 2 in-plant
manpower management. *sistem* **kenegaraan** the system of political institutions. *dr sudut* **ke-** usahaan from the
administrative point of view. **men-** to
organize, manage, put in order. ~ *meja*
table manners. ~ *pola* to regulate,
channel. **men-** laksanakan to manage.
men- (kan) *rambut* to do o's hair. **pen-:**
~ *boga* food manager (in hotel). ~
busana valet manager. ~ *graha* house-
keeper (in hotel). ~ *laksana* manager.
~ *laksana penjualan* sales manager. ~
minuman bartender. ~ *rambut* hairdresser. ~ *tari* choreographer. ~ *tehnik*
engineer, mechanic. **pen-an** *kembali*
restructuring (of the New Order). **pen-
layanan** *Kristen* Christian stewardship.
pen- usahaan administrating. - *adegan*
grouping (in theatrical life). - *air* irrigation. - *ajaran* curriculum. - *boga* food
management (in hotel). - *bunyi* phonology. - *busana* 1 costume, dress. 2 valet

management. 3 fashion designing. - *cara*
1 means, method. 2 standing operation
procedure. - *daerah* regional planning.
- *dunia baru* the new world order.
- *ejaan* orthography. - *fonem* pho-
nemics. - *gaul* (social) manners.
- *graha* housekeeping (in hotel). - *guna
biologi (,hayati)* bio-management. -
guna tanah land use. - *halaman* landscape gardening. - *kamar* housekeeping
(in hotel). - *kantor* office management.
- *kota* city planning, townscape.- *krama*
code of ethics, etiquette, proper social
conduct. - *lampu* lighting. - *letak* site
plan. - *meja* table setting (in hotel). -
moneter monetary system. - *muka*
cover layout. - *niaga* marketing. - *pelajaran* curriculum. - *pemerintahan* governmental system. - *pergaulan hidup*
way of life, life style. - *personalia* personnel management. - *perusahaan*
business administration. - *rias* decoration (of house), interior decoration.
- *ruang* interior (i.e. the inside of a
room or building). - *sopan* courtesies.
- *suara* sound system. - *taman* land-
scaping. - *tari* choreography. - *tempat*
layout. - *tentrem kertaraharja* the gold-
en age of peace and prosperity. - *tingkat*
hierarchy. - *titi* administrivia. - *udara*
air-conditioning. - *upacara* protocol.
dlm - *warna* in color (TV).
tatah men- to carve out (leather *wayang*
puppets). **pen-an** *wayang* the carving
out of leather *wayang* puppets.
tatak intrepid, undaunted, fearless.
tatanan 1 regulations, rules. *T- ekonomi
baru,* Regulations for a new economy.
2 structure.
tatangkalan trees.
tatap -**an** *mata* cynosure. - *muka* face to
face.
tatar men- to upgrade. **pen-** upgrader.
pen-an upgrading. -**an** 1 step (toward
a goal). 2 stage, level.
Tati 1 woman's proper name. 2 element
of woman's proper name, such as,
Hartati.
tatih ter-.- shaky. *karir pegawai negeri yg*

~ the shaky career of government
employees.
tato tattoo. **ment-** to tattoo. **pent-an**
tattooing.
Tat Twam Asi 1 'You are Me and I am
You.' 2 name of the women's association of the Department of Social Affairs.
tau (S.) TAHU -*lah* and -*lè* I don't know.
Nggak -lah! I don't know! - (pron.
tauk) I dunno (I don't know).
taufan - *pasir* sand storm.
tauk (s.) TAU.
taut ment-kan to bring in, involve in the
matter.
tawa menter-kan 1 (S.) MENERTAWA-
KAN. 2 ridiculous. **ter-** (S.) KETAWA.
meledak ~ to burst out laughing. ~
gelak.gelak to roar with laughter. ~
kecut to laugh out of the wrong side
of o's mouth. ~ *lebar* to laugh heartily.
~ *sendiri* to laugh to o.s.
tawadu 1 docile. 2 obedient. 3 modest.
4 humility.
tawaf (s.) THAWAF.
tawan men- *hati* charming.
tawang men-kan to hold (counterfeited
paper money) up to the light.
tawar I 1 flat (of taste). 2 fresh(water).
3 dull (of a translation, not flowery).
4 to become powerless (of a *mantera*).
Apa kabar? T- saja. How are you? Not
so good. **di- sedingini** to be refreshed.
men-i 1 to imbue (namely, *obats* with
manteras). 2 to treat with healing water
(*air obat,* etc., sprinkled over or rubbed
on sick persons, bride and groom, etc.).
pen- incantation, charm, spell; remedy
against a plague. *air* ~ *(,di-)* remedies
of a *dukun* given a healing power,
'elixir.' ~ *bisa* antidote. ~ *nyeri* analgesic. ~ *perut* s.t. to appease o's hunger.
- *bisa* antidote. - *hati* and - *saja pera-
saan(ku,* etc.) dejected, crestfallen,
despondent.
tawar II *tdk bisa di-.- (lagi)* 1 cannot be
faulted. 2 it's final! **pen-** *iklan* peddler,
hawker (working for a newspaper). **pen-
an:** ~ *perdamaian* sanction of composi-

tion. ~ *tak mengikat* offer without engagement. ~ *umum* tender. **-an** *tak mengikat* offer without engagement.

tawur -an to come to blows.

taypak banker, croupier.

tayub a dance peculiar to villages in Central and East Java; shows are only given in daylight, performed by two or three young women.

tc and **TC** [Training Center] training center. **men.tc.kan** and **men.TC.kan** to send to a training center.

téater theater. - *kendaraan (,mobil)* drive-in theater.

téater(a)wan actor, player.

tebak **men-** *harga (Rp. 2.000,-)* to pay a price (of Rp. 2,000.000).

tebal **ber-** *muka* impudent, insolent. **men-** to grow stronger (of confidence). - *keyakinannya* he is firmly convinced.

tebang *Gua - lu!* I'll knock you down!

tebu - *biasa* milling cane. - *bibit* seed cane. - *tunas* ratoons.

tebus **men-:** ~ *jiwa (,nyawa)* to save a man's life. ~ *kekalahan* to take (,have) o's revenge. ~ *waktu yg terbuang. buang* to make up for lost time. **men-i** *bon* to pay a charge account. **-an** *darah* vendetta.

tedak and **tedhak** to descend, move downward. *T- Siti* to set foot on the ground, i.e. the ceremony in which a baby of 7 x 35 days or 8 months old, for the first time touches the ground in order to learn to stand.

tedas vivid (of colors).

tèdèng and **tèdhèng** 1 peak (of cap). 2 Jav. sun hat. 3 fender. 4 railing (of bridge). *tdk pakai - aling.aling lagi, tdk dgn - aling.aling* and *tanpa - aling.aling* 1 plainly, overtly. 2 to make no bones about. **ber-an** on the sly.

téga - *hati* to have the heart. *kagak - hati* to feel sad. - *larané ora - patiné* to have the heart to see s.o.'s sufferings but not his death, the attempted blending of irreconcilable principles.

tegak **men-kan** *benang basah* to carry out a Sisyphean labor. **pen-** member of the

Pramuka Boy Scout Movement between 16 and 20 years, rover. ~ *hukum* law enforcement agency. - *lurus pd* at right angles to. - *sendiri* autonomous.

tegang to have an erection. **ke-an** erection. **men-** to have an erection. **men-kan** thrilling, exciting. **persi-an** stubbornness. - *syaraf* nervous, worried.

tegas **men-** to become firm.

tegel 1 strong. 2 to have the courage (to do s.t. abominable). - *hati* resolute.

tègel floor tile.

tégenprèstasi quid pro quo, compensation, (s.t. offered in) return, equivalent.

tegugu impetuous, violent.

teguh **ke-an** *hati* 1 stead-fastness. 2 perseverance. **memper-** to strengthen.

teguk **-an** gulp, swallow.

tegur *tiada* **bersi-an** *dgn* to be at variance with. *pandai* **men-** *orang* affable.

tèh - *bohèa* broken tea. - *daun* whole-leaf tea. - *pucuk* pekoe tea.

tèhnis - *militer* techno-military.

tèhnisi technicians.

tèhnokrasi technocracy.

tèhnokrat (s.) TEKNOKRAT.

tèhnokratis technocratic.

tèk.tèk *bakmi* - Chinese noodle dish sold by streetvendors who tap with a spatula on the deep-fry pan to attract customers. *penjual bakmi* - streetvendor who sells the above type of noodles.

Tékab [Team Khusus Anti Bandit] Anti-bandit Special Team (of the Mobile Brigade Investigation Unit).

tekan **ber-an** 1 stressed, accented. 2 pressured. **men-:** ~ *gas* to step on the gas. ~ *tombol klakson* to honk the horn. **pen-an** 1 accentuation. 2 reduction. **ter-** *jiwanya* to be depressed. **-an:** ~ *bunyi* stress. ~ *jiwa* psychological pressures. *dgn satu* ~ *knop* with a single push of the button.

tèkidanto (during the Jap. occupation) grenade hurler.

teklak.tekluk (s.) THEKLAK.THEKLUK.

tèklèk wooden shoes.

tèknokrat technocrat; in Indonesia the

term refers to the group of Western-trained economists called in by President Soeharto to halt inflation.

tékong ship's captain.

tèks di- bawahi to be subtitled.

tèktonis tectonic.

tekuk ber- *simpuh* to kneel down. **men-lututkan** to force to o's knees.

tekun concentrated. **ke-an** intensity. **men-i** to put o's mind to.

tekur men-i to bend over.

tèkwan (in the Karo area) chrysanthemum.

téla (S.) KETELA.

telaah pen-an *Alkitab* Bible study. - *keterlaksanaan* feasibility study.

teladan *kota* - model city.

telan di- *api* to go up in flames. **men-** to embezzle. ~ *biaya* to cost. ~ *korban* to claim victims. ~ *mentah.mentah* to devour bones and all. ~ *pil* to take a pill.

Telanaipura Jambi.

telanjang *dijual* - sold without tax stamp (of cigarettes). **ber-:** ~ *dada* topless. ~ *kaki* barefooted. **ke-an** nudity. - *bugil* (stark-)naked. - *kaki* barefoot.

telanjur *sdh* - 1 (to accuse) gratuitously. 2 too long. 3 let o's tongue run away with o. 4 (to commit an offense) by accident. 5 by mistake.

telantar (S.) TERLANTAR. **men-kan** to neglect s.t.

telapak *sbg* - *tangannya sendiri* at his finger tips.

telat ke-an overtime.

telatah region, territory.

telatèn (s.) TLATEN.

télé I ber-.- 1 to beat around the bush. 2 to drag (on). 3 long drawn out.

telédor ke-an 1 indifference. 2 sloppiness.

téléfonis telephone operator.

télégram men- to cable.

téléjènik telegenic.

telèk chicken droppings.

téléks telex. **di-kan** to be telexed.

télékomunikasi per-an telecommunications system.

telempap ber- to assess, measure.

télépon telephone call. **pen-** telephone caller. **per-an** telephone system. -.*hubungan.langsung* hot line.

téleprinter teleprinter.

téleprompter teleprompter.

télerama [tele (far) + ra (from: *irama* rhythm) + ma (from: *mata* eye)] a television program involving rhythmic music (pop, *kroncong* and regional) and dance.

télèskop telescope.

telètèk men-kan to drop (bombs).

télevisi di-kan to be televised. **per-an** television business. *(pesawat)* - *berwarna* a color television.

telikung di- to be bound (,tied) hand and foot.

telinga *masuk di - kanan keluar di - kiri* it goes in o. ear and out the other. *terangin.angin ke* - to have come to the knowledge of. *lebar* - good at picking up news, rumors. **ber-** *tipis* touchy, sensitive. **pen-** auditory.

teliti ke-an punctuality. **men-** to research. **pen-** researcher. **pen-an:** ~ *kelayakan* feasibility study. ~ *pembukuan* audit.

tèlor accent (in speech).

telor (S.) TELUR. **men-** to come out (of s.o.'s mouth). **men-kan** to hatch (plans). **n-** to lay eggs. - *burung puyuh* quail egg. - *kocok* scrambled eggs. - *penyu* turtle egg.

tèlpon - *umum* pay phone.

teluh the killing of people by persons possessing supernatural powers, voodoo. **men-** to kill people with supernatural powers. **pen-an** blackmagic spell put upon s.o.

teluk *T- Bayur* name of the port of Padang (West Sumatra). *T- Yos Sudarso* the new name for the former Humboldt Bay (in Irian Jaya).

telungkup (s.) JATUH (TERTELUNGKUP).

telunjuk - *lurus kelingking berkait* there's a catch to it.

telur head (of cabbage); (s.) TELOR. *spt* - *di ujung tanduk* to live on a volcano. **ber-** to spawn. *Uang yg ditanam dlm* *saham itu akan* ~, The money invested in those stocks will bear interest. - *asin* egg salted in the shell. - *busuk* rotten egg. - *mandi* poached egg. - *mata sapi* fried egg sunny side up. - *mata sapi matang* egg over well.

telus pe-an permeability. - *air* permeable.

telusur men- to unravel (s.t. complicated).

tèm nge- (busdriver's sl.) to wait for passengers.

teman *Cari -, tuan?* Looking for some company, Mr.? *dgn* **di-i** *semangkok teh* over a cup of tea. *meminta seseorang* **men-i** *berdansa* to ask s.o. for a dance. **per-an** friendship. - *bercakap* person with whom o. is conversing. - *bertanding* sparring partner. - *sepekerjaan* colleague. - *sepembuangan* fellow exile. - *serumah* housemate.

temaram dark (without light).

tèmbak bribe. - *di tempat* 'shot on the spot,' a term in use by the traffic police when a bus or cab driver has violated traffic rules and has to be replaced by another driver on the spot where the violation is made. **di-**: ~ *jatuh* to be shot down (of aircraft). ~ *mati* to be shot to death. **men-** to bribe. **men-kan** *kamera* to take pictures (a picture) with a camera. **pen-**: ~ *basoka* bazooka man. ~ *jitu* sharpshooter. ~ *mahir* marksman. ~ *mitralyur* machine gunner. ~ *sampai mati* the killer. ~ *tepat* sharpshooter. ~ *tersembunyi* sniper. ~ *titis* sharpshooter. ~ *ulung* shooter. **pen-an** *meriam* cannonade. **-an** bribe. *melepaskan* ~ to open fire, shoot. *melepaskan* ~ *dgn peluru tajam* to fire with live ammunition. *melepaskan* ~ *ke atas* to fire in the air (in order to intimidate). ~ *pantul* ricochet shot. ~ *peringatan* warning shot. ~ *sunyi* a single shot now and then. - *memusat* converging fire. *suatu* -.**men-** a shootout. - *mengaur* shots at random.

tembakau - *garang* dried tobacco. - *krosok* dried (uncut) tobacco-leaves. - *pepean* dried tobacco (in the sun). - *warning* shag tobacco.

tembang 1 k.o. herring. 2 sardine.

tèmbèl -an *musik* snatches of music.

tembelèk chicken (,bird) droppings.

tèmbok - *laut* breakwater.

tembus - *terkaannya* he guessed it (in o. go), he made a good shot. *surat itu juga* **di-kan** *ke* copies of the letter have also been sent to. **men-** *(jalan) ke* to thrust to. - *mata (,pandang ,penglihatan)* transparent. *tak* - *peluru* bulletproof.

Temenggung authority in charge of internal security.

temin (sl.) female friend.

temon pengantin the ceremony where the bride and groom meet o.a.

tempah -an deposit (of money).

tempat *pd suatu* - somewhere. *Firma Natuna & Co., di* - Messrs. Natuna & Co., of this city. **ber-** to happen, occur (in a certain place). **di-kan** 1 to be issued (of stocks). *sero yg tlh* ~ *oleh perseroan* the stocks that have been issued by the company. 2 to be placed. *Bangkok tlh* ~ *dlm keadaan siaga penuh*, Bangkok has been placed under a state of full alert. **men-kan** to plant (spies, etc.). ~ *seorang informan pd rumah tangganya* ... to plant an informant in the household of ... **pen-an**: ~ *kembali ke masyarakat* rehabilitation of discharged persons. ~ *sepeda* bicycle stand. **-an** local. **-nya**: *sdh pd* ~ 1 right. 2 with (good) reason. 3 fitting, proper. *tdk pd* ~ improper. *tdk pd* ~ *lagi* 1 no longer fitting. 2 out of place. - *berdiri* (in bus) standing room. - *ber(h)utang* creditor. - *buang hajat besar* toilet. - *cuci muka* washbasin. - *duduk* seat. - *hajat* toilet. - *hiburan malam* night club. - *indekos(t)* boardinghouse. - *jalan kaki* footpath. - *kediaman* abode. - *kontrol* check-point. - *labuh* berth. - *lada* pepper shaker. - *makan* (for cattle) manger. - *mayat* morgue. - *parkir pesawat* apron. - *pelarian* asylum. - *pelepas dahaga* refreshment stand. - *pembakaran mayat* crematorium. - *pemesanan tempat* booking

office. - *pemungutan suara* polling
station. - *penampungan* 1 relocation
center. 2 rehabilitation center. - *pendaratan helikopter* helipad. - *penitipan
pakaian* cloakroom. - *penjualan bensin*
gas station. - *penjualan karcis* ticket
counter. - *penyimpanan mesiu* muni-
tion dump. - *penyimpanan senjata
rahasia* arms cache. - *percontohan*
demonstration plot. - *perhentian (bis)*
(bus) stop. - *peristirahatan (,persema-
yaman)* resting place. - *persembunyian*
hideout. - *pondokan* housing accommodation. - *rapat* berth. - *rekreasi* a
resort. - *senjata* armory. - *tambatan*
berth. -.*temu* rendezvous. - *tidur
dorong* stretcher, litter. - *tidur susun*
bunk bed.

témpé a protein-rich savory cake of fermented soybeans. *bangsa* - a small and
insignificant nation. *pemuda* - a good-
for-nothing kid. - *gembos* fermented
beancake made from peanut residue.

tèmpèl men- to pull alongside (another
car). *Dia ~ sang ayah,* He clings to his
father.

tèmperamèn temperament.

temperas ber-an *masuk* to rush in (to a
house) in throngs.

tempil n- 1 to emerge, step forward. 2 to
be a match for, equal.

tèmplok n- to perch, alight.

tèmpo I and **tèmpoh** *sdh* - time is up. *tdk
tahu* - always (too) busy (to). **-nya:**
ada ~ 1 sometimes, now and then. 2
from time to time, at times, at inter-
vals. *(sdh) ~* it's time. *sdh sampai ~*
and *tlh lewat* - to expire (of agreement,
treaty, etc.). - *doeloe* (always written
with 'oe') in olden times, formerly, i.e.
(usually) during the Dutch col. period.

Tèmpo II name of an Indonesian magazine similar in format to "Time". **ment-
kan** to write a report about s.o. or s.t.
in "Tempo."

tempuh di- 1 acquired, gained. *pengalam-
an yg tlh ~* experiences acquired
(,gained). 2 (distance) covered (by a
vehicle). *Jaraknya tdk sampai setengah*

jam ~oleh taksi kami, The distance is
less than half an hour by our cab. **ke-
an** to pay the score, foot the bill. **men-
jalan tengah** to adopt a middle course.

tempur -an confluence (of two rivers).

temu I wild ginger (L. Scitamineoe). -
kunci a small cultivated ginger (L.
Koempferia pandurata). - *lawak* a
white turmeric, the zedoary (L. Curcuma zedoaria) (used in medicines).

temu II - *gelang* entirely round.

temu III ber- to find (a lost article, a
vacant *becak,* etc.). *Mereka berjalan
kaki sebentar sebelum ~ beca kosong,*
They went on foot a while before
they found a vacant pedicab. *~ dgn*
to come across. *Sampai ~ lagi!* See you!
Until we meet again! *~ jodoh dgn* to
marry. *~ hati* to fall in love. *~ muka*
(to meet) face to face. *~ muka dgn* 1 to
meet personally. 2 to see personally.
kami **men-kan** *pikiran* the idea struck
us. **per-an:** *~ di belakang pintu tertutup*
closed-door meeting, meeting held in
camera. *~ empat mata* tête-à-tête. *~
langit dan air* horizon, skyline. *~ perpisahan* farewell meeting. *~ ramah. tamah*
social get-together. *~ sungai* confluence.
~ tingkat atas top-level meeting. *~ utk
penglepasan* farewell meeting. **ter-kan**
to be found.

temukung (in Nusa Tenggara) village
elder.

tenaga *mengerahkan* - *dan dana* to mobilize funds and forces. **ber-** vigorous, active. *~ atom (,nuklir)* atomic-(,nuclear-)
powered. **ke-an** (adj.) energy, work.
ke- kerjaan (adj.) employee, labor. -
baru a new employee. - *beli* purchasing power. - *hayati* vitality, vital force.
- *kasar* unskilled labor. - *kerja* workman.
- *lama* an old hand. - *lepas* day worker,
part-time labor(er). - *matahari* solar
energy. - *operasionil* [term used
among members of the *PPD* (*,Peru-
sahaan Pengangkutan Djakarta:* Jakarta
Transportation Company)] operational
staff, consisting of bus drivers, conductors and mechanics. - *pejuang* fighter

(the person). - *pendorong* momentum. - *penentang* endurance. - *pengajar* teacher. - *pengukur* scaler.

Tenabang Tanah Abang (an area of Jakarta).

tenang ber- *diri* to calm (,quiet) down. **men-kan** *pikiran* to set (a person's mind) at ease.

tenar di-kan to be made popular. **ke-an** popularity.

tènda - *buka* convertible (automobile).

tendang -an *bebas 12 langkah* (in soccer) penalty.

tèndèns ber- to have a tendency.

tèndènsius tendentious.

tènder (a formal offer) tender. **di-kan** to be offered (to foreign-flag ships).

tengah (in soccer) center. **men-i** *pembicaraan* to interrupt, mediate. **per-an** center, axis, pivot. ~ *kedua (bln Agustus)* the second half (of August). **se-** 1 (a) half. ~ *baya* middle-aged. ~ *hari* a half day. ~ *jadi* half-finished (of a factory). ~ *sadar* half-conscious. 2 partly, to some extent, in some degree, not fully (,completely), imperfectly, semi-. ~ *kebal bakar* semifireproof. ~ *mengerti* to understand, but not fully. ~ *resmi* semiofficial. 3 half-witted, moronic, imbecile. *orang* ~ a half-wit, moronic, mentally aberrant person, an imbecile. 4 ~ *mati* extreme. *dia bekerja* ~ *mati (,mampus)* he worked himself to death. *panasnya* ~ *mati* the heat is insufferable. **se-.se-** halfhearted. *(wanita)* - *baya* a middle-aged (woman). - *kiri* (in politics) left of center.

tengahari noon, midday.

tèngèl.tèngèl and **thèngèl.thèngèl** to raise o's head for a moment (while lying down).

tenggak men- to swallow, gulp down.

tènggang I 1 time for consideration. 2 time limit. 3 length (of a limited time). - *penyerahan* time of delivery. - *waktu* grace period. *selama* - *waktu jabatannya* during o's term in office.

tènggang II share and share alike.

tenggel.tenggel do not give way an inch.

tenggelam pen-an (the) sinking (of a ship).

tènggèr men-kan to perch (s.t. on s.t.).

tenggiri k.o. sea fish, the Spanish mackerel.

tengik *ia* - *dan sombong* and *lagaknya* - he is very arrogant.

tengkar ber- to conflict.

tengkawang (L. Diptherocarpaceae) a fruit cultivated in the interior of Central Kalimantan.

tèngki tank car.

tenglang Chinese (person).

tèngtèng kacang sweet peanut brittle.

tènis pe- tennis player. ~ *meja* ping-pong player.

tènja faeces.

tenor tenor, i.e. the highest adult male voice.

tentang ber-an *dgn* as opposed to, in contrast with, contrary to. *tiada dpt* **di-** *lawan* irresistible. **men-** *kekuasaan* anti-establishment.

tentara ke-an (adj.) army. - *pembebasan* liberation army. - *pendudukan* army of occupation. - *sekutu* the allied forces. - *sewaan (,upahan)* mercenary army.

tèntèng -an portable. *lampu* ~ a portable lamp.

tentera soldier; (S.) TENTARA. **ke-an** the fighting services. - *darat* 1 army soldier. 2 infantryman.

tenteram ke-an a state of calm knowledge and acceptance, a feeling of harmony with nature.

tentu *blm* - it is not certain (that), it is not necessarily the case (that). *diundurkan sampai waktu yg blm* **di-kan** to be postponed indefinitely. **ke-an:** ~ *hukum* legal provision. ~ *larangan* prohibiting order. ~.~ *pelaksanaan* executory provisions. ~.~ *penutup* final provisions. ~.~ *peralihan* transitory provisions. *dgn* ~ *bhw* ... on condition that ... *tak* **men-** aimlessly. **men-kan** crucial. *fase yg* ~ a crucial stage. *faktor* **pen-** a decisive factor. **pen-an:** ~ *nasib sendiri* self-determination. ~ *pendapat rakyat* the act of free choice (in Irian Jaya, August 1969). ~ *waktu* timing. **-nya**

presumably.

téoritisi theoreticians.

tèp (s.) TIP.

tepa example. - *palupi* warning, model, example. - *slira* to put yourself in another's place, 'do onto others as you would have them do onto you.'

teparo neighbor.

tepat *menjadi* -an *pandangan orang* to attract the attention. - *guna* 1 effectiveness. 2 appropriate.

tepèkong Buddha statue in Chinese temple.

tepi ber-kan to border on. **men-** to pull over (a car). **men-kan** *kendaraan* to pull over a car. **-an** *laut* shore. -.**men-** on either side of.

tepo - *seliro* (s.) TEPA (SLIRA).

tepok (S.) TEPUK.

tèprekorder tape recorder.

tepuk ber-: ~ *sebelah tangan* one-sided love. *tak dpt* ~ *sebelah tangan* love cannot come from o. side.

tepung I - *kanji* tapioca. - *sari* pollen. - *susu* (S.) SUSU (BUBUK). - *tapioka* tapioca flour. - *tulang* bone meal.

tepung II - *tawar* a ceremony to honor a person (in Sumatra).

ter (from the prefix *ter-* to indicate a superlative) *gedung bioskop yg dikecapkan - apa saja* a movie theater boasted to be the best of all.

terabas shortcut. **men-** *ke* to take a shortcut to.

tèrakota terra-cotta.

teral *tenaga* -an excitation energy.

teralis (s.) TRALIS.

terampil skilled; (s.) TRAMPIL. *tenaga yg* - a skilled worker.

terang *sdh* - no question about it. **ber-bulan** to spend the time of the full moon. **ke-an** 1 data. 2 legend (on map). ~ *asas* (,*azas*) political program, statement of policy. ~ *atas sumpah* sworn statement. ~ *(ber)kelakuan baik* statement of good conduct. ~ *lisan* oral statement. ~ *mengemudi* driver's license. ~ *pakai* directions for use. *K*~ *Pemerintah* Government's Statement

(of Policy). ~ *saksi* deposition. *Maka atas* ~ *tersebut di atas akte ini diperbuat oleh saya ...,* (closing phrase under an Affirmation of Birth and other official documents) In witness whereof these presents have been drawn up by me ... ~ *waktu* (gramm.) adjunct of time. - *hati* clear-sighted. *di tengah. tengah* - in the bright daylight. *utk* -nya for the sake of.

terap apply, put into practice; (s.) TRAP I. **men-kan** to apply, put to use. **pen(t)** -an application.

teras I *(pejabat)* - key (,senior ,top) (official).

teras II ber- *ke dlm* inward-looking.

terawang men-: ~ *di angkasa angan.angan,* ~ *khayal* and ~.*mengukir jagat* to daydream.

terawèh (S.) TARAWIH.

terbang *tdk boleh* - (of aircraft) grounded. **di-i** to be flown to. *Tdk kurang dr 51 tempat di dlm negeri dan negara.negara tetangga* ~ *oleh Merpati,* The Merpati (Nusantara Airlines) fly to not less than 51 places within the country and neighboring countries. **pen-:** ~ *layang* glider pilot. ~ *pencoba(an)* and ~ *uji* test pilot. **pen-an:** ~ *angkasa bermanusia* manned space flight. ~ *borongan* charter flight. ~ *dlm negeri* domestic flight. ~ *dirgantara* aerospace flight. ~. *intai* reconnaissance flight. ~ *luar-negeri* international flight. ~ *niaga* commercial flight. ~ *percobaan* test flight. ~ *sipil* civil aviation. ~ *tamasya udara* joy flight. ~ *ujian* test flight. - *instrumen(t)* to fly by instrument. - *mengapung di tempat* to hover (of aircraft). - *rendah* low-level flight. - *sendirian* solo-flight. - *uji* test flight.

terbit men-kan: ~ *air liur* to make s.o.'s mouth water. ~ *ingatan kpd* to recall (to mind). - **an** *sore* evening edition (of newspaper).

terbosan break-through.

teri (fig.) an insignificant corruptor caught by the police, a small fish. *Kami ber-*

jubelan spt ikan -, We were all jammed together like sardines.

teriak ber-: ~ *kesakitan* to scream from pain. ~ *semampu urat lehernya* to shout at the top of o's voice, yell o's head off. ~ *spt cina kebakaran jenggot* to cry bloody murder. **ber-.-** *panik* to keep shouting in a panic-stricken way.

terik I *cahaya matahari yg -* and *panas (sedang) -(nya)* stifling hot.

terik II *(burung) -* k.o. heron.

terima di- *bekerja* to be hired (as an employee, etc.). **ke-** to be accepted. **men-:** *tdk bisa* ~ (fig.) can't accept that. ~ *kasih atas* to thank for. **pen-:** ~ *amanat* agent. ~ *darah* blood donee. ~ *kredit* borrower. ~ *muatan* consignee. ~ *perintah* agent. ~ *tamu* receptionist. ~ *tugas* agent. ~ *uang* cashier. **pen-an** 1 hiring, employment (of new personnel). 2 response (to s.t.). 3 opinion, view. ~ *dan pengeluaran* receipts and expenditures. - *kosong* (the house) is handed over vacated. - *nasib (,nasip)* to have to submit.

teritisan porch.

tèritorial territorial. *perairan -* territorial waters.

terjang men- *sebuah ranjau darat* to run into a land mine.

terjemah men-kan (s.) MENTERJEMAH-KAN. **pen-** (S.) PENTERJEMAH. **pent-** *bersumpah (,tersumpah)* registered (,attested) translator. **pen-an** (S.) PENTERJEMAHAN. **-an:** ~ *bebas* free translation. ~ *harfiah* literal translation. ~ *ilmiah* scientific translation. ~ *katawi (,menurut huruf)* literal translation. ~ *sastra* literary translation. **-.ment-kan** translating.

terjun pen- *payung* 1 parachutist. 2 para-trooper. **pen-an:** ~ *bebas* free fall. ~ *biasa* static fall. - *bebas* free fall (of paratrooper).

tèrminal terminal. *T- Bis (,Bus)* Bus Terminal.

tèrmodinamika thermodynamics.

tèrmonuklir thermonuclear.

ternak be(r)- *ayam* to raise chickens.

mempe-kan *sapi* to raise cattle. **pe-sapi** cattle breeder. **pe-an:** ~ *kuda* stud. ~ *lebah* (madu) apiary. - *potong (,sembelihan)* slaughter cattle. - *susu perah* dairy cattle.

terobos men- to go through a roadless area. ~ *masuk* to force an entrance. *tak* **ter-kan** impenetrable. **-an** shortcut.

teroka men- to do research. **pen-an** research.

terokmok *gemuk -* chubby.

tèrong eggplant.

tèrop temporary building.

tèror ment- to terrorize.

terowong -an *air* aqueduct.

terpal tarpaulin.

terpédo (s.) TORPEDO.

tèrsièr tertiary.

tertib pen-an sweeping. - *kembali* rearrangement.

terugval basis (mil.) redoubt.

teruk acute, severe, arduous.

teruni (s.) TARUNI.

terus berke-an continuous. **ke-an** continuity. **pen-an** continuation. **se-nya** further, then, for good (and all). - *mata* clear-sighted. **-.men-** sustained.

tès test. **men(ge)-** to test. **penge-an** testing.

tésala (s.) MINYAK (TESALA).

tésédé [from *T.C.D.:* typhus-cholera-dysentery] (in Indonesian: tipus-kolera-disenteri). *disuntik -* to be vaccinated against typhoid fever, cholera and dysentery.

tésis a scholarly paper.

tèst (s.) TES. **men-** to test.

tèsting a test, an examination.

tetabuhan musical instruments; (S.) TABUH. - *pedusunan* village orchestra.

tetangga - *duduknya* the person sitting next to o. **ber-** *dgn* to be located next to. **menen-** to visit the neighbors.

tétanus tetanus.

tetap men-kan *undang.undang* to enact a law. **pen-an** affirmation. ~ *berlakunya kembali Undang.Undang Dasar 1945* the reinstitution of the 1945 constitution. ~ *harga* price fixing. ~ *kelas* *negara* international ranking list. ~ *waktu* timing.

tetapi *ada* -**nya** there is a but in the question.

tetarub emergency construction for a festivity.

tètèk *masih bau* - quite young. **men-i** nursing (mothers). -.*bengek* odds and ends.

tételo newcastle disease (poultry).

tetenger - *nama: Podang Kentjonowati* named: Podang Kentjonowati.

tètès ber-(.-)an dropping, dripping.

tetoron a Jap.-made synthetic material (originally a brand name).

tétra(siklin) tetracycline.

tetuang - *udara* (in Malaysia) (radio) transmitter.

tetuban (S.) TUBAN.TUBAN.

Tètum a group and language of Timor Timur.

tévé TV, television.

tèwas men- *menjadi* to degenerate into.

tèwèl unripe jackfruit (a side dish).

téyol -**an** exhausted (from walking, etc.).

tgl. [tanggal] date.

Thailand Thailand.

thali (in Irian Jaya) single girl's skirt.

thaodèk (s.) TAODEK.

thawaf to circumambulate the *Ka'abah*.

theklak.thekluk - *ngantuk* to keep nodding drowsily.

thésaurir *T- Jenderal* Chief Treasurer (and Paymaster).

thibburruhany faith-healing.

thok (s.) TOK.

THT [Telinga, Hidung dan Tenggorokan] ENT; Ear, Nose and Throat.

tiada men-kan 1 to get rid of. 2 to undo, unfasten. 3 to abstain from. 4 to withdraw. **ke-an:** ~ *berat* weightlessness. ~ *jalan kembali* no return. -**nya** nonexistence, lack.

tiang se-*penuh* full mast. - *antena* antenna mast. - *gantungan* gallows. - *kili.kili* capstan. - *penyangga* cantilever, console.

tiap se- any (,every) time that. ~ *dia minta uang* ... every time he asks for

money ... *pd* ~ *ada pesta* at any time there's a party. ~ *kita* each of us.

tiban di-i to be struck by. *lagi nongkrong ia* ~ *beton* while squatting (a piece of) concrete fell on him. **ke-** be struck by. *Mereka blm* ~ *rezeki,* Luck has not yet befallen them.

tibang - *cukup (,pas)* just sufficient.

tibèr k.o. rubber mixed with material which looks like calfskin; synthetically prepared.

Tibum [(Pasukan) Ketertiban Umum] Public Order (Troops).

tidak berse-*tahu* to persist in not knowing a thing. **ke-** akuran disagreement. **ke-** aturan irregularity. **ke-** bahagiaan unhappiness. **ke-** bebasan lack of freedom. **ke-** becusan incompetence. **ke-** berangkatan non-departure. **ke-** beraturan disorder. **ke-** beresan disorder, mismanagement. **ke-** berhasilan unsuccessfulness. **ke-** bersalahan innocence (legal). **ke-** bertanggung-jawaban irresponsibility. **ke-** biasaan abnormality. **ke-bijaksanaan** lack of judgment. **ke-** cakapan incompetence. **ke-** cocokan disagreement. **ke-** cukupan insufficiency. **ke-** datangan nonarrival. **ke-disiplinan** non-disciplinary. **ke-** enakan uneasiness. **ke-** harmonisan disharmony. **ke-** imbangan imbalance. **ke-** kekalan instability. **ke-** kompakan non-solidarity. **ke-** lengkapan incompleteness. **ke-** mahiran lack of skill. **ke-** mauan unwillingness, obstinacy. **ke-** menentuan uncertainty. **ke-** mengertian misunderstanding. **ke-** mujuran bad luck. **ke-** mungkinan impossibility. **ke-** normalan abnormality. **ke-** nyamanan discomfort. **ke-** obyektipan lack of objectivity. **ke-** pastian insecurity. **ke-** patuhan disloyalty. **ke-** pengertian lack of understanding. **ke-** penghargaan lack of appreciation. **ke-** percayaan distrust, disbelief. **ke-perluan** non-necessity. **ke-** populeran unpopularity. **ke-** puasan dissatisfaction. **ke-** rasionilan irrationality. **ke-** rataan roughness, unevenness (of street surface). **ke-** relaan unwillingness. **ke-**

rukunan disharmony. **ke- sahan** illegality. **ke- sanggupan** inability, incompetence. **ke- sediaan** unwillingness, unpreparedness. **ke- sehatan** unhealthiness. **ke- seimbangan** disproportion, disequilibrium. **ke- senangan** displeasure, dissatisfaction. **ke- serasian** inadequacy. **ke- setujuan** disagreement. **ke- stabilan** instability. **ke- sukaan** dislike. **ke- sungguhan** untruthfulness. **ke- tahuan** ignorance. **ke- takutan** fearlessness. **ke- tenteraman** unrest. **ke- teraturan** disorder. **ke- terbatasan** limitlessness, unlimitedness. **ke- terikatan** lack of restraint. **ke- terlibatan** non-involvement. **ke- terpisahan** indivisibility. **ke- tertiban** disorder. **ke- wajaran** distortion. **ke- warasan** *jiwa* insanity. **-nya** or not. *baik* ~ whether it is good or not.

tidur to have sexual intercourse. - *dgn* to sleep with (sexual meaning). - *masih sendiri* still single (,unmarried). - *dgn sekenyang.kenyangnya* to catch up on o's sleep. **berseke-an** *dgn* to have sexual intercourse with, sleep with. **ke-an** to be overcome by sleep. **pen-** sleeper (agent). - *lelap (,senyap)* to be sound asleep.

tiga per-an T-intersection, three-corner, three-forked road. *T- Buta* 'the three forms of blindness,' i.e. *buta aksara, buta bahasa Indonesia dan buta pendidikan dasar* illiteracy, ignorance of the Indonesian language and lack of basic education. - *roda* (in Ujungpandang) pedicab. *T- Sejoli* Troika. *T- Tragedi Nasional* the Three National Tragedies for which President Soekarno must be held responsible: (a) the betrayal by the *Gestapu/PKI*, (b) the economic collapse and (c) the moral decline and/or moral decay which occurred during his regime.

tik ke-an typing work, typescript.

tikai per-an: ~ *bathin* pangs of conscience. ~ *pendapat* controversy.

tiké I opium.

tiké II water chestnut (L. Eleocharis dulcis).

tiktok *tukang - baso* vender.

tikung -an corner (of street). *mengambil* ~ *tajam* to take a sharp turn.

tikus I *macam - basah* with tail between legs. *spt - jatuh ke beras* to get a windfall. - *nyingnying* (s.) NYINGNYING.

tikus II thief.

ti kwee (s.) KUWE (KERANJANG).

tilang [bukti pelanggaran] k.o. ticketing system. **ment-kan** to ticket (in connection with a traffic violation). *para* **ter-** traffic violators (,offenders).

tilas pe-an remains of the past.

tilawah and **tilawat** reciting of a piece or pieces from the Koran at the graveside of a deceased person.

tilep di- to be relieved of o's office.

tilik *kalau di- seluruhnya* taken as a whole, on the whole.

tilpon a phone call. *Ada - utk anda,* You have a phone call. *percakapan liwat -* a telephone conversation. **ber-** (s.) BERTELPON. - *kepala* headphones. - *langsung* hotline.

tim I *nasi -* steamed rice.

tim II team.

TIM [Taman Ismail Marzuki] a subsidized cultural center on Jalan Cikini Raya (Jakarta) which offers plays, dances, music, art shows and films; inaugurated November 10, 1968.

timah *dahulu -, sekarang besi* from the frying pan into the fire. - *lempeng* tin plate. - *panas* hot lead, a bullet.

timang -an darling.

timba men- to get (knowledge). ~ *segala macam pengetahuan praktis ttg membuat film* to store up all k.o. practical knowledge about film making.

timbal ber- *balik* mutual, reciprocal. **ber-an** *dgn* commensurate with. *berdasarkan - balik* based on reciprocity. *komunikasi - balik* two-way communication.

timbang I ber- *rasa* considerate. *dpt di-dr* it can be derived from. **diper-kan** to be under consideration. **di-.terimakan** to be transferred. **men-:** *dpt (,tahu)* ~ *rasa* 1 sensitive. 2 ready to help. *tahu*

~ *buruk.baiknya* to know how to balance the good with the bad. **per-an:** *dlm* ~ to be under consideration. *dgn dasar* ~ based on the consideration. *menurut* ~ at the discretion of. *penuh* ~ deliberate. - *terima* 1 transfer of power. 2 transfer of office.

timbang II and **ka-** (,ke-) 1 compared to (,with), (better, more useful, etc.). than. *jauh lebih unggul* ~ *mereka* far more superior to theirs. 2 rather than. *K~ menunggu empat jam, lebih baik ke Yogya dgn naik bis,* Rather than waiting four hours, it would be better to go by bus to Yogya.

timbel lead.

timbris tamper (used in road construction). **di-** to be tampered with.

timbrung n- 1 to interfere, intervene. 2 jump down a person's throat. 3 to interrupt, interpose. 4 to participate in (a film, etc.). 5 to play (in a band).

timbul *habis gelap - terang* after rain comes sunshine. **men-kan** *perhatian* interesting.

Timor - *Dili* Portuguese Timor.

timpa **ber-an** overlapping. *barang.barang* -**an** stolen goods.

timpah -**an** (s.) TIMPAAN.

timpal I **men-i** to put in a word. **n-in** to agree with, consent. **se-** appropriate.

timpal II **men-i** to back s.o. (up), take s.o.'s side, concur with s.o.'s ideas (,views).

timpang **ke-an** inequality.

Timport [Timor Portugis] Portuguese Timor.

timpuh -(an) (s.) DUDUK [BERTIMPUH-(AN)].

Timtèng and **Tim.Tèng** [Timur Tengah] Middle East.

Timtim [Timor Timur] East Timor, i.e. the former Portuguese Timor.

timur *dr - datangnya an.nur* ex oriente lux.

tindak **ber-** *sendiri* to act in a high-handed manner. **di-** 1 to be dealt with. *Penimbun.penimbun beras akan* ~ *tegas,* Rice

hoarders will be dealt with firmly. 2 to be prosecuted. *Barang siapa yg mencoba menaikkan harga akan* ~, Those who try to jack up prices will be prosecuted. *Seorang anggota ABRI akan* ~ *secara hukum, apabila ...,* Legal action will be taken against a member of the Armed Forces, when ... **pe-** *pidana ulang* habitual criminal. **pen-an** (mil.) operations. -**an:** ~ *balasan* countermove. ~ *hukum* punitive measure. ~ *lanjutan* follow-up. - *laku* behavior. - *pidana ulang* recidivism.

ting lantern. - *pal* 1 streetlamp. 2 streetlighting.

tingak.tinguk to look bashfully from o. side to the other, as if searching (,puzzled).

tinggal 1 to live. *T- di mana?* Where are you living? What's your address? 2 nothing left to do but. *(Hanya) - memilih saja,* There's nothing left to do but select. 3 all (you) have to do is. *Sdr - ... saja,* All you have to do is ... 4 it's up to. *T- bagaimana lu!* It's up to you! *Hanya - lagi pd dia,* It's just up to him, it just depends on him! 5 pending. - *menunggu pembongkarannya saja* (of goods at a port) pending their clearance (from the warehouse). 6 to leave off, stop. *tak - berpuasa* to fast all along. **di-** to be left behind (by s.o. who ...). ~ *mati* left alone (due to s.o.'s death). *Dia* ~ *ke Amerika,* She was left behind by s.o. who went to America. *Perkampungan* ~ *mengungsi oleh penduduknya,* The village was abandoned by the evacuating population. *Dia* ~ *suaminya,* She was widowed. *Saya* ~ *tidur,* Everybody went to sleep on me. **di-kan:** ~ *oleh* to be surpassed (,outdone) by. ~ *tengah terbengkalai* to be left unfinished. **ke-an** 1 underdeveloped. 2 back (rent). 3 arrears. 4 in arrears. ~ *bis (,sepor)* to miss the bus (,train). ~ *waktu (,zaman)* out of date. *jauh* ~ *dr* cannot be compared to. *nggak* ~ *ikut* leave nothing undone in order to participate. **keter-an** backlog. **men-kan** to turn o's back on. ~ *hotel* to check-out. ~ *huruf* to omit a letter. ~ *landasan* to take off (aircraft). *usiaku sdh* ~ *8 th* I had passed my eighth birthday. **n-** to desert, leave. ~ *surat* to leave a note. **pe-** evader. **pen-an** relic. ~.~ *bersejarah* historical relics. **per-** (typed under a letter) file (copy). *Mereka - kelas* They were not promoted in school. *- landas-(an)* to take off (aircraft). *- muat* ready to load. *- pakai* ready for fitting. *- pilih!* (you can) take your pick!

tinggi I almost noon-time. *matahari sdh -* it's nearing high noon. *hendak - terlalu jatuh* pride goes before a fall. **berke-an** with a height of. **ke-an** height. *- hati* haughty. *- himmah* ambitious. *- kaji (,kecerdasan ,kepintaran)* advanced, on a high level. *- rendahnya* the standards (of that school).

tinggi II (bed)bug.

tingkah *membuang.buang -* to pose, attitudinize. *dgn tdk banyak -* without much ado. *-nya tambah diperbuat.buat* he became more and more bold. *- polah* way of acting.

tingkalak *- menghadap mudik, lukah menghadap hilir* you can tell a leopard by his spots.

tingkat social stratum. *Pasar ini mendapat kunjungan dr ibu.ibu segala -,* This market is frequented by housewives from all social strata. **ber-.-** gradually, by degrees, little by little. **men-:** *setelah* ~ *dewasa* after he grew up. ~ *melebihi* to reach a climax. ~ *menjadi* to develop into. ~.**mekarkan** to develop (a town). **men-kan** *mutu* to upgrade. **men-(tinggi)kan** to step up (production, etc.). **pen-an** 1 increase. 2 escalation. ~ *arti* (gramm.) amelioration. **-an** *hidup* standard of living. *- bawah tanah* basement. *- hidup (,kehidupan)* standard of living. *sanak.saudara dlm - kedua* relatives in the second degree. *- kecerdasan* 1 educational level. 2 intelligence quotient. *- kelahiran* fertility, fecundity. *- pengi-*

sian kamar occupancy rate (in hotel). *- sarjana* graduate level. *sampai pd - tertentu* to a certain extent. *- tinggi* high-level.

tingkepan ceremony held for a woman pregnant 7 months; the married couple is bathed in a traditional way and this is followed by eating *rujak gobet* or *rujak uyup* (dishes consisting of sliced fruits in a hot sauce).

tingwé [nglinting déwé] to roll o's own cigarette.

tinimbang (rather) than, compared with.

tinja (s.) TENJA. *mobil penyedot -* septic tank pump truck.

Tiongkok *- daratan* mainland China. *- Kuomintang* Nationalist China. *- Merah* Communist China.

tip I 1 (recording) tape. 2 tape recorder. 3 (Scotch) tape. *Pidatonya* **di-**, His speech was taperecorded. **(me)nge-** to record on tape.

tip II a tip. **di-** to be tipped (cab drivers, waiters, etc.).

tipa and **tipe** type.

tipi (s.) TIVI.

tipis **men-** 1 almost stop (of rain). *Hujan sdh agak* ~, It has almost stopped raining. 2 to become depleted. *-nya persediaan pangan* the depletion of food supplies.

tipu **di-** *bulat.bulat (,hidup.hidup ,mentah.mentah)* to be badly cheated (,swindled). **pen-** *ulung* con man. *- Aceh* Acehnese cunning moves. *- daya* artifice.

tipulogi the art of lying.

tirah **pe-an** convalescent center.

tirakat 1 to occupy o.s. with religious meditations. 2 trip to a site considered holy (to receive a revelation). **-an** 1 a feast (in particular, o. based on humility towards the host). 2 gathering for a night vigil. *malam* ~ evening of performing a night vigil.

tirani tyranny.

tirtamarta nectar.

tisor k.o. silk manufactured from an undomesticated Asian silkworm.

titel ber-kan *sarjana* with M.A. degree - *kesarjanaan* master's degree.

titi *diberi* **ber-an** bridged (over). **men-buih** to compromise, give and take.

titik ber- *tolak dr* starting from. **pen-**. **beratan** stressing. - *awal* initial point. - *balik* turning point. - *bertindih* colon (punctuation). - *impas* break-even point. - *jenuh* saturation point. - *kenal* check point. - *keseimbangan* break-even point. - *minat* points of interest. - *mula* starting point. - *penyatuan* rallying point. - *permati* critical point. - *permulaan* starting point. - *pertemuan* contact point. - *pulang pokok* break-even point. - *puncak* high point. - *seimbang* break-even point. - *terang* bright spot.

titinada pitch level.

titip to ask s.o. to do a favor, run an errand or buy s.t. for o. **di-kan:** ~ *menjualkan* to be taken on commission. ~ *tidur di* to be put to sleep at. *Saya* ~ *tidur di rumah tetangga,* I was put to sleep at a neighbors. **men-kan** to park (a car, bicycle, etc.), put s.t. some place for safekeeping. **pen-** (intelligence term) life drop. **pen-an** (intelligence term) dead drop. **-an** *sepeda* bicycle parking.

titis -.**men-** to reincarnate.

titit bulu - pubic hair.

tiup men- *mati* to blow out (a candle). **men-kan** *desas.desus* to start a rumor. **pen-:** ~ *selompret* bugler. ~ *trombon* trombonist.

tivi and **Tivi** TV (set), television. **di-kan** to be televised.

tiwul and **thiwul** 1 dried cassava. 2 snack made from dried cassave.

Tk [Tingkat] level.

TK [Taman Kanak kanak] Kindergarten.

tladung *tanpa* -.-**an** without attacking e.o.

tlatah (s.) TELATAH.

tlatèn unwearying, indefatigable, painstaking. **ke-an** painstakingness.

TLDM [Tentara Laut Diraja Malaysia] Royal Malaysian Navy.

tlècèk *pating* - scattered here and there.

tlèdèk and **tlèdhèk** female dancer and singer.

tlembuk whore.

tlétong and **tléthong** manure (cattle dung).

tlusub and **tlusur ke-an** infiltrated.

to *(ya)* -*?* isn't this the case? (asks the hearer for agreement), isn't it so? *Musti gitu,* -*?* It has to be that way, doesn't it? *Paké kaca mata,* -*?* (He's) wearing glasses, right? *Dekatnya alun.alun, ya* -*?* Near the square, right?

toa.pékong (s.) TEPEKONG.

tobat to be completely in the power of, at the mercy of.

toberos men- *(ke muka)* to press (,push) on forward.

tobong *perusahaan* - limekiln.

tobros (s.) TOBEROS.

todong pen- holdup-man. **pen-an** holdup.

toh I birthmark.

toh II however, on the other hand.

Toh Puan Malaysian title for the wife of a *Tun.*

toilèt toilet.

toji [moto siji] one-eyed person.

tok 1 pure. *kopi* - black coffee without sugar and milk. 2 purely, only.

tokh (s.) TOH II.

toko *pusat* **per-an** shopping center. - *barang seni* art shop. - *bebas.bea* duty-free store. - *makanan* grocery store. - *M dan M (,Makanan dan Minuman)* Food & Beverages Store. - *me(u)bel* furniture store. - *palèn* store which sells household utensils. - *P. & D.* (,Provisiën & Dranken) Food & Beverages Store. - *pangan serba ada* supermarket. - *penuntun* distributor. - *piringan hitam* disc shop, record store. - *radio* radio store. - *serba ada (,lengkap)* department store.

tokoh a leading (public) figure, person. **men-i** *film* to play the main role in a film. - *kunci* key figure. - *mobil* an automobile magnate. - *pahlawan nasional* a national hero. - *perdagangan obat.bius* drug trafficker. - *politik* politician. - *th ini* the man of the year.

toksis toxic.

tolak - *bala* to chase away evil spirits. - *landas* to take off (aircraft). - *peluru* shot-put.

tolbuk (in Madura) coconut beetle.

tolé and **tholé** boy, male infant.

toleran tolerant.

toleransi ber- to tolerate.

tolerir ment- to tolerate.

tolong *minta* - 1 to ask for a favor. *Bolehkah saya minta - saudara?* May I ask you a favor? 2 to cry for help. *(suara) jeritan minta* - a cry for help. *tdk* **ke-an** irretrievable. **pen-** auxiliary (in compounds).

tom indigo

tombok I **pen-an** increase.

tombok II **men-** to bet on.

tombol - *lift* elevator button. - *pintu* doorknob. - *putaran* winder (of watch).

tomplok **n-** to pile up. *rezeki* ~ a windfall, an unexpected good fortune.

tonaas 1 s.o. who uses magic incantations in fishing. 2 s.o. who has great influence, plays an important role in society and, for that reason, is honored.

tonarigumi (during the Jap. occupation) neighborhood association.

tonase tonnage.

tonéél (S.) TONIL.

tong - *kosong nyaring bunyinya* empty barrels make more noise.

tongak **n-** to look up at.

tongcay dried cabbage.

tonggèrèt a black tree-cricket.

tongkang lighter; large, open barge. - *laut* sea lighter. - *minyak* oil barge. - *pelabuhan* harbor lighter.

tongkat *tdk dua kali orang tua kehilangan* - and *jangan dua kali hilang* - once bitten twice shy. - *komando* swagger stick. - *penongkat* crutches. - *peramal* divining rod.

tongkrong **di-kan** to be put in mothballs. **men-i** to sit on top of. **n-** to lie in wait. *Tdk ada poltas* ~ *dgn jipnya,* There were no traffic policemen lying in wait in their jeep.

tongol **n-** to show up, rise (of the sun).

Petugas itu tiada ~, The functionary did not show up. *blm matahari* ~ *seluruhnya* the sun has not yet completely risen. **n-in** to show (s.t.), make s.t. visible.

tongpau mate, comrade, pal.

tongpès [kantong kempes] broke, penniless.

tongsan ancestral land.

tongsèng a dish prepared with sauteed foods, usually including lamb.

tonikum tonic.

tonjok boxing match. **men-** to punch, thrust a blow with the fist, box.

tonton **pen-:** *para* ~ 1 the audience. 2 the public. ~ *televisi* televiewer.

toos (pron. oo as o in go) to give a toast.

top top. *pendidik.pendidik Inggeris yg* - top British educationalists. **nge-** to be on top, at the top.

topan - *dlm segelas air* a tempest in a teacup. - *musim dingin* blizzard.

topang ber- *dagu* to twiddle o's thumbs.

topèng 1 to hide o's true feelings. 2 *wayang* - performance with masked living persons. **ber-:** ~ *alim (,dua)* hypocritical, sanctimonious. *Perampok* ~ *menyikat uang bank,* A masked bandit robbed a bank.- *Cirebon* a mask dance developed in the old Cirebon palaces of Kesepuhan and Kanoman. - *monyet* (s.) KOMEDI (KETEK).

topi condom. *si T- Merah* Little Red Riding Hood. - *lapangan* field cap (of army). - *pengaman* crash helmet. - *prop* a lightweight sun hat made of pith.

topik topic.

toplès jar.

topografi 1 topography. 2 topographic-(al).

toponima toponymy.

top.organisasi parent organization.

torak piston.

torani flying fish.

torèh **men-***getah* to tap rubber.

torpédo I torpedo.

torpédo II penis of a goat, in: *sop kaki kambing dan* - goat-leg and penis soup.

torti *bermain* - to play hide-and-seek.

tortor a Batak dance.

Toserba [Toko Serba Ada] Department
Store.

tosugik (in the southern Celebes) a rich
person.

total di- to be summed up, be totalled.
men-kan to aggregate.

totalisator soccer pool.

totemisme totemism.

Toto [Totalisator] sweepstakes. - *greyhound* sweepstakes linked to the greyhound races held in the *JCSC* (,Jakarta
Canidrome Sport Center); now prohibited. - *Koni* [Totalisator Komite Olahraga Nasional Indonesia] and - *Raga*
[Totalisator Olahraga] two k.o. sweepstakes.

totokromo (s.) TATAKRAMA.

totol -.- freckles.

tour of duty di-kan (the diplomat, member of the armed forces) was transferred
to another post, shunted into limbo.

towèl to touch slightly with a finger.

trada (S.) TIADA.

tradang ber-.- to speculate (in business).

tradisionil traditional.

tragikomis tragicomic.

trafo transformer.

trah pedigree, lineage.

traktor - *tangan* power tiller.

traktornisasi the introduction of tractors.

trakum trachoma.

tralis door (,window) bars; (s.) TERALI.

trampil berke-an skilled. *tenaga yg* ~
skilled workers.

trancam k.o. salad with hot sauce.

Transad [Transmigrasi Angkatan Darat]
relocation of army personnel; (s.)
TRANSMIGRASI.

Transau [Transmigrasi Angkatan Udara]
relocation of air force personnel; (s.)
TRANSMIGRASI.

transendèn transcendent.

transendèntal transcendental.

transfigurasi transfiguration.

transformator transformer.

transisi transition.

transito transit.

transkaryawan 1 settler. 2 migrant.

transkripsi transcription. ment- to trans-
scribe.

transliterasi transliteration.

transmigran a relocated resident, esp. o.
who has moved from the island of
Java to some other Indonesian island.
- *inti* a relocated resident with a high
school or higher education.

transmigrasi relocation (of families or the
population, esp. away from the island
of Java), interregional migration. ber-
to transmigrate, resettle. ment-kan to
relocate (families or the population,
esp. away from the island of Java).
pent-an relocation (also, of loiterers).
- *sisipan* relocation in which the
migrants are placed among an already
existing population.

transplantasi transplantation. ment-kan
to transplant (of human heart). - *jantung* heart transplant.

transportasi transportation.

Transwakarsa [Transmigrasi Swakarsa]
spontaneous relocation.

trap I (s.) TERAP. menge-kan to apply.
penge-an and pent-an 1 application.
2 enforcement.

trap II stairs (of a building).

trapel cèk (coll.) traveler's check.

tras trass, k.o. cement. *batu* - a brick
made from trass.

trasé (ground)plan.

tratak temporary bamboo or iron platform with thatched roof of palm leaves
or canvas roofing added to a building
to function as a seating structure for
spectators.

trawang n- transparent.

trawl (shrimp) trawl. nge- to catch shrimp
by using a trawl.

trayèk transportation line. - *pokok* trunk
line. - *sampingan* feeder line.

trèini trainee.

trèkbom land mine.

trembesi *pohon* - designation for trees,
belonging to the Pithecolobium family,
from which sometimes a rain of damp-
ness comes down, rain tree.

trèmos (S.) TERMOS.

trènd trend. **ber-** *naik* to show an upward trend. *- menurun* a decreasing trend.

trenggiling anteater (L. Manis javanica).

trengginas swift, quick. **ke-an** swiftness.

trenyuh 1 brokenhearted. 2 touched, moved, affected.

trèpès flat-chested.

tresna (pron. tresno) love, affection. *Ia* **di-ni** (pron. ditresnani) *oleh seseorang,* S.o. loves him.

TRI [Tebu Rakyat Intensifikasi] Smallholders' Sugarcane Intensification (Program). **di.-.kan** to be subjected to the Smallholders' Sugarcane Intensification (Program).

triangulasi triangulation.

Trias Politika The Legislative, Judicial and Executive Powers.

Tri Dharma Confucianism, Taoism and Buddhism.

Tri Karma Adhyaksa 'The Three Concepts of the Magistrate,' i.e. honesty, responsibility and wisdom.

triko tricot.

trilala ber- to sing.

trilyun a thousand billion.

trimasih (S.) TERIMA KASIH.

trimo n- 1 to be passive, be uncomplaining. 2 to be fatalistic. *(main)* ~ *saja* to acquiesce.

trim(s) (S.) TERIMA KASIH.

trinil common sandpiper.

TRIP [Tentara Republik Indonesia Pelajar] Students Army of the Republic of Indonesia.

trisula trident, a three-pronged spear.

tritik a piece of cloth.

Tritugas The Threefold Task (President Soekarno, Aug. 17, 1964): (1) Freedom, (2) Socialism and (3) A New World.

Tritunggal 1 Regional Triumvirate consisting of (a) the Head of the Civil Service, (b) the Chief of Police and (c) the Chief of the Regional Army Detachment. 2 (after Sep. 30, 1965) (a) the Great Leader of the Revolution/President/Supreme Commander of the

Armed Forces (Soekarno), (b) the Armed Forces and (c) the People.

Tri Tuntutan Ampera (abbrev. *Tritura*) *Ampera's* Three Demands: (a) The Banning of the Indonesian Communist Party, (b) The Purging of *Gestapu/PKI* elements from the *Dwikora* Cabinet and (c) The Lowering of Prices of Basic Necessities.

Tritura [Tri Tuntutan Rakyat] The People's Three Demands: (a) Getting Rid of the *Aspris,* (b) Lowering Prices and (c) Smashing Corruption.

triumvirat triumvirate.

triwikrama to assume a demonic form.

trobosan (s.) TERBOSAN.

trol patrol (boat).

tromol cannister.

trondol and **trondhol** almost destroyed. **ment-i** to squeeze s.o. dry of his money.

troondooloo (pron. oo as o in go) dummy, stupid person.

tropis tropical.

trotok *burung* - k.o. thrush.

trotskis trotskyite.

trubuk *ikan* - longtail shad, Chinese herring. *telor* - salted *trubuk* spawn, Indonesian caviar.

trucut ke- slip of the tongue.

truf trump.

truk per-an trucking. *- gandengan* trailer truck. *- jungkit* dumptruck. *- keran* crane truck. *- pengangkat sampah* garbage truck. *- tanki (bensin)* (gasoline) tank truck. *- yg diperlengkapi pengeras suara* sound truck.

trukbyangmu *- kocok!* a vulgar term of abuse referring to 'your dirty old mother!'

trundul (s.) TRONDOL.

Tsanawiyah (s.) SEKOLAH (TSANAWIYAH).

tsani second (chairman, etc.).

Tsar Czar.

TTS [teka-teki silang] crossword puzzle.

tua 1 classic. 2 aged. *budak lampau - tdk* young fellow, stripling, youth passing into manhood. *sdh terlampau -* obsolete. *orang -* 1 old person, elder. 2

parent(s). **berorang.**- to have parents. *yg tdk berorang. - (lagi)* parentless. **keorang.-an** parenthood. **men-** to grow old. **Penge-** Dean (of diplomatic corps). **-an** on the old side. *Orangnya gemuk, agak -,* The person in question is stout, elderly. -.- foster father. ~ *desa* village elder. - *muda* old and young. - *peot* decrepit.

tuah - *ada, untung tiada* he has luck but doesn't profit by it. - *melambung tinggi, malang menimpa* to be completely out of luck.

tuak fermented coconut milk. - *anggur* k.o. wine.

tualang kepe-an adventurous.

tuan boss. *tdk ber-* 1 no man's (land). 2 unclaimed (goods). *T- Besar* (col.) Governor General. *T- Guru* (in East Lombok) Moslem scholar. - *putri* wife.

tuang pen-an foundry.

tuas -an fish-lure.

Tubagus a hereditary title of nobility for the sons of the former Sultans of Banten.

tuberkulosa tuberculosis.

tubruk -an: ~ *beruntun* chain(-reaction) collision. ~ *yg membawa maut* fatal collision.

tubuh berse- *dgn* and **menye-i** to have sexual intercourse with. - *kendaraan bermotor* car body.

tuding men- to point, aim (with hand or stick).

TUDM [Tentara Udara Diraja Malaysia] Royal Malaysian Air Force.

tuduh *karena di-* on a charge of. **-an:** *atas* ~ on a charge of. *dgn* ~, *bhw...* on the charge that...

tugal pen- dibbler.

tugas assignment. **di- belajarkan** *ke* to be sent on a study assignment to. **pe-:** ~ *bali* employee who works in the front office (of a company, etc.). ~ *lapangan* field worker (of family planning). ~ *pimpinan* managing functionary. ~ *riset* research officer. **pen-an** assignment. - *belajar (,mengajar)* study (,teaching)

assignment. - *diselesaikan dgn baik!* mission accomplished!

tugu *T- Kemenangan* Arc de Triomphe. - *lembur* neighborhood association. - *peringatan* cenotaph.

tugur -an to stand guard (during the commemoration of a death ceremony).

tu(h) (S.) ITU.

Tuhan - *yg Kaya* the Almighty God. - *yg Kudrati* God the Almighty. - *yg Maha Esa* the One and Only God.

tuhu cuckoo (the male of the *kolik*).

tuing.tuing flying fish.

tuju ber-an purposeful. *tiada* ~ aimless. **berse-** to assent, consent. *kereta api* **men-** *ke* ... the train sets out for ... **ter-** *kpd* addressed to, aimed at.

tujuh *nyesel - rejeb (,turunan)* to regret forever. **T- belasan** the August 17 celebrations. - *keliling* 1 the seven rounds of the *Kabah.* 2 dizzy. 3 dizziness.

tukak - *lambung* ulcer.

tukang - *asut* agitator. - *besi kuda* farrier. - *bikin bersih jalan* street sweeper. - *bikin duit* moneylender. - *bikin kacau* troublemaker. - *bodor* clown, comedian. - *bonceng* freeloader. - *canai* (scissors) grinder. - *cari adpertensi* advertising salesman. - *catut* 1 black marketeer. 2 swindler. - *cicip* taster (of tea, etc.). - *cincang* film editor. - *cor* (metal-) founder. - *cungo* pickpocket. - *dagel* clown, comedian. - *derek* winch driver. - *diesel* diesel engine operator. - *dongkel* burgler. - *fitnah* slanderer, caluminator. - *gansir rumah* burglar. - *ganyang lampu mobil* automobile lamp thief. - *gedor* burglar. - *gendem* hypnotist. - *gergaji mesin* chain saw operator. - *gerogoti uang* corruptor. - *gigi* unlicensed Chinese dentist and dental technician. - *godot* corrupt government employee. - *gosok* intriguer. - *gunting rambut* hairdresser, barber. - *hambur uang negara* spendthrift of State money. - *hasut* (s.) TUKANG (ASUT). - *ijon* purchaser of paddy while still in the field. - *itung.itungan* astrologer. - *jamas* person who cleans *pusaka* with arsenic.

- *jambret* snatcher. - *jilat* ass kisser. - *jual obat* medicine man, quack. - *kacip* sniper. - *kaplok* person in the claque. - *kebut* irresponsible and reckless driver (teenager). - *keplok* (s.) TUKANG (KAPLOK). - *kepruk* member of a pressure group, member of a strong-arm squad. - *ketok* body repair technician (of automobile). - *kipas* (in volleyball) person who is known for his smashes. - *kisar* miller. - *kredit* creditor. - *lapor* informant. - *lumas* lubeman. - *mengiakan* yes man. - *mengocok* clown. - *nebeng* freeloader. - *ngadu* informant. - *ngamen* troubadour. - *ngentot* cocksman. - *ngeset* typesetter. - *ngobrol* chatterbox. - *nunut* freeloader. - *nyepom* shoplifter. - *obat* quack. - *pacak* dummy, puppet. - *pancing* angler. - *parkir* parking lot attendant. - *pateri* solderer. - *pelat* plate worker. - *pengkorankan* rumor monger. - *peras* blackmailer, extortionist. - *perkosa* rapist. - *pijat* masseur. - *plakat* o. who puts up posters. - *potong* cutter. - *pukul* hatchet man. -.- *pukul* pressure group, strong-arm squad. - *pungut puntung rokok* collector of cigaret butts. - *resensi* reviewer, critic. - *rias* make-up artist. - *royal* man about town. - *sabit rumput* grasscutter. - *samak* tanner. - *sambrah* dancing girl. - *sapu* trash collector. - *sepatu kuda* blacksmith. - *senjata* armorer. - *sepeda* bicycle repairman. - *sihir* hypnotist. - *sol sepatu* cobbler. - *spanduk* banner fastener. - *sulap* juggler, conjurer. - *sundut* arsonist. - *tambal ban sepeda* bicycle tire repairman (along the streets). - *taruhan* bettor, gambler. - *telepon* telephone installer. - *teluh* black magician. - *tepuk* claque. - *teriak* auctioneer. - *ternak uang* moneylender. - *tidur* sleepyhead. - *todong* gangster, holdupman. - *ukur jalan* vagabond, bum. - *ular* snake charmer. - *warang* person who cleans *pusaka* with arsenic.
tukar ber-: ~ *omong* to talk back and forth. ~ *pikiran* to change views (,o's

mind). **ber-.-** alternating. **di-** *tambah dgn* to be traded in for. **pe- pikiran** exchange of views. - *tambah* trade-in.
tukas pen- false accuser.
tukmis and **thukmis** [bat(h)uk klimis] philandering.
tul (S.) BETUL.
Tula Libra.
tulad di- to be imitated.
tulang rib (of leaf). *meraba - iga sendiri* to be introverted. *tinggal - terbalut kulit, tinggal kulit membalut -, tinggal - dgn kulit, - dan kulit saja lagi* and *hanya tinggal kulit dan - saja* nothing but skin and bones. **ber-** *belakang (,punggung)* backboned. **men-.punggungi** to support fully. - *babi panggang* barbecued spareribs.
tuli men-kan *telinga* to pretend not to hear.
tulis hand-done (batik). *surat yg* **ber-tangan** a handwritten letter. **ber-kan** ... to have ... written on it. *dgn di-tangan* handwritten. **kepen-an** (adj.) writing, authoring. **pen-**: ~*biografi* biographer. ~*ceritera panggung* playwriting, authoring. **men-kan** *resep* to write (out) a prescription. **pen-**: ~ *biografi* biographer. ~ *ceritera panggung* playwright. ~ *kepariwisataan* travel writer. ~ *komentar* commentary writer. ~ *kronik* chronicler. ~ *putri* authoress. ~ *rahasia* cryptographer. ~ *resensi* book reviewer. ~ *skenario* scenario writer. **pen-an** *sejarah* historiography. **-an** script. ~ *rahasia* cryptogram.
tulus ke-an candor. *dgn se-.- hatinya* 1 in all sincerity. 2 in good faith. 3 single-mindedly.
tuma *takutkan - dibuangkan kain* to throw the baby out with the bathwater.
tumang about 10 kilograms of sago.
tumbal ber- antidotal.
tumbang pen- *rekor* record breaker.
tumbèn nih ...? how come ...?
tumbila (bed)bug.
tumbu *spt - oleh tutup* well-matched.

tumbuh **ber-.-an** overgrown. **men-kan:** *Ini ~ cerita lain,* This leads (,gives birth) to another story. *~ minat thd* to arouse interest in. **men-.luaskan** to foster the growth of, spread. **-an** *pengganggu* weed.

tumbuk celebration of o's (8th, 16th, 24th, 32nd and 64th) birthday. **ter-:** *~ di (,ke ,pd) jalan* emerge on (the street, road). *~ dgn (,ke ,pd)* (your eyes will) immediately fall on. *~ pd batasnya* reach its utmost limit. *~ pd diri sendiri* thrown on o's resources. *~ pikiran* 1 to be at o's wits' end. 2 depressed. *T-Ageng* celebration of o's 64th birthday.

tumimbal *- lahir* 1 reincarnation. 2 to reincarnate.

tumis k.o. side-dish to the *rijsttafel,* made of stir-fry vegetables.

tumit **ber-** *tinggi* with high heel.

tumon to see (by accident), notice. *Apa -?* Did you ever see (,hear of) (such a thing)?

tumor **ber-** tumerous. *- ganas* malignant. *- tenang* benign.

tumpah **ber-** *ruah* abundant, plentiful, profuse, copious. *negara tempat darahnya* **ter-** his native land.

tumpak **n-** *becak* to ride a pedicab, go by pedicab.

tumpang **di-i** (all hopes) are pinned on. *Dara.dara Pulau Dewata yg ~ harapan sepenuhnya,* Balinese girls on whom all hopes are pinned. **men-:** *~ saja kpd* to trim o's sails to every wind. *~ dengar* 1 to listen too. 2 to overhear. *~ makan (,mandi ,telepon ,dll.)* to eat (,take a bath ,telephone ,etc.) in s.o. else's house. *~ mati* to die at the same time. **men-i** to make use of s.t. which belongs to s.o. else. **n-:** *~ di satu ruangan* housed (,accommodated) in a large space. *~ ketawa* to join in the laughter. *~ lewat* to ask permission to pass by. **pen-:** *~ gelap* stowaway. *~ yg berdiri* (in a bus, etc.) straphanger, standing passenger. *- suh* and *- tindih* overlap. **-.men-** overlapping.

tumpangsari (s.) TANAMAN (TUMPANGSARI).

tumpas **men-** to destroy.

tumpat *pikirannya sdh* - he's at his wits' end. **-an** filling (of tooth).

tumpeng(an) cone of cooked rice mixed with turmeric and meat.

tumplak ponjèn a Jav. ceremony related to the wedding of the youngest child; all the savings of the parents set aside earlier for the child's upbringing are now to be taken out.

tumplek **di-i** to be crawling with, be overrun with. **di-.blekkan** *kpd* to be centered (,focussed) on. **di-.ruek** to be piled up. **men-kan** to pour out. **ter-** *di* gathered, piled up in. *- bleg* be poured onto.

tumpu **ber-** to adjoin. **per-an** overlapping. **-an:** *~ gelombang* breakwater. *~ harapannya* the person on whom o. has pinned o's hope(s). *menjadi ~ jiwa (,kasih sayang rakyat jelata)* to enjoy great popularity. *~ pantai* beachhead. *menjadi ~ pusat nasihat* to be an oracle. *~ udara* airhead.

tumpuk **ber-** *sesak* piled up. **se-** *awan* cumulus. *menjadi* **-an** *perkataan* to be in the limelight.

tumpur broke, hard up. *jatuh -* to go bankrupt. **pen-** man about town.

tun I 1 guilder. 2 *rupiah.*

Tun II a Malaysian title.

tuna a loss, lack. **ke-.netraan** blindness. *- aksara* an illiterate person. *- anggota* an invalid. *(Direktorat Jenderal) T-Bina Warga* (Directorate General of) Correctional Institutions. *- busana* a barely-dressed person. *- deksa* a physically handicapped person. *- hasta* a o.-armed person. *- karna* a deaf person. *-karya* an unemployed person. *-karya biasa* able-bodied person who has neither job nor permanent housing. *-karya cacat* mentally and/or physically handicapped person who is unable or unwilling to work and who has no permanent housing. *- kawaca* a barely-dressed person. - *laras* an unsociable person. - *mental* a mentally retarded person. -*netra* a blind person. - *pidana* a convict. - *rungu* a deaf person. - *rungu dan wicara* a deaf-mute. - *sosial* an unsociable person. - *susila* a woman of loose morals, prostitute. - *tertib* a disturber. - *wicara* a stammerer. -*wisma* a roofless person. -*wisma biasa* person who has a job but no permanent housing.

tunai *ketiadaan* **per-an** and **per-an** *tdk sempurna* nonfulfillment.

tunak steady.

tunang **ber-an** *dgn* engaged to.

tunas - *bangsa (,muda)* the future generation.

tunawan term used by employees of the Jakarta-based "Dr. Tjipto Mangunkusumo" Hospital morgue when referring to the corpse of a person unable to pay for his burial, usually loafers, bums, etc.

tunda **di-**: ~ *keberangkatannya* to be canceled (of a flight). *sedang* ~ to be in abeyance.

tunduk - *kpd isteri* henpecked.

tunèt [tuna netra] a blind person.

tungau mites (infesting fowls and man). *meniup.niup* - *menjadi gajah* to make a mountain out of a molehill.

tunggak **n-** to be in arrears. **pen-an** delinquency (in repayment).

tunggal - *nada* monotonous.

tunggang **di-i** 1 to be exploited. 2 to be manipulated. *organisasi yg* ~ *kaum komunis* a communist-manipulated (,directed) organization. **men-** *indah* dressage (in horse riding). **pen-** *sepeda* cyclist.

tungging caudal.

tunggu - *dulu!* wait! stay! - *(tanggal) mainnya!* watch for the opening date! - *tempat di restoran* waiting to be seated in a restaurant. **di-** *kedatangannya* he is expected. **(me)n-**: ~ *gilirannya* to wait o's turn. ~ *sampai kiamat* to wait till

doomsday. *diminta* ~ *di luar sekolah* (euph.) to be fired (of teachers). **pen-** caretaker. ~ *dunia* men, people. ~ *lift* elevator operator.

tunggul I - *mati baharu ia berkata* to be (as) silent as the grave. - *kayu* tree stump.

tunggul II **pen-an** upgrading.

tungket (S.) PERSNELENG.

tungku - *pembakar* furnace.

tungkup *drpd* **ter-** *baik terteleng* half a loaf is better than no bread at all.

Tunisia Tunisia.

tunjang **pen-** *harga* price support. **-an** alimony. ~ *jabatan* official expense account. ~ *keluarga* child support. ~ *kerja* bonus.

tunjuk *sbg* **di-i** *Tuhan* as if inspired by God. **men-kan**: ~ *kesediaannya* to express o's willingness. *Jam* ~ *pukul sepuluh,* The clock is pointing to ten. **pe-**: ~ *memakai* directions (for use). ~ *perjalanan kereta api* railway timetable. **pen-**: ~ *arah* directional indicator (auto). ~ *jalan* guide (the person). ~ *kecepatan* speedometer. ~ *telepon* telephone directory. **per-an**: ~ *amal* benefit performance. ~ *perdana* première. **ter-**: *kpd (yg)* ~ to bearer. *Perdana Menteri.* ~ Prime Minister designate. - *hidung* (o. of *P.K.I.'s* political actions) fingerpointing, to name names.

Tunku (S.) TENGKU.

tuntas 1 drained. 2 completely emptied (,poured out). 3 thorough. 4 once for all. *keadaan di sana benar.benar* - the situation there is really secure, peaceful and stable. **pen-an** *air* drainage.

tuntut **men-**: ~ *di muka pengadilan (,hakim)* to summon to appear in Court. ~ *pelajarannya* to pursue o's studies. **men-.pulangkan** to request extradition. **-an**: ~ *jaksa* legal claim. ~ *ganti rugi* claim.

tupai *sepandai.pandai* - *melompat sekali akan gawal (,terjatuh)* it is a good horse that never stumbles.

tur tour. - *keliling* to take a tour through (,around).

turangga horse.

turba [turun ke bawah] 1 the go-down-to-the-people movement, grass-roots movement. 2 reconnoitering. *mengadakan* - 1 to integrate with the masses. 2 (fig.) to reconnoitre. **di-kan** (fig.) (the goods) have been unloaded.

turbin turbine.

turi name of a tree; o. variety with white flowers, another with red flowers. The white flowers are cooked and eaten as a vegetable, the red ones are bitter and used as medicine.

turinisasi encouragement to plant *turi* trees.

turta [turun tangan] to intervene.

turnoi tournament.

turun *sampai berita ini* **di-kan** until this news item went to press. *habis* **ke-an***nya* died out, extinct. **ke-** temurunan descent, lineage. **men-** tangga and **men-i** *anak tangga* to go down the stairs. **men-kan** 1 to publish (an article). 2 to disembark (passengers). ~ *pemain. pemain* to have players (,actors) appear on the scene. **pen-an:** ~ *harga* reduction in price, reduction of prices. ~ *ke air* launching (of ship). ~ *tingkat* phasing out. **se-an** cognate. **-an:** ~ *yg ditandai* certified copy. *yg mengambil* ~ copyist, transcriber. - *dr mobil* to get out of a car. - *kapal* 1 to go ashore. 2 debarkation. - *ke bawah* 1 go-down-to-the-people movement, grass-roots movement. 2 reconnoitering. - *ke jalan* to take to the streets. - *main* (in school) to have a break. - *meninggalkan kapal* to disembark. - *mesin* overhaul. *melakukan* - *mesin* to overhaul. - *minum* (in soccer) half-time. - *sebuah peraturan baru* a new regulation was issued. - *(dr) takhta* to abdicate. - *tangan* 1 to interfere. 2 to take action. - *tanpa konsep* to turn up without any ideas. - *warnanya* to fade (of colors). -.**men-** traditional.

turut **di-** sertakan (s.) DIIKUT.SERTA-KAN. **ke-** (along) with. **men-:** ~ *abjad* alphabetical. ~ *banyaknya* quantitatively. ~ *imbangan* proportionally. ~ *kias* on the analogy of. ~ *nilai* ad valorem. ~ *tingkat* gradually. ~ *usik hati* intuitive. **pen-** docile. - *berdukacita* to offer condolences. - *munding* to follow blindly. - *nafsu (,renyut hati)* impulsive.

tustèl - *foto* and - *kamera* camera. *dgn menyandang* - *Nikon* ... by strapping a Nikon camera over o's shoulder ...

tusuk awl. (**me)n-** to vote (in election). **men-** *hidung* penetrating (smell). **men-.n-** *tulang* penetrating (chill). -.*jarum* acupuncture. *ahli -.jarum* acupuncturist.

Tuti 1 woman's name. 2 female name element.

tutuk and **thuthuk** **di-** to be scolded. **-an** scolding.

tutup **keter-an** closeness, reticence. **men-.** **ikat** *matanya* to blindfold s.o. **men-.n-i** *(perkara Watergate)* to cover up (the Watergate case). **pen-** *lensa* shutter (of camera). **pen-an** lockout (of workers by company). **ter-:** ~ *bagi kendaraan* 1 no thoroughfare. 2 not a through street. *pertemuan di belakang pintu* ~ a meeting held in camera. *wilayah* ~ *a* bonded area. - *kejepit* flat broke. - *leher* scarf. - *usia* to pass away.

tutur **ber-.-** *seorang* to talk to o.s. *seorang* **pen-** *bahasa Indonesia* a speaker of Indonesian. **-an** utterance.

tuturuga Manadonese dish, mostly made from turtle.

tutut snail.

tutwuri to follow. - *(h)andayani* to follow (a person) but be influential. - *(h)andayani, ing madya karsa, ing ngarsa sung tulada* a description of Indonesian (village) life, meaning: stimulating from behind, in (their) midst arousing (their) will, and, in front providing (them) with an example.

tuwèk (joking) (s.) TUA. *sampek* - (s.) SAMPAI (TUA).

tuyul k.o. spirit who can be instructed
to hoard wealth; (s.) SETAN (KERDIL).
TV (pron. tévé or tivi) **di-kan** to be televised. *Nixon ke RRC akan* ~, Nixon
to the PRC will be televised. - *hitam.*

putih black and white TV. - *mata.mata*
closed-circuit television.
TVRI and **TV.RI** (pron. té-vé-èr.i) Republic of Indonesia Television.
twédehan second-hand.

U

ual meng- to break away (from).
uang - *itu pangkal segala kejahatan* money
is the root of all evil. *ada - abang
sayang, tak ada - abang melayang* fair-
weather friendship. **ke-an**: *yg kuat ~
nya* with sufficient capital, well sup-
plied with capital. *yg lemah ~nya*
lacking capital. **per-an** finance system.
- *bangku* bribe to gain school admission. - *bantuan* grant in aid. - *bedolan*
restitution for transportation costs.
- *berobat* medical expenses. - *besar*
large bills. - *cartal* money in circulation.
- *damai* damages paid in an out-of-court
settlement. - *hangus* (in banking) points
(it's the individual not the bank that
pockets the difference). - *ikhlas* k.o.
bribe. - *jempling* bribe paid to railroad
employees by s.o. who does not want
to pay full fare. - *kaget* money given
to s.o. who has experienced a shock
(due to a car collision, etc.). - *kartal*
money in circulation. - *kas* cash (on
hand). - *kehidupan* alimony. - *kelebihan
berlabuh* demurrage. - *kemeng* teacher's
overtime bonus. - *kertas bank* bank
note. - *kertas Pemerintah* Federal note.
- *kupatan* the epithet for the 1971-
Lebaran bonus, since the bonus was
very small, just enough to buy *ketupat.*
- *lelah* honorarium. - *lembur* bribes
(given to government officials for
them to 'stay overtime' to do some
work so as to obtain a needed document). - *logam peringatan* commemorative coin. - *mas ukon* a gold coin
(used as ornament). - *meja* an unofficial tax levied by officials of the Road
Traffic Service on newspaper boys
who sell their papers at the bus termi-

nal. - *nafkah* alimony. - *pakaian* clothing allowance. - *panas* 'hot money,' i.e.
money obtained from a loan shark. -
pandu pilotage. - *pangkal* admission
(,entrance) fee - *parkir* 1 parking fee.
2 aircraft ramp fee. - *pelancar (,pelicin)*
bribes. - *pemasukan pajak* tax reve-
nue(s). - *pembeli jarum* pin money. -
pencil keluarga family separation
allowance. - *pendaftaran* registration
fee. - *pendaratan* aircraft landing fees.
- *pengusiran* money given to s.o. to
vacate the house he is occupying. -
penyambung hidup 'money to extend
o's life.' *utk mendapatkan - penyambung hidup* to make (both) ends meet.
- *pesangon* severance pay. - *pitingan* (in
the Department of Education and
Culture) bribe a college student has to
pay in order to pass an examination.
- *sabun* bribes. - *semir* grease money.
- *siluman* (abbrev. *usil*) bribes. - *syukuran* (in the *Pendidikan Guru Agama
Negeri* State Training College for
Teachers of Islam Religion) a bribe
given to a member of the examining
board by an examinee. - *tambang*
freight. - *tandu* (in Semarang) demurrage. - *tanggungan botol* deposit. -
terima kasih k.o. bribe. - *tunjangan*
1 (unemployment) pay. 2 subsidy,
grant. - *tunggu* retainer. - *tutup mulut*
hush money. - *yg nganggur* idle money.
dgn - *yg terbatas* with limited funds.
ubah *tak - dr (,sbg ,spt)* and *tak -nya dgn
(,sbg, spt)* same as, similar to, identical
with. **ber-:** ~ *dr yg sudah.sudah* different from the past. ~ *kpd yg baik* and
~ *(men)jadi baik* to change for the better. ~ *kpd yg buruk* and ~ *(men)jadi*

buruk to change for the worse. ~ *setia* to become disloyal. *selalu boleh (,dpt)* **di-** and *sewaktu.waktu dpt* **di-** to be subject to change. **peng-** *arus listrik* rectifier (device to change alternating current into direct current). **peng-an** 1 change, alteration. 2 conversion. **per-an:** ~ *Anggaran Dasar* 1 constitutional amendments. 2 alteration of Articles of Association. ~ *haluan* 1 change of course. 2 change of policy.

ubek ng- to hang about. *Mula.mula ia hanya ~ di sekitar kampung,* At first he only hung about in the vicinity of his *kampung.*

ubel.ubel head scarf. *serdadu* - Indian soldier (Sikh) (with British army right after Jap. occupation).

uber peng- pursuer. *tukang - cewek* woman-chaser.

ubi *ada - ada talas (ada budi ada balas)* 1 tit for tat. 2 nothing for nothing. - *halia* artichoke. - *manis* sweet potato. - *pohon* cassava.

ubin - *porselen* wall tile.

ubleg (s.) NGUBLEG.

ucap ber- *kata* to say. **-an:** *dlm* ~ *dan perbuatan* in word and deed. ~ *penutup* closing address.

ucel (me)ng- to crumple, crush.

uda term of address for man.

udak.udak to chase o.a.

udal meng-.- to reveal.

udang - *api.api* (k.o. sea shrimp) endeavor. - *bago* tiger prawn. - *barong* lobster tails. - *basah* fresh shrimp. - *dogol* pink shrimps. - *jerbung* banana prawns, white shrimps. - *karang* lobster tails. - *kipas* Spanish lobster. - *menjangan* banana prawns, white shrimps. - *pancet* tiger prawn. - *penganten (,putih)* banana prawns, white shrimps. - *tokal* fresh water shrimp. - *windu* tiger prawn.

udan.iris k.o. batik design.

udara ke-an (adj.) air. *perjajian* ~ air treaty. **meng-** 1 to be in the air. 2 to be aired (on the radio). **meng-kan** 1 to broadcast. 2 to televise.

udik I *pulang* **m-** *ke kampung* to return to o's rural home or birth place.

udik II -.- a Jav. ceremony held in the afternoon before the two *Sekaten gamelans* are taken back to the *Kraton* in Yogyakarta.

udut ng- to smoke.

uged.uged and **uget.uget** caddis(-worms).

ugel.ugel(an) ankles.

uhau loyal to o's parents.

uitkéring payment.

uitklaring clearance (from Customs).

ujar -an speech.

uji meng-.coba to test (mil. equipment). **peng-** assayer. **peng-an** assay. **-an** to take an exam. *Dlm bln Oktober dia akan ~,* He'll take his examination in October. ~ *her* re-examination. ~ *kandidat* B.A. examination. ~ *kenaikan kelas* promotion examination (in school). ~ *praktek* practical examination. ~ *saringan* screening examination. ~ *sarjana muda* B.A. examination. -.*jalan* to test-drive.

ujug.ujug all of a sudden.

ujung *dr - dunia ke - dunia yg lain* from o. end to the other. *dr - kaki hingga - rambut* from head to toe. -.-**nya** it finally turned out (that). - *panah* arrowhead.

Ujung Pandang and **Ujungpandang** the new name for Makas(s)ar.

u/k [uang keluar] debits.

ukhrowi otherworldly, heavenly.

ukir -an design (on cloth).

ukon (s.) UANG (MAS UKON).

ukur ber-an to measure (v.i.). *16 meriam yg ~ 100 mm* sixteen 100-mm guns. **meng-:** ~ *bayang.bayang sepanjang badan* to cut your coat according to your cloth. ~ *keberanian* sizing e.o. up. ~ *tempat tidur* to go to bed. **peng-:** ~ *ampere (,arus)* ammeter. ~ *bunyi* audiometer. ~ *gigi perangko* perforation gauge (for stamps). ~ *jam ampere* ampere-hour meter. ~ *jarak* telemeter. ~ *kalori* calorimeter. ~ *suara* sound-finder (artillery). ~ *tinggi* altimeter.

peng-an *tinggi* altimetry. **-an:** ~ *kapal* admeasurement (of ship). ~ *vital* vital statistics. ~ *yg berlaku* accepted measure.

ulama (Moslem) clergyman.

ulang *verb* + - to re-(verb). **ber-:** ~ *kali* frequently, repeatedly, again and again. *Selamat* ~ *th dan semoga diberi umur panjang!* Many happy returns of the day and long life to you! **meng-.-** *kaji lama* to rake up old stories. -.*alik* commuting. *pelayanan* -.*alik* commuter service. **peng-.alik** commuter.

ulap I ng-in to beckon to.

ulap II young raw vegetables.

ular - *bukan ikanpun bukan* (neither) fish nor fowl. - *beludak* adder. - *puspokajang (,sanca)* python. - *tedung* cobra. - *tiung* k.o. poisonous snake.

ulas ber- *tangan* (s.) BERSAMBUNG (TANGAN).

ulayat *harto* - a form of property under the authority of the village, the *nagari*, as a whole; it consists mainly of forest tracts which had never been cultivated surrounding the village. *tanah* - the communal reserved land.

uli menguléni to mix, knead.

ulin *kayu* - ironwood.

ulos Batak traditional woven scarf.

ultah [ulang tahun] 1 anniversary. 2 birthday. **ber-** to celebrate the anniversary of s.t.

ultimatum ultimatum. **meng-** to deliver an ultimatum.

ultra- ultra-. -.*modern* ultramodern.

ulu.ulu a minor village officer in charge of irrigation.

uluk -an 1 shout. 2 loud greeting.

ulung ... *yg* - an arch-... *pencoleng* - a hard-boiled thief.

ulur meng- to put off, postpone. **meng-.-** *waktu* filibustering. **peng-an** *waktu* postponement. **-an** *tangan* gesture.

u/m [uang masuk] credits.

uma (among the people of Mentawai island, off Sumatra's west coast) longhouse.

umak.umik to quiver (of lips).

umara(k) and **umarok** 1 (Moslem) government (,authority). 2 official, functionary.

umbai - *cacing* appendix.

umbar ng- to let loose. ~ *hawa nafsu* emotional; to give vent to o's strong feelings.

umbul -.- *merah* k.o. folk art resembling the *doger* of Jakarta.

umpan - *balik* feedback. - *meriam* cannon fodder.

umrah and **umroh** the so-called minor haj to Mecca; (s.) HAJI (KECIL). *visa* - visa with a 2-week validity issued to persons who want to make the *umroh* by going via Saudi Arabia. (It turns out, however, that many of these persons did not want to return to Indonesia).

umum *di muka* - in public. *perang tak* **di-kan** an undeclared war.

umur *blm sampai (,cukup)* - underage. *cukup* - adult, mature. *Sdr. akan panjang -!* Talk of the devil and he will appear! **ber-:** ~ *separuh jalan* at the awkward age. *sdh* ~ advanced in years. *Dia sdh* ~ *lima puluh ke atas,* He is over fifty. **se-:** ~ *dunia* as old as the world. ~ *jagung* very young. ~ *manusia* a lifetime. ~ *zaman* for many years to come.

unanim unanimously.

uncèn watchman.

undag stairs.

undagi carpenter. **ke-an** and **per-an** carpentry.

undak -.-an podium.

undang I di-kan to be legislated. *U-. U-Pekaryaan* Employment Act.

undang II meng- 1 to invite (s.o. formally, to attend a party, etc.). 2 to provoke, cause. ~ *tawa* to provoke laughter.

undat meng- to hurl blame at s.o.

unduh ng-: ~ *mantu* to acquire a son- or daughter-in-law. ~ *pengantin (,temantèn)* the festive reception of the newlyweds by the bridegroom's family.

undur meng-kan *tanggal* to postdate. **peng-an** *pembayaran* moratorium.

- *diri* to resign.

uneg.uneg and **unek.unek** embitterment, exasperation, loathing. *mengeluarkan* - to say what is on o's mind, get it off o's chest.

unggah-unggah to show respect to o.a. or to others in conformity with e.o.'s position and dignity.

unggul di-kan (in sports) to be seeded.

ungkap meng-kan to disclose, reveal, make known.

ungkir meng-i (S.) MEMUNGKIRI.

ungsep ng- to crash. *Pesawat terbang* ~ *di gunung,* The aircraft crashed in the mountains.

unikum unique specimen.

unisèks unisex.

univèrsitas ber- to attend a university. **ke-an** (adj.) university. *kalangan* ~ university circles.

unjan (fish)lure.

unjuk - *gigi* to show o's teeth, show hostility, threaten angrily.

unsur meng-i to constitute the elements of.

untai -an circuitry.

untal ng- 1 to swallow (without chewing). 2 to annex. *Vested Interests* ~ *Pabrik,* Vested Interests annex Factories. **-.-an** to shake off.

untit meng- to pursue.

untu tooth.

untuk - *anak.anak (,ibu)* bribe.

untul (in Purwokerto, Central Java) assistant to the *tukang ogam.*

untung *mendapat banyak* - to make money. *ada yg -, ada yg buntung o.* man's meat is another man's poison. **ber-** 1 prosperous. 2 advantageous, helpful. **keber-an** good fortune. **se-.-nya** not exceeding, not more than. **-nya** fortunately, luckily. -.*buntungnya* the way it turns out.

unyeng k.o. roulette, practiced on a small scale, consisting of a black disc with numbers along its perimeter, running from 1 through 12. A needle is attached to the outside edge. The disc is spun, and if the number indicated

by the needle is the o. bet on by the player then the man will be paid 12 times the amount he bet.

upacara di-i to be made official with a ceremony. *U- Wishuda Para* Wing Day.

upah - *tempa.uang* mintage. - *tulis* legalization fee. - *yg dibawa pulang* take-home pay.

upakara take care of.

upasaka novice Buddhist priest.

upeti 1 (oil) royalties. 2 bribe.

upgrade **meng-** to upgrade. **peng-an** upgrading.

upil nasal mucus, snot. **ng-** to pick o's nose.

upleg to pile up.

uplek lively, busy, noisy.

ura.ura (s.) URO.URO.

urak -an boorish, ill-mannered. *orang* ~ person with crude boorish manners.

urang awak Minangkabau people (term used for themselves).

urap -.- vegetables mixed with grated coconut and spices. - *sari* miscellaneous.

urat ber-.berakar ingrained. - *bumi* train. - *nadi* (fig.) lifeblood.

urgèn urgent.

urgènsi urgency.

uro.uro to sing for o's own pleasure. *tukang becak yg jalannya lambat sambil* - a slow-peddling pedicab driver singing for his own pleasure.

urug and **uruk ke-(an)** overloaded, overburdened. **peng-an** *tanah* land reclamation. **ter-** *salju* buried in an avalanche of snow.

urun - *rembug* to state o's mind.

urung *kagak* - ultimately, eventually. *tak - dr* not exempt from. *tetapi tak -* yet, still.

urus *Saya* **ber-an** *banyak,* I'm busy. *tdk* **ke-an** neglected. **kepeng-an** management, administration. **meng-i** (s.) MENGURUSKAN. **peng-:** ~ *darurat* care taker. ~ *harian* executive (committee). ~ *pusat* general executive board. ~ *tata.usaha* administrator. **peng-an** maintenance. ~ *barang* cargo handling. ~ *ketata.usahaan* administrative management. **-an** section, department, division. *Itu 'kan ~ belakang,* That's after all a matter for later concern. *Saya banyak ~* I'm busy. *Departemen U~ Veteran* Department for Veteran Affairs. ~ *dinas* official duties. ~ *perburuhan* labor matters.

urut logical (of thought). **-nya** *surat kami tgl. 2 Mei* following our letter of May 2. **meng-:** ~ *dada* (fig.) to be nonplussed. *tinggal ~ dada* to look blank. ~ *muka* facial massage. ~ *rambut* cream rinse. **-an:** ~ *cerita* continuity, plot (of a movie, etc.). ~ *kata* (gramm.) word order. ~ *pertama (,terakhir)* first (,last) place in o's class. *Filem Indonesia jatuh ke ~ ketiga,* Indonesian films have fallen to third place.

usaha *atas -* 1 sponsored by. 2 at the instigation of. **ber-** *sendiri* to be self-employed. **kepeng-an** 1 entrepreneurial. 2 enterpreneurship. **meng-kan** to run (a business). **peng-:** ~ *pembuat kunci duplikat (,tiruan)* locksmith. ~ *rumah gelap* madam (female in charge of whore house). ~ *toko* shopkeeper. **per-an:** ~ *benah tubuh* figure salon. ~ *bongkar.muat* stevedoring company. ~ *campuran* joint enterprise. *P~ Dagang Negara* State Trading Company. ~ *gabungan* joint enterprise. ~ *guna (,jasa) umum* public utility company. ~ *kartu. kredit* creditcard company. *P~ Listrik Negara* State Electric and Power Company. ~ *manfaat umum* public utility company. ~ *mentega.keju (,kiju)* dairy factory. ~ *nasional WNI* non-native national enterprise. *P~ Negara* State Corporation. [The three types of State Corporations are: (a) *P~ Negara Jawatan* Departmental Agency, (b) *P~ Negara Umum* Public Corporation and (c) *P~ Negara Perseroan* Public/State Company]. ~ *pemasakan karet* remilling factory. ~ *pemborong dan bangunan* firm of building contractors. ~ *pencuci mobil* car wash, auto laundry. ~ *penerbangan* airline. ~ *pengangkutan* transport company. ~ *penjamin* underwriter

(i.e. an agent who underwrites insurance). ~ *penyosohan beras* rice hulling works. ~ *samping* subsidiary business, branch establishment. ~ *yg (bersifat) cepat (,lambat) menghasilkan* quick-(,slow-)yielding enterprise. *- asuransi* insurance business. *- gabungan (,kongsi ,patungan)* joint venture. *- pemerintah* government initiative. *- tempel.menempel* patchwork.

usahawati businesswoman.
usai *se-* ... after ... has finished, after finishing ...
usang obsolete, archaic.
usap **-an** caress.
Usdèkis supporter of the *Usdek.*
usia **ber-** at the age of. ~ *lanjut* advanced in years. *- pensiun* retirement age.
usiawan elderly person.
usik *blm pernah* **di-** (fig.) untouched, virgin. **ter-** troubled, annoyed. *- hati* intuition.
usil I *suka - mengurusi persoalan orang lain* to like to meddle in other people's business. *tdk mau -* 1 don't care about. 2 don't mind.
usil II [uang siluman] bribe, often referred to as 'invisible costs.'
usir **meng-** *rasa kantuk* to chase away sleep.
uskup **ke-an** *agung* archbishopric.
usreg 1 commotion. 2 busily engaged in.
ustana tomb (of the sovereigns of Pagarruyung).
ustaz 1 male Moslem religious teacher. 2 Lord. 3 (s.) GURU (MENGAJI). 4 professor in *madrasah.*
ustazah female Moslem religious teacher.
usul *ilmu - = usuluddin* knowledge of the tenets of Islam (based on the Koran, recommendations of the Prophet, analogy in Moslem theology and consensus of Moslem theological opinion). **peng-** *interpelasi* questioner.
usut **meng-** *jejak* to trace s.t.
usyah (S.) USAH.
utang (s.) HUTANG. **ng-** to be in debt, be in the red. ~ *kanan.kiri (,sana.sini)* to be everywhere in the red, be deeply

(,desperately) in debt, be up to o's ears in debt. **ng-in** to buy s.t. on credit. *Sayè ~ kaèn,* I bought cloth on credit.

utara ter- northernmost.

utik ng- to bother, pester. **ng-.-** to fiddle (around) with. **-.-an** tinkering, fiddling with.

Utopi(a) Utopia.

utuh in good condition.

uuuh pooh!

uwa.uwa gibbon.

uwak.uwak burrowing marine worm.

uwal - *dr* to depart from, turn aside from.

uwé I (personal pronoun).

uyel.uyelan to jostle e.o.

uzur I menstruation. *datang -nya* she has her period.

uzur II old.

V

vacum vacuum.

vakansi vacation, holiday. **ber-** to be (away) on vacation.

vaksin vaccine. **mem-** to vaccinate, inoculate.

vaksinasi vaccination. **mem-** to vaccinate, inoculate.

vasèktomi vasectomy.

VBS [Visa Berdiam Sementara] Temporary Resident Visa (an immigration document).

veem **di-kan** to be stored in a warehouse (in port areas). **per-an** wharfage business.

végétaris *seorang* - a vegetarian.

végétasi vegetation.

Vénésia Venice.

Vénésuéla Venezuela.

vèntilator ventilator.

verbalisan summoner.

Verklaring van Ingezetenschap Certificate of Inhabitantship.

vèrkoper salesman.

vermaak (s.) PERMAK.

Vèspa motor scooter.

vèsted interèst kaum - those with vested interests.

véteran di-kan to be retired from service.

vètsin monosodium glutimate.

viaduk viaduct.

vibrafon vibraphone.

vibrasi vibration. **ber-** to vibrate.

vidéo and **vidio** video. *pita* - video tape. - *kaset* video cassette.

Vietkong and **Vièt Kong** Vietcong, Viet Cong, V.C.

Vietnam Vietnam. - *Selatan (,Utara)* South (,North) Vietnam.

Vietsèl [Vietnam Selatan] South Vietnam.

Viètut [Vietnam Utara] North Vietnam.

vikaris vicar. - *apostolik* apostolic vicar.

viksi fiction.

vil(l)a villa.

violèt violet.

violis violist.

vipiawan and **VIPiawan** (male) V.I.P.

vipiawati and **VIPiawati** (female) V.I.P.

Virgi.Tab trade-mark of medicinal capsule to increase women's sexual potency (extract from the *tabat barito* root found in Central Kalimantan along the Barito River).

virologi virology.

virus virus.

visa - *dinas* service visa. - *diplomatik* diplomatic visa. - *kehormatan* courtesy visa. - *kunjungan* visitor's visa. - *transit* transit visa. - *turis* tourist visa.

visum post mortem. - *repertum* (doctor's) report on person's death for legal purposes.

vitamin vitamine. - *D* [vitamin Duit] (coll.) dough, money.

vivéré péricoloso **ber-** to live dangerously, pursue brinkmanship (under President Soekarno).

VOC [Verenigde Oostindische Compagnie] Dutch East India Company (1602–1800).

vokabulèr vocabulary.

vokatif vocativ.

vol volume control.
volontèr unsalaried clerk.
volt(a)mèter voltmeter.
Volksraad (col.) People's Council, k.o.
   embryonic parliament.
Volta.Hulu Upper-Volta.
voltase voltage.
von(n)is verdict. *menjatuhkan* - to pass
   a verdict. **di-** to be sentenced to. ~
   bebas to be acquitted (a prisoner of
   a charge). **memv-** to pass sentence on.

voorfinanciering pre-financing.
voorverkoop advance sale.
Vorstenlanden the Sultanates of Yogyakarta and Surakarta.
Vrisaba Taurus.
VS (pron. fé-ès) -*nya* her vital statistics.
vulkanisasi memv-kan to vulcanize.
vulkanit vulcanite.
vulkanolog volcanologist.
vuurcontact firefight.

W

wabah me- to be epidemic (of a disease).
   - *raya* pandemic.
wacana discourse.
wadag corporeal, physical.
wadah coalition (of political parties).
wadam [wanita adam] homosexual,
   transvestite.
wadat ber- unmarried.
wad(d)uh wow! (exclamation of surprise).
wadi I 1 secret that may not be disclosed.
   2 mysterious.
wadi II river basin.
wadon woman.
waduh(ai) wow!
waduk dam. - *listrik* condenser.
Wagé the fourth day of the five-day week.
wagon (S.) WAHON. - *restorasi* dining-
   car.
wah heavens! my! wow! *W- enaknya!*
   How delicious they were!
waha oasis.
wahab Giver (= God).
wahadah and **wahadat** unity (of God).
waham - *kebesaran* megalomania.
wahana vehicle.
wahdaniah 1 unity. 2 unanimity.
wahdat individually.
wahdatul Islamiah Islamic association.
wahèng (s.) WAING.
wahi revelation through vision or dream.
wahyu *W- kpd Yahya* the Revelation (of
   St. John the Divine). - *cakraningrat*
   1 godlike powers bestowed on mortals.
   2 the charisma of President Soekarno.

wai (in names of rivers of southern Sumatra) river.
Waicak Buddhist Holy Day of commem-
   orating the three important events in
   Buddha's life: his birthday, attainment
   of Buddhahood and his death.
wain(g) to sneeze.
Waisak (s.) WAICAK.
wajah ber- ... with a facade of ...
wajar plain, without embellishment.
wajib ke-an *membayar* 1 obligation to
   pay. 2 liabilities. **pe-** *militer* conscript.
   - *lapor* to have the obligation to report.
   - *latih (,tentara)* conscript. - *pajak*
   siluman tax evader.
waka [wakil kepala] assistant head.
wakaf pe- benefactor.
wakil me-kan to justify. **per-an** liaison
   unit. ~ *diplomatik* diplomatic representation. **ter-i** to be represented. -
   komandan second in command.
waktu - *malam (,pagi ,sore ,dll.)* in the
   evening (,morning ,afternoon ,etc.).
   dlm - singkat ini shortly, before (very)
   long, at an early date, in the near
   (,immediate) future, in the course of
   the next few days. *dlm - yg bersamaan*
   simultaneously. *dlm - yg sesingkat.*
   singkatnya (,sependek.pendeknya) in
   the shortest time possible. *dr - ke -*
   from time to time. *pd - ini* at this time
   (,moment). *pd - ini juga* right now,
   this very moment (,minute). *pd - itu*
   juga at the same time. *sampai - ini* up

till now. *sebarang* - 1 at any time. 2
always. *sedikit* - *lagi* in the near future.
setiap - any time. *tdk menurut* - 1
unpunctual. 2 irregular. *utk beberapa*
- *lamanya* for some time. *utk* - *yg tdk
ditentukan* indefinitely, for an indefinite time. *Dia mempunyai (,punya ,ada)*
-, He could afford the time. *(me)makan
(,menelan)* - time-consuming. *membuang* - to waste time. - *berarti duit*
time is money. *sang* - time. *sang* -
berjalan dgn cepatnya time flies. **-nya**:
sdh ~ it is time. *~ tlh sangat mendesak*
it is high time. *tepat pd ~* timely.
sebelum ~ 1 anticipated. 2 interim.
sdh lewat ~ expired, lapsed. - *belajar*
apprenticeship, period of study. -
bertelurnya kalkun the turkey's laying
season. - *datang* the future tense. -
dinas length of service. - *itu* in those
days. - *lampau* the past. - *luang* spare
time. - *menjenguk* visiting hours (in
hospital). - *penyerahan* time of delivery. - *telu (,tiga)* a modified form of
Islam found in parts of Lombok. -
tolok standard time. - *turun ke sawah*
period of rice field tilling. - *yg paling
sibuk* peak hours.

wakuncar [wajib kunjung pacar] (student sl.) 'duty to visit o's girl friend,'
i.e. visit. *Sok interview kalau ada
ceweq cantik, nanya alamat segala,
maksudnya biar bisa* **di-in,** Pretending
to carry out an interview when there
is a pretty girl, asking for her address
and all that jazz, with the intention
that he could pay her a visit.

walakhir finally.

walangsangit noxious bug for rice plant,
a stink beetle.

walat punishment from higher powers.

waledan arrears, balance.

walèh straightforward, plainspoken.

walèt swallow (the bird).

walhal notwithstanding.

wali 1 saint, apostle (of Islam in Java);
in full, - *Allah* and -*ullah.* 2 name of
the first preachers of Islam in Java
who as leaders commanded power

over the areas converted to Islam
under the title of *Sunan* and who at
present are still venerated as saints.
ke.W-kota.an mayoral. *W- Sanga
(,Songo)* the first nine (,*sanga* in Jav.)
walis who spread Islam over Java, the
Great Proselytizers; they were, among
others, *Sunan (Ng)ampel, Sunan Kali-
jaga, Sunan Giri* and *Sunan Gunung
Jati. Team W-songo* the team established by Presidential Decree #61 on
September 4, 1971; its official name
is *Tanjung Priok Port Control Team;*
purpose: to put an end to malversations
in the port area of Tanjung Priok. 3
male next of kin, and as such nearest
guardian whose consent is required for
the wedding of a girl or woman and
who represents her in person or writing during the solemnization of her
marriage before the *penghulu.* - *hakim*
authority (the *penghulu,* for instance)
who acts as *wali,* in the absence of
appropriate male nearest relative, appointed by Court. *surat* - the written
consent of the *wali* for the solemnization of the wedding of a girl or woman
for whom he is the guardian. - *murid*
(in school) guardian, i.e. the person to
whose care a student is committed.
- *nagari* (in West Sumatra) village head.
- *pemilih* elector. *W-yul Amri Daruri
Bisysyaukah* 'The President of the
Country though not Perfect should
be strong,' i.e. the designation conferred upon President Soekarno in the
1950s by the *NU*-party.

walik the green wild pigeon.

walikukun name of a tree with very hard
and tough wood (L. Scheutenia obo-
vata).

wallah God!

waloh and **waluh** pumpkin.

waluku ber- to plough.

wamilda [wajib militer darurat] emergency conscription.

Wan title given to descendants of chiefs
not of royal blood.

wana (s.) WANNA.

wanadri wilderness, terrain. *pendidikan* - terrain familiarization (for mountaineers).

Wanapati Forestry Minister.

wanda syllable.

wandu hermaphrodite, transvestite.

wanèh ka-an by chance, accidentally.

wangkang outrigger canoe, a Chinese ocean-going junk.

wangsa family, relatives.

wangsit inspiration from supernatural power, spiritual guidance.

wanita - *adam* (abbrev. *wadam*) transvestite. - *gituan* prostitute. - *metakil (,mutakil)* shrew, scolding woman. - *panggilan* call girl. - *plesiran* prostitute. - *tunasusila* prostitute.

wanna Chinese term for Indonesians. *Sama* - *boleh kasih makan tapi jangan kasih tahu cara cari makan,* (well-known saying among Chinese in Medan) You may give food to native Indonesians but don't tell them how to get it.

wantilan 1 o.-man sawmill operation. 2 sawmill for ironwood.

wanti.wanti to admonish, warn. **di-** to be repeatedly urged to.

wanua (in the southern Celebes) village.

Wapres [Wakil Presiden] Vice-President.

wara ber- abstinent.

warakawuri widow of an Armed Forces member.

warana screen.

waranggana 1 nymph. 2 female singer, lady crooner.

waras *kurang* - *otaknya, otaknya tiada* - *lagi* and *pikirannya tdk* - 1 mad. 2 frantic.

warembol bun, roll.

warga berke-an to have citizenship. *orang yg tdk* ~ a stateless person. **ke-an** *negara* 1 civic consciousness. 2 civics. **ke- duniaan** cosmopolitan(ism). **se-** allied, related. - *ABRI* member of the Armed Forces (of the Republic of Indonesia). - *dunia* cosmopolite. - *Eropa* European. *150* - *Eropa dibunuh pemberontak Zaire,* 150 Europeans were killed by Zairian rebels. - *jagat* cosmopolite. - *masyarakat* citizen (of a community). - *Nah(l)ijen [,Nah(l)ijin]* members of the NU party, NU'ers. - *negara asli* citizen by birth. - *negara bunglon* bipatride. - *negara kelas kambing* second-class citizen. - *negara tiri* second-class citizen. - *sekolah* pupil.

warkat - *niaga* commercial paper, such as, checks, promissory notes, bills of exchange and other negotiable paper used in business. - *pos udara* aerogram.

warmbol (s.) WAREMBOL.

warna ber-: ~ *gading* cream-colored. ~.*warni* colorful. - *keramat* 'sacred colors,' i.e. the national colors: red and white. - *hijau lapangan* fieldgreen (of army uniform). - *sawo* 1 brown. 2 flesh-colored. - *sawo matang (,tua)* dark brown. - *suara* timbre.

warok 1 master, expert. 2 leader. 3 village chief.

warsa year.

Warsawa Warsaw.

warta Pe- *Rahayu* the Gospel. - *yudha* war news.

wartawan - *amplop* 'envelope newsreporter,' i.e. a newsreporter who receives envelopes filled with money, for writing nicely about certain events. - *potret* photo journalist. - *tulis* newsman. - *yg tdk terikat kpd suatu suratkabar* freelancer.

waru spade (in card games).

waruga ancient grave.

warung a roadside food booth usually consisting of a small wood and straw hut with a central table. The customers sit on o. side, usually on a long bench, and the persons who prepare the food stand on the other. - *keliling* k.o. chuck wagon pushed by a man. - *pengecer* retail shop. - *pinggir jalan* roadside stall. - *remeng.remeng* 'obscure roadside stall,' i.e. a roadside stall which, besides selling food and drinks, also makes available waitresses to entertain male visitors; disguised brothel.

wasana end, close. - *kata* closing words.

wasangka - *yg jelek* fallacious ideas.

wasilkan to convey (a letter).

wasir (S.) BAWASIR.

wasit me-i to umpire, act as umpire of.
pe(r)-an arbitration.

wasi.wasiyat executor of an estate.

waskita and waskitha to foresee the future, be prophetic. orang - clairvoyant.

waspada.éling self-knowledge and self-
control.

Wastra Prèma the association of Indonesian batik and textiles lovers.

waswas - hati anxious.

wat I watt.

wat II Buddhist temple.

watak pe- character (in a play). pe-an
role, character.

watas me-i to modify.

wat(h)an native country.

wat(h)ania (adj.) native country.

waton - garang, sanajan garing all is not
gold that glitters.

watuna(s) (s.) WANITA (TUNASUSILA).

wawa and wauwau the long-armed black
gibbon.

wawancara ber- dgn and me-i to interview. pe- interviewer. - tivi (,tipi) TV-
interview.

wawankata dialogue.

wawanmuka face-to-face. komunikasi -
a face-to-face communication.

wawanrembug dialogue.

wawas ber-an to state o's viewpoint. -an
1 view(point). ~ Nusantara archipelagic
principle which will give Indonesia
control over use of what are now considered international waters; archipelagic state concept. 2 outlook.
3 vision.

Wayan (in Bali) name element placed
before personal names to indicate the
first born child, such as, Wayan Diya.

wayang - gedog performance using leather
puppets; gedog means 'horse,' because
Raden Panji, the prince of Janggala,
the hero of this show, bears titles which
signify 'horse,' e.g. Kuda Wanengpati,
Undakan Wasengsari, Inu Jaran, etc.
- golek performance in which clothed
three-dimensional wooden puppets are

used, with stories of the Amir Hamza
cycle in Central Java and the Ramayana
and Mahabharata stories in West Java.
- k(e)litik [,k(e)rucil] show in which
flat wooden puppets with leather arms
are used with stories of Damar Wulan
as themes. - madia (,madya) shadow
play with stories based on 19th century
poetry describing events connected with
the reign of the prophet-king Djojobojo.
- Pancasila shadow play in which the
five Pandawas are symbolically presented as the Pancasila. - pompa show with
puppets made of rubber; if used they
are inflated (,dipompa); the show using
this k.o. puppet was first put on by
students of the Gadjah Mada University, Department of Forestry, in Yogyakarta to disseminate information to
the people. - purwa performance in
which leather puppets project their
shadows on a canvas, which is tech-
nically called kelir; probably the oldest
of the wayang shows, with lakons based
on the Mahabharata and Ramayana.
- topeng (s.) TOPENG. - wong show
with living actors who are not masked;
they themselves speak.

wayuh 1 to have more than o. wife. 2
polygamy. ber- to commit bigamy.

wazir (S.) BAWASIR.

W.C. (pron. wésé) toilet, restroom. per-
an toilet (,restroom) system.

W.C.-nisasi the encouragement to install
restrooms.

wédang - kopi hot coffee.

Wedatama (Book of) Jav. ethics.

wedi pe-an (jur.) accession.

wedung and wedhung k.o. cleaver.

wegah averse.

wèger to misfire.

wekas the last. Rebo W-an the last
Wednesday in the month of Safar
(commemorated by the people
living at the southern edge of
Yogyakarta).

welas memelas pitiful, pitiable. - asih
pity, sympathy. - tanpo alis get no
thanks for earlier benefits.

wèlwèlan to tremble like a leaf.

wenang ber-: *pihak yg* ~ the competent
authorities. *sumber.sumber yg* ~ *mengatakan, bhw* ...competent circles
stated that ... **di-kan** to be authorized.
perse-.-an reign of terror.

wèrak and wèrèk di- to be recruited as a
laborer.

wereng 1 pitch-black, stony insect the
size of a rice kernel (L. Nilaparvata
lugens). 2 (in Banyuwangi, East Java)
prostitute.

werit 1 holy, awe-inspiring. 2 unsafe
(due to tigers or bandits). 3 weird
4 ominous, sinister.

Wèsak (s.) WAICAK.

wésé (s.) W.C.

wèsel short for *poswesel.* **me-kan** to
transmit (money) by postal money
order.

wèselbor switchboard.

wèselpos (s.) POSWESEL. **di-kan** to be
transmitted by postal money order.

wesi iron. - *aji* 'precious weapon,' such
as, the kris.

wèsminster (s.) JAM (WESMINSTER).

wèsternisasi westernization.

wèt law.

weton birthday determined by combin-
ing the five-day week and the seven-
day week, e.g. *Selasa Kliwon.*

wewangian perfumes.

wewarah instruction, teaching.

wewaton 1 rule, regulation. 2 yardstick.

wéwé (female) forest ghost.

weweja (in Java) (s.) ECENG.

wéwéka 1 precaution. 2 to take pre-
cautions. 3 cautious(ness).

wewengkon supremacy, control.

wewohan (in Java) (s.) ECENG.

wibawa ber- authoritative. **berke-an** *(utk)*
to have the authority (to).

wicaksana 1 to foresee. 2 with clear in-
sight. **ke-an** statesmanship, wisdom.

wicitra motion-picture theater, movie
house.

widya wisdom. **ber- wisata** to make a
study tour. - *iswara* lecturer. - *wisata*
study tour. *W- Yudha* 'War Wisdom,'

i.e. a training exercise for 3rd and 4th
year cadets of the General and Ground
Forces Department of the Armed Forces
Academy to test their ability in leadership and range of thinking in leading
a platoon to attack an enemy target.

wigah.wigih timid, diffident. *tdk* - undaunted.

wigih *tak* -.- not hesitate.

wihara Buddhist place of worship.

wijaya victorious. - *mala(,mulia,kesuma)*
a legendary flower (of the *sentolong*
plant, k.o. pisonia) which brought all
it touched to life. It is found on the
rocky islet of Majeti, east of *Nusakambangan* island off Java's southcoast.

Wiku Yudha Wirottama (motto of the
Infantry Training Center) Master of
Military Science.

wilahar lake.

wilayah per-an regional. - *industri* industrial estate. - *udara* air space.

wilis (dark) green.

Wil.Wo the system of 'to be touched (in
order to ask for o's attention; = *dijawil)*
and then to be dragged along *(= digo-
wo);'* this system has been introduced
into East Java to make family planning
a success.

winaya - *diri* self-discipline.

wingit impressive, inspiring.

wingking rear. *Wanita Indonesia bukan
konco -,* The Indonesian woman is not
just a friend who belongs in the back
of the house, i.e. the kitchen.

wiracarita epic.

wiraga swift in action.

wirama (S.) IRAMA.

wirapraja statesman. **ke-an** statesmanship.

wirasat 1 facial expression. 2 physiog-
nomy.

wiraswasta entrepreneur. **ke-an** enterpreneurship.

wirata(m)tama a handpicked soldier for
special services.

wirawati female soldier.

wira.wicara speaker.

wira.wiri to pace up and down.

wirid extra, personal prayers said after

the ritual prayers.

wisata excursion, tour. *bis - ber.AC* an air-conditioned tour bus. - *borongan* package tour. - *konvensi* convention tours.

wisatawati female tourist.

wi sèng palm wine.

wisésa powerful, mighty.

wishuda (s.) WISUDA. *W- Jurit* the promotion from Candidate Cadet to Cadet at the Armed Forces Academy.

wisik oracle.

wisit success.

wisma per-an housing. *W- Mulya Jaya* the rehabilitation center for prostitutes at Pasar Rebo (Jakarta) set up by the Department of Social Affairs. *W- Nusantara* a 30-story highrise accommodating various offices and a restaurant in Jakarta. - *ramah tamah* open house. *W-rini* the dormitory for coeds of the University of Indonesia at Bidaracina (Jakarta). - *tamu* guest house. *W- Warta* Press House. *W- Yaso* the Jakarta home in which President Soekarno died on October 5, 1972; now turned into the Armed Forces Struggle Museum.

Wisnu Vishnu, o. of the principal gods of Jav. mythology.

wisuda graduation, inauguration. **me-(kan)** to graduate (in university, college). **pe-an** *sarjana* commencement, graduation. *W- Purna Wira* ceremony at the end of o's assignment in army circles.

wisudawan male graduate (from university).

wisudawati female graduate (from university).

wisudha (s.) WISUDA.

witing tresno jalaran kulino a Solonese adage meaning: loves rises from proximity.

wiwaha ber- marriageable.

wiwéka (s.) WEWEKA.

wiwit a ritualistic ceremony before rice harvesting.

wiwitan beginning, origin.

wiyaga *gamelan* player.

wiyatapraja education service.

wiyatawan educationalist.

wiyatawisata study tour.

wiyosan birthday. *W- Dalem* Birthday of the *Sultan* (of Yogya).

wlijo middleman in the fishery industry who sells the fish he bought from another middleman directly to the wholesaler.

WNI *surat.surat* **ke.-.an** citizenship papers. **me.-.kan** *orang asing* to naturalize foreigners.

woki.toki *(alat)* - walkie-talkie.

wokwok ketekur the sound made by pigeons or doves. **ber-** to have a love affair.

wong man. - *angon bebek* boy who tends ducks. - *cilik* the little man, the small fry. - *ksamen* (in Bali) the Shudras. - *londo* Dutchman.

woreng lining.

wreda 1 old. 2 ex-, former.

wredatama a retired government employee.

wts [wanita tuna susila] prostitute. **per.-.an** (adj.) prostitute.

wudhu and **wudlu** (S.) WUDU.

wujud me-kan to accomplish, effect. **keter-an** realization.

wuku a 7-day cycle.

wulu - *wetu* agricultural products.

wungkul in full.

wungu purple, violet.

wuwu bow-net.

X

X (pron. èks) the letter x. *sinar X* X-ray. *perempuan X-2* a prostitute.

Y

ya 1 (at the end of the sentence) makes a statement, command or question less blunt. (I'm stating this, ordering this, or questioning this tentatively). *Apa -?* Really? *Bagaimana -?* What should I (,we) do? *Berapa -?* How much is it? Let me see, how much was it? *entah -* I don't know (polite). *Permisi -?* Excuse me, please. *Terima-kasih -,* Thank you. *Jangan nakal -,* Don't be naughty, OK? 2 (before the predicate) well (what should I say). *lauknya - masih perlu tambahan dr rumah* as for the side dishes, well they had to be supplemented from home (said by a prisoner). *Kalau tdk di Hong Kong, - di Singapura,* If he's not in Hong Kong, well he must be in Singapore. *Kalau mau kawin, - kawin,* If you want to get married, well get married. *Pegawai yg seharusnya dipensiun - dipensiun,* Employees who have to be retired, well they should be retired. *- ... - ...* (enumerating items) either ... or ..., (both) ... and ..., ... and ... *- pemandangan alamnya, - kesenian rakyatnya* its natural beauties and its folk arts. *- bawang, - kentang, - jeruk* onions, potatoes and oranges. *- Allah* Good Lord. *- halo* hello (said by person called to the phone).

yah long drawn out pronunciation of **ya**. *Y- kami ingin lihat.lihat dulu,* Weeell, we want to look around first.

yahud very good, fantastic.

yahudi peng-an judaisation.

yahut (s.) YAHUD.

Yahya John.

yais menopause.

yakin *harga yg cukup* **me-kan** a stiff price. *- se-.-nya* to be dead sure.

Yana Badra 'Salutary Path,' i.e. the initiation period students of the Basic School for Supply Officers of the Naval Supply School at Morokrembangan, Surabaya, have to undergo.

yang *Y- Di Pertuan Agung* title of the Malaysian Head of State. *- empunya* the haves; (s.) EMPUNYA. *- tak empunya* the have-nots. *- mana?* which o.? *buku - mana?* which book?

yan.oh edible bird's nest.

yargon jargon.

yarig (pron. yarikh) a year old; (s.) JARIG. *merayakan* **-nya** to celebrate o's birthday.

yasa 1 building. 2 structure, foundation.

yèl yell.

Yérus(s)alem Jerusalem.

Yésuit Jesuit.

yodisasi iodizing.

yodium *garam* **ber-** iodized salt.

yoga yoga. *ahli -* yogi.

yogia se-nya properly speaking, actually.

Yogya(karta) and **Yokya(karta)** = Jogja-(karta).

yok (s.) AYO.

yokal (in Irian Jaya) married woman's skirt.

yokwan k.o. Chinese *jamu* for increasing stamina.

you (the English) you, but only used to equals and persons of lower status than the speaker.... *kalau - gagal sekali ini, - tdk bisa motret saya lagi* ... if you fail this time (to take my picture), you can't shoot me again.

yoyo yo-yo (toy).

yubilium anniversary.

yuda (s.) YUDHA. *- kelana* straggler (in combat zone).

yudha *Y- Pratid(h)ina* Struggle without End, i.e. the slogan of the now defunct *Partai Nasional Indonesia;* in full: *Y-Pratid(h)ina Marhaenis* Marhaenist Struggle without End. *-warta* war news.

yudhya (s.) YUDHA.

yudisium announcement of passing and failing.

Yudistira *Prabu* - a *wayang* character also known as Puntadewa, the eldest of the *Pandawa* brothers.
yudo (s.) JUDO.
Yugo Yugoslavia.
yuk (s.) AYO.
yumèn [kayu.semèn] k.o. wallboard, a homogenous substance, mixture of waste lumber, cement and a chemical solution, cast in sheets of 2 meters x 1.5 meters x 25 millimeters, which after a one-week drying process be-

comes a component for walls in low-income housing projects; the sheets are fire, water, insect and soundproof.
yungyun ke- charmed, enchanted.
yunior junior.
yuridis legal.
Yustika Rini the women's organization under the jurisdiction of the Department of Justice and the Supreme Court.
yustisiil judicial.
yuyu rice paddy crab. - *kangkang* k.o. river crab.

Z

zaal (hospital) ward.
zadah *anak* - bastard.
zakat fitrah a religious tithe due on the last day of the fasting month (in proportion to o's ability to pay).
zakelijk (pron. sakelek) 1 businesslike. 2 practical.
zaman *manusia tiga* - o. who experienced the Dutch colonial period, the Jap. occupation and independence. - *sdh tua* the world is coming to an end. *menurut* - to keep up with the times. *sdh dimakan* -, *sdh tdk* men- *lagi* and *sdh lalu -nya* archaic, out of date. *sdh tdk sesuai dgn* - behind the times. - *atom* atomic age. - *baheula* the dim past. - *batu* the stone age. - *edan* 'crazy times,' times when order, security, norms and expectations are upset and at least temporarily suspended (mentioned in the *Djojobojo* prophecies). - *es* the ice age. - *kuda gigit besi* the olden days. - *normal* the period when prices were normal, i.e. the postwar Dutch period up to the transfer of

sovereignty (December 1949). - *purbakala* ancient times.
zat - *asam arang* carbon dioxide. - *lemas* nitrogen. - *pati* amylum. - *penangkal* antidote.
ziarah pe- 1 visitor (to a sacred place). 2 pilgrim.
zill ullah filalam (a sovereign is) the shadow of Allah (,God) on the world.
Zionis Zionist. *gerakan* - Zionism.
Zionisma and **Zionisme** Zionism.
zodiak zodiac.
zu 1 possessed of. *Iskander* - *l karnain* Alexander, the possessor of two horns, i.e. Alexander the Great. 2 endowed with.
Zulkaédah 1 the eleventh month of the Moslem year. 2 the month of the Truce (in which Arab feuds cease).
zus term of addressing a girl or woman about the same age as the male speaker. *Memang tas itu bagus sekali -!* Indeed the handbag is very nice, Miss!
zuster (S.) SISTER and SUSTER.
zuurzak (S.) SIRSAK.

SUPPLEMENT

A

abadi ke-an immortality.
acara kepeng-an advocacy.
acu meng-*(k)pd* to refer to.
adhi - *karya* masterpiece.
Adhimakayasa award for Armed Forces
  Academy Air Force cadets for excellent
  achievements.
adigang-adigung arrogant.
Adi.loka (in the Bina Graha, Jakarta)
  VIP-room.
adu - *ayu* beauty contest.
afdruk (of photo) print (made from a
  negative). **meng-** to have prints made.
agamis pertaining to religion, religious.
agèn - *samaran* undercover agent.
agènsi agency.
agribisnis agribusiness.
agung peng-.-an idolization.
ahli - *ekofertilitas* environmental fertility
  expert. - *fauna* zoologist. - *kandungan*
  gynecologist. - *kependudukan* demographer. - *urologi* urologist.
aib *tdk* **ber-** shameless.
Ai.con (in Malaysia) airconditioning.
air per-an *pedalaman* internal waters.
  - *kemih* urine. - *saringan* filtered
  water.
ajak -an persuasion.
ajudan di-i to be flanked by (two,
  three, etc.) adjutants.
akadémikus person who has obtained a
  diploma due to his passing the doctoral
  examination from a *fakultas;* (s.)
  SARJANA.
akaid, aka'id and **'akaid** dogma. *ilmu* -
  dogmatism.
akal *kehilangan* - to go crazy.
akan *tak* - and *takkan* isn't likely to.
  se-.- ostensibly.
akh (s.) AH.
akhir meng-i *masa lajangnya* to give up
  o's bachelorhood.
akidah 1 belief, faith. 2 confidence.
akréditasi accreditation. di-kan *kpd* to
  be accredited to.
akrobat *main* - to engage in sex.
aksèptor person, male as well as female,

who has expressed his (,her) willingness to apply birth control.
aktual topical. ke-an topicality.
aktuil meng-kan to actualize (v.t.).
alah *tdk* - *dgn* not less than.
alang *pak* - uncle between the eldest and
  the youngest.
alat per-an *dapur* kitchen utensils.
  - *pemanas air* water heater. - *pembakar*
  incinerator. - *penanak nasi* rice cooker.
  - *pencatat gempa* seismograph.
  - *pengering* dryer. - *penyembur api*
  flame thrower. - *penyemprot tangan*
  hand sprayer. - *penyuntik* injection
  syringe. - *perekam jantung* electro-
  cardiograph.
Ali Mohammad's cousin and
  son-in-law, the fourth Caliph.
aliènasi alienation.
alih -.- instead of. *Karena pengaruh
  bahasa Sunda "teu hasil" maka dlm BI
  pun dikatakan "blm hasil" ~ mengatakan "blm berhasil,"* Owing to the
  influence of Sundanese "teu hasil"
  also in Indonesian people say "blm
  hasil" instead of "blm berhasil."
alim ke-an *anak* (s.) KESALEHAN
  (ANAK).
alon.alon - *waton kelakon* slow but
  sure.
amariyah scenario.
ambil peng-alihan expropriation. peng-an
  suara voting.
amil -.*zakat* collector (,recipient) of
  religious tithes.
amit -.- I beg your pardon!
amplop meng-i to put in an envelope.
ampyang a delicacy using *gula Jawa*
  (brown sugar in lumps, half spheres,
  Jav. manufactured) and *kacang tanah*
  (ground nuts). *supermarket* - a supermarket which externally seems to be a
  native-run enterprise, but on closer
  look belongs to non-natives (usually
  Chinese); (cp.) ALIBABA and BABA.
  ALI.
anak - *isteri* children and wife. - *patung*
  doll. - *peliharaan* o. who gets special
  attention (,treatment) from a superior.

anéka meng-ragamkan to diversify.

ang ciu k.o. red Chinese liquor.

anggota - *sekutu* allied member (of an association, etc.).

angguk meng- to nod approvingly (,in approval).

anggurr graceful.

angin - *hantu* stroke (sudden attack of disease or illness, esp. of apoplexy or paralysis). - *limbubu* whirlwind. - *samirana* a soft breeze.

angka dial. - *kejahatan* crime rate.

angkasa meng- to rise.

angkat *sdh* ber- *remaja* to come of age. per-: ~ *keras* hardware. ~ *lunak* software. -an *kelima* the fifth column.

angkèt meng- to make use of the right of inquiry, inquire (into) (in *DPR* and *MPR*).

angon peng-an shepherding.

angpau Chinese red paper (in which money is wrapped for children during *Imlek* celebration).

anjing - *kurir* messenger dog. - *militer* war dog. - *pandu* scout dog.

anotasi annotation. ber- annotated.

antar -.*instansi* interagency.

antariksa 1 sky, firmament. 2 space.

anti meng-.karatkan to rustproof.

Antilla Belanda the Dutch Antilles.

apa *bukan* -.- 1 nothing. 2 there's no reason for it.

api *loncatan* - sparks.

arah penye- *arus* rectifier, i.e. a device which changes alternating current into direct current. se- *jarum jam* clockwise.

arang - *batok* charcoal made from coconut shells (an export commodity of the Northern Celebes).

arbitrèr arbitrary.

ardi I mountain.

ardi II, ardizi and arz earth.

arjuna boy friend, steady. - *idaman* idol.

asal *tdk* - *(ngomong)* not just (talk). *jangan* - *saja!* don't do it in a haphazard fashion! *penarikan* -.-an (the) symbolic withdrawal (of Russian troops from Afghanistan).

asap - *buangan* (from a bus, etc.) exhaust fumes (,gases).

asbun [asal bunyi] also, empty barrels make more noise.

asma - *bronkial* bronchial asthma.

asmaraloka world of love (,passion).

aspalisasi putting an asphalt surface on the streets.

asrar secret.

asuransi - *kebakaran* fire insurance. - *kecelakaan diri* personal accident insurance. - *kendaraan bermotor* motor vehicle insurance. - *kerusakan mesin.mesin* machinery breakdown insurance. - *ledakan ketel uap* boiler explosion insurance. - *pemasangan instalasi bangunan* construction all risks insurance. - *pembangunan gedung* contractor's all risks insurance. - *pengangkutan* cargo insurance. - *pengangkutan uang* cash-in-transit insurance. - *rangka kapal laut/udara* hull/aviation insurance.

atak meng- to arrange, order.

atraz 1 objection. 2 complaint.

atur keter-an regularity. *cara* meng- *pakaian* the way o. dresses. peng-: ~ *kamar* roomboy. ~ *redup terang lampu listrik* dimmer. -an *permainan* rule of the game.

avgas [aviation gasoline] aviation gasoline.

avtur [aviation turbo (fuel)] aviation fuel (for aircraft, helicopters, etc.).

awak - *darat* ground crew.

awang *angan (,cita. cita)* meng- to indulge in fantasies.

awas peng-an: ~ *pralaksana* pre-audit. ~ *purnalaksana* postaudit.

ayahan responsiblity, duty, task.

ayam - *negeri* (s.) AYAM (RAS); (opp.) - *kampung.* - *potong beku* frozen broiler. - *tukung* 1 a featherless chicken. 2 a tailless chicken. - *tulak* 1 a chicken with upright-standing feathers like a porcupine. 2 a spotted chicken.

Ayatollah Sign (,Miracle) of God; a religious teacher whose knowledge and piety is so highly respected that he is accepted as a special guide by believers. This is most common in the Shi'a community of Iran.

ayem to feel secure.

ayum meng- to abet. **-an** collision.

B

badminton badminton. **ber-** to play badminton.

baduta [(di) bawah umur dua tahun] under two years old. *anak* - toddler.

bagaimana 1 how shall I put it? 2 what do you mean? 3 how can it be! *Kamu ini -!* Oh you! How can you be like that! *jadi -?* get to the point! what do you think?

bagan lift net. - *gerak* movable lift net. - *tancap* unmovable lift net.

bagas sugar cane waste from sugar factory.

bagéa special Menadonese dish made from sago and wrapped in sagopalm leaves.

bagonjong (s.) RUMAH (BAGONJONG).

bahan - *madu* nectar. - *pencelup* dyestuffs.

bahasa - *lisan* spoken language. - *tubuh* body language.

bahaya - *primer* (of active volcano) eruption. - *sekunder* (of active volcano) cold lava stream.

baik *ada* **-nya** ... it would not be a bad idea to ...

bajidor (in Subang) (s.) KETUK (TILU).

bakar pem-an incinerator.

baku -nya the main ingredient.

bala *perang* - [perang rimba laut] lit. "jungle-and-sea war," i.e. a war waged to pursue the enemy in jungles and at sea.

baladupakan supernumerary (actor).

balai - *benih ikan (,udang galah)* fish (,lobster) hatchery. *B- Yasa* in Madiun for steam locomotives, *B- Yasa* in Yogyakarta for diesel locomotives, and *B- Yasa* in Bandung for bridges.

baldi (in Malaysia) bucket, basin. **se- a** bucketful.

balian (in the interior of South Kalimantan) (s.) DUKUN.

balik di- namakan to be transferred (of title).

bambu *sebilah* - a strip of bamboo used as a knife to cut the umbilical cord and for circumcision.

ban III - *serap* (pitying reference to) the Vice-President of the Republic of Indonesia.

ban IV (radio) band.

banci ke-an hermaphroditism.

bang *B- Noli* popular reference for Jakarta's governor H. Tjokropranolo.

bangkang pem- dissident.

bangkit ke-an *kembali* renaissance.

bangun (penis) is erect.

Banprès [Bantuan Presiden] Presidential Aid, i.e. special funds earmarked by the President.

bantal - *peluk* bolster, Dutch wife.

bantu pem-: ~ *all.in* (in the "Krakatau Steel" complex at Cilegon, West Java) a housemaid who next to taking care of the house of a 'bachelor,' has also to take care of her boss in the broadest sense of the word. ~ *Bupati* the former Wedana. ~ *Gubernur* the former *Residen*.

bapak *sifat* **mem-** (s.) BAPAKISME.

baru *(yg) tdk bisa* **diper-i** non-renewable.

barung the smallest unit in the *Pramuka* Boy Scout Movement consisting of *siagas;* membership maximum 10.

bas (in Malaysia) (S.) BIS and BUS.

basah -an (in Malaysia) common, of everyday occurrence. *bahasa* ~ colloquial language.

bata ter-.- halting (of speaking a language).

batang -an by the piece (of cigarettes, etc.).

bati m- 1 to favor o.s. at the cost of others. 2 to treat s.o. dishonestly.

batu renal calculus, kidney stone.

batuk - *teruk* tuberculosis cough.

bawa - *kendaraan sendiri* to go by o's own vehicle (usually, a car).

bawah di- komandokan *kpd* to be put under the command of.

bawang *bangsa pemakan* - thin-skinned, easily offended nation.

bayar - *kaul* to redeem a pledge.

bebalai (S.) BALAI(.BALAI).

becik - *ketitik, ala ketara* the good will make itself known, along with the bad.

bècuk (in Malaysia) noisy, loud (of talking).

bedebah (in Malaysia) wretch.

bedès monkey.

bedol *anak* -an a school dropout.

begitu *nah* - atta boy, that's the way it should be.

bekal ber-kan to be provided with.

bekel (s.) BEKAL II. **per-an** (in Bali) village.

bekicot escargot.

béla -.*paksa* jur. self-defense (necessary violence in defense of o's own or another's body, virtue or property).

belakang mem-i *lensa* (in caption of pictures) back to camera.

belampah (in Palangka Raya) to dig diamonds.

belantik (in Muncar, Banyuwangi) person who sells his services as a middleman between the fish owner and the buyer; (s.) BLANTIK.

beling (in Jakarta) eye glasses.

bélot **pem-an** defection.

bencèt I to push, press. - *knop* to push the button.

bencèt II mem- to single out (for criticism), pick on, browbeat.

benda -.- *padat* solids.

bendahari (fem.) treasurer.

bendung irrigation overseer. - *penangkap air* check-dam.

bengkoang (s.) BENGKUANG.

bengkung long wide woman's sash wound around the waist to hold the wraparound *(,jarik)* in place.

bengok (in Banten) (s.) ECENG.

bengung m- to speak inarticulately, mumble.

bentala the earth.

bentang mem- to extend, stretch (to).

bera *tanah* - uncultivated land.

bèrak -.- diarrhea.

berani - *sama* to dare to be disrespectful to. -.- *takut* ambivalent. *Banyak penulis*

Surat Pembaca masih ~ *takut,* Many writers of Letters to the Editor are still ambivalent.

berdikari **ke-an** standing on o's own feet, independence, self-reliance.

berèntang mem- to tug to get away (from embrace). **ter-** (to rise) with a jerk.

beri mem- *jalan* to yield the right-of-way. **pem-** *suara* voter.

berinda (in Singapore) se- *tubuh* over the whole body.

berisik *dgn suara* - in a loud voice.

berita *tdk* di-kan off the record. **ter-** heard as news.

Berkeley Mafia term used by the opponents of some American-educated economists asked by President Soeharto in 1966 to form a new economic policy for the government.

berkik (s.) BERKEK.

bersih mem-kan *diri* to clear o.s. (of an accusation). - *nagari* (in Tulungagung) the elimination from the city of all external and internal disturbances.

beru *anak* - son-in-law.

beruang - *madu* sun bear (L. Helarctos malayanus).

beruk the pigtail monkey.

bésan *memulangi* - to marry with o's cousin (i.e. the *anak mamak kandung*).

bésok *B- saja!* Wait till the time comes!

besus to know how to dress up.

besusu (s.) BENGKUANG.

betina 1 female animal. 2 female person. *si* - the hen.

betis *buah (,jantung ,perut)* - calf (of leg).

bhakti *B- Wisatastri* the women's organization under the jurisdiction of the Directorate General of Tourism.

biang - *rampok* ringleader of robbery.

biar - *bagaimana* come what may.

bibit **pem-an** (s.) KADERISASI.

bicokok 1 a small crocodile, alligator. 2 swindler.

biloh k.o. monkey.

bilon (in West Kalimantan) helicopter. *bapak* - helicopter pilot.

bimbit mem- to carry with the finger tips.

bina pem-: ~ *pramuka* (in the *Pramuka* Boy Scout movement) scout master. ~ *pramuka putri* den mother (for cub scouts). ~ *pramuka tuna raga* handicapped scout master. **pem-an** (in compounds) 1 guidance. 2 control. 3 administration. 4 development.

binatang - *berkuku ganjil* a perissodactyl(e), such as the Sumatran tapir (L. Tapirus indicus).

bingkas 1 sprung (of a trap). 2 - *bangun* to jump up quickly.

bintang *mulai terbuka -nya* his star is in the ascendant. *tdk* **se-** not go with. - *kutub* polar star. -.*mintang* all k.o. stars.

biosféra biosphere.

bis -*kota jangkung* the Leyland double-decker bus.

bismut bismuth.

bisnis mem-kan to deal in s.t.

blantik middleman, broker; (s.) BELAN-TIK.

bleketépé woven coconut leaves (for walls, roofs, temporary sheds).

bobot ber-kan to be weighted towards.

bocah *masa* - childhood.

bokong *main* -.-**an** (s.) MAIN (BACKING. BACKINGAN).

bokor *B- Kencana Astagina* the Octagonal Gold Cup, symbol of shadow-play performance supremacy.

bola - *dunia* globe. *menjadi* - *ping.pong* to send s.o. from pillar to post.

bonafid (s.) BONAFIDE. **ke-an** bona fides.

bonéka figurehead.

bowler bowler.

bowling bowling.

braok loud, shrill (of voice).

brèngsèk ke-an garbage (anything worthless).

buah - *enau (,atep)* sugar palm fruit eaten for dessert.

buang - *bom* to defecate.

buat ber- *cabul* to cohabit, live with.

buaya - *darat* 1 wolf, woman chaser.

2 komodo dragon. - *senyulong* a fresh-water crocodile (L. Crocodylus porosus).

budak - *belian* serf, slave, indentured labor. - *suruhan* servants, errand boys.

budaya pem-an institutionalization.

bujuk pem- persuader.

buku I - *jari (,lima)* knuckles. *beradu* - *jari (,lima)* to fist fight. - *lali* ankle.

buku II *tdk masuk* - does not count. - *pegangan* handbook. - *penunjuk telepon* telephone directory. - *pintar* vademecum. - *saku* diary, notebook.

bulé *Inggris* - a native-born Britisher.

Bulog [Badan Urusan Logistik] Logistics Management Board, i.e. a State agency with monopolistic powers in the production, purchase, and distribution of basic staples.

bumi *B- Perkemahan* Camping Ground (for boy scouts). *B- Sriwajaya* the South Sumatra Province.

buncang ter- blown away.

bungkem abstain.

bunting - *muda* in the first trimester of pregnancy.

buntut di- kuda to be tied in a pony-tail.

bunuh mem- *waktu* to kill time.

buru keter-.-an haste

buruhwati female worker.

butir(.butir) data, facts, details, points, items.

butuh ke-an: ~ *yg diperkirakan* assumed need. ~ *yg dirasakan* felt need. ~ *yg nyata* real need.

C

cacar - *ayam* fowl pox.

cadang -**an** *penyangga* bufferstock, i.e. a stock of commodities retained to offset price fluctuations.

cahaya - *laser* laser beam.

cair -**an** *pendingin* refrigerant.

cakal - *bakal* founding father(s).

cak.cek 1 active. 2 to make swift, sure motions.

calo canvasser. - *gituan (,WTS)* pimp.

calon - *tertanggung* (insurance) prospect.

cambah bean sprouts.

cambuk - *petir* thunder clap.

candu - *rokok* nicotin.

cangkang shell (of snail, etc.).

cantrik helper (of a *dukun*).

capai - *terbang* flying range (of aircraft).

capar bean sprouts.

carima [pemancar-penerima] a transceiver.

catur - *wulan* four-months'.

cawé *ikut* -.- to join in what others are doing.

cébong (s.) KECEBONG.

cèk - *pribadi* personal check.

cèker (in Medan) teller *(in bank)*.

ceklèk ny- to deviate.

celah - *kelengkang* crotch, area between the upper legs.

celurit (s.) CLURIT.

cendekiawati a female intellectual.

cendot (Sund.) (s.) ECENG.

cengkauw (s.) CENGKAU.

cengkèh clubs (in card games).

centèng bouncer.

centil meny- to give a rebuke (,scolding) to.

cepai (s.) CEPE(K).

ceramah presentation (something set forth for o's attention).

cerapan garbage dump.

ceroboh boorish.

cetya (Buddhist) altar.

ci.bie (pron. as English CB) citizen band.

cicek *jadi* -.*kering* to become as thin as a rail.

cidomo [cikar, dokar dan motor] a vehicle which is a combination of an ox-drawn cart (*ci*kar) and a two-wheeled horse-drawn cab (*do*kar) using motorcar (*mo*tor) wheels and tires, but pulled by a horse.

cidrajanji (jur.) non-performance.

cikal *proyek* - pilot project.

cikeruhan (in Sumedang) (s.) KETUK (TILU).

cilok delicacy made from seasoned tapioca flour; it tastes either sweet or salty.

cindan abbrev. of *kucindan*. - *celota* (in

Malaysia) jokes and chatter.

cingbok uncle's wife (younger sibling of father or mother).

cipoa (in Jakarta) bull shit!

citpè seven hundred (rupiahs).

citra -.*diri* self-image.

ciut men- to crumble.

clingkrak.clingkrik 1 to kick upstairs. 2 up and down.

coèl men- to touch slightly.

cokin (in Jakarta) the Indonesian-born Chinese.

col not proportionally divided.

comèl winsome, pretty.

congkèl men- to break open.

cor penge-an foundry.

cupang scar caused by a bite.

curah - *pendapat* brainstorming.

cuti men-.besarkan (euph.) to send s.o. to purgatory.

D

daérah - *belakang* hinterland. - *kandung beras* rice bowl, i.e. a rice-cultivated geographical region. - *kantong* enclave. - *penunjang* hinterland. - *rawan pangan* (s.) DAERAH (MINUS). - *serba kekurangan* (s.) DAERAH (MINUS).

daftar - *kepustakaan* bibliography, i.e. a list of sources of literary works of a given author, publisher, etc.

dagang pe-: ~ *batang* (in the fishery business) a trader who has about four retail dealers or ~ *kadal* under him. ~ *gerobak dorong* trader who uses a push cart to sell his merchandise. ~ *misbar* sidewalk salesman who has to leave his spot when it starts raining; (s.) MISBAR. ~ *pikulan* trader who uses a shoulder pole to sell his merchandise.

daging *nafsu* ke-an sexual desires.

dahwèn meddlesome, interfering.

damba -an (s.) PENDAMBAAN.

damen harvested, dried rice stalk.

dapra fender, i.e. a cushion of rope hung over a ship's side to protect it in docking.

dapur *utk membuat - berasap* to make ends meet.

darat **men-kan** to ground (aircraft).

darma *- bhakti* (fig.) contributions.

darmawisata *- kota* city tours.

dasbor dashboard.

datar monotonous.

daur **di-.ulang** to be recycled. *mesin* **pen-.ulang** recycling machine.

dawukbang blackish-brown colored mixed with white spots.

daya *- memproduksi* productivity. *- tahan* endurance. *- tarik seks* sex appeal.

dédikasi **ber-** dedicated.

degum sound like that of guns, roar (,boom ,booming) of guns.

demam *- panggung* stage fright.

dénok and **dhénok, dènok** and **dhènok** chubby, pleasantly plump.

dépok and **dhépok** **pa-an** 1 a holy man's shrine. 2 a complex, i.e. group of associated buildings.

derèbar (in Malaysia) driver.

dèrèk **men-** to tow (a car, etc.) away (from illegal parking lot, etc.).

désa *D- Praja* Village Government. *- swadaya* a traditional village. *- swakarya* a village in transition. *- swasembada* a progressive village.

désibèl decibel.

dèskripsi **pen-an** description.

déso **n-** to go to the villages (,rural areas); (s.) DESA.

déwan *D- Sesepuh* Council of Leaders.

dharma 1 religion. 2 (S.) KEBENARAN.

diagnosa diagnose. **men-** to diagnose.

diam **kepen-an** taciturnity.

diktator **men-i** to give orders arbitrarily.

diletan dilettante.

dinas **-an** schedule (for trains). ~ *baru (,lama)* the new (,old) schedule (for trains). *D- Giro dan Cekpos* Postal Check and Transfer Service.

dinding **ber-** *tembok* with a brick wall.

diplomasi *- selamat.muka* face-saving diplomacy.

diri **ke-an** egoistic(al). **pen-an** *fraksi* (s.) MINDERHEIDSNOTA.

disko **pe-** disco dancer.

diskusiwan discussant.

do first note in the musical scale.

dokter *- penerbangan* flight surgeon.

doktor *- kedokteran* medical doctor.

dolok log (a section of the trunk of a felled tree, in timber trade).

komplèng **n-** to be housed (,put up) temporarily.

dram drum.

duduk **pen-** *asing* resident alien.

dukuh small village under the administration of a different village.

dukun advisor in mysticism. *- pijat* practitioner specializing in massage. *- urut dukun* consulted for abortions.

dus a small (flimsy) box.

duyung (s.) IKAN (DUYUNG).

dwi *- fungsi* the dual function concept which states that the military's role is not simply to protect the nation in wartime, but also to undertake a nation-building task. **di-fungsikan** to be given a dual function. *- warna purwa cendekia wusana* [motto of Hankamnas (,National Defense and Security) training courses] emphasizing patriotism and fighting spirit above profession.

E

ècèk.ècèk maraca(s).

ècèr **peng-** *koran* newspaper streetvendor.

édar **peng-** *narkotika* (drug) pusher.

èdit **peng-** editor, a person who edits.

èk oak. *kayu* - oak-wood.

éka *E- Dasa Rudra* a ceremony, usually held every 100 years, in the largest temple, the Pura Besakih, located on the slope of Mount Agung (Bali). *E-dyasa* name of the women's organization of the Directorate General of Air Communications.

èkor **ber-** *panjang* to have a lot of consequences, cause a great number of problems.

èlak *tdk dpt* **di-kan** *(lagi)* inevitable, unavoidable.

èmangnya indeed.

emas - *hijau* lit. 'green gold,' i.e. the vanilla plant.

èmpèr -**an** open porch with roof.

èmporium emporium.

empunya *si* - *kemalangan* the unlucky person.

énak *merasa* -**an** (of a sick person) to feel better.

endap **peng-an** sedimentation.

énèrsi - *matahari (,surya)* solar energy.

enyèk **ng-** to humiliate, insult.

ès - *Apollo* (s.) ES (PLASTIK).

èselon - *III* (in a *Departemen* Ministry) the (Assistant) Inspectors.

èstapèt **meng-kan** to relay.

F

fa fourth note in the musical scale.

fakosan monkey soup.

fakultas - *non.eksakta* school of economics and law.

famili *tdk ada sangkut paut* - *dgn* not related to. - *pak anu* the system whereby s.o. is quickly hired for a job when he happens to be a relative of a certain big shot.

fantasi imagination. **ber-** to exercise o's imagination. *saputangan* - fancy handkerchief. *tenaga* - power of imagination.

favorit **pemf-an** favoritism.

fiksyen fiction.

filsafat - *ilmu pengetahuan* epistemology.

fisiotérapi physiotherapy.

Florida Pantai Suralaya at Merak, Banten, West Java.

folklor folklore.

fonologis phonological.

forum caucus.

fotokaméra camera.

G

gadis - *sampul* cover girl.

gadung *macan* -**an** human being in the form of a tiger.

Gaimusho Jap. Department of State.

gairah **ke-an** *angkasa* airmindedness. **meng-kan** to stimulate.

galau - *massa* mass hysteria.

gali [gerakan anak(-anak) liar] movement of outlawed children (in Semarang, Solo, Yogya and other large cities in Central Java). *oknum* -.- bodyguards, bouncers, paid killers.

galodo mud slide (from volcanic eruption).

galur variety (of *padi*).

gampang -.- *sulit (,susah)* (s.) GAMPANG (.GAMPANG ANGEL).

ganda *dua kali* - double the amount.

gandum -.-**an** grains.

ganjen coquettish.

ganti -*!* (in shortwave communications) over! *yg dpt* **di-** renewable.

garisah instinct.

garwo (s.) GARWA.

gas - *yg berdiri sendiri* nonassociated gas. - *yg bergabung dgn minyak* associated gas.

gasohol gasohol.

Gatutkaca and **Gatutkoco** the name of o. of Bima's sons in the *Mahab(h)arata*, called upon when the fighting gets rough.

gaul **ber-** to have social intercourse. **meng-** to roam about (a place). **per-an** *bebas* free sex, sexual intercourse outside of marriage.

gawat **ke-an** seriousness.

gaya *kalah* - to be less energetic.

gebah (Sund.) **meng-** to intimidate s.o.

gebrak **meng-** to intimidate, browbeat.

gebu **meng-** flamboyant.

gedung *G- Agung* (s.) ISTANA (KEPRESIDENAN "GEDUNG AGUNG"). *G- Sabahu* (col.) and (coll.) The War Department (Dutch: Department van Oorlog) in Insulinde Park, Bandung.

gelimpang -**an** *dlm uang* to be rolling in money.

gelitik tickle.

gelodok beehive made from pieces of coconut tree trunk.

gelugu coconut palm trunk.

gelung - *tekuk* a Central Javanese traditional hairdo.

gemar **peng-** *sulap* magic fan.

gemblep chubby-cheeked.

genang ter- covered with water. *mata ~*
eyes glistening with tears.
genit -.- flirtations.
gentar meng- deterring.
gentèngisasi tiling of roofs.
gènyèh meng- (in Malaysia) to rub,
massage.
geragal siliceous.
Gerakhas Malaysia's Special Forces.
gergaji - *mesin* chain saw.
gerimis ke-an to be caught in a drizzle.
gersang ke-an barrenness, aridity.
gèsèr - *ke pojok* to set aside (feelings).
getoktular di-kan to be spread by word
of mouth.
gim (in card playing) game.
gindé (in Bengkulu) village chief.
gini - *saja!* let's just do it like this!
-, *ya* it's like this, let me explain.
gizi *kaya-* nutritious.
glintir -an granular.
go.ban Rp. 50.000,-
golkaris a member of *Golkar*.
gombal -*!* shit! nonsense! rubbish!
shoot!
gondèl di-i to be talked out of it.
gondongan a gland infection on o's
neck (right or left), to have the mumps.
graita comprehension, mental grasp.
Grata.loka (in the *Bina Graha*, Jakarta)
showroom.
gula - *batak*, - *batu*, - *enau*, - *jawa*,
- *merah*, - *sakar* and - *tepak* sugars
made from the sugar palm.
gulung -an *pendingin* cooling coil.
gunting *kena* - laid off. peng-an lay off.
guring to sleep.
G.W. a covered freight car (in train
formation).

H

hablum - *minallah*, - *minannas* our ties
with Allah and our ties with our
fellow men.
hadang peng-an intercept.
hadap meng-kan to confront s.o.

hadrah tambourine.
Hadramaut a district of southern Arabia.
putra - an Arab.
hafidz, hafis and havidz well versed in
the Koran, knowing it by heart.
hak - *bungkam* right of silence.
halkum Adam's apple.
hamba - *abdi tebusan* slave.
hamburger hamburger.
hampir - *saja* almost (s.t. unpleasant)
happened.
hancur meng-kan destructive. *praktek ~*
destructive practices.
handal 2 reliable. 3 experienced, skilful.
handeuleum a plant (L. Praptophyllum
L. Griff) which can reach a height of o.
to three meters; seven leaves of this
plant mixed with turmeric, as large as
o's thumb, and brown palm sugar,
after boiling, seems to be an effective
medicine against hemorrhoids.
hantu meng- to hover around.
harap -an *hidup* life expectancy.
harbor hardboard.
harga - *dasar* floor price.
hari H- *Hak.Hak Asasi Manusia* Human
Rights Day (December 10). *H- Keuangan* (October 30; this was the first day
that republican money was circulated).
H- Koperasi Cooperative Day (July 12).
- *pengeposan* day a letter is mailed. *H-
Purnawirawan* Army Retirees' Day
(September 12).
hasil berpeng-an *rendah* (adj.) low-
income. - *karya* performance.
hati hearts (in card games).
he.e(h) yes, that's so.
hèibat (S.) HEBAT.
hématologi hematology.
héran ter-.- to become puzzled.
hias peng- *sampul depan* cover girl.
hidran *pompa* - hydrant.
hilang peng-an omittance.
himne hymn.
hincit to run away.
hirarkhi hierarchy.
Hispania Hispanic. *orang* - a Hispanic
(from Latin America).

hitung *tak* **ter-** innumerable.

hondanisasi the introduction of Honda outboard motors for fishing boats.

horoskop horoscope.

hu piece of paper placed over entrance door of a house, as a good luck charm.

huana lit. "barbarian;" (s.) WANNA.

hubung -an *bebas* free sex.

huffaz (s.) HAFIDZ.

humaniora arts and humanities.

hus exclamation of mild disgust.

hutan *tdk diketahui - rimbanya* he was nowhere to be seen, there was no sign of him (anywhere).

Huwi Blicki a plant (L. Dioscorea bulbi-ifera L.) with contraceptive powers.

I

ibu *- dapur* cook.

Idul Fitri k.o. Easter of Islam, the festival of the breaking of the Fast following a month of self-denial and atonement. **ber.-** to celebrate *Idul Fitri.*

igau -an (fig.) nightmare.

ijin *- kerja* work permit.

ikan *ibarat - dan air* hand in glove.

iklan *- tembak* a 'shotgun-approach' advertisement placed in a small newspaper without the consent of a business enterprise. Once the ad appears in the paper the newspaper then attempts to force that enterprise to pay for the advertisement.

ikut to do s.t. together with s.o. else. *- berbicara* to have o's say (on the matter), participate in offering an opinion.

ilmu *- belajar bahasa* language learning. *- gizi* science of nutrition, dietetics. *- kedokteran gigi kehakiman* forensic odontology. *-.- kelautan* maritime sciences. *- komputer* computer science. *- komunikasi massa* (s.) PUBLISISTIK. *- lingkungan manusia* human ecology. *- musik daerah* ethnomusicology. *- pemerintahan* science of government.

- pengajaran bahasa language teaching. *- pengetahuan khayali* science fiction. *- wiraniaga* salesmanship science.

imajinasi *penuh -* imaginative.

imbang meng- to offset.

imunitas immunity. *- diplomatik* diplomatic immunity.

inang female *jengek. - penularan* (in biology) vector.

indah ke-an *tunggang serasi* dressage.

indikasi *ada -* to be involved in the *G-30-S.*

Indopura [Indonesia-Singapura] Indonesia-Singapore. *Elang -* reference to the joint Indonesian-Singaporean Air Operations Maneuvers.

ini um, uh (representing a pause to collect o's thoughts; (cp.) ANU).

inkam income.

Inpres *Inpres* funds are allocated according to the instruction of the President, who is in charge of funds for development activities in the real sense of the words—mainly education, road building, etc.

insèk insect.

insès incest.

inspèktur *I-.Jenderal* Inspector-General; in a ministry he is the watchdog who keeps his eye on funding and performance.

intèr(e)n internal. *urusan -* internal affairs.

invèstasi peng-an *(kembali)* (re)investment.

IR-36 reference to a superior rice variety.

isi peng-an *bahan bakar kapal* bunker.

Islamisasi Islamization.

istana *I- Kepresidenan "Gedung Agung"* the Presidential Palace in Yogyakarta.

isteri ber- *dua kali* to have married twice (said of a man).

istihsan preference.

istisqa to ask for rain.

IUD [Intrauterine (Contraceptive) Device] Intrauterine (Contraceptive) Device. **meng.-.kan** to provide (an area) with IUDs in the framework of Family Planning.

J

jabat Pe-*Penyidik Sebab.Sebab Kematian* State Coroner.

Jadel [Jawa Deli] reference used by people from Northern Sumatra for Javanese who in the years 1926-28 were taken by the Dutch to Deli in order to work in the rubber, oilpalm, etc. estates.

jaga pen-*loket* window clerk. *gardu* pen-an guard post (for gate keeper at railway crossing).

jagal middleman between the trader and retailer.

jahat ke-an *terorganisasikan* organized crime. **pen-***kambuhan* recidivist, habitual criminal.

jajar -an *dlm* ~ among the rank and file.

jalan - *mengikuti peta* circuit.

jalin men-*kasih sayang* to make love.

jalur channel. *J- Gaza* Gaza Strip. - *gempa* seismic belt. - *laut* sea lane.

jam - *terbang* flight hours.

jaman - *sekarang* these days.

jamin pen-*emisi* underwriter.

jamu (fig.) cure-all.

jamur - *kulit* skin disease causing light-colored blemishes. - *merang* (L. Volvariella volvacean).

janji - *gombal* a promise which is not to be taken seriously.

jarab scabies.

jaring - *insang* gill net.

Jarkoni [pinter ngajar ora pinter nglakoni] (a Jav. acronym) clever in teaching but not smart in putting it into practice.

jarwodoso folk etymology.

jatah - *guru* 'teacher's allocation,' i.e. k.o. bribe to get a child enrolled in a certain school.

jatuh capitulation, fall. *sdh - tertimpa tangga* bad luck on top of bad luck.

jauh - *bumi sama laut* an immense difference.

jebulan surprise.

jelajah pen- explorer.

jembatan - *apung* pontoon bridge. - *laut* sea lift.

jèngèk [jenggo ekonomi] small business person who daily carries goods from Sabang Free Port to mainland Aceh (Ulee Lheu, the port of Banda Aceh) using the ferryboat, via the special port at Balohan.

jenjang -an hierarchy.

jeprèt men-i to staple (paper, etc.).

jera pen- deterrent.

jinlépis Levi's jeans.

joki -.*disko* disc jockey.

joli men-kan to squander money.

jorong *kepala* - (in West Sumatra) hamlet head.

juang kepe-an fighting spirit.

junjung men- *tinggi titah* to pay homage to the command of (royalty).

juragan - *darat* owner of fishing craft and gear who does not participate in catching fish at sea. - *laut* skipper (of fishing craft).

juru - *pengacara* beadle (in England, Holland, Indonesia, etc.), i.e. an official who leads university processions, carrying a mace used as a symbol of authority.

K

k-15-N (s.) K(E)NOP 15.

kabar peng-*Injil* evangelist.

kabayan hamlet headman.

kabin - *pengemudi* cockpit (of aircraft).

kaca ber-mata to wear glasses. ~ *min* to wear glasses to correct nearsightedness. ~ *plus* to wear glasses to correct farsightedness. -*mata.baca* reading glasses. - *nako* louver (,louvre) boards.

kadga poniard (of naval cadet).

kaji - *kelayakan* feasibility study.

kakak - *ipar* sibling-(,cousin-)in-law married to *kakak.*

kakerlak - *baju hijau* thugs in mil. uniform.

kaki 1 old man. 2 - *arak* drunkard.

kaku spastic.

kalui *(ikan)* - (Sund.) gourami (a fresh

water fish).

kalurahan (S.) KELURAHAN.

kambing - *hutan* serow (L. Capricornis sumatrensis).

kamérawati cameraman (female).

kampil peng-an packing (of cement in gunny sacks).

kampung - *kota* urban village.

kanan - *kiri, kiri* - to the right and the left.

kangkung swamp cabbage.

kantong - *empedu* gallbladder.

kapal - *angkut minyak* (oil) tanker.
- *pemadam tunda* fire tugboat.
- *semen bertulang baja* ferro-cement ship. - *trol* trawler.

kapan - *waktu saja* any time.

kapitan (at Banggai Laut) (s.) HUKUM (TUA).

karbon.monoksida carbon-monoxyde.

karya di-siswakan to be appointed as a trainee.

kasak.kusuk plotting and intrigues on the part of bureaucrats to elicit bribes.

kasih meng-i to love. *jatuh* **-an** to take pity on.

kata - *jabaran* (gramm.) derivative.

katub (s.) KATUP.

katup - *seleret* zipper.

kaum term used by the Chinese in Indonesia to refer to the natives.

kawin wedding. - *alam* natural mating (among cattle). - *berencana* hand mating (among cattle). - *emas* golden wedding, 50th anniversary of o's wedding. - *kontrak* (in the "Krakatau Steel" complex at Cilegon) k.o. contract agreed upon between a male foreign expert working for "Krakatau Steel" and a young local to the effect that the man is willing to marry the girl for the duration of his stay in Indonesia (5 years) and that he will divorce her after that period. - *perak* silver wedding, 25th anniversary of o's wedding. - *suntik (,slang)* artificial insemination (among cattle).

kaya ke-an assets. **pemer-an** enrichment.

kayu - *eben* ebony. - *gergajian* sawn timber. - *kelincung* (in Ampenan) ebony.

kebat - *kelewat, pinter keblinger* what is done in a hurry is seldom done well.

kebun per-an: ~ *padi* rice estate. ~ *tanaman pangan* food estate.

kecébong tadpole.

kecut kepeng-an cowardice.

kedai pe- shopkeeper. ~ *kopi* coffee house owner.

kedip meng-kan *sebelah matanya* to make eyes at, wink at s.o.

kedok meng- to cultivate (,till), plant and harvest the land for part of s.o. else's harvest (,rice paddy) agreed upon in advance. **peng-** land cultivator, planter and harvester who works for part of s.o. else's harvest (,rice paddy) agreed upon in advance.

Kekar Malindo [Keris Kartika Malaysia. Indonesia] name of the joint Indo-nesian-Malaysian Army Maneuvers; the *keris* and *kartika* are the emblems used by the Malaysian and Indonesian army respectively; the entire acronym means 'a solid *Malindo*.'

kèki dejected, irritated.

kelabu(h) ter-i deceived.

keladi *tua.tua -, makin tua makin jadi* dirty old man.

kèler di- to be thrown in jail.

kelètèk meng- *perangko* to peel off (stamps, from envelope).

kelontongisme consumerism.

keluar - *sidang* walk-out.

kemas mengk- dinikan to make early preparations.

kembang - *telon* a combination of three species of plants, used as an offering; usually used are the fragrant pandanus leaf, the frangipanni, and the hibiscus. Another frequently used combination is the magnolia, frangipanni, and rose. This flower combination is set out to avert calamity and ward off devils.

kembara peng-an (in *Pramuka* Boy Scout circles) hiking.

kemidi - *ombak* (in Jakarta) merry-go-round.

kemilan "in-between meals."

kemladéyan (S.) BENALU.

kemlandingan albizzia (tree with edible pods).

kemplang ng- 1 to refuse to pay for s.t. 2 to pay less than the asking price for s.t. 3 to fail to pay what o. owes.

kemudu.kudu *selak* - can hardly wait until, very anxious for s.t. to happen.

kena meng- relevant. **meng-kan** *penahanan* to put under arrest. - *air* get wet. - *flu* get the flu. - *hukum* be affected by the law of. - *jewer* be reprimanded. - *ketuk* be rapped (on the head). - *pandang* be stared at. - *piat* (in Malaysia) get a whipping. - *tanah* get mud on it. - *usik* be annoyed.

kencing *spt maling kesiram air* - 'like a thief s.o. emptied a chamber pot on,' i.e. not very happy; with a sour expression.

kendil earthenware or copper utensil for cooking rice. *menegakkan* - to make ends meet.

Kenop 15 [Kebijaksanaan Nopember 15] The November 15 Policy, i.e. the November 1978 devaluation of the *rupiah*.

kentut ter-.- to fart (,pass gas) unintentionally.

kepala *utk keselamantan -nya* to save his neck. -.- *botak* 'bald-headed ones,' experts, professors. - *bengkel* plant manager.

képang meng- *rambutnya* to wear o's hair in (matted-) cornrow dreadlocks. - *jagung* cornbraids.

keplok meng-i to clap for s.o.

keras ke-an *hati* steadfastness of purpose.

kercap -an smacking of the lips.

keréta (in Malaysia) motorcar. - *api peluru* the Jap. bullet train ("Shinkansen"). - *kabel* tramway.

kering ke-an *susu* have o's milk run dry.

kerio (in Palembang) hamlet head.

kerja be- *di belakang meja* to work in an office. **di-samakan** to be done in concert.

kertas - *berlapis* coated paper.

kerumut *penyakit* - morbilli, measles.

kètèng *secara* ng- (to sell) by the piece.

ketik I the sound of typing

ketik II *kios* - book stall.

kèts Keds (shoes; a trade mark).

ketua - *jurusan* department chairman in a university.

ketuk mengk-.k- *pipa rokoknya* to knock out o's cigarette pipe.

khamir peng-an fermentation.

khol *selamatan* - an annual ceremony in observance of a death anniversary (such as, for the late President Soekarno every June 21).

kiat art.

kibèrnétik cybernetics.

kibul *goyang* - to shake o's ass.

kilas - *balik* flashback.

kira per-an assumption.

kirap (s.) KIRAB. **di-** to be carried in procession.

kiri *kanan* -, - *kanan* to the right and the left.

kisah - *nyata* true story.

kisruh confused.

KKN [Kuliah Kerja Nyata] National Study Service Scheme, i.e. an interdisciplinary activity, k.o. public service performed by universities.

klomprot *berpakaian* ng- to be dressed in a sloppy way.

knol bulb (of plant).

Knop 15 (s.) K(E)NOP 15.

kocing (college sl.) coaching.

kodak -.meng- photography.

kode - *daerah pos* zip (,postal) code.

Koko the nickname for Dr. Soedjatmoko, the one-time Indonesian ambassador to the U.S.A.

kol III (s.) KHOL.

kolombi Menadonese dish made from an edible variety of snail, k.o. escargot.

kolt (s.) COLT. *pemilik* - Colt owner.

komodor *K- Muda Udara* Colonel (of the Air Force). *K- Udara* Major General (of the Air Force).

kompa (me)ng- to inflate (a tire).

Kompas 'Compass,' i.e. the name of a Catholic newspaper in Jakarta.

kompi and **komping** comfrey, a European plant of the borage family, with rough, hairy leaves, gaining large popularity in Indonesia for its medicinal faculties, used as k.o. *jamu.*

kompos di-kan to be stationed in a barracks, be housed (of prostitutes, pimps, etc.).

kompris crown prince.

komputerisasi computerization.

komsèn guard post (to charge tolls for trucks on some roads).

konsekuèn consistent.

konsèrvasi conservation. **mengk-** to conserve.

kontèiner container.

kontès di-kan to be made into a contest (,competition).

koplèt a stanza.

kor choir.

kordèn curtain, drape.

kornéa cornea.

kos *pak -* landlord.

kosong *- blong* completely empty.

kota *K- Banjir* Tulungagung. *K- Clurit* Semarang. *K- Hantu* Pontianak. *K- Ilmu Pengetahuan* Bogor. *K- Industri* Malang. *K- Jam Gadang* Bukittinggi. *K- Khatulistiwa* Pontianak. *K- Kembang* Malang. *K- Kenari* Bogor. *K- Mahasiswa* Yogyakarta. *K- Oncom* Bandung. *K- Pajajaran* Bogor. *K- Pariwisata* Malang. *K- Pelajar* Malang. *K- Pensiunan* Bogor. *K- Sanjai* Bukittinggi. *K- Sederhana* Yogyakarta. *K- Singa* Singapore. *K- Tri Arga* Bukittinggi.

kotamadya municipality, a city the government of which is independent of the *kabupaten.*

krédit *sepeda -an* bicycle that can be bought on easy terms. *- komando* credit issued at the command of an influential person; it has no collateral

and is issued over the telephone, k.o. illegal practice. *- lunak* soft credit.

krenggosan out of breath, panting.

kréosot creosote.

kriting *- daun* a plant disease (L. Macrophomina vilusexta) detrimental to clove trees.

kuat ke-an: ~ *penahan* restraining force. ~ *pendorong* driving force, pushing power.

kucindan joke.

kucing *- hutan* leopard cat (L. Felis bangalensis).

kuclak (in the Indramayu area, Cirebon) k.o. dice game using pictures of animals.

kuda *- besi* train.

kuli *- angkat* (at airports) porter, redcap.

kulo'ipus Menadonese dish made from a white-tailed rat.

kumbang bee, a symbol of a boy (with the girl symbolized as a flower). *- tiada bertali* a young bachelor.

kuping peng-an eavesdropping.

kurang ke- sempurnaan imperfection.

kurdin (s.) KORDEN.

kursus *- penataran (lanjutan)* (advanced) upgrading course.

kutil meng- to shoplift. **peng-** shoplifter. **peng-an** shoplifting.

L

la sixth note in the musical scale.

laboratorium *L- Angkasa* Skylab.

ladang per-an *ternak* and *- ternak* ranch.

lahan 1 soil. 2 agricultural land. 3 *- lapisan atas* topsoil.

lahir ke-an a native of.

lain *dan beberapa -nya* and some others.

lama *Sdh -? Baru sebentar.* Have you already been here for a long time? Just a few minutes. *Jangan -! Aku tak -.* Don't make it too long! I'll be back in a minute. *sdh berapa -* already for some time. *tiada berapa -nya* and *tak - kemudian* soon, not long thereafter. **se-.nya** *tdk* never (again).

lambang logo.

lampu - *baca* reading lamp. - *gaspom* k.o.
pressurized gasoline lamp. The lamp is
provided with a tank filled with
gasoline located at some distance from
the lamp and is connected to the lamp
by means of a very small wire pipe
through which the gasoline can flow
when put under pressure by a gasoline
pump.

lancar bersi- (s.) BERSELANCAR. **pesi-**
surfer.

landas me- to touch down (of aircraft).

langgan pe- customer.

langlang pe- *buana* globetrotter.

lansekap landscape.

lantur -an digression, temporary departure
from the main subject in talking or
writing.

lanun pirate (from the southern Philippines, usually operating in the months
of July and August as far as the Berau
Regency waters in eastern Kalimantan).

lapis di-i *seng* galvanized.

larang -an *terbang* grounded (of aircraft).

lari -.- *anjing* jogging.

latar pe-an *lapangan udara* apron.

laut - *bebas* the high seas.

lawa *tunjuk* - (in Malaysia) to show off.

lawak *dijadikan* - to be ridiculed, mocked.
me-(.-) to joke, jest. **me-** *cabul* to
crack smutty jokes.

lawan - *bicara* interlocutor.

layan pe-an *purna niaga* (s.) PELAYANAN
(PURNA JUAL).

layang se- *tinjauan* (S.) SELAYANG
(PANDANG). - *gantung* hang-gliding.

lecek crumpled, creased, wrinkled.

ledak pe-an blasting.

lèdèk - *ketek* (in Central and East Java)
(s.) KOMEDI (KETEK).

legawa gratification, pleasure.

légènda me- to become a legend.

lemah me- to weaken (v.i.).

lènsa - *tele* telephotolens.

lepas me- *topi* to raise o's hat. *tlh* **me-kan**

masa gadisnya to come of age. - *kangen*
reunion.

lès di-kan to be given … lessons.

lestari pe(ng)-an conservation.

letak me-kan *pesawat telponnya* to hang
up the phone. **pe-** *dasar* founder,
founding father.

libas (in Malaysia and northern Sumatra)
kena - to be cheated.

libat pe-an involvement.

lidi - *dupa* joss stick.

lift - *barang* freight elevator. - *berkecepat-
an tinggi* high-speed elevator. - *sampah*
trash chute.

likur se-an black-jack (the card game).

limbah waste.

lingkar - *roda* rim.

Li Niha the language of the island of Nias.

lintas *program* - crash program. **me-** *masuk
di* to ride into (of a train). *kota* -an a
transit town. *Kota ini merupakan sebuah
kota -an utk terus ke pulau dewata.*
This city is a transit town for continuing on to Bali.

lipat pe-gandaan augmentation.

liput (pe)-an *berita* news coverage.

lisan me-kan to put into words, express.

liurai (in East Timor) village chief.

lobster lobster.

loco me- to masturbate.

loklokbungaok (S.) PELESIT.

lolos pe-an escape.

lomba - *daya tahan* endurance competition. - *lintas medan* cross-country.
- *lompat berkuda* jumping competition
(on horseback). - *pacu rintangan*
steeplechase. - *tunggang serasi* dressage.

londo - *bule* any (pure) European or
American.

longong ter-.- agape, amazed, open-
mouthed.

lori - *gantung* overhead cableway.

luap -an (over)flow.

lugu simple. **ke-an** simplicity.

luhak the Minangkabau mother country
is divided into three *luhaks:* - Agam,
- Tanah Datar and - Lima Puluh.

lulus - *jarum*, - *kelindan* where o. sheep goes follows another.

lumpuh *penderita* ke-an paraplegic.

luncur bersi- to slip, slide down into the mud.

lutung the leaf monkey.

luwar ng- *nadar (,ujar)* to redeem a pledge.

M

macan - *dahan* clouded leopard (L. Neofelis nebulosa).

macapat reading of Jav. literary works in verse form, singing them without musical accompaniment.

maceki k.o. gambling peculiar to Bali.

macet ke-an deadlock.

mac(h)iok (s.) MAHYONG.

mahajutawan multimillionaire.

mahyong mah-jong.

main *ada yg* - persons who make use of the opportunity to acquire large material gains for their own purpose. per-an *kembali* playback (of cassettes, tapes, etc.). - *bowling* to go bowling, bowl. - *hakim sendiri* to take the law into o's own hands. - *pompa* to have sexual intercourse.

majemuk ke-an 1 complexity. 2 pluralism.

makan *mudah* di- *api* easily combustible (,inflammable).

makatana (in the Minahasa) traditional folk medicine to cure hypertension consisting of celery leaves boiled in water together with their stalks and roots.

Makbèt Macbeth (Shakespeare's tragedy).

makjun tonic for strengthening the body.

maklum -*lah* that's the way it is.

makna ber-*ganda* to have a dual meaning. ke-gandaan dualism. - *ganda* dual meaning.

malam ber- *Tahun Baru* to spend New Year's Eve.

malang - *yg timbul* and - *akan tumbuh* ... as ill luck would have it, he ...; unfortunately he ... (ber)-.*melintang* to have it all o's own way, have the game in o's own hands. se-.-nya if the worst comes to worst. -nya ... as ill luck would have it, he ...; unfortunately he ... -.- *mujur* misfortune is always accompanied by some luck.

malar ber- continuing. keber-an continuousness. ke-an continuity. keserba-an continuum. keter-an continuability. me-kan to continue. ter- continued. ter-kan continuable.

mamak the maternal uncle, customarily the eldest brother of the eldest woman.

mana - *ada!* inconceivable! - *tahan!* how could you resist it!

mandala M- *Krida* name of the stadium in Yogyakarta.

mandi I - *matahari* to sun(bathe), sit in the sun.

mandi II strong, powerful. me-kan to make (a fighting cock, keris, etc.) powerful.

mandiri ke-an self-reliance.

manfaat pe-an utilization.

manganranto (Batak) 1 to go and live somewhere while working. 2 to travel. 3 to wander and seek adventure (performs a function in Batak society similar to that of Minangkabau); (S.) MERANTAU.

manggala upgrader.

manol (in Muncar, Banyuwangi) person who sells his services by transporting fish from the fishing boat to the fish auction or processing site.

mantang sweet-potato plant.

mantap me-kan to reinforce.

manunggal me-kan to associate o.s. with.

mapan ke-an position.

marjajo (s.) MANGARANTO.

maro.tingal to split its outlook; two-faced.

mas ke-an goldsmith.

masa - *putar* (in movie theater) screening time.

masjid M-*il Aqsha* the mosque in Jerusalem. M-*il Haram* the mosque in Mecca.

masuk -kan *pos* to mail s.t. - *sekolah*
1 to enroll in school. 2 to go into a
school building.

mata I - *acara* agenda item.

mata II unit of weight for morphine,
etc.; internationally it equals 4 *cekak*,
but drug traffickers in Jakarta convert
it to 18 *cekak*.

mayat - *kering* mummy.

mbarang to tour about as a troubadour.

médan - *pertempuran* battle field.

méjar (in Malaysia) (army) major.
- *jenderal* major general.

mekidung (in Bali) k.o. classical verse.

mekobok k.o. gambling game in Bali.

melati *(bunga)* - jasmine (Indonesia's
national flower).

mèmang 1 yes that's so, (predicate) is
indeed the case. 2 actually, the case is
(so-and-so), but ...

memetri (s.) PEPETRI.

menara - *suar* (S.) MERCUSUAR.

mènijirial managerial. *berkeahlian* -
with managerial skill.

mèntal ber- *amplop* bribable.

menteri *M- Besar* (in Malaysia) comparable to a *Gubernur* (in Indonesia).

mentiko -*nya anak Medan* the showoffi-
ness of Medan people.

mentolo to be heartless enough (to ...);
to behave callously (toward ...). *tdk* -
could not bear (,stand) to.

mesin - *penyemprot* blower.

métajèn (in Bali) gambling on cockfight-
ing.

mèter -*.firkan* square meter, m².

métropolitan ke-an metropolitan character.

métrui k.o. gambling peculiar to Bali.

méwah sophisticated.

mi third note in the musical scale.

mikrobiologi microbiology.

mikrolèt k.o. microbus which is going
to replace the *op(e)let*.

mikul duwur mendem jero to respect o's
parents while alive and after their death.

milyar -an billions.

minum -an *segar* soft drink.

minus - *berapa kaca(mata)mu?* what is
the grade of your glasses (for short-
sightedness)?

minyak - *kopok gajah* and - *misik* oils
used to wash a *keris*.

mlandingan (s.) KEMLANDINGAN.

mocopat (s.) MACAPAT.

modèrnisasi me- to modernize

moluska mollusc.

momèn a trap set up by the police at a
certain point where all vehicles are
stopped to check whether they are in
compliance with a certain regulation.

montang.manting to run headlong.

montèl (in Malaysia) healthy and plump.

monyong di-kan to be protruded.

mori white cambric.

motif ber-kan with ... as its motif.

motorsikal (in Malaysia) motorcycle.

MPP [Masa Persiapan Pensiun] Retirement Preparation Period. di-.kan to
be retired.

mualaf convert to Islam.

mualim expert in religion.

muazam great, exalted (of rulers).

mubah neither good nor wicked.

muballigh (s.) MUBALIGH.

mubarat divorce due to a wife's request
(dowry unreturnable).

mubtadi beginner, novice.

mufarik separated, disentangled.

mufasal separated, detailed.

mufasir commentator (esp. of the Koran).

muflis bankrupt. ke-an bankruptcy.

muflisi insolvency.

mughayat supreme (in titles).

muhabbat love, affection.

muhajir 1 term used for the people who
fled together with Prophet Mohammed
to Medinah. 2 exile.

muhami lawyer.

muhit *al.*- the all-embracing (God).

muhsin virtuous, honest, pure.

muhsinat pure and honest woman.

muhtasyam highly respected.

mukim pe-an habitat.

mukimat female resident of a *pesantren*.

mukimin male resident of a *pesantren*.

mula pe- novice.

mumi (S.) MUMMI.

mungkin *termasuk* **ke-an** not ruled out.
sebab yg paling **me-kan** a probable
cause.
murtad ke-an apostasy.
mustahiq the poor and needy.
mutakhir ke-an sophistication.
mutt(h)ahidah (adj.) united.

N

nada - *sumbang* off-key notes.
nafsu - *seks* libido.
nagasari ironwood, Indian rose
chestwood.
naik - *ring* to enter the ring (in boxing).
nama - *sandi* alias. - *tempat* toponym.
napuh the larger chevrotin or mousedeer.
narasi narration.
narwastu spikenard, frankincense.
nasi - *jagung* ground corn.
Natali (adj.) Christmas.
ndoro 1 master. 2 mistress.
negara - *Bahari* Indonesia. - *kiwi* New
Zealand.
negeri - *Embun Pagi* Korea. - *Gajah
Putih* Thailand. - *Kincir Angin* Holland.
nelayan - *andon (,boro)* (in Muncar,
Banyuwangi) fisherman from outside
the Muncar area who comes and stays
in this area only during the fishing
season. - *pendega* (in Muncar, Banyuwangi) the fisherman who actually
catches fish at sea.
ngebut to exceed the speed limits.
ngendog (sl. in Bandung elementary
schools) to flunk.
ngenyèk (s.) ENYEK.
nglokro despondent, without hope.
ngluwari (s.) LUWAR.
ngocor to flow (of water). *tdk* - clogged
up.
ngomong -*!* (pron. in a somewhat long-
drown out tone on the first vowel)
Oh, that's merely hot air! - *dlm mulut*
to speak inarticulately, mumble.
ngorèk to croak (of frog during rain).
kodok - a croaking frog.
ngriwuki to disturb, interfere with.
ngudarasa prologue.

ni (S.) INI.
niat - *baik* goodwill.
nikah - *campur* mixed marriage.
nilai - *tunai* cash value (of whole life
insurance).
no I (Jav. particle) do it like that!
no II (in Eastern Indonesia) respectful
term of address to a man.
noda pe-an disgrace (the noun).
nol *jika dimulai dr* - if started from
scratch.
nomor - *penerbangan* flight number.
nonik (S.) NONI.
nusa *N- Lontar* another name for *Nusa
Tenggara Timur.*
nyali - *besar* courageous.
nyambut - *damel (,gawe)* to work.
nyata per-an: ~ *gugatan* statement of
claim. ~ *tertulis di bawah sumpah*
affidavit.
nyokor barefoot.
nyonya - *Menteri* the Minister's wife.
nyrepepek to stoop. *sikap* - a subservient
attitude.

O

obat peng-an *alamiah* physiotherapy.
- *penawar sakit* analgesic.
obor - *blencong* (lights on the outskirts
of an airstrip) gooseneck.
obral peng- bargain salesman. - *ketawa*
quick to laugh.
obrigado (in East Timor) thank you.
obrol peng- talker.
olah peng-an *tanah* land clearing.
om term of address or title for a respected
man of an ethnic group other than that
of the speaker.
ondé-ondé sesame balls; ingredients:
sweet-rice flour, potato, water, sugar,
green beans, sesame seeds, and vegetable oil.
operasi - *diam. diam* (intelligence term)
clandestine/under-cover operations.
- *lawan gerilya* counter insurgency.
opyak -.-**an** a drive (rounding up of
animals for killing).
orang -.-**an** *pengusir burung* scarecrow.

- *daerah anu* the system whereby an
applicant is quickly hired for a job
when he knows a certain big shot
who by chance comes from the same
region as the applicant. -.- *perahu*
boatpeople (Vietnamese refugees).
- *Wajo* coastal people of Malaysian
descent. *-utan* (S.) ORANG (HUTAN;
L. Pongo pygmaeus).

organisasi *O- Pembebasan Palestina*
Palestine Liberation Army, PLO.

orkèstrasi orchestration.

Orla [Orde Lama] the Old Order.

os [(in hospitals:) orang sakit] patient.

oton (in Bali) 2 years.

over meng- to change gears.

P

pacar mem-i to go steady with.

padan pem- *kata* and **-an** equivalent (of
a word).

padang - *penggembalaan* ranch.

padépokan (s.) D(H)EPOK.

padu ter- *dan melekat (dlm)* built-in.

pagar - *batu* a brick wall. *P- Baya* name
of the (Jakarta) village police, later
changed to *P- Praja* and then *Polisi
Pamong Praja.* - *gedeg (,gedek)* braided-
bamboo wall. - *kawat* wire fence.

paham kese-an understanding.

Pamardisiwi Correctional Institution for
Youth Delinquents, Juvenile Detention
Facility (in Jakarta).

panca *P- Agama* The five religions of
Indonesia: Islam, Christian Catholic,
Christian Protestant, Hinduism, and
Buddhism. *-warga* an ideal family
consisting of five persons: father,
mother, and three children.

pancong (s.) MACIOK.

pandu mem- (in Malaysia) to drive (a
car). **pem-an** *bakat* talent scouting.

panèn to have a field day.

panggung m- 1 to perform (on the stage).
2 to entertain. - *wayang* (in Malaysia)
movie, motion-picture theater.

pangkal -an *tolak* departure base (for
paratroopers).

pangku *Kesatuan* **Pem-an** *Hutan* Forest
District. **pem-** (in Bali) priest of the
common caste.

pangsit - *kuah* wonton soup.

pangsiun (S.) PENSIUN.

paniki Menadonese dish made from bats.

panitia - *perumus* drafting committee.

panjat mem-kan *doa* to say a prayer,
pray. **pem-an** *doa* the saying of a
prayer.

pantèk (s.) SUMUR (PANTEK).

papan *Perguruan Tinggi "P- Nama"*
an institution of higher education
(academy, university, college, etc.)
which is actively engaged in enrolling
students but which has not submitted
its name to the proper authorities for
the processing of its status. - *penunjuk.*
prestasi (in sports) score board.
- *reklame* bill board.

parade - *perpisahan* passing out parade.

parak approaching (daybreak, etc.).
- *pagi* at dawn (,daybreak ,the first
glimmer of dawn).

para.tifus paratyphoid.

pasang -an: ~ *yg dimabuk cinta* and ~ *yg
sedang asyik dilanda cinta.kasih* a
couple of lovers.

pasar pem- marketer, (insurance) agent.

pasca - *persalinan* postpartum.

pasu migraine.

patis pem-an the drawing of a rope
through the nose of a cow.

patungan ber- *dgn* to have a joint venture
with.

pawang - *laut* (in Aceh) person who
looks for fish and guides the catching
of fish at sea.

pé *(ikan)* - ray (variety of fish).

pecah - *nyalinya* to lose courage (,heart).

pedèl (s.) JURU (PENGACARA).

pegawai mem. *P-* Negeri.kan to make s.o.
a government employee. - *meja* white-
collar employee.

pekasèh (in Bali) chairman for contacts
with farmers.

péla *daerah (,masyarakat)* -.- area
(,community) of harmless drifters.

pèlak *tdk* - *lagi* indeed, sure enough, no

doubt, it cannot fail.

pelawa memp- (in Malaysia) to invite (,call) over.

pèlbak garbage dump.

Pelita [Pelajar, Industri dan Pariwisata] Students, Industry, and Tourism. *Kota* - The City of Students, Industry, and Tourism (i.e. Malang).

pèlor (s.) TORPEDO II.

pengambak (in Muncar, Banyuwangi) owner of money who invests his money in *juragan darats* and *(nelayan) pendegas* and has the right to sell the fish catch.

pengaruh *saling -*.**memp-** to interact.

pèngèn (S.) INGIN.

pentas ber- to stage, present.

pentil mem-.m- *gitar* to twang a guitar.

pepetri (s.) PETRI.

perabot - *dapur* kitchen utensils.

perawan ke-an virginity.

percaya ke-an fiduciary.

pergi - *haji* to make the pilgrimage to Mecca.

periksa pem-an *akuntan* auditing.

perintah pem-an *dlm negeri* civil service.

pernah - *apanya?* what relationship to him?

persaben excuse me, I can't give you anything (Sundanese; common in Bandung, when brushing off beggars).

Persatwi and **PERSATWI** [Persatuan Tenaga Wanita Indonesia] Indonesian Women (Government) Employees Association.

pèrsuasi di- to be persuaded.

peruan yard of mast or flagpole.

pesawat - *televisi hitam putih* a black-and-white TV set. - *tinggal landas tegak lurus* vertical-take-off plane.

petai - *cina* (s.) KEMLANDINGAN.

pethakil -an overacting.

peti - *ajaib* (in some far-flung villages) television set.

petik pem- *gitar* guitarist.

pètri mem- to honor. *upacara* ~ (in the Universitas Sarjana Wiyata of Taman Siswa, Yogyakarta) initiation ceremony consisting of sprinkling water from a

kendi over the head of new students; followed by having them wear a *peci* and uniform).

pétroléum petroleum.

pidana memp- to sentence (a criminal).

pidato - *kenegaraan* State of the Union Speech.

pikir *saya* - I believe that. **pem-** thinker.

pilih pem-an *tingkat permulaan* primary (election).

pilis powder put on forehead to relieve pain.

pimpin mem- leading. *posisi* ~ a leading position.

pincara (S.) PERAHU.

pindah per-an *besar.besaran* exodus. - *agama* to be converted (as to a religion).

pingat (in Malaysia) medal.

ping.pong di- *ke sana ke mari* to be sent from pillar to post.

pingsut 1 to draw lots by throwing out fingers to see who goes first. 2 to take a chance, risk o's luck.

pio(h) 1 k.o. (land) tortoise. 2 turtle soup.

pipi - *tempel* - cheek to cheek.

pipis to urinate.

piring - *terbang* (in Jakarta, also) merry-go-round.

pirsa to see.

pirsawan spectator, onlooker.

pisin saucer.

Pjs. [Pejabat sementara] **mem.-.kan** to make s.o. an acting office-holder.

plantar emergency mooring site (in port area).

plug - *malam* night shift.

polantas - *udara* (coll.) air traffic con-troller.

polisi *P- Hutan* Forest Rangers.

polos 1 innocent. 2 unbiassed. 3 honest. *pintu* - flush door. **ke-an** honesty.

pondan (in Malaysia) homosexual.

pos mem-kan to mail (a letter) - *bantuan hukum* legal clinic.

praduga presumption. - *tak bersalah* presumption of innocence.

pra.pengadilan pre-trial.

pra.Rapim [pra.Rapat Pimpinan] Preliminary Meeting of *Rapim*.
prayojana motivation.
prilaku - *manusia* human behavior.
profesor - *madya* (in Malaysia) associate
professor.
program pem-an programming.
proklamator proclaimer.
promovènda female candidate for
doctor's degree.
prosedur - *tetap* standing order.
proyèksi mem-kan to project.
psikoanalisa psychoanalysis.
psikotès psychotest.
puas - *diri* self-satisfied.
puasa - *mati.geni* not sleeping for several
nights.
Pudèk [Pembantu Dekan] (in university)
Deputy Dean.
puisi pem- poet.
pulang pem-an *kembali* repatriation.
pulas *penarikan* -an (the) symbolic
withdrawal (of Russian troops from
Afghanistan).
pulau - *bebas.bea* bonded island. *P-
Kapal* the new name for the island of
Onrust, o. of the islands belonging to
P-Seribu. *P-Kota* City Island, reference
to the island of Java that houses
65% of the entire Indonesian population.
pulsar recording device (in telephone
office) that produces electrical pulses
in order to be able to determine the
cost for a call placed by the subscriber.
puncak - *nafsu* orgasm.
punggawa rich fisherman.
pupa pupa.
pupuh a stanza.
pupuk - *fosfat alam* rock phosphate.
pura *penuh* -.- phony.
Purèk [Pembantu Rektor] (in university)
Deputy President.
purna *lulus* - to pass all subjects (in
university).
pusat mem-kan *pikiran* to concentrate.
pustaka Per-an *Kongres* The Library of
Congress (in Washington, D.C., U.S.A.).
putih pem-an *sapi Jawa* the improvement

of the quality of Java cattle through
the crossbreeding of local cows with
the *sapi putih* or white cows of Sumba
Island, also known as *Sumba Onggole
(S.O.)*.

Q

qath'i authoritative.
qias reasoning by analogy.

R

Rabitat Al Alam Al Islam Moslem
World League.
racana the smallest unit in the *Pramuka*
Boy Scout Movement consisting of
pandegas; membership maximum 10.
racun ke-an *darah* blood poisoning,
septicemia.
radang pe-an inflamation. - *otak* encephalitis.
rafaksi allowance for damage.
raga pe-an display.
rambut - *jangan putus, tepung jangan
terserak* in settling a matter it should
be done in a fair way, so that both
parties involved are pleased.
rancak (in Malaysia) hot (jazz music).
randai West Sumatra traditional theater.
ranjang - *lipat* folding bed (,cot).
ranking *menurut* - (in sports) seeded.
Rapim [Rapat Pimpinan] Leadership
Meeting of all Chiefs of Staff, *KODAM*
Commanders, and representatives of
the Armed Forces from institutions
under the jurisdiction of *Hankam*.
rata peme-an equity.
rawan 1 crucial. 2 critical. 3 dangerous
(full of thieves, etc.).
rawat pe-an *keluarga* home nursing.
ré second note in the musical scale.
rekam (pe)-an *pita* tape-recording.
rèmpèt tender (a boat for carrying
passengers, etc. to or from a large
ship close to shore).
rèncèkan dead (,fallen) wood, twigs
(used for firewood).

représèntasi representation. **di-kan** to be represented.

résètelmèn resettlement.

rèspons response.

ritslèting zip fastener, zipper.

rokok - *daun* cigarette with leaf (,corn husk) wrapper.

roling moving from place to place.

roman -.**-an** flirtation.

romo term of address for priests. *R-Prefek* Assistant to the Rector in seminary.

ronggèng - *kunyuk* (in Cirebon and Tegal); (s.) KOMIDI (KETEK).

rongsen di- to be X-rayed.

roti *R- Paskah* Easter Bread.

ruang -**an** *kelas* class room.

ruas section (of a road).

rubah fox.

rujuk me- silang *ke* to cross-refer to. *sistim* -**an** referral system.

rukun ke-an cooperation.

rumah - *bagonjong* the West Sumatra Governor's office. -.*contoh* model home. - *idaman* dreamhouse. - *paku* a house made of planks and nails. - *rangka* prefab. *R- Sakit NU* reference to the Islamic Hospital in Surabaya. - *sub inti* very simple housing earmarked for persons with irregular income, such as pedicab drivers, vegetable salesmen, etc. - *susun* an apartment building.

rumpil barely passable (of street).

rumpun - *aju* (mil.) advance group.

S

saat *suatu* - at some time (in the future).

sabdapraja dialect.

sadar ke-an feeling, sense.

sadran *musim* -**an** the season to pay homage to o's deceased ancestors, i.e. during the month of *Sadran* or eighth month of the Jav. (,Moslem) calendar.

sahang white pepper.

sahih ke-an validity. **peny-an** validation.

sak bag.

sakala concrete, material; (opp.) *niskala*.

sakit peny-: ∼ *gandongan* (,gondongan)

goiter. ∼ *kegemukan* adiposity. ∼ *mati bujang* 'Sumatra disease,' i.e. a disease attacking clove plants (L. Eugenia caryophilla), esp. in West Sumatra. - *pelupa* forgetfulness. - *pipi gemuk* goiter.

sal (in hospital) ward.

salah ke-.pengertian and **ke-terimaan** misunderstanding. **meny-kan** to blame, find fault with. *tdk ada* -**nya** ... there is no harm in ... - *ucap* slip of the tongue.

salèh ke-an *anak* filial piety.

salur -**an** *kemih* urinary tract.

sama keber-an (s.) SAMENLEVEN. *teman* **se-** *perampok* fellow bandit. - *rata - rasa* egalitarianism.

samada (in Malaysia) whether.

samapta ke-an preparedness, readiness for action.

sambang - *kerja* work visit.

samber *S- gledek!* (an oath) May I (,he ,she ,etc.) be struck by lightning if ...

sambung peny- *tilpon* telephone operator.

samen (sl. in Bandung elementary schools) ceremony and feast in connection with promotion to higher class.

sampai *S- nanti!* See you later!

samsèng bouncer.

sanak - *famili* relative(s).

sandera meny- to take as hostage(s), seize and keep as hostage(s). **peny-** hostage-holder (,taker). **peny-an** hostage-taking, the seizure and keeping as hostage(s).

Sandhyakara Murti the women's organization of the Department of Communications.

sangga peny- pylon (of aircraft).

sapi - *Banpres* cattle usually imported from Australia by the Indonesian government and distributed among farmers using special funds earmarked by the President. - *mirit* a large species of cow, considered a crossbreed between the *sapi Jawa* (Java cow) and the (Indian) Zebu. - *Peranakan.Onggole* (in Central and East Java) a white-grey colored cow with long legs and a

large hump over the shoulders; under
the neck hangs a large dewlap; the
animal is used to pull plows in villages
and carts in cities.

Sarinah 1 girl's name used to represent
the average female. 2 name of the
largest department store in Jakarta.

saring meny- selective.

sarwa - *sekalian alam* the whole world.
ber-makna meaningful.

satelit - *pengindra jarak jauh* remote-
sensing satellite.

Satriamandala the Armed Forces'
museum.

satu keber-an oneness.

satyalancana *S- Karya Satya* 'Medal for
Loyal Service,' awarded by the government in appreciation of o's continuous
service, loyalty, ability, and diligence
in carrying out o's duties as a civilian
government employee for 25 years or
more. *S- Peringatan Perjuangan
Kemerdekaan* 'Medal in Commemoration of the Struggle for Independence,'
awarded by the government in appreciation of o's merits, loyalty, and
struggle between the period August 17,
1945 through December 27, 1949 in
actively carrying out o's duties as a
civilian government employee.

saudara -.*sepengambilan* an adopted
child.

saur - *manuk* (to answer) in unison.

saus - *Inggris* Worcestershire sauce.
- *tiram* oyster sauce.

sawah - *geledug* (s.) SAWAH (TADAH
HUJAN).

sebar ter- scattered.

segi -*tiga* tripartite.

sekalor migraine.

sekolah - *mini* play group.

selamat *program* **peny-an** rescue program.
-an *hajat dalem malem selikuran*
ceremony held to commemorate the
end of the fasting month of Ramadhan.
S- Malam! Good Night! (said on
greeting as well as departing).

selawatan k.o. tambourine.

selenggara peny--*perjalanan* tour opera-

tor (in autobus for tourists).

selérak (S.) SERAK. **ber-** (S.)
BERSERAK.

selésa (in Malaysia) comfortable, pleasing,
agreeable. **ke-an** comfort, ease, pleasure.

sélibat celibate.

SELINDO [Selandia (Baru)-Indonesia]
New Zealand-Indonesia. *Latihan Laut* -
reference to the joint New Zealand-
Indonesian Naval Maneuvers.

selip *masih* **ny-** *di ketiak* ... still under
the jurisdiction of ...

selubung ter- hidden.

seluk - *bentuk* the shape in all its details.

semai per-an nursery.

semanggi clubs (in card games).

seminar pe- participant in a seminar.

sempit peny--*pembuluh darah* (heart)
infarct.

semut *dr* - *sampai gajah* from small to
big, from high to low.

sendiko - *dawuh* (a mental attitude)
only waiting for orders from superiors.

sèng sheet metal.

sengau per-an nasalizing.

sènggol - *lari* hit-and-run.

sengkèt (s.) SENGKEDAN.

senjang ke-an 1 gap. ~ *kepercayaan*
credibility gap. 2 discrepancy.

senjata - *pengejut listrik* electric stun gun.

seperti -nya it is as though ...

sepertimana (in Malaysia) such as.

sepet (S.) SEPAT. - *bila dipandang mata*
unpleasant to look at, unsightly.

serabut ber-an to stick up all over, bristle.

serahat (S.) ISTIRAHAT.

seranggasida insecticide.

serayang.seroyong to stagger.

serba -*bahasa* multilingualism.

sérémoni ceremony.

serpih flake. - *jagung* corn flakes.

serta kepe-an *dlm* participation in.
secara -.*merta* simultaneously.

sèt (in tennis) set.

setèl peny-an (car) tune up.

setil stylist; (s.) STIL.

séwa di-.belikan to be bought on the
lease-purchase plan. **meny-.borong** to
charter (an aircraft, etc.). -.*beli* lease-

purchase.

shalat - *Istisqa* prayer for rain.

si seventh note in the musical scale.

siap - *dipakai* ready for use.

siapa *tdk ada* -.- (there's) nobody.

sia.sia **peny-an** neglect.

sigako (during the Jap. occupation) school inspector.

sigaran - *nyowo* spouse.

silabus syllabus.

silang -.*dlm* inbreeding (of cattle). -.*garis* linebreeding (of cattle).

silhuèt silhouette.

simpang **ke-.siuran** zigzagging, crisscrossing.

sinambung **ke-an** continuity.

sinar *S- Harapan* 'The Ray of Hope,' i.e. the name of a Protestant newspaper in Jakarta.

sindap dandruff.

sinder plantation supervisor.

singgel single. *Masih* -? Are you still single?

sinonim synonym. **ber-** *dgn* synonymous with. **di-kan** *dgn* to be made a synonym of.

sirah (in Palembang) village head.

sisihan spouse.

sita **meny-** *seluruh waktunya* to take (up) all o's time.

sitrun lemon.

siwalan the palmyra palm and fruit.

SKM [Sarjana Kesehatan Masyarakat] Master of Public Health, M.P.H.

skripsi Master's thesis.

slébor drunk, intoxicated.

slintat.slintut to do s.t. on the sly.

soal *tdk menjadi* -! no big deal!

sogan red-brown color.

sogili Menadonese dish made from a water snake.

sol fifth note in the musical scale.

Solèman - *yg Bijak* King Solomon, the Wise.

solidaritas **ke-an** solidarity.

sono (S.) SANA. *dr* **-nya** by birth (,nature).

sopran *penyanyi* - soprano.

sorban turban. **ber-** turbaned.

soré *main* - to play vigorously (at the end of soccermatch).

sorolok k.o. sifting device to separate broken hulled rice from the grains.

spirit - *konco.koncoan* cronyism.

stasiun - *induk* base station. - *tenaga listrik* power station.

stater (s.) SETATER. **mens-** (s.) MENYE-TATER.

stèmpel - *pos* postmark.

stérilisasi sterilization. **di-** to be sterilized.

stofmap file for keeping papers in order.

sudah previous.

sufi a mystic. *ilmu* - mysticism.

sukar - *tidur* insomnia.

sukur *S- kowe!* It serves you right!

sulap **pe-** 1 conjurer, juggler. 2 magician. ~ *faqir* conjurer using mysticism. ~ *ilusi* conjurer by means of skill. ~ *manipulasi* conjurer using magical devices.

suluh **peny-an** educative information.

sumamburat **meny-** to scatter.

sumbat **peny-an** obstruction (in urinary tract, due to renal calculus).

sumber - *rujukan* reference sources.

sumpek to have o's head in a whirl because of problems.

sumur - *artesis* artesian well. - *pantek* a drilled well.

Sunni the tradition of the majority of Moslems who accept the historical experience of the early community as having been divinely guided. Sunnites emphasize the importance of the community and communal tradition.

sunting **peny-** editor, a person who edits. **peny-an** editing (of a book, etc.).

super **ke-an** superiority.

surat - *kepemilikan* title deed. - *muatan udara* airway bill. - *petok* (s.) GIRIK. - *rantai* chain letter. - *tauliah* credentials.

suru spoon made from a (banana) leaf.

survai survey. **mens-** to survey.

survéi (s.) SURVAI.

susu *saudara* **seper-an** sibling nurtured by the same breast. - *berlemak* whole milk. - *tak berlemak* skim milk.

susuk IUD.

swakelola self-management.
swa.layan self-serve. *toko* - self-service
store.
swarawati (S.) SUARAWATI.
Syiah *kaum* - the Islamic groups who
believe that leadership in the community should have passed directly
from Muhammad to *Ali* and then to a
line of divinely guided imams; the
Shi'ites emphasize the need for a personal focus for divine guidance.
Syuriah 1 Legislative. 2 Executive
Board (in the N.U. party structure)
consisting of prominent Moslem
scholars; now practically has been
replaced by the *Tanfidziah*.

T

tablèt - *bersalut gula* dragée.
tabrak pen- the person who collided
with.
tahan ke-an *di hutan (,laut)* jungle (,sea)
survival.
tahfidz memorization of 30 chapters of
the Koran.
tahi - *bintang* meteorite. - *burung* (fig.)
(S.) BENALU.
tahu - *nggak* you know (interjection).
-nya (S.) TAHU (.TAHU).
tahun *Toyoto Corolla* - *terbaru* the
latest Toyota Corolla model. - *kamariah*
lunar year. - *syamsiah* solar year.
tai - *tuwak* a liquid derived from *tuak*
having the qualities of yeast (makes
dough rise).
tak ke-berpihakan impartiality. ke-
terhinggaan infinity.
takut -nya *saya* what I'm afraid of is.
takziah condolence, mourning. ber- 1 to
grieve with, condole. 2 to feel (,express)
sympathy.
ta'lim non-formal education with religion
as the sole subject.
tamba - *kangen* s.t. to remember s.o. by.
tandak - *bedes* (in Surabaya) (s.) KEMIDI
(BEDES).
tanding per-an *pemanasan* (in sports)
tryout.

tangga - *pusing* spiral staircase.
tanggal - *merah* 'red-letter day,' official
holiday (marked red on the calendar).
tanggap responsive.
tanggulang ter-i warded off, held back.
tanggung halfway between, neither o.
nor the other. *randa* - a widow of
medium age, i.e. too old to be likely
to remarry but not yet very old.
Lagi -! said by s.o. who is engaged in
s.t., but does not want to finish it
halfway, since it is almost finished;
he wants to conclude the job first,
before doing s.t. else. *tdk mampu* ber-
jawab jur. not accountable (for).
-.bulan the period from the tenth of
the month.
tangis ter- burst into tears.
tangkap pair which fits together, such
as, two half spheres of Jav. brown
sugar, two hands of bananas. *mentega
di antara dua* - *roti* sandwich.
tangkar pen-an breeding.
tapak *orang yg putih* - *kakinya* a Japanese.
Tapianauli and Tapian Nauli Tapanuli.
taqwa ke-an piety, devotion.
tari pen- *strip* stripper.
tas - *belanja* shopping bag.
tata ke-negaraan public administration.
ke-niagaan business administration.
pen- *röntgen* radiologist. - *cahaya*
lights (in film). - *istilah* terminology.
- *kelola* management. - *kelola risiko*
risk management. - *kelola wiraswasta*
entrepreneurial management. - *kerajaan*
monarchy. - *krama* ethical code. - *loka*
lay-out. - *niaga* business administration.
- *pentas* setting (in film). - *rias surat
kabar* the lay-out (,make-up) of a newspaper. - *rupa* cover design (of magazine).
- *wiraniaga* salesmanship.
taudoa (in Gorontalo) (s.) HUKUM
(TUA).
tayang men-kan (in Malaysia) to show
(a film).
ta'ziah (s.) TAKZIAH.
téater -.restoran dinner-theater.
tebal pen-an *pembuluh darah* arteriosclerosis.

tédong (in Tana Toraja, Central Celebes) water buffalo. *mapasilaga* - water buffalo fight (held prior to a funeral).

teduh - *panasnya* his fever has dropped.

tegak **pen-an** *hukum* law enforcement.

tèhel (floor) tile.

teki a grass with an edible tuberous root. *emping* - chips made from this tuber, fried and eaten as snacks.

tekik cigarette butt.

teladan **ke-an** exemplariness.

telan **di**- *usia* out of date, antiquated.

teleng *jadi -nya* to be(come) the focal point of o's thoughts (,feelings, etc.).

télépon - *radio* wireless telephone.

tèlèr 1 (in Medan, Central and East Java) foul discharge from an infected ear. 2 (in Jakarta) intoxicated.

teluk *T- Cendrawasih* (the former) Geelvink Baai (in Irian Jaya).

telusur **men-i** to trace.

teman **men-i** to keep a person company.

Tembagapura 'Coppertown,' the site of Freeport Indonesia's mining operations.

tempat - *kejadian* scene (of the crime), - *kost* boardinghouse. - *parkir pesawat* apron. - *penyimpanan dingin* cold storage.

tempuh **ke-an** liable for damages.

temu **pen**- innovator. **per-an** *kekeluargaan* reunion.

tenaga - *yg bekerja penuh* full timer.

tèndanisasi the pitching of tents.

tenglang of Chinese descent.

tèntamèn test, exam.

tentang **per-an** *kepentingan* conflict of interest(s).

tèntèng *barang.barang* **-an** hand luggage.

tentu *sdh (barang)* - and *barang* - in all probability, very likely, quite probable.

tepas *T- Paniti Kismo* (in Yogyakarta) Office for the Control of Kraton Lands.

tepat -*.guna* effective.

tepi *jaga* - *kain orang* worry about other people's affairs instead of keeping o's own house in order.

tepok -*.bulu* badminton.

terbang I tambourine.

terbang II **pen**- *layang gantung* hangglider. - *berhenti* to hover (of aircraft).

teriak **di-(.-)kan** *(keras.keras)* to be bragged about.

terima **di**- *bekerja* to be hired (for a job). *tdk punya rasa -kasih* ungrateful.

teri(s)ka **(me)n**- to iron.

terjang **men-.n**- to have convulsions.

terjun **men-kan** *diri ke* (fig.) to participate in, take part in, join. - *payung* parachute jumping.

teroka **pen**- (in Malaysia) the equivalent of Indonesian *transmigran*.

terondol to be in low water.

tertib **di-kan** (of streetvendors) to be chased away from the site where they sell their goods. **pen-an** sweeping.

teruk aggravating.

terumbu - *karang* coral reef.

tetas **pen-an** hatchery.

tètès **ke-an** *darah ningrat* of noble descent, of princely stock.

tetumbuhan vegetation.

Thafizil Qur'an recitation of the Koran from memory.

thenguk -.- to sit around idly.

thiwul *nasi* - powdered dry cassava used as a rice substitute.

tiang - *bergantung* main source of hope. - *hidup* main source of income.

tidak **ke-.aktifan** inactivity. **ke-.hadiran** absence. **ke-ikutsertaan** non-participation. **ke-.lestarian** impermanence. **ke-.perawanan** loss of o's virginity. **ke-.samaan** disparity. **ke-.seragaman** disuniformity. **ke-.seriusan** lack of seriousness. **ke- terus terangan** dishonesty.

tidur II beating on the *beduk* at certain occasions before and during the fasting month of *Ramadhan*.

tifus typhus.

tigari three days.

tiker typist.

tiko (in Jakarta) the native Indonesian.

timbul -*.tenggelam* to bob up and down (as a drowning person, a ship during a storm).

tindak **-an** *sita jaminan* (jur.) seizure of

property (before judgment); (to apply
for an order of interim) custody of
property.

tinggal men-kan *ruang sidang* (in *DPR,*
etc.) walk-out. - *tunggu waktu saja*
it's just a matter of time.

tingkat *upacara penyelesaian - akhir*
topping-out ceremony. - *kegempaan*
seismicity.

Tionghwa (S.) TIONGHOA.

Tiongkok - *daratan* PRC.

tipis *keuntungan* - a small (,slight)
profit.

tiru pen- imitator.

titi *T-, Tataq, Tuntas* (motto of the
Pramuka Boy Scouts) Attentive,
Undaunted, Thorough.

titik - *leleh* melting point.

TNI [Tentara Nasional Indonesia] lit.
'Indonesian National Army,' Armed
Services. **TNI.AD** [Tentara Nasional
Indonesia.Angkatan Darat] Armed
Services-Army. **TNI.AL** [Tentara
Nasional Indonesia.Angkatan Laut]
Armed Services-Navy. **TNI.AU**
[Tentara Nasional Indonesia.Angkatan
Udara] Armed Services-Air Force.

tokoh - *masyarakat* informal leader.

tokolan short beansprouts.

tolak ber- *belakang* to go the opposite
direction.

tolok standard. -.*ukur* criterion.

tong *T- Setan* Hell Hole (i.e. a barrel
in which a daredevil rides his motorcycle against the wall).

tonggos prominent (of front upper teeth).

tongkat - *penopang* crutches. - *putih* cane
(for blind people).

tongkos (s.) TONGGOS.

tongkrong 1 to sit up high with the legs
drawn up. 2 to sit around idly. 3 to be
out of commission. *kedai (makanan
dan minuman)* -an roadside eating stall
where o. can sit in a relaxed way (with
the legs drawn up, etc.).

tongkrongan (in Jakarta) talent, aptitude.

topèng - *monyet* (in West Java and
Jakarta) (s.) KOMEDI (KETEK).

toto - *greyhound toto* linked to the

greyhound races held in the *JCSC*
(,Jakarta Caninedrome Sport Center);
now banned.

tradisi ment- to become a tradition.

trampil ke-an *lompat berkuda* show
jumping (on horseback).

tridasawarsa thirty years.

TRIPIDA [Tri Pimpinan Daerah]
Regional Leadership Trio, consisting
of the leaders of the Police Force,
Koramil, and village.

Tritura [Tri Tuntutan Rakyat] Three
People's Demands. This was the slogan
of the student activists who helped
overthrow Soekarno in the spring of
1966. The demands were: (1) dissolution of the Communist Party, (2) dismissal of the Cabinet, and (3) reduction
of prices.

trofoblas trophoblast. *penyakit* - trophoblast disease.

truck.lossing (in the Tanjung Priok port
area) the unloading of goods from the
ship directly to the truck.

tua ke- *kelas* class president. **pen-an**
aging.

tubir - *bibir* edges (,outlines) of the lips.

tugunisasi the erection of statues or
monuments.

tuju -an *menghalalkan segala cara* the end
justifies the means.

tujuh -*belasan* to celebrate August 17.

tukang - *angkut* (in Muncar, Banyuwangi)
(s.) MANOL. - *ledeng* bill collector
of the water supply company. - *pasang
sihir* black magician.

tukar di-.pikirkan (views) are exchanged.
~ *pesawat* to change planes. *terima
-.tambah* trading-in.

tukik young of a turtle.

tulung *sdh kagak* **ke-an** beyond help.

tumbèn I'm surprised. *Wah, kok - ke
sini!* What a surprise to see you here!

tumbuk - *yuswo* the seventy-second
birthday, = 9 *windu.*

tumpang *yg* **n-** *tinggal* boarder, paying
guest.

tumpangsari multiple cropping.

tuna -.*listrik* without electricity. - *mental*

mentally deficient person, retarded
person. -*warga* prisoner, captive.
tungau dermatophagoides.
tunjuk pen-*jalan* guide.
tuntas conclusive. **ke-an** conclusiveness.
men-kan to settle (a matter, etc.).
conclusively.
turun *bersifat* men- hereditary. **pen-an**
arti pejoration. *Ia masih ada* -**an**
ningrat, She is of aristocratic stock,
she has some aristocratic blood in
her veins.
tutor tutor.
tutur -*.bicara* subject of conversation.
tuxédo - *diplomat* diplomat who is
always well dressed and who makes an
impressive and neat appearance.

U

ubah meng-suai to adjust, adapt.
ucap ber- to express.
udang - *galah* lobster. - *satang* and
- *watang* species of fresh water shrimp.
- *papai* (S.) EBI.
udel navel. *dgn seenak* - in whatever way
I find it pleasant, to my heart's
content.
uji *maju* -**an** to stand for o's examination.
-.*coba* trial.
ukur -**an** *mini* in a small way, on a small
scale, in miniature.
ular - *patoa* Menadonese dish, made from
a rice paddy snake.
uli delicacy made from sticky rice that
has been crushed and steamed. *tapé* -
tapé and *uli* (eaten together).
umat - *manusia* mankind, the human
race.
umbalan (in Tanjungkarang, Lampung
Selatan) (S.) KAMPUNG
umbi - *bunga* bulb (of a plant).
umrah ber- to make the so-called minor
haj to Mecca.
uniformisasi peng-an uniformization.
unsur - *polusi* pollutant.
untung ke-an *yg tak diduga* windfall
profits.
urai -**an** *jenis pekerjaan* job description.

urologi urology.
usaha per-an: ~ *penukar uang* money
changer. ~ *sapi.perah* dairy farm.
usia - *sekolah* school age.
utang - *semahameru* mountainous debts.
utus *para* -**an** *Injil* messengers of the
Gospel.

V

vari(é)tas specimen.
vèlbak (s.) PELBAK.
voli to play volley-ball.
vooruitslag (Customs term) release of
goods from a warehouse anticipating
the settlement of the related
documents.
vrij (pron. frè) neutral gear.
VUTW [Vari(e)tas Unggul Tahan Wereng]
Wereng-proof Superior Variety; a rice
variety from the *Balai Penelitian Pertanian Bogor* (Bogor Agricultural
Research Institute).

W

wajib -.*putar* (in film business) the
obligatory showing of Indonesian films
in certain first-class movie theaters.
waktu - *senggang* slack-season.
wali -**an** (in North Celebes) (s.) TONAAS.
warangka (keris) sheath.
warga ke-negaraan *rangkap* dual citizenship.
waria [wanita pria] homosexual, transvestite.
warung - *kelap.kelip* (s.) WARUNG
(REMENG.REMENG).
waspada me-kan to put on the alert.
way (s.) WAI.
wayang (in Malaysia) play, theatrical
(,operatic) show.
wenang pe- person with the authority
(in that matter).
werda old. *golongan* - the senior citizens.
widyakarya workshop, experts' meeting.
Wihdatul Wujud Pantheism.
wira - *usaha* entrepreneur.
wiraniaga 1 salesman. 2 sales representa-

tive. **ke-an** salesmanship.

wiraswasta ber- to trade, do business (as
an entrepreneur).

wiski - *soda* whisky and soda.

wisuda mengw- (s.) MEWISUDA.

wisudha *W- Jurit* inauguration to become
a *Prajurit Taruna* (Cadet Soldier).

wolkayu woodwool.

Y

Yamaha - *bebek* the 79-cc V80 Yamaha
motorbike.

yang *Y- di.Pertuan Agong* (in Malaysia)
King (in all official Malaysian papers).

yokal (in Irian Jaya) woman's native
dress.

Yudha.loka (in the *Bina Graha*, Jakarta)
War-room.

yugèkitai (during the Jap. occupation)
guerrilla section of the *Peta (,Pembela
Tanah Air)*, the homeguard during
the Jap. period.

Y.W. an uncovered goods car (in train
formation).

Z

zona zone. - *ekonomi* economic zone.